LENIN'S STRUGGLE FOR A REVOLUTIONARY INTERNATIONAL

To the memory of Farrell Dobbs (1907–1983), who through sustained determination and tireless work over the past decade contributed to reconquering the political continuity of revolutionary workers today with the Communist International under Lenin's leadership. He more than any other person was the source of encouragement for launching this series of volumes.

The Communist International
in Lenin's Time

LENIN'S STRUGGLE FOR A REVOLUTIONARY INTERNATIONAL

Documents: 1907–1916
The Preparatory Years

Edited by John Riddell

PATHFINDER
New York London Montreal Sydney

ISBN 978-0-87348-928-7
Library of Congress Catalog Card Number 84-061519
Manufactured in the United States of America

First edition, 1984
Second edition, 1986
Eleventh printing, 2025

Pathfinder
pathfinderpress.com
Email: pathfinder@pathfinderpress.com

Contents

Maps

Photographs

Introduction

This is the first in a series of volumes on the Communist International. The series will encompass the preparatory years from 1907, through the Bolsheviks' call for a new International in 1914, until its foundation in 1919. It will then follow the political development of the Communist International (Comintern) until the end of 1923, the years during which the policies of the Comintern were shaped by V.I. Lenin and the team of Marxist revolutionaries led by him.

Forthcoming volumes will include further materials from the preparatory years shaped by the Russian revolution of 1917; resolutions and proceedings from the first four Comintern congresses; from the meetings of its Executive Committee; and from special conferences called under its auspices—conferences of revolutionary trade unionists, communist women, revolutionary nationalists from colonial countries, and young workers.

This series aims to make more accessible the example and lessons of the international communist movement that grew out of and was led by the Bolshevik Party. It will present the discussion and debates within this worldwide movement that were shaped by the great political upheavals of the first quarter of this century. It will include the key exchanges between the leaders of the new International and various reformist, centrist, and anarcho-syndicalist currents.

The *Collected Works* of Lenin, who was the dominant leader of the Comintern, have been in print in English for several decades. So, too, have been a few important works by other central Comintern leaders. But only a small portion of the debates surrounding the rise and development of the Comintern, or of the record of its proceedings, has ever been published in English. The editions that do exist are incomplete and often suffer from inadequate translation; most of them have been unavailable for many decades.

*

From the origins of the modern communist workers' movement in the middle of the nineteenth century, its leaders have worked to build an international organization to lead the worldwide struggle for socialism. The launching of the Communist International in 1919 was a continuation of that historic effort.

In taking the name "communist," the new International recalled the first international organization formed by revolutionary workers—the Communist League, founded in 1847 in London. Karl Marx and Frederick Engels, who were among the leaders of the League, accepted the assignment to draft its founding program. This document, the *Manifesto of the Communist Party,* published at the beginning of 1848, is the foundation of the program of the modern revolutionary workers' movement.

Marx, Engels, and other Communist League leaders threw themselves into the democratic revolutions that broke out in France, Germany, and much of Europe in early 1848. By the end of 1849 these revolutionary upsurges had been defeated, and by late 1850 it was clear to Marx and Engels that no early revival could be expected. In 1852, at their initiative, the Communist League was dissolved.

By the beginning of the next decade, the workers' movement in Europe had begun to show signs of recovery from the post-1849 reaction. In 1864 the International Working Men's Association was formed, which has become known as the First International. It included important workers' organizations from Britain, France, Germany, and elsewhere in Europe. Some of these were influenced by the communist current around Marx and Engels, who played a leading role in the organization from the outset, while others were influenced by anarchist and various petty-bourgeois socialist currents of the day.

Marx drafted what became the founding program of the new organization. Writing to Engels in November 1864, he commented that "it was very difficult to frame the thing so that our view should appear in a form acceptable from the present standpoint of the workers' movement," which was then only beginning to revive from more than a decade-long retreat under the blows of reaction. Contrasting this political situation in Europe to the revolutionary years of 1848–49, Marx explained that, "It will take time before the reawakened movement allows the old boldness of speech." (Marx and Engels, *Selected Correspondence,* pp. 139–40.) The early statements of the International were careful in tone but, from the very beginning, firm on principle.

The high point of the new period of struggles in Europe came in March 1871 with the establishment of the Paris Commune by the insurgent workers and other exploited producers of that city. Following the bloody crushing of that uprising the following May by the combined forces of the French and German exploiters, another period of reaction took hold throughout Europe. The First International, which had championed the Commune and worked tirelessly to generalize and spread its lessons, went into decline.

In 1874, two years before the final dissolution of the First International, Engels expressed the firm opinion that "the next International—after Marx's writings have exerted their influence for some years—will be directly communist and will candidly proclaim our principles." (*Selected Correspondence,* p. 271.) This was not to be the case as quickly as Engels had hoped. An International that was "directly communist" would not be launched until 1919.

The founding of the Second International in 1889, however, did mark an advance toward winning the workers' movement to a consistent revolutionary perspective. During the first two decades of this International, sharp debates among its divergent ideological currents were on the whole decided "in the spirit of revolutionary Marxism," as Lenin put it following the organization's 1907 congress.

The rise of world imperialism that coincided with the early years of the Second International brought new pressures to bear. Class-collaborationist currents gained ground in the International, challenging more and more directly the proletarian internationalist tenets of its program. On the other hand, the Russian revolution of 1905–1907 was the harbinger of a new period of worker and peasant uprisings in Europe and Asia, providing rich lessons for the revolutionary forces within the International.

As this volume documents, however, the majority of leaders in the International's most authoritative parties continued to move to the right. By the end of the first decade of the twentieth century, most of its parties were severely eroded from within by class-collaborationist practices. Business unionism, electioneering, and horse-trading in bourgeois legislatures were standard operating procedures for the majority of party leaders, trade-union officials, and parliamentary deputies in the Second International. In their daily practice, the parties of the International more and more placed the reform of capitalism through legislation, deals with the bosses, and cooperation with "their own" governments above any orientation toward educating and organizing the workers and farmers for a revolutionary struggle to conquer power. The International mobilized little active solidarity with the oppressed colonial peoples, and work to build parties in the colonial countries had a low priority.

The outbreak of the imperialist world slaughter in August

1914 revealed that the Second International had ceased to be an organization that reflected the interests of the broadest layers of the working class and others among the oppressed and exploited. The most prominent of its parties began openly acting as instruments of the ruling class in its attacks against the workers in their own countries and worldwide.

Three years of war brought European capitalism to the breaking point. The Russian revolution of February 1917 overthrew tsarism, and in October 1917 the workers and peasants under the leadership of the Bolshevik Party established a revolutionary government. The victory in October won millions of working people around the world to a revolutionary perspective, and won the best of their leaders to the international communist movement.

The establishment of the revolutionary workers' and peasants' republic in Russia transformed politics, shifting the world relationship of class forces to the advantage of the working class and its allies. The young Soviet republic was an ally of revolutionary struggles both in the industrially advanced capitalist countries and in the colonial nations oppressed by imperialism.

The triumph in Russia made possible the launching of the Communist International in March 1919 at a congress held in Moscow. The Marxist program could now be enriched to encompass the world's first experience of the successful overthrow of capitalism by the workers and peasants, and of a revolutionary government of the exploited.

The international working-class movement, Lenin explained, "now rests on an unprecedentedly firm base"—the conquest of power by the workers and peasants of Soviet Russia.

The new International's program was founded on its understanding of the imperialist epoch as a new phase of world capitalism: a period of interimperialist wars, of colonial uprisings, of civil war and socialist revolution.

The Comintern recognized the vanguard role that the colonially oppressed peoples of Asia, Africa, and Latin America were beginning to play in the world revolution. With aid from Soviet Russia, the Comintern held, the exploited peasants and small working classes in even the most economically backward countries could successfully organize soviets and follow the revolutionary road to power over the exploiters. It was vital to begin building communist parties in these oppressed nations, so that the working class could be organized to give consistent revolutionary leadership to the democratic revolution against imperialist domination and landlord-capitalist exploitation.

In line with this perspective, Lenin and other central Comintern leaders were determined that the new organization would break from the pattern of the Second International, which had, "in reality, only recognized the white race," as one Comintern document put it. The Second International had been largely limited to parties in the industrialized countries in Europe and North America, or with populations of European origin; even in these countries, its parties had few members from oppressed nationalities. The Comintern, on the other hand, gave assistance and encouragement to revolutionists in building parties in the colonial world. Its parties in the imperialist countries began to orient to recruiting Black and Asian working people, and toilers of other oppressed nationalities. It acted on the slogan, "Workers of the world and oppressed nations, unite!"

Millions of working people were attracted to the parties of the Communist International during these years. Delegates and observers at early Comintern gatherings came from divergent political backgrounds: some from the Bolshevik-led revolutionary left wing that had broken from the Second International, some who had held centrist views prior to the Russian revolution, some influenced by anarcho-syndicalism, and some just passing through on their way back toward reformism. The meetings of the International heard wide-ranging debates on the issues they were deciding that enriched the participants' understanding of Marxism.

The Communist International was guided by a team of leaders of the Soviet Communist Party politically led by Lenin. These included Nikolai Bukharin, Karl Radek, Leon Trotsky, Gregory Zinoviev, and others. Under this leadership, the International became a great school of revolutionary strategy and tactics.

The Comintern developed a transitional strategy for the working class and its allies, aimed at building a bridge between their present struggles and consciousness, and the revolutionary fight by the workers and farmers to conquer political power.

It discussed and adopted reports and resolutions on revolutionary work in the trade unions; on how communists use bourgeois elections and parliaments; on the fight against the exploitation of agricultural workers, peasants oppressed by landlordism, and working farmers; on the national liberation struggle of peoples oppressed by imperialism; on the fight for the emancipation of women; on the struggle of Blacks against racism in the United States and worldwide; and on many other questions important to revolutionary working-class strategy. Most importantly, the Comintern acted on these decisions.

The October 1917 revolution in Russia was followed by several years of upsurge in the international workers' struggle, with its high points between 1918 and 1920. With the defeat of revolutionary struggles in Germany and elsewhere in Central Europe during those years, however, the international workers' movement went into a period of retreat throughout the rest of the 1920s.

Lenin's death at the beginning of 1924 coincided with the end of the period during which the Communist International on the whole charted a revolutionary course along the lines developed by the Bolshevik team he had led. Over the next decade, the Comintern came to reflect the setbacks of the world revolution, an expansion of the world capitalist economy, and the rising influence of a privileged bureaucratic caste identified with Joseph Stalin in the Soviet Communist Party and workers' state. By the second half of the 1930s it had charted a class-collaborationist course, promoting "popular front" alliances between Communist and capitalist parties in the "democratic" imperialist countries. The Comintern was dissolved during the Second World War as a concession by the Soviet government to its imperialist allies in the war.

This counterrevolutionary course was the opposite of that charted by Lenin—the course that led to the founding of the Communist International and guided its activity from 1919 through 1923. The Comintern's achievements during these first five years, which will be recorded in these volumes, stand as an almost inexhaustible source of political lessons for revolutionary workers today.

*

This volume opens with proceedings from the 1907 Stuttgart congress of the Second International. The positions advanced by internationalists on three questions debated at that congress were to remain at the center of the Bolshevik-led fight for a revolutionary International throughout the next decade. These questions were posed by the opening of a new epoch in the history of world capitalism—the rise of modern imperialism.

The first question was how the International and its parties should respond to the growing threat of imperialist war. The second was how the International should respond to colonialism. The third was the position that Socialists should take on capitalist attempts to whip up racist sentiments against immigrant workers. As Lenin explained in his article on the Stuttgart congress, which appears in the first chapter of this volume, these debates revealed profound differences in the International, and showed that significant layers within it were giving ground to imperialist pressures.

The Stuttgart conference is also an appropriate place to begin a volume on Lenin's struggle for a revolutionary International, since it was there, following the 1905 revolution in Russia, that Lenin and the Bolsheviks began the process of drawing around them a revolutionary Marxist current in the Second International. This included efforts to deepen their collaboration with consistent internationalists in the German party such as Rosa Luxemburg. The rest of this volume traces the development of the initially small internationalist current through big tests in the world class struggle and a process of political debate, differentiation, and clarification. Lenin and the Bolshevik leadership team around him laid the programmatic foundations, led the political struggle, and took the organizational initiatives that guided this process forward over the next decade. Out of these efforts came the embryo of the Communist International.

The years after the 1907 Stuttgart congress saw the Second International increasingly dominated by its class-collaborationist wing. Seeking to reverse this process, the small left wing counted on further uprisings like that of 1905 in Russia, and above all on victorious revolutions, to provide the impetus that could make the Socialist International into a revolutionary instrument that would advance the historic interests of the exploited and oppressed.

Under the leadership of Lenin, the Bolsheviks during the decade before World War I built a workers' party in Russia with a strategy for the revolutionary overthrow of tsarist autocracy and landlordism, and the conquest of power by the proletariat and peasantry. This program had been tested in Russia's tumultuous revolutionary upheaval of 1905–1907, and in the subsequent rise of mass struggles after 1911. The party was firmly based in the industrial working class in

Russia, and it had developed an experienced cadre of party leaders.

During these years, a revolutionary left wing also began to emerge in the German party.

Overall, however, revolutionary forces remained a minority in the International, and were not able to halt its degeneration.

When the First World War broke out in August 1914, the opportunist leaders of Socialist parties broke with every proletarian internationalist principle that had been adopted by congresses of the Second International. Most of the International's best-known leaders now became open chauvinists.

These social-chauvinists—the term used by Lenin to describe them—rallied the toilers under the banners of the imperialist states and sent them into fratricidal combat against their brothers and sisters of other countries. They supported the repression by "their" governments of colonial revolts.

The Socialist International had collapsed. Bankrupt as a leadership of the world working class, it had become, in the words of Rosa Luxemburg, "a stinking corpse."

A minority of leaders in the Second International refused to go along with the chauvinist betrayal of August 1914. Russian and Serbian Socialist parliamentary deputies voted against financial appropriations for the war budget ("war credits") at the outbreak of the war. The German revolutionist Karl Liebknecht did the same in December 1914, as did the Italian Socialist Party when Italy entered the war in 1915.

Only the Bolsheviks, however, called for a complete, public, and definitive break with the Second International, as part of an uncompromising struggle not only against the open social-chauvinist majority, but against those centrist forces who sought to maintain ties with these betrayers in hopes that the bankrupt International could be revived at the war's end.

The Bolsheviks fought from the outset to bring together,

around a revolutionary program, the forces for a new International. While other revolutionary currents contributed cadres and important experiences to the movement that would accomplish this goal five years later, Lenin led the political struggle for that revolutionary perspective throughout the war. The Bolsheviks continued on their revolutionary course in Russia, which was to make possible the October 1917 victory and lay the foundation for a new, a communist, International.

The first international conferences of Socialists who sought to rally workers against the imperialist war took place in 1915. The most important, held in September 1915 in Zimmerwald, Switzerland, launched an international organization, often called the "Zimmerwald movement." This Zimmerwald conference brought together Socialist opponents of the imperialist war with sharply divergent positions. It included centrists who combined pacifist proposals for ending the war with continued support for "national defense" and who were still voting for war credits. It also included a left wing, led by the Bolsheviks.

Lenin responded to the call for the 1915 conference by organizing what became known as the Zimmerwald Left, the immediate forerunner of the Communist International. Composed of several revolutionary currents, its program advanced the struggle for the new International and called on workers and peasants to utilize the war crisis to advance the revolutionary struggle for the overthrow of capitalist rule. "Civil war not civil peace" was its slogan.

The appeal issued by the Zimmerwald conference for the workers of the world to unite in international solidarity against the war and for socialism helped inspire workers to resume their struggles. The Zimmerwald majority, however, refused to call for a definitive break with the Second International.

The Zimmerwald Left was led by the Bolsheviks as a

public alternative to this centrist course of the Zimmerwald majority. It published and circulated worldwide its own documents, which had been rejected at the 1915 conference.

By the end of 1916, where the collection of documents in this volume concludes, any progressive role of the Zimmerwald movement had been exhausted. As Lenin insisted, it had become an obstacle to rebuilding a proletarian internationalist leadership.

As the war raged on, the imperialist governments increased their attacks on working people, and the workers of warring and neutral countries mounted increasingly combative mass resistance. By the beginning of 1917, many Socialist parties, including the German party, had split under these pressures, and others were clearly headed in that direction. The revolutionary Socialists, taking advantage of growing class polarization, strengthened their links with the working masses and won new forces. The Zimmerwald Left made progress in convincing more revolutionists on the centrality of the political issues separating it from the centrist Zimmerwald majority.

Lenin waged a political struggle to influence and win the revolutionary Spartacist group in Germany led by Rosa Luxemburg and Karl Liebknecht. The Bolsheviks also made persistent proposals for collaboration to the Russian revolutionists around the left-centrist Paris newspaper *Nashe Slovo* edited by Leon Trotsky. These forces were not part of the Zimmerwald Left during the period covered in this volume. The majority of them, however, responded to the revolutionary events in Russia in 1917 by, for the first time, charting a course that turned toward the revolutionary perspectives that Lenin and the Bolsheviks had been fighting for throughout the imperialist war, and rallied to the Comintern in 1919. Many became members of the Comintern's leadership bodies.

The collection of documents in this volume ends on the eve of the Russian revolution of February 1917, which toppled tsarism and opened a European-wide revolutionary upsurge. The establishment of the workers' and peasants' republic in October 1917 showed millions of workers the way out of the death trap of imperialist war. The outbreak of the German revolution in November 1918 brought the war to an abrupt conclusion and led to the formation, the following month, of the Communist Party of Germany. After the Communist Party of Soviet Russia, the new German CP was the second large workers' party to rally to the banner of the new International.

When the Communist International was founded in March 1919, it received a declaration from participants in the Zimmerwald movement that "everything in [the Zimmerwald association] that was truly revolutionary is passing over to the Communist International." This first congress of the Comintern formally registered the dissolution of the Zimmerwald movement. (The statement heard by the congress and its resolution on Zimmerwald are appended to this introduction.)

*

The documents in this book present a representative selection of the debates and discussion through which the Bolsheviks began the process that culminated in the founding of the Comintern. Documents from the years before 1914 focus on the Stuttgart congress and the German party, where the conflicting positions in the Second International were most clearly expressed. After August 1914, its focus shifts to the forces that were to form the Zimmerwald Left, the debates among its components, and between it and other currents that were eventually to form part of the founding cadres of the Comintern.

Documents from these years are mainly drawn from the

debate among revolutionists in Germany and Russia. It was in these two countries that the most important attempts were made during the war to build revolutionary organizations. Emphasis has been given to the writings of those who were ultimately to join in launching the new International: the Bolsheviks themselves, who led the process; the Spartacists in Germany; Leon Trotsky among the left-centrist forces in Russia; and others.

The availability of documents in other English-language editions has been taken into account in selecting material for this volume. Selections from the extensive debate on the right of nations to self-determination that took place during this period, for example, have been limited because this material is readily available in several other forms. In the same way, Lenin's *Imperialism, the Highest Stage of Capitalism* has not been included since it is the most widely republished book of this period and is easily available. It is assumed that the present collection will be studied together with the corresponding volumes of Lenin's *Collected Works*.

A Marxist analysis of the evolution of the Second International and the U.S. Socialist Party in this period can be found in Farrell Dobbs's two-volume work, *Revolutionary Continuity*, also published by Pathfinder Press. Dobbs's two volumes served as a guide in preparing the present collection, and they can be profitably studied together with it.

*

New translations have been made of all the documents in this collection, with the exception of the writings of Lenin, where the standard translations in the most recent edition of the *Collected Works* have been reproduced without change. Occasional informational material by the editor has been inserted in square brackets in the documents.

A running commentary explains the historical background to the documents that have been selected, so that the documents can tell the story of Lenin's fight for a revolutionary International in a way understandable to readers who are not acquainted with the history of this period.

In some cases footnotes by the authors of selected documents have been preserved. These are indicated by asterisks (*) and are printed at the end of the selections. Endnotes by the editor, giving the source of selected material and some explanatory notes, are printed at the end of the book. A glossary of individuals, publications, and political currents mentioned in this volume is provided. The chronology lists important dates related to documents in this collection. Existing English-language editions of related material are indicated in the bibliography or the footnotes.

*

This book was made possible by a large number of collaborators who volunteered their time to collect source material and to translate it into English.

We wish in particular to acknowledge the assistance of Rudolf Segall, Lüko Willms, and the ISP-Verlag publishing house in Germany; the Socialist Workers Party and the *Berner Tagwacht* of Switzerland; Nat London in France; Aldo Lauria, Ethel Lobman, Alicia Muñoz, Art Sharon, and Bob Wilkinson in the United States, who shared in the research work and in obtaining source materials; and of Devon Parry.

The team of translators from Russian included Ron Allen, Robert Des Verney, Kenneth Eardley, Sonja Franeta, Joanne Holowchak, Jeff Jones, Steve Mitianin, and Marilyn Vogt.

Those sharing in the translation from German included Robert A. Cantrick, Robert Dees, Alex A. Koskinas, Ivan Licho, Markie Wilson, Peter Thierjung, Michael Tresidder, Duane Stilwell, Duncan Williams, and other collaborators in Canada, Switzerland, and the United States.

Will Reissner and Susan Wald helped translate from French, Ernest Harsch from Polish, and Mehdi Assar from Farsi.

John Riddell

EDITOR'S NOTE ON SECOND EDITION

Since the first edition of this work was published, many readers have pointed out errors and made suggestions for its improvement.

While the second edition of this book does not differ from the first in any substantial way, it does incorporate many such corrections. We wish to thank our readers for their suggestions.

MAY 1, 1986

DECLARATION TO THE FIRST CONGRESS OF THE COMMUNIST INTERNATIONAL ON ZIMMERWALD MARCH 1919

The Zimmerwald and Kienthal conferences were important at a time when it was vital to unify all the forces of the proletariat who were prepared to protest in any way against the imperialist slaughter. But along with the clearly communist forces, forces that were centrist, pacifist, and vacillating also entered the Zimmerwald Association. These centrist forces, as the Bern conference has shown, are now allying with the social patriots in the struggle against the revolutionary proletariat. Thus, they are exploiting Zimmerwald in the interests of reaction.

At the same time the communist movement is gaining strength in a number of countries. The struggle against the centrist forces who obstruct the development of the social revolution has become one of the most urgent tasks of the revolutionary proletariat.

The Zimmerwald Association has outlived its usefulness. Everything that was truly revolutionary in the Zimmerwald Association is passing over to the Communist International.

The undersigned participants in the Zimmerwald movement declare that they regard the Zimmerwald Association as dissolved, and call on the bureau of the Zimmerwald Conference to turn over all its documents to the Executive Committee of the Third International.

(Signed:) Christian Rakovsky, V.I. Lenin, Gregory Zinoviev, Leon Trotsky, Fritz Platten

RESOLUTION

Having received the report of Comrade Balabanoff, secretary of the Zimmerwald International Socialist Committee, and the declaration of comrades Rakovsky, Platten, Lenin, Trotsky, and Zinoviev, participants in the Zimmerwald Association, the First Congress of the Communist International resolves that the Zimmerwald Association be considered disbanded.

Chapter 1

The Stuttgart congress of 1907

Since the publication of the *Communist Manifesto* in 1848, its closing words, "Workers of the world, unite!" have inspired the struggle for international workers' unity. The manifesto had been written by Karl Marx and Frederick Engels for the Communist League and adopted as its program. The league, an international party, did not survive the decline of the workers' movement after the defeats of the revolutions of 1848–49. In 1864, however, a more ambitious attempt was made to establish the organizational unity of the international workers' movement through the launching of the International Working Men's Association, the First International. Under the leadership of Marx and Engels, the International brought together working-class socialists of different countries, provided an arena for testing different proposed working-class programs, and demonstrated in action the power of international solidarity. After the defeat in 1871 of the Paris Commune, the first attempt at a revolutionary dictatorship led by the working class, the International went into decline and split. It was ultimately dissolved in 1876.

The decades following the Paris Commune were a time of relative capitalist stability in Europe, free from major wars or social revolutions, and marked by rapid economic expansion. During the years 1870–1900 world oil output rose two and a half times, the railway network expanded four times, coal output five times, and steel production fifty-six times. Countries such as Germany and the United States joined Britain as major world industrial powers. The European and North American working class grew dramatically in size. In the United States and Russia, for example, the number of industrial workers grew more than three-fold during the last three decades of the nineteenth century. Workers were increasingly concentrated within large industrial enterprises.

These years witnessed a qualitative growth in the working-class movement in Europe and North America. The trade unions became mass organizations. In Britain trade union membership increased four times between 1876 and 1900, while in Germany union membership rose from the tens of thousands into the millions. Throughout Europe, Socialist parties were formed and gained mass influence. The most successful and politically authoritative of these was the Social Democratic Party of Germany (SPD), which came to encompass dozens of newspapers, hundreds of thousands of members, and millions of voters. Following Engels's death in 1895, international Social Democracy's most authoritative leaders came from the SPD: Wilhelm Liebknecht, August Bebel, and Karl Kautsky, all associates of Marx and Engels. The SPD won a reputation as the bastion of Marxist theory and practice within the international workers' movement.

During these years the working class in the leading capitalist countries was able to wage massive battles for political reforms and economic improvements, and win significant gains. During the last two decades of the 1800s their real wages rose by 30–50 percent.

With considerable help from Engels, several of the major Social Democratic parties in Europe launched the Second International at a congress in Paris on July 14, 1889—the 100th anniversary of the beginning of the Great French Revolution. For the next decade the International functioned only through party-to-party relations and through its congresses, which took place about every three years. In 1900 the International Socialist Bureau was established as the executive body to guide the work of the movement, although its decisions were only recommendations to the national parties.

From its inception, the Second International encompassed both revolutionary and opportunist trends. The long period of capitalist expansion and economic and political gains for sections of the working class strengthened the opportunist tendencies. In 1899 the debate between these currents won attention through two important events. The first was the entry of Alexandre Millerand, a French Socialist, into the capitalist government of France as minister of commerce. This provoked a sharp discussion on whether Socialists should share in governmental responsibility for administering the capitalist state. The second event was the open defense by German SPD leader Eduard Bernstein of the view that a gradual transition from capitalism to socialism could be achieved through the accumulation of electoral victories and legislative reforms. These reformist views, expressed in his book *Evolutionary Socialism,* became known as revisionism and stirred up a heated debate within the party. They were rejected by the SPD's 1899 congress.

Both these discussions were extended into the international arena, culminating in a debate and vote at the 1904 Amsterdam congress of the International, which decisively condemned both revisionism and the policy of participating in capitalist governments.

The outbreak of the Russian revolution in 1905 had an electrifying effect on the working class internationally. The first revolutionary uprising in Europe since 1871, its immediate aim was a democratic republic—the smashing of tsarist absolutism. The peasant masses threw themselves into that struggle, which promised them the land they wanted, and the upsurge quickly became countrywide in scope. The proletariat rapidly asserted its leadership as workers grasped the general strike as an effective means of struggle. Delegated councils of workers, called soviets, were established. An armed insurrection in Moscow brought the revolution to a climax at the end of 1905.

While the uprising was suppressed, and the blows of tsarist reaction led to the ebbing of the mass movement, the impact of the upsurge was felt throughout the world. Outside Europe, the reverberations were felt in revolutionary events over the next decade in Iran, China, and Turkey. In Austria, the Russian events helped spark a gigantic movement of mass demonstrations of hundreds of thousands which won the right of universal male suffrage. A strike wave spread across Europe that lasted until 1907, largely inspired by the Russian revolution. In Germany, it contributed to an upsurge of political and economic struggles by the working class, which had a radicalizing effect on a section of the Social Democratic Party. At its 1905 congress, the party adopted a resolution accepting mass protest strikes as a possible Socialist tactic.

❋

The congress of the International held in Stuttgart, Germany, August 18–24, 1907, was the largest and most imposing international Socialist gathering yet held. Organizing the congress in Germany was in itself a demonstration of strength against the despotic powers of the imperial government. (This challenge did not go without response. While the congress was still in session, the German government expelled British delegate Harry Quelch for referring to the Hague Peace Conference, which brought together the main imperialist governments, as a "thieves' kitchen.")

The congress began with an immense open-air rally attended by 60,000 people. Six speakers' platforms were set up so all might hear leaders of the International from different countries explain the aims of the congress and of the world Socialist movement.

In all, 884 delegates were registered; the largest delegations were from Germany (289), Great Britain (123), and France (78). Outside Europe, there were twenty-two delegates from the United States, three from Argentina, and one each from Japan, Australia, and South Africa.

On the agenda for debate at the congress were five topics: the colonial question, women's suffrage, the relationship between political parties and the trade unions, immigration and emigration of workers, and militarism and international conflicts. Delegates met in five commissions on August 20 and 21 for preliminary discussion of each of these topics.

The first point debated at the congress was the colonial question. The decades preceding 1907 had witnessed a feverish race by the imperialist powers to seize colonies and complete their division of the world's territories. This race had become one of the principal sources of the war danger. Most of the African continent and much of Asia was annexed outright by colonial powers in these years through many brutal wars against the colonial peoples. In addition, formally independent countries such as China and the Persian Empire were divided into "spheres of influence" that were economically controlled by the imperialist powers.

Of the main imperialist powers, Britain and France had long-established world empires while the United States, Germany, and Italy were now acquiring extensive colonial possessions. Austria-Hungary and Russia lacked overseas colonies, but in both of them a large section of the population was made up of subjugated nationalities.

The parties of the Second International were limited at this time to the advanced capitalist countries. After the Russian revolution of 1905 the first Socialist nuclei were established among the colonial peoples of Asia and Africa. Yet at the time of the Stuttgart congress the International remained by and large not a world, but a European movement, most of whose leaders thought of socialism in national or European terms.

Back in 1896 the London congress of the International had declared "in favor of the full autonomy of all nationalities and its sympathy with the workers of any country at present suffering under the yoke of military, national or other despotisms."[1] The

[NUMBERED ENDNOTES BEGIN ON PAGE 823.]

congress also had passed a resolution denouncing capitalist colonial expansion, but did not specify how its position for national autonomy applied to the colonial peoples.

The 1900 congress in Paris unanimously adopted a resolution from a special colonial commission, introduced by the Dutch Socialist Hendrick van Kol. The resolution stated that the exclusive objective of the colonial policy of the bourgeoisie was "to increase the profits of the capitalist class and to maintain the capitalist system by drawing blood and money from the proletarian producer via crimes and innumerable cruelties against peoples conquered by armed force." It declared that the proletariat had the duty to fight the bourgeoisie's colonial expansion by all the means at its disposal and to expose its atrocities. It also called on the International "to particularly further the formation of colonial Socialist parties affiliated to organisations in metropoles" and "to establish ties among the Socialist parties of different colonies."[2]

However, at the next congress, held at Amsterdam in 1904, van Kol argued for an opposing view. He presented a resolution that stated: "The new needs which will make themselves felt after the victory of the working class and its economic emancipation will make the possession of colonies necessary, even under the future socialist system of government." Van Kol asked the congress, "Can we abandon half the globe to the caprice of peoples still in their infancy, who leave the enormous wealth of the subsoil undeveloped and the most fertile parts of our planet uncultivated?"[3]

The resolution adopted by the Amsterdam congress neither endorsed nor clearly rejected van Kol's views. It proposed a series of measures to oppose the evils of colonialism and to reform colonial administration. It also indicated that the resolution of the colonial problem lay in the establishment of the self-government of the colonial peoples, and proposed that the indigenous inhabitants be provided with a degree of freedom and independence corresponding to their level of development, keeping in mind that the complete liberation of the colonies was the desired goal.

Linking independence with the colonies' level of development in this way was a retreat from the International's position, established in 1896, for national self-determination. Thus, while the congress gave an enthusiastic welcome to Dadabhai Naoroji, founder and president of the Indian National Congress, its resolution on India, while calling for Indian self-rule, specified that this was to be under continuing British sovereignty.

The same disagreements were quick to surface again three years later when discussion began in the colonial commission at Stuttgart. Eduard David and Georg Ledebour led off with introductory statements reflecting the two main contending views.

The commission on colonial policy[4]

EDUARD DAVID (GERMANY): . . . Our task here is to give clear direction for Social Democracy's practical work. We must condemn the kind of colonization carried out today by the bourgeois world. At the same time, we must use all of our influence to protect both the colonies' population and their natural resources from capitalist exploitation, in the same way that we struggle against capitalism for laws to protect workers in the civilized countries. Bebel expressed this thought in the German Reichstag, explaining that "it makes a big difference how colonial policy is conducted. If representatives of civilized countries come as liberators to the alien peoples in order to bring them the benefits of culture and civilization, then we Social Democrats will be the first to support such colonization as a civilizing mission."

I recommend that this point of view be taken into consideration in any resolution that we draft. . . .

Europe needs colonies. It does not have enough of them. Without colonies, we would be comparable from an economic standpoint to China. . . .

GEORG LEDEBOUR (GERMANY): Unfortunately I must speak against David and in a certain sense also against Bebel. Comrade David has missed the main point. As long as we have a capitalist world, colonial policy will exhibit the same abominable characteristics that we all condemn. David appears to believe that these atrocities are avoidable and are characteristic only of present-day colonial policies. That is a fundamental error.

To back up his viewpoint David read a supposed statement by Bebel. It does not come from an authoritative statement by Bebel, but from a remark made in passing in one of his many Reichstag speeches on colonial questions. As I understand Bebel's position, he would vigorously protest David's interpretation of his words. Simply picking a sentence out of context is unacceptable. In itself, the sentence certainly obliges me to polemicize against Bebel as well. It can be interpreted to mean that the existing horrors of colonialism can be avoided in today's capitalist states. But present-day colonialism is the inevitable result of capitalism. Only through the resistance of the exploited themselves can these brutalities be lessened, but the colonial peoples cannot accomplish this because their capacity to resist is virtually nonexistent.

The resolution must emphasize that we do not expect capitalist colonization to exercise any civilizing mission. We are principled opponents of all exploitation and oppression in our own countries, and as such must fight against the much greater exploitation in the colonies. With this declaration of principle at its head, our resolution can then further explain that as a minority of German society, we are for the greatest possible protection of the native peoples through the creation of colonial laws protecting their rights. We all agree on this. But here is the main thing: nobody must get the idea from our resolution that we think capitalism is compatible with any kind of colonialism except that marked by terror and atrocities. . . .

[Following Ledebour's remarks, a draft resolution was jointly introduced by Ledebour, van Kol, and Wibaut which, while condemning the colonial policy then being carried out by capitalism, made no statement on capitalist colonial policy in general.

[The Belgian delegate Terwagne then introduced an amendment to add this passage: "The congress therefore does not reject in principle every colonial policy. Under a Socialist regime, colonization could be a force for civilization."]

MODESTE TERWAGNE (BELGIUM): . . . I speak for the minority of my party. For us Belgians the question is: Should we leave the Congo in its current state, or do we want to better conditions there? . . .[5] Do not close the door to the future! If from one day to the next colonial production were ended, industry would be seriously damaged. It logically follows that men utilize all the riches of the globe, wherever they may be situated. . . . I therefore recommend the amendment which I introduced and which was, moreover, in the original draft of the text proposed by van Kol. . . .

An additional amendment, introduced by David, proposed to add the following sentence: "Whereas socialism aims to put the productive forces of the entire world in the service of humanity and raise peoples of all colors and languages to the highest level of civilization, the congress regards the colonial idea as such as an integral part of the Socialist movement's universal goals for civilization."

After further discussion, David's amendment was rejected and Terwagne's was incorporated into the draft resolution. This draft was submitted to the congress by the majority of commission members, whose reporter was van Kol.

A minority of the commission disagreed with this draft, and proposed amendments to delete the first and last paragraphs of the majority draft and add a substitute passage. The following is the text of the majority draft.

Draft resolutions on colonialism

COMMISSION MAJORITY PROPOSAL

Socialism strives to develop the productive forces of the entire globe and to lead all peoples to the highest form of civilization. The congress therefore does not reject in principle every colonial policy. Under a Socialist regime, colonization could be a force for civilization.

The congress reaffirms the resolutions on the colonial question of the Paris (1900) and Amsterdam (1904) congresses. It rejects once again the current methods of colonization, which are fundamentally capitalist in nature and serve no purpose other than conquering and subjugating alien peoples in order to relentlessly exploit them for the benefit of an insignificant minority. At the same time the proletariat in the capitalist countries must bear increasing burdens.

As opponents of all exploitation of man by man and as defenders of all the oppressed regardless of race, the congress condemns this policy of plunder and conquest, which shamelessly applies the principle that "might makes right," and tramples underfoot the rights of the conquered peoples.

This colonial policy increases the danger of military entanglements between the colonizing states and increases the burdens imposed by army and fleet.

The financial outlays for the colonies, whether accountable to imperialism or to colonial economic development, should be borne solely by those who profit from the plundering of these alien peoples and whose wealth originates from them.

Finally the congress declares that Socialist parliamentary deputies have the obligation to use the parliaments to fight against the merciless exploitation and bondage that prevails in all existing colonies.

To this end the deputies must advocate reforms in order to improve the lot of the native peoples. They must combat all infringements on the rights of the native peoples, including their exploitation and enslavement. They must work with all available means for the education of these peoples to independence.

The deputies of the Socialist parties should propose to their governments that they conclude a treaty and create a colonial law that would protect the rights of the native peoples and be guaranteed by all the treaty signatories.

The following amendments to the majority draft were proposed by the minority of the colonial commission.

AMENDMENTS BY THE COMMISSION MINORITY

1. Strike out the first paragraph.

2. Insert as the first paragraph:

The congress considers that by its inherent nature, capitalist colonial policy must lead to enslavement, forced labor, or the extermination of the native population of the colonized regions.

The civilizing mission that capitalist society claims to serve is no more than a veil for its lust for conquest and exploitation. Only Socialist society will offer the possibility to all peoples of developing fully to civilization.

Capitalist colonial policy, instead of increasing the world's productive forces, destroys the wealth of those countries where this policy is carried out by enslaving and impoverishing the native peoples as well as by waging murderous and devastating wars. It thus slows down and hinders even the development of trade and the export of industrial products of the civilized states.

The congress condemns the barbaric methods of capitalist colonization. In the interests of the development of the productive forces it demands a policy that guarantees peaceful, cultural development and that puts the natural resources of the earth at the service of the further development of all of humanity.

3. Strike out the last paragraph.

Submitted by: Comrades Georg Ledebour (Germany), Emanuel Wurm (Germany), Henri de la Porte (France), Alexandre Bracke (France), and Karski [Julian Marchlewski] (Poland).

A resolution on India was submitted by the British delegation. Bhikajee Kama, who represented the Indian National Congress at Stuttgart, introduced the resolution.

ON BRITISH RULE IN INDIA

Whereas it corresponds to our ideal of a social order that no people be subject to any despotic or tyrannical form of government, the congress states its conviction that the maintenance of English rule over India is a genuine misfortune for India and clearly and most seriously contradicts its real interests. The congress declares it the duty of all the friends of freedom throughout the world to aid the liberation movement of that fifth part of humanity who inhabit this unfortunate land.

Congress debate on colonial policy

HENDRICK VAN KOL (NETHERLANDS): . . . There were two opposing tendencies in the commission. One was negative and the other positive; one theoretical and the other practical and action-oriented.

Our duty is to pursue a policy of action. Before 1870 we were a small group and still believed in the theory of capitalist collapse. Then we thought it enough to simply protest against capitalism, point out to our followers their dreadful sufferings, and explain the sharp contrast between the reality they knew and the paradise of the future. Now we recognize we must also carry out actions against capitalism. We must have a program of reform, and that applies to colonial policy as well. . . . Surely Ledebour will agree that in Europe capitalism was unavoidable—a necessary and inevitable stage of development. Should not the same also be true about capitalism in the colonies? . . .

The horrors of colonialism are certainly frightful. But it is not true that we are unable to end them and improve colonial policy. We Dutch are one of the oldest colonizing peoples. But we have reached the point where murder, torture, burning, and plundering are no longer everyday occurrences in the Dutch colonies. Ledebour's plans for the future, by contrast, are quite utopian. He cannot be certain that a future colonial policy based on humane principles will always be entirely limited to peaceful means. . . .

The minority resolution also denies that the productive forces of the colonies can be developed through the capitalist colonial policy. I do not understand at all how a thinking person can say that. Simply consider the colonization of the United States of North America. Without it the native peoples there would today still be living in the most backward social conditions.

Does Ledebour want to take away the raw materials, indispensable for modern society, which the colonies can offer? Does he want to give up the vast resources of the colonies, even if only for the present? Do those German, French, and Polish delegates who signed the minority resolution want to accept responsibility for simply abolishing the present colonial system? As long as humanity has existed there have been colonies, and I think that they will exist for a long time yet. Surely there are few Socialists who think that colonies will be unnecessary in the future social order. Although we do not need to discuss this question today, I still ask Ledebour: does he have the courage now, under capitalism, to give up the colonies?

Perhaps he can also tell us what he would do about the overpopulation of Europe. Where would the people who must emigrate go, if not to the colonies? What does Ledebour want to do with the growing production of European industry if he does not want to create new export markets in the colonies? And does he as a Social Democrat want to shirk his duty to work continually for the education and further advancement of the backward peoples? . . .

Especially for Germany's sake, I regret that the Social Democracy there has limited itself to questioning the need for colonies and the benefits they bring. You saw in the last election campaign how the masses were hypnotized by the thought of the benefits to be gained from the colonies—not only the petty bourgeoisie but also the industrial workers. . . .[6]

The task of the congress is to see that the hope of a better future is offered to the millions of unfortunate peoples in the colonies through the practical work of the Social Democracy. *(British and Dutch delegates applaud)* . . .

EDUARD BERNSTEIN (GERMANY): . . . We must get away from the utopian notion of simply abandoning the colonies. The ultimate consequence of such a view would be to give the United States back to the Indians. *(Commotion)* The colonies are there; we must come to terms with that. Socialists too should acknowledge the need for civilized peoples to act somewhat like guardians of the uncivilized. Lassalle and Marx recognized this. In the third volume of *Capital* Marx wrote: "The earth does not belong to one people, but to all of humanity. Every people must administer it for the good of humanity."[7] And Lassalle once said: "The right of a people to its own development is as little an absolute right as any you will find. It is tied to the condition that there is some development. But peoples who do not develop may justifiably be subjugated by peoples who have achieved civilization." . . . Our economies are based, in large measure, on the extraction from the colonies of products that the native peoples had no idea how to use.

DAVID: . . . The minority says that there is absolutely no way to improve upon present colonial policy, that it invariably harms both the native peoples and the colonizing country. Then to be consistent the minority must advocate that the colonies be abolished. *("Quite right!")*

LEDEBOUR: That is what we want! *(Enthusiastic shouts of: "Hear! Hear!")*

DAVID: . . . Now if the partisans of this point of view were actually in the position to abolish colonies as such, it would mean giving them back to the native peoples. What then would occur in the colonies? They would not experience humane rule but a return to barbarism. *("Quite right!")* . . .

The colonies as well must go through a stage of capitalist development. There too you cannot simply leap from savagery to socialism. *("Very good!")* Nowhere is humanity spared the painful passage through capitalism. The scientific outlook of Karl Marx makes very clear that this stage is a precondition for the socialist organization of society.

KARSKI [JULIAN MARCHLEWSKI] (POLAND): . . . David has asserted the right of one nation to exercise tutelage over another. But we Poles know the real meaning of this tutelage, since both the Russian tsar and the Prussian government have acted as our guardians. *("Very good!")* . . . David quotes Marx to support his view that every nation must go through capitalism. But he is not right to do so here. What Marx said was that countries that had already begun capitalist development would have to continue the process through to completion. But he never said that this was an absolute precondition for all nations. . . .[8]

We Socialists understand that there are other civilizations besides simply that of capitalist Europe. We have absolutely no grounds to be conceited about our so-called civilization nor to impose it on the Asiatic peoples with their ancient civilization. *("Bravo!")* David thinks that the colonies would sink back into barbarism if left to themselves. In India's case that hardly seems likely. Rather I picture that if independent, India would continue to profit from the influence of European civilization in its future development and it would grow in this way to its fullest potential. Therefore I ask you to vote for the minority resolution. . . .

KARL KAUTSKY (GERMANY): . . . How is it that the notion of a "Socialist" colonial policy has found so many followers in our ranks here, when it appears to me to be a logical contradiction? Until now we have never heard anything about a "Socialist" colonial policy. I attribute its popularity to the newness of the idea, which has suddenly sprung up overnight. Further it is linked to other ideas that are quite correct and necessary but are connected only superficially with colonial policy and in reality have absolutely nothing to do with it.

Among these are two ideas which cannot be rejected out of hand. First is the idea that we cannot simply ignore the colonies. We have certain tasks to carry out there, and we must act as much as possible in a positive manner. As far as I know, nobody has disputed this. Our tasks in the colonies are fundamentally just the same as at home. They are to protect the people against capitalist exploitation and against the burden of bureaucracy and militarism; in other words, to advance policies for democracy and social welfare. That however is something quite different from colonialism. Colonial policy signifies the conquest and seizure by force of an overseas land. I contest the notion that democracy and social policy have anything to do with conquest and foreign rule. *("Bravo!")*

It was further said that we have a civilizing role to play and so must go out to these savage peoples as teachers and counselors. Yes, of course we must do that. I agree completely with what Bebel said in the Reichstag. We ourselves have an interest in seeing that these primitive peoples attain a higher level of civilization. But I disagree that a colonial policy, the conquest and seizure of foreign lands, is necessary for that. Indeed I maintain that a colonial policy is fundamentally detrimental to the ability to play a civilizing role. *("Quite right!")*

It is a widespread misconception that backward peoples are hostile to the civilization brought them by more advanced peoples. On the contrary all of our experience shows that when we approach the savages in a friendly manner, they willingly accept the tools and aid of the higher civilization. But if we come to oppress and enslave them, if they are to be brought under the tutelage of some despotism, no matter how benevolent, they will be mistrustful. Then they will reject the foreign civilization along with the foreign domination. Then it will come to wars and devastation. Everywhere we see this colonial policy practiced, it produces rebellion and degradation of the people. Even a Socialist regime could not change this at all. It would likewise be obliged to view the colonies as alien bodies and establish foreign domination over them. If we want to have a civilizing effect on the primitive peoples then it is first necessary to win their confidence. And we will only win it by giving them their freedom. *("Bravo.")*

Bernstein wants to persuade us that the policy of conquest is a law of nature. I am quite astonished that he defended here the theory that there are two groups of peoples, one destined to rule and the other to be ruled; that there are peoples who, like children, are incapable of governing themselves. That is only a variation on the old refrain, the postulate of all despotism, that some people are born into this world to be riders, with spurs on their feet, and others with saddles on their backs to carry them. . . .

Bernstein's reference to Marx is incorrect. Marx certainly said that the earth belongs to the human race. But it is not the human race that is carrying out a colonial policy today. *("Very good!")* Marx did not say that the earth belongs to the capitalist nations. *("Very good!" Speaking time has run out)* In conclusion I ask you not to accept the introductory paragraph. It is quite new, has not been given sufficient consideration, and contradicts our whole socialist and democratic way of thinking. *("Quite right!")* You must at least give us time to discuss it thoroughly and give it adequate consideration. . . .

VAN KOL: I had not planned to speak. But now that Kautsky has thrown the entire weight of his knowledge and international reputation into the scales, I must try to refute his arguments.

Various comrades have said that there is no way to improve the colonial economies. That is false and contradicts the history of colonial policy. Through our Socialist activity in the Dutch parliament we have achieved significant advantages for our colonies. Why should we help only the workers of Europe and not those of other parts of the earth? Arrayed against us in Europe are mighty forces of capitalism. Why should we not also take up the struggle against capitalism in other continents? Nowhere else could we achieve easier and bigger victories than there.

Ledebour said the majority's efforts are reactionary. I simply do not understand how he as a man of science can fail to recognize that the colonies must first pass through a stage of capitalist development before you can begin to think of socialism there. So we are working for the revolutionary development of the colonies in order to facilitate the transformation of the feudal state into a modern one, through capitalism to socialism. A leap from barbarism to socialism is impossible. *("Very true!")* To deny this is not only unscientific, but stupid and shortsighted. Why in God's name should we not be able to raise constructive demands for this development just as we do for the questions of militarism and the tax laws? . . .

Kautsky maintains the thesis that "colonial policy is conquest, is imperialism." This formula is completely wrong. You should learn better grammar! Today, to be sure, colonial policy is imperialist. But it does not *have to be.* It can be democratic as well. In any case it is a grave error of Kautsky's to put colonial policy conceptually on a par with imperialism. I hope he will see that this is unjustified and that he will strive to make good the error.

Kautsky said that we must win the confidence of the native peoples. How does he hope to win the confidence of millions of people of other skin colors if he does nothing for them? *("Very good!")* We in Holland have the duty and the right to tell the comrades of other countries about our experiences. We Dutch Socialists have gained the confidence of millions of Javanese. But in Africa the people know nothing about the German Social Democracy because until now it has not done its duty. If you want to win the confidence of the native peoples then you must actively engage yourselves in the colonial question.

The learned Kautsky made matters even worse with his advice on how to develop the colonies industrially. We are supposed to take the machines and tools to Africa! A theoretical pipedream. That's supposed to civilize the country! Suppose that we bring a machine to the savages of central Africa, what will they do with it? Perhaps they will start up a war dance around it *(Loud laughter)* or increase by one the number of their innumerable holy idols. *(Laughter)* Perhaps we should send some Europeans to run the machines. What the native peoples would do with them, I do not know. But perhaps Kautsky and I will make the attempt. Perhaps theory and practice will then go hand in hand into that savage land with the tools and machines. Perhaps the natives will destroy our machines. Perhaps they will kill us or even eat us and then I fear that *(Rubbing his belly)* given my superior corporeal development I would have precedence over Kautsky. *(Laughter)* If we Europeans go there with tools and machines, we would be defenseless victims of the natives. Therefore we must go there with weapons in hand, even if Kautsky calls that imperialism. *("Very true!" from a part of the hall)*

Furthermore the natives suffer now under the tyrannical rule of individual princes. They are nearly defenseless against these princes and are exploited in the most inhumane manner. I am dubious whether a fighting proletariat will arise there under such conditions. The natives are not aware of any needs. They run around naked, without clothes, and nourish themselves from what nature offers them. Consequently they have capitalism in its most dreadful form and no proletariat that can resist it. No, in such conditions, where no law offers protection either for the natives or for immigrants, it is impossible to develop the economy in Kautsky's fashion.

BHIKAJEE KAMA (INDIA): I bring the Socialists assembled here the fraternal greetings of countless thousands of Indians, who suffer under the brutal yoke of British despotism. India pays a heavy price for British capitalist rule. Much has been said here about economic questions. What then is the economic situation of India? Each year India must pay thirty-five million pounds sterling to Britain, and not a penny of it finds its way back to India. This economic relationship causes the hunger and desperate poverty of an immense population, countless epidemics, and a death rate that has risen to an unspeakable level.

I address here the tribunal of human justice. What is socialism, if not justice? And if there is justice, why must millions of unfortunate Indians endure such agony? *(Loud applause)* India is a possession of the British crown, a subjugated country ruled by despotism and unbearable tyranny, inhabited by a fifth of the world's population. I call on the congress to raise its protest against this vicious tyranny. *(Applause)* . . . India is too poor to be able to send delegates to the international congress. We extend our sympathy to the Russian people and offer the Russian freedom fighters our fraternal greetings. *(Stormy applause)* . . . I call on you to adopt our resolution. *(Applause)* Indians demand their human rights and their autonomy. We want the right to self-determination, we demand justice and the right to govern ourselves. *(Loud applause)*

PAUL SINGER (CHAIRMAN): We cannot consider the resolution on British rule in India because it was not previously submitted to the international bureau. But I believe I can say that both the bureau and the congress agree with the general direction of this resolution. *("Bravo!")* In addition, the proposed resolution would do no more than reaffirm the previous decisions of the Brussels and Amsterdam congresses.

That closes the discussion.

[The congress then proceeded to a vote. The amendments proposed by the commission minority were adopted 127 votes to 108. The resolution on India was not put to a vote.

[In the vote on the colonialism resolution as amended, the transcript continues:]

A commotion broke out in the German delegation, because David initially registered its votes *against* the resolution. This aroused loud protests, and Singer then took a vote of the German delegates. A large majority voted "yes."

The resolution was so adopted by the vote of all delegates except those from the Netherlands, who abstained.

Immigration and emigration

The attitude of Socialists to the peoples of the colonial world received further discussion under the agenda point on immigration and emigration. The parties of the Second International had always vigorously protested the mistreatment and exploitation of immigrants by capitalism, as well as the attempts to manipulate them to break the unity of the working class. However, many Socialists and trade unionists succumbed to the pressure of the capitalist class and fell in line with its efforts to promote antagonism against immigrants and racism against nonwhite peoples. Thus a resolution calling for restricting the immigration of "backward races" was submitted to the International's 1904 Amsterdam congress. Sponsored by Morris Hillquit, a prominent leader of the Socialist Party of the United States, along with delegates from Australia and the Dutch delegate van Kol, the resolution raised such an uproar that it was withdrawn.

U.S. Socialists were sharply divided on this question. Right-wing Socialist Victor Berger expressed the racism that infected the party when he warned in 1907 that the country would soon have five million "yellow men" invading the country every year. If something was not done at once, Berger said, "this country is absolutely sure to become a black-and-yellow country within a few generations."[9] The party's National Committee went on record for exclusionary measures against nonwhite immigrants.

Revolutionists carried out a stubborn struggle within the Socialist Party against this view. Eugene Debs later summarized their outlook as follows:

"Away with the 'tactics' which require the exclusion of the oppressed and suffering slaves who seek these shores with the hope of bettering their wretched condition and are driven back under the cruel lash of expediency by those who call themselves

Socialists in the name of a movement whose proud boast it is that it stands uncompromisingly for the oppressed and downtrodden of all the earth. These poor slaves have just as good a right to enter here as even the authors of this report who now seek to exclude them. The only difference is that the latter had the advantage of a little education and had not been as cruelly ground and oppressed, but in point of principle there is no difference, the motive of all being precisely the same, and if the convention which meets in the name of Socialism should discriminate at all it should be in favor of the miserable races who have borne the heaviest burdens and are most nearly crushed to earth."[10]

In March 1907 the Socialist Party National Executive Committee passed an immigration resolution, later adopted by the National Committee, for submission to the upcoming Stuttgart congress. While it urged the Socialist parties to educate immigrants about socialism and trade unionism, the resolution called on them "to combat with all means at their command the willful importation of cheap foreign labor calculated to destroy labor organizations, to lower the standard of living of the working class, and to retard the ultimate realization of socialism."[11]

The following is excerpted from the discussion on this question in the commission on immigration and emigration at the Stuttgart congress.

The immigration commission[12]

MANUEL UGARTE (ARGENTINA): We Argentine comrades raised the question of immigration and emigration at this congress for the following reasons. We want to combat only artificial immigration: that is, immigration carried out by capitalist government agencies to obtain cheap labor to compete with organized workers. Our comrades also demand measures against the shipping companies' exploitation of emigrants.

This is not a racial question, and the resolution is not anti-Chinese or anti-Japanese. Argentina should be open to all workers. But workers should be advised of the working and living conditions of any countries to which they wish to emigrate. The Argentine comrades are proposing two resolutions to this end. One demands that emigrating workers be informed about conditions of work, the other demands that the process of naturalization in the different countries be made easier so that workers can immediately acquire political rights in their new place of residence. . . .

MORRIS HILLQUIT (UNITED STATES): Immigration and emigration pose a very difficult, serious problem. Our resolution in no way infringes on the principle of internationalism, which has always been our guide in the United States. There are several kinds of immigration; the first is natural immigration, which arises from the very nature of the capitalist economy. For these immigrants we demand full freedom, and we consider it the workers' duty to assist the poor among them.

Another kind of immigration must be sharply distinguished from the first. Basically it amounts to capitalism's importation of foreign labor cheaper than that of native-born workers. This threatens the native-born with dangerous competition and usually provides a pool of unconscious strikebreakers. Chinese and Japanese workers play that role today, as does the yellow race in general. While we have absolutely no racial prejudices against the Chinese we must frankly tell you that they can not be organized. Only a people well advanced in its historical development, such as the Belgians and Italians in France, can be organized for the class struggle. The Chinese have lagged too far behind to be organized.

Socialism is by no means sentimentalism. A fierce struggle rages between capital and labor, and those who stand against organized labor are our enemy. Do we want to grant privileges to foreign strikebreakers, when they are locked in struggle with native-born workers? If we fail to take measures against the importation of Chinese strikebreakers, we will thrust the Socialist workers' movement backwards. While the French resolution undermines the principle of class struggle, ours holds it high. We do not insist on its every word, but we hope you will adopt a resolution with its general approach.

JÓZSEF DINER-DÉNES (HUNGARY): . . . Those countries that cannot be organized today will be organized tomorrow. Moreover in backward countries this evolution proceeds more rapidly than it did in countries that developed earlier, such as England and Germany. Only ten years ago our Hungarian workers emigrating to America were considered unorganizable. Today, only a few years later, they are being organized, and are inspired with the spirit of socialism.

You want to erect protective barriers around the workers. This will land you in the same fiasco as have the tariff-building efforts of the capitalists. If the wage question were merely one of supply and demand, we would have to oppose the importation of agricultural machinery, since it has replaced more workers than the Japanese and Chinese, especially in the Eastern European countries.

We must permit completely free immigration and emigration. A great many American workers are wage conscious but not yet imbued with a proletarian class consciousness. Of course we must fight against the abuses that stem from the mass importation of workers for the capitalists' benefit, but through explanation and organization. A good method would be to press for the establishment of a minimum wage—

where possible through political means, otherwise through trade union struggle. *(Enthusiastic applause)* . . .

CHARLES RAPPAPORT (FRANCE): . . . We cannot accept Hillquit's talk of predestined strikebreakers. So long as a worker has not acted as a strikebreaker, we treat him as a comrade. We too want to take a stand against immigration organized by the capitalists to break contracts, but not by fighting against the workers involved.

WILHELM ELLENBOGEN (AUSTRIA): The discussion is moving in two opposed directions. Some speak for the interests of the country of immigration and others for those of the emigrants. No reconciliation appears possible between the two points of view. . . . But we must combine them and make provisions for both sides. This is best done by excluding from the outset measures unacceptable to Socialists, such as guildlike regulations and discriminatory laws.

I hope Comrade Hillquit will not be offended, but I cannot accept his resolution because it is not clearly formulated. We should avoid distinctions such as those between "natural" and "unnatural" immigration which are slippery and hard to define. However, we do have a number of positive measures, in which the main tasks fall to the trade unions. The unions should reach out to the countries of emigration and educate the emigrants there, as the German trade unions have done in such an exemplary fashion. They must also try to prevent the export of strikebreakers. Most important, the trade unions of the country of immigration must make special efforts to attract the immigrant workers. Here I find it most regrettable that many American trade unions make it difficult for immigrants to join.

Social legislation poses a second set of tasks. The proposal of Diner-Dénes to demand a minimum wage should be supplemented with one for a limit on the hours of work. We must also demand supervision of recruitment, and above all, regulation of conditions on the emigration ships. A requirement of a certain air space per person in the cabins would make Chinese immigration in its worst form impossible, since their transportation would no longer produce a profit. . . .

KATO TOKIJIRO (JAPAN): As the representative of the Japanese Socialists, I must take the floor on this very important question. When the Americans excluded us from California they gave two reasons: first, that Japanese workers were depressing the wages and living standards of the indigenous workers, and second, that we were taking away their opportunity to work.[13] I disagree with this. Not only the Japanese, but also the Italians, Slovaks, Jews, and so forth do this. So why is it that only the Japanese are being excluded? The race question obviously plays a role here, and the Americans are clearly being influenced by the so-called yellow peril. The history of the United States confirms this opinion. Another factor is that the American capitalists want to flatter their workers.

The Japanese are under the heel of capitalism just as much as are other peoples. It is only dire need that drives them from their homeland to earn their livelihood in a foreign land. It is the duty of Socialists to welcome these poor brothers, to defend them, and together with them to fight capitalism. The founders of socialism, above all Karl Marx, did not address themselves to individual countries but to all humanity. Internationalism is inscribed on our banner. It would be a slap in the face to socialism if you were to exclude the poor, exploited Japanese. *(Enthusiastic, prolonged applause)*

DR. JULIUS HAMMER (UNITED STATES, SOCIALIST LABOR PARTY): There is no middle course in this question of immigration and emigration. Either you support restriction of immigration, or energetically combat it. Hillquit's resolution is an attempt at compromise that misses the mark. I especially oppose its third point that envisages possible restrictions on the immigration of Chinese and Japanese workers. This is completely antisocialist. Legal restriction of immigration must be rejected. Nothing can be gained for socialism through legislative action, or through collaboration with the bourgeois parties. *(The speaker cites several examples of how racial hatred in America blinds the workers and drives them to acts of violence)*

The Japanese and Chinese could be very effectively organized. They are not as unskilled as you might suppose. They are becoming quite well acquainted with capitalism and are learning how to fight it. I ask that you not approve any legal restrictions on immigration and emigration. We must create a great nation of the exploited.

The commission's resolution proposed measures to protect immigrants from exploitation and abuse, to grant them full political rights in their new homeland, and to assure them full membership rights in trade unions. It called for regulating shipboard conditions of passengers en route to their new country and for potential emigrants to receive full information about conditions in the countries of their destination.

Kautsky and Luxemburg had introduced an amendment to delete the demand for a minimum wage. Kautsky fully supported the struggle against the exploitation of immigrants, he later explained, but proposals for the state to legislate wage levels run counter to the laws of the capitalist economy and are therefore a waste of time. This amendment was defeated.

The resolution as a whole was unanimously adopted except for the British delegation, which abstained in protest over a procedural question.

Militarism and war

From its inception, the international workers' movement devoted much attention to the struggle against capitalist war and militarism.

The First International adopted resolutions on war in 1867 and 1868. It explained that efforts at disarmament would not end war, and called for an end to war through the abolition of standing armies and the creation of a new social order based on emancipation of the working class. On this basis the world's peoples could freely achieve unification. The First International also recommended international workers' solidarity and work stoppages in case of the outbreak of war as a means to promote "the peoples' war against war."

The epoch of bourgeois-democratic revolution, whose high point had been reached in the Great French Revolution of 1789, was in its final phase in Western and Central Europe when the First International was formed. Aspects of historically progressive struggles for national liberation and national unification were still sometimes mixed in to the wars between the European capitalist states.

Thus the Franco-Prussian War of 1870–71 was seen by the First International as a defensive struggle by Germany for its national unification against attempts by the French Emperor Napoleon III to block it by force. At the same time, the German Social Democrats attacked the Prussian monarchy's reactionary objectives and methods and its complicity in the outbreak of war, and they abstained on the vote for war credits. The war led to rapid German victories and to a revolutionary upheaval in France that ousted the emperor and established a republic in September 1870. The International then rallied to the defense of the French bourgeois republic against the Prussian armies and subsequently, when the working people of Paris rose up to establish their own government in 1871, the International led an international campaign of solidarity with the Paris Commune against the combined assault of French and German reaction.

As a result of this war, the German states (except Austria) joined together to form the German Empire, headed by the king of Prussia and dominated by the Prussian aristocracy. The French provinces of Alsace and Lorraine were forcibly annexed to the German Empire. This ended the period of struggles for national unification by the great nations in Western and Central Europe.

The first congress of the Second International was held in Paris in 1889. Europe's great powers were in the process of forming the two coalitions whose rivalry would lead to crises of increasing severity and, ultimately, to the outbreak of the First World War. Germany, Austria-Hungary, and Italy were linked in the Triple Alliance, and against them were allied France and Russia, later to be joined by Britain in the Triple Entente.

The International's first congress renewed the Socialists' long-standing call for replacing the standing army with the arming of the people as a whole. The Brussels congress of 1891 took note of the war danger in Europe, which was "growing more threatening every day, and the inflammatory chauvinist campaigns of the ruling classes," which threaten to bring on "the catastrophe of world war." This could only be opposed by "speeding the triumph of socialism through unceasing workers' agitation against the growing warlike desires and the alliances that promote war, and through the growing strength of the international workers' organization."[14]

The heightened war danger and increasing conflict between the major European powers pointed to at the Brussels congress flowed from a new fact in world politics—the rise of modern imperialism. A few huge banks came to dominate each of the major capitalist countries, and brought the rising industrial and trading monopolies under their wings. The rival national states ruled by the capitalist families who owned these giant trusts scrambled for colonies to guarantee access to cheap raw materials, labor power, and fields for investment and sales. Competition for imperialist superprofits became the drive wheel of international politics, diplomacy, and war.

The race of the imperialist powers to expand their colonial empires led at the turn of the century to a series of colonial wars. The Sino-Japanese war in 1895 established Japan as an imperial power and saw it gain de facto control over Korea. In 1898 the United States went to war against Spain and took over the remnants of Spain's colonial empire. In 1900 an anti-imperialist mass movement in China (often referred to as the "Boxers") occupied Peking with a force of 140,000. The imperialist powers leagued together to smash the uprising, sacked Peking, and imposed a huge indemnity on China and yet more restrictions on Chinese sovereignty. British imperialism succeeded in the Boer War of 1899–1902 in annexing the two independent Boer republics in southern Africa. The Second International viewed this as "a just war on the part of the Boers, and the world proletariat took their part,"[15] and its revolutionary wing endorsed that opinion.

The Paris congress of 1900 responded to the rising war danger with the following resolution:

"The congress declares that the workers' parties in every country must combat militarism and colonialism with redoubled energy and force. Above all it is absolutely necessary to respond to the world political alliance of the bourgeoisies and the governments to perpetuate war with an alliance of proletarians of all countries for perpetual peace.

"The congress resolves on the following practical means to this end:

"1. Socialist parties everywhere must take up the antimilitarist education and organization of the youth and conduct it with the greatest zeal;

"2. Socialist parliamentary representatives are obliged to vote against absolutely every expenditure for militarism, naval expansion, or colonial expeditions;

"3. Whenever the course of international events requires it, the permanent international Socialist commission is empowered to organize a protest movement against militarism, to be conducted simultaneously and through similar forms of action in all countries.

"The congress protests against the so-called peace conferences, such as that in The Hague, which in today's society are only a fraud and a delusion as has once again been revealed by the recent war in the Transvaal [the Boer War]." [16]

The French and German governments came close to blows in 1905 over possession of Morocco, and French and German Socialists worked together in their respective parliaments and through demonstrations and mass meetings to counter the threat of war. Revolutionary action by Russia's workers and peasants in 1905 helped force a rapid end to the Russo-Japanese war. These events helped place the debate on militarism and international conflicts at the center of the Stuttgart congress. The commission sessions which debated the draft resolutions on this topic extended over five days and were crowded with hundreds of delegates.

Four resolutions were submitted to the commission. For the most part they shared the common analysis that the growing danger of war resulted from the economic rivalries inherent in modern capitalism. They differed sharply, however, on whether to spell out the course of action that Socialists would follow should war appear imminent. Two resolutions, one proposed by Jean Jaurès and Edouard Vaillant and the other by Gustave Hervé, included mention of specific forms of action to avert an immediate threat of war, including use of a general strike. The resolutions proposed by August Bebel and Jules Guesde left this question entirely open.

The resolution proposed by Hervé, leading a minority of the French party, concluded that "in view of the diplomatic intrigues threatening the peace of Europe from various quarters," the congress "instructs all comrades to meet any declaration of war, no matter how it originates, with a military strike and with insurrection."

The resolution of the majority of the French delegation, presented by Jaurès and Vaillant, stated that "the working class must strive to prevent war through Socialist action in a national and international framework, using all means from action in parliament and public agitation, all the way to mass strike and insurrection. Proletarians and Socialists of all nations give expression to this solidarity by holding demonstrations on the First of May."

The resolution of another minority of the French delegation, led by Guesde, held that "the best means against militarism and for peace is the organization of workers of the entire world for socialism." In case of threatening political conflicts, it specified merely that "the International Bureau has the task of meeting according to its statutes and taking the appropriate measures."

The fourth resolution was presented by August Bebel for the Executive Committee of the German party. It concluded that "should war threaten to break out, the workers and their parliamentary representatives in the affected countries are duty bound to do everything possible to prevent the outbreak of war, using the means that they consider to be the most effective. Should war break out nonetheless, they will intervene for its rapid termination."[17]

Commission debate[18]

AUGUST BEBEL (GERMANY): We have debated and voted on the question of militarism and war at international congresses so often that simply reaffirming our previously adopted decisions would seem to be sufficient. *("Very true!")* But since the French comrades have asked that this question be put on the congress agenda again, prompted mainly by Hervé's so-called antimilitarist agitation, we cannot avoid discussing it once more. What Hervé says about militarism and patriotism in his book *Leur patrie* [Their fatherland] is not new. Domela Nieuwenhuis already said it to all of us at previous congresses, *("Quite right!")* and each one rejected his views by a large majority.[19] Today we maintain the same position.

Hervé says: "The fatherland is the fatherland of the ruling classes. It is not a concern of the proletariat." A similar idea is expressed in the *Communist Manifesto* which says: "The proletariat has no fatherland." But Marx's and Engels's students have declared that they no longer share the views of the manifesto. In addition, over the years they took positions that were very clear and in no way negative on the national questions in Europe, including that in Germany.[20]

We are not fighting against the fatherland in and of itself, for it belongs to the proletariat far more than to the ruling classes. Rather we combat the social relations that exist in this fatherland to serve the interests of the ruling classes. The fatherland in itself belongs far more to the proletariat than to the ruling classes. *("Quite right!")*

Parliament is also an institution of the ruling classes, established to maintain their class rule. But we participate in parliament not only to fight ruling class domination, but also to improve social conditions. We don't limit ourselves to being negative, but carry out positive work as well.

The cultural life and progress of a nation can develop only on the basis of complete freedom and independence and through the medium of an established national language. That is why peoples everywhere who suffer foreign domination are struggling for national independence and freedom. We see this, for example, in Austria and in the struggle of the Poles to restore their national independence. As soon as Russia becomes a modern state, the nationalities question will arise. *(Comrade Luxemburg disagrees)* I know that you have another viewpoint, but I think you are wrong.[21]

Every nation under foreign domination struggles first of all for its independence. Alsace-Lorraine fought against its separation from France [in 1871] because for centuries its cultural development progressed as a component part of France's and because it enjoyed and had equal rights to the achievements of the Great French Revolution. Thus its people possessed intimate cultural links to France without any disadvantages. Hervé thinks that it does not matter to the proletariat whether France belongs to Germany, or Germany to France—but that is absurd. *(Shouts of "That is not thinking at all!" Laughter)* I fear that if Hervé seriously explained this notion to his fellow compatriots, they would trample him underfoot. *("Very true!")*

In 1870 we saw what nationalist fever meant in time of war. The masses perceived Napoleon to be the troublemaker although it was not he but Bismarck who provoked the declaration of war by falsifying the Ems dispatch. This became known only later. But in 1870 the nationalist fever targeted us as well because we abstained on the vote to approve war credits. We held that both governments were to blame for the war, since the truth about the Ems dispatch was not yet public knowledge.[22]

I maintain that it is easy now to determine in any given case whether a war is defensive, or whether it is aggressive in character. While previously the causes leading to the catastrophe of war remained obscured, even to the trained and observant politician, today that is no longer the case. War has ceased to be a secret matter of cabinet politics.

But let us also evaluate the practical meaning of antimilitarism as posed by Hervé. I do not know if Hervé's tactics are possible in France. I am afraid, however, that in wartime we will have bad experiences there if we apply Hervé's methods of mass strike, desertion by the reservists and militia, and open insurrection. *(Agreement)* I must flatly state that for us these methods are not just impossible but totally beyond discussion.

The case of Karl Liebknecht shows how things stand today in Germany. Even though he clearly expressed his differences with Hervé in his book, and stated that Hervé's methods are unworkable, Liebknecht has been charged with high treason.[23] And I believe that the antimilitarist agitation Hervé is conducting may well be of dubious merit even from his own point of view. His activity is followed very closely by German military circles and by the German general staff. The pro-war party, which is small here and still has no adherents in government circles, welcomes any sign of weakness among possible opponents. *("Hear! Hear!")*

No one in the German ruling circles wants war. This is in large part due to the existence of the Socialist movement. Even Prince Bülow himself admitted to me that the governments know what would be at stake for the state and society in a great European war, and therefore would avoid it if possible.

Also, for the reasons already stated, we cannot vote for the Jaurès-Vaillant resolution. In its concluding sentence it makes grave concessions to Hervéism. In addition, we are not obliged to make public statements about such things.

We are in agreement on the issue before us, the struggle against militarism and war. In the last forty years we German Socialists have struggled against both militarism and war more consistently than has been done in any other country. *("Quite right!")* Jaurès is frequently held up, in contrast to us, as a model of patriotism.

JEAN JAURÈS (FRANCE): Just as you are to me in France!

BEBEL: Very true! In France I am presented as a "great patriot" who is for every war, even if it's not a defensive one.

In Germany, they sing quite a different tune.

During the Morocco crisis we did all we could both here and in France to prevent war. As Social Democrats we realize that we cannot completely do without military weaponry. So long as the relations among states have not fundamentally changed, we allow for armaments but only for purely defensive purposes and on a broad and democratic basis in order to prevent misuse by the military. In Germany, therefore, we struggle with all our strength against the prevailing militarism, as expressed in the army, the navy, or any other form. Beyond that, however, we must not allow ourselves to be pressured into using methods of struggle that could gravely threaten the activity and, under certain circumstances, the very existence of the party. I hope that, after the conclusion of the general debate, the subcommission will succeed in coming to an agreement. *(Enthusiastic applause)*

GUSTAVE HERVÉ (FRANCE): I was not aware that the general staff in Berlin had followed my agitation with such great interest and pleasure. But I do know one thing for certain. French socialism and the French republic have been anxiously awaiting Bebel's address—and it can only produce feelings of astonishment and grief. *(Objections)*

How is it that we have come to such brutal, reckless, and frenetic antimilitarist agitation in France? It was during the most feverish days of the Russian revolution, when we heard threats that Prussian bayonets would be used against the Russian revolutionaries. We asked ourselves what the German Social Democracy would do to oppose such an outrageous act, and feared it might do no more than throw the moral weight of its three million votes into the scales. *(Laughter)*

And then came the dreadful tension of the Morocco crisis when the clouds of war gathered over Germany and France. Once again we asked ourselves what German Social Democracy would do. Once again its response carried only the moral weight of its three million votes.

Bebel has most obligingly informed me that fatherlands exist today in Europe as a historical fact. But I have learned still more interesting things from Bebel. In the Amsterdam congress he told us: "Whether German monarchy or French republic: for us as Socialists it's all the same." I say the same thing to you today. For the capitalists, every fatherland represents the exploitation of the working majority by the bourgeois minority. The workers churn the butter for the rich man's table. Such a "motherland" is a harsh, evil stepmother indeed!

We aim to separate the capitalist wolves from their working-class prey by uniting the workers across national frontiers. Our class—that is our fatherland.

Bebel draws a fine distinction between an offensive and a defensive war. Thus when tiny Morocco is carved up, it is recognized as an offensive war of unconcealed brutality. But should war break out between the great powers, the only too powerful capitalist press will unleash such a storm of nationalism that we will not have the strength to counteract it. Then it will be too late to make your fine distinction.

When did you learn of the falsification of the Ems dispatch? Ten years after the murderous war. My antimilitarist agitation should act as a loud cry, a cry of warning to the German Social Democracy to do their duty to the International and make war impossible. My agitation in France had the greatest, most effective, and most outstanding success. *(Laughter)* I have been able to publicly explain my antimilitarist views in every city and village in France, confronting the bourgeoisie—and I have not been trampled on. Is that not a first-rate success?

In this year's French party congress at Nancy the much ridiculed Hervéists tipped the scales in favor of Jaurès and Vaillant and against Guesde on the question of militarism.[24]

(Objection from Jaurès) We thought that our splendidly successful agitation would set an example for you German Socialists, which would spur you onto our path. . . . Bebel has left us no illusions as to whether or not the German Social Democracy will follow our example.

I do not at all deny the great achievements of Marx, Engels, Lassalle, Kautsky, Bebel, and also Eduard Bernstein—the only one today with some courage. But you have now become an electoral and accounting machine, *(Laughter)* a party of cash registers and parliamentary seats. You want to conquer the world with ballots. But I ask you: When the German soldiers are sent off to reestablish the throne of the Russian tsar, when Prussia and France attack the proletarians, what will you do? Please do not answer with metaphysics and dialectics, but openly and clearly; practically and tactically, what will you do?

I know that in 1871 Bebel was imprisoned as a rebel. When Bismarck's government persecuted you, hundreds of you defied the German prisons.[25] You took risks in the face of Bismarck's iron laws because your political rights and electoral progress were being infringed upon. But today, when it would be a matter of preventing a clash that would cost the lives of hundreds of thousands of French and German workers, to judge from Bebel's speech, you are no longer able to take such risks.

ROSA LUXEMBURG (POLAND): That is not true!

HERVÉ: Naturally I do not mean you.[26] But we hear nothing more about defying the law.

BEBEL: You do not know that at all. We have endured ten times more prison terms than all the French antimilitarists put together!

HERVÉ: On the contrary, the whole German Social Democracy has now become bourgeois. Today Bebel went over to the revisionists when he told us: "Proletarians of all countries, murder each other!" *(Loud commotion)* If you do not want us to carry on antimilitarist propaganda, then we will not have worked for peace, but for war.

EMILE VANDERVELDE (BELGIUM): You are always working *pour le roi de Prusse!* [for the king of Prussia].[27] *(Laughter)*

HERVÉ: Well, in questions of national conflicts, Belgium is not really a factor. *(Commotion)*

I was eager to get to know the German Social Democracy personally. For years I knew it only when I shrugged my shoulders at those quibbling hairsplitting disputes over the interpretation of Karl Marx. Now I have seen the German proletarians here on the streets of Stuttgart. My naive illusions are destroyed. It turns out that they are all good, satisfied, and well-fed solid citizens. *(Resounding laughter)*

We have morally disarmed the French general staff, since they know that war would mean a rebellion by the proletariat. But the blind obedience of you German Social Democrats to "Kaiser Bebel" is a deathlike discipline. Your approach makes war very possible. And if you march into war for your kaiser, without offering resistance, you will be marching against revolutionary communes, thrusting your bayonets into the breasts of French proletarians, who are defending their barricades under the red flag of revolution. *(Commotion, laughter, and some applause)* . . .

JAURÈS: According to Hervé, the fatherland should be destroyed. We, instead, want to socialize the fatherland for the benefit of the proletariat by putting the means of production under common ownership. *(Applause)*

The nation is the treasure-house of human genius and progress; destroying these precious reservoirs of human culture would harm the proletariat. *("Very good!")* Our resolution has nothing to do with Hervéism. It did not accidentally pop up like the whim of some dreamer, but grew necessarily out of the big crises we experienced after the Fashoda incident and the Morocco crisis.[28] The proletariat must ask itself: Should we tolerate these crimes against humanity which are perpetrated for the benefit of a few capitalists? Should we not combat them through the great alliance of the powerful organized working masses? Is that a dream; is that a utopia?

Previously, national prejudices could make war unavoidable—as when Italy freed itself from Austria's domination or when Germany was only able to unify itself through blood and iron. But now these national pretexts have disappeared. Thus in the Morocco crisis the first thought of the French and German proletarians was to unite. After Fashoda the English trade unions came to a mighty peace demonstration in Paris, but only long after the danger of war had passed. And they told us that the danger of proletarian fratricide had taken them by surprise. In the future will we also let ourselves be taken by surprise? No! Preventive measures must be taken now to unite the proletarian forces into an invincible army.

Some say that the struggle against war is futile since capitalism inevitably engenders it. But capitalism has exactly the same inherent tendency to increase exploitation without limit and to endlessly lengthen the work day. And still we fight for the eight-hour day—and with success. *("Very good!")* . . .

In *Die Neue Zeit* [New Times] Kautsky called for direct action should German troops intervene in Russia to aid the tsar. Bebel repeated this statement from the tribune of the Reichstag. If you could say it then, you can say it in every international conflict. *("Very good!")* German military intervention on the tsar's behalf against the Russian Social Democracy would certainly be the most acute, most extreme form of the class struggle imaginable.

Alarmed by the growth of the Socialist movement, a government might attempt to create an external diversion rather than directly battle the Social Democracy. If a war breaks out in this way between France and Germany, would we permit the French and German proletariat to murder one another on behalf of the capitalists and for their benefit without the Social Democracy attempting to exert the greatest effort to stop it? *("Very good")* If we were not to make the attempt, we would all be dishonored. *(Stormy applause)*

Bebel has described for us the dangers of antimilitarist agitation in Germany. We definitely do not want to risk the destruction of the strongest branch of international socialism. But I think you are exaggerating. You have already gone through the test of the Anti-Socialist Laws, when a heavier hand came down upon you than that of some Prussian minister. The government can make an individual feel the severity of the law but it cannot crush the strength of three million. . . .

But if a conflict between France and Germany broke out, chauvinist brutality would be unleashed indiscriminately against all of us—even against the cleverest and most careful. *(Applause)* Therefore we should be frank enough to say that although we recognize the inviolability of every country and will not give up any country to the exploitation and oppression of another, we will not allow the international proletariat to be massacred. For thirty years the German party program has called for the resolution of international conflicts through arbitration courts. Given the increasing power of the Social Democracy, the bourgeois class has now made this slogan of international socialism one of their own demands. . . .

We can put every government in a real predicament if we demand that they submit to an international court of arbitration in the event of an international conflict. If they refuse we can denounce them as the biggest enemy of world peace. *("Very good!")*

Comrades! The whole bourgeois world is watching this congress. The strength of international socialism and its growth revealed by this congress surprise them. The immeasurable and inexhaustible proletarian forces represented by the 880 delegates here also surprises them. We, who have so proudly proclaimed the bankruptcy of the bourgeoisie, must never permit it to speak of a bankruptcy of the International on this vital question. *(Stormy, prolonged, and repeated applause)*

GEORG VOLLMAR (GERMANY): . . . It is not true that "international" means the same thing as "antinational." It is not true that we have no fatherland. And I use the word "fatherland" without adding some hairsplitting elucidation of the concept. I know why socialism must be international, but my love for humanity can never prevent me from being a good German, just as it cannot prevent others from being good citizens of France or Italy. We recognize the common cultural interests of all peoples, and condemn and fight against the incitement of nationalist hatreds. But we must also reject utopian chatter about the end of nations and their melting away into an amorphous porridge of peoples.

JAURÈS: So who wants that?

VOLLMAR: Comrade Jaurès . . . so long as the citizen Hervé is in your party, you cannot simply shrug your shoulders and refuse to take responsibility for him. . . . Wilhelm Liebknecht once said: "The bloodthirsty beast will be brought down by the spirit of socialism, by propaganda, by education, and by achieving influence both within parliament and with public opinion—but not by childish conspiracies in the barracks." The overwhelming majority of the German party has always supported this viewpoint. The same is also true for the other methods of struggle that are specified in the Jaurès-Vaillant resolution. . . .

As for Jaurès's reference to a statement by Kautsky, no one will fail to see the difference between an individual statement and the binding declaration of a whole party. Naturally I will not take up here Karl Liebknecht's statement concerning antimilitarist agitation because his case is now before the Supreme Court. But we do not argue against the methods outlined in the Jaurès-Vaillant resolution simply out of prudence. More importantly, we see the resolution as absurd on the basis of principles. *(Objection by a number of the French delegates, especially Hervé)* We believe it misconstrues the essence of Socialist politics. Instead of comprehending social reality in its essence and context, only its outward appearance is considered. It is just as foolish to believe the world can be rid of war through a military strike or something similar as it is to think that you could do away with capitalism overnight by means of a general strike. To choose such tactics would be a step away from the correct road. . . .

You can be sure that we German Social Democrats are as well acquainted with the whole misery of war as are the comrades in any other country. And we are just as prepared as they to use all possible means to put a stop to incitement of nationalist hatreds, and to use our growing influence on the ruling powers and on public opinion to prevent war. We are not going to insist on the wording of Bebel's resolution and we are quite willing to come to an agreement. But we urgently request that you not tie us to certain methods of struggle. This would take away our right to freely determine our own policies and imperil the basis of our existence. *(German delegates: "Bravo!")* . . .

VANDERVELDE: . . . We want a strong resolution but we also want to reach agreement. If we do not succeed, that is, if the French comrades declare themselves for the general strike and the German comrades against, then it will be an impossible situation for an international congress. The German delegates should think about that. I am an old friend of the German comrades and their comrade-in-arms for twenty years. I have learned a great deal from them, and I owe them so very much. I ask you German comrades, are you not willing to learn something this time from the experience of other countries? The majority of the congress thinks that it would be bad if the French comrades threw themselves into antimilitarist agitation while the German comrades held themselves entirely aloof. . . .

LUXEMBURG: I have asked for the floor in order to remind you, on behalf of the Russian and the Polish Social Democratic delegations, that at this point on the agenda we should all consider the great Russian revolution. At the opening of the congress when Vandervelde, with characteristic eloquence, duly expressed our gratitude to the martyrs, we all rendered homage to the victims, the fighters. But after hearing many speeches, and especially Vollmar's, it occurred to me that were the bloody ghosts of the revolutionaries here, they would say: "We give you back your homage, but learn from us!" And it would be a betrayal of the revolution for you not to do so.

The last congress, in 1904 at Amsterdam, discussed the mass strikes, and decided that we were too immature and unprepared for them. But materialist dialectics, so convincingly invoked by Victor Adler, has suddenly accomplished what we declared impossible. I must now speak against Vollmar and unfortunately against Bebel, too. They say we are not in a position to do more than we have done up to now. The Russian revolution, however, did not merely result from the Russo-Japanese War; it has also served to put an end to it. Otherwise tsarism would surely have continued the war. The dialectics of history does not mean that we wait with folded arms until it bears us ripe fruit.

I am a convinced adherent of Marxism, and for this very reason consider it very dangerous to mold the Marxist method into a rigid fatalistic form. This only calls forth in return such excesses as Hervéism. Hervé is an *enfant* [child], an *enfant terrible* to be sure. *(Laughter)*

Vollmar said of Kautsky that he spoke only in his own name. This is even more true of Vollmar. The fact is that most of the German proletariat has disavowed Vollmar's point of view. This happened at the Jena party congress, where a resolution was adopted almost unanimously that showed the German party to be a revolutionary party, which has learned from history.[29] In this resolution the party declared the general strike, which it had denounced for years as anarchistic, to be a method of struggle that could be applied under certain circumstances. It was not the spirit of Domela Nieuwenhuis, but the red ghost of the Russian revolution that hovered over the deliberations at Jena. Of course, we had in mind then a mass strike for suffrage rather than against the war. While we cannot swear to carry out a mass strike if we are deprived of suffrage, neither can we swear that it is only for suffrage that we will carry out such a strike.

In view of Vollmar's, and also to some extent Bebel's, speech we consider it necessary to sharpen Bebel's resolution. We have composed an amendment to submit later. I must also add that in it we go further, to a certain degree, than Comrades Jaurès and Vaillant. Our amendment contends that in case of war our agitation should aim at not merely ending the war, but also utilizing it to hasten the overthrow of class rule in general.[30] *(Applause)*

RUSSELL SMART (BRITAIN): Hervé's resolution is not at all suitable for Britain. No British government is capable of conducting a war without the consent of the overwhelming majority of the working class. But if the public were whipped up into a nationalist frenzy, then a military strike would be pure lunacy. In the struggle against war, therefore, under no circumstances can the British Social Democracy go beyond peaceful activity in Parliament, at conferences, and in the streets. . . .

British soldiers do not shoot at the people. That was clearly shown during the labor unrest in Belfast where unfortunately there were deaths, but two were not on the side of the strikers.[31] These figures prove that the British soldiers shoot into the air, not at the people. British freedom allows us to discuss this question without the least danger. Therefore we must alter the resolutions to adjust them to British conditions through an amendment against the demand for arming the entire people. That is the position of the Independent Labour Party. *(Applause)* . . .

BEBEL: . . . A Social Democrat could say that in a certain sense a great European war would advance our cause more than have decades of agitation and so we should hope for it. But we do not wish for such a dreadful means of reaching our goal. However if those who have the greatest stake in maintaining bourgeois society cannot perceive that such a war would uproot it, then we cannot object. Then I say: "Just keep right at it, we shall be your heirs." *(Enthusiastic applause, laughter from the Hervéists)* If the ruling class had not known this, we would long ago have had a Europe-wide war. Only the fear of Social Democracy has prevented it so far. *("Quite true!")* If such a war breaks out, then much more will be at stake than mere trifles like insurrection and mass strike. Then the entire civilized world will change, from the ground up. If we understand this, we do not need to argue over the methods of struggle to be used at such a moment.

The German resolution clearly and unequivocally states that we combat militarism with all the means that we deem effective. We cannot yet determine our tactics in advance; we cannot yet impose them on our enemy.

Earthshaking events can transform our minority into a majority. Never before in the history of the civilized world has a movement embraced the masses as profoundly as does the Socialist movement. Never before has a movement given the despised masses such an insight into the nature of our society. Never have there been so many who knew what they wanted from the state and society. Let us keep our eyes open and our heads clear, so that we are prepared for the moment, when it comes. *(Enthusiastic, prolonged applause)* . . .

A fourteen-person subcommission was set up to work out the text of a compromise resolution. V.I. Lenin nominated Luxemburg to represent the Russian Social Democratic Labor Party (RSDLP). She advanced there a series of amendments proposed jointly by herself, Lenin, and Julius Martov, and these were accepted. In the text of the resolution given below, the passages added by the Luxemburg-Lenin-Martov amendments and incorporated into the final draft are printed in italics.

Stuttgart resolution on war and militarism

The congress reaffirms the resolutions adopted by previous international congresses against militarism and imperialism and declares once more that the struggle against militarism cannot be separated from the Socialist class struggle as a whole.

As a rule, wars between capitalist states are the outcome of their competition on the world market, for each state seeks not only to secure its existing markets, but also to conquer new ones. In this, the subjugation of foreign peoples and countries plays a prominent role. *These wars result furthermore from the incessant arms race by militarism, one of the chief instruments of bourgeois class rule and of the economic and political subjugation of the working class.*

Wars are promoted by the prejudices of one people against

another, systematically cultivated among civilized peoples in the interest of the ruling classes. *This is done to distract the proletarian masses from their own tasks as a class as well as from their duties of international solidarity.*

Wars, therefore, are part of the very nature of capitalism. They will cease only when the capitalist system is abolished or when the enormous sacrifices in men and money required by advances in military technique, and the indignation aroused by the arms race, drive the peoples to abolish this system.

For this reason, the proletariat, which contributes most of the soldiers and makes most of the material sacrifices, is a natural opponent of war. War contradicts the proletariat's highest goal—the creation of an economic order on a socialist basis, which will bring about the solidarity of all peoples.

The congress, therefore, considers it the duty of the working class and in particular its parliamentary representatives to combat the naval and land armaments with all their might, explaining the class nature of bourgeois society and the motive for the maintenance of national antagonisms, and to reject measures to supply the means for these armaments. *It is their duty to work for the education of the working-class youth in the spirit of the brotherhood of nations and of socialism while developing their class consciousness.*

The congress sees the democratic organization of the army, the substitution of the people's militia for the standing army, as an essential guarantee that offensive wars will be rendered impossible and the overcoming of national antagonisms facilitated.

The International is not able to determine in rigid forms the antimilitarist actions of the working class. These naturally vary for different countries and for different circumstances of time and place. But it is its duty to coordinate and increase to the utmost the efforts of the working class against war.

In fact, since the international congress at Brussels [1891] the proletariat, in its indefatigable struggle against militarism, has employed the most diverse forms of action with increasing energy and success, including rejecting appropriations for armaments on land or sea, and working to democratize the military organization. In this way it works to prevent the outbreak of wars or put a stop to them, as well as to utilize the social convulsions caused by war for the emancipation of the working class.

This was especially evident in the agreement between the English and French trade unions following the Fashoda incident for the maintenance of peace and for the restoration of friendly relations between England and France; in the conduct of the Social Democratic parties in the German and French parliaments during the Morocco crisis; in the demonstrations organized by the French and German Socialists for the same purpose; in the concerted action of the Socialists of Austria and Italy, who met in Trieste in order to prevent a conflict between the two countries;[32] in the energetic intervention of the Socialist workers of Sweden in order to prevent an attack upon Norway;[33] finally, in the heroic, self-sacrificing struggle of the Socialist workers and peasants of Russia and Poland in order to oppose the war unleashed by tsarism, to put a stop to it, and to utilize the crisis of the country for the liberation of the working class.

All these efforts are evidence of the growing power of the proletariat and of its increasing ability to secure the maintenance of peace by resolute intervention. The preparation of workers' class consciousness by appropriate activity, and the spurring on and coordination by the International of the workers parties in different countries, will promote the success of this working-class campaign.

The congress is convinced that the pressure of the proletariat and a serious use of arbitration in place of the wretched machinations of the governments can secure the benefit of disarmament to all nations. This will make it possible to employ the enormous expenditures of money and energy, now swallowed up by military armaments and wars, for cultural purposes.

If a war threatens to break out, it is the duty of the working classes and their parliamentary representatives in the countries involved, supported by the coordinating activity of the International Socialist Bureau, *to exert every effort in order to prevent its outbreak. They must employ the means they consider most effective, which naturally vary according to the sharpening of the class struggle and the general political situation.*

In case war should break out anyway, it is their duty to intervene for its speedy termination and to strive with all their power to utilize the economic and political crisis created by the war to rouse the masses and thereby hasten the downfall of capitalist class rule.

[This resolution was presented to the congress on its final day, August 24. The debate was brief and harmonious, except for the contribution by Hervé, who pointed to the contradiction between the text of the resolution and the statements in the commission by Bebel and Vollmar. The congress proceedings describe the vote as follows:]

The resolution from the commission is thus unanimously adopted. *(Stormy, prolonged applause, renewed several times. The French delegation applauds with particular enthusiasm. Hervé climbs on a table and raises both arms to signal his affirmative vote.)*

Assessing the Stuttgart congress in the pages of *Die Neue Zeit*, Kautsky pointed to its spirit of political unanimity as its most significant feature. The disagreement on colonial policy constituted in his view the one significant area of disagreement. Also noteworthy, he added, was that the German Social Democracy was no longer playing its old leadership role in the International. Instead, the main Socialist parties now enjoyed roughly equal political authority—a sign of the rapid growth of the movement outside Germany. "This equality has not led to splits but to growing harmony and solidarity, because all parties are heading in the same direction," he said.

The adopted resolutions, however, did contain some weaknesses, Kautsky continued. He pointed in particular to the demand for a minimum wage contained in the resolution on immigration, and explained why he considered this a violation of the fundamentals of Marxism. His analysis concluded with an examination of the composition of international congresses.[34]

Lenin's assessment of the congress also noted the changed role of the German party:

"The remarkable and sad feature in this connection was that German Social-Democracy, which hitherto had always upheld the revolutionary standpoint in Marxism, proved to be unstable, or took an opportunist stand. . . . It is especially important for the Russian Social-Democrats to bear this in mind, for our liberals (and not only the liberals) are trying their hardest to represent the least creditable features of German Social-Democracy as a model worthy of imitation. The most thoughtful and outstanding minds among the German Social-Democrats have noted this fact themselves and, casting aside all false shame, have definitely pointed to it as a warning."

Lenin went on to quote from *Die Gleichheit* (Equality), the weekly magazine of the SPD for women. "'In Amsterdam,' writes Clara Zetkin's journal, 'the revolutionary *leitmotiv* of all the debates in the parliament of the world proletariat was the Dresden resolution;[35] in Stuttgart a jarring opportunist note was struck by Vollmar's speeches in the Commission on Militarism, by Päplow's speeches in the Emigration Commission, and by David's [and, we would add, Bernstein's] speeches in the Colonial Commission. On this occasion, in most of the commissions and on most issues, the representatives of Germany were leaders of opportunism.' And K. Kautsky, in appraising the Stuttgart Congress, writes: '. . . the leading role which German Social-Democracy has actually played in the Second International up to now was not in evidence on this occasion.'"[36]

Elsewhere Lenin took up the Stuttgart debate on patriotism:

"That 'working men have no country' was really said in the *Communist Manifesto*. That the attitude of Vollmar, Noske and Co. strikes at this basic principle of *international* socialism is also true. But it does not follow from this that Hervé and his followers are right in asserting that it is of no concern to the proletariat in what country it lives—in monarchical Germany, republican France or despotic Turkey. The fatherland, i.e., the given political, cultural and social environment, is a most powerful factor in the class struggle of the proletariat; and if Vollmar is wrong when he lays down some kind of 'truly German' attitude of the proletariat to 'the fatherland', Hervé is just as wrong when he takes up an unforgivably uncritical attitude on such an important factor in the struggle of the proletariat for emancipation. The proletariat cannot be indifferent to the political, social and cultural conditions of its struggle; consequently it cannot be indifferent to the destinies of its country. But the destinies of the country interest it only *to the extent* that they affect its class struggle, and not in virtue of some bourgeois 'patriotism', quite indecent on the lips of a Social-Democrat."[37]

Bolshevik leader Gregory Zinoviev tells of Lenin's initial attempt at this congress to draw together left forces in the International:

"Comrade Lenin recounted in his reports and in conversation that at the time of the Stuttgart congress he and Rosa Luxemburg made the first attempt to call together an illegal meeting of Marxists inclined to share their viewpoint—illegal not in the police sense of the word, but with respect to the Second International's leadership. There proved to be few people of that kind, but nonetheless, the initial foundation was laid for forming such a grouping."[38]

The following is a second article by Lenin analyzing the congress results:

The International Socialist Congress in Stuttgart[39]

by V.I. Lenin

A feature of the International Socialist Congress held in Stuttgart this August was its large and representative composition: the total of 886 delegates came from all the five continents. Besides providing an impressive demonstration of international unity in the proletarian struggle, the Congress played an outstanding part in defining the tactics of the socialist parties. It adopted general resolutions on a number of questions, the decision of which had hitherto been left solely to the discretion of the individual socialist parties. And the fact that more and more problems require uniform, principled decisions in different countries is striking proof that socialism is being welded into a single international force.

The full text of the Stuttgart resolutions will be found elsewhere in this issue. We shall deal briefly with each of them in order to bring out the chief controversial points and the character of the debate at the Congress.

This is not the first time the colonial question has figured at international congresses. Up till now their decisions have always been an unqualified condemnation of bourgeois colonial policy as a policy of plunder and violence. This time, however, the Congress Commission was so composed that opportunist elements, headed by Van Kol of Holland, predominated in it. A sentence was inserted in the draft resolution to the effect that the Congress did not in principle condemn all colonial policy, for under socialism colonial policy could play a civilising role. The minority in the Commission (Ledebour of Germany, the Polish and Russian Social-Democrats, and many others) vigorously protested against any such idea being entertained. The matter was referred to Congress, where the forces of the two trends were found to be so nearly equal that there was an extremely heated debate.

The opportunists rallied behind Van Kol. Speaking for the majority of the German delegation Bernstein and David urged acceptance of a "socialist colonial policy" and fulminated against the radicals for their barren, negative attitude, their failure to appreciate the importance of reforms, their lack of a practical colonial programme, etc. Incidentally, they were opposed by Kautsky, who felt compelled to ask the Congress to pronounce *against* the majority of the German delegation. He rightly pointed out that there was no question of rejecting the struggle for reforms; that was explicitly stated in other sections of the resolution, which had evoked no dispute. The point at issue was whether we should make concessions to the modern regime of bourgeois plunder and violence. The Congress was to discuss present-day colonial policy, which was based on the downright enslavement of primitive populations. The bourgeoisie was actually introducing slavery in the colonies and subjecting the native populations to unprecedented outrages and acts of violence, "civilising" them by the spread of liquor and syphilis. And in that situation socialists were expected to utter evasive phrases about the possibility of accepting colonial policy in principle! That would be an outright desertion to the bourgeois point of view. It would be a decisive step towards subordinating the proletariat to bourgeois ideology, to bourgeois imperialism, which is now arrogantly raising its head.

The Congress defeated the Commission's motion by 128 votes to 108 with ten abstentions (Switzerland). It should be noted that at Stuttgart, for the first time, each nation was allotted a definite number of votes, varying from twenty (for the big nations, Russia included) to two (Luxembourg). The combined vote of the small nations, which either do not pursue a colonial policy, or which suffer from it, outweighed the vote of nations where even the proletariat has been somewhat infected with the lust of conquest.

This vote on the colonial question is of very great importance. First, it strikingly showed up socialist opportunism, which succumbs to bourgeois blandishments. Secondly, it revealed a negative feature in the European labour movement, one that can do no little harm to the proletarian cause, and for that reason should receive serious attention. Marx frequently quoted a very significant saying of Sismondi. The proletarians of the ancient world, this saying runs, lived at the expense of society; modern society lives at the expense of the proletarians.

The non-propertied, but non-working, class is incapable of overthrowing the exploiters. Only the proletarian class, which maintains the whole of society, can bring about the social revolution. However, as a result of the extensive colonial policy, the European proletarian *partly* finds himself in a position when it is *not* his labour, but the labour of the practically enslaved natives in the colonies, that maintains the whole of society. The British bourgeoisie, for example, derives more profit from the many millions of the population of India and other colonies than from the British workers. In certain countries this provides the material and economic basis for infecting the proletariat with colonial chauvinism. Of course, this may be only a temporary phenomenon, but the evil must nonetheless be clearly realised and its causes understood in order to be able to rally the proletariat of all countries for the struggle against such opportunism. This struggle is bound to be victorious, since the "privileged" nations are a diminishing faction of the capitalist nations.

There were practically no differences at the Congress on the question of women's suffrage. The only one who tried to make out a case for a socialist campaign in favour of a limited women's suffrage (qualified as opposed to universal suffrage) was a woman delegate from the extremely opportunist British Fabian Society. No one supported her. Her motives were simple enough: British bourgeois ladies hope to obtain the franchise for themselves, without its extension to women workers in Britain.

The First International Socialist Women's Conference was held concurrently with the Congress in the same building. Both at this Conference and in the Congress Commission there was an interesting dispute between the German and Austrian Social-Democrats on the draft resolution. In their campaign for universal suffrage the Austrians tended to play down the demand for equal rights of men and women; on practical grounds they placed the main emphasis on male suffrage. Clara Zetkin and other German Social-Democrats rightly pointed out to the Austrians that they were acting incorrectly, and that by failing to press the demand that the vote be granted to women as well as men, they were weakening the mass movement. The concluding words of the Stuttgart resolution ("the demand for universal suffrage should be put forward *simultaneously* for both men and women") undoubtedly relate to this episode of excessive "practicalism" in the history of the Austrian labour movement.

The resolution on the relations between the socialist parties and the trade unions is of especial importance to us Russians. The Stockholm R.S.D.L.P. Congress went on record for *non-Party* unions, thus endorsing the neutrality standpoint, which has always been upheld by our non-Party democrats, Bernsteinians and Socialist Revolutionaries. The London Congress, on the other hand, put forward a different principle, namely, closer alignment of the unions with the Party, even including, under certain conditions, their recognition as Party unions.[40] At Stuttgart in the Social-Democratic subsection of the Russian section (the socialists of each country form a separate section at international congresses) opinion was divided on this issue (there was no split on other issues). Plekhanov upheld the neutrality principle. Voinov, a Bolshevik, defended the anti-neutralist viewpoint of the London Congress and of the Belgian resolution (published in the Congress materials with de Brouckère's report, which will soon appear in Russian). Clara Zetkin rightly remarked in her journal *Die Gleichheit* that Plekhanov's arguments for neutrality were just as lame as those of the French. And the Stuttgart resolution—as Kautsky rightly observed and as anyone who takes the trouble to read it carefully will see—puts an end to recognition of the "neutrality" principle. There is not a word in it about neutrality or non-party principles. On the contrary, it definitely recognises the need for closer and stronger connections between the unions and the socialist parties.

The resolution of the London R.S.D.L.P. Congress on the trade unions has thus been placed on a firm theoretical basis in the form of the Stuttgart resolution. The Stuttgart resolution lays down the general principle that in every country the unions must be brought into permanent and close contact with the socialist party. The London resolution says that in Russia this should take the form, under favourable conditions, of party unions, and party members must work towards that goal.

We note that the harmful aspects of the neutrality principle were revealed in Stuttgart by the fact that the trade-union half of the German delegation were the most adamant supporters of opportunist views. That is why in Essen, for example, the Germans were against Van Kol (the trade unions were not represented in Essen, which was a Congress solely of the Party), while in Stuttgart they supported him. By playing into the hands of the opportunists in the Social-Democratic movement the advocacy of neutrality in Germany has *actually* had harmful results. This is a fact that should not be overlooked, especially in Russia, where the bourgeois-democratic counsellors of the proletariat, who urge it to keep the trade-union movement "neutral," are so numerous.

A few words about the resolution on emigration and immigration. Here, too, in the Commission there was an attempt to defend narrow, craft interests, to ban the immigration of workers from backward countries (coolies—from China, etc.). This is the same spirit of aristocratism that one finds among workers in some of the "civilised" countries, who derive certain advantages from their privileged position, and are, therefore, inclined to forget the need for international class solidarity. But no one at the Congress defended this craft and petty-bourgeois narrow-mindedness. The resolution fully meets the demands of revolutionary Social-Democracy.

We pass now to the last, and perhaps the most important, resolution of the Congress—that on anti-militarism. The notorious Hervé, who had made such a noise in France and Europe, advocated a semi-anarchist view by naïvely suggesting that every war be "answered" by a strike and an uprising. He did not understand, on the one hand, that war is a necessary product of capitalism, and that the proletariat cannot renounce participation in revolutionary wars, for such wars are possible, and have indeed occurred in capitalist societies. He did not understand, on the other hand, that the possibility of "answering" a war depends on the nature of the crisis created by that war. The choice of the means of struggle depends on these conditions; moreover, the struggle must consist (and here we have the third misconception, or shallow thinking of Hervéism) not simply in replacing war by peace, but in replacing capitalism by socialism. The essential thing is not merely to prevent war, but to utilise the crisis created by war in order to hasten the overthrow of the bourgeoisie. However, underlying all these semi-anarchist absurdities of Hervéism there was one sound and practical purpose: to spur the socialist movement so that it will not be restricted to parliamentary methods of struggle alone, so that the masses will realise the need for revolutionary action in connection with the crises which war inevitably involves, so that, lastly, a more lively understanding of international labour solidarity and of the falsity of bourgeois patriotism will be spread among the masses.

Bebel's resolution (moved by the Germans and coinciding in all essentials with Guesde's resolution) had one shortcoming—it failed to indicate the active tasks of the proletariat. This made it possible to read Bebel's orthodox propositions through opportunist spectacles, and Vollmar was quick to turn this possibility into a reality.

That is why Rosa Luxemburg and the Russian Social-Democratic delegates moved their amendments to Bebel's resolution. These amendments (1) stated that militarism is the chief weapon of class oppression; (2) pointed out the need for propaganda among the youth; (3) stressed that Social-Democrats should not only try to prevent war from breaking out or to secure the speediest termination of wars that have already begun, but should utilise the crisis created by the war to hasten the overthrow of the bourgeoisie.

The subcommission (elected by the Anti-Militarism Commission) incorporated all these amendments in Bebel's resolution. In addition, Jaurès made this happy suggestion: instead of enumerating the methods of struggle (strikes, uprisings) the resolution should cite historical examples of proletarian action against war, from the demonstrations in Europe to the revolution in Russia. The result of all this redrafting was a resolution which, it is true, is unduly long, but is rich in thought and precisely formulates the tasks of the proletariat. It combines the stringency of orthodoxy—i.e., the only scientific Marxist analysis with recommendations for the most resolute and revolutionary action by the workers' parties. This resolution cannot be interpreted *à la* Vollmar, nor can it be fitted into the narrow framework of naïve Hervéism.

On the whole, the Stuttgart Congress brought into sharp contrast the opportunist and revolutionary wings of the international Social-Democratic movement on a number of cardinal issues and decided these issues in the spirit of revolutionary Marxism. Its resolutions and the report of the debates should become a handbook for every propagandist. The work done at Stuttgart will greatly promote the unity of tactics and unity of revolutionary struggle of the proletarians of all countries.

Nine years after the Stuttgart congress, when the Second International lay in ruins, Zinoviev wrote a reflective account of the International's policies on the question of war for the Bolshevik magazine *Sbornik Sotsial-Demokrata* (*Sotsial-Demokrat* Collection). The following selection analyzes the background to the Stuttgart debates. It is followed by a footnote by Lenin that appeared in the original text.

The tendency struggle at the Stuttgart congress[41]

by Gregory Zinoviev

The 1905 revolution, while not victorious, still showed the enormous revolutionary strength hidden in modern Russia. The events of 1905 also revealed the deeply reactionary role of the modern Western "democracies." They were ready and willing—as imperialist France showed in action—to rescue the predatory Romanov monarchy for the sake of a small group of capitalist magnates. The fortunes of the Russian bourgeois-democratic revolution proved to be linked very closely to the struggle of the Western European proletariat for socialist revolution.

The revolution of 1905 did not triumph. But it did awaken the peoples of Asia, and blew a fresh wind of freedom even into Europe.

At the same time decisive events were unfolding in the arena of international politics. The 1894–95 (Sino-Japanese), 1898 (Spanish-American), and 1900–1902 (Anglo-Boer and Sino-European) wars were openly imperialist in character and extended the imperialist web. An entire epoch of purely imperialist wars was approaching. . . .

The peace of Europe balanced on a razor's edge. The imperialist conflict between Britain and Germany ripened before everybody's eyes. The military buildup on land and sea took on ever more insane dimensions. Imperialism entered its highest phase. The outlines of the approaching Europe-wide war already stood out with total clarity: a war in which the two imperialist alliances would stake tens of millions of lives for the sake of their slaveholdings. Imperialist reaction grew more insolent every day. It became obvious that the impending war posed the question of life or death for the Second International.

This was the general outline of the situation in which the Stuttgart congress assembled. How would the Second International respond to it?

By 1907 it was no longer possible to make excuses about the weakness of the movement, and blame everything on inadequate strength. The number of Socialist voters and the membership of the Socialist trade unions had reached almost ten million.

By that time, however, opportunism had in essence already won the upper hand in the International. The existence of such a numerically enormous army standing for socialism only inspired the statesmen of opportunism all the more toward "positive," "organic" work in the capitalist framework and in "collaboration" with the bourgeoisie. . . .

The central debate on militarism and the struggle against war took place not in the congress itself but in the commission. But hundreds of delegates attended the commission, and all the parties sent their best representatives there. Everyone recognized that the commission would decide the most important question—was the International to be or not to be? . . .

The main struggle was between the majorities of the German and French parties: on the one hand, Bebel and Vollmar; on the other, Jaurès and Vaillant.

In fact the differences between these two camps were far narrower than they might appear to have been. Bebel, Jaurès, Branting, Vandervelde, Vollmar, and Vaillant all spoke about "the nation" and "the fatherland" in terms which the social patriots of all countries now find it easy to employ to justify their "new" tactics. Both Bebel and Jaurès spoke plainly about "defense of the fatherland." Neither explained the clear difference between genuine defense of the fatherland as in earlier national wars and the fraudulent character of this slogan in present-day imperialist wars.

The original proposals of Bebel (and of the German Social Democracy in general) aimed at ratifying the old decisions and leaving everything as it was in the past. But their key feature was their failure to state clearly that in the event of war Social Democracy would have to resort to certain revolutionary measures. "We will do what we can," he said, "but do not put us in an impossible position now. Do not bring things to the point where you put a weapon into the hands of the public prosecutor to use against the legality of our party." That was the meaning of the speeches of Bebel and his co-thinkers at Stuttgart.

And Jaurès and the French majority? Their resolution openly said that all means should be used to prevent war, "right up to mass strike and insurrection." The sacred words were spoken. Does this mean that Jaurès and his followers were better revolutionaries than Bebel and his supporters?

By no means!

We must search elsewhere for the key to Jaurès's position. Like Bebel, he did not draw a distinct line between defense of the fatherland in national wars and "defense of the fatherland" in capitalist wars. He too recognized defense of the fatherland in a "defensive" war. But he also sensed that his French fatherland was *weaker* than the Germans'. He realized that most likely it would be France that had to "defend itself"—his fatherland, "the birthplace of revolution," "the custodian of culture," and so on. Hence his efforts to secure the agreement of Socialists of other countries—first and foremost the Germans—to aid France if it were forced to wage a "just" war. Hence his striving to win from the German Socialists a clear commitment to resort not only to platonic protest, but to strike and insurrection. . . .

Both the French and German majority stood on *one and the same* principled position. The difference flowed only from the fact that one belonged to a country in a stronger military position, the other to a country in a weaker military position. . . .

We find more warnings of the danger threatening the proletariat from imperialist reaction in the speeches of Vaillant and Jaurès. "The danger exists that the bourgeoisie will resort to a world war merely to harm the proletarian movement," said Vaillant. But he completely failed to consider how, *in such a war, began for this purpose,* the theories of defensive war and of defense of the fatherland would be applied. . . .

Only one speech delivered at Stuttgart differed from both these positions *in principle*—Rosa Luxemburg's. This speech provided, although not yet in a fully finished form, the basis of the *revolutionary* Marxist position. It approached closest of all to the conception that now serves as the internationalists' basic position.

Rosa Luxemburg spoke "in the name of the Russian and Polish delegations." She attended the subcommission of the congress that worked out the text of the Stuttgart resolution as the delegate of the Russian Bolsheviks. . . .

An amendment signed by Lenin and Luxemburg among others was adopted by the congress and became the central passage of the Stuttgart resolution. It is much quoted today, for it alone clearly expresses the Marxist viewpoint.

An extraordinarily peculiar situation arose in drawing up the resolution. It was remarkable. The two main camps, *both* the German *and* the French majorities, stood on the principle of "defense of the fatherland." But while they were guaranteed an enormous majority in the congress, the resolution itself contained not one word about recognizing "defense of the fatherland." Neither did it express the basic position outlined above of Jaurès's followers endorsing defensive war and defense of the fatherland, a position on which the Germans were completely divided.

How this happened is a very important question. At first

glance it is completely inexplicable. But it is precisely this that gives us the key to the position of the entire Second International on this question. This position was ambiguous and contradictory.

The opportunists, who constituted the majority in the commanding heights of the party everywhere in Europe, quite consciously united reformism with "patriotism." . . . Fully aware of what they were doing, the opportunists led the Second International to social chauvinism.

For another wing of the International the matter was not so simple. The Marxist Center current in Germany and the revolutionaries of the old school in France (whose most typical representative was the late Vaillant) remained imprisoned by the old ideology generated by the period of national wars.[42] At the same time, they were sufficiently experienced politicians to recognize that the war actually approaching in Europe would be of another kind. If war broke out, it would be between the robbers themselves. In this war it would be impossible to distinguish between the attacking and the defending sides; it would be a mockery to speak of justice, rights, or morality.

In an article written immediately after the Stuttgart congress, Kautsky wrote:

"In today's world political situation a war in which a proletarian or democratic interest in defense or attack could arise, is out of the question. . . . The war danger today comes only from world colonial politics, which the proletariat decisively and fundamentally rejects."

With these words Kautsky undoubtedly expressed the conviction or attitude at that time of a whole layer of veteran leaders of the Second International, possibly even including the best of the opportunists.

The approaching war, toward which the bourgeoisie of the "great" powers was steadily leading Europe, could only be an imperialist war, a robber war. In this war, from the point of view of the proletariat and of democracy, there could be no talk of defense and attack. The Second International could not escape this idea; it was hammering relentlessly on the consciousness of all the leaders of the Second International for whom the workers' blood was not water and for whom proletarian interests were not empty words.

From the recognition of this was born the Stuttgart resolution. In it there is not a single word about "defense of the fatherland," but instead a Hannibalic oath to use the coming war to arouse the people and hasten the downfall of the bourgeois order. . . .

In 1907 to write a resolution in the name of an *international* congress that openly put forward the "defense of the fatherland" *was simply politically unthinkable.*

Imagine for a moment just how things stood. Jaurès, Bebel, Vaillant, Vollmar, Vandervelde, and Branting all approved equally of the principle of defense of the fatherland in a "defensive" war. But here they sit, as members of the commission, at one table, in order to draw up—in 1907!—a common resolution. If they didn't want to be up in the clouds they had to speak of the struggle between the Triple Alliance and the Triple Entente, about those real conflicts that had been occupying political center stage in Europe now for a number of years, about the competition between the two imperialist alliances which could lead only to war. The official leaders of the International took their standing on this, the only real ground. What could they say? Which side could they recognize as defending "civilization": the Triple Alliance or the Triple Entente?

When the war of 1914 began it was no longer necessary to advance closely reasoned arguments. When wartime passions were running high it was possible to stuff the workers full of phrases about "the struggle against tsarism," the overthrow of "Prussian militarism," about the basic principles of morality and right being defended by Tsar Nicholas II and the

"German humanity" being defended by Wilhelm II. *But in 1907 this was impossible.* Not a single honest socialist could then "take sides" with either of the coalitions. Everyone had to recognize that both groupings represented predatory and reactionary imperialism. . . .

This created a contradictory situation for the leaders of the Second International. That is why a small group on the left could exert such great influence on the adopted resolution. That is why instead of "defense of the fatherland" we find praise for the methods of struggle against war that were put into practice by the Russian workers in 1904–1905.

The revolutionary Marxists, whose representative was Rosa Luxemburg, were only a small minority at Stuttgart. The opportunists and "Center" indisputably made up the overwhelming majority. But the logic of the situation was on the side of the revolutionary Marxists. Only they consistently defended the interests of millions of workers of all countries. And the working masses, who were invisibly present at the congress, *compelled* the official leaders of the Second International to adopt much of what the revolutionary Marxists proposed through the words of Rosa Luxemburg.

FOOTNOTE BY LENIN

I remember clearly that before the final editing of this amendment we had extended negotiations with Bebel himself. The initial wording spoke far more frankly of revolutionary agitation and revolutionary action. When we showed it to Bebel, he told us, "I cannot endorse this, for if I did the prosecutor's office would outlaw our party organization, and we want to avoid that unless something really serious has happened." After consultation with lawyers and repeated alterations of the text so as to express the idea within the law, the final formula was arrived at which Bebel agreed to endorse.

Above, Jaurès speaking at public rally during 1907 Stuttgart congress; below; August Bebel, Hendrick van Kol.

1904 congress of the Second International at Amsterdam.

Chapter 2

Resisting the threat of imperialist war: 1907–1914

The debate in the Second International on imperialism and the war danger continued in the years after the Stuttgart congress, and was pursued most vigorously in the German party. Its predominant size and political authority guaranteed that controversies in the German Social Democratic Party would set the tone for the whole International. A few months before the Stuttgart congress, a dispute had broken out in the SPD on whether the party's parliamentary fraction had given ground to militarism in the April 1907 Reichstag debates on the military budget. The remarks by SPD deputy Gustav Noske provoked particular controversy.

SPD deputies came to this session of the Reichstag, the German parliament, smarting from a sharp electoral rebuff received in January 1907 in the so-called Hottentot elections. "Hottentot" was a racist term used by southern African whites for the Herero and Khoikhoi tribes. In 1904 these tribes rebelled against the cruelty of the German colonial administration in South-West Africa (now Namibia). The German troops sent to quell the uprising indiscriminately massacred the tribal peoples, and an estimated

60,000 Hereros were killed out of a total population of 80,000.

The German Socialists vigorously criticized the massacre and German colonial policy as a whole. The government, seeing an opportunity to attack the SPD, then transformed the content of the 1907 Reichstag elections into a referendum on German colonial expansion and world power status. It successfully rallied all the bourgeois parties in a chauvinist crusade, denouncing the SPD's opposition to German colonialism and militarism. For the first time since 1887, the ruling classes succeeded in halting the growth of the Socialist popular vote. By ganging up against the SPD candidates in run-off elections the bourgeois parties were able to cut the Socialist parliamentary fraction almost in half, from eighty-one deputies down to forty-three.

Socialists disagreed on what lessons to draw from the defeat. Bending to the pressure of the chauvinist crusade, the opportunists argued that the party should steer away from the contentious ground of Germany's foreign policy and emphasize instead economic and social questions. The left wing, on the contrary, saw the need to devote more agitation and propaganda to countering imperialist policies in an effort to overcome bourgeois influence among workers on this vital question.

The SPD fraction used the Reichstag debates on military preparations to reassert the SPD's commitment to national defense. SPD speakers stressed that the party's demands for institution of the militia system (the arming of the people as a whole) and an end to officers' mistreatment of the soldiers would strengthen Germany's military capacity. The government was quick to use this opening to drive a wedge between the position of the majority of the party leadership and the work of its most prominent antimilitarist spokesman, Karl Liebknecht.

August Bebel's main Reichstag speech presented the SPD's proposals for military reform as proposed improvements in Germany's capacity for national defense; one of his suggestions was that Germany follow the example of Japanese military education.

1907 Reichstag debate on the military budget[1]

AUGUST BEBEL: . . . After pointing out that the Japanese army to everyone's surprise has demonstrated a high degree of military excellence, a German reporter wrote, "These innate warlike virtues are further reinforced by an outstanding system of physical training of the young from earliest childhood on. In the great fencing schools of Osaka, Kobe, Yokohama, Tokyo, and others, countless children between the ages of eight and twelve can be seen practicing every day with wooden swords (shaped like the old two-handed kind) and wielding them with elegance and dexterity. You see these little tykes going after each other with an ardent zeal that often becomes fury. Every European would surely stand in awe of such gymnastic training of the future defenders of the fatherland." *("Hear! Hear!" from the Social Democrats)*

That's what a German paper has to say on the military upbringing of Japanese youth! Well now, Gentlemen, I am convinced that Germany, which long stood in the forefront of military training, has long since been surpassed by other nations. It really is becoming necessary that we deal with this question, because only after it has been thoroughly discussed will it then be possible to go into the other question: that of a truly significant reduction in the length of military service. . . .

LT. GEN. KARL VON EINEM (PRUSSIAN MINISTER OF STATE FOR WAR AND MEMBER OF THE FEDERAL COUNCIL): . . . Gentlemen, I have here a book by Mr. Liebknecht. On page forty-one there is a very odd sentence which I wish to call to the special attention of the gentlemen of the Social Democratic Party.

He discusses cases of mistreatment and says:

"But precisely because this form of disciplinary violence is built into the foundations of the army"—I have demonstrated with statistics that it is not built into the army at all—"provides us with a superb means of waging a fundamental and highly successful struggle against militarism and of arousing ever broader masses of the people against it. It provides a means of bringing class consciousness to layers that would otherwise still be difficult or impossible to reach."

Gentlemen, if that is correct, then one would have to assume that the grievances brought before the Reichstag by the Social Democrats serve less to combat the abuses than to make agitation. *("That's right!" from the right. Commotion and shouts from the Social Democrats)* Gentlemen, if those are not your motives, then fight against statements like these. Fight against this kind of book.

BEBEL: But we have done so in the congresses of our party!

VON EINEM: Well then, Mr. Bebel, keep it up and good luck. *(Much laughter)* . . .

BEBEL: The minister of war referred earlier to our motives in bringing up the abuses in the military. In my remarks I already indicated what our purpose was in doing so, and I stressed that our primary concern was that our comrades serving in the army have been treated in a manner which frequently gives cause for complaints. And I said that we had therefore brought up the matter in order to bring about some improvement. I must state that I reject any suggestion that we were guided by other motives. *("Very good!" from the Social Democrats)* I wish to make it very clear that whatever any third parties outside of these walls have said or may say in reference to this issue is not and cannot be authoritative. . . .

GUSTAV NOSKE: . . . Our position on the military system

flows from our conception of the principle of nationalism. We call for independence for every nation. But from this it follows that we also value preserving the independence of the German people. Our position, of course, is that it is damn well our duty and obligation to see to it that the German people are not shoved up against the wall by some other nations. *("That's right!" from the Social Democrats)* If anyone should try to do that, we would of course defend ourselves with as much resolution as could any of those gentlemen sitting on the right side of the house who act as though they had a hereditary title to patriotism. *("That's right!" from the Social Democrats)* . . .

Let our people have the best education, and let our youth receive the best possible physical training. Then we in Germany will have the best soldiers—even if we dispense with mindless drill and a whole range of other things that are still so revered today *("That's right!" from the Social Democrats)* as we have always proposed.

While the nationalist papers echoed Von Einem's pleasure at the stand of the SPD spokesmen, radical SPD newspapers thundered against compromise on the war question. Noske's emphasis on Social Democracy's willingness to fight for the kaiser came in for widespread criticism. Noske replied that he had done no more than restate the party's traditional stand in support of national defense, and the revisionists leaped to his defense.

The "Noske debate" raged on into the party's September 1907 congress at Essen. A resolution of Kiel Social Democrats, one of many on this topic at the congress, stated: "In debates on the military budget we should designate as speakers only those fraction members who offer a full assurance that they will take a firm position against militarism and defend the line of the resolution of the Stuttgart International congress."[2] This resolution was defeated by a large majority.

In the congress discussion, Clara Zetkin and Paul Lensch, speaking for the SPD's left wing, presented what they considered to be an internationalist line consistent with the Stuttgart resolution, yet one still in line with the SPD's traditional "national defense" policy.

Lensch and Zetkin on national defense[3]

PAUL LENSCH: . . . During the major European crisis of 1859, the one enemy of democratic institutions who could have posed a serious threat of national oppression was Napoleon III. And so at that time, both Engels and Lassalle spoke out in their pamphlets quite vigorously for war against him.[4] Engels wrote in his day almost word for word what today Noske claims to have merely said: if we are attacked, we will defend ourselves. The problem is, that was 1859. *(Laughter)*

Similarly, still in the 1870s, Bebel often said in the German Reichstag, "The mortal enemy of all European culture and also of German democracy, insofar as any exists, is Russian tsarism. If it should come to war against Russian tsarism, it goes without saying that German Social Democracy too will do its duty in the conflict." *("Very true!")* But that was in the seventies, eighties, and nineties. Since then, an event has taken place which Comrade Noske seems not to have noticed at all, and that is the outbreak of the Russian revolution. As a result, Russian tsarism has been eliminated as an effective, mortal enemy. It lies shattered on the ground. *(Objections)*

Russian militarism is completely incapable of waging a major war in Europe, because it has been transformed into an army to defend tsarism within its own borders. In such a political situation the same statement of readiness to go to war against Russia that was once an article of faith for revolutionists, has today, after the outbreak of the Russian revolution, been transformed into an article of faith for European reaction. To now declare support for such a war, means forgetting the great historic transformations that have taken place. . . .

Today there is no longer any state that threatens the independence of the German nation. I must emphasize that in earlier cases we always pointed to a specific danger. We referred to Russia or to France. But we never went so far as to give the ruling classes a blank check, so to speak, for any conceivable war of aggression. That would turn the working class into a kind of insurance agency for the ruling classes. In the present situation, there is no conceivable war that the Social Democracy could support. Noske's statement was therefore as superfluous as it was damaging.

CLARA ZETKIN: . . . These widespread objections are not directed solely against what Noske said. Rather they are primarily provoked by what our fraction failed to say on the question of the armed forces—what was not said, or at least not stressed strongly enough. A wide layer of party members have been unable to dismiss the feeling that Social Democratic criticisms in the last session were less sharp and vigorous than at earlier budget debates. Under the circumstances that was especially painful and distressing. Why? Because the January elections were just behind us, and our opponents were gloating over our defeat.

Party members felt then that we should expressly reject the

advice of our well-known, good friends in bourgeois circles to return from the elections chastened and respectful of bourgeois civilization. Comrades wanted us to maintain and defend our fundamental views unyieldingly and irreconcilably. *("Very true!")* But we noted the absence in Noske's speech of such a sharp emphasis on our basic ideas. His speech emphasized national solidarity much too strongly. At the same time it contained not one single reference to the existence of a class party of the proletariat which recognizes no national boundaries.

The difference between our patriotism and that of the ruling classes is not one of degree but of essence. *(Lively applause)* We do not want to keep this a secret or leave any doubt about it. The ruling classes' patriotism is conservative and reactionary. Its goal is clear—to maintain the fatherland as a domain for their class exploitation and domination and to extend this class exploitation beyond the borders to the proletariat of other countries. But the patriotism of the proletariat is revolutionary. It comes from the conception that the fatherland must first be conquered in struggle against the internal enemy, bourgeois class rule. This rule must be overturned in order for the country to be a fatherland for all. . . .

Inch by inch, step by step the proletariat conquers the fatherland in the proletarian class struggle. . . .

Two paths lead to the goal, and we must take both of them. One is that we work unceasingly for the democratization of the standing army, with the ultimate goal of arming the people as a whole. We do this not to render the fatherland defenseless before the enemy, but to make it strong. The other is that we undermine militarism from within through the revolutionizing of minds. A senior officer is supposed to have said that the government could no longer undertake an unpopular, frivolous war because the reserves are thoroughly imbued with socialism. We must see to it that the proletarian recruits enter the barracks so filled with the socialist spirit that they become unusable in battle against the external enemy.

Iranian Socialists and Kautsky discuss imperialism

For the most part, the SPD's 1907 debate on "national defense" took place in the old framework of a potential German war against tsarist reaction. Lensch noted that the Russian revolution had made this concept obsolete. But Germany's transformation into an imperialist power and its world expansion had done even more to change the context, bringing to the fore threats of war over colonial possessions, such as Morocco, or against the uprisings of colonial peoples, such as the Hereros.

The German ruling classes, like their counterparts in the other imperialist powers, justified these murderous wars against their colonial subjects by claiming to fulfill a civilizing mission in the non-European world. Some European Socialists stood very close to this view, twisting to their own ends statements by Marx and Engels on the progressive and revolutionary role of mid-nineteenth century capitalism in precapitalist societies. Some Socialist cadres of Asia and Africa also discussed whether imperialism, the force that was creating the first elements of a modern proletariat in their countries, was not thereby a progressive force.

The massive uprising against foreign domination that broke out in Iran in 1906 raised this question for Iran's Social Democrats—among the first in Asia to rally to the Second International. Many workers and intellectuals there had been influenced by their contact with the Russian revolution and the Social Democrats in Russia. Under the rule of the Qajar dynasty, the Persian Empire had fallen victim in the nineteenth century to Russian and British domination. The empire was politically fragmented and economically extremely backward; modern industry had not yet appeared, although tens of thousands of Iranians were employed in industry within the tsarist empire. Following the outbreak of the Russian revolution in 1905, Iran underwent its Constitutional Revolution of 1906–11—a massive popular upheaval to modernize and democratize the state and to free it from foreign rule. Only in 1911, with the aid of Russian military intervention, was Iran finally brought back under imperialist control.

A Social Democratic Party had been formed in 1904 among Iranians living in Baku, part of the Russian Empire. Soon after the outbreak of the Iranian revolution, a Social Democratic group formed inside the country. This new group, in Tabriz, began to discuss the questions that had aroused such heated debate at Stuttgart: Was imperialist penetration a force for progress or for reaction? Should a struggle led by bourgeois forces to free the country from imperialist control be supported?

The Iranian Socialists wrote to two leaders of the International, Karl Kautsky and a leading Russian Marxist, Georgi Plekhanov, soliciting their opinions on these questions. No reply from Plekhanov has been published. The letter to Kautsky and his reply are printed below.

On October 16, 1908, a meeting of the Tabriz group voted 28–2 to constitute a Social Democratic organization there, with goals that included participating in the revolutionary democratic movement, while heightening the class consciousness of the proletariat.

IRANIANS' LETTER TO KAUTSKY[5]

TABRIZ, JULY 16, 1908

Citizen Karl Kautsky
Dear Citizen,

We recognize your great competence in the economic and social sciences, and we would like to pose a few questions in this letter. As the answers to these are important to us, we would appreciate an immediate reply.

The Tabriz Social Democratic Group has recently been

formed by some of this city's intellectuals. . . . Our group has already drafted its program of action. But the recent turmoil in Iran has forced us to change our next meeting, scheduled for September, into a general assembly to reconsider our program and to discuss our participation in the Iranian democratic movement.

Industrial capitalism has not yet come into existence in Iran, and an industrial proletariat (in the European sense of the word) does not exist on which our group could base itself. However, despite this some of our comrades correctly believe that the group can go beyond its limited educational work, and that we can and must actively participate in the democratic movement. We can work for democracy and for the country's economic and social progress at the same time, without abandoning our fundamental principles. Social Democrats naturally do not abstain from a democratic movement, because they are not only Socialists but also democrats—and the most consistent democrats at that. Therefore the group agreed in principle to participate in this movement. Some comrades disagree with this. They are not completely opposed, but raise partial and conditional criticisms, which stem from their unclear conception of the nature of the Iranian revolution.

As you may know, there are two views among us concerning the nature of the movement in our country. According to the first, the Iranian revolution has no progressive content. This view contends that the thrust of the movement is against foreign capital, which is the only factor that can help develop the economy of the country. In other words, that the aim of this movement is to block the road to European civilization.

By contrast, those who support the second view claim that the movement is progressive because it is aimed against the feudal order, and because it is a movement of the masses, who are exploited by the landlords.

The democratic movement includes the big and commercial bourgeoisie. They are struggling against the big landowners, who keep the population in poverty through hoarding, and so on, and who bar the development of trade. Although the movement in its initial stage contains retrogressive tendencies arising from reactionary elements, and inclined toward nostalgia for the past, these tendencies will be destroyed as the movement develops. Supporters of this view stress that despite the so-called struggle against foreign capital, imports of European products increased during the tax year 1906–1907, the year Iran had a parliament, and when the democratic movement was ascendant. . . .

We hope that you will be in a position to answer the following theoretical and scientific questions, which we must discuss in our next general assembly. We will be very grateful for your answer, as it will make our decisions much easier.

1) What in your view is the character of the Iranian revolution? Is it retrogressive? Please explain your view.

2) How should Social Democrats participate in a democratic and progressive movement? What if the movement is reactionary? We recognize that such participation should not violate our fundamental principles. Please explain your views. . . .

Arshavir Chalangarian

KARL KAUTSKY'S REPLY

AUGUST 1, 1908

Dear Comrade,

I apologize for not responding to your letter earlier. The delay was not because of a lack of interest on my part; on the contrary, I consider your letter very important. But I have been traveling and received your letter only yesterday.

Since I am traveling and do not possess the necessary documents, it is not possible for me to write a complete answer to your letter. Therefore I will limit myself to a few lines. Turning to your question: it is difficult for me to pass judgment on a country about which I know very little, a country, furthermore, where new forces and social layers, previously unknown even in their own country, have suddenly emerged, and where sharp oscillations occur every day.

I can say without hesitation, however, that Iranian Socialists have the duty to participate in the democratic movement. Like simple democrats, Socialists take part in this struggle alongside bourgeois and petty-bourgeois democrats. But for Socialists the fight for democracy is a class struggle. The triumph of democracy will not end the political struggle, but will open new struggles that were virtually impossible to wage under the previous despotic rule.

In a democratic movement supported by all classes of the country's toilers there are always reactionary tendencies brought in by small peasant and petty-bourgeois layers. This is not a reason to stay out of the struggle; on the contrary it poses the need to combat such tendencies inside the democratic movement. This was Marx's tactic in 1848 when there was no chance of establishing a strong proletarian party in Germany.

A hostile attitude toward foreign capital is not necessarily reactionary, even though heavy industry and railroads are as important for Iran as for other countries. Capitalist development has now begun in Iran and perhaps it will develop even faster if it is not exploited by foreign capital. This capital appears in Iran not only as industrial capital, but also, and to a greater extent, as capital for moneylending. In this form it exploits the whole nation, including the peasants, whose taxes pay the interest on the government's debts. Consequently, the peasants become poorer and are unable to buy industrial goods. This is why foreign capital in Iran, as in Russia, obstructs the development of the home market, the essential precondition for industrial development.

When Iran's exploitation by foreign capital is ended, the extra surplus value remaining inside the country will help develop the internal market and domestic capital. For the proletarian movement, democracy means not only political freedom, but also independence of the country from foreign influence—both economic and political. By fighting to overthrow capitalism, the peoples of the East weaken European capitalism and therefore strengthen the European proletariat. Thus they fight for socialism not only in their own countries, but also for us in Europe.

If the 1905 revolution in Russia had been able to stop interest payments on the government loans, a revolution in France would have resulted. If British India and Egypt were strong enough to achieve their independence, that would deliver a mighty blow to English capital and intensify the contradictions between British capitalism and the proletariat.

Iran and Turkey, in their struggle for liberation, fight for the freedom of the international proletariat.

Dear Comrade! I hope this short letter will satisfy you. When I return to Berlin, if time allows, I will study the Iranian situation in depth.

In any case, it is important for us to be informed of the revolutionary movement in Iran, its causes, tendencies, and the classes that support it.

I will be happy to publish an article by you on this topic in *Die Neue Zeit,* a newspaper distributed internationally. Your Marxist viewpoint would enrich your article and allow us to see the problems more clearly than would that of a simple democrat.

Although your country is in a revolutionary situation, I hope these lines will reach you. I shake your hand and wish success for you and your comrades.

With comradely greetings,
K. Kautsky

New opportunities in Germany

The workers' movement in Germany grew steadily in the years before World War I. By 1914, the SPD's membership had climbed to more than one million, the circulation of its press to two million, and the party's voting strength to four million. SPD-led trade unions organized workers in basic industry and led many militant and successful struggles.

Yet despite this power, the working class made no headway in the prewar years in achieving its most strongly felt demands. Despite Germany's burgeoning capitalist wealth, most of the working class achieved no further improvement in its living standards after the turn of the century. There was no reform of Germany's semi-absolutist political structure. The danger of war was increasing, and workers were burdened with rising taxes to finance the growing cost of Germany's military machine. Democratic rights faced new attacks. New limits were imposed on the right of assembly and association; a 1908 law, for example, prohibited those under eighteen years of age from attending political meetings, and restricted meetings held in languages other than German. Social Democrats were barred from many jobs, including on the railways, and continued to be jailed for public expression of their political views. The prewar years thus saw increasing class antagonisms and significant waves of workers' mass action in 1905–1906 and after 1910.

Socialists took the offensive in 1910 for democratic rights, demanding universal, equal suffrage in the parliamentary elections held in each of the component states of the German Empire. Nationally, the Reichstag was elected by universal male suffrage, although it had very little power. But the Kingdom of Prussia, which included Berlin and was the most important component state by far, stubbornly maintained an electoral system rigged to ensure a mechanical parliamentary majority for the propertied classes.

When the government introduced a new electoral law in February 1910 maintaining the voting privileges of the capitalists and landowners, Prussia exploded in mass demonstrations organized by the Social Democrats. The police attacked many of these actions, and banned the giant rally planned by Berlin Socialists for March 6. The Berlin party organization responded by announcing a "suffrage promenade" in Treptow Park—observing that there was no law against a walk in the park. As the police massed to block access to the park, party cadres quietly spread the word that the demonstration would be held at an entirely different location. An estimated 150,000 demonstrated in the Tiergarten park, undisturbed, and the outwitted police arrived only near the close of proceedings.

All social classes viewed this Socialist show of force as a portent of revolutionary struggles to come. Its impact encouraged Social Democrats to come to grips with the growing problem of opportunism in their ranks, which had acquired its greatest influence in the south German states. In Baden, especially, the opportunist-led party organizations had been collaborating with ruling-class forces for many years and had regularly voted for the government's budget proposals since 1894. The SPD leadership under Bebel had condemned this practice as a violation of principle and had passed many resolutions against it, but they had never taken any action to halt it.

Encouraged by the mass suffrage campaign, the left decided that it was time to act against the opportunists. At the September 1910 party congress in Magdeburg, 211 delegates signed a resolution proposing the automatic expulsion from the SPD of anyone who voted in the future for government budget proposals. While the Bebel leadership did not accept this resolution, it did join in the assault on the opportunists, and a resolution was adopted threatening the opening of expulsion proceedings should the opportunists vote for a budget again.

The congress also debated the lessons of the suffrage campaign. Many workers felt this campaign showed the need for more vigorous action in the future, and motions for the use of mass protest strikes were passed in many party branches. Half-day demonstration strikes were held in Kiel and Frankfurt. Rosa Luxemburg, who had popularized the notion of mass protest strikes at the time of the 1905–6 Russian revolution, pressed the leadership to carry the movement forward in this direction. This course was not adopted. Kautsky, indeed, refused to print Luxemburg's proposal in the party journal *Die Neue Zeit,* and instead urged a course of patience, reliance on traditional tactics, and a strategy of gradually wearing down the enemy's resistance through attrition.

By the time of the party congress, the suffrage movement had ebbed, hampered by the tradition-bound leadership's orientation to parliamentary action. Sixty-two congress delegates, headed by Luxemburg, signed a resolution which declared "that the fight for the suffrage in Prussia can be waged to victory only through great, determined mass actions in which all means must be employed, including the political general strike if necessary."[6] It also proposed the opening of a discussion of the mass strike in the party press and party meetings. After a vigorous polemic, the statement of principle in the resolution was adopted, while the specific proposal for party discussion was dropped.

Lenin commented on the meaning of the SPD's Magdeburg conference in the following article in the November 16, 1910, issue of the Bolshevik newspaper *Sotsial-Demokrat* (Social Democrat).

Two worlds[7]

by V.I. Lenin

Much has been written in all the newspapers about the Magdeburg Congress of the German Social-Democratic Party. All the main events of this Congress, all the vicissitudes of the struggle are sufficiently known. The outward aspect of the struggle of the revisionists with the orthodox, the dramatic episodes of the Congress overmuch engaged the attention of the readers, to the detriment of a clarification of the principles involved in this struggle, the ideological and political roots of the divergence. Yet the debates in Magdeburg—above all on the question of the Badenites voting for the budget—provide exceedingly interesting material for characterising the two worlds of ideas and the two class tendencies *within* the Social-Democratic Labour Party of Germany. The voting for the budget is but one of the manifestations of this division into two worlds, a division which is so deep that it is undoubtedly bound to be expressed on much more serious occasions, much more profound and important. And now, when, as everybody can see, a great revolutionary storm is *impending* in Germany, the Magdeburg debates should be regarded as a small review of forces covering a small fraction of the army (for the question of voting for the budget is only a small fraction of the fundamental questions of Social-Democratic tactics) *before* the beginning of the campaign.

What has this review shown as to how different sections of the proletarian army understand the tasks that confront them? How, judging by this review, will these different sections of the army conduct themselves when the time comes?—these are the questions on which we intend to dwell. . . .

Bebel . . . said in his closing remarks at Magdeburg: "The masses cannot understand that there are Social-Democrats who support with a vote of confidence a government which the masses would much prefer to do away with altogether. I often get the impression that a section of our leaders has ceased to understand the sufferings and afflictions of the masses *(thunderous applause)*, that the position of the masses has become alien to them." Yet "all over Germany an enormous resentment has accumulated among the masses."

"We are living through a time," said Bebel in another part of his speech, "when rotten compromises are particularly impermissible. Class contradictions are not subsiding, but growing more acute. We are on the threshold of very, very grave times. What will happen after the forthcoming elections? We shall wait and see. If matters come to the outbreak of a European war in 1912 you will see what we are in for, where we shall have to take our stand. It will probably not be where the Badenites are standing today."

While some people are becoming smugly content with the state of affairs which has become customary in Germany, Bebel himself turns all his attention to the inevitable change which is impending and advises that the Party's attention should be turned to it. "All our experiences so far have been skirmishes at the outposts, mere trifles," said Bebel in his closing remarks. The main struggle lies ahead. And from the standpoint of this main struggle, the whole tactics of the opportunists are the height of spinelessness and short-sightedness.

Bebel only speaks in hints about the coming struggle. Never once does he say outright that revolution is impending in Germany, although such, undoubtedly, is the idea in his mind—all his references to the aggravation of contradictions, the difficulty of reforms in Prussia, the inextricable position of the government and the classes in command, the growth of resentment among the masses, the danger of a European war, the intensification of the economic yoke as a result of the high cost of living, the amalgamation of the capitalists in trusts and cartels, etc., etc.—all are clearly intended to open the eyes of the Party and the masses to the inevitability of a revolutionary struggle.

Why is Bebel so cautious? Why does he confine himself to pointed references? Because the maturing revolution in Germany encounters a special, peculiar political situation that does not resemble other pre-revolutionary periods in other countries and for that reason requires from the leaders of the proletariat the solution of a somewhat *new* problem. The chief feature of this peculiar pre-revolutionary situation consists in the fact that the coming revolution must inevitably be incomparably more profound, more radical, drawing far broader masses into a more difficult, stubborn and prolonged struggle than all previous revolutions. Yet at the same time this pre-revolutionary situation is marked by the greater (in comparison with anything hitherto) domination of *legality,* which has become an obstacle to those who introduced it. There lies the peculiarity of the situation, there lies the difficulty and novelty of the problem.

The irony of history has brought it about that the ruling classes of Germany, who have created the strongest state known in the whole second half of the nineteenth century, who have consolidated conditions for the most rapid capitalist progress and conditions for the most stable constitutional legality, are now most unmistakably coming to a point when this legality, *their* legality, *will have to be* shattered—so that the domination of the bourgeoisie may be preserved.

For about half a century the German Social-Democratic

Labour Party has made exemplary use of bourgeois legality, having created the best proletarian organisations, a magnificent press, having raised to the highest pitch (that is possible under capitalism) the class-consciousness and solidarity of the proletarian socialist vanguard.

Now the time is drawing near when this half-century phase of German history *must,* by force of objective causes, be replaced by a different phase. The era of utilising the legality created by the bourgeoisie is *giving way* to an era of tremendous revolutionary battles, and these battles, *in effect,* will be the destruction of *all* bourgeois legality, the *whole* bourgeois system, *while in form* they must begin (and are beginning) with panicky efforts on the part of the bourgeoisie to get rid of the legality which, though it is their own handiwork, has become unbearable to them! "You shoot first, Messieurs the Bourgeoisie!"—with these words, spoken in 1892, Engels summed up the peculiarity of the position and the peculiarity of the tactical problems of the revolutionary proletariat.

The socialist proletariat will not forget for a moment that it is confronted, inevitably confronted, with a revolutionary mass struggle that must sweep away all the legalities of the doomed bourgeois society. But, at the same time, a party which has magnificently utilised a half-century of bourgeois legality *against* the bourgeoisie has not the slightest reason to renounce those conveniences in the struggle, that advantage in battle afforded by the fact that *the enemy is caught in the toils* of his own legality, that the enemy is compelled to "shoot first", is compelled to shatter his own legality.

There lies the peculiarity of the pre-revolutionary situation in modern Germany. That is why old Bebel is so cautious, fixing all his attention on the great struggle which is to come, exerting all the power of his vast talent, his experience and authority against the short-sighted, spineless opportunists, who do not understand this struggle, who are not fit to lead it, who during the revolution will probably find themselves degraded from the *leaders* to the *led* or even cast aside.

In Magdeburg these leaders were remonstrated with, they were censured, they were given an official ultimatum as the representatives of all that was unreliable that had accumulated in the great revolutionary army, of all that was weak, infected with bourgeois legality and stupefied by pious prostrations before this legality, before all the limitations of what is *one* of the eras of slavery, i.e., one of the eras of bourgeois supremacy. In condemning the opportunists, threatening them with expulsion, the German proletariat thereby expressed its condemnation of all the elements in its mighty organisation personifying stagnation, diffidence, flabbiness and inability to break with the psychology of moribund bourgeois society. In condemning the bad revolutionaries in its own ranks the vanguard class held one of the last reviews of its forces before entering upon the path of social revolution.

*

While the attention of all revolutionary Social-Democrats throughout the world was concentrated on seeing how the German workers were preparing for action, selecting the moment for action, keeping a watchful eye on the enemy and *purging* themselves of the weaknesses of opportunism—the opportunists throughout the world were gloating over the differences which had arisen between Luxemburg and Kautsky in their estimate of the present situation, on the question whether one of those turning-points like the Ninth of January in the Russian revolution was due now *or not just yet*,[8] this very minute *or the next*. The opportunists gloated. They did their utmost to make a burning issue of these differences, which were not of prime importance, in the columns of *Socialist Monthly, Golos Sotsial-Demokrata* (Martynov), *Zhizn, Vozrozhdeniye* and suchlike liquidationist papers and *Neue Zeit* (Martov).* The shabbiness of these methods of the opportunists in all countries was indelibly registered in Magdeburg, where differences of opinion among the revolutionary Social-Democrats of Germany did not play any appreciable role. The opportunists however gloated too soon. The Magdeburg Congress *adopted* the first part of the resolution proposed by *Rosa Luxemburg*, in which there is direct reference to the mass strike as a means of struggle.

* In *Neue Zeit* Martov was met with an emphatic rebuke from Comrade Karski. [Footnote in original.]

The Copenhagen congress

The International's 1910 Copenhagen congress discussed the question of war and militarism once again, this time in an atmosphere heavy with the menace of the imperialist arms buildup and the growing threat of war in the Balkans. Keir Hardie, perhaps the most prominent leader of British socialism, joined with Vaillant in pressing for a commitment to more vigorous antiwar action along the lines of the French majority resolution of 1907. However, their resolution was defeated in commission by a vote of 119 to 58. The resolution finally adopted restated the conclusions of the Stuttgart text, adding only a number of immediate proposals to lessen the war danger.

Resolution against militarism[9]

The congress notes that despite the peace congresses and the pacific protestations of the governments, military armaments have increased enormously in the last few years. Furthermore the naval arms race in particular, whose latest phase is the construction of dreadnoughts, signifies more than just the demented squandering of public funds for unproductive purposes and the consequent shortage or absence of funds for the provision of social welfare and workers' relief. It also threatens all peoples with material exhaustion through intolerable burdens of indirect taxation and all states with financial ruin. These armaments imperiled world peace very recently, and they will threaten it again and again. In view of the danger that the arms race poses to human civilization, the well-being of the peoples, and the lives of the masses, the congress reaffirms the resolutions of previous congresses, in particular that of the Stuttgart congress, and reiterates that:

There are neither differences nor discords among the workers of all countries that could lead to war. Today's wars are caused by capitalism, especially the international competition of capitalist states for world markets, and by militarism, which is a central instrument of bourgeois class domination in domestic affairs and of the economic and political subjugation of the working class. Wars will cease once and for all only when the capitalist economic order is abolished. The working class, which carries the main burden of war and is hardest hit by its consequences, has the greatest interest in abolishing war. The organized Socialist proletariat of all countries is therefore the sole reliable guarantor of world peace. Therefore the congress again urges the workers' parties of all countries to carry on energetic work among the entire proletariat, and above all among the youth, to expose the causes of war and to educate the workers and the youth in the spirit of the brotherhood of peoples.

Socialist parliamentary representatives have repeatedly affirmed their duty to refuse funds for armaments and to use all their strength to combat them. The congress stands by this position and expects these representatives:

A) continually to reiterate the demand for compulsory international courts of arbitration in all conflicts between states;

B) continually to renew proposals aimed at general disarmament and, first and foremost, at an agreement for limitation of naval armaments and abolition of the right of seizure at sea;

C) to demand the abolition of secret diplomacy and the publication of all the existing and future treaties and agreements between governments;

D) to intervene in favor of the peoples' right of self-determination and in their defense against armed attack and forcible subjugation.

The International Socialist Bureau will provide material assistance to all Socialist representatives in the struggle against militarism and if necessary will work to bring about common action on their part. Should military conflicts arise, the congress confirms the Stuttgart resolution which states:

"If a war threatens to break out, it is the duty of the working classes and their parliamentary representatives in the countries involved, supported by the coordinating activity of the International Socialist Bureau, to exert every effort in order to prevent its outbreak. They must employ the means they consider most effective, which naturally vary according to the sharpening of the class struggle and the general political situation.

"In case war should break out anyway, it is their duty to intervene for its speedy termination and to strive with all their power to utilize the economic and political crisis created by the war to rouse the masses and thereby hasten the downfall of capitalist class rule."

The congress instructs the bureau to implement these measures, should war be threatened, by at once taking the steps necessary so the workers' parties of the affected countries can examine how best to bring about common action to prevent war.

Gregory Zinoviev recounted in 1924 that "Lenin undertook once again at the Copenhagen congress to form a left wing by trying to call an international meeting of revolutionary Marxists. The meeting was haphazardly organized. About ten people met, and half of them had cold feet. They regarded Comrade Lenin with a fair dose of skepticism. He was not well known, and prominent representatives of the International had spoken against him on the question of uniting Russian Social Democrats. The Copenhagen attempt to pull together a left wing within the Second International ended in fiasco."[10]

Rosa Luxemburg's article below, published in May 1911 in a left-wing SPD paper, the *Leipziger Volkszeitung* [Leipzig peoples's paper], criticized the pacifist illusions reflected in the action proposals of the Copenhagen resolution and in many earlier Socialist statements.

Peace utopias[11]

by Rosa Luxemburg

Our task on the question of peace does not consist merely in vigorously and continually demonstrating the Social Democrats' love of peace. First and foremost it is to expose the nature of militarism to the masses of people and to bring out sharply and clearly the differences in principle between the Social Democrats' standpoint and that of the bourgeois peace lovers.

What are these differences? Certainly not merely that the bourgeois apostles of peace rely on the influence of pretty words, while we do not depend on words alone. Even our starting points are diametrically opposed. The friends of peace from bourgeois circles believe that world peace and disarmament can be realized within the framework of the present social order, while we, who base ourselves on the materialist conception of history and on scientific socialism, are convinced that militarism can be banished from the world only with the destruction of the capitalist state.

From this follows our entirely different policy for propagating the idea of peace. The bourgeois friends of peace take pains—and from their point of view this is perfectly logical and explicable—to conjure up all sorts of "practical" projects for gradually restraining militarism. They are naturally inclined to take every superficial sign of a tendency toward peace for good coin, to take every expression of the rulers' diplomats in this vein at face value, to exaggerate it into a basis for earnest activity. The Social Democrats, on the other hand, must consider it their duty here, just as in all matters of social criticism, to expose bourgeois attempts at restraining militarism as pitiful half measures, and the expressions of such sentiments, from government circles in particular, as diplomatic hocus-pocus, and to oppose the bourgeois prattle and pretense with a ruthless analysis of capitalist reality. . . .

From this same standpoint the task of Social Democrats with regard to declarations of the kind made by the British government can only be to expose the idea of a partial *limitation* of armaments, as an impracticable half measure.[12] We must argue it through to the end, explaining to the people that militarism is intimately linked up with colonial, trade, and international politics. We show that the existing nations, if they seriously and honestly wish to call a halt to the arms race, would therefore have to begin by dismantling their weapons of commercial warfare, giving up campaigns of colonial robbery and for controlling spheres of influence in all parts of the world. In a word, in their foreign as well as in their domestic politics they would have to do the exact opposite of everything that is essential to the political character of a capitalist state today. The heart of the Social Democratic conception is therefore that militarism in both its forms—as war and as armed peace—is a legitimate child and a logical result of capitalism, and can only be overcome with its destruction. Hence whoever honestly desires world peace and liberation from the tremendous burden of armaments must also desire socialism. Only in this way can real Social Democratic education and recruitment be conducted on the armaments question.

This work, however, will be rendered somewhat difficult and the position of the Social Democrats will become unclear and vacillating if, by some strange exchange of roles, our party tries to convince the bourgeois state that this state itself can quite well limit armaments and bring about peace and that it can do this from its own standpoint, that of a capitalist class state. . . .

Until now, the pride of our party—and its firm scientific grounding—has been that we do not pull slogans out of a hat, whether in the general lines of our work or in our day-to-day activity. Rather, we have always relied on our understanding of the tendencies of social development and made the objective lines of this development the basis of our position. For us the determining factor until now has not been what was possible in terms of the current relationship of forces within the state, but what was possible in terms of the tendencies of social development. . . .

Arms limitation and curbing militarism are not part of international capitalism's further development. In fact they could result only from the *stagnation* of capitalist development. Only those who hope for a halt to [imperialist] world politics—and this is the highest and last stage of capitalist development—can consider a halt to the further development of militarism likely. World politics and militarism, its servant on land and at sea and during war and peace, are nothing other than capitalism's specific method for both developing and resolving international contradictions. With the further development of capitalism and of the world market, these contradictions, together with internal class antagonisms, increase and intensify without limit until they become intolerable and bring about the social revolution.

Only those who believe that class antagonisms can be softened and be blunted, and that capitalist economic anarchy can be contained, can think it possible that these international conflicts can subside, ease, or dissolve. For the international antagonisms of the capitalist states are only the complement of class antagonisms, and world political anarchy is but the reverse side of the anarchic system of capitalist production. Only together can they grow and only together can they be overcome. "A little peace and order" is, therefore, impossible, a petty-bourgeois utopia, as much so in the capitalist world market as in world politics, in the limitation of economic crises as in the limitation of armaments.

Let us glance at the events of the last fifteen years of international development. Where do they show any tendency toward peace, disarmament, or settlement of conflicts by arbitration?

During these fifteen years we had the following: the 1895 war between Japan and China, the prelude to the East Asiatic period of imperialism; the 1898 war between Spain and the United States; Britain's 1899–1902 Boer War in South Africa; the European great powers' 1900 campaign in China; the 1904 Russo-Japanese War; the 1904–7 German Herero War in Africa; Russia's 1908 military intervention in Persia; and at the present moment France's military intervention in Morocco.[13] This does not even mention the incessant colonial skirmishes in Asia and in Africa. The bare facts alone show that for fifteen years hardly a year has gone by without a war.

But more important still is the enduring aftereffect of these wars. The war with China was followed by a military reorganization in Japan which made it possible ten years later for Japan to undertake the war against Russia and become the predominant military power in the Pacific. The Boer War resulted in a military reorganization of Britain and the strengthening of her land forces. The war with Spain inspired the United States to reorganize its navy and made it a colonial power with imperialist interests in Asia. Thus the germ of the clash of interests between the United States and Japan in the Pacific was created. The Chinese campaign was accompanied in Germany by a thorough military reorganization—the great Navy Law of 1900, which marks the beginning of Germany's competition with Britain on the sea and the sharpening of the antagonisms between these two nations.

But to this we must add yet another and extremely important factor: the social and political awakening to independent life of the hinterlands, of the colonies and the "spheres of interest." The revolution in Turkey, in Persia, the revolutionary ferment in China, in India, in Egypt, in Arabia, in Morocco, in Mexico, all these are points of departure for world political antagonisms, tensions, military activities, and armaments.[14] Just in the course of these fifteen years the points of friction in international politics increased to an unparalleled degree, a number of new states stepped forward into active struggle on the international stage, and all the great powers undertook a thorough military reorganization.

As a result of all these events, the antagonisms have reached an unprecedented acuteness. This process is going further and further, since on the one hand the ferment in the Orient increases daily, and on the other every agreement between the military powers unavoidably becomes the starting point for fresh conflicts. The Reval [Tallinn] Entente between Russia, Great Britain, and France, which Jaurès hailed as a guarantee for world peace, sharpened the crisis in the Balkans, accelerated the outbreak of the Turkish revolution, and encouraged Russia to take military action in Persia. It also led to a rapprochement between Turkey and Germany which, in its turn, sharpened the Anglo-German antagonisms. The Potsdam agreement resulted in the sharpening of the crisis in China and the Russo-Japanese agreement had the same effect.[15]

These facts signify anything but a tendency toward mitigation of international conflicts, or toward world peace. This is plain to anyone with open eyes.

In view of all this, how is it possible to speak of tendencies toward peace in bourgeois development, which supposedly neutralize and overcome its tendencies toward war? How do they find expression?

In Sir Edward Grey's declaration and that of the French parliament?[16] In the "armament weariness" of the bourgeoisie? But the middle and petty-bourgeois sections of the bourgeoisie have always groaned about the burden of militarism, just as they groan about the devastation caused by free competition, the economic crises, the unscrupulousness of stock exchange speculation, the terrorism of the cartels and trusts. The tyranny of the tycoons in America has even led to a rebellion of broad masses of the people and protracted legal proceedings against the trusts by the government authorities. Do the Social Democrats interpret this as a sign that the trusts are beginning to be curtailed, or do they not rather give a sympathetic shrug of the shoulders for the petty-bourgeois rebellion and a scornful smile for the government's legal campaign?

The "dialectic" of the tendency of capitalist development toward peace, which supposedly cuts across and prevails over its tendency toward war, simply confirms the old truism that the roses of capitalist profit-making and class domination have thorns even for the bourgeoisie. But the bourgeoisie prefers to wear its thorns round its long-suffering head, in spite of all pain and woe, rather than get rid of them—and its head as well—in response to the well-intentioned advice of the Social Democrats.

Explaining this to the masses, ruthlessly dispelling all illusions about the bourgeoisie's sham moves for peace, and declaring the proletarian revolution to be the first and only step toward world peace—these are the tasks of the Social Democrats with regard to all disarmament farces, whether produced in Petersburg, London, or Berlin. . . .

In July 1911, while French troops were establishing a protectorate over Morocco, a German warship steamed into the Moroccan harbor of Agadir to land troops against the French, provoking the second Morocco crisis. Britain sided with France and for a while war seemed imminent. The crisis was settled in November when Germany recognized France's protectorate in Morocco, in return for territorial concessions from France in Equatorial Africa.

The secretary of the International Socialist Bureau, Camille Huysmans, responded to the crisis by sending out a letter on July 6 asking all sections of the International whether they thought an emergency meeting of the bureau should be held. The German party's confidential reply was sent by Hermann Molkenbuhr, one of the secretaries of the SPD Executive Committee.

The Molkenbuhr letter on Morocco[17]

BERLIN
JULY 8, 1911

Esteemed comrades,

I have not yet been able to submit your letter to a meeting of the Executive Committee. For the moment, I want to convey my personal opinion, which I also expressed in a meeting on Tuesday.

I see the whole affair as something cooked up by the heads of our government to divert attention from the domestic situation and create a mood favorable to them for the Reichstag elections. Our government's domestic policy has led it into a mess that would wring tears from a stone. It is resorting to the familiar methods that Bismarck used with Boulanger in 1887 and Bülow, with the Hottentots in 1906.[18]

Now I give credit to Bethmann-Hollweg and Kiderlen-Wächter for every kind of stupidity, sufficient even to lead to serious European conflicts. But in the case of Morocco I don't think these gentlemen have a free hand. Conflicting capitalist interests come into play here, and in Germany the "pro-French" group is the stronger. . . .

I don't believe the managers of our foreign policy will go any further. The biggest capitalists are keenly aware that this would harm their interests, and they will order a timely "halt."

Even if we were to rapidly launch a very active campaign, subordinating all questions of domestic policy and so permitting our opponents to concoct an effective election slogan against us, it is still not clear that we would achieve anything. For [the industrialists] Krupp and Thyssen are just as afraid of Socialists as Bethmann-Hollweg. We are vitally concerned that domestic issues in this discussion (tax policy, the privileges of great landowners, the social insurance system, and so on) not be driven into the background. And this could well happen, even if we speak on the Morocco question in every village, and build up a movement of opposition. Given the notorious clumsiness of Bethmann and his colleagues, it is very likely they will suffer a well-deserved defeat in their game, which will provide us with one more argument in the elections.

Best wishes,
H. Molkenbuhr

As a member of the International Socialist Bureau representing the Social Democracy of Poland and Lithuania (SDKPiL), Rosa Luxemburg received a copy of the Molkenbuhr letter. On July 24, at the height of the crisis, she published it in the *Leipziger Volkszeitung* along with a comment on the policy it embodied.

On Morocco[19]

by Rosa Luxemburg

We must confess that the conclusions drawn by Molkenbuhr from the Morocco affair, which he has portrayed with such specialized competence, have very little merit. They boil down to the following exalted political approach: "Leave it to the grandees of the steel monopolies to order a halt to the German action in Morocco at the appropriate moment. As for us, we will pay as little attention as possible to the entire affair, since we have other business to attend to, namely the Reichstag elections." . . .

It is quite likely that our opponents, now in a painfully difficult spot, will try and utilize the Morocco uproar to fashion an election slogan against the Social Democracy in order to create some sort of "patriotic" carnival atmosphere in the elections. But if we assume this and even consider that this absurd and frivolous adventure could provide them with "an effective slogan" against us, it seems completely illogical to avoid discussing this question in our agitation. . . .

If [Molkenbuhr's] position errs by showing too little confidence in the power of our slogans, we believe it also fails by greatly overestimating the weight of capitalist interests as a guarantee of peace. . . .

The future course of the Morocco adventure will not be determined by Mannesmann and Thyssen alone. Like every sudden thrust in world power politics, it can easily escape the control of its originators. Starting as a silly game with matches it can flare up into a world holocaust. "Concessions" of some sort can easily shift the center of gravity to southern Africa or some other part of the world, and there give birth to completely new conflicts. We therefore hold that it is not Social Democracy's duty to soothe public opinion, but rather to arouse it and warn it of the dangers lurking behind every such adventure in present-day world politics.

It is best to rely not on the commitment to peace of any particular capitalist clique, but on the resistance of the enlightened masses as a force for peace. Moreover, the decision to keep quiet plays into the hands of the architects of the government's Morocco policy. [French Ambassador] Cambon and [German State Secretary] Kiderlen, the two high priests of colonial policy, insisted that we all maintain a respectful silence so they could carry out their hocus-pocus unhindered behind the backs of the parliamentary deputies and the public. What better proof that the workers' parties must do just the opposite. Where the government aims to present the public with a fait accompli, we must vigorously appeal to the public to intervene. The demand for convocation of the Reichstag, which first appeared in *Vorwärts,* was therefore a step in the right direction. Unfortunately, if we are not mistaken, our central party organ no longer advances this demand.

Finally, the general conception of an election campaign as expressed by the party's Executive Committee is, we believe, open to objection. They would have us confine our agitation exclusively to questions of domestic policy like taxes and social legislation. But questions of financial policy, junker rule,[20] and the paralysis in social reform are organically tied to militarism, naval expansion, colonial policy, the kaiser's personal rule, and his foreign policy. Any artificial separation of these domains can only produce a fragmentary, one-sided picture of our present circumstances.

Above all we must carry out *socialist education* in the Reichstag elections. This cannot be accomplished, however, if we aim our criticism exclusively at Germany's internal political conditions, and fail to portray the overall international context—capital's deepening domination over all parts of the world, the obvious anarchy everywhere you look, and the prominent role of colonialism and world power politics in this process. We must not fashion our electoral agitation as some simplistic political primer cut down to a couple of catchy slogans, but as the Socialist world view in its all-encompassing totality and diversity.

The publication of the Molkenbuhr letter raised an uproar within the SPD. A wave of criticism of the Executive Committee forced it to initiate a protest campaign and, on September 3, 1911 more than 200,000 took part in a rally in Berlin against the government's aggressive policies.

At the SPD congress later that month the Executive Committee faced more criticism for its tardy and limited response. The party leadership attempted to shift the axis of discussion to criticism of Luxemburg's publication of the Molkenbuhr letter, a confidential document.

The issue was taken to the International Socialist Bureau meeting of September 23–24, where a motion of censure against Luxemburg was introduced. After some discussion, in which Lenin protested the idea of censure, the motion was withdrawn and a compromise proposal passed, stating that in the future such correspondence should be regarded as confidential.

Luxemburg and the left, however, had succeeded in spurring the German party leadership to action, and thus enabled mass opposition to the war danger to find expression.

The SPD debate on imperialism

The SPD adopted a resolution on imperialism at its 1912 congress in Chemnitz (Karl-Marx-Stadt), which helped prepare the party for its mobilization that year against the Balkan War.

While the debate at the 1912 congress in Chemnitz marked, on the whole, a step forward for the SPD, it also witnessed a renewal of the division between the party's "Center" current, whose main theorist was Kautsky, and the revolutionary left wing. This division had surfaced at the 1910 Magdeburg congress, and had subsequently deepened in written discussion. Anton Pannekoek, a leader of the party's radical Bremen organization, had conducted a lengthy debate with Kautsky in 1911 in the pages of *Die Neue Zeit*. Pannekoek had argued that the party should aim to rally the masses in action on issues like suffrage reform, using measures like mass protest strikes, instead of relying on Kautsky's policy of attrition, and had urged that mass action be emphasized instead of subordinating the party's tactics to parliamentary maneuvers. In 1912 Karl Radek, a collaborator of the Bremen radicals, debated Kautsky on imperialism in the pages of *Die Neue Zeit,* challenging Kautsky's theory that forces existed within capitalism that could counteract and overcome imperialism's tendency toward war.

A view similar to Kautsky's was expressed at the Chemnitz congress by Hugo Haase, the reporter for the Executive Committee. Haase explained the economic forces within capitalism that drove it to increase armaments and to an imperialist policy. "Imperialism is not peaceable," he concluded, "its tendency is to generate conflict and war." However, he said, it is wrong to view war as inevitable. "Marx and Engels correctly warned us again and again against a fatalistic conception of history. While we must keep sight of imperialism's violent character, which whips the states into war against each other in their eagerness for booty, this is countered by other tendencies."

Haase pointed to what he viewed as these tendencies within the ruling class itself: "Capitalist groupings in different countries intertwine and are tied together by international links of many kinds, and rather than conduct wars, which are exhausting, uncertain in outcome, and dangerous to profits, they hold it to be more advantageous to divide the world's markets among themselves." He recalled the agreement to share the coal resources of Morocco between the powerful French and German monopolies, Schneider-Creuzot and Krupp, which had led them to work against the war danger in the Morocco crisis of 1911. Haase also quoted protestations for peace by other magnates of German heavy industry, and argued "indeed trade relationships between Germany and England have proliferated and grown so dense that the outbreak of war between the two states would bring with it economic crisis of truly annihilating scope."

"Stronger than the cohesion of international capital," Haase continued, is the "solidarity and fraternity of the international proletariat," pointing in particular to the links between the British and German working classes. Moreover, military experts agreed that the modern war machine was dependent on the morale of the soldiers, he contended, and although they could be forced to the front lines, they could not be forced to fight with enthusiasm. Finally, he stated, the ruling classes must reckon with the consequences of war for the class struggle, particularly should the war lead to defeat. The masses would blame capitalism for the suffering brought on by the war: "Would this not mean that the hour had struck for the Social Democracy to win political power and assume the place of the present ruling classes?"[2]

In the discussion, Eduard Bernstein accepted the framework of Haase's report, emphasizing that militarism was by no means inevitable under capitalism. Karl Liebknecht called for a heightening of the class struggle as the only way to show the capitalists the price they would pay for war. Ludwig Quessel, speaking for the pro-imperialist current on the party's extreme right wing, supported the continued independence of countries such as China and Iran as the best way to secure access to them for German products. It is not enough to call for abolition of tariff barriers, he continued, "Wherever the German government intervenes to ensure that our industry is truly granted equal access to markets, we must stand behind it."[22]

Rosa Luxemburg had not been elected as a delegate to the congress—an indication of the party establishment's success in isolating the left wing. Speaking for the left, Paul Lensch and Anton Pannekoek explained some of the revolutionists' disagreements with Haase and their hesitations about the resolution.

Lensch and Pannekoek on imperialism[23]

PAUL LENSCH (LEIPZIG): My misgivings chiefly concern the passage in the resolution dealing with arms reduction. . . . Our difference of opinion on the evolution of imperialism is most clearly expressed precisely on the disarmament question. Let there be no mistake, I consider a temporary agreement between two capitalist states on questions of arms policy by no means excluded. On the contrary, I have always stressed this possibility. But that is something completely different from what is called for in the resolution and was earlier proposed by the Reichstag fraction. Here it is a question of an "international agreement for general arms reduction." And as before, I certainly consider that to be utopian.

Comrades! How did the international arms buildup which we have witnessed these last ten years come about? Is it really just a case of an international misunderstanding, which could be resolved by an international agreement? That would mean that world history had made a mistake, as it were; that a capitalism without resort to force, without colonies and fleets is also feasible. No doubt that is true, but only in a vacuum! Perhaps in your imagination, or on paper, you can conceive of a capitalism without violence. But we deal with the real capitalism here on earth. Our task cannot be to correct World History's homework, and say, "Dear World History, here is your work back! It's swarming with mistakes. I marked them all for you in red. In the future I expect better work from you." *(Laughter)* That's not how it works! We must deal with capitalism as it is, and in so doing we must admit that the arms race grows naturally and inevitably out of the given economic relations.

Protected by tariffs, imperialism has shut out free competition in the internal market and replaced it with monopoly. In the process it has demolished the economic foundations of liberalism—an event of great political importance!—but only to unleash free competition all the more in the world market. The struggle for the world market brings as its necessary complement the international arms race. The one is unthinkable without the other. War is the continuation of politics by other means, says Clausewitz. By the same token the international arms race is the continuation of international economic competition by other means. . . .

The arms race is a symptom of imperialism, which we must not view in isolation. We have no special weapons for our fight against imperialism, only the great but simple slogans: agitate and organize! We say to the masses that imperialism is the last expression of the existing society, that it opens up all the well-springs of social revolution. Because it subjugates the entire earth to its domination, imperialism taps the last reservoir of the earth's life-giving springs, and blocks up the channels through which the powerfully increased productive forces can be discharged. But even at home it drives all contradictions to the breaking point. While the tables of the capitalist magnates groan under the weight of their gold, the specter of hunger haunts the alleyways of the working people. The class struggle sharpens visibly, and in the collosal struggles of the modern unions, the organized classes stand so close to each other that they can see the whites of their opponents' eyes.

We are approaching a time of great mass struggles and sharp conflicts, which will make the highest demands on the understanding and energy of the proletarian organizations. We must arm ourselves for these struggles. I completely agree with Haase's conclusions that if we extend our organization, our political education, if we prepare ourselves—then all we must do is to be ready! *(Lively applause)* . . .

ANTON PANNEKOEK (BREMEN): While you can demonstrate that imperialism damages the interests of broad layers, even of the bourgeoisie, the fact remains that the whole bourgeoisie supports this policy. . . .

We have not only the arms industry to fight. The circle of those whose interests are directly at stake is much bigger. All big business and finance capital has a stake in imperialism and consequently in the arms race. Therefore imperialism is more than the product of bourgeois pressure groups lobbying for extra profits. It is more like a way of thinking, an ideology. Only for big business is it a question of the lobbying for profits. The bourgeoisie as a whole allows itself to be taken in tow for many material and ideological reasons.

We often hear talk of imperialism as a sort of mental derangement of the bourgeoisie and in the party congress issue of the *Chemnitzer Volksstimme* [Chemnitz people's voice] Bernstein speaks of a spiritual epidemic. But we should not conceive of it in such an un-Marxist manner, as if it were an accident. Our literature exposes all the threads that tie each bourgeois group to the imperialist policy. That is why we consider it utopian to count on its reversal. . . .

The ruling class cannot adopt the course of disarmament because it is an exploiting class, because the politics of looting and brutality are part of its soul. Each of the different powers wants to be in as powerful a position as possible to pursue this policy. Power alone determines the outcome of each and every one of their conflicts. Even when it does not lead to war, the arms race is useful for large-scale capital, which uses it to force concessions from its competitors, the other world powers. That is why the arms race is pursued so zealously. Haase mentioned that the capitalist magnates are already organizing internationally, but he added that this process will not rid the world of war. If that is so, and the capitalists know that wars are unavoidable, then the arms race will not disappear either.

HUGO HAASE: Ending the arms race is not the same thing as disarmament.

PANNEKOEK: We emphasize that the arms race is inevitable, not to justify it in any way, but to direct our fight against imperialism.

We want to struggle the most vigorously against this brutal, dangerous form of capitalism. But not by trying to drive capitalism back to an earlier form. That is impossible. There is only one way: beyond imperialism to socialism.

The resolution on imperialism itself was adopted with only three votes against and two abstentions, and it helped rally the party ranks for the massive antiwar actions of the coming year. It was reprinted by the Bolsheviks in 1915 in their theoretical journal *Kommunist* (Communist) as a reminder of the SPD's prewar stand against imperialism.

1912 SPD resolution on imperialism[24]

Given the exploited proletariat's stunted standard of living, the enormous expansion of capitalist production requires an extension of its markets. The immense accumulation of capital is driven to find new areas of investment and new possibilities of turning a profit.

With the growing exports of commodities and capital, of production and transportation equipment, world trade grows ever more and the global economy expands. The employers' organizations, cartels, and trusts, strongly reinforced by the tariff system, increasingly dominate economic life. They use their influence on their countries' governments to harness the powers of the state to their drive to expand, to enclose large parts of the world's productive areas in their spheres of influence and power, and to exclude foreign competitors. They willingly resort to the most brutal violence, whenever it promises to bring success. The Mainz congress [of the SPD] in 1900 denounced the unscrupulous policy of robbery and conquest that results from imperialist expansionism. To carry out their plunder expeditions successfully and bring the booty to safety, the imperialists perfect and stockpile their weapons of murder as never before.

In every state where the capitalist class has this need to

expand, the same means are employed. This leads to deep antagonisms and severe entanglements that further augment and intensify the arms race to the point of madness.

The resulting danger of devastating world war is further increased through shameless incitement by the capitalist magnates and the junkers, who have a special interest in the provision of war materiel and in the expansion of the upper state bureaucracy and the officer corps.

Imperialism strengthens the power of the war-mongers, endangers the right of association, and hinders the further development of social reform. Military expenditures place an unbearable burden on the masses of the people, while the increasing cost of all necessities undermines their health.

The bourgeois parties are completely under imperialism's spell. They approve without resistance all appropriations for the army and navy. The Social Democracy most emphatically opposes all imperialist and chauvinist endeavors wherever they appear. With firm resolve it nurtures international proletarian solidarity, which never entertains hostile feelings toward another people.

Imperialism is a product of the capitalist economic system and can only be completely overcome along with it. Nothing must be left undone, however, to lessen its dangerous consequences.

This congress proclaims its resolute will to make every effort to bring about an understanding among the nations and maintain the peace.

The congress demands international agreements to put an end to the arms race, which threatens the peace and is driving humanity into a terrible catastrophe.

The congress demands freedom of world trade, in place of the policy of conquest, that hunger for plunder. It further demands the abolition of the tariff system, which only serves to enrich the capitalist magnates and big landlords.

The congress expects that party comrades will work tirelessly to build the political, trade union, and cooperative organizations of the class-conscious proletariat in order to fight against brutal imperialism with greater force until it is overcome. It is the task of the proletariat to transform capitalism, now brought to its highest stage, into socialist society, thus securing lasting peace, independence, and freedom for the peoples.

The Balkan Wars

The following month a coalition of the governments of Serbia, Greece, Montenegro, and Bulgaria attacked Turkey. This launched a devastating conflict that threatened for a time to expand into a world war. In the First Balkan War (October 1912–May 1913) Turkey was defeated and forced to cede most of its European territories. During the peace negotiations held in London under the supervision of the European imperialist powers, the victorious Balkan states fell out over a division of the spoils. Behind these differences were the imperialist powers, which had their own interests in the Balkans. This conflict led to the Second Balkan War (June–August 1913) in which the Serbian, Greek, and Romanian governments defeated Bulgaria and forced it to cede some of its territory. Also Turkey seized the opportunity to retake some territory from Bulgaria.

The Balkan governments justified the first war as a national liberation struggle to free compatriots still under the Turkish yoke. Balkan Socialists, however, opposed the war and voted against war credits.

In October 1912 the Central Committee of the Russian Social

Democratic Labor Party (Bolsheviks) issued the following manifesto, drafted by Lenin, which was circulated in leaflet form and also published in German, French, and Belgian Socialist newspapers.

To all the citizens of Russia[25]

Comrades workers and all citizens of Russia!

A war of four powers against Turkey has started in the Balkans. War threatens the whole of Europe. Despite their lying government denials, Russia and Austria are preparing for war. Italy is becoming more brazen in her policy of plundering the Turkish lands. The stock-market panic in Vienna and Berlin, in Paris and London shows that the capitalists of all Europe see no possibility of preserving European peace.

All Europe wants to take part in the events in the Balkans! Everyone favours "reforms" and even "freedom for the Slavs". Actually, Russia wants to snatch a piece of Turkey in Asia and to seize the Bosporus. Austria has designs on Salonika, Italy on Albania, Britain on Arabia, and Germany on Anatolia.

The crisis is mounting. Hundreds of thousands and millions of wage slaves of capital and peasants downtrodden by the serf-owners are going to the slaughter for the dynastic interests of a handful of crowned brigands, for the profits of the bourgeoisie in its drive to plunder foreign lands.

The Balkan crisis is a link in the chain of events which since the turn of the century has everywhere been leading to sharper class and international contradictions, to wars and revolutions. The Russo-Japanese war, the revolution in Russia, a series of revolutions in Asia, mounting rivalry and hostility between the European states, the threat to peace over Morocco, and Italy's plunderous campaign against Tripoli[26]—such has been the preparation of the current crisis.

Wars and all their calamities are produced by capitalism, which keeps millions of working people in bondage, sharpens the struggle between nations, and turns the slaves of capital into cannon fodder. A world-wide socialist army of the revolutionary proletariat is alone capable of putting an end to this oppression and enslavement of the masses and to these massacres of slaves in the interests of the slave-owners.

In Western Europe and America, there is a sharpening struggle by the socialist proletariat against imperialist bourgeois governments, who are increasingly inclined to plunge into desperate escapades as they see the working-class millions inexorably marching to victory. These governments are preparing for war but at the same time are afraid of war in the knowledge that world-wide war means world-wide revolution.

In Eastern Europe—the Balkans, Austria and Russia—alongside areas of highly developed capitalism, we find the masses oppressed by feudalism, absolutism and thousands of medieval relics. Like tens of millions of peasants in Central Russia, the peasants in Bosnia and Herzegovina, on the Adriatic coast, are still ground down by the landowning serf-masters. The piratical dynasties of the Hapsburgs and the Romanovs support this medieval oppression and try to stoke up hostility between the peoples in an effort to strengthen the power of the monarchy and perpetuate the enslavement of a number of nationalities. In Eastern Europe, the monarchs still share out the peoples between them, exchange and trade in them, putting together different nationalities into patchwork states to promote their own dynastic interests, very much as the landowners under the serf system used to break up and shuffle the families of their subject peasants!

A federal Balkan republic is the rallying cry that our brother socialists in the Balkan countries have issued to the masses in their struggle for self-determination and complete freedom of the peoples, to clear the way for a broad class struggle for socialism.

It is the rallying cry of true democrats and real friends of the working class and we must take it up with especial vigour in face of the Russian tsarist monarchy, one of the most vicious supporters of reaction throughout the world.

The foreign policy of Russian tsarism is an unbroken chain of unprecedented crimes and acts of violence, and the dirtiest and basest intrigues against the freedom of nations, against democracy and against the working class. With the aid of Britain's "liberal" rulers, tsarism is crushing and choking Persia; tsarism has been undermining the republic in China; tsarism is sneaking up to seize the Bosporus and extend "its" own territory at the expense of Turkey in Asia. The tsarist monarchy was the gendarme of Europe in the 19th century, when Russian serf-peasant troops put down the uprising in Hungary. Today, in the 20th century, the tsarist monarchy is the gendarme of both Europe and Asia.

Tsar Nicholas the Bloody, who has dispersed the First and Second Dumas, who has drowned Russia in blood, enslaved Poland and Finland, and is in alliance with out-and-out reactionaries conducting a policy of stifling the Jews and all "aliens", the tsar whose loyal friends shot down the workers on the Lena[27] and ruined the peasants to the point of starvation all over Russia—that tsar pretends to be the champion of Slav independence and freedom!

Since 1877, the Russian people have learned a thing or two, and they are now aware that worse than all the Turks are our *"internal Turks"*—the tsar and his servants.

But the landowners and the bourgeoisie, the Nationalists and the Octobrists give their utmost support to this vile and provocative lie about a freedom-loving tsarism. Such papers as *Golos Moskvy* and *Novoye Vremya* are at the head of a whole army of government newspapers brazenly baiting and badgering Austria, as though Russian tsarism was not a hundred times more sullied in dirt and blood than the Hapsburg monarchy.

And it is not only the Right-wing parties, but even the opposition, liberal bourgeoisie that has been strident in its chauvinistic imperialist propaganda, scarcely covered up with diplomatically evasive and hypocritical phrases. Not only the non-party liberal *Russkoye Slovo,* but even *Rech,* the official organ of the Party of "Constitutional-Democrats" (actually counter-revolutionary liberals), has been zealous in attacking the tsarist Minister Sazonov for his alleged "tractability", for his "concessions" to Austria and for inadequate "protection" of Russia's "great power" interests. The Cadets have been blaming the wildest nationalist reactionaries not for their imperialism, but on the contrary for minimising the weight and the importance of the "great" idea of the tsarist conquest of Constantinople!!

For the sake of the vital interests of all the working people, the Russian Social-Democratic Labour Party raises its voice in resolute protest against this base chauvinism and brands it as a betrayal of the cause of freedom. A country with 30 million starving peasants and with the wildest arbitrary rule by the authorities, including the shooting of workers in their hundreds—a country where tens of thousands of fighters for freedom are being tormented and tortured through hard labour—what such a country needs above all is liberation from tsarist oppression. The Russian peasant must think about emancipating himself from the landowning serf-masters and from the tsarist monarchy, and not allow himself to be diverted from this vital cause by the false speeches of landowners and merchants about Russia's "Slavonic tasks".

Imperialist liberalism, desirous of tolerating tsarism, may insist on "peaceful constitutional" action, promising the people both external victories and constitutional reforms under a preserved tsarist monarchy, but the Social-Democratic proletariat indignantly rejects this fraud. The only thing that can ensure free development for Russia and the whole of Eastern Europe is the revolutionary overthrow of tsarism. Only the victory of a federal republic in the Balkans, together with the victory of a republic in Russia, can release hundreds of millions of people from the calamities of war and the torments of oppression and exploitation in the so-called "time of peace".

In the first five months of 1912, more than 500,000 workers in Russia rose to political strikes, restoring their strength after the most trying years of the counter-revolution. In some places, sailors and soldiers rose up in revolt against tsarism. Our call is for revolutionary mass struggle, for more steadfast, stable and extensive preparation for resolute joint action by the workers, peasants and the best section of the army! That is the only salvation for Russia, which has been oppressed and ruined by tsarism.

The socialists of the Balkan countries have come out with a sharp condemnation of the war. The socialists of Italy and Austria and the whole of Western Europe have given them unanimous support. Let us join in their protest and unfold our agitation against the tsarist monarchy.

Down with the tsarist monarchy! Long live the democratic republic of Russia!

Long live the federal republic of the Balkans!

Down with war! Down with capitalism!

Long live socialism, long live international revolutionary Social-Democracy!

R.S.D.L.P. Central Committee

To meet the war crisis, the International held an international day of mass actions for peace on November 17, and convened an emergency congress in Basel, Switzerland, November 24–25, 1912. It was an impressive demonstration of Socialist unity against the Balkan War and against the imperialist war drive as a whole. Applause was particularly enthusiastic when the Bulgarian delegate, Janko Sakazov, rose to describe the stand of Bulgarian Socialists against the war:

"It is said that the war is popular in our country and that it has evoked overwhelming enthusiasm. It is true that the war was very popular—before the war. When war was declared, it was greeted with cries of joy in the streets and in public gatherings. But we also saw concern on the faces of the soldiers, and consciences were never so troubled as in the days of the mobilization. As we well know the enthusiasm, quite marked in the streets, was artificial. Furthermore, it was superficial rather than deeply felt. The women, the elderly, and the young people who followed the army did not do so in the spirit of the old warlike nations, but rather more out of concern for their loved ones. Keep in mind that in Bulgaria the war now claims everything. Out of a population of four million, 360,000 men are at the front and 100,000 are engaged in war duty in the provisioning of food, supplies, and sanitation.

"And the enthusiasm has disappeared quickly! It is true that in Sobraniya [parliament] the Socialist who read out our antiwar declaration was assaulted by the enraged majority. But when the people saw the indescribable misery, they did not follow this majority. How many women have come crying to me with their forsaken children and told me of their suffering. Even the wives of officers—including General Staff officers, who had waited so long for the war—have expressed agreement with me. When the people begin to see what war is, the change in consciousness will soon be complete."[28]

The French Socialist Party had held an extraordinary congress November 21, which adopted proposals for the Basel congress. Its resolution stated:

"In case of war [Socialists] must make use of the entire energy and efforts of the laboring class and the Socialist Party to prevent the war by every means, including parliamentary intervention, open agitation, manifestoes, as well as a general strike and insurrection."[29] They decided however not to renew the debate on this question at Basel, given the urgency of a united stand against the war danger.

The manifesto of the Basel congress, which was unanimously approved, outlined the specific tasks of Socialists in all major countries to combat the war danger. It also further developed the general socialist position on the war danger.

Basel manifesto[30]

At its Stuttgart and Copenhagen congresses the International formulated these guiding principles for the proletariat of all countries in the struggle against war:

"If a war threatens to break out, it is the duty of the working classes and their parliamentary representatives in the countries involved, supported by the coordinating activity of the International Socialist Bureau, to exert every effort in order to prevent its outbreak. They must employ the means they consider most effective, which naturally vary according to the sharpening of the class struggle and the general political situation.

"In case war should break out anyway, it is their duty to intervene for its speedy termination and to strive with all their power to utilize the economic and political crisis created by the war to rouse the masses and thereby hasten the downfall of capitalist class rule."

Recent events oblige the proletariat more than ever to devote the utmost force and energy to planned and concerted action. On the one hand, the general craze for armaments has aggravated the high cost of living, thereby intensifying class antagonisms and creating in the working class an implacable spirit of revolt. The workers want to put a stop to this system of panic and waste. On the other hand, the incessantly recurring threats of war have a more and more inciting effect. The major European peoples are constantly on the verge of being driven against one another. Yet these assaults on humanity and reason cannot be justified by even the slightest pretext of service to the peoples' interest.

If the Balkan crisis, which has already caused such terrible disasters, should spread further, it would pose the most frightful danger to civilization and the proletariat. It would also be the greatest outrage in all history, because of the crying discrepancy between the immensity of the catastrophe and the insignificance of the interests at stake.

The congress records with satisfaction the complete unanimity of the Socialist parties and of the trade unions of all countries in declaring war against war.

The proletarians of all countries have risen simultaneously in a struggle against imperialism. Each section of the International has rallied the resistance of the proletariat against the government of its own country and mobilized the public opinion of its nation against all desires for war. This has produced a mighty cooperation of the workers of all countries, which has already contributed a great deal toward saving the threatened peace of the world. The ruling classes' fear of a proletarian revolution resulting from a world war has proved to be an essential guarantee of peace.

The congress, therefore, calls upon the Social Democratic parties to continue their campaign by every means that seems appropriate to them. . . .

The congress records that the entire Socialist International is unanimous on these principles of foreign policy. It calls upon the workers of all countries to rally the power of international proletarian solidarity against capitalist imperialism. It warns the ruling classes of all states not to increase by acts of war the misery of the masses brought on by the capitalist system of production. It emphatically demands peace. Let the governments remember that, given the present condition of Europe and the mood of the working class, they cannot unleash a war without danger to themselves. Let them remember that the Franco-German War was followed by the revolutionary outbreak of the Commune; that the Russo-Japanese War set into motion the revolutionary energies of the peoples of the Russian Empire; that the military and naval arms race gave the class conflicts in England and on the continent an unheard-of sharpness and unleashed an enormous wave of strikes. It would be insanity for the governments not to realize that the very idea of a monstrous world war must inevitably call forth the indignation and the revolt of the working class. Proletarians consider it a crime to fire at each other for the profits of the capitalists, the ambitions of dynasties, or the greater glory of secret diplomatic treaties.

If the governments cut off every possibility of normal progress, and thereby drive the proletariat to desperate steps, they themselves will have to bear the entire responsibility for the consequences of the crisis they bring about.

The International will redouble its efforts to prevent this crisis; it will raise its protest with greater vigor and make its propaganda more and more energetic and comprehensive. The congress therefore directs the International Socialist Bureau to follow events even more closely, and, no matter what may happen, to maintain and strengthen the bonds uniting the proletarian parties.

The proletariat is conscious that at this moment it is the bearer of the entire future of humanity. The proletariat will exert all its energy to prevent the annihilation of the flower of all peoples, threatened by all the horrors of mass murder, starvation, and pestilence.

The congress therefore appeals to you, proletarians and Socialists of all countries: Make your voices heard in this decisive hour. Proclaim your will everywhere and in every form; raise your protest in the parliaments with all your force; unite in great mass demonstrations; use every means that the organization and the strength of the proletariat place at your disposal. See to it that the governments are constantly kept aware of the proletariat's vigilance and its passionate desire for peace. Counterpose the proletarian world of peace and fraternity of peoples to the capitalist world of exploitation and mass murder.

The following analysis of the Basel congress appeared in the January 25, 1913, issue of the Bolshevik newspaper *Sotsial-Demokrat.*

On the Basel congress[31]

by L.B. Kamenev

The Socialist International greeted the new tide of the Russian proletarian movement, and also declared that the task now before the Russian proletariat is one of the most important at this time. By the second decade of the twentieth century conditions that had developed in Europe and Asia thrust the Russian proletariat into the center of international events. Proletarian Europe and Asia, which are becoming revolutionary, now listen attentively to the voice of the Russian proletariat and much depends on it. It must resound ever louder in the struggle against the Romanov monarchy. . . .

Revolution in Russia is the Achilles' heel of the entire system of relations in Europe and Asia. Only a new revolution in Russia can open a fresh period of victories for the proletarian cause in Europe and the democratic cause in Asia. Unless it occurs the resolution of all questions will be postponed for a long time, and in particular, the resolution of the question that brought proletarian representatives of all countries to assemble at Basel. The Basel congress could not help but recognize that the task of assuring peace in Europe demands at least one *war*—a victorious war of all the peoples of Russia against the Romanov monarchy.

But just as this war is inevitable as a precondition for solving the problem of a stable peace, it was also clear to the congress that a number of similar "wars" might be required for its actual solution. The French section of the International, at its extraordinary congress held before the Basel congress, passed a resolution pointing directly to the general strike and insurrection as the ultimate weapons of struggle against the European war. These words, "general strike and insurrection," were omitted from the manifesto adopted by the Basel congress because of the same theoretical and practical considerations which determined the resolutions of the Stuttgart and Copenhagen congresses. However, this does not minimize the fact that the congress was imbued with the understanding that the proletariat, in struggling against war, would have to develop its energy to the utmost, even to an open civil war. The references made in the manifesto to the Commune which followed the Franco-Prussian War of 1870–71 and to the Russian revolution of 1905 point this out unequivocally.

Events the following year in Germany, however, were cause for strong doubts over whether Social Democratic leaders there would put the Basel congress manifesto into practice in case of war. When the German government asked the Reichstag for massive new appropriations to expand the armed forces, SPD deputies voted for the first time in favor of new taxes to raise the funds. The debate at the SPD's 1913 Jena congress that resulted from this action contributed to the growing polarization between the main currents in the SPD.

Since the previous SPD congress, Bebel had died and the party leadership had passed into the hands of Friedrich Ebert and Philipp Scheidemann. A mood of unease gripped the party, caused in part by the onset of stagnation in its membership and activity, and in part by disagreements of growing sharpness between its three main tendencies.

As at previous congresses, the left wing at Jena advanced

a resolution on the use of the mass strike as the way out of the party's stagnation. This was counterposed to a resolution by the Executive Committee relegating the use of the mass strike to the distant future. The Executive Committee's resolution carried by a vote of 333 to 142.

The other major debate at the congress centered on the Reichstag vote on the military appropriations bill. When the government proposed a bill in March 1913 calling for a vast expansion in military expenditures, there was agreement in the SPD Reichstag fraction to oppose the bill. The government decided, however, to separate out the question of how the funds were to be raised, proposing a direct income tax to finance the appropriations, instead of the indirect taxes that bore down most heavily on the poor, and on which the government had previously relied. Institution of such an income tax had been a longstanding SPD demand, and the income tax bill could not pass without the SPD's backing. Yet the SPD had hitherto stood by its principle: "not one man, not one penny for the system." The fraction divided sharply, and after a heated debate it decided by a vote of 52 to 37, with 7 abstentions, to support the military tax bill.

The fraction's declaration on this bill was read out in the Reichstag by Hugo Haase.

The SPD's 1913 declaration on taxes for war[32]

HUGO HAASE: The majority of this house has approved a new, monstrous, and completely unjustified increase in the military budget. As we have conclusively shown, this is not the way to protect our country from war or to guarantee peace among the civilized nations. . . . At the same time, militarism as an instrument of class rule is a constant threat to domestic freedom.

Our proposals, directed at redressing the grievous wrongs of the military system and preparing its transformation into a people's army, have been rejected. The military bill has become law. Now we must face the question: Who will pay the costs? We have always demanded that the burden of military spending not be borne by the poor. In this we are in complete harmony with international Social Democracy and in particular with our party comrades in the French Chamber of Deputies. Together with them we put forward our views in a manifesto on March 1 of this year: "If, despite our most determined resistance, the peoples are saddled with new military expenditures, the Social Democracy of both countries will fight with every ounce of strength to shift the financial burden onto the shoulders of the rich and well-to-do.". . .

We are prepared to approve these two bills so that they won't be replaced by others that would tax the poorer layers of the population. We proceed from the conviction that, by making the property-holders more liable for the costs of military spending, this measure will cool their ardor for a continuation of the arms race and will make the fight against militarism easier for us.

The SPD leadership rallied support for the fraction's stand at the party congress, winning over some members of the fraction minority, including Emanuel Wurm and Karl Liebknecht. Wurm submitted the majority resolution and gave the main Executive Committee report to the congress.

A resolution was introduced, however, signed by eighty-one Social Democrats, which concluded as follows:

"Militarism, the ruling classes' strongest weapon of domination, must be fought to the utmost.

"Any legislation to strengthen militarism submitted to the Reichstag must be rejected, regardless of whether it calls for direct or indirect taxes.

"The position of the Social Democratic parliamentary fraction on other tax bills is determined by point ten of the party program, which reads: 'Existing indirect taxes must be replaced by direct taxes.'"[33]

Friedrich Geyer, Arthur Stadthagen, and Rosa Luxemburg were among the speakers for this resolution. In her speech, Luxemburg gave a clear warning of what was to happen eleven months later, on August 4, 1914.

SPD Left on war taxes

FRIEDRICH GEYER:[34] I agree with the statement that once the party has become a power, it should exert its influence to relieve the working class of its burdens. But the party must not make it easier for the rulers to strengthen their methods of domination, as we are doing by the approval of taxes for military spending. Our resolution seeks to protect the party from the charge that its struggle against militarism is not in earnest. From many quarters we have heard the reproach: What good is all this energetic agitation against militarism, when we are voting for the appropriations to carry it out? Resounding speeches, even the rejection of the military bill, are worthless if militarism is promoted by approving the appropriations. Some have even pointed out that, if we approve the military appropriations, our protestations against the military bill are just so much hot air. . . .

It is unmistakably clear that by voting for the taxes to finance the military bills, we make it easier for the government to put new military bills before the Reichstag as soon as possible. *("Very true!")* Then it's no trouble at all for the government to demand the military appropriations. *("Very true!")* We have to assume that much when we are told the government has so much respect for the power of the Social Democracy that it will demand direct taxation and will tailor its military bills to the effect they have on our party. The more we grant militarism, even with direct taxation, the sooner will there be new burdens for the workers and new military appropriation bills. . . .

ARTHUR STADTHAGEN:[35] Professor Abbé gave a lecture on tax reform here in Jena on March 7, 1894, giving the line of the Progressives against the Social Democracy.[36] His proposal was that wages remain completely untaxed and that all taxes be levied only on surplus value. He thus went even further than Wurm's resolution. Similar proposals were made in the 1850s. In response, Karl Marx explained that in the final analysis, all taxes are raised from the workers and that the workers cannot be emancipated by means of any tax policy, and that proposals to do so represent a liberal view.[37] In a conflict between our fight against militarism and our fight against indirect taxation, the former weighs heavier. We must reject anything that can aid militarism, whether through direct or indirect taxation. Our tactics must start from this foundation. . . .

Our main focus ought to have been to counter the enormous strengthening of militarism, not to settle the question of how to finance it. *("Very true!")* We should have taken the position: no expenditures without appropriations. If a bourgeois party had followed this principle, we should have supported it. The rejection of the military appropriations bill would have presented us with the only possibility to obtain dissolution of the Reichstag and a new election. That's what we should have worked for. But several comrades held the view that we would not have much luck with a dissolution, because of the patriotic uproar. If such considerations lead you to wish to avoid a dissolution and an election campaign, you must have very little faith indeed in our principles and our demands. *("Very true!")*

ROSA LUXEMBURG:[38] Some comrades are trying to defend the Reichstag fraction majority's position by claiming it had to choose between permitting indirect taxation for military expenditures or voting in favor of direct taxation. Leave aside the question of whether such a take-it-or-leave-it situation really existed. While it is quite correct for us to choose the lesser of two evils, which is the lesser evil for Social Democrats? To allow a chance to support a limited reform to pass by, or to abandon a fundamental principle? *("Very good!")* . . .

If you base yourself on the majority's position, what will happen if war breaks out and we can do nothing more to avert it? The question will then arise whether the costs should be covered by indirect or direct taxes, and you will then logically support the approval of war credits. *(Shouts of "Very true!" and disapproval)* As Emanuel Wurm said in Leipzig, this position will lead us onto a slippery slope where there is no way to stop. Let our resolution therefore put an end to such cheating on principles by proclaiming, "So far and no further!" *(Loud applause)*

The congress voted to approve the stand of the Reichstag fraction by a vote of 336 to 140.

This was the last congress of the united Social Democratic Party, and it clearly showed the lines of cleavage along which the split was soon to occur. Shortly after the congress, Rosa Luxemburg analyzed the division of the SPD into three clearly defined currents.

After the Jena congress[39]

by Rosa Luxemburg

We have absolutely no reason to suppose that the revisionists' usual one-third at party congresses—the conscious and consistent advocates of opportunism—grew in any way at this congress. The majority was formed by the joining together of this revisionist third with the undecided and vacillating layer in the middle. At the 1904 Dresden congress Bebel called this middle layer the "swamp," employing the well-known terminology of the Convention in the Great French Revolution.[40]

"It is ever and always the same old struggle: here left, there right, and in between the swamp. These are the elements that never know what they want, or rather, never say what they want. Like sharp-eyed chameleons they are always glancing about to right and left, asking, 'Which way is he going to go?' They sense who has the majority and head that way. We have this sort in our party too. A whole number of them have come to light in these proceedings. We must denounce these comrades. *('Denounce them?')* Yes, denounce them I say, so that the comrades know just what kind of weaklings they are. The man who at least openly puts forward his point of view lets me know where I stand. I can fight with him, and either he wins or I do. But the rotten elements always shirk their duty and avoid any clear decisions. They always say, 'We are all united, we are all brothers.' They are the worst of all! Against them I fight the hardest."

In spite of the indecisiveness of its individual members, the "swamp" plays a very particular role in every political body and in our party as well. During the entire last period of the struggle with revisionism, the swamp supported the left wing and with it created a solid majority in opposition against revisionism. Together with the left, the swamp dealt revisionism one resounding defeat after another. It was moved to do this by the apparent conservatism of this struggle. The "old policies, tried and true"[41] had to be protected against revisionist innovations. And this defensive campaign appeared particularly sacred in the eyes of all the middle elements because at its head stood the top echelons, the acknowledged authorities. The party Executive Committee, the party's main theoretical organ, trusted names like Singer, Liebknecht, Bebel, and Kautsky all fought in the front ranks. So the forces of the swamp received every reassuring guarantee that they were on the side of all that was traditional and customary.

The imperialist period and the more tense circumstances of the last few years have put new situations and tasks before us. The whole party must be instilled with greater flexibility, sharpness, and aggressiveness; the masses must be mobilized, their weight thrown directly on the scales. All this requires more than clinging desperately to the external forms of the "old policies, tried and true." In particular it demands the understanding that these tried and true revolutionary policies now require new forms of mass action. They must now also be maintained in new situations such as, for example, the introduction of the property tax for militarism in Germany.

At this point the "swamp" fails us. As a conservative element it now turns against the left wing, which is striving to move forward, just as it had previously opposed the right wing that was striving to move backward. It thus goes from being the party's shield against opportunism to being a dangerous element of stagnation. In its tepid waters opportunism, until now contained, can shoot up like weeds. The decision on the tax question shows, upon closer inspection, how the triumphant swamp unconsciously prepared the way for a victory for parliamentary opportunism, the very force it had routed in a dozen party congresses. Even more, the whole style of the swamp's struggle against the left and its entire argumentation was taken chapter and verse from the arsenal of the revisionist wing. That includes the systematic distortion of the other side's views and the stubborn "misunderstandings" over its opponents' supposed contempt for painstaking day-to-day work, underestimation of parliamentarism and the cooperatives, putschist tendencies, and whatever else was dreamed up, in short, its whole method of operating. In its struggle against the left the swamp used exactly the same arguments that the right had hurled against it for years.

What finally determined the swamp's attitude was that the party establishment turned against the left. The party Executive Committee, which for years under Bebel's leadership had fought against the right, now accepted the support of the right in order to defend conservatism against the left. The Executive Committee finally made this about-face in 1910, together with the theoretical journal, *Die Neue Zeit.* The expression "Marxist Center" has become popular lately among their friends. To be more precise, the supposed "Marxist Center" is the theoretical expression for the present political function of the swamp. Supported by the swamp and allied with the right, the party Executive Committee and the parliamentary fraction majority achieved victory in the decisive questions at the Jena party congress. And Kautsky, rejoicing over the victory of the "old policies, tried and true" at Jena, forgot to reflect upon the curious circumstance that old war-horses like Südekum, David, Noske, and Richard Fischer stepped forward as his allies this time—the very people against whom he had defended these same policies for more than a decade. . . .

The Jena party congress shows that the next task is to go on a systematic offensive against the "swamp," that is, against theoretical conservatism in the party. Here too the only effective method is to mobilize the broad masses of party comrades, and challenge them to think through the discussion on the mass strike and the tax question (and all the tactical differences) in party and trade union meetings, and in the press. With historic inevitability the march of events proves more and more each day the correctness of the left's policies. If events themselves lead to overcoming the forces of stagnation in the party, then the minority at the Jena party congress can look to the future with optimism.

The Jena party congress clarified the relationship of forces today within the party. For the first time the left closed ranks against an alliance of the right and the swamp. We should greet this as an auspicious beginning.

The colonial revolution

While the main parties of the Second International were gripped with a sense of stagnation and deadlock at this time, a revolutionary upsurge of immense power was taking shape in Asia. It received little or no attention from the majority of the Second International's leaders. The Bolshevik Party, however, followed these struggles closely, and stressed their significance. They considered the struggle of colonial peoples against imperialist oppression to be a progressive force, spurring on the economic and social development of their societies. In a 1911 letter to Maxim Gorky, Lenin explained:

"It would be quixotism and whining if Social-Democrats were to tell the workers that there could be salvation somewhere apart from the development of capitalism, not through the development of capitalism. But we do not say this. We say: capital devours you, will devour the Persians, will devour everyone and go on devouring until you overthrow it. That is the truth. And we do not forget to add: except through the growth of capitalism there is no guarantee of victory over it. . . .

"If it devours, say the Marxists, if it strangles, fight back. *Resistance* to colonial policy and international plunder *by means* of organising the proletariat, *by means* of defending freedom for the proletarian struggle, *does not retard* the development of capitalism, but *accelerates* it, forcing it to resort to more civilised, technically higher methods of capitalism. There is capitalism and capitalism. There is Black-Hundred-Octobrist capitalism and *Narodnik* ("realistic, democratic", full of "activity") capitalism. The more we expose capitalism before the workers for its "greed and cruelty", the more difficult it is for capitalism of the first order to persist, the more surely it is bound to pass into capitalism of the second order. And this just suits us, this just suits the proletariat."[42]

The following three articles from the Bolshevik press in 1913 describe how the democratic revolutions of the oppressed nations and the proletarian socialist revolutions in the advanced capitalist countries are combined in the struggle against world imperialism.

The awakening of Asia[43]

by V.I. Lenin

Was it so long ago that China was considered typical of the lands that had been standing still for centuries? Today China is a land of seething political activity, the scene of a virile social movement and of a democratic upsurge. Following the 1905 movement in Russia, the democratic movement spread to the whole of Asia—to Turkey, Persia, China. Ferment is growing in British India.

A significant development is the spread of the revolutionary democratic movement to the Dutch East Indies, to Java and other Dutch colonies, with a population of some forty million. . . .

World capitalism and the 1905 movement in Russia have finally aroused Asia. Hundreds of millions of the downtrodden and benighted have awakened from medieval stagnation to a new life and are rising to fight for elementary human rights and democracy.

The workers of the advanced countries follow with interest and inspiration this powerful growth of the liberation movement, in all its various forms, in every part of the world. The bourgeoisie of Europe, scared by the might of the working-class movement, is embracing reaction, militarism, clericalism and obscurantism. But the proletariat of the European countries and the young democracy of Asia, fully confident of its strength and with abiding faith in the masses, are advancing to take the place of this decadent and moribund bourgeoisie.

The awakening of Asia and the beginning of the struggle for power by the advanced proletariat of Europe are a symbol of the new phase in world history that began early this century.

Backward Europe and advanced Asia[44]

by V.I. Lenin

The comparison sounds like a paradox. Who does not know that Europe is advanced and Asia backward? But the words taken for this title contain a bitter truth.

In civilised and advanced Europe, with its highly developed machine industry, its rich, multiform culture and its constitutions, a point in history has been reached when the commanding bourgeoisie, fearing the growth and increasing strength of the proletariat, comes out in support of everything backward, moribund and medieval. The bourgeoisie is living out its last days, and is joining with all obsolete and obsolescent forces in an attempt to preserve tottering wage-slavery.

Advanced Europe is commanded by a bourgeoisie which

supports everything that is backward. The Europe of our day is advanced not *thanks to*, but *in spite of*, the bourgeoisie, for it is only the proletariat that is adding to the million-strong army of fighters for a better future. It alone preserves and spreads implacable enmity towards backwardness, savagery, privilege, slavery and the humiliation of man by man.

In "advanced" Europe, the *sole advanced* class is the proletariat. As for the living bourgeoisie, it is prepared to go to any length of savagery, brutality and crime in order to uphold dying capitalist slavery.

And a more striking example of this decay of the *entire* European bourgeoisie can scarcely be cited than the support it is lending to *reaction* in Asia in furtherance of the selfish aims of the financial manipulators and capitalist swindlers.

Everywhere in Asia a mighty democratic movement is growing, spreading and gaining in strength. The bourgeoisie there is *as yet* siding with the people against reaction. *Hundreds* of millions of people are awakening to life, light and freedom. What delight this world movement is arousing in the hearts of all class-conscious workers, who know that the path to collectivism lies through democracy! What sympathy for young Asia imbues all honest democrats!

And "advanced" Europe? It is plundering China and helping the foes of democracy, the foes of freedom in China! . . .

All the commanders of Europe, all the European bourgeoisie are *in alliance* with all the forces of reaction and medievalism in China.

But all young Asia, that is, the hundreds of millions of Asian working people, has a reliable ally in the proletariat of all civilised countries. No force on earth can prevent its victory, which will liberate both the peoples of Europe and the peoples of Asia.

The historical destiny of the doctrine of Karl Marx[45]

by V.I. Lenin

The chief thing in the doctrine of Marx is that it brings out the historic role of the proletariat as the builder of socialist society. Has the course of events all over the world confirmed this doctrine since it was expounded by Marx?

Marx first advanced it in 1844. The *Communist Manifesto* of Marx and Engels, published in 1848, gave an integral and systematic exposition of this doctrine, an exposition which has remained the best to this day. Since then world history has clearly been divided into three main periods: (1) from the revolution of 1848 to the Paris Commune (1871); (2) from the Paris Commune to the Russian revolution (1905); (3) since the Russian revolution.

Let us see what has been the destiny of Marx's doctrine in each of these periods.

I

At the beginning of the first period Marx's doctrine by no means dominated. It was only one of the very numerous groups or trends of socialism. The forms of socialism that did dominate were in the main akin to our Narodism: incomprehension of the materialist basis of historical movement, inability to single out the role and significance of each class in capitalist society, concealment of the bourgeois nature of democratic reforms under diverse, quasi-socialist phrases about the "people", "justice", "right", and so on.

The revolution of 1848 struck a deadly blow at all these vociferous, motley and ostentatious forms of *pre*-Marxian socialism. In all countries, the revolution revealed the various classes in society *in action*. The shooting of the workers by the republican bourgeoisie in Paris in the June days of 1848 finally revealed that the proletariat *alone* was socialist by nature. The liberal bourgeoisie dreaded the independence of this class a hundred times more than it did any kind of reaction. The craven liberals grovelled before reaction. The peasantry were content with the abolition of the survivals of feudalism and joined the supporters of order, wavering but occasionally between *workers' democracy and bourgeois liberalism*. All doctrines of *non*-class socialism and *non*-class politics proved to be sheer nonsense.

The Paris Commune (1871) completed this development of bourgeois changes; the republic, i.e., the form of political organisation in which class relations appear in their most unconcealed form, owed its consolidation solely to the heroism of the proletariat.

In all the other European countries, a more tangled and less complete development led to the same result—a bourgeois society that had taken definite shape. Towards the end of the first period (1848–71), a period of storms and revolutions, pre-Marxian socialism was *dead*. Independent *proletarian* parties came into being: the First International (1864–72) and the German Social-Democratic Party.

II

The second period (1872–1904) was distinguished from the first by its "peaceful" character, by the absence of revolutions. The West had finished with bourgeois revolutions. The East had not yet risen to them.

The West entered a phase of "peaceful" preparations for

the changes to come. Socialist parties, basically proletarian, were formed everywhere, and learned to use bourgeois parliamentarism and to found their own daily press, their educational institutions, their trade unions and their cooperative societies. Marx's doctrine gained a complete victory and *began to spread*. The selection and mustering of the forces of the proletariat and its preparation for the coming battles made slow but steady progress.

The dialectics of history were such that the theoretical victory of Marxism compelled its enemies to *disguise themselves* as Marxists. Liberalism, rotten within, tried to revive itself in the form of socialist *opportunism*. They interpreted the period of preparing the forces for great battles as renunciation of these battles. Improvement of the conditions of the slaves to fight against wage slavery they took to mean the sale by the slaves of their right to liberty for a few pence. They cravenly preached "social peace" (i.e., peace with the slave-owners), renunciation of the class struggle, etc. They had very many adherents among socialist members of parliament, various officials of the working-class movement, and the "sympathising" intelligentsia.

III

However, the opportunists had scarcely congratulated themselves on "social peace" and on the non-necessity of storms under "democracy" when a new source of great world storms opened up in Asia. The Russian revolution was followed by revolutions in Turkey, Persia and China. It is in this era of storms and their "repercussions" in Europe that we are now living. No matter what the fate of the great Chinese republic, against which various "civilised" hyenas are now whetting their teeth, no power on earth can restore the old serfdom in Asia or wipe out the heroic democracy of the masses in the Asiatic and semi-Asiatic countries.

Certain people who were inattentive to the conditions for preparing and developing the mass struggle were driven to despair and to anarchism by the lengthy delays in the decisive struggle against capitalism in Europe. We can now see how short-sighted and faint-hearted this anarchist despair is.

The fact that Asia, with its population of eight hundred million, has been drawn into the struggle for these same European ideals should inspire us with optimism and not despair.

The Asiatic revolutions have again shown us the spinelessness and baseness of liberalism, the exceptional importance of the independence of the democratic masses, and the pronounced demarcation between the proletariat and the bourgeoisie of all kinds. After the experience both of Europe and Asia, anyone who speaks of *non*-class politics and *non*-class socialism, ought simply to be put in a cage and exhibited alongside the Australian kangaroo or something like that.

After Asia, Europe has also begun to stir, although not in the Asiatic way. The "peaceful" period of 1872–1904 has passed, never to return. The high cost of living and the tyranny of the trusts are leading to an unprecedented sharpening of the economic struggle, which has set into movement even the British workers who have been most corrupted by liberalism. We see a political crisis brewing even in the most "diehard", bourgeois-Junker country, Germany. The frenzied arming and the policy of imperialism are turning modern Europe into a "social peace" which is more like a gunpowder barrel. Meanwhile the decay of *all* the bourgeois parties and the maturing of the proletariat are making steady progress.

Since the appearance of Marxism, each of the three great periods of world history has brought Marxism new confirmation and new triumphs. But a still greater triumph awaits Marxism, as the doctrine of the proletariat, in the coming period of history.

Lenin's prognosis was rapidly confirmed. The following year, 1914, the European "barrel of gunpowder" exploded, and the continent was plunged into political crisis and war. Under the impact of the conflict, the Second International shattered, as the majority of Social Democratic leaders, abandoning the Basel congress decisions, rushed to support their respective governments' war efforts. August 4, 1914, the date of the German SPD's vote for war credits, stands as the symbol of the old International's collapse.

After 1914, some revolutionists suggested that the Second International's principled statements and resolutions had been a sham, and that by the time of the Basel congress the old organization had long since rotted out. The Bolsheviks, however, sought to build on the positive achievements of the old International, publicizing its decisions on the war question. In his 1916 article on the Second International and the war question, Gregory Zinoviev reexamined the Basel congress, and assessed in its light the heritage of the struggle of revolutionists within the Second International.

The legacy of the Second International[46]

by Gregory Zinoviev

The best proof that the Second International—for all its enormous concessions to opportunism—could not yet officially proclaim "defense of the fatherland" and "defensive" war as its point of view is provided by its attitude toward the Balkan wars of 1912–1913. In these wars the national question played a role; but it was completely drowned out by imperialist themes. The small nations were playthings in the hands of the imperialist cliques.

No one in the International ever thought of viewing these clashes from the perspective of "defensive war" and "defense of the fatherland." The Balkan Socialists all voted *against* war credits and struggled against war. The European Socialists all applauded them for this and never thought of reminding them of their obligation to "defend the fatherland."

Why? Because everybody understood that the culprit in the war was imperialism. . . .

The Basel manifesto was written in anticipation of precisely *the very Europe-wide war* that has now broken out. Basing itself on the fact that the war would be imperialist in character, provoked by the clashes of different cliques of European finance capital, the manifesto analyzed in detail the position of Socialists in each country. It laid out a program of action for the Socialists of all nations. What kind of program? Does it contain the slightest suggestion that the Socialists of even one of the countries that will be dragged into the war will have to "defend the fatherland" and apply the criterion of "defensive" war? No. *Not a word, not a murmur of this!* You find in it an appeal to organize civil war, and references to the Paris Commune, to the 1905 revolution, and so forth. But you will *not* find in it a single thing about "defensive" war. . . .

The Basel resolution was not worse, but better than that of Stuttgart. Every word in it is a slap in the face to the present tactics of the "leading" parties of the Second International.

Nevertheless, the cup of August 4, 1914, did not pass us by. The Second International, such as it was, was a hopeless case—however many excellent resolutions it passed. But that did not mean at all that those resolutions had no importance. . . .

In his excellent little book, *Imperialism, the World War and Social Democracy,* the Dutch Marxist Hermann Gorter says:

"Whoever knew the situation in international Social Democracy close at hand had already seen for a long time that it [the crisis, the policy of August 4—GZ] was drawing near. The Stuttgart congress was the last to take a serious stand against imperialism. At Copenhagen the International had already started wavering, and at Basel it took to flight.

"It turned out that the stronger imperialism became, the greater the danger of war and the nearer it approached, the more timid was the International. At Basel it was still sounding trumpet calls. But through the loud phrases of Jaurès, through the empty threats of Keir Hardie, through Victor Adler's cowardly sobbing about the destruction of culture, through the empty, pallid words of Haase, through the self-satisfied din and racket of the entire congress—through all of this, there was already clearly no desire, no striving, no strength for any kind of action. The bourgeoisie, which, thanks to its own putrefaction, has a better nose for moral rottenness in general, immediately sniffed out the scent of the rottenness of the congress and the International. It sensed that it had nothing to fear from this congress."

There is much truth in this Dutch Marxist's words. The bourgeoisie, in fact, smelled the weakness of the Second International and knew that no danger of any kind threatened them from the opportunist majority so truly devoted to them. The present-day government minister Sembat, in his book, *Faites un roi* (Make a king), published not long after Basel, recounts the irony with which the French bourgeois spoke of the Basel congress, calling it "le Grand Pardon de Bâle" (the general absolution of Basel). Many Socialists shared the foreboding that something was rotten in the state of Denmark. But we shall not be wise in hindsight. We honestly admit: the possibility of anything even remotely resembling what we witnessed on August 4, 1914, occurred to none of us. It is incorrect to say that the International took flight at Basel. The official Social Democratic parties of Europe only took to flight on August 4, 1914. At Basel not a word was said to the worker masses about "defense of the fatherland" in the impending war. On the contrary, at Basel the proletarians of the whole world were told about the examples of the Paris Commune, and the Russian revolution of 1905, that "to shoot one another is a crime," that the approaching war is a war in the interests of a small group of capitalists. . . .

The Second International's weakness lay in its failure to say clearly and precisely that while defense of the fatherland is legitimate and essential in the epoch of national wars, in the epoch of imperialism the concept of "defense of the fatherland" does not apply to *imperialist* war.

The Second International's calamity, misfortune, and collapse came because opportunism, which was strong for reasons we cannot discuss here, got the upper hand. Opportunism objectively subordinated the main parties of the Second International to the politics of the bourgeoisie, which has a vital interest in passing off dishonorable imperialist war to the workers as just and progressive.

In proclaiming the necessity to found a Third International, must we renounce utterly and completely the legacy of the Second International?

The task of revolutionary Marxists lies in showing how in the course of the entire twenty-five-year existence of the Second International two fundamental tendencies struggled within it with varying degrees of success: the Marxist and the opportunist. We are *not* erasing the entire history of the Second International. We are not renouncing what was Marxist in it.

A *layer* of theoreticians and "leaders" have departed from revolutionary Marxism; the Kautskyites of all nations have turned away from revolutionary Marxism. In the last years of the Second International's existence the opportunists and the "center" obtained a majority over the Marxists. But in spite of everything, a revolutionary Marxist tendency always existed in the Second International. *And we are not renouncing its legacy for one minute.*

Social Democratic antiwar rally in Berlin of 100,000, 1910.

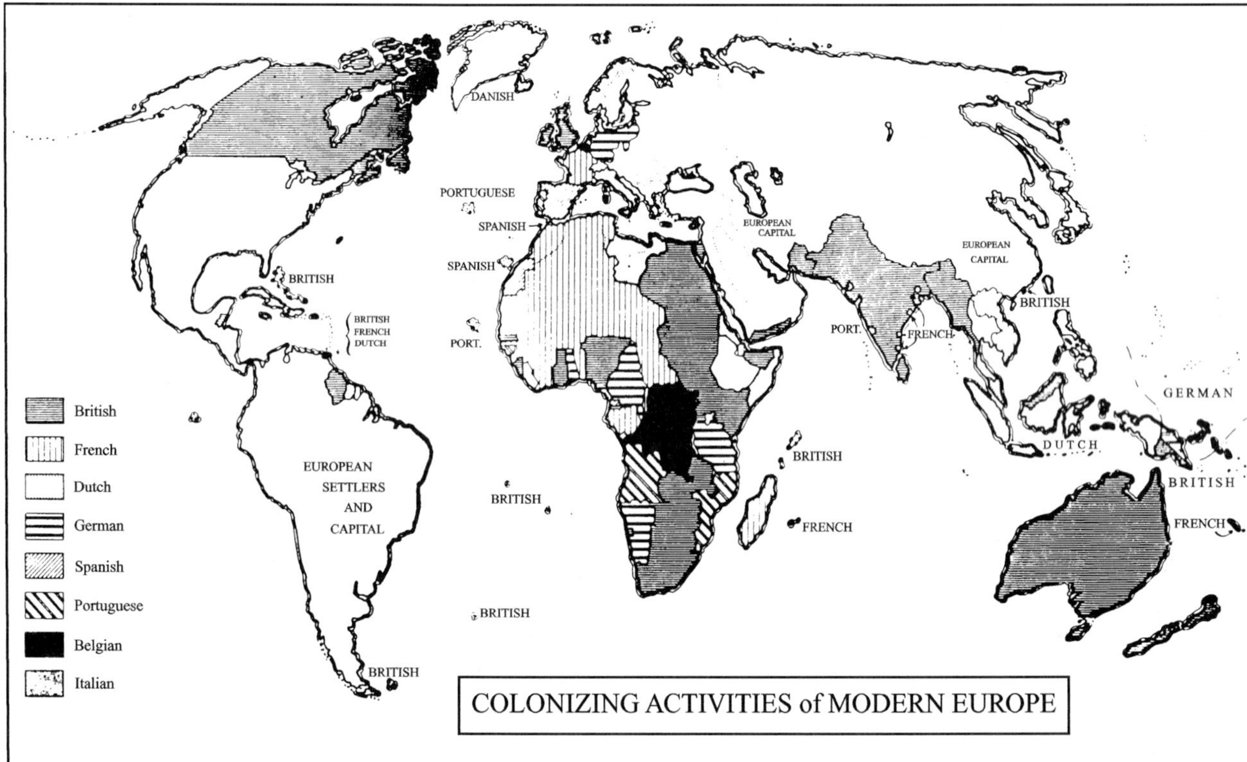

COLONIZING ACTIVITIES of MODERN EUROPE

Chapter 3

1914: The collapse of the Second International

On June 28, 1914, Archduke Francis Ferdinand, heir to the throne of Austria-Hungary, was assassinated in Sarajevo by a Serbian nationalist. The archduke had been visiting Bosnia, a nationally oppressed region inhabited by south Slavs within the Austro-Hungarian Empire. Austria and Serbia had sharply conflicting designs for the Balkans. While Serbia hoped to achieve political unity with Bosnia as part of a larger south Slavic nation-state, Austria desired to crush south Slavic national aspirations and expand its power in the Balkans.

On July 23 the Austro-Hungarian regime issued an ultimatum to the Serbian government holding it responsible for the conditions that led to the assassination and demanding concessions that would have virtually destroyed Serbian independence. When Serbia rejected the ultimatum, Austria moved rapidly toward war. Each side then turned to its more powerful allies for assistance: Serbia to Russia, and thereby to Russia's Entente partners, France and Britain; Austria-Hungary to Germany.

With the assassination as a pretext, the rival imperialist coalitions set out to settle on the battlefield their competing claims to world domination. An Austrian victory over Serbia would give Austria-Hungary dominance over the Balkans, which tsarism—already shaken by a great workers' upsurge in July—could not permit. Furthermore, such an upheaval in the Balkans could change the relationship of forces between the two great imperialist coalitions. On the Entente side, Britain and France resolved to defend their positions as the dominant imperialist powers. On the other, the German ruling classes sought to expand Germany's holdings in Europe and overseas and achieve a world-power status at least equal to Britain's.

On July 28 Austria-Hungary declared war on Serbia. Two days later Russia ordered a mobilization against both Austria-Hungary and Germany. The other powers followed suit. On August 1 Germany declared war on Russia and invaded Luxemburg; by August 4 Britain and France had formally entered the conflict. That same day German troops invaded Belgium.

At first, leaders of the Second International had not thought it likely that the assassination in Sarajevo would lead to war. Most of them shared the confidence of conventional "public opinion" that the great powers would shrink from risking war over such a small incident. The International's leaders continued their preparations for a planned August congress in Vienna. On its agenda, among other points, was to be the question of imperialism and the war danger.

The French Socialist Party had held a congress July 14–16 where the main discussion was on war. A resolution sponsored by Vaillant and Jaurès was passed that called on the workers to stage a general strike in the event of war. Yet the discussion did not deal with the specific threat of war that was shaping up at that very moment.

Following Austria's ultimatum, however, most Socialists realized that war was imminent. Antiwar demonstrations were organized across Europe, and party newspapers denounced militarism and secret diplomacy. Reflecting the growth of class-collaborationist currents in the Second International, many Socialist leaders, however, believed that the capitalist governments of their own countries wanted peace, and expected them to act to prevent the Austro-Serbian dispute from escalating into more than a localized conflict. The demonstrations they organized in countries such as Germany, France, and Britain therefore rarely took issue with the war preparations of their own governments.

With Austria now at war, and the real possibility of all Europe being drawn into the conflict, the International Socialist Bureau (ISB) met in emergency session in Brussels July 29–30. Most of the authoritative leaders of the Second International participated, although Lenin, working at the party center in Poronin, Galicia, did not attend. The moment of crisis of which the International had so often warned had at last arrived.

Much of the ISB discussion concerned where and how to organize the planned congress, displaced from Vienna by the war. Rosa Luxemburg and others successfully argued that it be an emergency congress on the war danger, like that in Basel in 1912. Several leaders of the International spoke about the political significance of the war and how it might yet be averted.

The July 1914 session of the International Socialist Bureau[1]

VICTOR ADLER (AUSTRIA): I will not tell you things that you all know. But let me say that Austria's provocative note was as much a surprise to us as to everyone else. We should have been on our guard because of the diplomatic moves, but we could not have expected war. Even though Serbia accepted the principal points of the Austrian ultimatum except for a few items, war is upon us.

The party is disarmed. To say anything else would mean deceiving the bureau. We must not be misled by the news reports. We now see the result of years of [ruling-]class agitation and demagogy. Street demonstrations in support of the war are taking place. Our country, with its many national problems and contrasts, will face a new situation. What this will be nobody knows. The south Slav question, Serbian agitation in Bosnia—all this has naturally turned people against Serbia. In our country, hostility to Serbia is almost second nature. I personally do not believe that there will be a generalized war. In Austria people want to get Serbia out of the way.

Let us examine how the situation affects the party. We cannot ward off the threat. Demonstrations have become impossible. You risk your life in the process; you risk going to prison. So be it. We have been through that before. But our whole organization and our press are threatened, and we run the danger of destroying thirty years' work without any political result.

Is it not dangerous to encourage Serbia from inside our own country? Are we not taking on a great responsibility in trying to lead the Serbs to think that Austria is threatened by revolution? We must protect the proletariat against such a virus. We must protect our institutions. Ideas of a strike and so forth, are mere fantasies. It is a very serious question and our only hope is that we will be the only victims and that the war will not spread. Even if it remains localized, the party will be in dismal straits. Our enemies will be strengthened and encouraged by their successes.

We have had the pleasure of being allowed to organize the international congress in our country, and we made diligent preparations for it. The Austrian proletariat of all nationalities was eagerly looking forward to it. It is sad, but there is nothing we can do about it. We hope that the bureau believes us when we say that we could not have acted differently. We want to save the party. What the bureau and we can do together is to condemn those responsible and try to contain the conflict.

Our industry may well be militarized; every refusal to work will be dealt with under martial law.

In spite of everything, we hope that the great war will be avoided. To believe this may mean believing in a miracle, but we hope nevertheless.

HUGO HAASE (GERMANY): I want to make a very important announcement. People ask what the proletariat is doing at this critical moment. If you believed the bourgeois press, you would think the proletariat remains chauvinistic. But the following telegram I have just received from Berlin clearly proves the contrary.

(*Haase* then read a telegram signed by Braun saying that in Berlin on the previous day thousands of workers had demonstrated against the war and for peace at twenty-seven crowded meetings and in the streets. . . .)

PAVEL AXELROD (RUSSIA, ORGANIZING COMMITTEE [MENSHEVIKS]): It is unnecessary to discuss Russia's position vis-à-vis Austria and the possibility of a clash. The main task is to find out whether Russian Social Democracy is capable of antiwar action. For about ten years Russia has been in a revolutionary situation and it will not be necessary to wait much longer for the second act of the affair. In my opinion, the masses will rise again to oppose the war. What is the party's position now? A few days ago, there were strikes of a revolutionary character. On the one hand, the party is weakened. The organization has suffered big losses because of the present strike. But the prestige of socialism has risen enormously. We can say with certainty that revolution will break out if there is a war. . . .

ILYA RUBANOVICH (RUSSIA, SOCIALIST REVOLUTIONARIES): The

Russian situation is different from that in Austria. We are a secret, unorganized party. Therefore, our concerns are not the same. Tsarism is isolated in Europe and seeks diversions. What is its aim? The mobilization shows that its designs are warlike. A farce has been acted out in Russia, which we shall foil one day with the help of part of the bourgeoisie. We cannot enter into formal commitments. The Russian proletariat is more revolutionary than the party. There is no doubt that if there is a war the situation will become still more revolutionary. And then, if necessary, the party will have recourse to highly effective means.

HAASE: We know the Austrians well enough to understand their attitude. We know their policies. They are too close to the situation to view it with perspective. Their attitude of passivity and resignation is wrong, first because this passivity does not help Social Democracy, and second because it does nothing to solve the present crisis. If they oppose the war now, they will have public opinion on their side after the war. The people will realize that the Social Democracy did not lose its head at the critical moment. I cannot believe that proletarian demonstrations strengthen the governments' warlike stance. If anything, in my opinion, they will weaken it. I know that that entails great difficulties, nonetheless, that is my opinion. We hope that the decisions taken at this session and in Paris will not cause further trouble for the Austrians.

The German government, for its part, says it was not consulted. That may be so. But two weeks before the publication of Austria's note to Serbia we knew that Austria would in the end present Serbia with an ultimatum. We can be blamed for not having spoken out then. We did not do so because we could not believe that this would happen. The German government closed its eyes so as to have a free hand when the conflict came. The *Temps* telegram suggests that Germany influenced Austria. We know that Germany wants peace, but if Russia intervenes, Germany in turn will have to intervene.

The story about the conversation I am alleged to have had with the chancellor is a pure fabrication. The government did not try to influence the Social Democrats, who were notified by a government representative. Everything that might lead to war is being avoided. Nor have we stopped our activities. Our demonstrations have even been treated somewhat neutrally [by the police]. Our rallies were tolerated. The most warlike element is the liberal bourgeoisie, which is anti-Serb and pro-Austrian. But the ruling class and the great industrialists are opposed to the war. The press of the war party declares that Germany has no reason to go to war. But if Russia attacks, Germany will intervene. There is no doubt about that. The Social Democrats are utilizing the present situation. We shall not desist. We shall hold more demonstrations and sharpen their tone of protest against the war. . . .

JEAN JAURÈS (FRANCE): I want to examine the question of what pressure can be exerted. France is unanimous in condemning Austria's action and the hypocritical pretexts used by Austria to reject Serbia's reply, which was already too accommodating. Austria wanted to go to war and destroy this small nation. That fact has created universal indignation. Even the militant Catholics who, as Catholics, had considerable sympathy for Austria, are expressing disapproval.

As regards Germany, not one person in a hundred thousand in France will concede that Germany was not aware of the facts. Germany might not have been handed the text of the note, but there is no doubt that it was determined to take Austria's side as soon as the first incident occurred. Two days before the note was handed over, a German journalist attached to the German embassy in Paris said: "I am leaving because there will be a big to-do over the Austro-Serbian incident." The conclusion was therefore that Germany knew everything. We will thus receive a display of the Triple Entente's powers of resistance. "If we give way, Germany's prestige will be enhanced without war." That is also how people argued in Germany. Have the governments sunk to such a level of weakness that they fail to see the danger? We all agree: the greatest misfortune awaits us.

The French government wants peace. It will support Britain in its attempts to mediate. It has exerted pressure on Russia to avoid a worsening of the situation. All we can do now is be on guard against new unfavorable influences. Our theme should be: we are not committed to any action nor bound by any treaty. I rejoice to hear about the German comrades' peace demonstrations, and I thank them sincerely for their efforts. In France it is thought that Germany would attack France even if the French did not follow Russia. This attitude implies no hidden plans for war on our part. We wish to prove that to you, and we ask you to believe us. If we succeed in preventing that terrible situation, we will be satisfied.

ODDINO MORGARI (ITALY): Italy has not remained loyal to the Triple Entente. The national rivalries are sufficiently well known. It is impossible to predict the attitude of the Italian proletariat to a general strike, etc. I understand the Austrians' difficulties, but they are of no consequence. The Italian Socialists went through similar difficulties during the Tripoli war. They were insulted and slandered, but after the war their prestige increased.

The meeting was adjourned at 8:30 p.m.

Thursday morning, 30 July

BRUCE GLASIER (BRITAIN): I regret the absence of Keir Hardie, who together with the other British comrades, was very disappointed by yesterday's debate. Too much attention was given to the French and Germans, and not enough was paid to the British. The capitalist world regards Britain as a power but the International Socialist Bureau does not.

People in Britain at present are not seriously concerned with the consequences of the Austro-Serbian war. It is true we felt the economic repercussions of the Balkan War, but we do not think we will be affected by the present war. The British want peace. The whole of the cabinet wants peace; so does the working class. Militarism and war have been attacked at every trade union congress. Even if part of the population is caught up in it, the trade union and Socialist movements will continue to fight that trend. . . .

TWO RESOLUTIONS ADOPTED BY THE ISB

At its meeting of July 29, the International Socialist Bureau heard delegates from all the nations threatened by the World War describe the political situation in their respective countries. It unanimously calls upon the proletarians of all countries concerned not merely to continue but to intensify their demonstrations against war, for peace, and for a settlement of the Austro-Serbian conflict by arbitration.

The German and French proletarians must put more pressure than ever before on their governments to ensure that Germany restrains Austria and that France persuades Russia not to intervene in the conflict. The proletarians of Great Britain and Italy will support these efforts with all their strength.

The emergency congress convened in Paris will be a powerful expression of the world proletariat's desire for peace.

*

The International Socialist Bureau warmly welcomes the revolutionary attitude of the Russian proletariat, urging it to persevere in its heroic actions against tsarism, which provide the most effective guarantee against the threat of a world war.

The only action decided upon by the International Socialist Bureau was to organize an emergency congress to begin on August 9 in Paris. It made no plans to meet again. Plans for the Paris congress were quickly swept away in the storms of war, however. The ISB's secretariat moved to The Hague. No further meetings of the ISB were called during the war.

ISB members participated in a giant rally against the war on the evening of July 29 at the Brussels Cirque Royale. Angelica Balabanoff, an Italian representative on the ISB, recalls the impact of Jaurès's address—his last, since he was assassinated by a chauvinist fanatic on his return to Paris.

"It is no exaggeration to say that the Cirque Royale shook at the end of Jaurès' magnificent speech. Jaurès himself was quivering, so intense was his emotion, his apprehension, his eagerness to avert somehow the coming conflict. Never had he spoken with such fervour as on this the last time in his life he was to address an international audience.

"A few minutes after the close of the meeting, thousands of workers were swinging through the streets of Brussels, intoxicated with the enthusiasm engendered by the revolutionary songs they were singing. The slogans: 'Down with war; long live peace!', 'Long live International Socialism!' echoed for hours throughout the city and its suburbs."[2]

In his address, Jaurès outlined more fully the French Socialists' attitude to their government's policy:

"As French Socialists, our duty is clear. We do not have to force a peace policy on our government. It is carrying out such a policy. I, who have never hesitated to expose myself to the hatred of our jingoists because of my stubborn and unflagging desire for French-German reconciliation, can tell you that at present the French government wants peace and works to maintain peace. It is the best ally of the peace efforts of the splendid British government, which took the initiative for conciliation. And it advises Russia to be prudent and patient.

"As regards us, our duty is to press it to speak forcefully to Russia so that Russia stays out. But if, unfortunately, Russia were not to pay heed, our duty would be to say: 'We recognize only one treaty, the treaty that binds us to the human race.'"[3]

The German Socialists held well-attended demonstrations against the war danger across the country, several of which were attacked by the police. Mass meetings passed antiwar resolutions, and the party press thundered against the war threat. Tens of thousands attended demonstrations in Berlin on July 28. The following resolution, passed at all twenty-seven Berlin rallies, stopped short of attacking the policies of the German government, but pressed it to act as a force for peace.

Berlin Socialist resolution for peace[4]

With its brutal ultimatum Austria has declared war on Serbia. The peoples of Europe now recognize with stark clarity the sinister peril brought upon them by the pernicious policy of secret treaties concluded without their consent.

The flames of war manifestly threaten to engulf yet more countries and to set all Europe ablaze, bringing untold suffering to humanity and destroying everything that civilization has created through decades of arduous labor.

In keeping with the resolutions of the international congresses in Stuttgart, Copenhagen, and Basel, the class-conscious proletarians of all countries involved consider it their most pressing and sacred duty at this moment to summon all their strength to prevent this catastrophe.

The Russian proletariat has acted heroically, showing

tsarism the fateful handwriting on the wall. The workers of Russia do not submit passively to exploitation, or to their misuse as a pliant tool of tsarist policies of aggression.

Through ardent protest, the French and German workers have vigorously expressed their horror at the criminal dealings of the warmongers.

The Austrian proletariat, which is most directly involved, also resolutely rejects any responsibility for the actions of its government.

It is therefore not true that the broad masses in these countries are in a warlike mood. In defiance of all the chauvinists, they strive only for peace on earth.

The warmongers should know that when world war breaks out bringing untold grief and horror, political and economic crises will follow inexorably. This will arouse those layers of the masses who have been deluded by imperialism and drive them into the ranks of the Social Democracy. It will enormously accelerate the transition from the capitalist social order to socialism.

Nevertheless in the name of humanity and civilization, the proletariat vehemently confronts all the warmongers with its demand for peace.

Like the proletariat of the other countries involved, we firmly demand that our government not only stand aside from any involvement in war, but also that it do everything possible to quell the war hysteria. To this end it should immediately join with the other governments and work to resolve this calamitous conflict as quickly as possible.

Great is the danger! There is no time to lose!

Just like the French workers, the German workers now have a special duty to influence their government to prevent the sacrifice of these peoples to the hunger for conquest and glory of Austrian or Russian policy.

Down with all warmongers! Long live the international brotherhood of peoples!

The SPD's Berlin daily, *Vorwärts,* warned the government on July 30 against the consequences of war. "Workers know that for them, new life will bloom out of the ruins. The responsibility for war falls on today's rulers. For them the question is: To be or not to be." *Vorwärts* called again on the government to press Austria for peace, and in terms reminiscent of Jaurès, praised their rulers' credentials in carrying out this task:

"*We have always been and always will be* open, *principled* opponents of the monarchy. Frequently we have had to carry out bitter struggles against the high-spirited bearer of the crown. But we candidly recognize, and not for the first time, that through his actions, particularly in the last few years, Wilhelm II has proved himself to be a sincere partisan of international peace. Insofar as human ability and good will have any power to determine the fate of many millions in a humane and rational spirit, there is no great need for fear about the present situation. But even the most forceful person is susceptible to influence. And unfortunately evidence is at hand that the *cabal of warmongers is once again at its unscrupulous work,* seeking to trip up the government at every step and tumble us into that monstrosity: *international war, a world conflagration, the devastation of all Europe.* . . . Germany must therefore use its influence on Austria—that is the prime necessity." [5]

As part of its war preparations, the imperial government reached out to the SPD's leadership, collaborating with its right-wing and centrist majority to subvert the membership's antiwar stand. SPD leader Albert Südekum was granted a private audience with Chancellor Bethmann-Hollweg and was asked to convey a message to the SPD Executive Committee. He then made this confidential report to the chancellor.

Südekum's report to the chancellor[6]

JULY 29, 1914

First of all I reported on the briefing I had received, as accurately as possible. I did not mention those remarks about the personalities and views of princes and statesmen that had been designated to me as confidential.

In the discussion that followed I immediately received confirmation of my statement that no actions of any kind (general or partial strike, sabotage, and the like) are planned or even to be feared, precisely because of our desire for peace.

Entirely conscious of its responsibility, the party Executive Committee further acknowledges the necessity of avoiding ambiguous or misleading statements in the press that could be used in either good or bad faith by the war parties in the various countries. It is endeavoring to convey this viewpoint to the editors of the party newspapers as well. Concerning the paragraphs from today's issue of *Vorwärts* that Your Excellency pointed to, they seem in fact to originate in a somewhat peculiar interpretation of the saying that "people use words to hide their thoughts." That is to say, they actually mean nothing; or rather, they are only supposed to express the desire that those who advocate peace be on guard so as not to abandon the field to others. . . .

[Südekum then asked that the government revoke a deportation order against SPD leader Rudolf Hilferding, an Austrian national and editor of *Vorwärts,* explaining that Hilferding was a force for caution on the *Vorwärts* editorial staff, trusted by the party leadership, and sympathetic to Austria's grievance against Serbia. Hilferding did in fact remain in Germany during the war.]

Finally may I express the conviction, derived from the discussion with party Executive Committee members, that Your Excellency's step in communicating with us directly in critical moments was gratefully received and met with complete and sympathetic understanding.

Hoping that this report has rendered a modest service to Your Excellency and to the cause, and holding Your Excellency in high esteem, I remain,

Very respectfully yours,
Dr. A. Südekum

The following day Chancellor Bethmann-Hollweg assured the Prussian Ministry of State that nothing was to be feared from the Social Democratic antiwar agitation.

That same day an article appeared in many SPD papers that set a new tone in their treatment of the war. Headlined "To Be Or Not To Be," it was written by Friedrich Stampfer, another adherent of the right-wing faction striving to rally the SPD to the war. Although the German people had not wanted the war, he explained, they must now wage it with all their strength, since defeat would mean catastrophe and unspeakable suffering for them. Playing on fears of the brutality of the tsarist army, he cried, "We must not let our women and children be sacrificed to Cossack atrocities."[7]

On July 31 an agent of the War Ministry informed the military high command that "reliable reports show that the Social Democratic Party has the firm intention of conducting itself under present circumstances in a manner worthy of every German. It is my duty to make this known to military authorities so they can take it into account in the measures they take."[8]

The chauvinist campaign within the SPD took another step forward on August 1, with an article by Ernst Heilmann in a provincial SPD newspaper. "We stood on guard for peace until the last moment," he wrote. "In vain! . . . Work for peace is over now. Other concerns come to the fore. And a single question now holds us all in its grip: Will we strive for victory? Our answer is, 'Yes!'" Calling on the Russian workers to pursue their revolutionary struggle against tsarism, Heilmann repeated the warnings against Cossack atrocities, and continued, "that is why we must now defend the entirety of German civilization and German freedom against the relentless barbarian foe."[9]

Even SPD members who had been identified with the party's left wing were affected by the tremendous patriotic propaganda barrage. Konrad Haenisch, one such party member, recounted his experience:

"The conflict of *two souls* in one breast was probably not easy for any of us. May the author try here for once to overcome a certain inner reserve and speak for a moment of himself; may he be permitted to pass over from the impersonal 'we' to the immediate 'I,' that comes from the heart? Well, then I'd only like to say that not for anything in the world would I want to live through those days of inner struggle once again! Such a driving, burning desire to throw yourself into that powerful current, the universal tide of national feeling, and on the other hand, the terrible spiritual fear of giving way without restraint to that longing, of surrendering fully to that feeling that roared and raged about you and which, if you looked deeply into your heart, had long since taken possession of your soul. This fear: will you not be betraying yourself and your cause? Can you feel as your heart feels? And then, suddenly—I recall the day and the hour—the terrible tension was resolved.

"You dared to be what you really were, and despite all rigid principles and wooden theories you could, for the first time in almost a quarter century, join wholeheartedly and with a clean conscience, and without any fear of becoming a traitor, in the sweeping, stormy song: '*Deutschland, Deutschland über alles*' [Germany, Germany before all else]!"[10]

Chancellor Bethmann-Hollweg invited the SPD fraction chairmen, Hugo Haase and Philipp Scheidemann, together with representatives of the bourgeois parties, to a meeting August 3 to hear the government's statement on the war. The SPD representatives undertook that once the SPD response was drafted, it would be circulated to the bourgeois party leaders before it was read in the Reichstag. According to Scheidemann, Haase promised that there would be nothing in it to which the other parties would feel compelled to take exception.

SPD Deputy König later recalled the pressures he felt as he travelled to the fateful Reichstag session, where he would vote on the proposed war credits, the financial appropriations for the war effort.

"On 3 August Dittmann and I travelled from Dortmund to Berlin to attend the party meeting on that day, at which the question of voting the war-credits was to be decided. . . . I shall never forget the crowded incidents of those days. I saw reservists join the colours and go forth singing Social Democrat songs! Some Socialist reservists I knew said to me: 'We are going to the front with an easy mind, because we know the Party will look after us if we are wounded, and that the Party will take care of our families if we don't come home.'

"Just before the train started for Berlin, a group of reservists at the station said to me: 'König, you're going to Berlin, to the Reichstag: think of us there: see to it that we have all that we need: don't be stingy in voting money.' In the train I told Dittmann what a deep impression all this had made upon me. Dittmann confessed that things had happened to him, too, which affected him in the same way. For hours, as the train carried us towards Berlin, we discussed the whole situation, what our attitude should be to national defence, whether the party would vote the credits. We came to the final conclusion that the Party was absolutely bound to vote the credits, that, if any difference of opinion came up in the meeting, that was the line we should have to take. Dittmann wound up by saying: 'The Party could not act otherwise. It would rouse a storm of indignation among men at the front and people at home against the Social Democrat Party if it did. The Socialist organization would be swept clean away by popular resentment.'"[11]

The diary of the exiled Russian revolutionist Alexandra Kollontai gives a different picture of the mood of the working-class ranks in Germany:

"8 August: . . . Yesterday a friend called to see me. Her husband has gone to the front. She cried bitterly; she does not understand in the least why the war is being fought. Who needs the war? And her husband was not at all keen to go to war. The workers of the Charlottenberg district were waiting for the party to initiate action. They were prepared to come out, they were not in favour of the mobilisation. Many decided not to go to the call-up centre. But they received notices from the regional committees [of the party] urging them to fulfil their duties as citizens. . . .

"13 August: Night: The proletariat does not support the war. I heard at the Liebknechts' how during the first days of the war the workers besieged the regional committees in expectation of the signal to action. Everyone believed that the party would put up a fight. Now the atmosphere has changed considerably. But even so, if you talk to workers on their own they usually do not approve of the war."[12]

Karl Liebknecht later recalled that when the SPD Reichstag fraction met August 3, "its so-called radical wing was shown to have collapsed. In all haste—for we had only minutes—three comrades, Ledebour, Lensch, and Liebknecht, drafted an inadequate draft declaration that closed with rejection of war credits."

When the fraction met, David took the floor and declared that the moment had come to discard previous conceptions and change course, proposing on behalf of the Executive Committee that the party vote for the war credits. References to "the Russian peril" dominated the discussion, and speakers for the minority were greeted with impatience and unease. The majority position was adopted by 78 votes to 14, with a few abstentions.

Haase, of the minority, agreed under pressure to read the declaration to the Reichstag. The fraction further decided to rise, for the first time, during the ceremonial cheering of the kaiser, which this time would take the form of "three cheers for the kaiser, the people, and the fatherland." The declaration was submitted to the chancellor for censorship before being read to the Reichstag. According to Kautsky, a passage opposing transformation of the conflict into a German war of conquest was removed on Bethmann-Hollweg's request.[13]

It did not prove possible in the few hours remaining to organize the minority deputies to vote against the war credits Liebknecht later concluded that he had had illusions on August 4 that the majority had merely been seized by a temporary panic and could soon get back on a class-struggle course. The SPD left wing had still not grasped the new reality. The left's dedication to party discipline, he recalled, built up in long years of struggle against the opportunists' defiance of party decisions, now paralyzed it.[14]

SPD Reichstag declaration, August 4, 1914[15]

A fateful hour is upon us. *Imperialism brought into being the epoch of the arms race and heightened the antagonisms between the nations. Now its consequences have broken over*

Europe like a tidal wave. The responsibility for this rests upon those who have carried out imperialist policies; not with us. The Social Democracy has fought against this fateful development with all its strength. Even up until the last few hours we held mighty demonstrations in all countries, especially in close collaboration with our French brothers, working to maintain peace. Our efforts were to no avail.

The cold reality of war is upon us. *We are threatened with the horror of enemy invasion. Today we have to decide not whether we are for or against the war, but what steps must be taken to defend the country.*

Now we must think of the millions of our compatriots swept up into this calamity through no fault of their own. They will bear the main brunt of the war's devastation. Our best wishes accompany our brothers who have been called to arms, no matter what their party. *(Applause from all parties)*

We are also mindful of the mothers who have given their sons, of the women and children, robbed of their providers and now threatened not only by anxiety for their loved ones, but also by the horrors of hunger. They will soon be joined by tens of thousands of wounded and maimed fighters. We consider ourselves duty-bound to stand by them, to ease their suffering, and to lighten their immeasurable burden.

Russian despotism is stained by the blood of the best of its own people. Its triumph would put much if not everything in question for our nation and its future freedom. It is necessary to fend off this danger and to secure the culture and independence of our own country. Therefore we are going to make good on what we have always said: We will not forsake our fatherland in its hour of need. In this we feel that we are in accord with the International, which has always recognized the right of every people to national independence and self-defense, just as we agree with it in condemning all wars of conquest.

We demand that the war be ended as soon as our security has been guaranteed and our foes are so inclined, through a peace that will make friendly relations possible with our neighboring countries. We demand this not only in the interest of international solidarity, which we have always defended, but also in the interest of the German people.

We hope that the merciless school of war will awaken an abhorrence of war in ever more millions of people and will win them to the ideal of socialism and international peace.

Guided by these principles, we approve the required credits.

The Social Democrats of German Austria responded to the SPD's August 4 declaration with a hymn of praise for "the holy cause of the German people," and beat the drums for the crusade against the tsar. Most other Social Democratic organizations in Austria-Hungary also fell into line.

French and Belgian Socialist leaders employed similar arguments of "national defense" to justify support to the war policies of the capitalist governments in those two countries. A statement of ISB members of the two countries, dropped from aircraft behind German lines, claimed that:

"We have every certainty of defending the independence and autonomy of our nation against German imperialism.

"We do not fight against the German people, whose autonomy and independence we equally respect.

"It is with the certainty of supporting the principle of liberty, the right of the people to dispose of themselves, that the French and Belgian Socialists suffer the hard necessity of war.

"They are certain that once the truth shall be established their action will be approved and they will be joined by the Socialists of Germany."[16]

The signatories included Guesde, Vaillant, and Vandervelde. Meanwhile, Gustave Hervé, lamenting the collapse of "our beautiful dream of an international general strike against war," became one of the most frenzied of French pro-war chauvinists.

One wing of the British labor movement, the Independent Labour Party, refused to rally to the war drive. However the Labour Party as a whole pledged itself to build the war effort, explaining:

"The Labor Party in the House of Commons . . . recognized that Great Britain, having exhausted the resources of peaceful diplomacy, was bound in honor, as well as by treaty, to resist by arms the aggression of Germany. The party realized that if England had not kept her pledges to Belgium, and had stood aside, the victory of the German army would have been probable, and the victory of Germany would mean the death of democracy in Europe.

"Working-class aspirations for greater political and economic power would be checked, thwarted, and crushed, as they have been in the German Empire. Democratic ideas cannot thrive in a state where militarism is dominant; and the military state with a subservient and powerless working class is the avowed political ideal of the German ruling caste."[17]

No Socialist party was subjected to as strong a pressure of patriotic feeling as were the Serbian Social Democrats. Socialists recognized that the south Slavic peoples in Austria-Hungary, whom the Serbian regime claimed to defend, were nationally oppressed. Moreover Serbia's own national independence was threatened by the Austrian attack. Yet the Socialist representative Lapčević explained to the Serbian parliament on July 31 (18) that the Socialists could not support war credits. He expressed confidence that Austrian and Serbian Socialists took a common stand against the war and that the Austrian party defended Serbia's independence and its people's right to self-determination. He recalled the fearful sacrifices of the "unhappy years of the Balkan wars," and challenged the government with its failure to do everything possible to avert the war.

"I fear that the Serbian government is being manipulated right now as a pawn of the great powers," Lapčević continued, explaining that the colonialist and imperialist policies of these powers had led Europe into this war. He stated that these imperialist powers saw the Balkans as just another field for their insatiable lust for conquest. "When the costs of the war are assessed, the Great Powers will of course treat the small nations of the Balkans and Asia as mere objects to be handed out as compensation." Lapčević demanded that Serbia "cease to be a tool of the great powers, and pursue instead the goal of a Balkan federation."[18]

Russian workers against the war

Besides the two Socialist members of the Serbian parliament, the only Socialist deputies in belligerent countries to vote against war credits at that time were those in Russia, which was in the grip of a renewal of the revolutionary crisis that had shaken it in 1905–07.

Following the defeat of this revolution, Russia had experienced a period of political reaction. Trade unions were repressed and strikes became infrequent. Socialist political parties were driven underground and their leaders arrested or forced into exile. The tsar set up a parliamentary body, the State Duma, but it had no real power.

This political situation began to change with a wave of student protests against tsarist repression in 1910 and 1911. Strikes by workers increased significantly in 1911 and then shot up dramatically following the April 1912 massacre of striking miners in the Lena goldfields. Many of these strikes took on a political character from the start, raising the demand for a democratic republic, which had been a central slogan of the 1905 revolution.

The influence of the Social Democratic parties grew rapidly in this upsurge. In the spring of 1912, the Bolsheviks launched a legal newspaper, *Pravda* (Truth), whose circulation grew to 40,000 a day, despite continual government harassment. The main Menshevik paper, *Luch* (Ray), sold up to 16,000 copies a day. Despite election laws that excluded most workers from voting, thirteen Social Democrats were elected to the 442-member Duma—seven Mensheviks and six Bolsheviks, with the Bolsheviks strongest in the areas with the highest concentration of industrial workers.

In the spring of 1914 repression of an oilworkers' strike in Baku set off protests across the country. The Bolsheviks played a leading role in the protests, which were centered in their stronghold of St. Petersburg. In the first half of 1914, 1.5 million workers took part in strikes, most of them for political demands, a level of strike activity comparable to the revolutionary upsurge of 1905.

In July, a series of massive strikes took place in St. Petersburg, which led to pitched battles between the workers and the police. Barricades began to appear in working-class districts. The employers responded by locking out the workers, and the government unleashed a wave of repression, closing down workers' organizations and newspapers and making mass arrests.

By the time that factories returned to normal in St. Petersburg, the outbreak of war was only a few days away. The conflict between Austria and Serbia seemed distant; the main topic of discussion was the strike wave, which the workers considered a success.

Then war came, and the workers were back out on the streets. As Russia mobilized for war, July 31 (18), an estimated 27,000 people in St. Petersburg went on strike in protest against the war, and strikes broke out in Moscow, as well. Mass antiwar actions were organized to oppose demonstrations called in support of the government and the war. During the first days of the war all the large workplaces in Riga stopped functioning. Actions by workers, peasants, and draftees spread throughout the industrial centers and to Byelorussia, the Ukraine, the Caucasus, and the Urals, with battles breaking out between draftees and the police or the Cossacks. According to official tsarist figures there were disturbances and antiwar protests in seventeen provinces and thirty-one districts. Five hundred and five draftees and 106 officials were wounded and killed in twenty-seven provinces in the two weeks following the declaration of war.[19]

This was not to be like the July 1914 strike upsurge, however. The patriotic fever built up by the government soon shifted the relationship of forces against the working class and influenced some workers. So too did the attacks on the workers' actions and the brutal repression of their movements. Many of the workers' leaders were in jail and many more were being called to arms.

A Bolshevik leader in St. Petersburg, Alexander Shlyapnikov, wrote in the Bolshevik magazine *Kommunist* in 1915 about how the workers of the capital responded to the war.

The working class of Petersburg and the war[20]

by Alexander Shlyapnikov

Events unfolded so rapidly that they took the organized workers by surprise. Although the workers all opposed the war in principle, the complexity of the situation was beyond the comprehension of many and so there was a multitude of "personal opinions."

The general mobilization of the Petersburg District (and of all European Russia) was decreed for August 1 [July 19] at 6:00 a.m. The police stations worked all night delivering the call-up notices.

In the morning the dark-red mobilization notices stood out all over the city, alongside the white leaflets with the prices being offered for requisitioned items such as jack-boots, linen, etc.

Knots of people crowded around the leaflets, talking over the events in an anxious, despondent mood. Hundreds of workers' families thronged the police stations, which had been converted into recruiting offices. Women wept, wailed, and cursed the war. In the workshops, factories, and mills the mobilization created great havoc since as many as 40 percent of the workers were taken from their machines and benches. Helplessness and despair arose everywhere. . . .

The factory owners demanded that the ministry return the skilled workers, since otherwise they would not be able to fill government orders. Their request was later granted and within several days all the mobilized metalworkers from factories holding government contracts returned. But they were still on the "inventory" of the military command.

On the morning of the day of mobilization, however, nobody gave any thought to work. Without changing into their work clothes the workers assembled at the workshops, came to an agreement, and went out into the streets singing revolutionary songs. At several factories there were general meetings, which the mobilized men attended. There they pledged to not forget the struggle at home and to try at the first opportunity to win the "liberation of the Slavs in Russia itself" with arms in hand.

The suburban streets were filled with people just as they were in the days of the mobilization of labor's power to protest the regime's oppression. Crowds of thousands demonstrated in the streets, singing revolutionary songs and crying out "Down with the war!"

Tear-stained and grief-stricken women stood near the police stations and often shouted through their tears: "Down with the war!" and urged others to do the same. . . .

During the first days of the war the conscious workers were convinced that Western European democracy, headed by the organized proletariat, would not permit this carnage, this mutual self-destruction. . . .

What we then learned staggered us with its absurdity. Telegrams and newspaper articles reported that the leaders of German Social Democracy were trying to justify the war and were voting for war credits. At first we thought that the government telegrams were false, that they wanted to win over the Russian Social Democrats. But soon there was verification as hundreds of refugees from Germany and people returning from abroad brought confirmation.

As monstrous as this news was, we had to accept it as true. The workers bombarded us with questions: What did this behavior of the German Socialists mean, those Socialists whom we had always depicted as our model? Where was world solidarity?

It was particularly painful to learn that the German army, composed of so many organized workers, had ravaged Belgium, and that the Belgian soldiers had defended their country to the strains of the "Workers' International."

All these questions and serious charges had to be answered. We had to explain that the leaders of German Social Democracy had betrayed the workers' cause, and had betrayed international socialism. We gave the workers an account of the German workers' movement, explaining that in recent years it had been led by reformists, or "liquidators," as we say in Russia.

This "burial of the German leaders" did not turn out to be an easy task for us. In the broad circles supporting the Social Democrats a conception emerged of "not doing worse for Russia than the German Socialists were doing for Germany." It was a big job for us to explain to the conscious workers that betrayals by some should not lead to a betrayal by all, since that way only the capitalists would gain. It was essential for workers to restore their international ties over the heads of the leaders.

As the conflict developed, the Russian government itself helped to clarify the foggy situation. It had barely finished the mobilization in Petersburg when it began a campaign against the "internal enemy." New repressions rained down on the working class in the form of arrests, exile under martial law, and the closing of associations, clubs, and the remaining trade union journals. That was the way the government had resolved "to unite all classes and nationalities."

A.Y. Badayev, a Bolshevik deputy in the Duma, writing of these events in the 1920s, gave more emphasis to the chauvinist mobilization's impact in limiting the scope of workers' protests.

The outbreak of war[21]

by A.Y. Badayev

In Petersburg the first days of the war were marked by strikes and even by some scattered demonstrations. On the day that army reservists were mobilized, workers at more than twenty Petersburg enterprises went on strike to protest the war. In some places the workers met the reservists with shouts of "Down with the war" and revolutionary songs.

But the demonstrations now took place under conditions different from those two or three weeks earlier. The crowds of onlookers, especially in the center of the city, were stirred up by patriotic shouts. Now they not only did not maintain a "friendly" neutrality, but fell upon the demonstrators, and helped the police arrest and beat them. One incident typical of this time was the "patriotic" outburst that took place the same day as the mobilization in the city center, at the City Duma building on the Nevsky Prospect.

Just as a batch of reservists were passing by here, a crowd of demonstrating workers appeared. With shouts of "Down with the war" the demonstrators closed in on the reservists. The public on the Nevsky Prospect, mainly philistines and all sorts of idle loafers, usually scurried away and hid in the side streets during workers' demonstrations. Sometimes, as a last resort, they huddled timidly in porches and gateways and observed the demonstrators from afar. But this time the public displayed "activism," and took on the role of tsarist police. Crying "Betrayers, traitors" they rushed from the sidewalk onto the avenue and began to beat up the demonstrating workers. The police then arrested the demonstrators and dispatched them to nearby police stations.

Under these conditions any broad development of a protest movement against the war was impossible. The individual heroic actions of the workers were drowned in the broad sea of militant patriotism.

The two Socialist fractions in the State Duma, representing the Menshevik and Bolshevik parties, joined to make a common statement in the State Duma on August 8 (July 26) explaining their rejection of the war credits. Their statement did not entirely close the door to some form of "national defense," however.

Joint Socialist statement in the Russian Duma[22]

A terrible and unprecedented calamity has befallen the people of the entire world. Millions of workers have been torn from peaceful labor, thrown into the bloody maelstrom, and condemned to ruin. Millions of families have been delivered over to famine. The war has begun.

When the governments prepared to launch the war, the European proletariat, headed by that of Germany, unanimously protested. Many circumstances prevented the workers of Russia from demonstrating openly against the war in the same way. But their hearts were with the European proletariat as it conducted its immense antiwar demonstrations.

This war grew out of the aggressive and expansionist policies of the rulers of the belligerent countries and they bear the responsibility for it. The proletariat, constant partisan of freedom and of the peoples' interests, will always defend the cultural well-being of the people against any encroachments, no matter where they originate.

The class-conscious proletariat of the warring countries could not prevent the war's outbreak and the rampage of barbarism that it brings. But we are deeply convinced that the proletariat will find in the international solidarity of the world's working masses the means to bring the war to an early end. The terms of the peace treaty must be dictated by the masses themselves, and not the diplomats.

We also express our deep conviction that this war will finally open the European masses' eyes to the real source of the violence and oppression they suffer, and that this outbreak of barbarism will also be the last.

No such hesitation on the question of "national defense" was found in the resolution of the Bolshevik Party's Petersburg organization published at about the same time as the Duma declaration, and circulated underground in the factories of the capital.

Petersburg Bolshevik appeal against the war[23]

Workers of the World, Unite!
To all workers, peasants, and soldiers.
Comrades!

A bloody specter is haunting Europe. The capitalists' greedy competition, their politics of violence and plunder, dynastic calculations, and fear for their privileges in the face of the growing international workers' movement are pushing the governments of all countries onto the road of militarism and expansion of the armed forces. The cost of this expansion crushes the working people of all lands and all colors.

In recent years the "armed peace" of Europe frequently threatened to turn into general war. But under the pressure of popular protests in Germany, France, England, and other countries, the sabre-rattling capitalists and landowners were forced to settle their affairs without bloody collisions between the peoples. The International Socialist Workers Association [Second International], which stands guard over the interests of all the world's toilers, has led this movement for peace. It now calls on the working class of all countries to protest against the war. "Down with the war! War on the war!" must roll mightily through the towns and villages of the wide Russian land.

The workers must remember that they have no enemies on the other side of the border. Everywhere the working class is oppressed by the rich and by the power of the property-owners. The yoke of exploitation and the shackles of poverty oppress it the world over.

The tsarist government has proclaimed itself the "protector and liberator" of the Slavic peoples in the coming conflict, but this is not protection but rather a craving for the seizure of new possessions. Pushed back in the East by Japan, our irresponsible, bloody rulers now try to fish in the troubled waters of the Near East through secret diplomatic agreements.

In this bloody hour, the workers' press has been completely stifled and cannot utter a word of truth. Meanwhile the bourgeois and police-run newspapers, claiming to speak on behalf of working people, talk of a collectivity of interests. *"Off with the mask!"* must be the response of the workers and of all the working people—look our bashibazouks[24] in the face. The government of the oppressors of the Russian workers and peasants, the government of the landlords, cannot be a liberator. Everywhere it penetrates it brings with it servitude, the whip, and bullets. It has not yet had time to wash the workers' blood off the streets of Petersburg. Only yesterday the government declared the workers of Petersburg and all the working people of Russia to be *internal enemies* and unleashed savage Cossacks and mercenary police against them. Now it calls on them to defend the fatherland.

Soldiers and workers! You are being summoned to die for the glory of the Cossack whip, for the glory of the fatherland of the executioners of hungry peasants and workers, which strangles its best sons in prison. "No, we don't want the war," you must declare. "We want the freedom of Russia!"—that must be your cry.

Long live world-wide workers' solidarity! Long live the constituent assembly, which can give the peasants all the land and the working people the freedom to fight for a better world, for socialism, where all the peoples can live and work in peace. *Down with the war, down with the tsarist government! Long live the revolution! Amnesty to all the martyrs for freedom! Long live the equality of nations!*

Petersburg Committee,
Russian Social Democratic Labor Party (RSDLP)

The Latvian Social Democracy, affiliated to the Bolshevik Central Committee of the RSDLP, was cut off by the war from the central leadership of their party. Deeply rooted in the Latvian working class, they developed on their own many of the key revolutionary slogans against the imperialist war in their initial antiwar manifestos.

Their first proclamation on the war predicted that the Russian people "will turn their weapons against their oppressors and fight not for tsarist Russia but for a free homeland. The war of the governments must be converted into an uprising of the peoples against the perpetrators of the war." A further resolution declared that "the tasks of the 1905 revolution have still not been accomplished. Nor can they be carried out by the present war, which is being conducted by the reactionary landlords and the big capitalists. . . . The only war we favor is revolution. . . . This will be a war in which the people themselves determine their own destiny." The resolution also called for an international conference of Social Democratic parties, but sought to free the International from the grip of the chauvinists by specifying that only "parties that have agitated and worked against the war should be invited with decisive vote. Others will have only consultative vote."[25]

The "Revolutionary Faction" of the Polish Socialist Party (PPS), which had always adapted to bourgeois and petty-bourgeois nationalism in Poland, supported the German side in the war, viewing it as a war of liberation against tsarist oppression. The Left PPS (PPS Lewica), however, joined with the other three major socialist organizations in Russian-held Poland to publish an internationalist manifesto. One of these, the Social Democracy of Poland and Lithuania, was the party of Rosa Luxemburg and Julian Marchlewski; a split in this movement had given rise to the Warsaw-based opposition (here the "National Executive Committee") with which Karl Radek was associated.

Joint Polish appeal against the war[26]

Down with the war—that cry rises from the breasts of millions of demonstrating workers in all countries and nations. The policy of war pits everyone against everyone else. To this the proletariat counterposes international solidarity, based on the revolutionary spirit of fraternity and the common aim of abolishing the present system of exploitation and oppression and establishing a socialist order. The proletariat proclaims a struggle against its own governments and against its own oppressors. The specter of workers' revolution is looming, as the powerful march of the revolutionary workers' battalions resounds in the trenches of the present capitalist system.

Workers! You are part of the great proletarian family. In the historic period now opening, we must realize our revolutionary responsibility to step forward, with all our strength, as part of the international revolutionary army.

The beginning of the tsarist war against Germany and Austria draws our country, above all, into the turbulent vortex of war. Hundreds of thousands of working people have already been wrenched from their jobs and many workplaces have fallen silent. Already the dispossessed stare hunger in the face and starvation threatens.

The proletariat lacks the strength to prevent the outbreak of war. In the present-day states, the vicissitudes of war and peace and the fate of millions depend on the handful of people who comprise the ruling circles. Huge military forces confront each other, and the proletariat is not strong enough, with its own hands, to stop the warfare.

But the proletariat knows that its revolutionary position must remain intact and its revolutionary action be further developed and strengthened as much as possible.

The proletariat's political demands are independent of the shifting fortunes of war. Guided by the revolutionary aim of overthrowing the existing governments and establishing people's governments, the revolutionary initiatives of our country's proletariat will be coordinated with those of the proletariats of Russia and Europe.

While it fights for national rights, the Polish proletariat will elaborate its demands based on working class policies as a whole. Free from nationalism, these demands will advance revolutionary struggle, opposing all diplomatic schemes and bargains.

In the struggle between social forces engendered by the outbreak of war and the country's economic situation, the proletariat must counterpose its class consciousness to the bourgeois and landowning circles. As an organized force and the only champion of freedom, it must stand guard for the future and advance its will in the coming historic events.

Comrades! Workers! The revolutionary policy and action of the proletariat must be expressed strongly and clearly.

The proletariat must remain an independent force in the struggle against governments, against capital, against nationalism.

The proletariat must strive to defend its class interests against all enemy forces. For a victorious realization of its aims, it must take power and place the reins of government in its own hands.

Comrades! Workers! Stand shoulder to shoulder. Let all proletarians find a place in the ranks of the struggle.

Let international socialism lead us to struggle and victory.

Down with the war!

Long live the fraternity of peoples!

Down with oppression and exploitation! Long live socialism!

Down with tsarism! Long live revolution!

National Executive Committee of the Social Democracy of the Kingdom of Poland and Lithuania[27]

Central Executive Committee of the Social Democracy of the Kingdom of Poland and Lithuania
Central Workers Committee of the Polish Socialist Party
Central Committee of the Bund
WARSAW, AUGUST 2, 1914

When the war broke out, Lenin was living in Galicia in Austrian-held Poland. He was arrested there on August 8 and released eleven days later through the intervention of Austrian Social Democrats. He then moved to neutral Switzerland, where many exiled Bolsheviks were located. On September 6, the day after his arrival in Bern, he met with the local Bolshevik group in a three-day conference.

The meeting adopted theses on the tasks of Socialists in the war that contain the central ideas associated with the Bolsheviks in the following years, including the proposition that the military defeat of tsarism was a lesser evil for Russian working people, the call to turn the imperialist war into a civil war against the exploiting classes, and to respond to the collapse of the Second International by building a new International, freed from opportunism and chauvinism. These theses were circulated among exiled Bolsheviks and smuggled into Russia for discussion by the Central Committee members in Russia, by party organizations, and by the Duma fraction. They were also submitted to a conference on the war of Italian and Swiss Socialists in Lugano, September 27. The following is the text of the theses.

The tasks of revolutionary Social-Democracy in the European war[28]

by V.I. Lenin

RESOLUTION OF A GROUP OF SOCIAL-DEMOCRATS

1. The European and world war has the clearly defined character of a bourgeois, imperialist and dynastic war. A struggle for markets and for freedom to loot foreign countries, a striving to suppress the revolutionary movement of the proletariat and democracy in the individual countries, a desire to deceive, disunite, and slaughter the proletarians of all countries by setting the wage slaves of one nation against those of another so as to benefit the bourgeoisie—these are the only real content and significance of the war.

2. The conduct of the leaders of the German Social-Democratic Party, the strongest and most influential in the Second International (1889–1914), a party which has voted for war credits and repeated the bourgeois-chauvinist phrases of the Prussian Junkers and the bourgeoisie, is sheer betrayal of socialism. Under no circumstances can the conduct of the leaders of the German Social-Democratic Party be condoned, even if we assume that the party was absolutely weak and had temporarily to bow to the will of the bourgeois majority of the nation. This party had in fact adopted a national-liberal policy.

3. The conduct of the Belgian and French Social-Democratic party leaders, who have betrayed socialism by entering bourgeois governments,[29] is just as reprehensible.

4. The betrayal of socialism by most leaders of the Second International (1889–1914) signifies the ideological and

political bankruptcy of the International. This collapse has been mainly caused by the actual prevalence in it of petty-bourgeois opportunism, the bourgeois nature and the danger of which have long been indicated by the finest representatives of the revolutionary proletariat of all countries. The opportunists had long been preparing to wreck the Second International by denying the socialist revolution and substituting bourgeois reformism in its stead, by rejecting the class struggle with its inevitable conversion at certain moments into civil war, and by preaching class collaboration; by preaching bourgeois chauvinism under the guise of patriotism and the defence of the fatherland, and ignoring or rejecting the fundamental truth of socialism, long ago set forth in the *Communist Manifesto,* that the workingmen have no country; by confining themselves, in the struggle against militarism, to a sentimental philistine point of view, instead of recognising the need for a revolutionary war by the proletarians of all countries, against the bourgeoisie of all countries; by making a fetish of the necessary utilisation of bourgeois parliamentarianism and bourgeois legality, and forgetting that illegal forms of organisation and agitation are imperative at times of crises. One of the organs of international opportunism, *Sozialistische Monatshefte,* which has long taken a national-liberal stand, is very properly celebrating its victory over European socialism. The so-called Centre of the German and other Social-Democratic parties has in actual fact faintheartedly capitulated to the opportunists. It must be the task of the future International resolutely and irrevocably to rid itself of this bourgeois trend in socialism.[30]

5. With reference to the bourgeois and chauvinist sophisms being used by the bourgeois parties and the governments of the two chief rival nations of the Continent—the German and the French—to fool the masses most effectively, and being copied by both the overt and covert socialist opportunists,

who are slavishly following in the wake of the bourgeoisie, one must particularly note and brand the following:

When the German bourgeois refer to the defence of the fatherland and to the struggle against tsarism, and insist on the freedom of culture and national development, they are lying, because it has always been the policy of Prussian Junkerdom, headed by Wilhelm II, and the big bourgeoisie of Germany, to defend the tsarist monarchy; whatever the outcome of the war, they are sure to try to bolster it. They are lying because, in actual fact, the Austrian bourgeoisie have launched a robber campaign against Serbia, and the German bourgeoisie are oppressing Danes, Poles, and Frenchmen (in Alsace-Lorraine); they are waging a war of aggression against Belgium and France so as to loot the richer and freer countries; they have organised an offensive at a moment which seemed best for the use of the latest improvements in military matériel, and on the eve of the introduction of the so-called big military programme in Russia.

Similarly, when the French bourgeoisie refer to the defence of the fatherland, etc., they are lying, because in actual fact they are defending countries that are backward in capitalist technology and are developing more slowly, and because they spend thousands of millions to hire Russian tsarism's Black Hundreds gangs for wars of aggression, i.e., the looting of Austrian and German lands.

Neither of the two belligerent groups of nations is second to the other in cruelty and atrocities in warfare.

6. It is the first and foremost task of all Russian Social-Democrats to wage a ruthless and all-out struggle against Great-Russian and tsarist-monarchist chauvinism, and against the sophisms used by the Russian liberals, Cadets, a section of the Narodniks, and other bourgeois parties, in defence of that chauvinism. From the viewpoint of the working class and the toiling masses of all the peoples of Russia, the defeat of the tsarist monarchy and its army, which oppress Poland,

the Ukraine, and many other peoples of Russia, and foment hatred among the peoples so as to increase Great-Russian oppression of the other nationalities, and consolidate the reactionary and barbarous government of the tsar's monarchy, would be the lesser evil by far.

7. The following must now be the slogans of Social-Democracy:

First, all-embracing propaganda, involving the army and the theatre of hostilities as well, for the socialist revolution and the need to use weapons, not against their brothers, the wage slaves in other countries, but against the reactionary and bourgeois governments and parties of all countries; the urgent necessity of organising illegal nuclei and groups in the armies of all nations, to conduct such propaganda in all languages; a merciless struggle against the chauvinism and "patriotism" of the philistines and bourgeoisie of all countries without exception. In the struggle against the leaders of the present International, who have betrayed socialism, it is imperative to appeal to the revolutionary consciousness of the working masses, who bear the entire burden of the war and are in most cases hostile to opportunism and chauvinism.

Secondly, as an immediate slogan, propaganda for republics in Germany, Poland, Russia, and other countries, and for the transforming of all the separate states of Europe into a republican United States of Europe.

Thirdly and particularly, a struggle against the tsarist monarch and Great-Russian, Pan-Slavist chauvinism, and advocacy of a revolution in Russia, as well as liberation of and self-determination for nationalities oppressed by Russia, coupled with the immediate slogans of a democratic republic, the confiscation of the landed estates, and an eight-hour working day.

A group of Social-Democrats,
members of the Russian Social-
Democratic Labour Party

Rosa Luxemburg speaks at SPD mass meeting in 1907, flanked by portraits of Ferdinand Lassalle and Karl Marx.

The Balkan peninsula after the wars of 1912-13.

Chapter 4

National defense or social revolution

As the war began, Germany threw the bulk of its army into a great western offensive, hoping to take Paris and score a rapid and decisive victory over France. After quickly overrunning Belgium and pressing deep into France, the German forces were turned back in early September 1914 in the Battle of the Marne. The rival armies entrenched across northern France, and the war in the west settled into a stalemate that was not to be broken for four years. Attacks by either side produced little gain, and took a prodigious toll in human lives.

Nor did the battles in the east give either side a decisive advantage. A Russian victory in Galicia was balanced by a German triumph in East Prussia. At sea, the British navy quickly swept German surface ships from the world's oceans, and imposed a naval blockade against Germany and Austria-Hungary. For its part, Germany attempted to blockade Britain and France with submarines.

The warring powers mobilized all their human and economic resources for the slaughter and prepared for a protracted test of strength. Enormous casualties required more and more replacements on the front, cutting deeply into the labor force. The demands of the war economy further disorganized production of basic necessities. Throughout Europe this rapidly resulted in food shortages. Britain and France, however, were able to call on the resources of their world empires and the support of U.S. imperialism's financial and productive strength. Thus they acquired the economic preponderance that over time would prevail against the blockaded Central Powers. The primitive economy of Russia, the most backward of the imperialist powers, was exposed to the most extreme strain of all.

The size of the armies and the scale of the death toll far exceeded anything the world had seen. The battle of Verdun in 1916 alone cost the lives of over six hundred thousand French and German soldiers in a contest for a few dozen square miles of soil. Generals sacrificed the lives of tens of thousands in hopeless attacks, and could offer no perspective for an end to the conflict.

Virtually all the Social Democratic and trade union leaders in Germany, France, Britain, and Belgium (and eventually many of their counterparts in the United States and Canada) joined in an alliance with their capitalist rulers to prosecute the war. They agreed to call off mass struggles, strikes, and political opposition to the government—to subordinate the workers' struggles to the demands of the bosses—for the duration.

The German version of this betrayal was called the *Burgfrieden* (civil peace). This German term originally referred to a ban on feuding and private warfare within the walls of a medieval city. Now it was revived in an effort to cloak the real nature of the agreement between the leaders of the trade unions and the majority Socialist leadership on the one side and the ruling classes on the other. This accord enabled the government to send hundreds of thousands of working people to their deaths, while assaulting the living standards and political rights and organizations of those left at home, with the assistance of the official leaders of the workers' movement. Similar agreements were put in force in Britain, France, and Austria-Hungary. Attempts by workers at independent action met brutal repression. In many cases the officials of their own trade unions helped break their struggles.

The prospect of a long and costly war and the enormous toll this would take on the proletariat did not shake the opportunist majority wing of the Socialist leadership in its support to the war. Its only answer was to call on the workers to make even greater sacrifices, to "hold out to the end." That was the message that German Social Democratic Party leader Philipp Scheidemann, chairman of the SPD parliamentary fraction, had in his New Year's greetings to his Solingen constituents for 1915.

New Year's greetings for 1915[1]

by Philipp Scheidemann

Best wishes for the New Year!

Grave concerns burden us all. . . . In agony we spend sleepless nights, remembering our loved ones at the front. Cruelly grief tears at the hearts of those who have already lost those closest to them. . . .

Hats off to the heroes who have fallen for the fatherland!

But greater than our pain and sorrow is our unbending will and our unwavering determination. We want not only to live through these terrible times with open eyes and a clear understanding, but also to thwart the intentions of our enemies. *We will triumph!*

And so at year's end I wish you all *the strength* to overcome your pain and sorrow. I wish you all *the unshakeable will to hold out until victory!*

I wish our wounded and sick soldiers a speedy and complete recovery and extend my heartfelt greetings to you and your comrades in the trenches, at sea, or on guard for the fatherland!

To you I especially say: *Hold out!* You will determine what becomes of our country and *what becomes of the German working class.*

May the new year bring us a *speedy victory* and a lasting peace!

BERLIN, END OF 1914
Philipp Scheidemann

Wolfgang Heine, of the party's openly pro-imperialist right wing, struck a similar theme in his remarks on the war at a public rally in Stuttgart two months later.

'Confidence in the Kaiser'[2]

by Wolfgang Heine

If we want peace, a peace that serves our needs, then we must now above all have confidence in German arms, in the combative German people. Similarly we must also have confidence in the German kaiser's desire and will for peace. Twice in recent years he personally and resolutely intervened to insure peace for us. Notwithstanding our disagreements with the kaiser's policies we must state that today we can have confidence in him.

The statement in the *Norddeutsche Allgemeine Zeitung* (North German Universal News) on negotiations over peace terms bears the mark of the imperial chancellor and we know his point of view conforms to the kaiser's will. If it should become necessary, German Social Democracy will stand by the chancellor and the kaiser, when it is the question of ending the war through a peace free from the seeds of new conflicts, returning the world to peaceful endeavor.

Confronted with the alliance between the majority Socialist leaders and the capitalist ruling class, many workers looked to Karl Kautsky for an alternative perspective. In his widely read 1909 pamphlet, *The Road to Power,* Kautsky had predicted that "a world war is ominously imminent, and war means also revolution." Laying out the full meaning of the final sentence of the International's Stuttgart resolution, he wrote then that he could "quite definitely assert that a revolution that war brings in its wake, will break out either during or immediately after the war."[3]

The spirit of the Stuttgart resolution, however, was not to be found in Kautsky's first wartime article in *Die Neue Zeit,* written four days after the war credits vote. Instead, he expressed the hope that the party could survive the strains of war untouched. "We must preserve the organization and publications of the party and the unions intact," he wrote, "and protect their members as much from rash deeds as from cowardly desertion." He continued, "we are a party of self-criticism, but in conditions of war this must cease."

The party could not possibly adopt a position to everyone's liking, Kautsky argued, because it was caught, as in every war, in the "fatal dilemma of choosing between the necessity of defending home and hearth, and international solidarity. . . . We well understand that many disagree with this or that step of the party, but it would be wrong, indeed it would be a fatal error, to unleash internal discord because of some such disagreement. In this respect too, the weapon of criticism must be silent. In wartime, discipline comes first, not only in the army but in the party too. . . . The most vital condition of our success today is not *criticism,* but *trust.*"[4]

Kautsky attempted to soft-pedal the fact that the French and German Socialist parties were now on opposite sides of the trenches, while both still claimed to stand firmly on the same fundamental proletarian socialist principles. In an October 2 article he called for confidence that the rift would be closed in due course.

French Socialists, he explained, had good reason to believe they were defending against the autocratic German Empire the republican institutions that had created better conditions for the struggle of French workers. Similarly, German Socialists were aiming to defend the democratic rights that workers had achieved within the German Empire in a war against tsarist despotism. Both were correctly using the criterion of advancing the class interests of the workers, he argued, yet it threw them into conflict with one another. "Their opposition flows not from a difference in criteria or in basic outlook, but from contrasting assessments of the situation, which flow from their contrasting geographical positions. This opposition can hardly be overcome while the war rages on," Kautsky concluded, but it will end with the conclusion of the war.

In Kautsky's view, the criterion of proletarian class interests had thus led Socialists in the two warring camps to opposite conclusions. So too had the criterion of "offensive or defensive war," for Socialists on each side held their state to be on the defensive. Kautsky saw a third criterion, however, one that could bring Socialists of all countries to common conclusions: "Each people, and the proletariat of each country as well, has an urgent interest in preventing the enemy of its country from crossing its frontiers, since that would convert the horror and devastation of war into its most terrible form, an enemy invasion. And in each national state the proletariat must also commit its full energy to assure that the independence and unity of the national territory remains intact. That is a fundamental part of democracy, which in turn is the necessary basis for the proletariat's struggle and victory." According to Kautsky's argument Russian Socialists had opposed the war with Japan back in 1905, and U.S. Socialists the war with Spain in 1898 only because their national frontiers were secure. But now, in 1914, the two warring camps were evenly balanced, and no frontiers were secure.

Kautsky's line of argument implied that the division among Socialists was inevitable. Responsibility for these differences fell simply on objective conditions—a military situation where all belligerents were threatened with invasion. Should one side gain the upper hand, Socialists of all countries would then surely unite in defending the weaker country from invasion. Should the war tend toward stalemate, on the other hand, Socialists could reckon with a compromise peace whose terms would most closely correspond with the Socialist point of view.[5]

Socialists, then, had grounds for hope, Kautsky asserted. But did they have a basis for action? How could they act on their internationalist convictions during the war? Kautsky explored this question in an article in the November 28 *Die Neue Zeit*.

Internationalism and the war[6]

by Karl Kautsky

The outbreak of war brought bitter disappointment for the Social Democracy, particularly in those countries where it was strong and closely tied to the masses. Everywhere the masses and the Socialist organizations rallied to support their governments.

While almost every previous war had led us to disagree on which side to support, never had we seen such sharply defined national alignments in our ranks. Taking sides in a war according to your national point of view clearly endangers the International. This is not because such a course violates our principles. We certainly can rally behind a war fought to fend off enemy invasion.

It is true that this criterion of national defense must be subordinate to that of world proletarian interests, and that theoreticians and party leaders must understand this subordination if they are to avoid being swept along by the tide. But in the present war this criterion of world proletarian interests has broken down almost completely. Even in the past it never had much of a historical impact. It has never decisively influenced the masses, whose most tangible, immediate, and urgent concern was to defend themselves and their livelihoods.

Proletarian internationalism would be in a grievous state if it were not compatible with national defense. Of course that is not the case, for this is expressly sanctioned.

Yet this is not to say that taking a stand for national defense does not endanger the spirit of proletarian internationalism. Proletarians have been brought into hostile conflict with one another, and the social contradictions in each country have been temporarily forced into the background.

This internationalist patriotism is difficult to distinguish in practice from nationalist and chauvinist patriotism. And it becomes even more difficult to distinguish between them when martial law makes it hard to clarify the difference before public opinion. The uninformed, both in the enemy's country and in our own, could easily conclude that a turn had taken place to real nationalism, further aggravating the situation.

Thus, a great danger is posed for internationalism. Under these circumstances it is doubly important for us to arm ourselves against this danger, to avoid every utterance that could be interpreted in a nationalist sense, and to fight against every real manifestation of chauvinism in our own ranks.

This danger should only summon us to greater vigilance in our work. But it is not so great as to give grounds for discouragement.

Some party comrades, carried away by the tide of events, have seriously infringed on our internationalist convictions. But I have seen no sign from any country of a leading comrade advancing a demand that would violate internationalism. . . .

The war will not kill the International. Rather it will lead to a better understanding of the limits of the International's effectiveness than we had before it began.

What people can accomplish greatly depends on their awareness of their own limitations. They should neither set themselves tasks beyond their strength, nor have expectations that they cannot fulfill. By concentrating their efforts on what they can realistically attain they will reach the highest possible achievements. . . .

So too the present war has exposed the limits of the International's effectiveness. We deluded ourselves in expecting that the International would be able to bring about a united stance of the whole world Socialist proletariat during a world war. Only in isolated and particularly simple cases has such a united stance been possible. The World War has divided Socialists into different camps, for the most part into different national camps. The International cannot prevent that.

In other words the International is not an effective tool in wartime; *in essence it is an instrument of peace.* Only in peacetime can it develop its full strength, and insofar as it is able to bring this strength to bear, it always works for peace.

The International is a product not only of the proletarian class struggle but also of international commerce, which makes the situation of the proletariat of every country completely dependent on that of the proletariat of other countries. The situation of the proletariat tends to rise and fall in a common rhythm with international trade. Only the closest international collaboration among proletarians protects them from being played off one against another, thereby aiding the capitalists to oppress them.

Socialism is the intellectual heir of revolutionary bourgeois-democratic idealism and of the inclination of free-trade industrialism to promote international peace—a heritage which has certainly not been taken over unchanged. Therefore it strives from the outset to achieve international unity against the worldwide solidarity of reaction and protectionism. This international unity acquires a firm material foundation only when it is recognized that the achievements of the proletarian class struggle cannot be made secure in a national framework when international unity is absent. Even trade unions, which have kept aloof from any kind of socialist ideology, have finally seen the necessity of international organization.

When a war reaches the point where it forces the class struggle into the background and paralyzes international commerce, then the strongest sources of internationalism will temporarily dry up. The International will be most weakened precisely when it needs to be strongest, when national antagonisms rage the loudest and crush all resistance.

The International is at its strongest in peacetime and its weakest in wartime. While we must certainly regret this, it does not lessen in the slightest the International's importance in times of peace, that is, in times of normal social development.

The International is not merely at its strongest in peacetime. It is also the most powerful instrument to keep the peace.

The present war shows the significance already achieved by the proletariat, most clearly in the appointment of Socialist ministers in France and Belgium. Even before the war the proletariat's attitude had an influence on the governments. Of course this influence was not yet strong enough to prevent the outbreak of war. Still it would not be wrong to say it was strong enough to cause the governments to hold off and delay the World War for years.

Certainly the proletariat was the weightiest of all the factors that contributed to the maintenance of peace, a capacity that was increased enormously by the International. It drew together all the proletarian movements of the individual countries and gave them a common goal—a policy that would have maintained the peace had it prevailed. The International has shown that a policy is possible for the world that guarantees every nation its economic development and does not oppress any. The Socialist parties of the belligerent countries have now amply shown that the supporters of this international policy did not intend by this to abandon their national interests.

Has the International's policy proven itself to be a shimmering soap bubble, burst by the hard realities of the war? Not at all. This policy is deeply rooted in the conditions in which the proletariat lives and works; as soon as the possibility of action for peace reappears the International's policy will assume new life and effectiveness. Then it will be able once again to act as an instrument for peace, and to show whether or not the war has impaired its strength. Then we will see whether our "national convulsion" has weakened our internationalist thought and sensibility, or whether on the contrary we have triumphantly maintained its strength and can give it unanimous expression in an international program for peace.

If we succeed it will be a great achievement. And we have every reason to expect success. . . .

A nation's victory in war is never an end in itself. Rather it is simply the means to a prosperous peace. Amid all the division, delusion, confusion, and catastrophe of war, preoccupation with the means for war must not blind us to the goals we seek. Amid the pervasive concern for national prosperity, we must always uphold international solidarity and never allow it to come into question.

If we do this, then our partisanship in the war will not prevent the International, firm and united, from fulfilling its great historical tasks: Struggle for peace, class struggle in peacetime.

It was several months before German revolutionists were able to break through censorship and circulate their answers to Heine, Scheidemann, and Kautsky. Russian revolutionists, however, were quick to print their replies, and these circulated inside Germany. Leon Trotsky's pamphlet, *War and the International,* was serialized in the Paris Russian-language daily *Golos* (Voice), edited by Menshevik leader Julius Martov, starting in November

1914. Trotsky, the chairman of the 1905 Petersburg Soviet and a prominent Socialist writer, held a middle position between the Bolshevik and Menshevik wings of the Russian movement. When a German translation of his pamphlet began to circulate underground in Germany in December, the imperial government prosecuted its distributors, and sentenced Trotsky *in absentia* to several months in prison.

Trotsky's pamphlet strongly criticized the German SPD majority leadership's stand; its introductory and concluding sections, excerpted here, discussed the overall perspectives for socialism and for the rebirth of its international organization. In contrast to Kautsky, Trotsky did not call for the revival of the Second International, with all the faults that had led to its collapse, but for a new International, to lead to revolutionary victory.

War and the International[7]

by Leon Trotsky

The fundamental question

The present war is basically a revolt of the productive forces developed by capitalism against the nation-state form of their exploitation. Today the entire globe—its dry land and water, its surface and interior—has become the arena of a *worldwide* economy; the dependence of each part on the other has become indissoluble.

While capitalism completed this task, it also forced the capitalist states into a struggle for the subjection of this world economy to the profit interests of each national bourgeoisie. The politics of imperialism provide clear proof that the old European nation-states that were created in the revolutions and wars of 1789, 1815, 1848, 1859, 1864, 1866, and 1870 have outlived themselves and become intolerable obstacles to the further development of the productive forces.[8] The war of 1914 is, above all, the downfall of the *nation-state* as an independent economic arena. Nationality may continue as a cultural, ideological, and psychological fact, but the economic basis has been pulled out from under its feet. All talk about the present free-for-all being an affair of "national defense" is either hypocrisy or blindness. On the contrary, the objective meaning of the war consists of the destruction of the present national economic enclaves in the name of a world economy. Imperialism, however, is not striving to solve this task on the basis of intelligently organized, productive cooperation, but on the basis of exploitation of the world economy by the capitalist class of the victorious country, a country that must achieve through this war the transformation from a great power into a world power.

The war proclaims the downfall of the nation-state, but at the same time the downfall of the *capitalist form* of economy. By means of the nation-state capitalism revolutionized the entire world economy. It divided the entire globe among members of an oligarchy of great powers, around which the small states were arranged as satellites, living off the rivalry of the great ones. The further development of the world economy on a capitalist basis means a continuous struggle of the world powers to constantly redivide the earth's surface as the object of capitalist exploitation. Under the banner of militarism, economic rivalry gives way to world robbery and devastation, disorganizing the very foundation of human economic life. World production revolts not only against the chains of the nation-state but also against the economy's capitalist organization, or rather, now, its barbaric disorganization.

The war of 1914 is the greatest convulsion in history of an economic system perishing from its own contradictions.

All the historical forces that were called on to guide bourgeois society, to speak in its name and to exploit it—the monarchies, the ruling parties, diplomacy, standing armies, the churches—have announced with the war of 1914 their historical bankruptcy. They defended capitalism as a system of human culture, and the catastrophe born of this system is primarily *their* catastrophe. The first wave of events raised the national governments and armies to an unprecedented height. For the moment the entire nation rallied around them. But all the more terrible will be the rulers' fall when, in the face of the cannons' deafening roar, the peoples realize the meaning of the current events in their full truth and horror.

The revolutionary response of the masses will be all the more powerful the more monstrous are the jolts that history gives them now.

Capitalism has created the material preconditions for a new socialist economy. Imperialism has taken the peoples of the capitalist world into a historical blind alley. The war of 1914 is showing the way out of this blind alley, violently forcing the proletariat onto the road of a socialist revolution. . . .

It has become intolerable for capitalism to remain in the grip of the nation-state. The national great power must be replaced by the imperialist world power.

In these historical conditions it is not the business of the European proletariat to defend the outlived national "fatherland," which has become the main brake on economic progress, but rather to create a new, more powerful, and more stable fatherland—the republican *United States of Europe* as the transition to the united states of the world. The proletariat can oppose the imperialist dead end of capitalism only through the socialist organization of the world economy as the practical program for today. War is the method by which capitalism, at the peak of its development, tries to solve insoluble contradictions. The proletariat must oppose war with its own method—socialist revolution.

The collapse of the Second International is a tragic *fact,* and it would be blindness or cowardice to close our eyes to it. The conduct of French and the greater part of English socialism is just as much a part of this collapse as are the actions of German and Austrian Social Democracy.

The war of 1914 proclaims the downfall of the nation-states. The Socialist parties of the period now concluding were *national* parties. They had become entwined with the national states in all the ramifications of their organizations, activities, and psychology. And in spite of the solemn pledges of their congresses, when imperialism, nurtured on national soil, began to demolish outdated national barriers, sword in hand they rose to the defense of conservative state formations. In their historic fall the national states are dragging along with them the national Socialist parties.

It is not socialism that is perishing, but only its temporary historical expression. The revolutionary idea is moulting, casting off its dried-out skin. This skin is made up of living people, of an entire Socialist generation that in selfless agitational and organizational work during several decades of political reaction petrified into the outlooks and habits of national "possibilism."[9]

As the nation-states became a brake on the development of the productive forces, so too the old national Socialist parties became the main obstacle for the revolutionary working-class movement. They revealed their total backwardness, discredited all their inadequate, limited methods, and brought on the proletariat the disgrace and horror of internecine warfare. Only then could the proletariat liberate itself, through terrible disillusionments, from the prejudices and slavish habits of the preparatory period and become at last that which the voice of history is now calling it to be: a revolutionary class fighting for power.

The Second International did not live in vain. It carried out an enormous cultural work, the likes of which the world has never seen: the education and rallying of an oppressed class. The proletariat does not now need to begin all over again. It does not set out on its new road with empty hands. The period now concluded bequeathed it a rich arsenal of ideas. The new epoch is forcing it to combine the old weapon of criticism with the new criticism of weapons.[10]

This pamphlet was written with extreme haste, under less than favorable conditions for systematic work. A considerable part of it is devoted to the old International which has fallen. But the entire pamphlet, from the first to the last page, was written with the idea of the new International which must be born out of the present world upheaval, of the International of the last conflict and the final victory. . . .

The revolutionary epoch

The awakening, enlightenment, and organization of the proletariat in the past period uncovered vast sources of revolutionary energy, which were not adequately employed in the daily struggle. Social Democracy not only awakened the most conscious layers of the proletariat, it also restrained their revolutionary energy, necessarily imparting a *delaying* character to party tactics. The extended reactionary character of the period did not summon the proletariat to the kind of tasks that would have demanded its all—its full selflessness and heroism. Imperialism has now presented such demands to the proletariat.

Imperialism attained its goal of drawing the proletariat

over to support a position of "national self-defense." For the workers themselves this could only mean the defense of everything that they had created with their own hands, not only the colossal wealth of the nation, but also their own class organizations, treasuries, and presses—all of the things the workers had achieved in tireless and painstaking struggle over several decades. Imperialism violently knocked society out of a state of unstable equilibrium. It blew up the sluice gates that had been erected by Social Democracy to channel the flow of the proletariat's revolutionary energy, and directed this flow into *its own* stream.

This colossal historical experiment smashed the spine of the Socialist International at one blow. However, it conceals in itself a mortal danger for bourgeois society. The hammer is knocked out of the workers' hands and a rifle is put in its place. The worker, formerly bound hand and foot by the mechanism of capitalist economic life, suddenly escapes from its constrictions and accustoms himself to place collective goals higher than worldly blessings, higher than life itself. With the gun in his hands that he himself created, the worker is put in the position where the immediate political destiny of the state depends on him. Those who oppressed and scorned him in normal times now flatter him and try to ingratiate themselves with him. At the same time he comes into intimate contact with the cannons which, according to Lassalle, make up one of the most consequential parts of a constitution. He steps over borders, participates in forced requisitions; through his action cities switch hands.

Changes are taking place such as the present generation has never seen before. Even if the advanced worker knew theoretically that *might makes right,* his political thinking remained permeated through and through with the spirit of possibilism and conformity to bourgeois law. Now he is being taught in life to despise that conformity to law and to forcibly violate it. Dynamic elements are replacing static ones in his psychology. The big guns are pounding the idea into his head that if it is impossible to go around an obstacle, it is possible to smash it. Almost the entire adult male population is going through this school of war, terrible in its realism, which is forming a new human type. Iron necessity is now raising its fist against all the norms of bourgeois society, with its rights, morals, and religion. "Not kennt kein Gebot" [necessity knows no law], said the German chancellor on August 4. Monarchs walk about in the public squares calling each other liars in the street language of market-women; governments violate solemnly recognized obligations; the national church chains its god to the national cannon like a condemned criminal.

Is it not clear that this environment must generate the most profound changes in the psychology of the masses of workers, radically curing them of that hypnosis of legality which is a reflection of a period of political immobility? The propertied classes, to their horror, will soon be convinced of this. A proletariat that has graduated from the school of war inevitably feels the necessity to speak the language of force when the first serious obstacle presents itself within its own country. "Necessity knows no law!", it responds to whomever tries to restrain it with the commandments of bourgeois legality.

And necessity, the terrible material want that prevails during wartime and after the cessation of hostilities, will push the masses into violating many commandments. The general economic exhaustion of Europe is affecting the proletariat the most immediately and sharply of all. The state's material resources will be exhausted by the war and the possibility of satisfying the demands of the working masses will prove to be extremely limited. This must lead to the most profound political conflicts which, widening and deepening, can take on the character of a social revolution, the pace and outcome of which no one, of course, can now predetermine.

On the other hand, the war with its armies of millions and its hellish implements of destruction can exhaust not only the material resources of the state, but also the moral forces of the proletariat itself. This war does not have definite, politically limited aims; it no longer appears either offensive or defensive, in a literal sense, to any of the participants. It has become mutually destructive for all of them. If it does not encounter internal resistance it could last several more years with changing fortunes on both sides until the main participants are completely exhausted. All the fighting energy of the international proletariat, now called forth by imperialism's bloody incantation, may be entirely used up in the terrible work of mutual exhaustion and destruction. As a result our entire culture could be thrown back for many decades.

A peace arising not from the will of the awakened peoples but from the mutual exhaustion of the participants would be a repetition for all of Europe of the Bucharest peace that ended the Balkan War. It would patch together again all the contradictions, antagonisms, and incongruities that led to the present war. And with many other things, the socialist work of two human generations would be utterly drowned in rivers of blood.

Which of these two prospects is the more probable? It is impossible to predetermine this theoretically. The outcome depends on the activity of living social forces—first and foremost, of revolutionary Social Democracy.

"An immediate cessation of the war!"—that is the slogan under which Social Democracy can once again rally its scattered ranks both in individual parties and in the International as a whole. The proletariat cannot make its will to peace dependent on the strategic considerations of the general staffs. On the contrary, it must resolutely oppose these considerations with its demand for peace. What the warring

governments call a struggle for national self-preservation is in actual fact mutual extermination. True national self-defense now lies in the struggle for peace.

For us this means not only a struggle to save humanity's material and cultural birthright from further reckless destruction, but above all a struggle to preserve the proletariat's revolutionary energy.

Gathering the ranks of proletarians in the struggle for peace means opposing a frenzied imperialism all along the line with the forces of revolutionary socialism. The conditions upon which we demand the conclusion of peace—a peace of the peoples themselves, not a deal between the diplomats—must be identical for the whole International.

No annexations!

No reparations!

The right of every nation to self-determination!

The United States of Europe—without monarchies, without standing armies, without ruling feudal castes, without secret diplomacy!

Agitation for peace, which must be conducted simultaneously with all the means that Social Democracy now has at its disposal, as well as with those which, with a will, it can acquire, not only liberates the workers from the hypnosis of nationalism, but above all stimulates the salutary work of internally cleansing the present official parties of the proletariat. The national revisionists and social patriots, who are exploiting for national militarist aims the influence that socialism has won over the years among the working masses, must be thrust back into the camp of the proletariat's class enemies by our uncompromising revolutionary agitation for peace.

Revolutionary Social Democracy does not have to be in the least bit afraid of becoming isolated. The war is conducting a very terrible agitation against itself. Every day will bring new masses under our banner, if it is the honest banner of peace and democracy. Using the slogan of peace, revolutionary Social Democracy will most readily isolate militant reaction in Europe and force it to take the offensive.

ZÜRICH, OCTOBER 31, 1914

While Trotsky was preparing his pamphlet, Lenin's draft theses on the war ("The Tasks of Revolutionary Social-Democracy in the European War"—see Chapter 3) were under discussion by the Bolshevik Party leadership. The theses arrived in Petrograd in August, recalls Alexander Shlyapnikov, and "they responded to the mood of party workers at the time, but the question of 'defeatism' did cause perplexity. Comrades did not want to link their tactics to the army's strategic situation," as "defeatism" seemed to do. "But at the same time nobody wished Nicholas II the smallest victory, as it was clear that a victory would strengthen the vilest reaction." [11]

The theses met with general agreement, and were expanded and strengthened in the statement issued by the Central Committee of the Russian Social Democratic Labor Party (Bolshevik). While its call for a new, Third International resembled that in Trotsky's pamphlet, it differed by stressing that the new International could only be constructed by a definitive break not just with the pro-war chauvinists like Scheidemann and Guesde but with those opportunists who covered up the role of the chauvinists in the August 1914 collapse and sought at all costs to maintain unity with them. The manifesto, drafted by Lenin, was published November 1 in the first wartime issue of *Sotsial-Demokrat* (Social Democrat), the newspaper of the RSDLP (Bolshevik) Central Committee, published approximately every month in Switzerland. The following is the text of the manifesto.

The war and Russian Social Democracy[12]

Central Committee, RSDLP

SEPTEMBER 1914

The European war, which the governments and the bourgeois parties of all countries have been preparing for decades, has broken out. The growth of armaments, the extreme intensification of the struggle for markets in the latest—the imperialist—stage of capitalist development in the advanced countries, and the dynastic interests of the more backward East-European monarchies were inevitably bound to bring about this war, and have done so. Seizure of territory and subjugation of other nations, the ruining of competing nations and the plunder of their wealth, distracting the attention of the working masses from the internal political crises in Russia, Germany, Britain and other countries, disuniting and nationalist stultification of the workers, and the extermination of their vanguard so as to weaken the revolutionary movement of the proletariat—these comprise the sole actual content, importance and significance of the present war.

It is primarily on Social-Democracy that the duty rests of revealing the true meaning of the war, and of ruthlessly exposing the falsehood, sophistry and "patriotic" phrase-mongering spread by the ruling classes, the landowners and the bourgeoisie, in defence of the war.

One group of belligerent nations is headed by the German bourgeoisie. It is hoodwinking the working class and the toiling masses by asserting that this is a war in defence of the fatherland, freedom and civilisation, for the liberation of the peoples oppressed by tsarism, and for the destruction of reactionary tsarism. In actual fact, however, this bourgeoisie, which servilely grovels to the Prussian Junkers, headed by Wilhelm II, has always been a most faithful ally of tsarism, and an enemy of the revolutionary movement of Russia's workers and peasants. In fact, whatever the outcome of the war, this bourgeoisie will, together with the Junkers, exert every effort to support the tsarist monarchy against a revolution in Russia.

In fact, the German bourgeoisie has launched a robber campaign against Serbia, with the object of subjugating her and throttling the national revolution of the Southern Slavs, at the same time sending the bulk of its military forces against the freer countries, Belgium and France, so as to plunder richer competitors. In fact, the German bourgeoisie, which has been spreading the fable that it is waging a war of defence, chose the moment it thought most favourable for war, making use of its latest improvements in military matériel and forestalling the rearmament already planned and decided upon by Russia and France.

The other group of belligerent nations is headed by the British and the French bourgeoisie, who are hoodwinking the working class and the toiling masses by asserting that they are waging a war for the defence of their countries, for freedom and civilisation and against German militarism and despotism. In actual fact, this bourgeoisie has long been spending thousands of millions to hire the troops of Russian tsarism, the most reactionary and barbarous monarchy in Europe, and prepare them for an attack on Germany.

In fact, the struggle of the British and the French bourgeoisie is aimed at the seizure of the German colonies, and the ruining of a rival nation, whose economic development has been more rapid. In pursuit of this noble aim, the "advanced" "democratic" nations are helping the savage tsarist regime to still more throttle Poland, the Ukraine, etc., and more thoroughly crush the revolution in Russia.

Neither group of belligerents is inferior to the other in spoliation, atrocities and the boundless brutality of war; however, to hoodwink the proletariat and distract its attention from the only genuine war of liberation, namely, a civil war against the bourgeoisie both of its "own" and of "foreign" countries—to achieve so lofty an aim—the bourgeoisie of each country is trying, with the help of false phrases about patriotism, to extol the significance of its "own" national war, asserting that it is out to defeat the enemy, not for plunder and the seizure of territory, but for the "liberation" of all other peoples except its own.

But the harder the governments and the bourgeoisie of all countries try to disunite the workers and pit them against one another, and the more savagely they enforce, for this lofty aim, martial law and the military censorship (measures which even now, in wartime, are applied against the "internal" foe more harshly than against the external), the more pressingly it is the duty of the class-conscious proletariat to defend its class solidarity, its internationalism, and its socialist convictions against the unbridled chauvinism of the "patriotic" bourgeois cliques in all countries. If class-conscious workers were to give up this aim, this would mean renunciation of their aspirations for freedom and democracy, to say nothing of their socialist aspirations.

It is with a feeling of the most bitter disappointment that we have to record that the socialist parties of the leading European countries have failed to discharge this duty, the behaviour of these parties' leaders, particularly in Germany, bordering on downright betrayal of the cause of socialism. At this time of supreme and historic importance, most of the leaders of the present Socialist International, the Second (1889–1914), are trying to substitute nationalism for socialism. As a result of their behaviour, the workers' parties of these countries did not oppose the governments' criminal conduct, but called upon the working class to *identify* its position with that of the imperialist governments. The leaders of the International committed an act of treachery against socialism by voting for war credits, by reiterating the chauvinist ("patriotic") slogans of the bourgeoisie of their "own" countries, by justifying and defending the war, by joining the bourgeois governments of the belligerent countries, and so on and so forth. The most influential socialist leaders and the most influential organs of the socialist press of present-day Europe hold views that are chauvinist, bourgeois and liberal, and in no way socialist. The responsibility for thus disgracing socialism falls primarily on the German Social-Democrats, who were the strongest and most influential party in the Second International. But neither can one justify the French socialists, who have accepted ministerial posts in the government of that very bourgeoisie which betrayed its country and allied itself with Bismarck so as to crush the Commune.

The German and the Austrian Social-Democrats are attempting to justify their support for the war by arguing that they are thereby fighting against Russian tsarism. We Russian Social-Democrats declare that we consider such justification sheer sophistry. In our country the revolutionary movement against tsarism has again assumed tremendous proportions during the past few years. This movement has always been headed by the working class of Russia. The political strikes of the last few years, which have involved millions of workers, have had as their slogan the overthrow of tsarism and the establishment of a democratic republic. During his visit to Nicholas II on the very eve of the war, Poincaré, President of the French Republic, could see for himself, in the streets of St. Petersburg, barricades put up by Russian workers. The Russian proletariat has not flinched from any sacrifice to rid humanity of the disgrace of the tsarist monarchy. We must, however, say that if there is anything that, under certain conditions, can delay the downfall of tsarism, anything that can help tsarism in its struggle against the whole of Russia's democracy, then that is the present war, which has placed the purses of the British, the French and the Russian bourgeois at the disposal of tsarism, to further the latter's reactionary aims. If there is anything that can hinder the revolutionary struggle of Russia's working class against tsarism, then that is the behaviour of the German and the Austrian Social-Democratic leaders, which the chauvinist press of Russia is continually holding up to us as an example.

Even assuming that German Social-Democracy was so weak that it was compelled to refrain from all revolutionary action, it should not have joined the chauvinist camp, or taken steps which gave the Italian socialists reason to say that the German Social-Democratic leaders were dishonouring the banner of the proletarian International.

Our Party, the Russian Social-Democratic Labour Party, has made, and will continue to make great sacrifices in connection with the war. The whole of our working-class legal press has been suppressed. Most working-class associations have been disbanded, and a large number of our comrades have been arrested and exiled. Yet our parliamentary representatives—the Russian Social-Democratic Labour group in the Duma—considered it their imperative socialist duty not to vote for the war credits, and even to walk out of the Duma, so as to express their protest the more energetically; they considered it their duty to brand the European governments' policy as imperialist. Though the tsar's government has increased its tyranny tenfold, the Social-Democratic workers of Russia are already publishing their first illegal manifestos against the war, thus doing their duty to democracy and to the International.

While the collapse of the Second International has given rise to a sense of burning shame in revolutionary Social-

Democrats—as represented by the minority of German Social-Democrats and the finest Social-Democrats in the neutral countries; while socialists in both Britain and France have been speaking up against the chauvinism of most Social-Democratic parties; while the opportunists, as represented, for instance, by the German *Sozialistische Monatshefte,* which have long held a national-liberal stand, are with good reason celebrating their victory over European socialism—the worst possible service is being rendered to the proletariat by those who vacillate between opportunism and revolutionary Social-Democracy (like the "Centre" in the German Social-Democratic Party), by those who are trying to hush up the collapse of the Second International or to disguise it with diplomatic phrases.

On the contrary, this collapse must be frankly recognised and its causes understood, so as to make it possible to build up a new and more lasting socialist unity of the workers of all countries.

The opportunists have wrecked the decisions of the Stuttgart, Copenhagen and Basel congresses, which made it binding on socialists of all countries to combat chauvinism in all and any conditions, made it binding on socialists to reply to any war begun by the bourgeoisie and governments, with intensified propaganda of civil war and social revolution. The collapse of the Second International is the collapse of opportunism, which developed from the features of a now bygone (and so-called "peaceful") period of history, and in recent years has come practically to dominate the International. The opportunists have long been preparing the ground for this collapse by denying the socialist revolution and substituting bourgeois reformism in its stead; by rejecting the class struggle with its inevitable conversion at certain moments into civil war, and by preaching class collaboration; by preaching bourgeois chauvinism under the guise of patriotism and the defence of the fatherland, and ignoring or rejecting the fundamental truth of socialism, long ago set forth in the *Communist Manifesto,* that the workingmen have no country; by confining themselves, in the struggle against militarism, to a sentimental, philistine point of view, instead of recognising the need for a revolutionary war by the proletarians of all countries, against the bourgeoisie of all countries; by making a fetish of the necessary utilisation of bourgeois parliamentarianism and bourgeois legality, and forgetting that illegal forms of organisation and propaganda are imperative at times of crises. The natural "appendage" to opportunism—one that is just as bourgeois and hostile to the proletarian, i.e., the Marxist, point of view—namely, the anarcho-syndicalist trend, has been marked by a no less shamefully smug reiteration of the slogans of chauvinism, during the present crisis.

The aims of socialism at the present time cannot be fulfilled, and real international unity of the workers cannot be achieved, without a decisive break with opportunism, and without explaining its inevitable fiasco to the masses.

It must be the primary task of Social-Democrats in every country to combat that country's chauvinism. In Russia this chauvinism has overcome the bourgeois liberals (the "Constitutional-Democrats"), and part of the Narodniks—down to the Socialist-Revolutionaries and the "Right" Social-Democrats. (In particular, the chauvinist utterances of E. Smirnov, P. Maslov and G. Plekhanov, for example, should be branded; they have been taken up and widely used by the bourgeois "patriotic" press.)

In the present situation, it is impossible to determine, from the standpoint of the international proletariat, the defeat of which of the two groups of belligerent nations would be the lesser evil for socialism. But to us Russian Social-Democrats there cannot be the slightest doubt that, from the standpoint of the working class and of the toiling masses of all the nations of Russia, the defeat of the tsarist monarchy, the most reactionary and barbarous of governments, which is oppressing the largest number of nations and the greatest mass of the population of Europe and Asia, would be the lesser evil.

The formation of a republican United States of Europe should be the immediate political slogan of Europe's Social-Democrats. In contrast with the bourgeoisie, which is ready to "promise" anything in order to draw the proletariat into the mainstream of chauvinism, the Social-Democrats will explain that this slogan is absolutely false and meaningless without the revolutionary overthrow of the German, the Austrian and the Russian monarchies.

Since Russia is most backward and has not yet completed its bourgeois revolution, it still remains the task of Social-Democrats in that country to achieve the three fundamental conditions for consistent democratic reform, viz., a democratic republic (with complete equality and self-determination for all nations), confiscation of the landed estates, and an eight-hour working day. But in all the advanced countries the war has placed on the order of the day the slogan of socialist revolution, a slogan that is the more urgent, the more heavily the burden of war presses upon the shoulders of the proletariat, and the more active its future role must become in the re-creation of Europe, after the horrors of the present "patriotic" barbarism in conditions of the tremendous technological progress of large-scale capitalism. The bourgeoisie's use of wartime laws to gag the proletariat makes it imperative for the latter to create illegal forms of agitation and organisation. Let the opportunists "preserve" the legal organisations at the price of treachery to their convictions—revolutionary Social-Democrats will utilise the organisational experience and links of the working class so as to create illegal forms of struggle for socialism, forms appropriate to a period of crisis, and to unite the workers, not with the chauvinist bourgeoisie of their respective countries, but with the workers of all countries.

The proletarian International has not gone under and will not go under. Notwithstanding all obstacles, the masses of the workers will create a new International. Opportunism's present triumph will be short-lived. The greater the sacrifices imposed by the war the clearer will it become to the mass of the workers that the opportunists have betrayed the workers' cause and that the weapons must be turned against the government and the bourgeoisie of each country.

The conversion of the present imperialist war into a civil war is the only correct proletarian slogan, one that follows from the experience of the Commune, and outlined in the Basel resolution (1912); it has been dictated by all the conditions of an imperialist war between highly developed bourgeois countries. However difficult that transformation may seem at any given moment, socialists will never relinquish systematic, persistent and undeviating preparatory work in this direction now that war has become a fact.

It is only along this path that the proletariat will be able to shake off its dependence on the chauvinist bourgeoisie, and, in one form or another and more or less rapidly, take decisive steps towards genuine freedom for the nations and towards socialism.

Long live the international fraternity of the workers against the chauvinism and patriotism of the bourgeoisie of all countries!

Long live a proletarian International, freed from opportunism!

Accompanying the Central Committee manifesto in *Sotsial-Demokrat* was an article by Lenin explaining why the Bolsheviks rejected "national defense" and advocated efforts by the revolutionary workers' movement in each country to turn the imperialist war into a civil war to overturn the rule of the exploiters.

The position and tasks of the Socialist International[13]

by V.I. Lenin

The question of the fatherland—we shall reply to the opportunists—cannot be posed without due consideration of the concrete historical nature of the present war. This is an imperialist war, i.e., it is being waged at a time of the highest development of capitalism, a time of its approaching *end.* The working class must first "constitute itself within the nation", the *Communist Manifesto* declares, emphasising the *limits and conditions* of our recognition of nationality and fatherland as essential forms of the bourgeois system, and, consequently, of the bourgeois fatherland. The opportunists distort that truth by extending to the period of the end of capitalism that which was true of the period of its rise. With reference to the former period and to the tasks of the proletariat in its struggle to destroy, not feudalism but capitalism, the *Communist Manifesto* gives a clear and precise formula: "The workingmen have no country." One can well understand why the opportunists are so afraid to accept this socialist proposition, afraid even, in most cases, openly to reckon with it. The socialist movement cannot triumph within the old framework of the fatherland. It creates new and superior forms of human society, in which the legitimate needs and progressive aspirations of the working masses of *each* nationality will, for the first time, be met through international unity, provided existing national partitions are removed. To the present-day bourgeoisie's attempts to divide and disunite them by means of hypocritical appeals for the "defence of the fatherland" the class-conscious workers will reply with ever new and persevering efforts to unite the workers of various nations in the struggle to overthrow the rule of the bourgeoisie of all nations.

The bourgeoisie is duping the masses by disguising imperialist rapine with the old ideology of a "national war". This deceit is being shown up by the proletariat, which has brought forward its slogan of turning the imperialist war into a civil war. This was the slogan of the Stuttgart and Basel resolutions, which had in mind, not war in general, but precisely the present war and spoke, not of "defence of the fatherland", but of "hastening the downfall of capitalism", of utilising the war-created crisis for this purpose, and of the example provided by the Paris Commune. The latter was an instance of a war of nations being turned into a civil war.

Of course, such a conversion is no easy matter and cannot be accomplished at the whim of one party or another. That conversion, however, is inherent in the objective conditions of capitalism in general, and of the period of the end of capitalism in particular. It is in that direction, and that direction alone, that socialists must conduct their activities. It is not their business to vote for war credits or to encourage chauvinism in their "own" country (and allied countries), but primarily to strive against the chauvinism of their "own" bourgeoisie, without confining themselves to legal forms of struggle when the crisis has matured and the bourgeoisie has itself taken away the legality it has created. Such is the *line* of action that *leads* to civil war, and will bring about civil war at one moment or another of the European conflagration.

War is no chance happening, no "sin" as is thought by Christian priests (who are no whit behind the opportunists in preaching patriotism, humanity and peace), but an inevitable stage of capitalism, just as legitimate a form of the *capitalist* way of life as peace is. Present-day war is a people's war. What follows from this truth is not that we must swim with the "popular" current of chauvinism, but that the class contradictions dividing the nations continue to exist in wartime and manifest themselves in conditions of war. Refusal to serve with the forces, antiwar strikes, etc., are sheer nonsense, the miserable and cowardly dream of an unarmed struggle against the armed bourgeoisie, vain yearning for the destruction of capitalism without a desperate civil war or a series of wars. It is the duty of every socialist to conduct propaganda of the class struggle, in the army as well; work directed towards turning a war of the nations into civil war is the only socialist activity in the era of an imperialist armed conflict of the bourgeoisie of all nations. Down with mawkishly sanctimonious and fatuous appeals for "peace at any price"! Let us raise high the banner of civil war! Imperialism sets at hazard the fate of European culture: this war will soon be followed by others, unless there are a series of successful revolutions. The story about this being the "last war" is a hollow and dangerous fabrication, a piece of philistine "mythology" (as *Golos* aptly puts it). The proletarian banner of civil war will rally together, not only hundreds of thousands of class-conscious workers but millions of semi-proletarians and petty bourgeois, now deceived by chauvinism, but whom the horrors of war will not only intimidate and depress, but also enlighten, teach, arouse, organise, steel and prepare for the war against the bourgeoisie of their "own" country and "foreign" countries. And this will take place, if not today, then tomorrow, if not during the war, then after it, if not in this war then in the next one.

The Second International is dead, overcome by opportunism. Down with opportunism, and long live the Third International, purged not only of "turncoats" (as *Golos* wishes), but of opportunism as well.

The Second International did its share of useful preparatory work in preliminarily organising the proletarian masses during the long, "peaceful" period of the most brutal capitalist slavery and most rapid capitalist progress in the last third of the nineteenth and the beginning of the twentieth centuries. To the Third International falls the task of organising the proletarian forces for a revolutionary onslaught against the capitalist governments, for civil war against the bourgeoisie of all countries for the capture of political power, for the triumph of socialism!

These initial statements on the war by the Bolshevik leadership and by Trotsky shared a common internationalist opposition to the war but proposed different courses of action for Socialists. A debate developed, in which Trotsky's viewpoint was advanced by the Paris daily *Golos*, and its successor, *Nashe Slovo* (Our Word). Trotsky arrived in Paris in late 1914, assuming co-editorship of the paper with Martov.[14] The editorial team also included internationalist Mensheviks like V.A. Antonov-Ovseenko and dissident Bolsheviks like S.A. Lozovsky and D.Z. Manuilsky.

Golos and *Nashe Slovo* criticized the Bolsheviks for rejecting the potential of the peace slogan for mobilizing the masses against their governments.

"Social Democracy certainly must not ignore the movement

to end the war now taking shape," replied Zinoviev in *Sotsial-Demokrat.* This movement should be utilized to deepen the masses' hatred for the war, he said, but that did not mean adopting the peace slogan as the Socialists' own. "Social Democrats will participate in a peace demonstration. But they should raise their own slogans there, and proceeding from the masses' simple desire for peace, they will call for revolutionary struggle."

There is nothing inherently revolutionary about the "peace" slogan, Zinoviev continued, as can be seen from the spectrum of forces who raise it: Socialists opposed to the war and renegades who support it, Kautsky and the SPD majority leadership, pacifists and the Catholic hierarchy, and in Britain and Russia a wing of the bourgeoisie itself. The "peace" slogan "only becomes revolutionary when it is linked to our explanation of a policy of revolutionary struggle, and accompanied by a call to revolution, and a revolutionary protest against the government of one's own country." [15]

Zinoviev argued that Trotsky's stress on the objective conditions that led to the collapse of the Second International also tended to obscure the responsibility of the opportunist current that led it and reflected his unwillingness to carry out a full break with these opportunists. "Trotsky considers the opportunist current and its leaders somewhat as victims of circumstances," Zinoviev wrote in 1915. "It is not a question of the opportunist leaders or of their current, if you please, but of the 'possibilism' of the entire preceding period. Such a counterposition is inherently a lawyer's defense of opportunism. There is no doubt that opportunism, like all else in the world, has its objective causes in external conditions," he continued. "But in politics more than anywhere else, to understand is not to forgive." [16]

According to Lenin, Trotsky's analysis of the period before 1914 seriously distorted reality. The impression is produced, Lenin wrote in 1915, that Social Democracy in that period "remained a single whole, which, generally speaking, was pervaded with gradualism, turned nationalist, was by degrees weaned away from breaks in gradualness and from catastrophes, and grew petty and mildewed." In reality other tendencies were operating, however, and class contradictions were growing more acute.

Lenin pointed to the way colonialism permitted broad petty-bourgeois sectors, many labor officials, as well as a layer of privileged workers—the "aristocracy of labor"—to share in the crumbs of imperialist superprofits. This helped generate "an entire opportunist *trend* based on a definite social stratum" within the working-class movement, linked to its own bourgeoisie "by numerous ties of common economic, social, and political interests." Trotsky's unwillingness to recognize the maturity of this opportunist trend was at the root of many of his errors, Lenin concluded.[17]

Writing in *Nashe Slovo,* Trotsky criticized the Bolshevik conception that Russian workers should favor the defeat of their government in the war. Lenin and Trotsky continued the debate in the following two articles, written in the summer of 1915 as the tsar's armies were in full retreat under the blows of a German offensive.

The defeat of one's own government in the imperialist war[18]

by V.I. Lenin

During a reactionary war a revolutionary class cannot but desire the defeat of its government.

This is axiomatic, and disputed only by conscious partisans or helpless satellites of the social-chauvinists.[19] Among the former, for instance, is Semkovsky of the Organising Committee (No. 2 of its *Izvestia*), and among the latter, Trotsky and Bukvoyed, and Kautsky in Germany. To desire Russia's defeat, Trotsky writes, is "an uncalled-for and absolutely unjustifiable concession to the political methodology of social-patriotism, which would replace the revolutionary struggle against the war and the conditions causing it, with an orientation—highly arbitrary in the present conditions—towards the lesser evil" (*Nashe Slovo* No. 105).[20]

This is an instance of high-flown phraseology with which Trotsky always justifies opportunism. A "revolutionary struggle against the war" is merely an empty and meaningless exclamation, something at which the heroes of the Second International excel, *unless* it means revolutionary action against *one's own government* even in wartime. One has only to do some thinking in order to understand this. Wartime revolutionary action against one's own government indubitably means, not only desiring its defeat, but really facilitating such a defeat. ("Discerning reader": note that this does not mean "blowing up bridges", organising unsuccessful strikes in the war industries, and in general helping the government defeat the revolutionaries.)

The phrase-bandying Trotsky has completely lost his bearings on a simple issue. It seems to him that to desire Russia's defeat *means* desiring the victory of Germany. (Bukvoyed and Semkovsky give more direct expression to the "thought", or rather want of thought, which they share with Trotsky.) But Trotsky regards this as the "methodology of social-patriotism"! To help people that are unable to think for themselves, the Berne resolution (*Sotsial-Demokrat* No. 40) made it clear that in *all* imperialist countries the proletariat must now desire the defeat of its own government.[21] Bukvoyed and Trotsky preferred to avoid this truth, while Semkovsky (an opportunist who is more useful to the working class than all the others, thanks to his naïvely frank reiteration of bourgeois wisdom) blurted out the following: "This is nonsense, because either Germany or Russia can win" (*Izvestia* No. 2).

Take the example of the Paris Commune. France was defeated by Germany but the workers were defeated by Bismarck and Thiers! Had Bukvoyed and Trotsky done a little thinking, they would have realised that *they* have adopted the viewpoint on the war held by *governments and the bourgeoisie,* i.e., that they cringe to the "political methodology of social-patriotism", to use Trotsky's pretentious language.

A revolution in wartime means civil war; the *conversion* of a war between governments into a civil war is, on the one hand, facilitated by military reverses ("defeats") of governments; on the other hand, one *cannot* actually strive for such a conversion without thereby facilitating defeat.

The reason why the chauvinists (including the Organising Committee and the Chkheidze group) repudiate the defeat "slogan" is that *this slogan alone* implies a consistent call for revolutionary action against one's own government in wartime. Without such action, millions of ultra-revolutionary phrases such as a war against "the war and the conditions, etc." are not worth a brass farthing.

Anyone who would in all earnest refute the "slogan" of defeat for one's own government in the imperialist war should prove one of three things: (1) that the war of 1914–15 is not reactionary, or (2) that a revolution stemming from that war is impossible, or (3) that co-ordination and mutual aid between revolutionary movements in *all* the belligerent countries are impossible. The third point is particularly important to Russia, a most backward country, where an immediate socialist revolution is impossible. That is why the Russian Social-Democrats had to be the first to advance the "theory and practice" of the defeat "slogan". The tsarist government was perfectly right in asserting that the agitation conducted by the Russian Social-Democratic Labour group in the Duma—the *sole* instance in the International, not only of parliamentary opposition but of genuine revolutionary anti-government agitation among the masses—that this agitation has weakened Russia's "military might" and is likely to lead to its defeat. This is a fact to which it is foolish to close one's eyes.

The opponents of the defeat slogan are simply afraid of themselves when they refuse to recognise the very obvious fact of the inseparable link between revolutionary agitation against the government and helping bring about its defeat.

Are co-ordination and mutual aid possible between the Russian movement, which is revolutionary in the bourgeois-democratic senses, and the socialist movement in the West? No socialist who has publicly spoken on the matter during the last decade has doubted this, the movement among the Austrian proletariat after October 17, 1905, *actually* proving it possible.[22]

Ask any Social-Democrat who calls himself an internationalist whether or not he approves of an understanding between the Social-Democrats of the various belligerent countries on joint revolutionary action against all belligerent governments. Many of them will reply that it is impossible, as Kautsky has done (*Die Neue Zeit*, October 2, 1914), thereby *fully proving* his social-chauvinism. This, on the one hand, is a deliberate and vicious lie, which clashes with the generally known facts and the Basel Manifesto. On the other hand, if it were true, *the opportunists would be quite right in many respects*!

Many will voice their approval of such an understanding. To this we shall say: if this approval is not hypocritical, it is ridiculous to think that, in wartime and for the conduct of a war, some "formal" understanding is necessary, such as the election of representatives, the arrangement of a meeting, the signing of an agreement, and the choice of the day and hour! Only the Semkovskys are capable of thinking so.

An understanding on revolutionary action even in a *single* country, to say nothing of a number of countries, can be achieved *only* by the force of the *example* of serious revolutionary action, by *launching* such action and *developing* it. However, such action cannot be launched without desiring the defeat of the government, and without contributing to such a defeat. The conversion of the imperialist war into a civil war cannot be "made", any more than a revolution can be "made". It *develops* out of a number of diverse phenomena, aspects, features, characteristics and consequences of the imperialist war. That development is *impossible* without a series of military reverses and defeats of governments that receive blows from their *own* oppressed classes.

To repudiate the defeat slogan means allowing one's revolutionary ardour to degenerate into an empty phrase, or sheer hypocrisy.

What is the substitute proposed for the defeat slogan? It is that of "neither victory nor defeat" (Semkovsky in *Izvestia* No. 2; also the *entire* Organising Committee in No. 1). This, however, is nothing but a paraphrase of the *"defence of the fatherland"* slogan. It means shifting the issue to the level of a war between governments (who, according to the content of this slogan, are to *keep* to their old stand, "retain their positions"), and not to the level of the *struggle* of the oppressed classes against their governments! It means justifying the chauvinism of *all* the imperialist nations, whose bourgeoisie are always ready to say—*and do say to the people*—that they are "only" fighting "against defeat". "The significance of our August 4 vote was that we are not for war *but against defeat,"* David, a leader of the opportunists, writes in his book. The Organising Committee, together with Bukvoyed and Trotsky, stand on *fully* the same ground as David when they defend the "neither-victory-nor-defeat" slogan.

On closer examination, this slogan will be found to mean a "class truce", the renunciation of the class struggle by the oppressed classes in all belligerent countries, since the class struggle is impossible without dealing blows at one's "own" bourgeoisie, one's "own" government, whereas dealing a blow at one's own government in wartime *is* (for Bukvoyed's information) high treason, *means* contributing to the defeat of one's own country. Those who accept the "neither-victory-nor-defeat" slogan can only be hypocritically in favour of the class struggle, of "disrupting the class truce"; *in practice*, such people are renouncing an independent proletarian policy because they subordinate the proletariat of all belligerent countries to the *absolutely bourgeois* task of safeguarding the imperialist governments against defeat. The only policy of actual, not verbal disruption of the "class truce", of acceptance of the class struggle, is for the proletariat *to take advantage* of the *difficulties* experienced by its government and its bourgeoisie *in order to overthrow them*. This, however, cannot be achieved or *striven for*, without desiring the defeat of one's own government and without contributing to that defeat.

When, before the war, the Italian Social-Democrats raised the question of a mass strike, the bourgeoisie replied, no doubt correctly from their *own* point of view, that this would be high treason, and that Social-Democrats would be dealt with as traitors. That is true, just as it is true that fraternisation in the trenches is high treason. Those who write against "high treason", as Bukvoyed does, or against the "disintegration of Russia", as Semkovsky does, are adopting the bourgeois, not the proletarian point of view. A proletarian *cannot* deal a class blow at his government or hold out (in fact) a hand to his brother, the proletarian of the "foreign" country which is at war with "our side", *without committing* "high treason", *without contributing* to the defeat, to the *disintegration* of his "own", imperialist "Great" Power.

Whoever is in favour of the slogan of "neither victory nor defeat" is consciously or unconsciously a chauvinist; at best he is a conciliatory petty bourgeois but in any case he is an *enemy* to proletarian policy, a partisan of the existing governments, of the present-day ruling classes.

Let us look at the question from yet another angle. The war cannot but evoke among the masses the most turbulent sentiments, which upset the usual sluggish state of mass mentality. Revolutionary tactics are *impossible* if they are not adjusted to these new turbulent sentiments.

What are the main currents of these turbulent sentiments? They are: (1) Horror and despair. Hence, a growth of religious feeling. Again the churches are crowded, the reactionaries joyfully declare. "Wherever there is suffering there is religion," says the arch-reactionary Barrès. He is right, too. (2) Hatred of the "enemy", a sentiment that is carefully fostered by the bourgeoisie (not so much by the priests), and is of economic and political value *only to the bourgeoisie.* (3) Hatred of one's *own* government and one's *own* bourgeoisie—the sentiment of all class-conscious workers who understand, on the one hand, that war is a "continuation of the politics" of imperialism, which they counter by a "continuation" of their hatred of their class enemy, and, on the other hand, that "a war against war" is a banal phrase unless it means a revolution against their *own* government. Hatred of one's own government and one's *own* bourgeoisie cannot be aroused unless their defeat is desired; one *cannot* be a sincere opponent of a civil (i.e., class) truce without arousing hatred of one's own government and bourgeoisie!

Those who stand for the "neither-victory-nor-defeat" slogan are in fact on the side of the bourgeoisie and the opportunists, for they do not believe in the possibility of international revolutionary action by the working class against their own governments, and *do not wish* to help develop such action, which, though undoubtedly difficult, is the only task worthy of a proletarian, the only socialist task. It is the proletariat in the most backward of the belligerent Great Powers which, through the medium of their party, have had to adopt—especially in view of the shameful treachery of the German and French Social-Democrats—revolutionary tactics that are quite unfeasible unless they "contribute to the defeat" of their own government, but which alone lead to a European revolution, to the permanent peace of socialism, to the liberation of humanity from the horrors, misery, savagery and brutality now prevailing.

Defeat and revolution[23]

by Leon Trotsky

War is a historical test of a class society, verifying by force its material basis, the strength of the material links between classes, and the stability and flexibility of the state organization. In this sense it can be said that *victory*—all other conditions being equal—demonstrates the relative strength of a given state structure, increases its authority, and thereby strengthens it. *Defeat,* on the contrary, discredits the state organization and thereby weakens it.

Before the war no sensible Social-Democrat believed that Russia, having undergone the triumph of a counterrevolution, would be able to generate a victorious imperialism. None doubted that war would open wide all the existing fissures in society and the state. At that time our party was unalterably *against* war. It never entered our heads to link our political hopes, whether revolutionary or reformist, to tsarism's military misfortunes, which seemed to us inevitable beyond any doubt in case of war. This was not because we regarded it as "morally unacceptable" for the revolutionary class to be interested in the military defeat of its government, as do today's social-patriotic sycophants. Nor was it due to blind national-state instincts, which in Russian revolutionary circles are heavily counterbalanced by an adequately strong hatred of tsarism. Nor, finally, was it due to general humanitarian considerations regarding the miseries unavoidably associated with war.

The "normal" life of class society for centuries and millennia has been based on the most frightful miseries of the masses—war merely concentrates these miseries in time. And if the surest or shortest road to emancipation led through war, revolutionary Social Democracy would not have hesitated to take it, with the resolution of a surgeon not intimidated by the prospect of suffering and blood when he considers that resorting to the knife is expedient.

If we refused to speculate upon war and the defeats it could bring, this was not for national or humanitarian reasons but for revolutionary political considerations, both international and internal.

Other things being equal, a defeat that shatters one state structure implies the corresponding strengthening of that of its opponent. And we do not know of any European social and state organism which it would be in the interest of the European proletariat to strengthen. At the same time, we do not assign to Russia the role of the state chosen to have its interests subordinated to those of the development of other European peoples. It is hardly necessary to dwell on this aspect of the question, which has been adequately clarified in the columns of our paper.

But even within the narrow framework of the prospects for national development, Russian Social Democracy could not link its political plans to the revolutionizing effect of military catastrophe.

Defeats can serve as the indisputable and irreplaceable driving force of development only under certain historical conditions. That is, when the necessity for internal transformation has matured and is not matched by the presence in the depths of society of new historical classes capable of bringing about these transformations or compelling their accomplishment. In such circumstances, reforms introduced from above as the result of defeat can give a serious impetus to the development of progressive social classes. But war is far too contradictory and double-edged a factor of historical development. Thus, a revolutionary party that feels a firm class foundation under its feet and is sure of its future cannot see the road of defeat as the road of its political success.

Defeats disorganize and demoralize the ruling reaction, but at the same time war disorganizes the whole of social life, and above all the working class.

In addition, war is not an "auxiliary" factor over which the revolutionary class can exert control. It cannot be eliminated at will after it has given the revolutionary impetus expected of it, like some historical "Moor" who "has done his work."[24]

Finally, a revolution which grows out of a defeat inherits an economic life utterly disordered by war, exhausted state finances, and extremely strained international relations.

Adventuristic speculation on war remained quite foreign to Russian Social Democracy even in the darkest years of the counterrevolution's unlimited triumph. This was because war, while it may give an impetus to revolution, can at the same time create a situation that will make the social and political utilization of a revolutionary victory extremely difficult.

Now, however, we have not only to *estimate* the direction in which war and defeat affect the course of political development, we have, above all, to *act* on the basis that defeat has actually created. For, whatever the subsequent ups and downs of military events may be, one thing can be said with complete certainty: there is no serious possibility of Russia restoring and increasing her power quickly enough to still be able to realize her plans for world conquest in the present war. The tsarist army has been smashed. It may have isolated successes, but it has lost the war. The recent defeats mark the beginning of a military catastrophe.

We must repeat once more that Social Democracy does not create at will the historical situation in which it operates. It is only one of the forces in the historical process. It is obliged to operate on the terrain created for it by history . . .

Social Democracy is now discovering inexhaustible opportunities for revolutionary agitation, every word of which will meet with a tremendous echo. But we must also take clearly into account that military catastrophe, exhausting as it does the economic and spiritual forces and resources of the population, retains only a *limited* capacity to arouse active indignation, protest, and revolutionary action. Beyond a certain point, exhaustion can be so great as to suppress energy and paralyze the will. Despair, passivity, and moral disintegration set in. The link between defeats and revolution is not mechanical but dialectical in character.

The hopes of Lloyd George and others that the pressure of defeats alone will be sufficient to "enlighten" Russia's rulers in the direction of liberalism only reflects the latter's hopeless banality. But it would be a childish delusion to conclude on the basis of a false interpretation of the Russo-Japanese "experience" that military defeats automatically have a revolutionizing effect on the masses. The gigantic dimensions of the present war—*with its indefinitely prolonged character*—may for a long period clip the wings of all social development, and consequently, first and foremost, that of the revolutionary movement of the proletariat.

This shows the need to struggle to end the war as soon as

possible. The revolution is not interested in a further accumulation of defeats. On the contrary, the struggle for peace is dictated to us by revolutionary self-preservation. The more powerfully the toilers are mobilized against the war, the more fully will the experience of defeat prove politically instructive to the working class, and the sooner will it be transformed into a force stimulating the revolutionary movement.

It was several months before revolutionary Socialists in Germany were able to make known their views. Left-wing Socialist leaders there were shaken by their party's sudden rallying to the bourgeois camp, muzzled by censorship, and cut off from the party ranks. They lacked at first any underground network through which their real views might be heard.

A few left-wing leaders had met at Rosa Luxemburg's home in Berlin after the August 4 Reichstag vote and decided to send telegrams to 300 left-wing party functionaries, inviting them to a discussion on how to respond to the SPD's support of the war credits. Only one clearly positive reply was received—from Clara Zetkin.

Karl Liebknecht continued to call on the party leadership to speak out against ruling-class agitation for annexations, but without response. Meetings where he and Luxemburg were to speak on this theme were blocked by the party Executive Committee. Liebknecht wrote to Socialist newspapers explaining that the SPD Reichstag fraction's vote for the war credits had not been unanimous, but his letters were published only outside Germany.

More success was achieved in party membership organizations where the left had traditionally been strong. In Stuttgart, for example, a meeting of SPD elected leaders condemned the war credits stand by a vote of eighty-one to three. Liebknecht met with a group of party leaders there on September 21. Jacob Walcher, a participant, later recalled that after Liebknecht's report, ten of the eleven speakers, almost all of them industrial workers, strongly supported Liebknecht's stand. They also argued that there was no reason for the minority to have bent to discipline and voted with the majority in the Reichstag.

"Comrades openly said they could not understand why Liebknecht and the others had not voted against the war credits and thus at least saved the honor of German Social Democracy," Walcher wrote. "They considered that by giving way at this historic hour, the minority had made a very serious error and had almost irremediably damaged the cause of peace and revolutionary socialism."

Walcher recounted that in his summary, Liebknecht explained that "what comrades had said here had deeply shaken and gratified him. The criticisms of the minority and of him personally were quite correct. . . . He added, 'You are quite right in criticizing me. Even if alone, I should have called out my "No!" in the Reichstag and so informed the whole world that the talk of unanimity of the Reichstag and the German people is a lie. I have committed a serious error. . . . I can only promise you to conduct in the future an uncompromising struggle against the kaiser's war and against the kaiser's Socialists.'"[25]

This rethinking can also be seen in an analysis by left-wing leaders circulated by the SPD organization in the Berlin suburb of Niederbarnim. Probably written in November 1914, it suggested the need for underground work and for a new party: "No one could have foreseen that the whole organized power of the German Social Democratic Party and the trade unions would be committed to support of the war government and utilized to subdue the revolutionary energy of the masses. With the August 4 vote of the Social Democratic fraction it was settled that a different position, even though deeply rooted in the masses, could not have prevailed under the leadership of the experienced party [the SPD]. It could have prevailed only against the will of the leading party bodies, and by overcoming the resistance of the party and the trade unions."

"Had the Social Democratic fraction done its duty on August 4," the Niederbarnim circular continued, "the external form of the organization would probably have been destroyed, but the spirit would have remained, the spirit that animated the party during the Anti-Socialist Laws and enabled it to overcome all obstacles. Then the German working class would have carried out its historic mission—of that we can be sure. Now we have the party organization and its press acting as a most efficient counterrevolutionary agency, as a reliable tool of the government."[26]

These views unexpectedly reached a wider working-class audience when Carl Legien, an opportunist and the president of the trade union federation, made a speech attacking them. Quoting extensively from the Niederbarnim circular, Legien ridiculed the proposal "to wreck the organisation in order to bring about a solution of the problem by the masses." His speech, including the quotations, was published in pamphlet form. That is how Lenin first received word of the views of German revolutionists, which he enthusiastically applauded.[27]

In December the minority view in the SPD broke through the censorship with a dramatic action. In late November the SPD Reichstag fraction had voted to approve the second set of war credits, this time with seventeen voting no in the fraction meeting. While Paul Lensch went over to the chauvinist side, four other deputies, including Arthur Stadthagen, joined the minority. However, once again Liebknecht was unable to convince the minority to take a united *public* stand against the credits. Thus, when the Reichstag voted on December 2, Liebknecht cast the sole vote against the war appropriations. The Reichstag refused to hear an explanation of his vote, or to receive it in the minutes. But his declaration was distributed as an illegal leaflet across Germany, and by his action he became a symbol of resistance to the war in Germany and internationally.

Explanation of war credits vote[28]

by Karl Liebknecht

BERLIN, DECEMBER 2, 1914

I am voting against the War Credits bill today for the following reasons: None of the peoples involved desired the war nor was it kindled for their welfare—in Germany or anywhere else. It is an imperialist war, fought for the capitalist domination of the world market and for the political domination of important territories for settlement of industrial and finance capital. In the framework of the arms race, it is a pre-emptive war, cooked up jointly by the pro-war forces of Germany and Austria in the shadowy corridors of semiabsolutism and secret diplomacy. It is, furthermore, a Bonapartist undertaking, aimed at demoralizing and demolishing the growing workers' movement. All this has become increasingly clear in the last few months, despite the official tactic of recklessly sowing confusion.

The German slogan: "Against Tsarism," like the present English and French slogans "Against Militarism," serves to enlist the noblest instincts and revolutionary traditions and ideals of the people in the cause of nationalist hatred. Germany is the accomplice of tsarism and remains to this very day the model of political backwardness. It has no vocation as liberator of the peoples. Both the Russian and the German peoples must carry out their own liberation.

This war is not for the defense of Germany. Its historical character and evolution preclude placing any trust whatsoever in this capitalist government's claim that war credits will be used to defend the fatherland.

We must demand a speedy peace, a peace without conquest, a peace that humiliates no one. We must welcome every effort to this end. Only the simultaneous and continuous strengthening of currents in all the belligerent countries fighting for such a peace can put a stop to the bloody slaughter before the complete exhaustion of the nations involved. The only secure peace is one based on the international solidarity of the working class and the freedom of all peoples. Therefore the proletariat of all countries must continue today, in wartime, its united socialist action for peace.

I agree to the relief credits in the amount requested, although this sum is completely inadequate. Similarly, I will vote for everything that may relieve the cruel fate of our brothers at the front, of the wounded, and of the sick, all of whom have my unbounded compassion. In this there is no demand that goes far enough for me.

However, in protest against the war; against those who launched it and those who direct it; against the capitalist policies that brought it about; against the capitalist objectives for which it is waged; against the plans of annexation; against the violation of Belgian and Luxemburgian neutrality; against the military dictatorship; and against the continuing neglect by the government and ruling classes of their social and political obligations, I reject the requested war credits.

This declaration was circulated as the first of the underground circulars that after 1916 carried the title *Spartacus.* The government responded with a fierce campaign of repression and arrests; Liebknecht was drafted into the army February 7, 1915, as a construction laborer, and Luxemburg was jailed February 18 of the same year. Yet their underground circulars penetrated widely, and their movement was later known as the "Spartacists." Supporters in each major city were chosen to be responsible for circulation; these individuals, in turn, passed on copies to a comrade in each major factory who recruited co-workers. In this fashion the Spartacists constructed the embryo of a proletarian party, capable of underground work.

The "Spartacists" went far beyond opposition to the war and a call for peace. Their basic stand was contained in the final words of their underground leaflet of May 1915, printed below. It was written on the occasion of Italy's entry into the war on the Entente side, and hailed the Italian Social Democrats' clear stand against the war and against the government.

The main enemy is at home[29]

by Karl Liebknecht

The senseless slogan "Hold out to the end" is bankrupt and only leads deeper into the genocidal maelstrom. The task of the hour for Socialists is the international proletarian class struggle against international imperialist slaughter.

Every people's main enemy is in their own country!

The main enemy of the German people is in Germany: German imperialism, the German war party, and German secret diplomacy. Here in our own land is the enemy that the German people must combat. We must wage this political struggle alongside the proletariat of other countries, as they struggle against their own imperialists.

We know we are one with the German people. We have nothing in common with the Tirpitzes and Falkenhayns of Germany,[30] or with the German government of political repression and social enslavement. Nothing for them; everything for the German people! Everything for the international proletariat, for the sake of German workers and of downtrodden humanity!

The enemies of the working class count on the masses' forgetfulness—we must prove they are mistaken! While they wager on the patience and leniency of the masses, we raise the fervent cry:

How much longer will the imperialist gamblers abuse the patience of the people? Enough and more than enough of the slaughter. Down with the warmongers on both sides of the border!

End the genocide!

Proletarians of all countries, follow the heroic example of your Italian brothers. Unite in international class struggle against the conspiracies of secret diplomacy, against imperialism, against the war, and for a peace in the socialist spirit.

The main enemy is at home!

Revolutionary workers in each belligerent country found ways to express this outlook. The following is from a Bolshevik leaflet circulated about the same time in Petrograd.

Where is the main enemy?[31]

Who is it that threatens the Russian people? Who should we combat? They say it is the Germans. . . .

But it is the landlords, the factory owners, the big proprietors and merchants who steal from us; it is the police, the tsar, and his hangers-on who rob us. And when we have had enough of this robbery, and call a strike to protect our interests, then the police, the soldiers, and the Cossacks are unleashed upon us. They beat us and they throw us in prison; they deport us to Siberia, persecute us, and treat us like mad dogs. These are our real enemies—enemies who fight against us ruthlessly and irreconcilably. . .

Now they try to mislead us and make us believe that our enemy is "the German" whom we have never seen. They want to incite us against Germany. Now when they need our fists, they sing a song of "unity." They try to lull us to sleep, saying we should forget every internal conflict and all unite into one patriotic stream. They say we must forget our own working-class cause and instead make their cause our own and march off to conquer new lands for the tsar and his landlords.

But will we Russian workers really be so stupid as to take these lying phrases seriously? Will we really give up our own fight? No! If we must sacrifice our lives, we will do so for *our own* cause and not for that of the Romanovs and their rustic landlords. They put guns into our hands. Good. We will show our courage and use these guns to fight for better living conditions for the Russian working class.

Petersburg Committee,
RSDLP

As the war-caused death toll and social crisis mounted, leaflets such as these, calling on workers to turn the imperialist war into a civil war began to win a wider hearing. The widespread fraternization by French and German soldiers at the front lines at Christmas 1914 was cited by Lenin as further proof that the Bolshevik slogan corresponded to the working people's line of march in resisting the imperialist war.

The slogan of civil war illustrated[32]

by V.I. Lenin

On January 8 (New Style), Swiss papers received the following message from Berlin: "Of late the press has repeatedly carried reports of peaceable attempts made by men in the German and French trenches to enter into friendly relations. According to *Tägliche Rundschau,* an army order dated December 29 bans any fraternisation and any kind of intercourse with the enemy in the trenches. Disregard of this order is punishable as high treason."

Thus, fraternisation and attempts to enter into friendly relations with the enemy are a fact. The German military authorities are showing concern over the matter, which means that they attach considerable importance to it. The British *Labour Leader* of January 7, 1915, published *a series* of quotations from the British bourgeois press on instances of fraternisation between British and German soldiers, who arranged a "forty-eight-hour truce" at Christmas, met amicably in no-man's land, and so on. The British military authorities issued a *special order forbidding* fraternisation. And yet, with the utmost complacency and the comfortable feeling that the military censorship will protect them against any denials, the socialist opportunists and their vindicators (or lackeys?) have assured the workers, through the press (as Kautsky has done), that *no* understanding on anti-war action by the socialists of the belligerent countries is possible (the expression literally used by Kautsky in *Die Neue Zeit*)!

Try to imagine Hyndman, Guesde, Vandervelde, Plekhanov, Kautsky and the rest—instead of aiding the bourgeoisie (something they are now engaged in)—forming an international committee to agitate for "fraternisation and attempts to establish friendly relations" between the socialists of the belligerent countries, both in the "trenches" and among the troops in general. What would the results be several months from now, if today, only six months after the outbreak of the war and *despite* all the political bosses, leaders and luminaries who have betrayed socialism, opposition is mounting on all sides against those who have voted for war credits and those who have accepted ministerial jobs, and the military authorities are threatening that "fraternisation" carries the death sentence?

"There is only one practical issue—victory or defeat for one's country", Kautsky, lackey of the opportunists, has written, in concord with Guesde, Plekhanov and Co. Indeed, if one were to forget socialism and the class struggle, that would be the truth. However, if one does not lose sight of socialism, that is untrue. Then there is another *practical* issue: should we perish as blind and helpless slaves, in a war between slaveholders, or should we fall in "attempts at fraternisation" between the slaves, with the aim of casting off slavery?

Such, *in reality*, is the "practical" issue.

Kautsky, however, posed the "practical" issue in different terms. He denied that workers had to choose between perishing in imperialism's wars or struggling to overthrow it. In his view, imperialism could well be transformed into what he termed "ultraimperialism." In such a system, the rival powers would join together in a kind of cartel, agreeing on a division of the world among them, in order to exploit the world without risk of major wars.

The struggle for peace could then be completely severed from any struggle against imperialism as such. Kautsky's concept of "ultraimperialism" could suggest a course of pressure on the imperialist governments to go over to new policies that would bring peace. Kautsky developed the conception of "ultraimperialism" in an article written shortly before the war's outbreak and published August 28, 1914.

Imperialism[33]

by Karl Kautsky

Does imperialism represent the last possible manifestation of capitalist world policy, or is another still possible? In other words, does it offer the only remaining possible form in which to expand the exchange between industry and agriculture within capitalism? This is the basic question.

The construction of railways, the exploitation of mines, the increased production of raw materials and foodstuffs in the agrarian [colonial] countries have, without a doubt, become necessities of life for capitalism. The capitalist class is as little likely to renounce them as it is to commit suicide: and the same is true of all the bourgeois parties. None of these parties can sincerely oppose domination over the agrarian zones and the reduction of their populations to slaves without rights, because these features are too closely bound up with the economic efforts. The subjugation of these zones will come to an end only when either their populations or the proletariat of the industrialized capitalist countries have grown strong enough to throw off the capitalist yoke. This side of imperialism can only be overcome by socialism.

But imperialism has another side. The tendency toward occupation and subjugation of the agrarian zones has produced sharp rivalries between the industrialized capitalist states. The result is that the arms race, which previously was only a race for land armaments, has now also become a naval contest, and the long prophesied world war has now become a fact. Is this side of imperialism, as well, a necessity for capitalism's continued existence, one that can be overcome only along with capitalism itself?

There is no *economic* necessity for continuing the arms race after the World War, even from the standpoint of the capitalist class itself, with the possible exception of certain armaments interests. On the contrary, the capitalist economy is seriously threatened precisely by these disputes. Every far-sighted capitalist today must call on his fellows: capitalists of all countries, unite! Because, first of all, the growing opposition of the more developed of the agrarian zones threatens not just one or another of the imperialist states, but all of them together. This is true of the awakening of Eastern Asia and India as well as of the Pan-Islamic movement in the Near East and North Africa.

The growing opposition of the proletariat of the industrial countries to every new increase in their tax burden accompanies this upsurge. Even before the war, it was clear that the arms race and the costs of colonial expansion since the Balkan War had reached a level that threatened the rapid continuation of capital accumulation and thereby the export of capital that is the basis of imperialism itself.

While industrial accumulation at home still advanced continuously, thanks to technical progress, capital no longer rushed to be exported. That is why even in peacetime the European states had difficulty in covering their own loans and the rates of interest they were forced to grant rose. . . . If, after the war, the arms race and its demands on the capital market continue to grow this trend will not get better, but worse.

Imperialism thus digs its own grave. From a force for the development of capitalism, it becomes a hindrance to it. Nevertheless, capitalism may not yet be at the end of the line. Purely from the economic standpoint, it can continue to develop as long as the growing industries of the capitalist countries can generate a corresponding expansion of agricultural production. This becomes more and more difficult, of course, as the growth of world industry increases yearly and still unexploited agrarian zones become fewer and fewer. Until this limit has been reached, while capitalism may be wrecked on the reef of the rising political opposition of the proletariat, it need not come to an end in economic collapse.

However, continuing the present imperialist policy would bring just such an economic bankruptcy prematurely. This policy cannot therefore be continued much longer. Of course, if imperialism were indispensable to the maintenance of the capitalist system of production, then the factors I have referred to might make no lasting impression on the ruling class, and would not convince them to alter the direction of their imperialist tendencies. This change will be possible, however, if imperialism, the striving of every great capitalist state to extend its own colonial empire in opposition to all the other colonial empires, represents only one among various possibilities for the expansion of capitalism.

What Marx said about capitalism can also be applied to imperialism: monopoly creates competition and competition, monopoly. The frantic competition among the huge firms, giant banks, and multimillionaires compelled the great financial groups, who were absorbing the small ones, to devise the cartel. Similarly the World War between the great imperialist powers may result in a federation of the strongest, who renounce their arms race.

From the purely economic standpoint it is therefore not impossible for capitalism to live through yet another phase, the transferral of this process of forming cartels into foreign policy; a phase of *ultraimperialism*. Of course we would have to struggle against it as energetically as we do against imperialism. But its perils would lie in a different direction than in the arms race and the threat to world peace.

In Lenin's view, Kautsky was "exploiting the *hope* for a *new* peaceful era of capitalism so as to justify the adhesion of the opportunists and the official Social-Democratic parties to the bourgeoisie."[34] Lenin's response is contained in "The Collapse of the Second International," printed below in this chapter.

Left-wing Socialists also disputed Kautsky's views on the cause of war, and argued that it lay not in the rulers' policies, but in the character of imperialism as a world system. War, therefore, was an inevitable product of imperialism itself. That conviction, the theme of internationalist leaflets in every country, was summarized in the following theses, distributed on November 17, 1914, by Käte Duncker, a close colleague of Rosa Luxemburg, to leaders of women's evening study classes in Germany.

The economic causes of the war[35]

1. The present World War was caused neither by the arbitrary actions of individuals nor by racial hatred between nations. Rather it is a result of the capitalist economy's *drive for profits on a world scale* and of *imperialist antagonisms.*

2. The concentration of capital, the development of large-scale industry and its increasing and one-sided specialization, and increasing productivity, together with the anarchy of the whole capitalist economy lead to chronic overproduction. Cartels, tariffs, and indirect taxes hold down workers' wages and inflate the prices of commodities, limiting the expansion of the internal market. This produces a continual and growing need for *foreign markets.* The enormous accumulation of capital originating in capitalist exploitation is driven to seek profitable *fields for investment,* and finds particularly lucrative outlets in countries where capitalist development is only beginning or has yet to begin (colonies, half-civilized states). In this race to monopolize markets to sell their products, sources of raw materials, and fields for capital investment, the capitalist cliques of the various great powers poach on each other's preserves.

3. This capitalist drive to expand is expressed politically in the *world power politics* of the large modern states, in *imperialism.* The conquest of colonies, the protection of capital invested abroad, and the exclusion of troublesome competitors require powerful armaments both at sea and on land. Competition in the colonial regions and for so-called spheres of influence and the arms race create constant tension between the capitalist states, a tension that increases to the breaking point—the launching of war.

4. The Balkans, Asian Turkey,[36] Persia, Africa, and East

Asia are the main focuses for the crises and wars of modern imperialism. Austria vies with Russia; Germany rivals England for possession of these regions, all fortifying themselves for defense and defiance. The continuation of capitalism after the end of this war will in all probability bring forth new world wars for world markets and world power.

5. The class-conscious German proletariat fights against capitalism as the deadly enemy of the socialist liberation of the working class. Therefore it cannot view the advancement of German imperialism as an *advance for the class interests of the proletariat.* Also, in the present stage of capitalism, the *development of the internal market* is more important to the proletariat than is that of the external market. An expansion of the internal market would both presuppose and guarantee higher wages. On the other hand the export of capital increases the exploitation essential to capitalism by keeping wages low and prices high. The miserable plight of the proletariat is made worse by the burden of military armaments and the terrible misery of war.

6. The vital interests of the proletariat thus demand a tireless struggle against imperialism, conducted in the understanding that *socialism* alone can end and supersede this imperialist stage of capitalist development and the constant danger of world war.

In order to reply to the falsification of Marxism by Kautsky and other SPD leaders, and to achieve clarity on proletarian tasks in the class struggle, leaders of the German Socialist opposition current decided at a March 1915 conference to launch a new Marxist magazine. Called *Die Internationale* (The International), it listed as its founders

Rosa Luxemburg and the Marxist historian and political writer Franz Mehring.

Taking advantage of a legal loophole that permitted publication in one part of the Prussian state without prior censorship, they brought out an edition of 9,000 copies of the new journal on April 14, 1915. The police moved quickly to seize all copies of the magazine, but arrived too late—the press run was already distributed, and the printing type spirited off to Robert Grimm in Switzerland, who published a second edition for international circulation.

"This monthly magazine owes its existence to Comrade Luxemburg," *Die Internationale* explained. "She had already written the lead article, 'The Reconstruction of the International,' and recruited many collaborators, when she fell victim to the celebrated 'civil peace.'"

The reconstruction of the International[37]

by Rosa Luxemburg

I

On August 4, 1914, German Social Democracy abdicated politically; at the same time the Socialist International collapsed. Every attempt to deny these facts or to gloss them over, regardless of its motive, in reality serves only to perpetuate the disastrous self-deception of the Socialist parties and the internal sickness that led to their collapse. Denying these facts only accepts this collapse as the normal state of affairs, and so in the long run transforms the Socialist International into mere illusion and hypocrisy.

The collapse itself is unprecedented in all of history. Socialism or imperialism—this alternative sums up completely the political orientation of the workers' parties in the last decade. Especially in Germany this was formulated in countless political speeches, mass meetings, pamphlets, and newspaper articles as the slogan of the Social Democracy, as its conception of the present historical period and its development.

With the outbreak of the World War the word has become flesh. The alternative is now posed not as a historical tendency but as the present political situation. Faced with this alternative, which it was the first to recognize and bring to the attention of the broad masses, Social Democracy backed down and, without a struggle, conceded victory to imperialism. Never before in the history of the class struggle, since political parties appeared, has a party collapsed in this way. After fifty years of uninterrupted growth, after achieving a first-rate position of power, and after drawing millions to its banner, it completely dissolved into thin air as a political force within twenty-four hours. Precisely because it was the best organized and most disciplined vanguard contingent of the International, the case of the German Social Democracy provides the clearest proof of the current collapse of socialism.

Kautsky, the representative of the so-called Marxist Center—politically speaking, the theoretician of the "swamp"—made a sincere contribution to the party's present collapse. Many years ago he degraded theory to the role of obliging hand-maiden of the official practice of the party establishment. Already he has thought up an opportune new theory to justify and whitewash the collapse. He holds that Social Democracy is an instrument for peace but not for the fight against the war. Or, as Kautsky's loyal pupils of the Austrian *Der Kampf* (The Struggle) put it, sighing profusely at the present aberrations of German Social Democracy, the only policy befitting socialism during the war is "silence." Only when the bells of peace ring out can it begin to function again.

This theory proposes the voluntary assumption of a eunuch's condition. It argues that socialism's virtue can be upheld only if it ceases to be a factor in the decisive moments of world history. But it makes the basic mistake of all theories of political impotence: it does not take into account those who can bring real power to bear.

Social Democracy faced the choice: for or against the war. From the moment it abandoned opposition to the war, the iron laws of history forced it to throw its entire weight into the scales in support of the conflict. In the memorable parliamentary fraction debate of August 3 Kautsky pleaded the case for approving the war credits. Nevertheless both he and the self-styled "Austro-Marxists"[38]—who now write in *Der Kampf* that the Social Democratic fraction's approval of the war credits was a matter of course—occasionally shed a few tears over the nationalist excesses of the Social Democratic Party organs and their insufficient theoretical training. In particular they split hairs over the idea of "nationality" and other "concepts" which are supposedly responsible for these aberrations. But events have their own logic, even when human beings do not. Once the Social Democracy's parliamentary fraction had decided to support the war, everything else followed automatically with the inevitability of historical destiny.

On August 4 the German Social Democracy, far from being silent, assumed a very important historical function: that of shield-bearer for imperialism in the present war. Napoleon once said that two factors decide a battle's outcome. One is the "earthly" factor—the terrain, quality of the weapons, the weather, and so forth. The other, the "spiritual" factor, incorporates the moral state of the army, its enthusiasm, and its faith in its own cause. The "earthly" factor on the German side was largely taken care of by the Krupp firm in Essen. The "spiritual" factor can primarily be charged to the account of the Social Democracy.

Since August 4 it has daily rendered immeasurable services to the German war effort. The trade unions suspended all struggles for higher wages when the war broke out and now invest all the security measures undertaken by the military authorities to prevent mass protests with the aura of socialism. The Social Democratic women withdrew all their time and energy from Social Democratic agitation and, arm in arm with the patriotic bourgeois women, tend the needy families of the soldiers. The Social Democratic press uses its daily papers and weekly and monthly periodicals, with a few exceptions, to promote the war as a cause both for the nation and for the proletariat. Following the war's twists and turns, it graphically portrays the Russian danger and the dreadful tsarist regime; abandons the perfidious Albion [Britain] to the people's hatred; rejoices at the uprisings and revolutions in the colonies of other states; prophesies that after the war Turkey will grow strong again; promises freedom to the Poles, the Ruthenians, and all peoples; imparts courage and heroism to the proletarian youth; and in short completely manipulates public opinion and the broad masses to win them to the ideology of the war.

Finally the Social Democratic parliamentarians and party leaders not only approve funds for the war effort, but they also condemn as "intrigue" every stirring of doubt and criticism in the masses and try to suppress it decisively. They also support the government with discreet personal services and with pamphlets, speeches, and articles displaying the most pure-bred German nationalist patriotism. When in world history was there a war in which anything like this happened?

Where and when has the suspension of all constitutional rights been accepted so submissively as a matter of course? Where has severe press censorship ever received such a hymn of praise from the ranks of the opposition as it has in the newspapers of the German Social Democracy? Never before has a war found such Pindars, and a military dictatorship met with such obedience. Never has a political party so fervently sacrificed all that it stood for and possessed on the altar of a cause that it had sworn before the world a thousand times to combat to the last drop of blood. Compared with this metamorphosis, the National Liberals stand out as real Roman Catos, real *rochers de bronze* [pillars of strength].

A body four million strong allowed a handful of parliamentarians to turn it around in twenty-four hours and harness it to a wagon going in a direction opposite to its aim in life. Thus was the organizational power and much-praised discipline of German Social Democracy confirmed in life. The fruit of fifty years of preparatory work by the Social Democracy is revealed in this war in the claim by the trade unions and party leaders that Germany's impetus and victorious strength largely flows from the "training" the masses received in the proletarian organizations. Marx, Engels, and Lassalle; Liebknecht, Bebel, and Singer trained the German proletariat so that Hindenburg could lead it. And the superiority of the trade unions and workers' press in Germany as compared to France—in training, organization, size, and development—serves only to render the Social Democratic contribution to the German war effort more effective than that of its French counterpart. Despite their governmental ministers, the French Socialists are revealed as rank amateurs in the unfamiliar trade of nationalism and waging war, when you compare their deeds to the services the German Social Democracy and trade unions provide to their imperialist fatherland.

II

Official theory, whose organ is *Die Neue Zeit*, misuses Marxism any way it pleases to serve the party officials' current domestic requirements and to justify their day-to-day dealings. It attempts to explain the minor discrepancy between the workers' party's current role and its previous statements by explaining that international socialism worked hard on the question of what to do to prevent the war, but not with what to do after its outbreak!

Like a loose woman who obliges all, this theory assures us that the most wonderful harmony prevails between socialism's present practice and its past. It says that none of the Socialist parties need to reproach themselves for having done anything that would call into question their membership in the International. At the same time, however, this pliant theory also has at hand an adequate explanation for the contradiction between the present position of the international Social Democracy and its past, a contradiction not lost on even the most dim-witted. The International, it is said, debated only the question of how to prevent the war. But then "war was upon us," as the formula goes, and it turned out that quite different rules of conduct were required of Socialists after the outbreak of war than before it.

Once the war was upon us, the only question left for the proletariat in every country was—victory or defeat. Or, as Friedrich Adler, another "Austro-Marxist," explained more scientifically and philosophically: Like any organism the nation must above all ensure its survival. Frankly stated, this means: There is not one set of rules for the proletariat, as scientific socialism has always maintained, but two: one for peace and one for war. In peacetime the class struggle applies inside each country and international solidarity outside. In wartime it is class solidarity internally, between the workers and the capitalists, and externally the struggle between the workers of the various countries.

The world historic call of the *Communist Manifesto* has been substantially enriched and, as corrected by Kautsky, now reads: "Proletarians of all countries, unite in peacetime and cut each other's throats in wartime!" Today our slogan is: "May every bullet find a Russian; every bayonet a Frenchman." Tomorrow, after peace is declared, it will be: "We embrace the millions of the whole world." For the International is "essentially a peace instrument" but "an ineffective tool in wartime."

This obliging theory opens up charming perspectives for Social Democratic practice. Not only does it elevate the fickleness of the weathercock parliamentary fraction, coupled with the Jesuitism of the Center,[39] virtually to a fundamental dogma of the Socialist International. In addition, it inaugurates a completely new "revision" of historical materialism compared to which all of Bernstein's previous attempts look like innocent child's play. Proletarian tactics before and after the outbreak of war are supposed to be based on completely different, in fact directly opposed lines of march. This presupposes that social conditions, the basis of our tactics, are also fundamentally different in war than in peace. According to historical materialism, as Marx laid it out, all of previously recorded history is the history of class struggle. According to Kautsky's revision of materialism, that must be amended to read: "except in time of war."

According to this, historical development, which for thousands of years has been periodically interspersed with wars, proceeds along the following schema: A period of class struggle followed by a pause in which the classes join together to wage a national war. Then again a period of class struggle, again a pause and the classes unite, and so on in this charming fashion. Every time that war breaks out, the peacetime foundations of social life are turned upside down. Then when peace is achieved, they are overturned once again. As you can see this is no longer a theory of social development "in catastrophes," which Kautsky and other such "intriguers" once had to refute. Rather this is a theory of development—in somersaults. Society moves in somewhat the same manner as an iceberg caught by spring waters: after a time, when its base has been melted away on all sides by the tepid stream, it topples over, after which this delightful little performance periodically repeats itself.

This revised historical materialism flies in the face of all accepted facts of history. Instead of this newly concocted antithesis between war and class struggle, history on the contrary clearly shows its essential inner unity in the constant dialectical alteration of wars into class struggle and class struggle into wars. So it was in the history of the cities of the Middle Ages, in the wars of the Reformation, in the Dutch war of liberation, in the wars of the Great French Revolution, in the United States Civil War, in the uprising of the Paris Commune, and in the great Russian revolution of 1905.

A moment's reflection shows that Kautsky's theory of historical materialism, even in purely abstract theoretical terms, does not leave a single stone of Marxist theory standing. According to Marx neither the class struggle nor war fall from the sky, but rather arise out of deep-seated social and economic causes. Thus neither of the two can periodically disappear unless their causes also vanish into thin air. The proletarian class struggle is simply a necessary consequence of both the wage system and the political class rule of the bourgeoisie. And during a war the burdens of the wage system do not diminish in the least. On the contrary, they are increased enormously through the feverish activities of speculators and promoters, which flourish in the luxuriant atmosphere of the war industries and through the pressure on the workers of the military dictatorship. Nor does the political class rule of the bourgeoisie cease in times of war.

On the contrary, through the suspension of constitutional rights it is converted into a naked class dictatorship. If the economic and political sources of the class struggle in society gush forth with ten times the force, then how can their inevitable result, the class struggle, cease?

Wars in the present historical period result from the competing interests of rival groups of capitalists and from capitalism's need to expand. But these two driving forces do not operate only when the cannons roar, but also in peacetime, when they prepare and make inevitable the outbreak of new wars. War is indeed, as Kautsky is fond of quoting from Clausewitz, only "the continuation of politics by other means." And it is precisely the imperialist stage of capitalist domination whose arms race has made peace illusory, by declaring what is in essence the dictatorship of militarism and permanent war.

Thus an either-or question is posed for this revised historical materialism. Either in wartime the class struggle remains the paramount condition of the proletariat's existence, and the party establishment's proclamation of class harmony is an outrage against the vital interests of the proletariat. Or in peacetime too the class struggle must be a crime against "national interests" and the "security of the fatherland." Either class struggle or class harmony is the fundamental factor of social life in war as well as in peace.

In practice the alternative is even clearer. On the one hand, the Social Democracy can say *pater peccavi* [Father, I have sinned] to the patriotic bourgeoisie, as has already been done by yesterday's young enthusiasts, now today's old fogies. This would mean Social Democracy fundamentally changing its entire tactics and principles in peacetime so that they conform to its present social imperialist policies. Or, on the other hand, it can say *pater peccavi* to the international proletariat and bring its conduct in wartime into line with its peacetime principles. And what is true for the German workers' movement is obviously also true for the French.

Either the International remains a heap of rubble after the war or its resurrection will begin on the basis of the class struggle, the unique source of its life's blood. It will not revive after the war simply by retelling the same old stories, being fresh, pious, cheerful, and bold as though nothing had happened, and playing the same melodies that captivated the world until August 4. Only by "pouring merciless scorn on all our half-measures and weaknesses," on our own moral collapse since August 4, and on the liquidation of our entire system of tactics employed since August 4 can the reconstruction of the International begin. The first step in this direction is to take action for a speedy end to the war as well as for the conclusion of a peace in accordance with the common interests of the international proletariat.

III

Two different tendencies on the question of peace have come to the fore so far in the ranks of the party. One is represented by party Executive Committee member Scheidemann and several other parliamentary deputies and party newspapers. It echoes the government's slogan to "hold out" and opposes the peace movement as inopportune and dangerous to the military interests of the fatherland. This tendency advocates the continuation of the war, and thus objectively ensures that the war is in fact continued in line with the wishes of the ruling classes "until a victory is won that accords with sacrifices made," until a "secure peace" is guaranteed. In other words the supporters of this policy of "holding out" are seeing to it that the war's actual development is as closely as possible in step with the imperialist conquests which *Die Post,*[40] Rohrback, Dix, and the other prophets of Germany's world domination openly proclaim as the goal of the war.

If all these wonderful dreams do not become reality and if the trees of this fledgling imperialism do not grow all the way to the heavens, it will be as little the fault of the *Post* people as of their pacesetters in the ranks of the German Social Democracy. It is obviously not the solemn "declarations" in parliament "against any policy of conquest" that are conclusive for the war's outcome, but rather support for the policy of "holding out." The war, whose continuation is advocated by Scheidemann and others, has its own logic. Its real sponsors are the capitalist-agrarian elements who are in the saddle in Germany today, not the modest figures of the Social Democratic parliamentarians and editors who merely hold the stirrups for them. This tendency is the clearest expression of the party's social-imperialist position.

In France too the party leaders—admittedly in a completely different military situation—cling to the slogan, "hold out until victory." However, a movement to rapidly end the war is making itself gradually but increasingly felt in all countries. The most striking single characteristic of all these aspirations for peace is a very meticulous preparation of peace guarantees to be demanded when the war ends. Not only the universal demand for no conquests, but also a whole series of new demands are appearing: universal disarmament, or more modestly, systematic limitation of the arms race; abolition of secret diplomacy; free trade in the colonies for all nations; and other such wonderful proposals.

The admirable aspect of all these stipulations for the future happiness of humanity and for the prevention of future wars is their irrepressible optimism, emerging intact from the terrible catastrophe of the present war, which on the grave of old hopes plants new resolutions. If the collapse of August 4 has proven anything, it is the historic lesson that pious hopes, cleverly devised prescriptions, and utopian demands directed at the ruling classes are not an effective guarantee of peace nor a real bulwark against war. On the contrary, only the proletariat's resolute determination to remain loyal to class politics and to international solidarity through all the turmoil of imperialism can achieve these.

Before 1914 there was no lack of demands and formulas on the part of the Socialist parties in the decisive countries, especially in Germany. But the capacity was lacking to back up these demands with determination and action in the spirit of the class struggle and internationalism. If today, after all that we have gone through, we viewed the campaign for peace as a process of devising the best formula against war, it would signify the greatest danger for international socialism. Despite all the cruel lessons we would have learned nothing and forgotten nothing.

Here again we find the prime example in Germany. In a recent issue of *Die Neue Zeit,* parliamentary deputy Hoch put forward a peace program which, as a party organ attested, he fervently supported. Nothing was missing from this program—neither an enumerated list of "demands" that are to painlessly and reliably prevent future wars, nor a very convincing demonstration that a speedy peace was possible, necessary, and desirable. The only thing missing was an explanation of what we should do to achieve this peace, and that we should work for it with actions, not with "wishes." The author belongs to the solid caucus majority that not only twice voted for war credits, but also on each occasion defended its action as a political, patriotic, socialist necessity. Excellently drilled in its new role, it is ready as a matter of course to approve further credits for the continuation of the war. This group supports the provision of material means to prosecute the war and, in the same breath, extols the desirability of a speedy peace with all of its blessings. "With the one hand it presses the sword into the government's hand, while with the other it waves the soft palm branch of peace over the International." This is a classic example of how the politics of the swamp, propagated theoretically by *Die Neue*

Zeit, are put into practice.

When Socialists of the neutral countries participate in the Copenhagen Conference[41] and seriously consider that concocting peace proposals and formulas on paper contributes to the speedy termination of the war, this is a relatively harmless error. An understanding of the salient points in the International's current situation and the causes of its collapse can and must be the common property of all the Socialist parties. Redeeming action to restore peace and the International can come only from the Socialist parties of the belligerent countries, and its first step must be to reject the road of social imperialism. If the Social Democratic parliamentarians continue to approve funds for the war, then their desires and formulas for peace and their solemn declarations "against any policy of conquest" are a hypocrisy and, worse still, a grand delusion. They are exactly like the Kautskyist International, whose members "have not done anything to reproach themselves for" and who periodically embrace one another fraternally or, as the case may be, cut each other's throats.

Here again events have their own logic. By approving the war credits, people like Hoch surrender control of the reins and thus bring about the virtual opposite of peace, namely a policy of "holding out." In the same way, the advocacy of "holding out" by people like Scheidemann in fact hands over the reins to the *Post* people and thus brings about the opposite of their solemn declarations against "any policy of conquest." It gives free rein to imperialist instincts until the country bleeds to death. Here again there is only an either-or choice: either Bethmann-Hollweg—or Liebknecht. Either imperialism or socialism, as Marx understood it.

In Marx himself the sharp historical analyst was inseparably bound up with the bold revolutionary; the man of ideas supported and complemented the man of action. In the same way the socialist teachings of Marxism, for the first time in the history of the modern workers' movement, have brought theoretical understanding together with the revolutionary might of the proletariat. The one illuminates and gives impetus to the other. Both are equally essential elements of Marxism. If one is separated from the other, then Marxism is turned into a sad caricature of itself.

In the course of half a century the German Social Democracy reaped the most abundant fruits from its theoretical understanding of Marxism and, nurtured on its milk, grew into a powerful organization. Put to the greatest historical test, one which moreover it had foreseen with scientific precision and predicted in all its essential features, the Social Democracy defaulted completely in the second essential principle of the workers' movement—the resolute determination not only to understand history, but to make it. With all exemplary theoretical understanding and organizational strength, it was swept away in the current of history, turned around in a flash like a rudderless wreck, and left to the winds of imperialism, against which it was supposed to make its way forward to the redeeming isle of socialism. Even without the mistakes of others, the defeat of the entire International was sealed by the failure of its "vanguard," its best trained and most powerful elite.

It was a historic collapse of the first order, which dangerously complicates and delays the liberation of humanity from capitalist rule. But it did not come to this because of any flaw in Marxism. All attempts to make Marxism conform to the present transitory decrepitude of Socialist practice, to prostitute it to the level of a mercenary apologist for social imperialism, are in themselves more dangerous than all the blatant and shrill excesses of the nationalist confusion in the ranks of the party. Such attempts tend not only to conceal the real causes of the International's profound failure, but also to discard the lessons from this experience necessary for its future construction.

An International and a peace that correspond to the proletariat's interests can be born only from the self-criticism of the proletariat, from reflecting upon its own power. It was this power that on August 4 snapped like a frail reed lashed by the storm. But raised to its true stature, it is historically destined to uproot thousand-year-old institutions of social injustice—to move mountains. The road to this power, not one of paper resolutions, is at the same time the road to peace and to the reconstruction of the International.

The new journal *Die Internationale* was warmly received by left-wing Socialists. "We are happy to convey the news to Russian workers that a mighty voice of protest and revolt will now be heard on the other side of the front lines as well," wrote Yuri Pyatakov in the Bolshevik journal *Kommunist.* While *Die Internationale*'s denunciation of "the treasonous conduct of the official Socialist parties of Germany, France, and other countries" is not the only voice of left protest in Germany, Pyatakov added, it is "without a doubt the sharpest and the clearest."[42]

That same issue of *Kommunist,* published in September 1915, also contained an extended reply by Lenin to Kautsky's articles on the war. (A German translation of this reply was published in 1916.)

Kautsky had continued to develop his theoretical justification for the pro-war policies of the majority Socialist party leaderships. He now argued in *Die Neue Zeit* that the antiwar resolutions of the Basel and other congresses of the old International had been proven inapplicable by the workers' failure to rise in revolution when the war broke out. In his reply in *Kommunist,* printed below, Lenin reviewed the meaning of the 1912 Basel resolution. Lenin's original footnotes follow the article.

The collapse of the Second International[43]

by V.I. Lenin

But perhaps sincere socialists supported the Basel resolution in the anticipation that war would create a revolutionary situation, the events rebutting them, as revolution has proved impossible?

It is by means of sophistry like this that Cunow (in a pamphlet *Collapse of the Party?* and a series of articles) has tried to justify his desertion to the camp of the bourgeoisie. The writings of nearly all the other social-chauvinists, headed by Kautsky, hint at similar "arguments". Hopes for a revolution have proved illusory, and it is not the business of a Marxist to fight for illusions, Cunow argues. This Struvist,[44] however, does not say a word about "illusions" that were shared by all signatories to the Basel Manifesto. Like a most upright man, he would put the blame on the extreme Leftists, such as Pannekoek and Radek!

Let us consider the substance of the argument that the authors of the Basel Manifesto sincerely expected the advent of a revolution, but were rebutted by the events. The Basel Manifesto says: (1) that war will create an economic and political crisis; (2) that the workers will regard their participation in war as a crime, and as criminal any "shooting each other down for the profit of the capitalists, for the sake of dynastic honour and of diplomatic secret treaties", and that war evokes "indignation and revolt" in the workers; (3) that it is the duty of socialists to take advantage of this crisis and of the workers' temper so as to "rouse the people and hasten the downfall of capitalism"; (4) that all "governments" without exception can start a war only at "their own peril"; (5) that governments "are afraid of a proletarian revolution"; (6) that governments "should remember" the Paris Commune (i.e., civil war), the 1905 Revolution in Russia, etc. All these are perfectly clear ideas; they do not *guarantee* that revolution will take place, but lay stress on a precise characterisation of *facts and trends*. Whoever declares, with regard to these ideas and arguments, that the anticipated revolution has proved illusory, is displaying not a Marxist but a Struvist and police-renegade attitude towards revolution.

To the Marxist it is indisputable that a revolution is impossible without a revolutionary situation; furthermore, it is not every revolutionary situation that leads to revolution. What, generally speaking, are the symptoms of a revolutionary situation? We shall certainly not be mistaken if we indicate the following three major symptoms: (1) when it is impossible for the ruling classes to maintain their rule without any change; when there is a crisis, in one form or another, among the "upper classes", a crisis in the policy of the ruling class, leading to a fissure through which the discontent and indignation of the oppressed classes burst forth. For a revolution to take place, it is usually insufficient for "the lower classes not to want" to live in the old way; it is also necessary that "the upper classes should be unable" to live in the old way; (2) when the suffering and want of the oppressed classes have grown more acute than usual; (3) when, as a consequence of the above causes, there is a considerable increase in the activity of the masses, who uncomplainingly allow themselves to be robbed in "peace time", but, in turbulent times, are drawn both by all the circumstances of the crisis *and by the "upper classes" themselves* into independent historical action.

Without these objective changes, which are independent of the will, not only of individual groups and parties but even of individual classes, a revolution, as a general rule, is impossible. The totality of all these objective changes is called a revolutionary situation. Such a situation existed in 1905 in Russia, and in all revolutionary periods in the West; it also existed in Germany in the sixties of the last century, and in Russia in 1859–61 and 1879–80, although no revolution occurred in these instances. Why was that? It was because it is not every revolutionary situation that gives rise to a revolution; revolution arises only out of a situation in which the above-mentioned objective changes are accompanied by a subjective change, namely, the ability of the revolutionary *class* to take revolutionary mass action *strong* enough to break (or dislocate) the old government, which never, not even in a period of crisis, "falls", if it is not toppled over.

Such are the Marxist views on revolution, views that have been developed many, many times, have been accepted as indisputable by all Marxists, and for us, Russians, were corroborated in a particularly striking fashion by the experience of 1905. What, then, did the Basel Manifesto assume in this respect in 1912, and what took place in 1914–15?

It assumed that a revolutionary situation, which it briefly described as "an economic and political crisis", would arise. Has such a situation arisen? Undoubtedly, it has. The social-chauvinist Lensch, who defends chauvinism more candidly, publicly and honestly than the hypocrites Cunow, Kautsky, Plekhanov and Co. do, has gone so far as to say: "What we are passing through is a kind of *revolution*" (p. 6 of his pamphlet, *German Social-Democracy and the War*, Berlin, 1915). A political crisis exists; no government is sure of the morrow, not one is secure against the danger of financial collapse, loss of territory, expulsion from its country (in a way the Belgian Government was expelled). All governments are sleeping on a volcano; all are *themselves* calling for the masses to display initiative and heroism. The entire political regime of Europe has been shaken, and hardly anybody will deny that we have entered (and are entering ever deeper—I write this on the day of Italy's declaration of war) a period of immense political upheavals. When, two months after the declaration of war, Kautsky wrote (October 2, 1914, in *Die Neue Zeit*) that "never is government so strong, never are parties so weak as at the outbreak of a war", this was a sample of the falsification of historical science which Kautsky has perpetrated to please the Südekums and other opportunists. In the first place, never do governments stand in such need of agreement with all the parties of the ruling classes, or of the "peaceful" submission of the oppressed classes to that rule, as in the time of war. Secondly, even though "at the beginning of a war", and especially in a country that expects a speedy victory, the government *seems* all-powerful, nobody in the world has ever linked expectations of a revolutionary situation exclusively with the "beginning" of a war, and still less has anybody ever identified the "seeming" with the *actual*.

It was generally known, seen and admitted that a European war would be more severe than any war in the past. This is being borne out in ever greater measure by the experience of the war. The conflagration is spreading; the political foundations of Europe are being shaken more and more; the sufferings of the masses are appalling, the efforts of governments, the bourgeoisie and the opportunists to hush up these sufferings proving ever more futile. The war profits being obtained by certain groups of capitalists are monstrously high, and contradictions are growing extremely acute. The smouldering indignation of the masses, the vague yearning of society's downtrodden and ignorant strata for a kindly ("democratic") peace, the beginning of discontent among the "lower classes"—all these are facts. The longer the war drags on and the more acute it becomes, the more the governments themselves foster—and must foster—the activity of the masses, whom they call upon to make extraordinary effort and self-sacrifice. The experience of the war, like the experience of any crisis in history, of any great calamity and any sudden turn in human life, stuns and breaks some people, *but enlightens and tempers others*. Taken by and large, and considering the history of the world as a whole, the number and strength of the second kind of people have—with the exception of individual cases of the decline and fall of one state or another—proved greater than those of the former kind.

Far from "immediately" ending all these sufferings and all this enhancement of contradictions, the conclusion of peace will, in many respects, make those sufferings more keenly and immediately felt by the most backward masses of the population.

In a word, a revolutionary situation obtains in most of the advanced countries and the Great Powers of Europe. In this respect, the prediction of the Basel Manifesto has been *fully* confirmed. To deny this truth, directly or indirectly, or to ignore it, as Cunow, Plekhanov, Kautsky and Co. have done, means telling a big lie, deceiving the working class, and serving the bourgeoisie. In *Sotsial-Demokrat* (Nos. 34, 40 and 41) we cited facts which prove that those who *fear* revolution—petty-bourgeois Christian parsons, the General Staffs and millionaires' newspapers—are compelled to admit that symptoms of a revolutionary situation exist in Europe.

Will this situation last long; how much more acute will it become? Will it lead to revolution? This is something we do not know, and nobody can know. The answer can be provided only by the *experience* gained during the development of revolutionary sentiment and the transition to revolutionary action by the advanced class, the proletariat. There can be no talk in this connection about "illusions" or their repudiation, since no socialist has ever guaranteed that this war (and not the next one), that today's revolutionary situation (and not tomorrow's) will produce a revolution. What we are discussing is the indisputable and fundamental duty of all socialists—that of revealing to the masses the existence of a revolutionary situation, explaining its scope and depth, arousing the proletariat's revolutionary consciousness and revolutionary determination, helping it to go over to revolutionary action, and forming, for that purpose, organisations suited to the revolutionary situation.

No influential or responsible socialist has ever dared to feel doubt that this is the duty of the socialist parties. Without spreading or harbouring the least "illusions", the Basel Manifesto spoke specifically of this duty of the socialists—to rouse and to stir up the people (and not to lull them with chauvinism, as Plekhanov, Axelrod and Kautsky have done), to take advantage of the crisis so as to *hasten* the downfall of capitalism, and to be guided by the *examples* of the Commune and of October–December 1905. The present parties' failure to perform that duty meant their treachery, political death, renunciation of their own role and desertion to the side of the bourgeoisie. . . .

The most subtle theory of social-chauvinism, one that has been most skilfully touched up to look scientific and international, is the theory of "ultra-imperialism" advanced by Kautsky. Here is the clearest, most precise and most recent exposition of this theory in the words of the author himself:

> The subsiding of the Protectionist movement in Britain; the lowering of tariffs in America; the trend towards disarmament; the rapid decline in the export of capital from France and Germany in the years immediately preceding the war; finally, the growing international interweaving between the various cliques of finance capital—all this has caused me to consider whether the present imperialist policy cannot be supplanted by a new,

ultra-imperialist policy, which will introduce the joint exploitation of the world by internationally united finance capital in place of the mutual rivalries of national finance capital. Such a new phase of capitalism is at any rate conceivable. Can it be achieved? Sufficient premises are still lacking to enable us to answer this question . . . (*Die Neue Zeit* No. 5, April 30, 1915, p. 144).

The course and the outcome of the present war may prove decisive in this respect. It may entirely crush the weak beginnings of ultra-imperialism by fanning to the highest degree national hatred also among the finance capitalists, by intensifying the armaments race, and by making a second world war inevitable. Under such conditions, the thing I foresaw and formulated in my pamphlet, *The Road to Power,* would come true in horrifying dimensions; class antagonisms would become sharper and sharper and with it would come the moral decay [literally: "going out of business, *Abwirtschaftung*", bankruptcy] of capitalism. . . . [It must be noted that by this pretentious word Kautsky means simply the "hatred" which the "strata intermediary between the proletariat and finance capital", namely, "the intelligentsia, the petty bourgeois, even small capitalists", feel towards capitalism.] But the war may end otherwise. It may lead to the strengthening of the weak beginnings of ultra-imperialism. . . . Its lessons [note this!] may hasten developments for which we would have to wait a long time under peace conditions. If it does lead to this, to an agreement between nations, disarmament and a lasting peace, then the worst of the causes that led to the growing moral decay of capitalism before the war may disappear." The new phase will, of course, bring the proletariat "new misfortunes", "perhaps even worse", but "for a time", "ultra-imperialism" "could create an era of new hopes and expectations within the framework of capitalism" (p. 145).

How is a justification of social-chauvinism deduced from this "theory"?

In a way rather strange for a "theoretician", namely as follows:

The Left-wing Social-Democrats in Germany say that imperialism and the wars it engenders are not accidental, but an inevitable product of capitalism, which has brought about the domination of finance capital. It is therefore necessary to go over to the revolutionary mass struggle, as the period of comparatively peaceful development has ended. The "Right"-wing Social-Democrats brazenly declare: since imperialism is "necessary", we too must be imperialists. Kautsky, in the role of the "Centre", tries to reconcile these two views.

> "The extreme Lefts," he writes in his pamphlet, *The National State, the Imperialist State and the League of States* (Nuremberg, 1915), wish to "contrapose" socialism to inevitable imperialism, i.e., "not only the propaganda for socialism that we have been carrying on for half a century in contraposition to all forms of capitalist domination, but the immediate achievement of socialism. This seems very radical, but it can only serve *to drive* into the camp of imperialism *anyone* who *does not believe* in the immediate practical achievement of socialism" (p. 17, italics ours).

When he speaks of the immediate achievement of socialism, Kautsky is resorting to a subterfuge, for he takes advantage of the fact that in Germany, especially under the military censorship, revolutionary action cannot be spoken of. Kautsky is well aware that the Left wing is demanding of the Party *immediate* propaganda in favour of and preparation for, revolutionary action, not the "immediate practical achievement of socialism".

From the necessity of imperialism the Left wing deduces the necessity of revolutionary action. The "theory of ultra-imperialism", however, serves Kautsky as a means *to justify the opportunists,* to present the situation in such a light as to create the impression that they have not gone over to the bourgeoisie but simply "do not believe" that socialism can arrive immediately, and expect that a new "era" of disarmament and lasting peace "may be" ushered in. This "theory" boils down, and can *only* boil down, to the following: Kautsky is exploiting the *hope* for a new peaceful era of capitalism so as to justify the adhesion of the opportunists and the official Social-Democratic parties to the bourgeoisie, and their rejection of revolutionary, i.e., proletarian, tactics in the *present stormy era,* this despite the solemn declarations of the Basel resolution!

At the same time Kautsky does not say that this new phase follows, and necessarily so, from certain definite circumstances and conditions. On the contrary, he states quite outspokenly that he cannot yet even decide whether or not this new phase is *"achievable"*. Indeed, consider the "trends" towards the new era, which have been indicated by Kautsky. Astonishingly enough, the author has included among the economic facts "the trend towards disarmament"! This means that, behind innocent philistine talk and pipedreaming, Kautsky is trying to hide from indisputable facts that do not at all fit in with the theory of the mitigation of contradictions. Kautsky's "ultra-imperialism"—this term, incidentally, does not at all express what the author wants to say—implies a tremendous *mitigation* of the contradictions of capitalism. We are told that Protectionism is subsiding in Britain and America. But where is there the least trend towards a new era? Extreme Protectionism is now subsiding in America, but Protectionism remains, just as the privileges, the preferential tariffs favouring Britain, have remained in that country's colonies. Let us recall what the passage from the previous and "peaceful" period of capitalism to the present and imperialist period has been based on: free competition has yielded to monopolist capitalist combines, and the world has been partitioned. Both these facts (and factors) are obviously of world-wide significance: Free Trade and peaceful competition were possible and necessary as long as capital was in a position to enlarge its colonies without hindrance, and seize unoccupied land in Africa, etc., and as long as the concentration of capital was still weak and no monopolist concerns existed, i.e., concerns of a magnitude permitting domination in an *entire* branch of industry. The appearance and growth of such monopolist concerns (has this process been stopped in Britain or America? Not even Kautsky will dare deny that the war has accelerated and intensified it) have rendered the free competition of former times *impossible;* they have cut the ground from under its feet, while the partition of the world *compels* the capitalists to go over from peaceful expansion to an armed struggle for the *repartitioning* of colonies and spheres of influence. It is ridiculous to think that the *subsiding* of Protectionism in two countries can change anything in this respect. . . .

[Kautsky had ridiculed the notion that the SPD's leadership could be held responsible for the party's reversal on August 4, as if "an order given by a handful of parliamentarians is sufficient to make four million class-conscious proletarians turn right-about-face."]

Every word uttered here is a lie. The German Party organisation had a membership of one million, not four million. As is the case with any organisation, the united will of this mass organisation was expressed *only* through its united political centre, the "handful", who betrayed socialism. It was this handful who were called upon to vote; they were in a position to vote; they were in a position to write articles, etc. The masses were not consulted. Not only were they not permitted to vote, but they were disunited and coerced *"by orders"*, not from a handful of parliamentarians, but from the military authorities. A military organisation existed; there was no treachery among the leaders of *this* organisation. It called up the "masses" *one by one*, confronted the individual with the ultimatum: either join the army, as your leaders advise you to, or be shot. The masses could not act in an organised fashion because their previously created organisation, an organisation embodied in a "handful" of Legiens, Kautskys and Scheidemanns, had betrayed them. It takes time to create a *new* organisation, as well as a determination to consign the old, rotten, and obsolete organisation to the scrap heap.

Kautsky tries to defeat his opponents, the Lefts, by ascribing to them the nonsensical idea that the "masses", "in retaliation" to war, should make a revolution "within twenty-four hours", and institute "socialism" as opposed to imperialism, or otherwise the "masses" would be revealing "spinelessness and treachery". But this is sheer nonsense, which the compilers of illiterate bourgeois and police booklets have hitherto used to "defeat" the revolutionaries, and Kautsky now flaunts in our faces. Kautsky's Left opponents know perfectly well that a revolution cannot be "made", that revolutions *develop* from objectively (i.e., independently of the will of parties and classes) mature crises and turns in history, that without organisation the masses lack unity of will, and that the struggle against a centralised state's powerful terrorist military organisation is a difficult and lengthy business. Owing to the treachery of their leaders, the masses *could not* do anything at the crucial moment, whereas this "handful" of leaders *were in an excellent position* and in duty bound to vote against the war credits, take a stand against a "class truce" and justification of the war, express themselves in favour of the defeat of *their own* governments, set up an international apparatus for the purpose of carrying on propaganda in favour of fraternisation in the trenches, organise the publication of illegal literature* on the necessity of starting revolutionary activities, etc.

Kautsky knows perfectly well that it is precisely such or rather *similar* actions that the German "Lefts" have in mind, and that under a military censorship they cannot talk about these things *directly*, openly. Kautsky's desire to defend the opportunists at all costs has led him into unparalleled infamy: taking cover behind the military censors, he attributes patent absurdities to the Lefts, in the confidence that the censors will protect him from exposure.

The serious scientific and political question, which Kautsky has deliberately evaded by means of subterfuges of all kinds, thereby giving enormous pleasure to the opportunists, is this: how was it *possible* for the most prominent representatives of the Second International to betray socialism?

This question should not, of course, be considered from the standpoint of the biographies of the individual leaders. Their future biographers will have to analyse the problem from this angle as well, but what interests the socialist movement today is not that, but a study of the historical origins, the conditions, the significance and the strength of the social-chauvinist *trend*. (1) Where did social-chauvinism spring from? (2) What gave it strength? (3)How must it be combated? Only such an approach to the question can be regarded as serious, the "personal" approach being in practice an evasion, a piece of sophistry.

To answer the first question we must see, first, whether the ideological and political content of social-chauvinism is *connected* with some previous trend in socialism; and second, in what relation—from the standpoint of actual political divisions—the present division of socialists into opponents and defenders of social-chauvinism stands to divisions which historically preceded it.

By social-chauvinism we mean acceptance of the idea of the defence of the fatherland in the present imperialist war, justification of an alliance between socialists and the bourgeoisie and the governments of their "own" countries in this war, a refusal to propagate and support proletarian-revolutionary action against one's "own" bourgeoisie, etc. It is perfectly obvious that social-chauvinism's basic ideological and political content fully coincides with the foundations of opportunism. It is *one and the same* tendency. In the conditions of the war of 1914–15, opportunism leads to social-chauvinism. The idea of class collaboration is opportunism's main feature. The war has brought this idea to its logical conclusion, and has augmented its usual factors and stimuli with a number of extraordinary ones; through the operation of special threats and coercion it has compelled the philistine and disunited masses to collaborate with the bourgeoisie. This circumstance has naturally multiplied adherents of opportunism and fully explains why many radicals of yesterday have deserted to that camp.

Opportunism means sacrificing the fundamental interests of the masses to the temporary interests of an insignificant minority of the workers or, in other words, an alliance between a section of the workers and the bourgeoisie, directed against the mass of the proletariat. The war has made such an alliance particularly conspicuous and inescapable. Opportunism was engendered in the course of decades by the special features in the period of the development of capitalism, when the comparatively peaceful and cultured life of a stratum of privileged workingmen "bourgeoisified" them, gave them crumbs from the table of their national capitalists, and isolated them from the suffering, misery and revolutionary temper of the impoverished and ruined masses. The imperialist war is the direct continuation and culmination of this state of affairs, because this is a war for the *privileges* of the Great-Power nations, for the repartition of colonies, and domination over other nations. To defend and strengthen their privileged position as a petty-bourgeois "upper stratum" or aristocracy (and bureaucracy) of the working class—such is the natural wartime continuation of petty-bourgeois opportunist hopes and the corresponding tactics, such is the economic foundation of present-day social-imperialism. And, of course, the force of habit, the routine of relatively "peaceful" evolution, national prejudices, a fear of sharp turns and a disbelief in them—all these were additional circumstances which enhanced both opportunism and a hypocritical and a craven reconciliation with opportunism—ostensibly only for a time and only because of extraordinary causes and motives. The war has changed this opportunism, which had been fostered for decades, raised it to a higher stage, increased the number and the variety of its shades, augmented the ranks of its adherents, enriched their arguments with a multitude of new sophisms, and has merged, so to say, many new streams and rivulets with the mainstream of opportunism. However, the mainstream has not disappeared. Quite the reverse.

Social-chauvinism is an opportunism which has matured to such a degree that the *continued* existence of this bourgeois abscess within the socialist parties has become impossible.

Those who refuse to see the closest and unbreakable link between social-chauvinism and opportunism clutch at individual instances—this opportunist or another, they say, has turned internationalist; this radical or another has turned chauvinist. But this kind of argument carries no weight as far as the development of *trends* is concerned. Firstly, chauvinism and opportunism in the labour movement have the same economic basis: the alliance between a numerically small upper stratum of the proletariat and the petty bourgeoisie—who get but morsels of the privileges of their "own" national capital—against the masses of the proletarians, the masses of the toilers and the oppressed in general. Secondly, the two trends have the same ideological and political content. Thirdly, the old division of socialists into an opportunist trend and a revolutionary, which was characteristic of the period of the Second International (1889–1914), *corresponds*, by and large, to the new division into chauvinists and internationalists. . . .

By and large, if we take the trends and tendencies, we must admit that it was the opportunist wing of European socialism that betrayed socialism and deserted to chauvinism. What is the source of its strength and its seeming omnipotence within the official parties? Now that he himself is involved, Kautsky, who is well versed in raising questions of history, especially with reference to ancient Rome or similar matters that do not have a direct bearing on problems of our times, hypocritically pretends a lack of understanding. But the whole thing is crystal-clear. The immense strength of the opportunists and the chauvinists stems from *their alliance* with the bourgeoisie, with the governments and the General Staffs. This is often overlooked in Russia, where it is assumed the opportunists are a *section* of the socialist parties, that there always have been and will be two extreme wings within those parties, that "extremes" should be avoided, etc., etc.—and plenty of similar philistine copybook maxims.

In reality, the opportunists' formal membership in workers' parties by no means disproves their objectively being a political detachment of the bourgeoisie, conductors of its influence, and its agents in the labour movement. . . .

At the crucial moment, Südekum alone, actually proved stronger in the policies of the German Social-Democratic Party than a hundred Haases and Kautskys (Just as *Nasha Zarya* alone is stronger than all the Brussels bloc trends,[45] which are afraid to break away from that paper).

Why is that so? It is because behind Südekum are the bourgeoisie, the government, and the General Staff of a Great Power. These support Südekum's policy in a thousand ways, whereas his opponents' policy is frustrated by every means, including prison and the firing squad. Südekum's voice reaches the public in millions of copies of bourgeois newspapers (as do the voices of Vandervelde, Sembat, and Plekhanov), whereas the voices of his opponents *cannot* be heard in the legal press because of the military censorship!

It is generally agreed that opportunism is no chance occurrence, sin, slip, or treachery on the part of individuals, but a social product of an entire period of history. The significance of this truth is not always given sufficient thought. Opportunism has been nurtured by legalism. The workers' parties of the period between 1889 and 1914 had to take advantage of bourgeois legality. When the crisis came, they should have adopted illegal methods of work (but this could not be done otherwise than with the greatest vigour and determination, combined with a number of stratagems). A *single* Südekum was sufficient to prevent the adoption of illegal methods, because, speaking in a historico-philosophical sense, he had the whole of the "old world" behind him, and because he, Südekum, has always betrayed, and will always betray, to the bourgeoisie all the military plans of its class enemy, speaking in the sense of practical politics.

It is a fact that the entire German Social-Democratic Party (and the same holds for the French and *other* parties) does *only* that which pleases Südekum or can be tolerated by Südekum. *Nothing else* can be done legally. Anything *honest* and really socialist that takes place in the German Social-Democratic Party, is done in *opposition* to its centres, by *circumventing* its Executive and Central Organ, by *violating* organisational discipline, in a *factional* manner, on behalf of new and anonymous centres of a new party, as was the case, for instance, with the German Lefts' manifesto published in *Berner Tagwacht* on May 31 of this year. As a matter of fact, a *new* party is growing up, gaining strength and being organised, a real workers' party, a genuinely revolutionary Social-Democratic Party, unlike the old and corrupt national-liberal party of Legien, Südekum, Kautsky, Haase, Scheidemann and Co.**

It was, therefore, a profound historical truth that the opportunist "Monitor" blurted out in the conservative *Preussische Jahrbücher* when he said it would be bad for the opportunists *(i.e., the bourgeoisie)* if present-day Social-Democracy were to *swing to the right*—because in that case the workers would desert it. The opportunists (and the bourgeoisie) need the party as it is today, a party *combining* the Right and the Left wings and officially represented by Kautsky, who will be able to reconcile everything in the world by means of smooth, "thoroughly Marxist" phrases. In word, socialism and the revolutionary spirit for the people, the masses, the workers; in deed, Südekumism, adhering to the bourgeoisie in any grave crisis. We say: *any* crisis, because in any serious political strike, and not only in time of war, "feudalist" Germany like "free and parliamentary" Britain or France will *immediately* introduce martial law under one name or another. No one of sound mind and judgement can have any doubt about this.

Hence logically follows the reply to the question raised above, viz., how is social-chauvinism to be combated? Social-chauvinism is an opportunism which has matured to such a degree, grown so strong and brazen during the long period of comparatively "peaceful" capitalism, so definite in its political ideology, and so closely associated with the bourgeoisie and the governments, that the existence of *such a trend within* the Social-Democratic workers' parties *cannot* be tolerated. Flimsy, thin-soled shoes may be good enough to walk in on the well-paved streets of a small provincial town, but heavy hob-nailed boots are needed for walking in the hills. In Europe socialism has emerged from a comparatively peaceful stage that is confined within narrow and national limits. With the outbreak of the war of 1914–15, it entered the stage of revolutionary action; there can be no doubt that the time has come for a complete break with opportunism, for its expulsion from the workers' parties.

This definition of the tasks the new era of international

development confronts socialism with does not, of course, immediately show how rapidly and in what definite forms the process of separation of the workers' revolutionary Social-Democratic parties from the petty-bourgeois opportunist parties will proceed in the various countries. It does, however, reveal the need clearly to realise that such a separation is inevitable, and that the entire policy of the workers' parties must be directed from this standpoint. The war of 1914–15 is such a great turn in history that the attitude towards opportunism *cannot* remain the same as it has been. What has happened cannot be erased. It is impossible to obliterate from the minds of the workers, or from the experience of the bourgeoisie, or from the political lessons of our epoch in general, the fact that, at a moment of crisis, the opportunists proved to be the nucleus of those elements within the workers' parties that deserted to the bourgeoisie. Opportunism—to speak on a European scale—was in its adolescent stage, as it were, before the war. With the outbreak of the war it grew to manhood and its "innocence" and youth cannot be restored. An entire social stratum, consisting of parliamentarians, journalists, labour officials, privileged office personnel, and certain strata of the proletariat, has sprung up and has become *amalgamated* with its own national bourgeoisie, which has proved fully capable of appreciating and "adapting" it. The course of history cannot be turned back or checked—can and must go fearlessly onward, from the preparatory legal working-class organisations, which are in the grip of opportunism, to revolutionary organisations that know how *not* to confine themselves to legality and are capable of safeguarding themselves against opportunist treachery, organisations of a proletariat that is beginning a "struggle for power", a struggle for the overthrow of the bourgeoisie.

This, incidentally, proves how wrong are the views of those who befog both their own minds and those of the workers with the question as to what should be done with such outstanding authorities of the Second International as Guesde, Plekhanov, Kautsky, etc. In fact, no such question arises. If these persons fail to understand the new tasks, they will have to stand aside or remain as they are at present, in captivity to the opportunists. If these persons free themselves from "captivity" they are hardly likely to encounter *political* obstacles to their return to the camp of the revolutionaries. At all events, it is absurd to substitute the question of the role of individuals for the question of the struggle between trends and of the new period in the working-class movement. . . .

The building of a revolutionary organisation must be begun—that is demanded by the new historical situation, by the epoch of proletarian revolutionary action—but it can be begun only *over the heads* of the old leaders, the stranglers of revolutionary energy, *over the heads* of the old party, through its *destruction.*

Of course, the counter-revolutionary philistines cry out "anarchism!", just as the opportunist Eduard David cried "anarchism" when he denounced Karl Liebknecht. In Germany, only those leaders seem to have remained honest socialists whom the opportunists revile as anarchists. . . .

Take the army of today. It is a good example of organisation. This organisation is good only because it is *flexible* and is able at the same time to give millions of people *a single will.* Today these millions are living in their homes in various parts of the country; tomorrow mobilisation is ordered, and they report for duty. Today they lie in the trenches, and this may go on for months; tomorrow they are led to the attack in another order. Today they perform miracles in sheltering from bullets and shrapnel; tomorrow they perform miracles in hand-to-hand combat. Today their advance detachments lay minefields; tomorrow they advance scores of miles guided by airmen flying overhead. When, in the pursuit of a single aim and animated by a single will, millions alter the forms of their communication and their behaviour, change the place and the mode of their activities, change their tools and weapons in accordance with the changing conditions and the requirements of the struggle—all this is genuine organisation.

The same holds true for the working-class struggle against the bourgeoisie. Today there is no revolutionary situation, the conditions that cause unrest among the masses or heighten their activities do not exist; today you are given a ballot paper—take it, learn to organise so as to use it as a weapon against your enemies, not as a means of getting cushy legislative jobs for men who cling to their parliamentary seats for fear of having to go to prison. Tomorrow your ballot paper is taken from you and you are given a rifle or a splendid and most up-to-date quick-firing gun—take this weapon of death and destruction, pay no heed to the mawkish snivellers who are afraid of war; too much still remains in the world that *must* be destroyed with fire and sword for the emancipation of the working class; if anger and desperation grow among the masses, if a revolutionary situation arises, prepare to create new organisations and *use* these useful weapons of death and destruction *against* your *own* government and your *own* bourgeoisie.

That is not easy, to be sure. It will demand arduous preparatory activities and heavy sacrifices. This is a *new* form of organisation and struggle that also *has to be learnt,* and knowledge is not acquired without errors and setbacks. This form of the class struggle stands in the same relation to participation in elections as an assault against a fortress stands in relation to manoeuvring, marches, or lying in the trenches. It *is not so often* that history places this form of struggle on the order of the day, but then its significance is felt for decades to come. *Days* on which *such* methods of struggle can and must be employed are equal to *scores of years* of other historical epochs. . . .

"We would have been arrested," one of the Social-Democratic deputies who voted for the war credits on August 4 is alleged to have declared at a workers' meeting in Berlin. The workers shouted in reply: "Well, what would have been bad about that?"

If there was no other *signal* that would instil in the German *and the French* working masses revolutionary sentiments and the need to prepare for revolutionary action, the arrest of a member of parliament for a courageous speech would have been useful as a call for *unity* of the proletarians of the various countries in their revolutionary work. It is *not easy* to bring about such unity; all the more was it the duty of members of parliament, whose high office made their purview of the entire political scene so extensive, *to take the initiative.*

Not only in wartime but positively in any acute political situation, to say nothing of periods of revolutionary mass action of any kind, the governments of even the *freest* bourgeois countries will threaten to dissolve the legal organisations, seize their funds, arrest their leaders, and threaten other "practical consequences" of the same kind. What are we to do then? Justify the opportunists on these grounds, as Kautsky does? But this would mean sanctifying the transformation of the Social-Democratic parties into national liberal-labour parties.

There is only one conclusion a socialist can draw, namely, that pure legalism, the legalism-and-nothing-but-legalism of the "European" parties, is now obsolete and, as a result of the development of capitalism in the pre-imperialist stage, has become the foundation for a bourgeois labour policy. It must be augmented by the creation of an illegal basis, an illegal organisation, illegal Social-Democratic work, without, however, surrendering a single legal position. Experience will show *how* this is to be done, if only the desire to take this road exists, as well as a realisation that it is necessary. In 1912–14, the revolutionary Social-Democrats of Russia proved that this problem can be solved. Muranov, the workers' deputy in the Duma, who at the trial behaved better than the rest and was exiled to Siberia, clearly demonstrated that—besides *"ministeriable"* parliamentarism (from Henderson, Sembat and Vandervelde down to Südekum and Scheidemann, the latter two are also being completely "ministeriable", although they are not admitted further than the anteroom!)—there can be *illegal and revolutionary* parliamentarism. Let the Kosovskys and Potresovs admire the "European" parliamentarism of the lackeys or accept it—we shall not tire of telling the workers that *such* legalism, *such* Social-Democracy of the Legien, Kautsky, Scheidemann brand, deserves nothing but contempt.

To sum up.

The collapse of the Second International has been most strikingly expressed in the flagrant betrayal of their convictions and of the solemn Stuttgart and Basel resolutions by the majority of the official Social-Democratic parties of Europe. This collapse, however, which signifies the complete victory of opportunism, the transformation of the Social-Democratic parties into national liberal-labour parties, is merely the result of the entire historical epoch of the Second International—the close of the nineteenth century and the beginning of the twentieth. The objective conditions of this epoch—transitional from the consummation of West-European bourgeois and national revolutions to the beginning of socialist revolutions—engendered and fostered opportunism. During this period we see a split in the working class and socialist movement in some European countries, which, in the main, was cleavage along the line of opportunism (Britain, Italy, Holland, Bulgaria and Russia); in other countries, we see a long and stubborn struggle of trends along the same line (Germany, France, Belgium, Sweden and Switzerland). The crisis created by the great war has torn away all coverings, swept away conventions, exposed an abscess that has long come to a head, and revealed opportunism in its true role of ally of the bourgeoisie. The complete organisational severance of this element from the workers' parties has become imperative. The epoch of imperialism cannot permit the existence, in a single party, of the revolutionary proletariat's vanguard and the semi-petty-bourgeois aristocracy of the working class, who enjoy morsels of the privileges of their "own" nation's "Great-Power" status. The old theory that opportunism is a "legitimate shade" in a single party that knows no "extremes" has now turned into a tremendous deception of the workers and a tremendous hindrance to the working-class movement. Undisguised opportunism, which immediately repels the working masses, is not so frightful and injurious as this theory of the golden mean, which uses Marxist catchwords to justify opportunist practice, and tries to prove, with a series of sophisms, that revolutionary action is premature, etc. Kautsky, the most outstanding spokesman of this theory, and also the leading authority in the Second International, has shown himself a consummate hypocrite and a past master in the art of prostituting Marxism. All members of the million-strong German party who are at all honest, class-conscious and revolutionary have turned away in indignation from an "authority" of this kind so ardently defended by the Südekums and the Scheidemanns.

The proletarian masses—probably about nine-tenths of whose former leaders have gone over to the bourgeoisie—have found themselves disunited and helpless amid a spate of chauvinism and under the pressure of martial law and the war censorship. But the objective war-created revolutionary situation, which is extending and developing, is inevitably engendering revolutionary sentiments; it is tempering and enlightening all the finest and most class-conscious proletarians. A sudden change in the mood of the masses is not only possible, but is becoming more and more probable, a change similar to that which was to be seen in Russia early in 1905 in connection with the "Gaponade",[46] when, in the course of several months and sometimes of several weeks, there emerged from the backward proletarian masses an army of millions, which followed the proletariat's revolutionary vanguard. We cannot tell whether a powerful revolutionary movement will develop immediately after *this* war, or during it, etc., but at all events, it is *only* work in this direction that deserves the name of socialist work. The slogan of a civil war is the one that summarises and directs this work, and helps unite and consolidate those who wish to aid the revolutionary struggle of the proletariat against its own government and its own bourgeoisie.

FOOTNOTES BY LENIN

* Incidentally, it would not have been at all necessary to close *all* Social-Democratic papers in reply to the government's ban on writing about class hatred and class struggle. To agree not to write about this, as *Vorwärts* did, was mean and cowardly. *Vorwärts* died *politically* when it did this, and Martov was right when he said so. It was, however, possible to retain the legal papers by declaring that they were non-Party and *non-Social-Democratic,* and served the technical needs of a section of the workers, i.e., that they were *non-political papers.* Underground Social-Democratic literature containing an *assessment* of the war, and legally published working-class literature *without that assessment,* a literature that does not say what is not true, but keeps silent about the truth—why should this not have been possible?

** What happened before the historic voting of August 4 is extremely characteristic. The official party has cast the cloak of bureaucratic hypocrisy over this event, saying that the majority decided and that all voted unanimously *in favour.* But this hypocrisy was exposed by Ströbel who told the truth in the journal *Die Internationale.* The Social-Democratic members of the Reichstag split into *two* groups, each of whom came with an *ultimatum,* i.e., a dissentient decision, i.e., one signifying a split. One group, the opportunists, who were about thirty strong, decided to vote *in favour, under all circumstances;* the other and Left group numbering about fifteen, decided—less resolutely—to vote against. When the "Centre" or the "Marsh", who never take a firm stand, voted with the opportunists, the Lefts sustained a crushing defeat and—submitted! Talk about the "unity" of the German Social-Democrats is sheer hypocrisy, which actually covers up the inevitable submission of the Lefts to ultimatums from the opportunists.

Lenin continued the debate with Kautsky in a polemical answer to Kautsky's pamphlet *Internationalism and the War* (excerpted earlier in this chapter). Kautsky and other SPD leaders who supported the war frequently cited the positions of Marx and Engels in defense of the German side in the national wars of the mid-nineteenth century. Kautsky said that, while Marx had condemned wars, when, despite the will of the Socialists war became a fact, Marx in 1854–76 took sides with one of the belligerents.

"That is the main contention and the chief trump card in Kautsky's pamphlet," Lenin wrote. "It is also the stand of Mr. Potresov, who by 'internationalism' understands finding out the *success of which side* in the war is more desirable or less harmful from the standpoint of the interests of the proletariat, not in a particular country but *the world over.* The war, he says, is being conducted by governments and the bourgeoisie; it is for the proletariat to decide *which* government's victory presents the least danger to the workers of the world.

"The sophistry of this reasoning consists in a bygone period of history being substituted for the present. The following were the main features of the old wars referred to by Kautsky: (1) they dealt with the problems of bourgeois-democratic reforms and the overthrow of absolutism or foreign oppression; (2) the objective prerequisites for a socialist revolution had not yet matured, and *prior to the war,* no socialist could speak of utilising it to 'hasten the downfall of capitalism', as the Stuttgart (1907) and Basel (1912) resolutions do; (3) in the countries of *neither* of the belligerent groups were there any socialist parties of any strength or mass appeal, and tested in the struggle.

"In short, it is not surprising that Marx and the Marxists confined themselves to determining *which* bourgeoisie's victory would be more harmless to (or more favourable to) the world proletariat, at a time when one could not speak of a general proletarian movement against the governments and the bourgeoisie of all the belligerent countries.

"Long before the war and for the first time in world history, the socialists of all the countries now engaged in hostilities gathered together and declared that they would make use of the war 'to hasten the downfall of capitalism' (the Stuttgart resolution, 1907). In other words, they recognised that objective conditions had matured for that 'hastening of the downfall' i.e., for a socialist revolution. That is to say, they threatened the governments with a revolution. In Basel (1912) they said the same thing in still clearer terms, referring to the Commune and to October–December 1906, i.e., civil war."[47]

The Bolsheviks summed up their position on the war in the pamphlet *Socialism and War.* Originally published in German for circulation to the delegates at the September 1915 International Socialist Conference at Zimmerwald, it was also secretly distributed in German, French, and Russian editions, and translated and published by the Swedish-Norwegian Social Democratic youth league. It began by placing the First World War in the context of both the Marxist position on war in general and of the historical period in which the war occurred.

Socialism and war[48]

by V.I. Lenin and Gregory Zinoviev

The attitude of socialists toward wars

Socialists have always condemned wars between nations as barbarous and brutal. Our attitude towards war, however, is fundamentally different from that of the bourgeois pacifists (supporters and advocates of peace) and of the anarchists. We differ from the former in that we understand the inevitable connection between wars and the class struggle within a country; we understand that wars cannot be abolished unless classes are abolished and socialism is created; we also differ in that we regard civil wars, i.e., wars waged by an oppressed class against the oppressor class, by slaves against slaveholders, by serfs against landowners, and by wage-workers against the bourgeoisie, as fully legitimate, progressive and necessary. We Marxists differ from both pacifists and anarchists in that we deem it necessary to study each war historically (from the standpoint of Marx's dialectical materialism) and separately. There have been in the past numerous wars which, despite all the horrors, atrocities, distress and suffering that inevitably accompany all wars, were progressive, i.e., benefited the development of mankind by helping to destroy most harmful and reactionary institutions (e.g., an autocracy or serfdom) and the most barbarous despotisms in Europe (the Turkish and the Russian). That is why the features historically specific to the present war must come up for examination.

The historical types of wars in modern times

The Great French Revolution ushered in a new epoch in the history of mankind. From that time down to the Paris Commune, i.e., between 1789 and 1871, one type of war was of a bourgeois-progressive character, waged for national liberation. In other words, the overthrow of absolutism and feudalism, the undermining of these institutions, and the overthrow of alien oppression, formed the chief content and historical significance of such wars. These were therefore progressive wars; during *such* wars, all honest and revolutionary democrats, as well as all socialists, always wished success to that country (i.e., that bourgeoisie) which had helped to overthrow or undermine the most baneful foundations of feudalism, absolutism and the oppression of other nations. For example, the revolutionary wars waged by France contained an element of plunder and the conquest of foreign territory by the French, but this does not in the least alter the fundamental historical significance of those wars, which destroyed and shattered feudalism and absolutism in the whole of the old, serf-owning Europe. In the Franco-Prussian war, Germany plundered France but this does not alter the fundamental historical significance of that war, which liberated tens of millions of German people from feudal disunity and from the oppression of two despots, the Russian tsar and Napoleon III.

The difference between wars of aggression and of defence

The period of 1789–1871 left behind it deep marks and revolutionary memories. There could be no development of the proletarian struggle for socialism prior to the overthrow of feudalism, absolutism and alien oppression. When, in speaking of the wars of *such* periods, socialists stressed the legitimacy of "defensive" wars, they always had these aims in mind, namely revolution against medievalism and serfdom. By a "defensive" war socialists have always understood a *"just"* war in this particular sense (Wilhelm Liebknecht once expressed himself precisely in this way). It is only in this sense that socialists have always regarded wars "for the defence of the fatherland", or "defensive" wars, as legitimate, progressive and just. For example, if tomorrow, Morocco were to declare war on France, or India on Britain, or Persia or China on Russia, and so on, these would be "just", and "defensive" wars, *irrespective* of who would be the first to attack; any socialist would wish the oppressed, dependent and unequal states victory over the oppressor, slave-holding and predatory "Great" Powers.

But imagine a slave-holder who owns 100 slaves warring against another who owns 200 slaves, for a more "just" redistribution of slaves. The use of the term of a "defensive" war, or a war "for the defence of the fatherland," would clearly be historically false in such a case and would in practice be sheer deception of the common people, philistines, and the ignorant, by the astute slave-holders. It is in this way that the peoples are being deceived with "national" ideology and the term of "defence of the fatherland", by the present-day imperialist bourgeoisie, in the war now being waged between slave-holders with the purpose of consolidating slavery.

The war of today is an imperialist war

It is almost universally admitted that this war is an imperialist war. In most cases, however, this term is distorted, or applied to one side, or else a loophole is left for the assertion that this war may, after all, be bourgeois-progressive, and of significance to the national-liberation movement. Imperialism is the highest stage in the development of capitalism, reached only in the twentieth century. Capitalism now finds that the old national states, without whose formation it could not have overthrown feudalism, are too cramped for it. Capitalism has developed concentration to such a degree that entire branches of industry are controlled by syndicates, trusts and associations of capitalist multi-millionaires and almost the entire globe has been divided up among the "lords of capital" either in the form of colonies, or by entangling other countries in thousands of threads of financial exploitation. Free trade and competition have been superseded by a striving towards monopolies, the seizure of territory for the investment of capital and as sources of raw materials, and so on. From the liberator of nations, which it was in the struggle against feudalism, capitalism in its imperialist stage has turned into the greatest oppressor of nations. Formerly progressive, capitalism has become reactionary; it has developed the forces of production to such a degree that mankind is faced with the alternative of adopting socialism or of experiencing years and even decades of armed struggle between the "Great" Powers for the artificial preservation of capitalism by means of colonies, monopolies, privileges and national oppression of every kind. . . .

[Reviewing the political positions of the Bolshevik Party, *Socialism and War* stressed its commitment to struggle, come what may, for a revolutionary International.]

The Russian Social-Democratic Labour Party and the Third International

The Russian Social-Democratic Labour Party has long parted company with its opportunists. Besides, the Russian opportunists have now become chauvinists. This only fortifies us in our opinion that a split with them is essential in the interests of socialism. We are convinced that the Social-Democrats' present differences with the social-chauvinists are in no way less marked than the socialists' differences with the anarchists when the Social-Democrats parted company with the latter.[49] The opportunist Monitor was right when he wrote in *Preussische Jahrbücher,* that the unity of today is to the advantage of the opportunists and the bourgeoisie, because it has compelled the Lefts to submit to the chauvinists and prevents the workers from understanding the controversy and forming their own genuinely working-class and genuinely socialist party. We are firmly convinced that, in the present state of affairs, a split with the opportunists and chauvinists is the prime duty of revolutionaries, just as a split with the yellow trade unions, the anti-Semites, the liberal workers' unions, etc., was essential in helping speed up the enlightenment of backward workers and draw them into the ranks of the Social-Democratic Party.

In our opinion, the Third International should be built up on that kind of revolutionary basis. To our Party, the question of the expediency of a break with the social-chauvinists does not exist, it has been answered with finality. The only question that exists for our Party is whether this can be achieved on an international scale in the immediate future.

It is perfectly obvious that to create an *international* Marxist organisation, there must be a readiness to form independent Marxist parties in the *various* countries. As a country with the oldest and strongest working-class movement, Germany is of decisive importance. The immediate future will show whether the conditions are mature for the formation of a new and Marxist International. If they are, our Party will gladly join such a Third International, purged of opportunism and chauvinism. If they are not, then that will show that a more or less protracted period of evolution is needed for that purging to be effected. Our Party will then form the extreme opposition within the old International, pending the time when the conditions in the various countries make possible the formation of an international workingmen's association standing on the basis of revolutionary Marxism.

We do not and cannot know what road world developments will take in the next few years. What we do know for certain and are unshakably convinced of is that *our* Party will work indefatigably in the above-mentioned direction, in *our* country and among *our* proletariat, and through its day-by-day activities will build up the Russian section of the *Marxist* International.

Iranians protest tsarist invasion to crush revolution, 1911.

Chapter 5

Russian internationalists discuss unity: 1914–15

The outbreak of war in 1914 put all the currents of the Russian Social Democratic Labor Party (RSDLP) to a decisive test. The most cohesive and proletarian group was the Bolsheviks. It originated as a public faction following the 1903 congress of the RSDLP, which had resulted in a split between the Bolsheviks ("majority") and Mensheviks ("minority"). From then on—with the exception of two periods, the last of them in 1911—the Bolsheviks functioned as a separate organization. Although a few Bolsheviks, particularly among those in exile, broke with the party in 1914 and went over to chauvinist positions, the organization took a united stand against the war.

The Mensheviks were not a centralized or homogeneous party, and they held quite divergent views on the war question. The official Menshevik leadership, the Organizing Committee, and the Menshevik Duma fraction, led by N.S. Chkheidze, both initially opposed a vote for war credits, although their subsequent courses were not identical. *Nasha Zarya* (Our Dawn), later relaunched as *Nashe Dyelo* (Our Cause), an influential Menshevik periodical inside Russia, supported

Russian "self-defense" and adopted an openly chauvinist position. A group around Georgi Plekhanov had an even more extreme pro-war stance.[1]

The most important expression of the smaller currents standing between the Mensheviks and Bolsheviks were the Paris newspaper *Golos* (later *Nashe Slovo*), and the Mezhrayontsi (Interdistrict Organization) in Petrograd. These forces took a stand against the imperialist war. *Golos* was initially edited by Julius Martov, who was a member of the Menshevik Organizing Committee.

Socialist organizations in the oppressed nations of the tsarist empire also formed part of the Social Democratic movement in Russia. Among these were the Social Democracy of Latvia and the two wings of the Polish-Lithuanian Social Democracy (SDKPiL), which adopted firmly antichauvinist positions.

"Practically all Social-Democrats in Russia realise that the old divisions and groups are, if not obsolescent, then at least undergoing a transformation," Lenin wrote in May 1915. "In the forefront is the division on the main issue raised by the war, viz., the division into 'internationalists' and 'social-patriots'."[2]

Many divergent currents in Russian Social Democracy held an antichauvinist position on the war. The question was thus posed of the desirability for the consistent internationalist forces of consummating their break from the social chauvinists, uniting in common action, and conducting a discussion of their many persisting differences.

Many political problems had to be overcome, however, in order for this to be achieved. An early indication of these problems was the divergent response of Social Democrats to a maneuver of the Entente powers to rally Social Democratic support for the war.

Soon after the declaration of war, Second International leader Emile Vandervelde, now a minister in the Belgian king's government, sent a letter to the RSDLP through the tsarist ministry of foreign affairs. Vandervelde appealed to his Russian comrades to rally behind the war effort against "Prussian militarism." While the Mensheviks in the Duma fraction, led by Chkheidze, did not reply, the chauvinist wing of the Menshevik forces in Petrograd issued an answer assuring Vandervelde that "your cause in this war is a legitimate one of self-defense against the danger posed to the proletariat's democratic rights and to its freedom struggle by the aggressive policies of the Prussian junkers.

"Whatever the past and future goals of the great powers participating in this war," the Petrograd Mensheviks continued, "the objective course of events puts in question the very existence of Prussian junkerism, that citadel of militarism today, which bears down with its heavy weight against the liberation struggle of the German proletariat as well. We are strongly convinced that in the struggle to eliminate this power, the Socialists of those countries obliged to participate in this war will come together with the glorious vanguard of the international proletariat—German Social Democracy.

"Yet, to our regret, the Russian proletariat does not find itself in a situation similar to that of the proletariats of other countries warring against Prussian junkerism," they wrote, pointing to the reactionary character of tsarism, and its repression of every attempt by Russian workers at political self-expression. "This deprives Russian Social Democracy at this time of the possibility of taking the stand of Belgian, French, and British Socialists, and actively participating in the war, assuming responsibility for the actions of the Russian government before the country and before international socialism."

The Menshevik document added, "We assure you that our activity in Russia does not oppose the war. We consider it necessary, however, to draw your attention to the necessity of now preparing an energetic opposition to the great powers' policy of conquest that is already taking shape, and to demand the holding of plebiscites before any annexations are carried out."[3]

The Bolsheviks reproduced this statement in *Sotsial-Demokrat,* along with the comment by Gregory Zinoviev that his worst expectations about the Mensheviks had proven justified. "Martov's stand against chauvinism has remained an isolated voice among the liquidationists," Zinoviev said. He concluded, "This credo of the liquidators stands as a shameful disgrace for their entire current."[4]

While some Menshevik leaders, such as Martov and Pavel Axelrod, of the Secretariat of the Organizing Committee Abroad, disagreed with this chauvinist position, they rejected a break with these forces. Indeed, when the Secretariat received this statement, according to Bolshevik leader Alexander Shlyapnikov, it did not publicly criticize it, but instead, after a period of time, published it with two small changes.[5]

Sotsial-Demokrat also printed a statement of the Bolshevik Central Committee, drafted by L.B. Kamenev and other party leaders inside Russia, which rejected any alignment of Russian workers with the Entente powers. "While fully bearing in mind the antidemocratic nature of Prussian hegemony and Prussian militarism," the Central Committee declared, "we Russian Social Democrats cannot forget that no less dangerous enemy of the working class and democracy, namely, Russian absolutism."

Russian victory in the war would bring only misfortune to Russian workers, the Central Committee continued: "Under no circumstances, therefore, can the Russian proletariat march hand in hand with our government, conclude any truce with it, however temporary, or support it in any way." The immediate task during the war could only be to strengthen the independent power of the proletariat and the democratic movement and "utilize the war crisis to prepare the people's awareness, so as to assist the quickest possible realization of the tasks of 1905 by the masses of the people. . . .

"That is why we have the immediate duty of exploiting in every way [tsarism's] difficult situation in the interests of Russian liberty. . . . The true interests of European and world democracy cannot be guaranteed by Russian tsarism, but only by the growth and strengthening of the democratic movement in Russia.

"Thus, from every point of view, history sets us the task of continued struggle against the régime ruling in Russia and for immediate revolutionary slogans. Only in this way will we render a true service to the Russian working class, world democracy, and the Socialist International, whose role must, we are profoundly convinced, inevitably grow in the near future. . . . This war will without doubt open the eyes of backward layers of laboring masses and force them to seek salvation from the horrors of militarism and capitalism only through the realization of our common socialist ideal."[6]

The congress of Swedish Social Democrats that opened November 24, 1914, afforded an opportunity for a face-to-face confrontation between the Bolsheviks and the Organizing Committee. Shlyapnikov, a leader of the Bolshevik organization in Petrograd, and Y. Larin, a Menshevik representing the Organizing Committee, gave greetings to the gathering.

Shlyapnikov and Larin address Swedish Socialists[7]

GREETINGS BY ALEXANDER SHLYAPNIKOV

Respected comrades!

I bring you greetings from the organized proletariat of Russia, and from its class organization, the Russian Social Democratic Labor Party. I wish the Swedish Social Democratic Labor Party success in its work. At the present moment of general collapse, the bourgeoisie of almost the whole of Europe—Western and Eastern—is conducting a policy of armed aggression under the guise of "national self-defense." We Socialists must now raise high our red international revolutionary banner. We must not allow ourselves to be washed away by the waves of reformism, which, in the present criminal war, is putting into practice its theory of the "unity of classes." . . .

We conscious workers did not believe in the possibility of a world war. We turned our hopeful gaze to the West, to our organized brothers: German, French, and Austrian. There we expected to find support and to hear a powerful appeal for struggle against the bourgeoisie's diabolical plot. But bitter reality brought us something else. The government press and the bourgeois newspapers, as well as our countrymen fleeing from abroad, informed us of the betrayal of the leaders of the powerful German Social Democracy and later of many others as well who had considered the matter from the "point of view of national self-defense."

But the general conflagration did not consume our Social Democratic Labor Party. It did not forget the true causes of the present war, which results from the imperialist policy carried out by the bourgeois governments of all countries. By refusing to vote for the war budget the Duma fraction has correctly expressed the will of the organized proletariat. The fraction underscored its opposition to the war by walking out of the session. Many local organizations (Petersburg, Moscow, Riga, Warsaw, the Caucasus, and others) have issued illegal leaflets on the war.

Our party's Central Committee and its central organ, *Sotsial-Demokrat,* have joined battle against international opportunism. We appeal to all the revolutionary proletarian elements of all countries to join this struggle in the name of the common interests of the world proletariat.

In conclusion, I wish our fraternal party success in the work of its congress. Long live the Swedish proletariat and its class party, the Social Democracy! Long live the International!

GREETINGS BY Y. LARIN

Dear Comrades!

We greet you in the name of the Organizing Committee of the Russian Social Democratic Labor Party, which unites the Jewish Social Democratic Workers' League, the League of Ukrainian Social Democrats, and the Social Democracy of the Caucasus with the Russian organizations led by Plekhanov, Axelrod, and Trotsky, and maintains organizational relations with the Social Democracy of Poland and Lithuania.

However great the material and moral losses the war that has broken out in Europe may bring, we face the future with hope. Life does not end today or this year, and the great cause of the working class will, in the final analysis, undoubtedly surmount every internal and external obstacle in its path. It may well be that during the present war and in its future development the beginnings of a strong upsurge of energy and solidarity will come about in the ranks of the international working class.

The present serious and crucial moment demands from the working class of every country the greatest energy and resoluteness in the face of future chance and circumstance. We Russian Social Democrats, who know from personal experience the bitter fruits of a party split, wish our fraternal Swedish party victory and success. And we trust that in the future it will hold its banner of solidarity and proletarian activity high in all the questions of the day and also the banner of its organization, which constitutes the party's highest blessing and guarantees its further development and final victory.

Long live the Swedish Social Democracy!

Long live international Social Democracy!

Larin's enumeration of the forces supposedly united by the Menshevik Organizing Committee brought a disclaimer from Polish Social Democrats and also from Trotsky, who published a statement in *Nashe Slovo* denying any responsibility for Larin's use of his name or for the politics of the Organizing Committee. The Secretariat of the Organizing Committee Abroad also stated that it did not agree with Plekhanov's position.

Taking up Larin's view on Socialist unity, Lenin called for "unflagging caution against fictitious 'unity', as long as there is an irreconcilable cleavage in practice." Instead what was needed was unity based on revolutionary principles, he believed. "The mighty crisis of socialism as a result of the world war has evoked a supreme effort in all groups of S.D.s [Social Democrats] and a striving to muster the forces of all who *can* draw together on the fundamental issues of the attitude towards the war."[8]

In an article in the January 9, 1915, issue of *Sotsial-Demokrat,* Lenin noted the contrast between the two statements to the Swedish congress, and explained that the Bolsheviks did not favor unity with opportunists.

What next?[9]

by V.I. Lenin

For the first time since the outbreak of war, a representative of our Party, of its Central Committee, and a representative of the liquidationist Organising Committee met at a congress of socialists of a neutral country. What did their speeches differ in? Belenin [Shlyapnikov] took a most definite stand regarding the grave, painful but momentous issues of the present-day socialist movement; quoting *Sotsial-Demokrat,* the Party's Central Organ, he came out with a resolute declaration of war against opportunism, branding the behaviour of the German Social-Democratic leaders (and "many others") as *treachery.* Larin took no stand at all; he passed over the essence of the question in silence, confining himself to those hackneyed, hollow and moth-eaten phrases that always win hand-claps from opportunists and social-chauvinists in all countries. But then, Belenin said nothing at all about our attitude towards the other Social-Democratic parties or groups in Russia, as though intimating: "Such is our stand; as for the others, we shall not express ourselves as yet, but shall wait and see *which course* they will take." Larin, on the contrary, unfurled the banner of "unity", shed a tear over the "bitter fruit of the split in Russia", and depicted in gorgeous colours the "work of unification" carried on by the Organising Committee, which, he said, had united Plekhanov, the Caucasians, the Bundists, the Poles, *and so forth.* . . .

We have before us two slogans. One is: war against the opportunists and the social-chauvinists, who are traitors. The other is: unity in Russia, in particular with Plekhanov (who, we shall state parenthetically, is behaving with us in exactly the same way as Südekum with the Germans, Hyndman with the British, etc.). Is it not obvious that, though he is afraid to call things by their proper names, Larin has in fact come out as advocate of the opportunists and social-chauvinists?

Let us, however, consider in general and in the light of present-day events the meaning of the "unity" slogan. The proletariat's unity is its greatest weapon in the struggle for the socialist revolution. From this indisputable truth it follows just as indisputably that, when a proletarian party is joined by a considerable number of petty-bourgeois elements capable of *hampering* the struggle for the socialist revolution, unity with such elements is harmful and perilous to the cause of the proletariat. Present-day events have shown that, on the one hand, the objective conditions are ripe for an imperialist war (i.e., a war reflecting the last and highest stage of capitalism), and, on the other hand, that decades of a so-called peaceful epoch have allowed an *accumulation* of petty-bourgeois and opportunist junk *within* the socialist parties of all the European countries. Some fifteen years ago, during the celebrated "Bernsteiniad"[10] in Germany—and even earlier in many other countries—the question of the opportunist and *alien* elements within the proletarian parties had become a burning issue. There is hardly a single Marxist of note who has not recognised many times and on various occasions that the opportunists are in fact a non-proletarian element hostile to the socialist revolution. The particularly rapid growth of this social element of late years is beyond doubt: it includes officials of the legal labour unions, parliamentarians and the other intellectuals, who have got themselves easy and comfortable posts in the legal mass movement, some sections of the better paid workers, office employees, etc., etc. The war has clearly proved that at a moment of crisis (and the imperialist era will undoubtedly be one of all kinds of crises) a sizable mass of opportunists, supported and often directly guided by the bourgeoisie (this is of particular importance!), go over to the latter's camp, betray socialism, damage the workers' cause, and attempt to ruin it. In every crisis the bourgeoisie will always aid the opportunists, will always try to suppress the revolutionary section of the proletariat, stopping short of nothing and employing the most unlawful and savage *military* measures. The opportunists are bourgeois enemies of the proletarian revolution, who in peaceful times carry on their bourgeois work in secret, concealing themselves within the workers' parties, while in times of crisis they *immediately* prove to be open allies of the *entire* united bourgeoisie, from the conservative to the most radical and democratic part of the latter, from the free-thinkers, to the religious and clerical sections. Anyone who has failed to understand this truth *after* the events we have gone through is hopelessly deceiving both himself and the workers. Individual desertions are inevitable under the present conditions, but their significance, it should be remembered, is determined by the existence of a *section* and *current* of petty-bourgeois opportunists. Such social-chauvinists, as Hyndman, Vandervelde, Guesde, Plekhanov and Kautsky, would be of no significance whatever if their spineless and banal speeches in defence of bourgeois patriotism were not taken up by the entire social strata of opportunists and by swarms of bourgeois papers and bourgeois politicians.

Typical of the socialist parties of the epoch of the Second International was one that tolerated in its midst an opportunism built up in decades of the "peaceful" period, an opportunism that kept itself secret, adapting itself to the revolutionary workers, *borrowing* their Marxist terminology, and evading any clear cleavage of principles. This type has outlived itself. If the war ends in 1915, will any thinking socialist be found willing to begin, in 1916, restoring the workers' parties *together* with the opportunists, *knowing from experience* that in any new crisis all of them *to a man* (plus many other spineless and muddle-headed people) will be for the bourgeoisie, who will of course find a pretext to ban any talk of class hatred and the class struggle?

In Italy, the party was the exception for the period of the Second International; the opportunists, headed by Bissolati, were expelled from the party. In the present crisis, the results have proved *excellent:* people of various trends of opinion have not deceived the workers or blinded them with pearls of eloquence regarding "unity"; each of them followed his own road. The opportunists (and deserters from the workers' party such as Mussolini) practised social-chauvinism, lauding (as Plekhanov did) "gallant Belgium", thereby shielding the policies, not of a gallant, but of a bourgeois Italy, which would plunder the Ukraine and Galicia . . . I mean, Albania, Tunisia, etc., etc. Meanwhile, the socialists were waging *against them* a war against war, in preparation of a *civil* war. We are not at all idealising the Italian Socialist Party and in no way guarantee that it will stand firm should Italy enter the war. We are speaking not of the future of that party, but only of the present. We are stating the indisputable *fact* that the workers in most European countries have been *deceived by the fictitious unity* of the opportunists and the revolutionaries, Italy being the happy exception, a country where no such deception exists at present. What was a happy exception for the Second International should and *shall* become the rule for the Third International. While capitalism persists, the proletariat will always be a close neighbour to the petty bourgeoisie. It is sometimes unwise to reject temporary alliances with the latter, but *unity* with them, unity with the opportunists can be defended *at present* only by the enemies of the proletariat or by hoodwinked *traditionalists* of a bygone period. . . .

Some Russian socialists seem to think that internationalism consists in readiness to welcome a resolution containing an international vindication of social-chauvinism in all countries, such as is to be drawn up by Plekhanov and Südekum, Kautsky and Hervé, Guesde and Hyndman, Vandervelde and Bissolati, etc. We permit ourselves the thought that internationalism consists only in an unequivocal internationalist policy within one's party. A genuinely proletarian internationalist policy cannot be pursued, active opposition to the war cannot be preached, and forces for such action cannot be mustered while we are in the company of the opportunists and the social-chauvinists. To find refuge in silence, or to wave this truth aside which, though bitter, is necessary to the socialist, is detrimental and ruinous to the working-class movement.

A fuller statement of the view of the Menshevik Organizing Committee was made to a conference of Scandinavian and Dutch Social Democratic parties meeting in Copenhagen, January 17–18, 1915. Its survey of the views of Russian Social Democrats, while omitting the positions of the Bolsheviks, details several Menshevik viewpoints.

Russian Social Democrats and the war[11]

Organizing Committee [Mensheviks], RSDLP

The conditions under which Russian Social Democrats live must be considered, particularly now that the country is ruled by martial law. This is necessary in order to understand the difficulty of speaking about the attitude of the party as a whole toward the new questions generated by the war. That is why we are compelled to concentrate on the clearly expressed sentiments and opinions of separate organizations and groups.

First, it can be definitely stated that the overwhelming majority of Russian Social Democrats are convinced that only the re-establishment of the International and the organized international proletariat's efforts can solve the questions raised by the war in the interests of the proletariat and the democracy. Only in this way can the proletariat assure its interests when the war ends. Consequently, the ranks of Russian Social Democracy have been warmly sympathetic toward the calling of an international Socialist conference as the first step along that road. It is only political conditions in Russia that prevent Russian Social Democrats from taking as active a part in this conference as they would wish.

An overwhelming majority of Russian Social Democrats likewise support the demand for an early end to the war and the conclusion of peace. As far as can be determined, two currents exist on the question of the demands the international proletariat should advance when the war ends. One current proposes as a slogan that the people's democratically elected representatives participate in working out peace terms. It also calls for disarmament, arbitration courts, repudiation of forcible seizure of foreign territories, and self-determination of different regions through plebiscites. The second current, while supporting these slogans, considers that the International should resolve the question of the fate of disputed areas and the state formations of the various powers (Austria, Germany, Russia).

It is the assessment of the causes of this war and the evaluation of its possible consequences that arouses the most disputes. Some advance general causes resulting from capitalist competition among various countries as being the most important. From that point of view they consider unimportant the degree of responsibility of the individual nations for the outbreak of the war. Others, without denying the general causes, consider it necessary to emphasize the specific characteristics of German militarism and Prussian junkerism, which they believe to be chiefly responsible for the war. The adherents of this view believe Germany's defeat will guarantee a democratic revolution in Germany and clear the way to further conquests by democracy and by the Social Democratic movement in all Europe. Accordingly, they consider that this war, to the extent it inflicts blows on German militarism and Prussian junkerism, has progressive elements.

Meanwhile the adherents of the first point of view, who include the majority of the Organizing Committee, consider it impossible to connect the success of the democratic and socialist movements with the victory or defeat of one or another coalition in the present war. They emphasize that a Russian victory over Germany would entail the danger of strengthening Russian reaction and thus be a menace to the European labor movement. It must be noted that there is also a minority among Russian Social Democrats who, proceeding from this latter view, consider a German victory over Russia desirable in the interests of progress. . . .

PETERSBURG,
JANUARY 12, 1915 (DECEMBER 31, 1914)

The Organizing Committee's open call for the revival of the Second International and avowal of its ties to the Russian social-chauvinists confirmed for the Bolsheviks that merely professing internationalist views was an insufficient basis for Socialist collaboration against chauvinism. Lenin was quick to explore, on the other hand, the possibility of collaboration with non-Bolshevik forces who showed signs of developing a consistent internationalist position. Alexandra Kollontai, formerly a prominent Menshevik, was soon working as part of the Bolshevik team, accepting responsibilities for its work in Scandinavia.

Lenin also remarked favorably in *Sotsial-Demokrat* on Martov's initial stand against chauvinism in the columns of *Golos*. However, Lenin told Shlyapnikov that "I am in deadly fear that Martov (and others akin to him) will go over . . . to the position taken by Kautsky and Troelstra."[12] Lenin's misgivings were well-founded, and he discovered no openings for collaboration with Martov.

Nashe Slovo, which now included both Martov and Trotsky among its editors, took an initiative in February 1915 to explore the possibilities for uniting with the Organizing Committee and the Bolsheviks around a common internationalist platform. On February 6, 1915, a few days before a conference of Socialists of the Entente countries in London, the *Nashe Slovo* group wrote to the Bolshevik Central Committee and to the Organizing Committee proposing a joint stand of Russian internationalists at the conference and a meeting of these forces to prepare such a declaration. Both organizations replied positively.

Welcoming *Nashe Slovo*'s initiative, the Bolshevik reply sought to determine the program on which such a common action could be based.

To the editors of 'Nashe Slovo'[13]

by V.I. Lenin

BERNE, 9.2.1915

Dear Comrades:

In your letter of February 6 you proposed to us a plan of struggle against "official social-patriotism", in connection with the proposed London conference of socialists of the "allied countries" of the Triple Entente. As you have, of course, seen from our newspaper *Sotsial-Demokrat,* we support that struggle in general, and are conducting it. That is why we are very glad to have received your message, and accept with pleasure your proposal for a discussion of a plan of joint action. . . .

For our part and in view of the desire you have expressed, we propose the following draft declaration: . . .

"The undersigned representatives of the Social-Democratic organisations of Russia (Britain, etc.) proceed from the conviction:

"that the present war is, on the part, not only of Germany and Austro-Hungary, but of Britain and France (acting in alliance with tsarism), an imperialist war, i.e., a war of the epoch of the final stage in the development of capitalism, an epoch in which bourgeois states, with their national boundaries, have outlived themselves; a war aimed exclusively at the grabbing of colonies, the plundering of rival countries, and the weakening of the proletarian movement by setting the proletarians of one country against those of another.

"Consequently it is the absolute duty of the socialists of all belligerent countries immediately and resolutely to carry out the Basel resolution, viz.:

"(1) the break-up of all national blocs and the *Burgfrieden* [civil peace] in all countries;

"(2) a call to the workers of all the belligerent countries to wage an energetic class struggle, both economic and political, against the bourgeoisie of their country, a bourgeoisie that is amassing unparalleled profits from war deliveries and makes use of the military authorities' backing so as to gag the workers and intensify oppression of the latter;

"(3) decisive condemnation of any voting for war credits;

"(4) withdrawal from the bourgeois governments of Belgium and France, and recognition that entry into governments and voting for war credits are the same kind of treachery to the cause of socialism as the entire behaviour of the German and Austrian Social-Democrats;

"(5) that the hand be stretched out to internationalist elements in German Social-Democracy that refuse to vote for war credits, and that an international committee be set up, together with them, for the conduct of agitation for the cessation of the war, not in the spirit of the pacifists, the Christians, and the petty-bourgeois democrats, but in inseparable connection with the propaganda and organisation of mass revolutionary action by the proletarians of each country, against the governments and the bourgeoisie of that country;

"(6) support for any attempts by the socialists of the belligerent countries to bring about contacts and fraternisation in the fighting forces and the trenches, despite the bans imposed by the military authorities of Britain, Germany, etc.;

"(7) a call to women socialists of the belligerent countries to intensify agitation in the direction indicated above;

"(8) a call for support by the entire world proletariat of the struggle against tsarism, and for support for those Social-Democrats of Russia who have not only refused to vote for credits, but have shown disregard of the danger of persecution and are conducting socialist work in the spirit of internationalist and revolutionary Social-Democracy."

The Bolsheviks and *Nashe Slovo* were unable to agree on joint action at the London conference, which took place February 14, 1915. Discussion of unity among Russian internationalists, however, continued after the London conference.

An obstacle to this unity was disagreement on how to define the range of "internationalists" to be invited to *Nashe Slovo*'s projected conference. *Nashe Slovo* had invited the Organizing Committee, but not open chauvinists like Plekhanov. The Organizing Committee, however, refused to be separated from its chauvinist allies in the Menshevik camp.

The Secretariat of the Organizing Committee Abroad replied to *Nashe Slovo* that "invitations to the conference should be sent to . . . all party centers and groups that attended . . . the Brussels Conference of the International Socialist Bureau before the war." This proposal would have included even Plekhanov, an open and outspoken Russian chauvinist.[14]

On the other hand, *Nashe Slovo* rejected the Bolsheviks' proposals of how to define the internationalists to be invited to such a conference. While the "internationalists" of the Organizing Committee and the Bund rejected any notion of regroupment that would exclude their chauvinist allies, *Nashe Slovo* rejected a regroupment that would exclude the Organizing Committee. The following exchange of letters sets out the contrasting views of Lenin and *Nashe Slovo*.

Letter from the Central Committee of the R.S.D.L.P. to the editors of 'Nashe Slovo'[15]

by V.I. Lenin

Dear Comrades:

We fully agree with you that the rallying of all genuine Social-Democratic internationalists is one of the most pressing tasks of the moment. . . . Before replying to your practical proposal, we consider it necessary to clarify with frankness certain preliminary questions, so as to know whether we are at one in the main issue. You are quite right in feeling indignant about Alexinsky, Plekhanov and the like having come out in the foreign press, claiming that theirs is "the voice of the Russian proletariat or of influential groups therein". This *must* be fought against. To carry on the struggle, the root of the evil has to be got at. There cannot be the least doubt that there has not been, and there is not, any greater vice than the so-called system of representation of the notorious "trends" abroad. . . . This evil cannot be countered with the aid of some declaration or another. What is needed is a long struggle. For that struggle to be successful, we must say to ourselves, once and for all, that we recognise only those *organisations* which for years have been linked up with the working masses, and have been empowered by recognised committees, etc., and that we brand, as deception of the workers, a system under which a half-dozen intellectuals who have brought out two or three issues of a newspaper or journal declare themselves a "trend", or lay claim to "equal rights" with the Party.

Does agreement exist between us on this, comrades?

Then, about the internationalists. In one of your recent editorials, you enumerated those organisations which, in your opinion, hold an internationalist stand. High on that list is—the Bund. We would like to know what grounds you have to number the Bund among the internationalists. The resolution of its Central Committee does not contain a single definite word on the major problems of socialism. It breathes a most unprincipled eclecticism. The Bund's organ *(Information Bulletin)* indubitably adheres to the standpoint of Germanophile chauvinism, or else gives a "synthesis" of French and German chauvinism. It was with good reason that an article by Kosovsky adorned the pages of *Die Neue*

Zeit, a journal which (we hope you agree with us on this) is now among the most disreputable of the so-called "socialist" press organs.

We stand heart and soul for unity among all internationalists. We would very much like their number to be greater. We must not, however, go in for self-deception; we cannot count among the internationalists people and organisations whose internationalism exists only on paper.

What should be understood by internationalism? Is it, for instance, possible to number among the internationalists those who stand for the International being restored on the principle of a mutual "amnesty"? As you know, Kautsky is the leading representative of the "amnesty" theory. Victor Adler has come out in the same vein. We consider the adherents of an amnesty the most dangerous opponents of internationalism. Restored on the basis of an "amnesty", the International would cheapen socialism. All concessions and all agreements with Kautsky and Co. are inexcusable. A most determined struggle against the "amnesty" theory is a *conditio sine qua non* of internationalism. It is vain to speak of internationalism if there is no desire and no readiness to make a complete break with the defenders of an "amnesty". The question arises: does agreement on this fundamental issue exist between us? A negative attitude towards the "amnesty" policy seems to have been hinted at in your newspaper. You will, however, agree that before any practical steps can be made we are entitled to ask you to let us know in detail how you regard this issue.

Connected with this is the question of the attitude towards the Organising Committee. In our very first letter to you, we considered it necessary to tell you quite frankly that there are serious grounds to doubt the internationalism of that body. You have not made any attempt to dispel that opinion. We again ask you: what facts do you possess to consider that the Organising Committee adheres to an internationalist stand? It cannot be positively denied that Axelrod's stand, set forth on several occasions in print, is patently chauvinist (almost Plekhanovite). Axelrod is without doubt the Organising Committee's leading representative. Further, consider the Organising Committee's official statements. Its report to the Copenhagen Conference was couched in a vein that led to its being published by the most extreme chauvinists in Germany. Statements by the Organising Committee's "Secretariat Abroad" are much the same. At best, they say nothing that is definite. On the other hand, Larin—officially, on behalf of the Organising Committee and not of some kind of secretariat abroad—has made statements designed to defend chauvinism. What is there internationalist about this? Is it not clear that the Organising Committee adheres completely to the standpoint of a mutual "amnesty"?

Furthermore, what guarantees are there that the Organising Committee represents some force in Russia? Today, following the statement in *Nasha Zarya,* this question is most pertinent. For years, the *Nasha Zarya* group conducted their line; they brought out a daily paper, and went in for mass agitation of their own brand. But what about the Organising Committee?

We all acknowledge that the issue will be settled, not by the alignment of forces in groups abroad—in Zurich, Paris, etc.—but by the influence enjoyed among the workers of St. Petersburg and of all Russia. This should be kept in view, whatever the steps we take.

Such are the considerations we have wanted to inform you of. We shall be very glad to get a detailed and clear reply to all these questions. Then we shall be able to think of what is to come next.

Letter of the editorial board of 'Nashe Slovo' to the Central Committee of the RSDLP[16]

Respected comrades,

Your letter of March 23 recognized in principle the usefulness of coordinating the activities of those Russian Social Democratic organizations that have taken an internationalist position in the present crisis. This principled agreement gives us a reason to hope that we shall succeed in dispelling your doubts about our proposal for action.

This proposal did not put questions of party building or organizational unification on the order of the day. It did not even touch on them. In essence it boils down to calling a conference of those organized forces of Russian Social Democracy that advance in the International the true position of our party, a position that the social patriots are distorting. In order to simplify and facilitate this process of coordination we proposed to start it with the Russian groups (in the narrow sense of the word "Russian").[17] We believe that the success of this first attempt will facilitate extending this agreement to include the groups representing other nationalities. As you can see, the Secretariat of the Organizing Committee Abroad speaks out resolutely in the enclosed letter against this limitation. We still stand by our opinion, but, of course, do not attach any vital importance to this difference.

You ask about our attitude toward the established method for representing various "currents." This method arose in response to the disturbances within the life of our party, and is, of course, abnormal. Certainly the fact that it has been practiced for so long makes it easy for certain irresponsible individuals to speak before the outside world in the name of the Social Democratic proletariat of Russia, and to distort its actual position. Incidentally, for our part we posed the question of a joint declaration in order to prevent such abuse. A declaration of this kind would counterpose what unifies us and what we hold in common to the distorted statements of separate individuals. The areas of agreement have created a common approach among a majority of the Russian organizations in their attitude toward the war and toward social patriotism, despite continuing nuances of difference and persisting estrangement in our ranks.

You express doubt as to whether the Organizing Committee and the Bund, organizations whose activities we propose to coordinate, hold a revolutionary internationalist position. We proceed from the opinion that such coordination is made possible by the principled agreement that exists on the general and basic implications of recent events for Social Democracy. We believe this general and basic framework to be a resolute and unequivocal war against the war and an equally resolute rejection of "civil peace" imposed in the name of so-called national defense, and also the adherence to the Stuttgart resolution with its call for the revolutionary utilization of the war and the crisis it has brought about. The organizations we have approached satisfy these demands and have proved it, both by their activity in Russia and by their unequivocal declarations before the International.

We believe that the Organizing Committee, in the report of its Secretariat Abroad to the Copenhagen conference, gave an entirely incorrect evaluation of the position of the *Nasha Zarya* group, as if this position were not moving inevitably toward a weakening of the revolutionary struggle against tsarism. In saying this, however, we must add that we consider extremely incorrect the viewpoint expressed in *Sotsial-Demokrat* that is ready to turn a partial disagreement on shadings of meaning into a reason for classifying Social Democrats among the social chauvinists. This, for example, has been done with respect to the Duma fraction,[18] even though the fraction did not hesitate to expel Mankov from its ranks for his militarist declaration, when this was required in the interests of political action.

With regard to Russian Social Democracy, as with all the Socialist parties which have generally withstood the chauvinist wave, it is undoubtedly possible to note certain frequent unclear formulations, and insufficiently precise answers to a series of questions raised by life. This is all the more natural, to be sure, since even among those whose internationalism is clearly defined there are vital differences, as for example, on the question of the significance of Russia's defeat. *Sotsial-Demokrat* reveals an unclarified position on the slogan of the struggle for peace, under whose banner all the effective actions of internationalists are now being carried on. But it would be inexpedient for our struggle for an internationalist policy, if we were to apply the same methods to influence an internationalism that lacks definition as we apply to fully defined social patriotism.

It remains for us to explain our attitude toward all those who are already talking about a "general amnesty" after the war. You should not doubt that *Nashe Slovo* considers that the International's revival cannot consist of unifying internationally the nationalist parties which have mutually recognized the fight to furl the revolutionary banner in the name of "national defense." Our newspaper, as you yourselves indicate, has already expressed itself to that effect.

In the interest of the cause that it serves, however, we assume that any far-left group that took a clear stand from the very beginning of the crisis must not hurry to harden organizationally at this early stage those relations from which the group must inevitably benefit, because of the logic of events and of the effects of its own work. Thus when Liebknecht and Rühle went along with the majority of the

German Social Democracy at the beginning of the war,[19] we believe it would have been a mistake had we judged there to be an unbridgeable abyss between them and us and built our party tactics on that estimation.

We cannot, therefore, make a question of principle at the present moment out of one's attitude toward granting a future "amnesty" to the elements that now defend a nationalist position. That would be the basis for splitting with elements that are struggling against social patriotism in practice and as a matter of principle. We stand for the most consistent and *ideological* demarcation of revolutionary socialism from nationalist and seminationalist tendencies, and we assume that revolutionary action today must not be weakened, not even by considerations of organizational unity and of party discipline. Therefore, we think that the revolutionary minority faction, which we internationalists presently represent, must decide the question of preserving or sacrificing unity in each case from the point of view of expediency. That is, the decision must depend on what kind of organizational development would assure it, in every single case, the maximum revolutionary influence on the progress of the working-class movement.

We should like to think that our explanation will clear up your doubts about our initiative, whose success, as we see it, could only promote our common cause of struggle for the triumph of internationalist principles in the workers' movement.

Despite their inability to arrive at a common internationalist program with Trotsky and *Nashe Slovo*, the Bolsheviks made another, more direct attempt to develop joint work with Trotsky. They invited him to become a collaborator in the new theoretical journal, *Kommunist* (Communist), which they were then preparing to launch. Trotsky wrote an open letter in reply, which was printed in the June 4, 1915, issue of *Nashe Slovo,* rejecting the proposal.

Open letter to the editorial board of 'Kommunist'[20]

Respected Comrades,

You invite me to collaborate on the journal you are launching, *Kommunist.* I greatly regret I must decline your offer—all the more so because I consider it extremely important and urgent to work out theoretically the new problems posed by the war and the crisis of the International. And at the same time I am deeply convinced that we Russian internationalists have a general theoretical and political basis entirely adequate for joint work, and in particular, for the struggle against social patriotism in both the Russian workers' movement and the International.

In saying this I do not wish to close my eyes to the serious differences that divide us. Thus I cannot reconcile myself to the vagueness and evasiveness of your position on the question of mobilizing the proletariat under the slogan of the *struggle for peace.* It is under this slogan that the working masses are now in fact coming back to their senses politically, and the revolutionary forces of socialism are rallying in all countries. Under this slogan an attempt to restore the international ties of the Socialist proletariat is now being made.

Furthermore, I cannot possibly agree with your view, now concretized in a resolution, that the defeat of Russia is the "lesser evil." This uncalled for and unjustified position represents a concession in principle to the political methodology of social patriotism, which substitutes an orientation, extremely arbitrary under present circumstances, toward a "lesser evil" in place of the revolutionary struggle against the war and the conditions that generated it. Neither can I agree with the way you pose the question of social patriotism organizationally, which seems to me to be utterly vague and shapeless. It only seems clear and precise because it evades all the practical questions faced by internationalists in their struggle against the social patriots for influence over the working masses.

However, these very serious disagreements, as well as others not mentioned here, would by no means prevent me from collaborating with you on a common theoretical journal. On the contrary, I consider that such a journal, while maintaining a united front in the common struggle against social patriotism, would have to remain open for discussion on questions about which internationalists have no uniformly worked out opinion or where differences exist.

But such collaboration presupposes, in my view, that we share a common interest in truly uniting all internationalists, regardless of their factional origins or of this or that nuance in their internationalism. This would surely rule out in advance any attempt to exploit the crisis in the workers' movement for factional or group ends not flowing out of the needs of the movement or the necessity to influence it in a revolutionary internationalist direction. However, your printed announcement of the publication of the journal *Kommunist* represents for me very regrettable evidence that you subordinate your struggle against social patriotism to other considerations and aims, for which I have no right to assume responsibility.

You declare that you are not alone in the struggle against social patriotism. You identify as your allies in this struggle the journals *Lichtstrahlen* [Rays] and *Die Internationale* [The International] in Germany; comrades Nicod, Monatte, and Merrheim in France; the minority of the British Socialist Party; the majority of the Independent Labor Party in England, and so on. Passing on to Russia, you refer only to the manifesto of the Central Committee and to the conduct of the five convicted deputies [Bolsheviks]. Beyond this you see only "an incipient opposition that expresses sympathy for internationalism and to that extent merits a greeting."

Both this list and this characterization are a clear factional distortion of the real state of affairs. Not only the five convicted deputies, but all the other Social Democratic deputies of the State Duma signed one and the same declaration and defended it jointly. The conduct of the five deputies did not differ from that of the other half of the fraction on any principled question. It goes without saying that no one could perceive in their statements at the trial any step forward in principle compared to the joint declaration of the Social Democratic Duma fraction.[21]

I agree that this first declaration, while an act of true political courage, was not sufficiently precise. But the responsibility for this—if we are to speak of responsibility at all—falls on both halves of the fraction. Meanwhile, the latest actions of our deputies (the speeches of Chkheidze, Chkhenkeli, and Tulyakov) and their voting undoubtedly represent steps forward toward political definition and revolutionary irreconcilability. After the actions of Plekhanov and of *Nasha Zarya*, the Duma fraction [the Menshevik deputies] scathingly rejected all attempts to introduce patriotic corruption into the workers' ranks.

We can and must protest that the Organizing Committee did not find it necessary or possible to totally and categorically separate itself from the influential social patriots in its ranks who had gone over its head in sending declarations to Vandervelde and the Copenhagen conference. We must protest even more vigorously that the Secretariat of the Organizing Committee Abroad undertook the mission of whitewashing this social-patriotic group before the International. But we must not overlook the Duma fraction's expulsion from its ranks of a deputy who drew a practical conclusion from the position of Plekhanov and *Nasha Zarya* [and voted for war credits].

I am proud of the conduct of our deputies as are all the revolutionary elements of the International. I see in them the most important agency today for the internationalist education of the proletariat of Russia. That is why I consider it to be the duty of every revolutionary Social Democrat to support them to the utmost and to strengthen their authority in the International. At best you ignore them, as if they did not exist in Russia's political life; as if after the arrest of the five deputies of your persuasion (I consider them *our* deputies) no authentic and worthy representatives of the working class of Russia were left in the State Duma. While naming and saluting Nicod, Monatte, and the independent English socialists as your allies, you avoid, you pass over in silence, you ignore Chkheidze, Tulyakov, and their comrades.

This way of functioning does not flow from either the requirements of political accuracy or the interests of internationalism. I cannot support those conceptions which lay beneath it.

It is understandable why you include neither *Golos* nor *Nashe Slovo* in the list of your allies along with *Lichtstrahlen*, Nicod, Monatte, Merrheim, and the independent English Socialists. *Sotsial-Demokrat*, with which you declare yourself in complete solidarity, has already recorded the "bankruptcy" of *Nashe Slovo*. Within the limits of this letter I cannot appraise the considerations which permit you to speak of the "failure" of our newspaper. However, suffice it to say that on those questions that separate *Nashe Slovo* from your position, all the groups in the International listed by you are incomparably more distant from you.

This leads to one of two conclusions. First, if the independent English Socialists, Nicod, and Merrheim are your allies, then *Nashe Slovo* is all the more so, and you are silent about it for unprincipled reasons. Second, if they are not your allies, then it may be that you have no allies at all in the International. I am in complete solidarity with the positions of *Nashe Slovo*. I clearly cannot lend my name to an enterprise that starts by appraising our paper as one that has hardly begun "to express sympathy for internationalism" and is already a "failure."

In conclusion, let me express my firm confidence that close contact with the revolutionary elements of the International—and we are moving toward establishing such contact—will prompt you or compel you to broaden your criteria and change many of your evaluations. Upon this new basis, collaboration in common literary undertakings, as well as in common political organizations, will become possible and fruitful.

With comradely greetings.
N. [Leon] Trotsky

Trotsky's letter to *Kommunist* closed for the time being the discussion of direct organizational collaboration between the Bolsheviks, *Nashe Slovo*, and Trotsky. The political discussion among the internationalists in the Russian Social Democracy continued at the

September 1915 Zimmerwald conference and after. The contrast between Bolshevik and Menshevik conduct and perspectives inside Russia under the pressure of war gradually impelled the consistent internationalists outside the Menshevik and Bolshevik groups toward the Bolsheviks. Following the February 1917 revolution, a large number of them, including Trotsky and other key figures from *Nashe Slovo* and the Mezhrayontsi, fused with the Bolshevik Party.

A few weeks before receiving Trotsky's letter to *Kommunist,* Lenin wrote of the challenge facing *Nashe Slovo,* now that the Organizing Committee had clearly rejected participation in a regroupment of Russian Socialist antichauvinists. Lenin emphasized the importance of advancing the movement inside Russia which, in fact, turned out to be the force which would bring about the convergence of revolutionists two years later.

In his article, "The Question of the Unity of Internationalists," Lenin wrote:

"We should be thankful to the Organising Committee for its letter to *Nashe Slovo,* confirming the correctness of our opinion of that body.

"Does that mean that *Nashe Slovo's entire idea* of uniting the internationalists has been wrecked? No, it does not. While there exist ideological solidarity and a sincere desire to combat social-patriotism, no failure of any conferences can check unity among internationalists. At the disposal of the editors of *Nashe Slovo* is the great instrument of a daily paper. They can do something immeasurably more businesslike and serious than calling conferences and issuing declarations; they can invite *all* groups, and themselves start: (1) to immediately evolve full, precise, unequivocal and perfectly clear definitions of the content of internationalism (it being a fact that Vandervelde, Kautsky, Plekhanov, Lensch, and Haenisch also call themselves internationalists!), of opportunism, the collapse of the Second International, the tasks and the methods of combating social-patriotism, etc.; (2) to rally forces for a severe struggle for certain principles, not only abroad, but mainly in Russia.

"Indeed can anyone deny that there is no *other* way towards the victory of internationalism over social-patriotism, and that there can be none? Half a century of Russian political emigration (and thirty years of *Social-Democratic* emigration)—have these not shown that all declarations, conferences, etc., abroad are powerless, insignificant, and empty, *unless* they are supported by a *lasting* movement of some social stratum in Russia? Does not the present war also teach us that everything that is immature or decaying, everything that is conventional or diplomatic, will collapse at the first blow?

"During the eight months of war, *all* Social-Democratic centres, groups, currents and shades of opinion have held conferences with all and sundry, and have come out with 'declarations', i.e., made their opinions known to the public. Today the task is different, and *closer to action:* more distrust of *resonant* declarations and *spectacular* conferences; more energy in evolving precise replies and advice to writers, propagandists, agitators, and all thinking workers, written in a way that *cannot but be* understood; more clarity and purposefulness in mustering the forces for a long-term effort to give effect to such advice.

"Much has been given to the editors of *Nashe Slovo*—after all, they are a daily paper!—and they will have much to answer for if they fail to carry out even this 'minimum programme'."[22]

EUROPE IN 1914
European Allied countries in World War I
The Central Powers in World War I
Neutral countries
ATLANTIC
OCEAN
NORTH SEA
UNITED KINGDOM
London
NORWAY
SWEDEN
Stockholm
DENMARK
Copenhagen
BALTIC SEA
FINLAND
St. Petersburg
NETHERLANDS
BELGIUM
LUX.
Paris
FRANCE
Bordeaux
Geneva
SWITZ.
Marseille
GERMAN EMPIRE
Berlin
Frankfurt
Munich
AUSTRIA-HUNGARY
Vienna
BOSNIA
Belgrade
SERBIA
MONTENEGRO
ALBANIA
RUMANIA
BULGARIA
Sofia
GREECE
Athens
CRETE (Gr.)
POLAND
Warsaw
Vilna
RUSSIA
Moscow
Samara
Kiev
Kharkov
UKRAINE
Rostov
Tzaritsyn
Aral Sea
CASPIAN SEA
TURKESTAN
BLACK SEA
Constantinople
OTTOMAN EMPIRE
Aleppo
Baghdad
SYRIA
Damascus
CYPRUS
PERSIA
Lisbon
PORTUGAL
Madrid
SPAIN
Barcelona
Gibraltar (U.K.)
Tangier
MOROCCO (Fr.)
ALGERIA (Fr.)
Algiers
Tunis
CORSICA (Fr.)
SARDINIA (It.)
ITALY
Rome
Naples
MEDITERRANEAN

Chapter 6

The Bolsheviks in the first year of war

The tsarist military machine suffered a stinging defeat in East Prussia soon after the outbreak of war in August 1914; its losses in prisoners alone came to more than 150,000 men. Other costly defeats followed. Millions of workers and peasants were mobilized as replacements; ultimately, nearly 16 million would be called to arms. Ill-fed, ill-equipped, and ill-officered, the massive Russian army excelled only in staggering casualty statistics. By the end of the war, 1.8 million of its soldiers were dead.

The massive call-up created a labor shortage in industry and agriculture. And it was not only men that were enlisted into the war effort. By 1917 the number of draft horses on Russian farms was reduced by 5 million. The territory under cultivation decreased and food production fell. The army's demands also strained the country's inadequate transport system, causing severe disruption in civilian commerce.

By early 1915 there were food shortages in the cities. Prices shot up. By 1917 the price of bread would almost double; that of meat would increase three times. In 1916 workers' consumption was estimated at only 57 percent of the prewar level.

The tsarist government and the employers utilized the outbreak of war to strike hard blows at the workers and their organizations.

Many workers were drafted at the start, and those exempted because of their skills were placed under military discipline in the factories. The composition of the working class was considerably changed, as those called up for military service were replaced in industry by peasants or others not previously exposed to working-class political ideas. The few unions not banned outright were put under close police surveillance. Most of the workers' social and cultural organizations were closed down. Workers who went on strike were frequently handed over to the police and sometimes sent immediately to the front lines, along with a police letter that was virtually a death sentence. The most militant workers' leaders were in jail or in hiding.

Under these conditions, the number of strikes dwindled sharply: official statistics noted only seventy strikes in the five first months of war, compared to about a thousand strikes in the preceding month of July.

The Bolsheviks were the only party calling for the defeat of tsarist Russia in the war, and so came under especially heavy repression. Simply maintaining the party structure was a constant struggle. Leading bodies of the party, both at the local and national levels, were repeatedly shut down by arrests. In Samara, for example, six successive party executive committees were established and then arrested in one year.

Although driven deep underground, the Bolsheviks continued to function in many parts of the country. In Petersburg, they handed out leaflets in crowded sections of the city. At the railway stations they circulated handbills or stuffed them into the pockets of reservists called to active duty.

The Bolshevik deputies in the Duma helped reestablish the party organization in the early days of the war, using their parliamentary immunity to travel around the country and meet with party members. This ended in November 1914 when the police arrested the five deputies—A.Y. Badayev, M.K. Muranov, G.I. Petrovsky, F.N. Samoilov, and N.R. Shagov—along with six other Bolsheviks.

Despite their supposed immunity, the deputies were charged, along with other arrested Bolshevik leaders, with participating in an illegal organization aimed at the overthrow of the existing system.

At first the government seemed intent on securing the execution of the Bolshevik leaders. Party members conducted a vigorous defense campaign, circulating protest statements in the factories. A few thousand workers were able to hold protest strikes. There were also several mass student meetings. The government was forced to retreat, and content itself with sentencing the accused to exile for life in Siberia.

The conduct of the Bolshevik defendants in court, under such enormous pressure, increased the party's authority. The party leadership, however, felt that there were deficiencies in how the defendants handled themselves. L.B. Kamenev, a member of the Central Committee, and several of the deputies had disavowed the party's position that the defeat of tsarism in the war would aid the struggle of Russian workers. Lenin took up this matter in a review of the trial the following month in *Sotsial-Demokrat*.

What has been revealed by the trial of the Russian Social-Democratic Labour Duma group?[1]

by V.I. Lenin

The trial, by the tsar's court, of five members of the R.S.D.L. Duma group and six other Social-Democrats seized on November 4, 1914 at a conference near Petrograd has ended. They have all been sentenced to life exile in Siberia. The censor has deleted from accounts of the trial published in the legal press all the passages that may be unpleasant to tsarism and the patriots. The "internal enemies" have been rapidly dealt with and again nothing is to be seen or heard on the surface of public life except the savage howling of a pack of bourgeois chauvinists, echoed by some handfuls of social-chauvinists.

What, then, has the trial of the Russian Social-Democratic Labour group proved?

First of all, it has shown that this advance contingent of revolutionary Social-Democracy in Russia failed to display sufficient firmness at the trial. It was the aim of the accused to prevent the State Prosecutor from finding out the names of the members of the Central Committee in Russia and of the Party's representatives in its contacts with workers' organisations. That aim has been achieved. To continue achieving that aim in the future, we must resort to a method long recommended officially by the Party, i.e., refuse to give evidence. However, to attempt to prove one's solidarity with the social-patriot Mr. Yordansky, as Rosenfeld [Kamenev] did, or one's disagreement with the Central Committee, is a wrong method, one that is inexcusable from the standpoint of a revolutionary Social-Democrat.

We shall note that, according to a *Dyen* report (No. 40)—there is no official or complete record of the trial—Comrade Petrovsky stated: "In the same period [November] I received the Central Committee resolution . . . and besides I was given resolutions adopted by workers in seven various places concerning their attitude towards the war, resolutions *coinciding with the Central Committee's attitude.*"

This declaration does Petrovsky credit. The tide of chauvinism was running high on all sides. In Petrovsky's diary there is an entry to the effect that *even* the radical-minded Chkheidze spoke with enthusiasm of a war for "liberty". This chauvinism was resisted by the R.S.D.L. group deputies when they were free, but it was also their duty, at the trial, to draw a line of distinction between themselves and chauvinism.

The Cadet *Rech* had servilely "thanked" the tsar's court for "dispelling the legend" that the Russian Social-Democratic deputies wanted the defeat of the tsar's armies. Taking advantage of the fact that in Russia the Social-Democrats are tied hand and foot in their activities, the Cadets are pretending to take seriously the so-called "conflict" between the Party and the Duma group, and declare that the accused gave their evidence without the least compulsion. What innocent babes? They pretend ignorance of the threat of a court-martial and the death sentence that hung over the deputies in the early stage of the trial.

The comrades should have refused to give evidence concerning the illegal organisation, and, in view of the historic importance of the moment, they should have taken advantage of a public trial to openly set forth the Social-Democratic views, which are hostile, not only to tsarism in general, but also to social-chauvinism of all and every shade.

Let the government and bourgeois press wrathfully attack

the R.S.D.L. group; let the Social-Revolutionaries, liquidators and social-chauvinists (who must fight us somehow, if they cannot fight us on the issue of principles!) with gleeful malice "discover" signs of weakness or of fictitious "disagreement with the Central Committee". The Party of the revolutionary proletariat is strong enough to openly criticise itself, and unequivocally call mistakes and weaknesses by their proper names. The class-conscious workers of Russia have created a party and have placed in the forefront an advance contingent which, during a world war and the worldwide collapse of international opportunism have revealed more than anyone else the ability to perform their duty as internationalist revolutionary Social-Democrats. The road we have been travelling has been tested by the greatest of all crises, and has proved, over and over again, the only correct road. We shall follow it still more firmly and resolutely; we shall throw out fresh advance contingents, and shall see to it that they not only carry out the same work, but carry it through more correctly.

Secondly, the trial has revealed a picture without precedent in world socialism—that of *revolutionary* Social-Democracy making use of parliamentarianism. More than any speeches, this example will appeal to the minds and hearts of the proletarian masses; more convincingly than any arguments, it will refute the legalist opportunists and anarchist phrase-mongers. The report on Muranov's illegal work and Petrovsky's notes will long remain a model of *that* kind of work carried out by our deputies,[2] which we have had diligently to conceal, and the meaning of which will give all class-conscious workers in Russia more and more food for thought. At a time when nearly all "socialist" (forgive the debasement of the word!) deputies in Europe have proved chauvinists and servants of chauvinists, when the famous "Europeanism" that once charmed our liberals and liquidators has proved an obtuse habitude of slavish legality, there was to be found in Russia a workers' party whose deputies excelled, not in high-flown speech, or being "received" in bourgeois, intellectualist salons, or in the business acumen of the "European" lawyer and parliamentarian, but in ties with the working masses, in dedicated work among the masses, in carrying on modest, unpretentious, arduous, thankless and highly dangerous duties of illegal propagandists and organisers. To climb higher, towards the rank of a deputy or minister influential in "society" such has been the *actual* meaning of "European" (i.e., servile) "socialist" parliamentarism. To go into the midst of the masses, to help enlighten and unite the exploited and the oppressed—such is the slogan advanced by the examples set by Muranov and Petrovsky.

This slogan will acquire historic significance. In no country in the world will a single thinking worker agree to confine himself to the old legality of bourgeois parliamentarism, when that legality has been abolished with a stroke of the pen in all the advanced countries, and has led to merely a closer actual alliance between the opportunists and the bourgeoisie. Whoever dreams of "unity" between revolutionary Social-Democratic legalists of yesterday, and *of today*, has learned nothing and forgotten everything, and is in fact an ally of the bourgeoisie and an enemy of the proletariat. Whoever has to this day failed to realise why the R.S.D.L. group broke away from the Social-Democratic group that was making its peace with legalism and opportunism can now learn a lesson from the activities of Muranov and Petrovsky as described in the report on the trial. It was *not only* by these two deputies that this work was conducted, and only hopelessly naïve people can dream of a compatibility between such work and a "friendly and tolerant attitude" towards *Nasha Zarya* or *Severnaya Rabochaya Gazeta*, towards *Sovremennik*, the Organising Committee, or the Bund.

Does the government hope to intimidate the workers

by sending the members of the R.S.D.L. group to Siberia? They will find themselves mistaken. The workers will not be intimidated, but will the better understand their aims, those of a workers' party as distinct from the liquidators and the social-chauvinists. The workers will learn to elect to the Duma only men such as the members of the R.S.D.L. group, and for similar and ever more extensive work, such that will be conducted among the masses with still more *secrecy*. Does the government intend to do away with "illegal parliamentarianism" in Russia? They will merely consolidate the links between the proletariat *exclusively* with that kind of parliamentarism.

Thirdly, and most important, the court proceedings against the R.S.D.L. group have, for the first time, produced open and objective material, disseminated all over Russia in millions of copies, concerning the most fundamental, the most significant and most vital questions of the attitude of the *various classes* in Russian society towards the war. Have we not had enough of nauseating intellectualist jabber about the compatibility between "defence of the fatherland" and internationalism "in principle" (i.e., purely verbal and hypocritical internationalism)? Has not the time come to examine the *facts* that bear upon *classes*, i.e., millions of living people, not some dozens of phrasemongers?

Over half a year has passed since the outbreak of war. The press, both legal and illegal, and expressing all trends, has had its say; all the party groups in the Duma have defined their stands—a highly insufficient index of our class groupings, but the only objective one. The trial of the R.S.D.L. group and the press comment on it have summed up all this material. The trial has shown that the finest representatives of the proletariat in Russia are not only hostile to chauvinism in general but, in particular, share the stand of our Central Organ. The deputies were arrested on

November 4, 1914. Consequently, they had been conducting their work for over two months. How and with whom did they carry it on? Which currents in the working class did they reflect and express? The answer is found in the fact that the "theses" and *Sotsial-Demokrat* provided the material for the conference, and that, on several occasions, the Petrograd Committee of our Party issued leaflets of the same nature. There was no other material at the conference. The deputies had no intention of reporting to the conference on other currents in the working class, because no other currents existed.

Perhaps the members of the R.S.D.L. group were expressing the opinion of a mere minority of the workers? We have no grounds to suppose so, since, in the two and a half years, between the spring of 1912 and the autumn of 1914, four-fifths of the class-conscious workers of Russia rallied around *Pravda,* with which these deputies were working in complete ideological solidarity. That is a fact. Had there been a more or less appreciable protest among the workers against the Central Committee's stand, that protest would have surely found expression in the resolutions proposed. Nothing of the kind emerged at the trial, though the latter, it might be said, did "reveal" much of the work done by the R.S.D.L. group. The corrections made in Petrovsky's handwriting do not reveal even the slightest hint at any difference of opinion.

The facts show that, in the very first months after the outbreak of the war, the class-conscious vanguard of the workers of Russia rallied, *in deed,* about the Central Committee and the Central Organ. However unpleasant this fact may be to certain "groups", it is undeniable. Thanks to the trial, the words cited in the indictment: "The guns should be directed, not against our brothers, the wage slaves of other countries, but against the reactionary and bourgeois governments and parties of all countries"—these words will spread—and have already done so—all over Russia as a call for proletarian internationalism, for the proletarian revolution. Thanks to the trial, the class slogan of the vanguard of the workers of Russia has reached the masses.

An epidemic of chauvinism among the bourgeoisie and a certain section of the petty bourgeoisie, vacillation in the other section of the latter, and a working-class call of this nature—such is the actual and objective picture of our political divisions. It is to this actual situation, not to the pious wishes of intellectuals and founders of grouplets, that one must gear one's "prospects", hopes, and slogans.

The Pravdist papers and the "Muranov type" of work have brought about the unity of four-fifths of the class-conscious workers of Russia. About forty thousand workers have been buying *Pravda;* far more read it. Even if war, prison, Siberia, and hard labour should destroy five or even ten times as many—this section of the workers *cannot* be annihilated. It is alive. It is imbued with the revolutionary spirit, is antichauvinist. It *alone* stands in the midst of the masses, with deep roots in the latter, as the champion of the internationalism of the toilers, the exploited, and oppressed. It *alone* has held its ground in the general *débâcle*. It alone is leading the semi-proletarian elements *away* from the social-chauvinism of the Cadets, the Trudoviks, Plekhanov and *Nasha Zarya,* and *towards* socialism. Its existence, its ideas, its work, and its call for the "brotherhood of wage slaves of other countries" have been revealed to the whole of Russia by the trial of the R.S.D.L. group.

It is with this section that we must work, and its unity must be defended against social-chauvinists. That is the only road along which the working-class movement of Russia can develop towards social revolution, and not towards national-liberalism of the "European" type.

The Bern conference of Bolsheviks abroad

Only with the greatest difficulty did the central leadership of the Bolsheviks, in exile, maintain contact with the party inside Russia. Couriers were required to smuggle material across the border by long and dangerous routes. Yet *Sotsial-Demokrat,* published in Switzerland, filled a high proportion of its columns with news, resolutions, and leaflets from the underground party. The groups of Bolsheviks scattered across Western Europe were alive with debate over the course of party work in Russia.

Delegates representing seven of these exile groups and two comrades who had escaped from Siberia via Japan met in Bern, Switzerland from February 27 to March 4, 1915. One achievement of the conference was to unite the exile groups in support of the party's central organ, *Sotsial-Demokrat;* the group in Baugy-en-Clarens, Switzerland, had been moving to launch its own publication. The other main goal was to take up some disagreements that had surfaced on tasks in the war, and to adopt a resolution on that topic.

One delegate at the conference, Nikolai Bukharin, submitted theses proposing that the outbreak of the imperialist war signaled a new epoch in which slogans for democratic rights would be much less important, at least in the advanced countries of the West. "The center of gravity of the proletarian struggle must shift from the sphere of struggle in favor of general democratic demands to the sphere of socialist demands of the proletariat—socialist in the narrow sense of the word," Bukharin said.[3] While these theses did not suggest such a shift for Russia, Bukharin did propose to reject one key democratic slogan there: self-determination of oppressed nations in the tsarist empire.

Bukharin found no support for his viewpoint at the conference, although discussion on these questions continued until the 1917 revolution. He joined with two other delegates from Baugy-en-Clarens to present a proposal on party tasks. It contained only a hint of the criticisms in Bukharin's theses, but raised strong hesitations around the way in which Lenin had presented the slogan of "civil war" and objected to the "so-called 'defeat of Russia' slogan."

Baugy resolution on party tasks[4]

I. The Baugy group agrees fully with the slogan of "civil war." It is the only correct proletarian slogan that answers the conditions of the new period of imperialist war now opening. We consider it vitally necessary, however, to define the limits within which we can advance and defend it both as an agitational slogan and as a slogan for today.

1. Our group by no means agrees with a conception of this slogan that would reduce its entire content to simply replacing the prevailing policy of "national unity" with a policy of "class struggle" in general. In a revolutionary period the class struggle must take on revolutionary forms. We will consider any other conception of this slogan or any attempt to interpret it differently as its direct repudiation and will strongly protest against it.

2. At the same time, however, our group cannot agree with any interpretation of this slogan that would advance it as the only one possible and to *the exclusion of all others.*

We agree fully with the interpretation of this slogan that appeared in No. 33 of [*Sotsial-Demokrat*], in the article, "The Position and Tasks of the Socialist International."[5] It read:

"The proletarian banner of civil war will rally together . . . hundreds of thousands of class-conscious workers. . . . And this will take place, if not today, then tomorrow, if not during the war, then after it, if not in this war then in the next one." However we cannot agree at all with the following words in the same article: "Down with mawkishly sanctimonious and fatuous appeals for 'peace at any price.' Let us raise high the banner of civil war!"

In the first passage quoted, and developed later in many other articles in [*Sotsial-Demokrat*], Social Democracy's tasks are formulated as *a line of preparatory work leading toward civil war.* "For the capture of political power, for the triumph of socialism" are the concluding words of the same article. This not only does not exclude, *but, on the contrary, includes* other revolutionary slogans, as, for example, the slogan of "peace" and the slogan of a "United States of Europe."

Our group considers that these last two slogans can have very great agitational and revolutionary significance. First, they are not advanced abstractly, but rather connected to the slogan of "civil war" and represent its first stage and initial goal. Second, they are slogans directed *against the governments.* They are aimed at destroying the *Burgfrieden* [civil peace] and transferring the existing proletarian struggle from the realm of mutual hatred and national enmity to the *realm of the proletariat's class conflict with its own government in each country and to civil war with it.* This is especially true of the slogan of "peace" *since none of the governments now desire peace.* (Compare this with the Stuttgart resolution, which also advances the struggle for "peace" as the first form of the proletariat's revolutionary intervention into the war.)

Our group welcomes, therefore, the Central Committee's correct step toward *combining both slogans* in the declaration it sent to the London conference.[6] At the same time, we protest strongly against the simple substitution of one slogan for the other, as occurred in the statement on that conference published in the February 20 issue of *Berner Tagwacht* (Bern Reveille) which caused some perplexity in our group.

We consider that in Russia the slogan of "civil war" cannot be combined with any slogans other than the old fighting slogans of the 1905 revolution.

II. However, our group categorically rejects advancing for Russia the so-called defeat of Russia slogan, particularly in the way it was explained in [*Sotsial-Demokrat*] No. 38.[7]

In the Central Committee's manifesto, as well as in the reply to Vandervelde, this latter slogan is depicted only as a "lesser evil," in the broad framework of an objective appraisal of possible outcomes of the war. The editorial in issue No. 38 says that every revolutionary ought to *wish for* this defeat. Our group believes that this way of posing the question lacks any practical meaning, and introduces quite an undesirable confusion.

If a revolutionary is obliged only to "wish for" defeat, then there is nothing to write about in the editorials of the party's central organ. But if he is obliged to do more than just "wish for" defeat, then he is no longer simply making an objective appraisal. Rather, he is advocating active participation in the war, which would hardly be approved by the editorial board.

Even more unsatisfactory, in our opinion, is the way this question is posed in the third and final section of the article. It argues that defeat is desirable because it may lead to a revolutionary uprising. It is absolutely impossible to carry out this line of argument in life, and we must therefore reject *à limite* [completely] this kind of agitation for defeat. We find this article's evaluation of the situation to be objective, fully acceptable, and correct, but note that it fails to draw a line between this and *agitation for defeat*. We think this is urgently needed to eliminate decisively any confusion and unclarity on this question.

III. In the *realm of organization,* we consider that now the most urgent task is to strengthen contacts with Russia as much as possible and to begin reconstruction work immediately and not after the war. In the sphere of *international policy* the immediate task is to begin the work of reconstruction to found the Third International, initiating and strengthening ties with the left forces of Socialist organizations. We consider this last task so important that we fully accept and welcome agreements with other sections of the Russian Social Democracy that are defending an internationalist position, agreements similar to the one that has already been attempted with the group that puts out the newspaper *Nashe Slovo.*

submitted by Nikolai Bukharin,
N.V. Krylenko, and
Yelena Fedorovna Rozmirovich

A major discussion at the conference was on the "United States of Europe" slogan raised in earlier statements of the Central Committee. G.L. Shklovsky, a delegate from Bern who opposed the slogan, recalled later how the conference set about to resolve the question.

The United States of Europe debate[8]

by G.L. Shklovsky

Our objections to the slogan of a United States of Europe can be summarized as follows: (1) Under imperialism a true democracy is impossible. Therefore, a United States of Europe is also impossible. (2) Furthermore, it is impossible in view of the conflict of interests of European capitalist countries. (3) If it is constituted, it will be formed only for the purpose of attacking the more advanced United States of America.

During the discussion Ilyich [Lenin] answered us that proceeding on the basis of our reasoning it would be necessary to discard a whole series of points from our minimum program as being impossible under imperialism. While it is true that genuine democracy can be realized only under socialism, we still do not discard these points, he said. Further, he criticized us for not dealing in any way with the economic side of the question.

We answered him that the formation of a United States of Europe under imperialism would not be the highest form of democracy but a reactionary union of the belligerent countries—which were unable to conquer each other in the war—for the struggle against America. . . .

Ilyich completely convinced the conference and it voted unanimously for the theses. But he did not succeed in convincing himself. That evening he saw Comrade Radek, who was then living in Bern but did not belong to our group, and questioned him in detail about the opinion of different European comrades on this question.

When the conference convened the next morning, Vladimir Ilyich took the floor and made a statement. "Although we settled the question of a United States of Europe yesterday," he said, "considering that this question has led to differences of opinion within our ranks, and furthermore, that the discussion was one-sided and did not touch upon the economic side of the question, which remained quite unclear; therefore, this question must not be considered as resolved."

He also mentioned his meeting with Radek, who had told him that Rosa Luxemburg also was opposed to a United States of Europe. He therefore proposed to delete from the theses for the time being the point concerning a United States of Europe and to open a discussion on this question in the Central Organ [*Sotsial-Demokrat*], giving special attention to the economic side of the question.

Another conference participant, Yevgeniya Bosh, recalled that it took two days for the conference to work out a common resolution. "Heated disputes took place with Comrade Bukharin," she said. He was elected to a commission along with Lenin and Zinoviev to edit Lenin's draft resolution. "Vladimir Ilyich strove to come to an understanding with him, and finally the resolution of the Commission was adopted unanimously."[9]

Under the impact of the Baugy criticisms on the question of "defeatism," the draft of the resolution was clarified to spell out that the workers not only of Russia but of every belligerent country "must not falter at the possibility of that country's defeat," an outcome that would "facilitate the civil war against the ruling classes."

Another participant considered that the conference "put an end to the ideological deterioration within the ranks of revolutionary Social Democracy which had resulted from the collapse of the Second International. Here at the Conference other principles were elaborated which formed the platform of the Zimmerwald Left and which later on become the basis of the Third International."[10] The following is the text of the Bern conference resolution.

Resolution of the Bern conference[11]

On the character of the war

The present war is imperialist in character. This war is the outcome of conditions in an epoch in which capitalism has reached the highest stage in its development; in which the greatest significance attaches, not only to the export of commodities, but also to the export of capital; an epoch in which the cartelisation of production and the internationalisation of economic life have assumed impressive proportions, colonial policies have brought about the almost complete partition of the globe, world capitalism's productive forces have outgrown the limited boundaries of national and state divisions, and the objective conditions are perfectly ripe for socialism to be achieved.

The 'defence of the fatherland' slogan

The present war is, in substance, a struggle between Britain, France and Germany for the partition of colonies and for the plunder of rival countries; on the part of tsarism and the ruling classes of Russia, it is an attempt to seize Persia, Mongolia, Turkey in Asia, Constantinople, Galicia, etc. The national element in the Austro-Serbian war is an entirely secondary consideration and does not affect the general imperialist character of the war.

The entire economic and diplomatic history of the last few decades shows that both groups of belligerent nations were systematically preparing the very kind of war such as the present. The question of which group dealt the first military blow or first declared war is immaterial in any determination of the tactics of socialists. Both sides' phrases on the defence of the fatherland, resistance to enemy invasion, a war of defence, etc., are nothing but deception of the people.

At the bottom of genuinely national wars, such as took place between 1789 and 1871, was a long process of mass national movements, of a struggle against absolutism and feudalism, the overthrow of national oppression, and the formation of states on a national basis, as a prerequisite of capitalist development.

The national ideology created by that epoch left a deep impress on the mass of the petty bourgeoisie and a section of the proletariat. This is now being utilised in a totally different and imperialist epoch by the sophists of the bourgeoisie, and by the traitors to socialism who are following in their wake, so as to split the workers, and divert them from their class aims and from the revolutionary struggle against the bourgeoisie.

The words in the *Communist Manifesto* that "the workingmen have no country" are today truer than ever before. Only the proletariat's international struggle against the bourgeoisie can preserve what it has won, and open to the oppressed masses the road to a better future.

The slogans of the revolutionary Social-Democrats

"The conversion of the present imperialist war into a civil war is the only correct proletarian slogan, one that follows from the experience of the Commune, and outlined in the Basel resolution (1912); it has been dictated by all the conditions of an imperialist war between highly developed bourgeois countries."[12]

Civil war, for which revolutionary Social-Democracy today calls, is an armed struggle of the proletariat against the bourgeoisie, for the expropriation of the capitalist class in the advanced capitalist countries, and for a democratic revolution in Russia (a democratic republic, an eight-hour working day, the confiscation of the landowners' estates), for a republic to be formed in the backward monarchist countries in general, etc.

The appalling misery of the masses, which has been created by the war, cannot fail to evoke revolutionary sentiments and movements. The civil war slogan must serve to co-ordinate and direct such sentiments and movements.

The organisation of the working class has been badly damaged. Nevertheless, a revolutionary crisis is maturing. After the war, the ruling classes of all countries will make a still greater effort to throw the proletariat's emancipation movement back for decades. The task of the revolutionary Social-Democrats—both in the event of a rapid revolutionary development and in that of a protracted crisis, will not consist in renouncing lengthy and day-by-day work, or in discarding any of the old methods of the class struggle. To direct both the parliamentary and the economic struggle against opportunism, in the spirit of revolutionary struggle of the masses—such will be the task.

The following should be indicated as the first steps towards converting the present imperialist war into a civil war: (1) an absolute refusal to vote for war credits, and resignation from bourgeois governments; (2) a complete break with the policy of a class truce *(bloc national, Burgfrieden);* (3) formation of an underground organisation wherever the governments and the bourgeoisie abolish constitutional liberties by introducing martial law; (4) support for fraternisation between soldiers of the belligerent nations, in the trenches and on battlefields in general; (5) support for every kind of revolutionary mass action by the proletariat in general.

Opportunism and the collapse of the Second International

The collapse of the Second International is the collapse of socialist opportunism. The latter has grown as a product of the preceding "peaceful" period in the development of the labour movement. That period taught the working class to utilise such important means of struggle as parliamentarianism and all legal opportunities, create mass economic and political organisations, a widespread labour press, etc.; on the other hand, the period engendered a tendency to repudiate the class struggle and to preach a class truce, repudiate the socialist revolution, repudiate the very principle of illegal organisations, recognise bourgeois patriotism, etc. Certain strata of the working class (the bureaucracy of the labour movement and the labour aristocracy, who get a fraction of the profits from the exploitation of the colonies and from the privileged position of their "fatherlands" in the world market), as well as petty-bourgeois sympathisers within the socialist parties, have proved the social mainstay of these tendencies, and channels of bourgeois influence over the proletariat.

The baneful influence of opportunism has made itself felt most strongly in the policies of most of the official Social-Democratic parties of the Second International during the war. Voting for war credits, participation in governments, the policy of a class truce, the repudiation of an illegal organisation when legality has been rescinded—all this is a violation of the International's most important decisions, and a downright betrayal of socialism.

The Third International

The war-created crisis has exposed the real essence of opportunism as the bourgeoisie's accomplice against the proletariat. The so-called Social-Democratic "Centre", headed by Kautsky, has in practice completely slid into opportunism, behind a cover of exceedingly harmful and hypocritical phrases and a Marxism falsified to resemble imperialism. Experience shows that in Germany, for instance, a defence of the socialist standpoint has been possible only by resolute opposition to the will of the majority of the Party leadership. It would be a harmful illusion to hope that a genuinely socialist International can be restored without a full organisational severance from the opportunists.

The Russian Social-Democratic Labour Party must support all and every international and revolutionary mass action by the proletariat, and strive to bring together all anti-chauvinist elements in the International.

Pacifism and the peace slogan

Pacifism, the preaching of peace in the abstract, is one of the means of duping the working class. Under capitalism, particularly in its imperialist stage, wars are inevitable. On the other hand, however, Social-Democrats cannot overlook the positive significance of revolutionary wars, i.e., not imperialist wars, but such as were fought, for instance, between 1789 and 1871, and with the aim of doing away with national oppression, and creating national capitalist states out of the feudal decentralised states, or such wars that may be waged to defend the conquests of the proletariat victorious in its struggle against the bourgeoisie.

At the present time, the propaganda of peace unaccompanied by a call for revolutionary mass action can only sow illusions and demoralise the proletariat, for it makes the proletariat believe that the bourgeoisie is humane, and turns it into a plaything in the hands of the secret diplomacy of the belligerent countries. In particular, the idea of a so-called democratic peace being possible without a series of revolutions is profoundly erroneous.

The defeat of the tsarist monarchy

In each country, the struggle against a government that is waging an imperialist war should not falter at the possibility of that country's defeat as a result of revolutionary propaganda. The defeat of the government's army weakens the government, promotes the liberation of the nationalities it oppresses, and facilitates civil war against the ruling classes.

This holds particularly true in respect of Russia. A victory for Russia will bring in its train a strengthening of reaction, both throughout the world and within the country, and will be accompanied by the complete enslavement of the peoples living in areas already seized. In view of this, we consider the defeat of Russia the lesser evil in all conditions.

The attitude towards other parties and groups

The war, which has engendered a spate of chauvinism, has revealed that the democratic (Narodnik) intelligentsia, the party of the Socialist-Revolutionaries (with complete instability of the oppositional trend, which is centred in *Mysl*), and the main group of liquidators *(Nasha Zarya)* which is supported by Plekhanov, are all in the grip of chauvinism. In practice, the Organising Committee is also on the side of chauvinism, beginning with Larin and Martov's camouflaged support of chauvinism and ending with Axelrod's defence of the principle of patriotism; so is the Bund, in which a Germanophile chauvinism prevails. The Brussels bloc (of July 3, 1914) has disintegrated, while the elements that are grouped around *Nashe Slovo* are vacillating between a Platonic sympathy with internationalism and a striving for unity, at any price, with *Nasha Zarya* and the Organising Committee. The same vacillation is manifest in Chkheidze's Social-Democratic group. The latter has, on the one hand, expelled the Plekhanovite, i.e., the chauvinist, Mankov; on the other hand, it wishes to cover up, by all possible means, the chauvinism of Plekhanov, *Nasha Zarya*, Axelrod, the Bund, etc.

It is the task of the Social-Democratic Labour Party in Russia to consolidate the proletarian unity created in 1912–14, mainly by *Pravda,* and to re-establish the Social-Democratic Party organisations of the working class, on the basis of a decisive organisational break with the social-chauvinists. Temporary agreements are possible only with those Social-Democrats who stand for a decisive organisational rupture with the Organising Committee, *Nasha Zarya* and the Bund.

Six months later the party's central organ published an article by Lenin explaining that the slogan of the "United States of Europe" had to be assessed in a world framework, and in light of the movement of colonial peoples.

On the slogan for a United States of Europe[13]

by V.I. Lenin

In No. 40 of *Sotsial-Demokrat* we reported that a conference of our Party's groups abroad had decided to defer the question of the "United States of Europe" slogan pending a discussion, in the press, on the *economic* aspect of the matter.

At our conference the debate on this question assumed a purely political character. Perhaps this was partly caused by the Central Committee's Manifesto having formulated this slogan as a forthright political one ("the immediate *political* slogan . . .", as it says there); not only did it advance the slogan of a republican United States of Europe, but expressly emphasised that this slogan is meaningless and false "without the revolutionary overthrow of the German, Austrian and Russian monarchies".

It would be quite wrong to object to such a presentation of the question *within the limits* of a political appraisal of this slogan—e.g., to argue that it obscures or weakens, etc., the slogan of a socialist revolution. Political changes of a truly democratic nature, and especially political revolutions, can under no circumstances whatsoever either obscure or weaken the slogan of a socialist revolution. On the contrary, they always bring it closer, extend its basis, and draw new sections of the petty bourgeoisie and the semi-proletarian masses into the socialist struggle. On the other hand, political revolutions are inevitable in the course of the socialist revolution, which should not be regarded as a single act, but as a period of turbulent political and economic upheavals, the most intense class struggle, civil war, revolutions, and counter-revolutions.

But while the slogan of a republican United States of Europe—if accompanied by the revolutionary overthrow of the three most reactionary monarchies in Europe, headed by the Russian—is quite invulnerable as a political slogan, there still remains the highly important question of its economic content and significance. From the standpoint of the economic conditions of imperialism—i.e., the export of capital and the division of the world by the "advanced" and "civilised" colonial powers—a United States of Europe, under capitalism, is either impossible or reactionary.

Capital has become international and monopolist. The world has been carved up by a handful of Great Powers, i.e., powers successful in the great plunder and oppression of nations. The four Great Powers of Europe—Britain, France, Russia and Germany, with an aggregate population of between 250,000,000 and 300,000,000, and an area of about 7,000,000 square kilometres—possess colonies with a population of *almost 500 million* (494,500,000) and an area of 64,600,000 square kilometres, i.e., almost half the surface of the globe (133,000,000 square kilometres, exclusive of Arctic and Antarctic regions). Add to this the three Asian states—China, Turkey and Persia, now being rent piecemeal by thugs that are waging a war of "liberation", namely, Japan, Russia, Britain and France. Those three Asian states, which may be called semi-colonies (in reality they are now 90 per cent colonies), have a total population of 360,000,000 and an area of 14,500,000 square kilometres (almost one and a half times the area of all Europe).

Furthermore, Britain, France and Germany have invested capital abroad to the value of no less than 70,000 million rubles. The business of securing "legitimate" profits from this tidy sum—these exceed 3,000 million rubles annually—is carried out by the national committees of the millionaires, known as governments, which are equipped with armies and navies and which provide the sons and brothers of the millionaires with jobs in the colonies and semi-colonies as viceroys, consuls, ambassadors, officials of all kinds, clergymen, and other leeches.

That is how the plunder of about a thousand million of the earth's population by a handful of Great Powers is organised in the epoch of the highest development of capitalism. No other organisation is possible under capitalism. Renounce colonies, "spheres of influence", and the export of capital? To think that it is possible means coming down to the level of some snivelling parson who every Sunday preaches to the rich on the lofty principles of Christianity and advises them to give the poor, well, if not millions, at least several hundred rubles yearly.

A United States of Europe under capitalism is tantamount to an agreement on the partition of colonies. Under capitalism, however, no other basis and no other principle of division are possible except force. A multi-millionaire cannot share the "national income" of a capitalist country with anyone otherwise than "in proportion to the capital invested" (with a bonus thrown in, so that the biggest capital may receive more than its share). Capitalism is private ownership of the means of production, and anarchy in production. To advocate a "just" division of income on such a basis is sheer Proudhonism,[14] stupid philistinism. No division can be effected otherwise than in "proportion to strength", and strength changes with the course of economic development. Following 1871, the rate of Germany's accession of strength was three or four times as rapid as that of Britain and France, and of Japan about ten times as rapid as Russia's. There is and there can be no other way of testing the real might of a capitalist state than by war. War does not contradict the fundamentals of private property—on the contrary, it is a direct and inevitable outcome of those fundamentals. Under capitalism the smooth economic growth of individual enterprises or individual states is impossible. Under capitalism, there are no other means of restoring the periodically disturbed equilibrium than crises in industry and wars in politics.

Of course, *temporary* agreements are possible between capitalists and between states. In this sense a United States of Europe is possible as an agreement between the *European* capitalists . . . but to what end? Only for the purpose of jointly suppressing socialism in Europe, of jointly protecting colonial booty *against* Japan and America, who have been badly done out of their share by the present partition of colonies, and the increase of whose might during the last fifty years has been immeasurably more rapid than that of backward and monarchist Europe, now turning senile. Compared with the United States of America, Europe as a whole denotes economic stagnation. On the present economic basis, i.e., under capitalism, a United States of Europe would signify an organisation of reaction to retard America's more rapid development. The times when the cause of democracy and socialism was associated only with Europe alone have gone for ever.

A United States of the World (not of Europe alone) is the state form of the unification and freedom of nations which we associate with socialism—until the time when the complete victory of communism brings about the total disappearance of the state, including the democratic. As a separate slogan, however, the slogan of a United States of the World would hardly be a correct one, first, because it merges with socialism; second, because it may be wrongly interpreted to mean that the victory of socialism in a single country is impossible, and it may also create misconceptions as to the relations of such a country to the others.

Uneven economic and political development is an absolute law of capitalism. Hence, the victory of socialism is possible first in several or even in one capitalist country alone. After expropriating the capitalists and organising their own socialist production, the victorious proletariat of that country will arise *against* the rest of the world—the capitalist world—attracting to its cause the oppressed classes of other countries, stirring uprisings in those countries against the capitalists, and in case of need using even armed force against the exploiting classes and their states. The political form of a society wherein the proletariat is victorious in overthrowing the bourgeoisie will be a democratic republic, which will more and more concentrate the forces of the proletariat of a given nation or nations, in the struggle against states that have not yet gone over to socialism. The abolition of classes is impossible without a dictatorship of the oppressed class, of the proletariat. A free union of nations in socialism is impossible without a more or less prolonged and stubborn struggle of the socialist republics against the backward states.

It is for these reasons and after repeated discussions at the conference of R.S.D.L.P. groups abroad, and following that conference, that the Central Organ's editors have come to the conclusion that the slogan for a United States of Europe is an erroneous one.

The Russian retreat and the workers' upsurge

Events in Russia in 1915 quickly confirmed the Bern resolution's prediction that military defeat would aid the revolutionary struggle. For the tsarist regime the war had provided a long-awaited opportunity to settle accounts with all its foes—not only the workers' movement, but all proponents of democracy. Even the few trappings of democracy that the tsarist government had accepted in the prewar period were largely discarded. The Duma was permitted to meet for only one day in August 1914 and another three days in early 1915. The tsar assumed the power to rule by fiat.

However, from May to September 1915 a German military offensive inflicted a catastrophic military defeat on Russia. The Russian forces were driven back 300 miles, surrendering an area greater than all of France, and including most of Russian Poland. Three-quarters of a million Russian soldiers were taken prisoner. Ten million civilian refugees fled the battle zones, helping to spread word of the debacle.

Under pressure, the tsar shuffled the most notorious reactionaries out of his cabinet and called the Duma into session in August. Most of the capitalist parties united in a "Progressive Bloc," which held a majority in the Duma and demanded internal reforms and a reorganization of the government to allow a more effective war effort. The tsar responded in September by dismissing the Duma and, for the first time since its creation, setting no date for it to reconvene. Some currents in the bourgeoisie now began toying with the notion of a patriotic revolution to replace tsarist rule with a strong government they hoped could win the war.

In May 1915, the capitalists set up what were called War Industries Committees to step up production for the war effort, and in July it was decided to include workers' representatives. While the Mensheviks and Socialist Revolutionaries decided to participate in these committees, the Bolsheviks called for a boycott, in line with their refusal to support the war effort in any way. The Bolsheviks did, however, run candidates in the elections for delegates to the committees to explain their antiwar views to the workers.

The military defeats and obvious government bungling, the shortages and price increases, the enormous casualties, and the repression all fed the workers' anger. Strikes increased. The September 30, 1915, issue of *Sotsial-Demokrat* printed the following account of the workers' upsurge, written by a party correspondent within Russia.

On the workers' movement in Russia[15]

The general picture of the workers' movement since March [1915] is as follows:

March. Large-scale arrests in Petersburg and in other localities, among the supporters of both the Central Committee and the Organizing Committee; *Proletarskii Golos* [Proletarian Voice] closed down.

April. Large protest strikes on the anniversary of the Lena events; four hundred are arrested in Petersburg.

May 1. Thirty-five thousand go on strike in Petersburg; 300 are arrested.

June. Economic strikes in Petersburg, mainly among metalworkers; use of the "Italian" strike[16]; about 15,000 go on strike, 400 are arrested, 300 later released, and the remaining 100 sentenced to various punishments, additionally, thirty were sent to the front.

Kostroma. Strike of the weavers, shootings; fourteen killed and many wounded [on June 18 (5), 1915].

Moscow. Disturbances; twenty killed and wounded.

July. The movement takes on a sharply political character; in *Ivanovo-Voznesensk* a strike (led by supporters of the Central Committee), accompanied by large demonstrations with banners, singing of revolutionary songs, slogans: "Down with the government!" "General amnesty!", etc.; 100 killed and forty wounded [on August 23 (10), 1915].

Beginning of August. Large protest strikes against the massacre in Ivanovo-Voznesensk; 15,000 strike in Petersburg; continuous meetings at all the factories concerning the "mobilization of industry," and other questions. The gendarmes and police often do not dare to disperse them, despite their openly "antigovernment" character. At the Putilov Works more than 15,000 workers attend these meetings, at Lessner 6,000 to 7,000; similar meetings at Aivaz, Ericsson, and so forth. In most cases the workers decide against participation in the War Industries Committees. The Liquidators [Mensheviks] (and recently even some "unifiers" [Mezhrayontsi]) stood for and still stand for participation in these committees, with the aim of "utilizing them in the interests of the working class." But the workers saw in these proposals only the aim of drawing them into the alien business of "defense of the fatherland," that is, defense of the economic interests of Russian capital.

Just before the [September 16 (3), 1915] dissolution of the Duma there were many arrests and searches, even in the health insurance fund committees (Putilov Works)[17]; at the same time massive searches in Moscow.

When the Duma was dissolved, the Petersburg Committee and others called a general protest strike, which was intended as a response not only to the dissolution, but also to the government's policy in general. The bourgeois press spread totally false information that this was a display of "solidarity with the Duma" or with the liberals. The slogan was not "Convocation of the Duma," but "Down with the government"; and it was also said that there are no real workers' representatives in the Duma. The strike was to have continued for three days, but when General Frolov issued an order for the strikers to be brought before field court-martials, and so on, the Petersburg Committee resolved to strike for one more day to demonstrate that the workers were not ending the strike on the general's orders. The Liquidators were against this and their supporters returned to work; ours returned to work one day later, as had been decided. Altogether, 150,000 went on strike in Petersburg (not 75,000 as the bourgeois press reported), 25,000 in Nizhni Novgorod [Gorki]; there were big strikes in Moscow, Kharkov, and Ekaterinoslav [Dnepropetrovsk] (in Nizhni Novgorod they struck for only one day).

After these strikes the liberals went on a concerted "pacification" drive, but the workers were not about to be pacified at all. The repression carried out against them, the incredible rise of inflation, and so on, heighten the revolutionary mood.

Recently the Petersburg Committee decided to carry out agitation for the convocation of a workers' parliament as a counterweight to the various bourgeois organizations. The factory representatives and others, elected on the basis of proportional representation in all the cities, must create an all-Russian soviet of workers' deputies, where we think we can obtain a majority. Everyone senses that the revolution is drawing near. We are moving toward a general strike under the slogan of the "Constituent Assembly" and the "three whales."[18]

The Bolsheviks, feeling the rising tide of the coming revolution, called for the establishment of a revolutionary government of the workers and peasants. A resolution of the party organization in the industrial region of the Ural mountains, adopted at its September 1915 conference, defined these central tasks of the revolution as follows:

"The immediate political tasks facing all the democratic classes of Russia—the proletariat, the peasantry, and the urban democratic forces—are to bring the war to an end on democratic principles and to fully democratize Russia's political structure (a democratic republic, the eight-hour workday, the confiscation of the landlords' estates, and so on).

"This raises the struggle for power, for the dictatorship of the proletariat and the peasantry as the next tactical task. This can be accomplished only by a popular revolutionary insurrection, for only the victory of the revolutionary people (a provisional revolutionary government, a constituent assembly) guarantees them both the end of the war on a democratic basis and a democratic republic within the country. Only a victorious revolutionary people embodied in a provisional revolutionary government, or, even more, in an all-people's constituent assembly, can come to an agreement with the peoples of Central Europe over the heads of the German and Austro-Hungarian governments on the terms for a democratic peace. And at the same time only an all-people's constituent assembly can organize and consolidate a democratic republic in Russia.

"Thus the slogan 'All-People's Constituent Assembly,' is the immediate slogan of the political struggle of the working class and of all the democratic forces for ending the war on the basis of a democratic peace and organizing a democratic republic within the country."[19]

The conclusion of a leaflet by the Petersburg Bolshevik Party committee from the summer of 1915 reflects the spirit of anticipation of those days.

"Comrades workers and soldiers! The moment is approaching when the betrayers of the people will for a second time face our terrible justice. The time is coming when the people will assemble their mighty regenerative strength and strike against their age-old foe: the government and the capitalists. We must swiftly undertake preparations in every part of our native land to carry out this great and glorious task. Since the beginning of the war the Russian Social Democratic Labor Party has tirelessly summoned you to this work. . . .

"It calls on you, comrades workers and soldiers, to organize revolutionary cells and groups in the army, the factories, and everywhere where there is the slightest possibility. The time is coming when all the cells scattered through the army and the working masses will unite in the powerful and terrible army of revolution, which as it marches forward will sweep away from the face of the land the bloodthirsty tsarist government and the thousands of parasitical bureaucrats. . . .

"Comrades, remember that with every hour the fateful hour of decisive struggle and of the peoples' just retribution draws near. On you, comrade soldiers, the success of the second Russian revolution will depend.

"Down with the war, down with the autocracy! Long live civil war! Long live the democratic republic, the eight-hour working day, and the confiscation of the landlords' estates! Long live the second Russian revolution and its demands! Long live the mighty Social Democratic Labor Party!"[20]

Lenin composed the following draft statement in August 1915 for circulation to party cadres inside Russia as a guide in explaining the imperialist nature of the war and the tasks of revolutionary workers.

Appeal on the war[21]

by V.I. Lenin

Worker Comrades:

The European war has been in progress for over a year. All things considered, it will last a long time, because, while Germany is best prepared and at present the strongest, the Quadruple Entente (Russia, Britain, France and Italy) has more men and money, and besides, freely gets war material from the United States of America, the world's richest country.

What is this war being fought for, which is bringing mankind unparalleled suffering? The government and the bourgeoisie of each belligerent country are squandering millions of rubles on books and newspapers so as to lay the blame on the foe, arouse the people's furious hatred of the enemy, and stop at no lie so as to depict themselves as the side that has been unjustly attacked and is now "defending" itself. In reality, this is a war between two groups of predatory

Great Powers, and it is being fought for the partitioning of colonies, the enslavement of other nations, and advantages and privileges of the world market. This is a most reactionary war, a war of modern slave-holders aimed at preserving and consolidating capitalist slavery. Britain and France are lying when they assert that they are warring for Belgium's freedom. In reality, they have long been preparing the war, and are waging it with the purpose of robbing Germany and stripping her of her colonies; they have signed a treaty with Italy and Russia on the pillage and carving up of Turkey and Austria. The tsarist monarchy in Russia is waging a predatory war aimed at seizing Galicia, taking territory away from Turkey, enslaving Persia, Mongolia, etc. Germany is waging war with the purpose of grabbing British, Belgian, and French colonies. Whether Germany or Russia wins, or whether there is a "draw", the war will bring humanity fresh oppression of hundreds and hundreds of millions of people in the colonies, in Persia, Turkey and China, a fresh enslavement of nations, and new chains for the working class of all countries.

What are the tasks of the working class with regard to this war? The answer to this question is provided in a resolution unanimously adopted by the socialists of the whole world, at the Basel International Socialist Congress of 1912. This resolution was adopted in anticipation of a war of the very kind as started in 1914. This resolution says that the war is reactionary, that it is being prepared in the interests of "capitalist profits", that the workers consider it "a crime to shoot each other down", that the war will lead to "a proletarian revolution", that an example for the workers' tactics was set by the Paris Commune of 1871, and by October–December 1905, in Russia, i.e., by a revolution.

All class-conscious workers in Russia are on the side of the Russian Social-Democratic Labour group in the Duma, whose members (Petrovsky, Badayev, Muranov, Samoilov, and Shagov) have been exiled by the tsar to Siberia for revolutionary propaganda against the war and against the government. It is only in such revolutionary propaganda, and in revolutionary activities leading to a revolt of the masses, that the salvation of humanity from the horrors of the present and the future wars lies. Only the revolutionary overthrow of the bourgeois governments, in the first place of the most reactionary, brutal, and barbarous tsarist government, will open the road to socialism and peace among nations.

The conscious or unwitting servants of the bourgeoisie are lying when they wish to persuade the people that the revolutionary overthrow of the tsarist monarchy can lead only to victories for and consolidation of the German reactionary monarchy and the German bourgeoisie. Although the leaders of the German socialists, like many leading socialists in Russia, have gone over to the side of their "own" bourgeoisie and are helping to deceive the people with fables of a war of "defence", there is mounting among the working masses of Germany an ever stronger protest and indignation against their government. The German socialists who have not gone over to the side of the bourgeoisie have declared in the press that they consider the tactics of the Russian Social-Democratic Labour group in the Duma "heroic". In Germany, calls against the war and against the government are being published illegally. Tens and hundreds of the finest socialists of Germany, including Clara Zetkin, the well-known representative of the women's labour movement, have been thrown into prison by the German Government for propaganda in a revolutionary spirit. In all the belligerent countries without exception, indignation is mounting in the working masses, and the example of revolutionary activities set by the Social-Democrats of Russia, and even more so any success of the revolution in Russia, will not fail to advance the great cause of socialism, of the victory of the proletariat over the blood-stained bourgeois exploiters.

The war is filling the pockets of the capitalists, into whose pockets gold is pouring from the treasuries of the Great Powers. The war is provoking a blind bitterness against the enemy, the bourgeoisie doing its best to direct the indignation of the people into such channels, to divert their attention from the *chief* enemy—the government and the ruling classes of their *own* country. However, the war which brings in its train endless misery and suffering for the toiling masses, enlightens and steels the finest representatives of the working class. If perish we must, let us perish in the struggle for our own cause, for the cause of the workers, for the socialist revolution, and not for the interests of the capitalists, the landowners, and tsars—this is what every class-conscious worker sees and feels. Revolutionary Social-Democratic work may be difficult at present, but it is possible. It is advancing throughout the world, and in this alone lies salvation.

Down with the tsarist monarchy, which has drawn Russia into a criminal war, and which oppresses the peoples! Long live the world brotherhood of the workers, and the international revolution of the proletariat!

Revolutionary Social Democratic work in Russia in 1915 still faced difficulties, but was recovering from the blows it received in the first months of the war. One area where it began to make important gains was among women, who were being drawn into the industrial work force in large numbers. By the outbreak of the war, women made up roughly one-third of the industrial workers, and a still larger portion of those in the textile industry. This increased even further during the war as men were mobilized for military service.

Social Democrats had begun consistent work among women workers during the 1912–14 upsurge. The Bolsheviks organized the first International Women's Day meeting in Russia in 1913. The same year *Pravda* began regularly publishing a page devoted to questions facing women.

The Bolsheviks launched a women's newspaper, *Rabotnitsa* (Woman Worker), in 1914, with the first issue appearing on International Women's Day, when the party again organized demonstrations. The paper was suppressed in July along with the rest of the workers' press. The Mensheviks also began a women's paper during that year.

The Bolshevik paper was supported financially by women factory workers and distributed by them in the workplaces. It reported on the conditions and struggles of women workers in Russia and abroad, and encouraged women to join in struggle with their male co-workers. It urged them to reject the women's movement initiated by bourgeois women following the 1905 revolution.

The situation of women worsened during the war as many became the sole support of their families and necessities became scarcer and more expensive. Women workers took part in many strikes and demonstrations against the economic hardships created by Russia's involvement in the war.

While the Bolshevik Party remained overwhelmingly male in composition, recruitment of women workers in significant numbers began with the 1912–14 upsurge. At the Bolsheviks sixth congress in August 1917, women made up about 6 percent of the delegates.[22]

When the Kiev Bolsheviks distributed their leaflet for the March 8 (February 23), 1915, women's celebration, the workers' movement was only beginning to recover from the blows received since the outbreak of war. Their appeal linked the oppression of women to the suffering of male workers, and to a program for the liberation of all working people.

To the working women of Kiev[23]

Workers of the World, Unite!

Comrades, working women, listen to us, for this matter concerns you deeply. The third anniversary since the Russian working woman followed the example of her comrades abroad and organized her working woman's holiday is approaching. This is the third anniversary since the Russian working woman awakened from a deathlike lethargy, threw off the chains of age-old slavery, and began a resolute struggle for her liberation. For the third year now she loudly proclaims her rights. On her holiday she assembles and reviews her forces, and arouses her backward friends, summoning and organizing them in the struggle for freedom and the brotherhood of the people, for the freedom of women.

Pitiful as the lot of the worker is, the status of the woman is far worse. In the factory, in the workshop, she works for a capitalist boss, at home—for the family.

Thousands of women sell their labor to capital; thousands drudge away at hired labor; thousands and hundreds of thousands suffer under the yoke of family and social oppression. And for the enormous majority of working women it seems this is the way it must be. But is it really true that the working woman cannot hope for a better future, and that fate has consigned her to an entire life of work and only work, without rest night and day?

Comrades, working women! The men comrades toil along with us. Their fate and ours are one. But they have long since found the only road to a better life—the road of organized labor's struggle with capital, the road of struggle against all oppression, evil, and violence. Women workers, there is no other road for us. The interests of the working men and women are equal, are one. Only in a united struggle together with the men workers, in joint workers' organizations—in the Social Democratic Party, the trade unions, workers' clubs, and cooperatives—shall we obtain our rights and win a better life.

Now, in the hard times of world war, the yoke still rests on your shoulders, woman workers. The capitalists, in their pursuit of riches, have started a bloody war, a carnage in which they have incited the workers of different countries against each other. Millions of proletarians have been forced to abandon their personal affairs, their wives, children, and relatives to go and destroy their fellow-workers. Your fathers, husbands, and brothers have perished by the thousand in this cruel, bloody war, a war such as the world has never seen.

They are destroying one another mercilessly, spilling blood not for the freedom and happiness of the working class but in the interests of the ruling clique—the government and the capitalists—for whose benefit millions of people perish, villages and cities are annihilated, and industrial life is obliterated. Thanks to them, hungry families of workers flee by the thousands; flee in vain, searching for bread and work.

"Down with the war!"—the working woman declares on Women's Day.

Down with the war, long live the international brotherhood of the workers!

Comrades, working women, let's get to work! Wake all who are still sound asleep; unite those who are still weak and divided. Call them to the road of struggle for the demands of the whole working class:

The eight-hour workday; the legislative protection of labor; high wages; state insurance for illness, old age, disability, accidents, and unemployment;

Benefits for pregnancy and maternity, full equality of civil and family rights for men and women;

Universal and equal suffrage, direct elections and the secret ballot; a democratic republic.

These must be the slogans of the working woman on Women's Day. Around them she must organize her forces, she must struggle resolutely to carry them through to the end.

So comrades, working women, let's get organized! May Women's Day be the pledge for the further development of the workers' movement. Long live the democratic republic, the eight-hour workday, the confiscation of the land and its distribution to the peasants!

Long live the international brotherhood of the workers against the chauvinism and nationalism of all countries!

Long live the revolution and socialism!

Long live the Russian Social Democratic Labor Party!

Kiev Committee RSDLP

With the military defeats of 1915 and the revival of the workers' movement, the tsarist regime entered into crisis. Lenin wrote the following analysis of the decisive turn in Russia in November 1915.

The defeat of Russia and the revolutionary crisis[24]

by V.I. Lenin

The dissolution of the Fourth Duma in retaliation for the formation of an Opposition bloc consisting of liberals, Octobrists and nationalists, is one of the most vivid manifestations of the revolutionary crisis in Russia. The defeat of the armies of the tsarist monarchy; the growth of the strike movement and the revolutionary movement of the proletariat; the discontent of the masses and the formation of the liberal-Octobrist bloc for the purpose of reaching an understanding with the tsar on a programme of reforms and mobilising industry for the victory over Germany—such is the sequence and texture of events at the end of the first year of war.

There is obviously a revolutionary crisis in Russia, but its significance and the attendant tasks of the proletariat are not correctly understood by all.

History seems to be repeating itself: again there is a war, as in 1905, a war tsarism has dragged the country into with definite, patently annexationist, predatory and reactionary aims. Again there is military defeat, and a revolutionary crisis accelerated by it. Again the liberal bourgeoisie—in this case even in conjunction with large sections of the conservative bourgeoisie and the landowners—are advocating a programme of reform and of an understanding with the tsar. The situation is almost like that in the summer of 1905, prior to the Bulygin Duma, or in the summer of 1906, after the dissolution of the First Duma.

There is, however, actually a vast difference, viz., that this war has involved all Europe, all the most advanced countries with mass and powerful socialist movements. The imperialist war has *linked up* the Russian revolutionary crisis, which stems from a bourgeois-democratic revolution, with the growing crisis of the proletarian socialist revolution in the West. This link is so direct that no individual solution of revolutionary [problems] is possible in any single country—the Russian bourgeois-democratic revolution is now not only a prologue to, but an indivisible and integral part of, the social revolution in the West.

In 1905, it was the proletariat's task to consummate the bourgeois revolution in Russia so as to kindle the proletarian revolution in the West. In 1915, the second part of this task has acquired an urgency that puts it on a level with the first part. A new political division has arisen in Russia on the basis of new, higher, more developed and more complex international relations. This new division is between the chauvinist revolutionaries, who desire revolution so as to defeat Germany, and the proletarian internationalist revolutionaries, who desire a revolution in Russia *for the sake of* the proletarian revolution in the West, and simultaneously with that revolution. This new division is, in essence, one between the urban and the rural petty bourgeoisie in Russia, and the socialist proletariat. The new division must be clearly understood, for the impending revolution makes it the prime duty of a Marxist, i.e., of any class-conscious socialist, to realise the position of the *various classes,* and to interpret general differences over tactics and principles as differences in the positions of the various classes.

There is nothing more puerile, contemptible and harmful, than the idea current among revolutionary philistines, namely, that differences should be "forgotten" "in view" of the immediate common aim in the approaching revolution. People whom the experience of the 1905–14 decade has not taught the folly of this idea are hopeless from the revolutionary standpoint. Those who confine themselves, at this stage, to revolutionary exclamations, without analysing which classes have *proved* their ability to adopt, and have indeed adopted, a definite revolutionary programme, do not really differ from "revolutionaries" like Khrustalyov, Aladyin and Alexinsky.

We have before us the clear-cut stand of the monarchy and the feudal-minded landowners—"no surrender" of Russia to the liberal bourgeoisie; better an understanding with the German monarchy. Equally clear is the liberal bourgeoisie's stand—exploit the defeat and the mounting revolution in order to wrest concessions from a frightened monarchy and compel it to share power with the bourgeoisie. Just as clear, too, is the stand of the revolutionary proletariat, which is striving to consummate the revolution by exploiting the vacillation and embarrassment of the government and the bourgeoisie. The petty bourgeoisie, however, i.e., the vast mass of the barely awakening population of Russia, is groping blindly in the wake of the bourgeoisie, a captive to nationalist prejudices, on the one hand, prodded into the revolution by the unparalleled horror and misery of war, the high cost of living, impoverishment, ruin and starvation, but on the other hand, glancing *backward* at every step towards the idea of defence of the fatherland, towards the idea of Russia's state integrity, or towards the idea of small-peasant prosperity, to be achieved through a victory over tsarism and over Germany, but without a victory over capitalism.

This vacillation of the petty bourgeois, of the small peasant, is no accident, but the inevitable outcome of his economic position. It is foolish to shut one's eyes to this bitter but profound truth; it must be understood and traced back in the existing *political currents and groupings,* so as not to deceive ourselves and the people, and not to weaken and paralyse the revolutionary party of the Social-Democratic proletariat. The proletariat will debilitate itself if it permits its party to vacillate as the petty bourgeoisie does. The proletariat will accomplish its task only if it is able to march unfalteringly towards its great goal, pushing the petty bourgeoisie forward, letting the latter learn from its mistakes when it wavers to the right, and utilising all the petty bourgeoisie's forces to the utmost when life compels it to move to the left.

The Trudoviks, the S.R.s, [Socialist Revolutionaries] and the Organising Committee's liquidationist supporters—these are the political *trends* in Russia which have taken shape during the past decade, have proved their links with the various groups, elements and strata in the petty bourgeoisie, and shown vacillation from extreme revolutionism in word, to an alliance with the chauvinist Popular Socialists, or with *Nasha Zarya,* in deed. On September 3, 1915, for instance, the five secretaries of the Organising Committee abroad issued a manifesto on the tasks of the proletariat, which said not a word about opportunism and social-chauvinism, but called for a "revolt" in the rear of the German army (this after a whole year of struggle against the slogan of civil war!) and proclaimed a slogan praised so highly in 1905 by the Cadets, viz., a "constituent assembly for the liquidation of the war" and for the "abolition of the autocratic [June 3] regime"! People who have failed to understand the need for a cleavage between the party of the proletariat and these petty-bourgeois trends so that the revolution may be successful, have assumed the name of Social-Democrats in vain.

No, in the face of the revolutionary crisis in Russia, which is being accelerated by defeat—and this is what the motley opponents of "defeatism" are afraid to admit—it will be the proletariat's duty to carry on the struggle against opportunism and chauvinism, or otherwise it will be impossible to develop the revolutionary consciousness of the masses, and to assist their movement by means of straightforward revolutionary slogans. Not a constituent assembly, but the overthrow of the monarchy, a republic, the confiscation of landed estates, and an eight-hour day will, as hitherto, be the slogans of the Social-Democratic proletariat, the slogans of our Party. In direct connection with this, and to make it possible really to single out the socialist tasks and contrast them with the tasks of bourgeois chauvinism (including the Plekhanov and the Kautsky brands) in all its propaganda and agitation, and in all working-class action, our Party will preserve the slogan of "transform the imperialist war into a civil war", i.e., the slogan of the socialist revolution in the West.

The lessons of the war are compelling even our opponents to recognise in practice both the stand of "defeatism" and the necessity of issuing—at first a spirited phrase in a manifesto, but later more seriously and thoughtfully—the slogan of "a revolt in the rear" of the German militarists, in other words, the slogan of a civil war. The lessons of the war, it appears, are knocking into their heads that which we have been insisting on since the very outset of the war. The defeat of Russia *has proved* the lesser evil, for it has tremendously enhanced the revolutionary crisis and has aroused millions, tens and hundreds of millions. Moreover, in conditions of an imperialist war, a revolutionary crisis in Russia could not but lead people's thoughts to the only salvation for the people—the idea of "a revolt in the rear" of the German army, i.e., the idea of a civil war in *all* the belligerent countries.

Life teaches. Life is *advancing,* through the defeat of Russia, towards a revolution in Russia and, through that revolution and in connection with it, towards a civil war in Europe. Life has taken this direction. And, drawing fresh strength from these lessons of life, which have justified its position, the party of the revolutionary proletariat of Russia will, with ever greater energy, follow the path it has chosen.

Above, Leon Trotsky, Nikolai Bukharin; below, Karl Kautsky, Emile Vandervelde.

Chapter 7

Birth of the Zimmerwald Left

The secretariat of the International Socialist Bureau (ISB) took no action in the first months of the war to regroup the deeply divided International. The chauvinist leaderships of the Social Democratic parties of belligerent countries obstinately refused to meet in the same room with their counterparts from the other side. Initial probes from outside the ISB at convening conferences of all Socialist parties also foundered. Conferences were organized of Social Democratic leaders from the Entente countries, from Germany and Austria, and from nonbelligerent countries, but no way was found to bring together the parties from nations on opposite sides of the trenches.

The first successful effort to assemble Socialists from the warring nations came from the Socialist women's movement. In November 1914, both Inessa Armand, acting on behalf of the Bolsheviks' women's paper *Rabotnitsa,* and Alexandra Kollontai wrote letters to German Socialist Clara Zetkin, proposing an international conference of left-wing Socialist women. Zetkin was the secretary of the International Bureau of Socialist Women of the Second International and editor of the German Socialists' women's fortnightly, *Die Gleichheit* (Equality).

Die Gleichheit had responded to the declaration of war by reprinting the final two paragraphs of the Stuttgart resolution on militarism and war in large type on its front page. Thereafter, within the limits imposed by government censorship, it continued to speak out against the war. When the censors cut Zetkin's antiwar "Appeal to proletarian women of all countries" from the November 27 issue of *Die Gleichheit,* she had it printed in a Swiss Socialist paper and distributed in Germany as an illegal leaflet.

Zetkin responded positively to *Rabotnitsa*'s proposal. Moreover, she wrote to Armand that women had to "demonstrate decisive influence in the preparation of the founding of the Third International."[1] Few of the prospective delegates, however, were prepared to limit the conference to those ready to break once and for all with the chauvinists and opportunists, so the invitation was made without restrictions.

The ISB and the chauvinist party leaderships reacted to the project with hostility. The German leadership went so far as to prohibit members from attending. The conference had to be organized in secret, as an informal gathering, and kept small. Twenty-nine delegates met in Bern March 26–28, 1915; six women came from Germany, and others came from England, France, Italy, the Netherlands, Poland, and Russia.

The Bolshevik delegates to the conference criticized the draft resolution, for its failure to go beyond a pacifist framework or to condemn the betrayal of socialism by the majority leaders of the old International.

The Bolsheviks proposed an alternate draft. It attacked the leadership of "most socialist parties of the belligerent countries" for "succumbing to the pressure of circumstances" and having "committed a real betrayal in respect of socialism, supplanting it with nationalism." It noted that "imperialism threatens the world with a series of wars, unless the proletariat musters enough strength to put an end to the capitalist system by the final overthrow of capitalism," and that the objective conditions were ripe for socialism in the advanced countries of Europe. "The working woman will attain her aim" of ending the suffering caused by imperialist wars "only through a revolutionary mass movement, and a strengthening and sharpening of the socialist struggle."[2]

Only the Bolshevik delegates—Inessa Armand, Nadezhda Krupskaya, Zina Lilina, Olga Ravich, and Yelena Rozmirovich—and Anna Kamienska, of the Polish-Lithuanian Social Democracy, supported this proposal. The Bolsheviks and Kamienska subsequently voted against the majority resolution. Nevertheless they helped edit its final text and declared their readiness to participate in common actions to promote revolutionary struggle and the fight against chauvinism. The conference manifesto was widely circulated, with 200,000 copies distributed underground in Germany alone. It helped win many women to the struggle against the war and for international solidarity.

Women of the working people![3]

International conference of Socialist women in Bern

MARCH 1915

Where are your husbands? Where are your sons?

For eight months they have been at the front. They have been torn from their work and their homes: youths, the support and the hope of their parents, men in the prime of life, men with graying hair, the providers of their families. They all wear uniforms, live in the trenches, and are ordered to destroy what industrious labor has created.

Millions already lie in mass graves. Thousands upon thousands lie in the hospitals—with mangled bodies, with shattered limbs, with blinded eyes and destroyed minds, seized by epidemics or prostrated from exhaustion.

Burned villages and towns, demolished bridges, destroyed forests, and cratered fields form the trail left by their deeds.

Proletarian women! They told you that your husbands and sons departed to defend you, the frail women, your children, your hearth, and your home. What is the reality? A double burden has been heaped on the shoulders of you "weak" women. Defenseless, you have been delivered up to grief and misery. They threaten to take the roof from over your head. Your children starve and freeze. Your hearth is cold and empty.

They spoke to you of one great brotherhood and sisterhood between the noble and the humble, of a "civil peace" between poor and rich. But the "civil peace" now shows its true face. The boss lowers your wages, the merchant and unscrupulous speculator increase prices, and the landlord threatens to put you out onto the street. The state is miserly toward you and bourgeois charity sets up its soup kitchens while advising you to be thrifty.

What is the purpose of this war which brings you such dreadful suffering? They say it is for the well-being and the defense of the fatherland. But what is the well-being of the fatherland? Should it not be the well-being of the many millions? The well-being of the millions whom the war turns into corpses, into cripples, into unemployed, into beggars, into widows, and into orphans?

Who endangers the well-being of the fatherland? Is it the men of other countries in different uniforms who wanted the war just as little as did your husbands and who know just as little why they should murder their brothers? No! The fatherland is endangered by all those who derive their wealth from the misery of the broad masses and who base their rule upon oppression.

Who benefits from the war? In every nation it is only a small minority, above all, the manufacturers of rifles and cannon, armor plate and torpedo boats, the owners of the docks, and the suppliers of the army. To feed their profits they aroused nationalist hatred among the peoples and so contributed to the outbreak of war. Moreover, the war benefits the capitalists in general. Has not the labor of the disinherited and exploited masses accumulated goods that are denied to those who created them? Denied to them, of course, because they are poor. They cannot pay for them! The sweat of the workers created these goods and now the blood of the workers must conquer new export markets for them abroad. Foreign lands must be colonized where the capitalists can rob the earth of its treasures and exploit the cheapest labor power.

Not the defense of the fatherland, but its expansion is the purpose of this war. Such are the requirements of the capitalist order, for without the oppression and exploitation of one human being by another, it cannot exist.

The workers have nothing to gain from this war but everything to lose—all that is dear to them.

Women of the working class! The men of the belligerent countries have been brought to silence. The war has dulled their consciousness, paralyzed their wills, and deformed their entire beings.

But you women who endure misery and deprivation at home, in addition to the gnawing concern for your loved ones at the front, why should you hesitate to voice your desire for peace, to raise your protest against the war? Why do you recoil? Until now you have endured for the sake of your loved ones. Now it is time to act for the benefit of your husbands, for the benefit of your sons.

Enough of the slaughter! This cry resounds in all languages. Millions of proletarian women sound this call. It echoes back from the trenches where the conscience of the sons of the people rebels against the slaughter.

Women of the laboring people! In these difficult days Socialist women from Germany, England, France, and Russia have come together. Your misery, your suffering have touched their hearts. For the sake of the future—yours and that of your loved ones—they call upon you to work for peace. Just as the will of Socialist women is united across the battlefields, so you in all countries must close ranks in order to raise the call—peace, peace!

The World War has imposed the greatest sacrifice upon you. It robs you of your sons to whom you gave birth in pain and suffering and whom you have raised with effort and worry. It robs you of your husbands who are your companions in life's hard struggle. In comparison to these sacrifices all others are small and insignificant. All of humanity looks to you, proletarian women of the belligerent countries. You must become the heroines, the deliverers!

Unite in one will and in one action! Proclaim a millionfold that which your husbands and your sons cannot yet assert.

The working people of all countries are brothers. Only the united determination of the people can stop the slaughter. Socialism alone is the future peace of humanity!

Down with capitalism, which sacrifices untold multitudes of humanity to the wealth and power of the propertied!

Down with the war! Onward to socialism!

The International Socialist Youth Conference, April 1915

Although the Socialist Youth International had campaigned actively against militarism since its formation in 1907, its bureau ceased functioning when the war broke out. The initiative to call an international conference against the imperialist slaughter came from the Swiss Socialist youth league, in collaboration with the Socialist youth of Italy and those of the Stuttgart region of Germany.

When the official youth bureau declined to organize the gathering, the initiators proceeded on their own. Fourteen delegates—from Bulgaria, Denmark, Germany, Italy, the Netherlands, Russia, Switzerland, and one delegate representing Norway and Sweden—met in Bern, April 5–7, 1915. Youth leagues with a total membership of nearly thirty-four thousand were represented, not counting Germany, where the official youth leadership opposed the conference, and Russia, where no membership figures existed.

The debate focused on the same alternative positions that faced the women's conference. Bolshevik delegates pressed their proposal for a revolutionary course in the fight against the war—but to no avail. By a nine-to-five vote a proposal by the Scandinavian delegates was adopted that youth organizations work to obtain the "recognition of the demand for disarmament in the program of the workers' movement of their country."[4]

The final resolution was passed by a vote of nineteen to three, with the Russian Bolsheviks and the Polish delegate voting no.[5] The conference reconstituted the Socialist Youth International on the basis of this resolution.

A new international youth secretariat was established in Zürich with a young German Socialist, Willi Münzenberg, as secretary. An international day of youth protest against militarism was organized, held for the first time on October 3, 1915, and subsequently on the first Sunday in September. The "Liebknecht fund" was launched to finance the secretariat's work.

Shortly after the conference the secretariat published the first issue of its quarterly magazine, *Jugend-Internationale,* (Youth International). It contained discussion articles by leaders of the revolutionary Socialist current, including Liebknecht and Lenin, as well as news and debate from the Socialist youth movement.

The reconstituted Socialist Youth International did not adopt the positions of Lenin and the Bolshevik Central Committee, positions that were to lay the programmatic foundations for the formation of the Communist International in 1919. Its break from the chauvinist ISB and Social Democratic leaderships in Europe, however, did create a framework for international anti-imperialist actions, and for an international discussion of revolutionary strategy during the war. In a number of European countries the cadres of the Socialist Youth International formed a decisive component of the leaderships of the Communist parties established after 1918. The Socialist Youth International itself was won politically and organizationally to the Communist International.

The following is the resolution of the Bern youth conference.

The war and the tasks of the Socialist youth organizations[6]

The International Socialist Youth Conference held at Bern on April 5, 6, and 7, 1915, and attended by delegates from nine countries, renews the decisions of the International Socialist Youth Conferences in Stuttgart, Copenhagen, and Basel calling on the laboring youth of all countries to struggle against militarism and against war, which massacres the people.

The conference notes with profound regret that the Socialist youth organizations in most countries, like the Socialist organizations of the elders, did not act in accordance with these decisions at the outbreak of war.

The present war results from the imperialist policy of the ruling classes of all the capitalist countries. Even where the ruling classes and their governments characterize it as a defensive war, it is still the result of that same policy, hostile to the people and inseparable from capitalism. *The war is irreconcilably counterposed to the interests of the working class, whose activity against international exploitation it hampers, whose organizations it cripples, and whose vital energy it endangers and destroys.*

The policy of "civil peace" signifies class reconciliation and the abdication of the Social Democracy as a party of proletarian class struggle. Abandonment of the class struggle means renunciation of the vital interests and ideals of the proletariat.

For these reasons the International Socialist Youth Conference raises the call for an immediate termination of the war. It heartily welcomes the attempts made by groups in the parties in belligerent countries and the resolution of the International Proletarian Women's Conference in particular to *compel the ruling classes to conclude peace through the resumption of class struggle by the working class.* The International Socialist Youth Conference declares that young men and women comrades in the belligerent countries have the duty of vigorously supporting this ever-growing movement for peace. The conference expects active support of this campaign for peace from the youth organizations in the neutral states.

The conference protests emphatically the attempts to place

Socialist youth organizations at the service of the bourgeois military youth guards. The sole purpose of these attempts is to divert the working-class youth from their real task: socialist education and the struggle against capitalist exploitation and militarism.

Confronted by the horrible results of this war, which callously uses even young people scarcely past school age for cannon fodder, the conference stresses the need to explain more energetically than ever to the young men and women workers of all countries the causes and nature of the war and of militarism, which always accompany a capitalist social order; to educate them in the spirit of international class struggle; and thus to rally them more firmly and in greater numbers around the banner of revolutionary socialism.

Preparing the Zimmerwald conference

In April 1915 the Italian Socialist Party, in consultation with its Swiss counterpart, sent its parliamentary deputy Oddino Morgari to France and Britain. His mission was to convince majority Socialist leaders in those countries to convene the ISB and to hold an international Socialist conference. He was not successful.

Emile Vandervelde and the French Socialist leaders refused to meet with German Socialists. They argued that an international Socialist conference would obstruct the war for liberty and justice in which their countries were engaged. When Morgari hinted at one meeting that Italian Socialists might proceed without the

ISB, Vandervelde interrupted dramatically, "We shall prevent it."[7] Morgari received a positive response, however, from opposition Socialist currents in Britain and France.

The Italian Socialists' Executive Committee decided May 15 to convene the conference despite ISB opposition. The organizational work was entrusted to Robert Grimm, editor of the Swiss Socialist newspaper *Berner Tagwacht,* and Angelica Balabanoff.

A preliminary organizational meeting was called for July 11. Grimm sent invitations only to those party leaders and party bodies with official standing in the old International. In Germany, for example, he contacted Hugo Haase and Karl Kautsky who had recently made their first limited statement of pacifist dissent from SPD policy. Haase and Kautsky rejected the invitation, explaining that they did not want to act outside the framework of the ISB. Grimm did not invite Julian Borchardt, editor of the German revolutionary Socialist publication *Lichtstrahlen* (Rays).

Gregory Zinoviev attended the July conference and sent the following report to the Bolshevik Party leadership.

Report on July, 1915 preliminary conference[8]

by Gregory Zinoviev

On Sunday, July 11, a preliminary conference took place in Bern to prepare an international conference of the left. We were invited by Robert Grimm. Present were: Grimm (representing the *Berner Tagwacht* newspaper), A. Balabanoff (?),[9] Morgari (of the Italian party), Axelrod (representing the so-called Organizing Committee), Warski [Adolf Warszawski] (representing the so-called Central Committee of the Polish party), Walecki (representing the Left Polish Socialist Party—"Lewica"), and Zinoviev (representing our organization).

Even the composition of this gathering seemed to me (Zinoviev) to be rather strange. Where were the *genuine lefts* of the International? I asked whether invitations had been sent, for example, to the Dutch Marxists,[10] the Polish Social Democratic opposition, the Latvian Social Democracy, the German *Lichtstrahlen* group, and so on. They answered: No, only organizations with official representatives on the International Socialist Bureau had been invited. I asked, why so? After all, this is not an official conference, but a conference of the left! I received the answer to this later, in the course of the meeting as a whole. . . .

Our representative, Comrade Zinoviev, introduced the following three motions:

First Motion: Those assembled declare that they fundamentally agree with the resolution of the Executive Committee of the Italian party.

The assembly resolves: to invite those parties or sections of parties (as well as unions and other workers' organizations) which are prepared: (1) to struggle resolutely against "civil peace," that is, against taking ministerial posts, voting for war credits, and so on; (2) to lead a struggle against chauvinism; (3) to strive for the resumption and continuation of the class struggle and its development into revolutionary mass actions.

Second Motion: To invite to the second conference one representative each from (1) Holland (the Marxists), (2) Bulgaria (Blagoev), (3) Scandinavia (Höglund and one of the Norwegians), (4) Germany—the *Lichtstrahlen* group (in addition to Zetkin's group and others),[11] (5) the Polish Social Democratic Party (opposition), and (6) the Social Democracy of Latvia.

Third Motion: (1) To refer the question of inviting Haase's group to the German lefts (the *Internationale* and *Lichtstrahlen* groups) for their consideration.

Zinoviev proposed the following agenda:

1. Reports.

2. Pacifism or the revolutionary struggle of the proletariat to end the war.

3. Imperialist wars and the revolutionary mass actions of the proletariat.

4. Is a common International possible with the social chauvinists? (The principled basis of a third International.)

After many hours' discussion, the assembly adopted only the first paragraph of the first motion, rejected the second, and tabled the rest. The rejection of the second motion seems especially noteworthy to us. In fact the left forces of various parties are not being invited at all to the decisive preliminary conference. On the contrary, the assembly stated very distinctly that they unconditionally intend to invite people like Troelstra, Branting, and Haase to the conference. Axelrod said that if they did not want to invite Haase, then for him, Axelrod, the question arose as to whether *he* ought to participate in such a conference. Walecki also interceded energetically for Haase.

They did not want to establish contact with the *Lichtstrahlen* group, yet Warski was allowed to repeat the well-known gossip of the gentlemen of the party Central Committee about Borchardt and Radek (Parabellum). In all probability, said Warski, Zetkin will not want to sit in the same room with Borchardt, and Pannekoek has no influence whatsoever on the German lefts. The speaker did not even wish to waste any words on Radek. After all of this, it was clear that the so-called conference of the left will in reality be a conference of the "conciliators" of the "center" with the social chauvinists. It is clear that no one seriously wants to call such a conference.

The final decision on invitations was referred to a second preparatory conference, which was never held. Grimm approached oppositional Socialist groups with invitations, while persisting in his efforts to draw in the German centrists. Kautsky would not come in, but the current led by Georg Ledebour agreed to participate.

Like Kautsky, Ledebour opposed the call for a Third International. Also like Kautsky, he had a pacifist policy toward the war, demanding that the German government move rapidly to negotiate a settlement, but not repudiating national defense. A Reichstag deputy, he had still not voted against war credits. He represented, however, the more active wing of the German centrists. Together with ten other deputies, Ledebour had joined Liebknecht in signing the June 9, 1915, appeal of over 1,000 SPD members, initiated by the Spartacists, which called on the party to break with "civil peace" and resume the class struggle for workers' interests.

According to Zinoviev, Grimm's plan was to convene "not so much a left conference as a conference of the center, with a certain admixture of lefts."[12] The Bolsheviks undertook a vigorous effort to bring the left oppositional groupings to the conference, and to unite them around a common statement that could be proposed there. Karl Radek was enlisted to write a draft. Alexandra Kollontai organized the participation of the Swedish and Norwegian left Socialists. The Marxist group around the Dutch paper *De Tribune* (The Tribune) was contacted.

The Bolsheviks published a pamphlet in German for circulation to delegates to the forthcoming conference. It contained Lenin and Zinoviev's article *Socialism and War,* as well as the Central Committee and Bern conference resolutions. It also included the Bolsheviks' 1913 resolution on the national question, an area where the Russian revolutionists had differences with many of their left allies.[13]

The Polish and Russian left delegates to the conference met beforehand to discuss the left's resolution, and the discussion continued at a meeting of eight left delegates on September 4 in Zimmerwald, near Bern, where the International Socialist Conference was to open the following day. The September 4 meeting established the "Zimmerwald Left," the first stable organizational expression of the revolutionary socialist current coming out of the old International, and the political forerunner of the Communist International.

Eight conference delegates joined in supporting the Zimmerwald Left's resolution: Lenin and Zinoviev for the Bolsheviks, Radek for the Polish-Lithuanian opposition, Jan Berzin (Winter) for the Latvian Social Democrats, Julian Borchardt for *Lichtstrahlen* in Germany, Zeth Höglund and Ture Nerman for the Swedish and Norwegian left, and Fritz Platten of Switzerland. Several other delegates, including Trotsky, attended this meeting, but did not join in supporting the Zimmerwald Left statement.

Both Radek and Lenin had prepared draft resolutions for consideration by the left delegates. On the question of the liberation struggle of oppressed nations, Lenin's draft said the following:

"The socialists, who seek to liberate labour from the yoke of capital and who defend the world-wide solidarity of the workers, are struggling against any kind of oppression and inequality of nations. When the bourgeoisie was a progressive class, and the overthrow of feudalism, absolutism and oppression by other nations stood on the historical order of the day, the socialists, as invariably the most consistent and most resolute of democrats, recognised 'defence of the fatherland' in the meaning implied by those aims, and in that meaning alone. Today too, should a war of the oppressed nations against the oppressor Great Powers break out in the east of Europe or in the colonies, the socialists' sympathy would be wholly with the oppressed."[14]

The left delegates agreed to present Radek's draft, rewritten to encompass many of Lenin's points. Lenin's paragraph on wars of the oppressed nations, printed above, was not included. In addition, Lenin's phrase that Socialists will not shy away "from considerations of the defeat of their 'own' country" was also absent from the Zimmerwald Left's final proposal.[15] The text of this draft resolution is included in the conference proceedings below.

The Zimmerwald conference

Forty-two delegates met September 5–8, 1915, in Zimmerwald, a small town near Bern, Switzerland. There were ten delegates from Germany: seven from the "Center" current led by Georg Ledebour, Berta Thalheimer and Ernst Meyer from the Spartacist current, and Borchardt from *Lichtstrahlen*. Delegates of the Independent Labour Party and the British Socialist Party were not permitted to leave Britain. The French revolutionists Alfred Rosmer and Pierre Monatte were also blocked from attending; two more moderate French trade unionists did attend. The Italian delegates were official representatives of their party; the Swiss came as individuals. The Swedish and Norwegian delegates represented the youth organization of their two countries, and through it, the Socialist Youth International. The Dutch "Tribune" group sent no delegate; Henriette Roland-Holst represented a small independent Dutch Socialist publication. The other countries represented were Bulgaria, Latvia, Poland, Romania, and Russia.[16]

The conference opened with a report by Robert Grimm.

September 5: Opening remarks[17]

by Robert Grimm

The international relationships uniting the proletariat have been abruptly destroyed by the war. This was not simply a superficial break in our previously existing relations; rather, Socialist parties and workers' organizations of various countries abandoned the principles not only of the class struggle but also of internationalism. Today they are marching to the beat of a nationalist drummer.

With the outbreak of the war, national rivalries, which had determined the policies of the bourgeois governments and against which the proletariat had always fought, began to infect the working class itself. This newly created antagonism in our ranks was intensified by the stance of the working-class press, which in various countries put itself at the service of the ruling class and its war policies. These papers have supported the rulers' war policies and, at times, even their goals of conquest. In place of the international solidarity of the proletariat, they have preached a new social gospel—the solidarity of the working class with the nation.

Under these circumstances the International Socialist Bureau could no longer carry out its functions. Normal relations between it and its affiliated parties and associations have ceased. Today the bureau leads a sham existence.

Socialist parties of the neutral countries have attempted repeatedly to reestablish our international ties. They aim in this way to bring the Socialist parties together and lead them toward joint actions against the war and for peace, as laid down in the Stuttgart, Copenhagen, and Basel congress resolutions. . . .

On May 15, 1915, the Italian party Executive Committee met in Bologna to consider the facts at hand. It heard an informational report by the parliamentary deputy, Comrade Morgari, who had conferred with party comrades from both belligerent and neutral countries. The Executive Committee resolved to take the initiative, in agreement with Socialists of other countries, and convene an international conference.

Invitations were sent to all parties and workers' organizations, or groups within them, that were known to have held firm to the original principles and resolutions of the Internationals. These we could assume would be prepared to oppose the policy of "civil peace" and to support simultaneous antiwar action of Socialists in the various countries on the basis of the proletarian class struggle. Backed up by the resolutions of the Italian party Executive Committee, the Swiss and Italian parties entered into negotiations. These led first of all to a preliminary conference among representatives from the belligerent and neutral countries, which took place on July 11, 1915, in Bern.

This preliminary discussion laid out the general guidelines of the proposed conference. It was agreed that it would not aim in any way to create a new International. Rather its tasks would be to appeal to the proletariat for a joint peace action, to create an action center for this purpose, and to work to win the working class back to its historic mission. It was therefore agreed to invite all organizations and groups that are willing to take up the struggle against the war, regardless of principled differences in general social outlook.

[Following Grimm's address, the conference adopted an agenda consisting of procedural points, "reports on the situation in each country; the proletariat's peace campaign; building an action center; financial resources; and new business."

[Grimm, Constantino Lazzari, and Christian Rakovsky were elected as a bureau to lead the conference, and Angelica Balabanoff and Henriette Roland-Holst were elected secretaries.

[Grimm chaired the conference, except for the first two sessions on September 7, which were chaired by Rakovsky.

[Under the credentials report, Ledebour challenged the presence of Borchardt in the German delegation. The matter was referred to the bureau.

[A telegram was read from F.W. Jowett and J.B. Glasier of the Independent Labour Party, saying they had been denied passports by the British government and could not attend.

[A letter from Karl Liebknecht was then read, and received with great enthusiasm.]

Liebknecht's letter to the conference

Dear Comrades,

Forgive me for these few, hurried lines.

I am imprisoned and fettered by militarism and so am unable to join you. Nonetheless, my heart, my mind, and my whole spirit is with you.

You have two serious tasks—a hard one of grim duty and

a sacred one of enthusiasm and hope:

A settling of accounts—an inexorable settling of accounts with the deserters and turncoats of the International in Germany, England, France, and elsewhere. Mutual understanding, encouragement, and inspiration among those who remain true to our banner, who are determined to yield not one inch before international imperialism, even if they fall victim to it. And order in the ranks of those who are determined to hold out—to hold out and to fight, with their feet firmly planted on the foundation of international socialism.

It is necessary to briefly clarify the principles of our attitude to the World War as a special case of our attitude to the capitalist social order. Briefly, I hope, for in this we are, and must all be, united.

It is above all a matter of drawing the tactical conclusions from these principles—ruthlessly, and for all countries.

Civil war, not civil peace!

International solidarity of the proletariat above and *against* pseudonational, pseudopatriotic class harmony. International class war above war among states, against war among states. International class war for peace, for the socialist revolution.

How to wage the struggle must be determined. But only through cooperation, only in actions reinforcing each other from one country to another, building up each other's strength, can the greatest possible forces be unleashed. Only in this way can successes be achieved that are within our grasp.

Our friends in each country hold in their hands a share in responsibility for the hopes and prospects of their friends of every other country. You in particular, Socialists of France and Germany, share one and the same fate. Friends in France, I implore you! Don't let yourselves be caught up in the slogan of national unity. Against that slogan you are immune. But also be careful of the equally dangerous slogan of *party* unity. Every protest against this; every demonstration of your rejection of the semiofficial government policy; every bold avowal of the class struggle, of solidarity with us, of the proletarian will to peace strengthens our fighting spirit. It increases tenfold our strength to work in the same way in Germany for the world proletariat, for its economic and political liberation, its liberation from the fetters of capitalism—but also from the fetters of tsarism, kaiserism, junkerism, and militarism, which is no less *international.* To fight in Germany for the political and social liberation of the German people against the German imperialists' lust for power and territory. To fight for a speedy peace without conquest or the subjugation of peoples. For a peace that would also restore unfortunate Belgium, wedged into Europe's heart, to freedom and independence, and give France back to the French.

French brothers, we are aware of the exceptional difficulties of your tragic situation and bleed with you as with the tormented and tortured masses of all the peoples. Your misfortune is our misfortune, just as we know that our pain is your pain.

Let our struggle be your struggle. Help us as we vow to help you.

The new International will arise on the ruins of the old. It can only arise on these ruins, on newer and firmer foundations. Friends—Socialists from all countries—you must lay the foundation stone today for the future structure. Pass irreconcilable judgement upon the false Socialists. Ruthlessly urge on those in all countries, and especially in Germany, who vacillate and hesitate.

The greatness of our goal will help you overcome the daily trials and tribulations and the misery of these horrendous days.

Long live the future peace among peoples! Long live internationalist, people-liberating, revolutionary socialism!

Proletarians of all countries—unite once again!

Karl Liebknecht[13]

Delegates' reports

[Written reports were received from the Social Democratic Youth League of Sweden and Norway and the left Social Democrats of Württemberg.

[Lazzari and Merrheim gave oral reports.]

GEORG LEDEBOUR (GERMANY): The German opposition is inspired by the idea of carrying out a joint action—especially with the French comrades. Before the war, I personally stressed the necessity for an agreement. At my request, Müller was sent to Paris on September 2 in order to propose a similar declaration in the name of both parliamentary fractions.[19]

The war took the party comrades in Germany by surprise. Demonstrations were held until the last moment. When the party and fraction executive committees met on Thursday and Friday [July 30–31], the predominant opinion was to reject the war credits. The situation changed after Scheidemann and Haase met with representatives of the government. In a highly charged and heated meeting the fraction split into a majority, and a minority of fourteen. The minority did not want to jeopardize the party by engaging in a separate action and so submitted to the majority decision in the plenary session. That is also why Haase read the declaration in the Reichstag.

On his return from Paris, Müller reported that Sembat had said he could give no declaration about how the French fraction would vote. No one knew whether they would agree to grant the war credits or reject them. But they would probably vote in favor. This made the position of the German minority more difficult. We had supposed that the murder of Jaurès would have aroused antiwar sentiments in the French proletariat.

ARTHUR MERRHEIM (FRANCE): I also heard that Müller came to bring about an agreement, but I didn't hear anything about issuing a declaration.

LEDEBOUR: It was definitely a matter of making a joint declaration of both fractions. Of course it was not voted on, but it was more or less the purpose of Müller's mission.

Relations in the fraction became more and more strained. The minority did not want to participate in drafting a declaration. Because of that, Belgium was not mentioned, or rather, Germany's violation of Belgium's neutrality was not mentioned. When the imperial chancellor spoke on the violation of Belgium's neutrality—of which no one knew anything—the declaration of the Social Democratic fraction had already been presented to the government.

(In response to an interruption) It was not possible for the minority to speak out in the Reichstag unless we established a new fraction, and we avoided that in order not to split the party. In wartime it is especially necessary to hold together so that we don't lose influence over the masses. The correctness of this course is shown by the growth of the opposition. In Berlin nine-tenths of the comrades support the opposition. The same holds true among the functionaries. The work of the opposition is made more difficult because of the press censorship, which is continually carving up *Vorwärts* and other organs of the opposition. It is impossible to publish accurate reports about the minority movement. If the press were not so muzzled, the minority in Germany would already have become a majority. On the lower Rhine, in Stuttgart, in Dresden, in Hamburg, in Frankfurt am Main, and elsewhere, the opposition is strong. Most party members in Stuttgart support the opposition, but the majority leadership has a firm grip on the party organization.

In reference to the Südekum affair: a vehement dispute with the party Executive Committee took place because it sent Dr. Südekum to Italy in the assumption that he could do useful work there for the German nation. Earlier, he had been to Sweden privately. A Romanian comrade told us that Südekum had also been in Romania. On behalf of the Ministry of War he spoke with French prisoners of war who knew about the opposition in the German Social Democracy and told them that Karl Liebknecht's position was of no consequence. Südekum refused to give the party Executive Committee further information about the incident, saying that it involved a "discreet mission." Incensed by these events, the minority of the fraction demanded a fraction Executive Committee meeting. When this was refused, I resigned my position as a member of the fraction Executive Committee.

The opposition in the fraction is also growing steadily: from fourteen votes it has grown to seventeen, twenty-five, thirty-three (budget resolution), and thirty-six.[20] The struggle is also being conducted outside of parliament, and rallies are being held. The main thing now is agreement—collaboration with the French opposition. Merrheim is quite correct to stress that it's a time for action, not for recriminations over the past. *(Applause)*

BERTA THALHEIMER (GERMANY): Comrade Ledebour has not spoken here for the whole opposition. There is also a minority within the minority, grouped around Liebknecht. It supports his stance of placing principles above party discipline.

As for action, it is obvious that every struggle for peace carried out today is both a mass and a class struggle. The enumeration of the methods of struggle in Radek's resolution is unnecessary. When you act, you do not enumerate every single method of struggle. It's a matter of what you do, not what you say.

ADOLPH HOFFMANN (GERMANY): There is not a *Liebknecht opposition* and some other one. Nevertheless, it is true that Ledebour has not expressed the entire opinion of the opposition.

JOSEF HERZFELD (GERMANY): Liebknecht belongs to the opposition as a whole. What separates us is simply a question of tactics—of discipline. Liebknecht also has discussed the present conference repeatedly with the opposition. We must emphasize what unites us, not what divides us. . . .

[Ewald Vogtherr also spoke, denying the existence of a Liebknecht tendency. The conference then adjourned.]

September 6

[The second day of the conference began with a discussion of allocation of voting rights. It was agreed that each country should receive five votes, although no vote was actually conducted on that basis. The conference then continued with delegates' reports.]

HOFFMANN: I would like to say a few things in response to Ledebour. He said that we were completely taken by surprise. I dispute this. The masses, however, were taken by surprise—by the fraction's vote. The population had been incited to fear an invasion by "Russian barbarians." It certainly would not have been easy to refuse the war credits in face of such general excitement. Party members took fright before the wrath of the population, and feared for the destruction of the People's Centers. I say, better that our People's Centers be destroyed than our principles. *(Agreement)*

The great majority of the opposition is completely in agreement with Liebknecht, and he should have come to an understanding with it. Had he done this, the number of those rejecting the war credits when they were introduced for the fourth time would undoubtedly have been much greater. It is almost incomprehensible that the minority did not vote against the war budget.[21]

The fraction minority wants above all to avoid an open split with the majority. But they forget that a split in the fraction is not the same thing as a split in the party. *("Very true")* The majority of the masses are with us. Whether or not this will be displayed depends on whether it is possible, after the conclusion of the peace negotiations, to postpone the party congress until after the last man is discharged from the trenches. We must especially avoid holding the next party congress during the initial period of postwar jubilation since it would be controlled by the paid functionaries then. They are simply people who cannot overcome the influences of their social environment. If we can avoid this, we will win.

We should not be working towards a split. It is not necessary in Germany because the masses are radical. It would be therefore foolish to act in a way that would give the party Executive Committee the possibility and the justification to throw us out.

The last vote on war credits, after the annexationist desires of the government had clearly come out into the open, contributed greatly to strengthening the opposition. It was the last straw. The opposition felt that it was impossible for the majority of the fraction to consent again to war credits under these circumstances. Likewise, we thought it impossible that the minority would not now vote against them. . . .

If the German Reichstag fraction had rejected the war credits right at the start of the war, there would certainly have been no ministerialism in France.[22] And even if credits had initially been granted, this shouldn't have occurred repeatedly. We should have simply accepted the unpleasant consequences just as the Italians have done.

If we are successful here in arriving at an agreement then

the International will awaken within a year to a new and effective life. *(Applause)*

PAVEL AXELROD (RUSSIA, ORGANIZING COMMITTEE [MENSHEVIKS]): . . . The German party has always been our teacher. When we got word of the German fraction's vote we couldn't believe it.

LEON TROTSKY (RUSSIA, NASHE SLOVO): We thought that the August 4 issue of *Vorwärts* had been produced by the German general staff.

AXELROD: After that vote, everyone asked, "What can we believe in now?" We were afraid that the German example would influence the Russian workers, but the demoralizing effect proved to be not very strong. Then we heard that Plekhanov had also become nationalist-minded. I myself was affected for some time by the danger for France and the occupation of Belgium, and so, *for a moment,* hoped for some military successes of the Entente, "for Russia." . . .

There is a literary group which believes that a victory of the West over Germany would spell the collapse of European reaction. This group, around *Nasha Zarya,* is inconsistent, but has in no way abandoned an internationalist perspective. Since the beginning of the war, the various groups within Russian socialism have all come out in opposition to the nationalist currents. . . .

An oppositional mood is surfacing again now in Russia. In Moscow, for example, patriotic demonstrations are being turned into antipatriotic demonstrations; everywhere there are strike movements. Even today, after the big victories of the German army, the question of national defense is not at all prominent in party circles.

Nevertheless today there are two different currents within the movement. One current demands that a constituent assembly be convened in order to end the war, and that until such time we must defend ourselves. The other considers it dangerous to combine to some extent the goal of a constituent assembly with support for national defense. It thinks that the main emphasis should be put on the constituent assembly. . . .

We think that the rebuilding of the International on a much firmer basis than before cannot be achieved overnight, through resolutions passed at a conference such as this. Only an international agreement of the proletarian parties for joint peace action will create the necessary preconditions for the rapid restoration and regeneration of the International. . . .

The International will revive and develop, in all probability, through a process of intense, inner-party struggles and the splitting off of some forces. But we put great emphasis on ensuring that this is not accompanied by major changes and splits. . . .

In its September 3 letter to the comrades in Russia, the Secretariat of the Organizing Committee Abroad took a position on these questions. The secretariat sharply criticized the liberal opposition and refused to subordinate the interests and tasks of proletarian democracy to "national defense." It characterized the slogan "war until victory" as not only incompatible with our internationalist principles, but also, at the same time, as a corrupting, misleading illusion. The letter also declared the slogan "national defense" to be an illusion. Russia can be saved from decline only through the destruction of the reactionary regime and the establishment of democratic rule—not through military means. The battle cry of our party should be, "A democratic constituent assembly to end the war and the absolutist regime of June 3."[23] . . .

P.L. LEMANSKY (RUSSIA, THE BUND): . . . All the leaflets which the Central Committee of the Bund has put out in Russia take a position against the war and demand peace without annexations or indemnities, or in other words, with neither victors nor vanquished. In the Entente states it is said that tsarism shed its old skin during the war; however, it is actually more bloodthirsty than ever. For example, the Jewish people, blamed for the military defeat, are being expelled from Poland and southern Russia with unheard-of cruelty. Sometimes these unfortunates are packed into a closed railroad car and sent long distances. In Nosovleisk these railroad cars were kept shut a full ten days; naturally there were dozens of sick among them. This continues in exactly the same manner today.

GREGORY ZINOVIEV (RUSSIA, CENTRAL COMMITTEE [BOLSHEVIKS]): It is presented as if we wanted to create a special Russian policy, but that is not true. We only want to apply Marxist policies to Russian conditions. The legal *Nasha Zarya* is more of a factor in Russia than the *Sozialistische Monatshefte* in Germany, and it is completely in the camp of social patriotism. Axelrod has said that his most fervent desire is a united Russian party. We also want that, but on the basis of internationalism. We cannot possibly fight alongside the social patriots. No one says to the Italians, "build a party together with Bissolati." So no one should say it to us either. Although the mass of the conscious workers in Russia are not infected with nationalism, the position of the German party has had a terrible effect. It was the greatest misfortune that the Russian movement could have encountered.

The movement in opposition to the war is growing. Our Central Committee has staged huge strikes, as in the Putilov works. Although the press is muzzled, many leaflets are published. The social patriots use the slogan, "Revolution in order to triumph over the Germans." In response we say, "Revolution as the first step towards the international revolution."

PAUL WINTER [JAN BERZIN] (LATVIAN SOCIAL-DEMOCRACY): No one abroad has any idea of the extent to which the situation in Russia immediately before the war had taken on revolutionary dimensions. We had four mass strikes in Riga in the last six months before the war, including one of more than 80,000 workers. There were also many mass demonstrations in the streets.

We've carried out extensive work during the war. In twelve months of war we have distributed tens of thousands of copies of forty leaflets. Every recruit who went to war has read them. The party has put out eleven issues of an illegal paper in Riga, and we have opposed the war in the legal trade union and scientific press, as well.

The actions of the German party were the worst blow that could have befallen us. The workers said, "that is the result of bureaucracy."

[After Victor Chernov and Oddino Morgari reported, Leon Trotsky declined to report, explaining that *Nashe Slovo*'s position was well known.]

STANISLAW LAPINSKI ([LEFT] POLISH SOCIALIST PARTY): The conditions under which the revolutionary Polish proletariat works are exceptionally difficult. It is cut in half by the massive armies and its ties to the Central Committee abroad are severed. The economic situation is unprecedented in history; industry has been completely paralyzed for the last year. Half a million factory workers and a million rural laborers are in an indescribable plight. Austrian Poland has been turned into a bloody wasteland. A territory inhabited by thirteen million people is completely ruined—trampled over by armies of millions. Certain cities pass over again and again from one side to the other. This happened to Lodz three times, to other cities as many as five times. The situation in our country is a thousand times worse than in Belgium. *("Very true")*

Nevertheless our working people have remained conscious of their position in capitalist society. They know that tsarism is the same as ever. But they also know that German rule would not change their social situation much. Our proletariat has remained true to its principles and its past, and, in contrast to what occurred in Belgium, has continued to voice its opposition to the imperialist ideologues.

I want to describe briefly for you how we have organized

our work in Poland. In order to fend off the constant threat of starvation, it was necessary to organize the procurement of food, the opening of communal kitchens, and so forth. Above all, however, it was necessary to sustain the consciousness of the Polish proletariat against the various dangers which threatened it. We had to sustain this consciousness against the demagogy of the Polish bourgeoisie as well as against the proclamations of the Russian grand dukes and the enticements from the German side. . . .

At the beginning of the war, the Polish proletariat was astounded to learn of the British and French Socialists' glorification of tsarism. Today it is no less astounded to learn of the position of the German party. Neither David, in his Reichstag speech,[24] nor the party press as a whole has taken a clear stand on the question of the annexation of Poland. . . . It is true that much is said in the Social Democratic press on the annexation of Belgium. The reason for that is that a great imperialist empire raised this to the level of a first-rank question. *("Very true!")* Another reason for this silence is that you cannot speak clearly and specifically on Poland without touching on the question of Alsace-Lorraine. So we find that everyone, ministers and journalists alike, is talking about annexing Poland—except the Social Democracy. It remains silent. . . .

[Lapinski's report closed with the reading of a joint declaration of the three Polish organizations represented at the conference, the Left Polish Socialist Party (Lewica) and the two wings of the Social Democracy of Poland and Lithuania.

[The declaration said that the talk by both warring camps of "freeing" Poland is merely a screen for their goals of imperialist robbery. It continued:]

The revolutionary class-conscious Polish proletariat opposes the coalitions of the Polish ruling classes on both sides of the front lines. In pursuit of their class interests and imperialist ambitions, they support the belligerent governments and justify this war, doubly fratricidal for the Poles, by ascribing to it supposedly "Polish" goals.

The Polish territories have been transformed into a giant cemetery and a bloody wasteland. They face today the immediate danger of new experiments in annexation and partition. . . .

The struggle of the revolutionary international proletariat which is now impending will break the chains of national oppression and eliminate every form of foreign domination. The Polish Social Democracy is convinced that only by participating in this struggle can the Polish people secure the possibility of full and free development as a member with equal rights of the International of all peoples.

[Ernst Meyer replied that Lapinski's criticism of the SPD was correct, and was shared by the minority, which had just published a pamphlet against annexationism. Ledebour said he had attacked the government several times for permitting army leaders to talk of burning Polish or Russian villages.

[Reports by Christian Rakovsky, Vasil Kolarov, Zeth Höglund, Ture Nerman, and Henriette Roland-Holst closed the second day's proceedings.]

September 7: The proletariat's peace campaign

KARL RADEK (POLAND): (Motivating the resolution he introduced together with Lenin) Our resolution on principles, and the call to action based on it, are submitted by the representatives of the Polish Regional Executive Committee, the

Russian Central Committee, the Latvian Committee Abroad, and the Swedish and Norwegian Youth League.

Unless the conference clarifies its position on the World War and the collapse of the International, it will be difficult, if not impossible, to issue a call to action. We must be *clear* on the preconditions for the peace campaign and on its goals. Clarity is necessary not only for the conference, but also for the masses of the workers, because, except for spontaneous popular outbursts, they can undertake the struggle for peace only after they have broken from the bourgeois policy of holding out to the end.

The methods and content of this struggle must be revolutionary. As long as the governments still hope that continuing the war will bring success, only resolute pressure by the workers can be effective. Only by attacking the insatiable beast head-on, through street demonstrations, political strikes, and yes, even insurrections, can the workers hope to subdue it. That means revolution. But revolution doesn't just happen because you decide on it. Its outbreak depends on the contradictions sharpening to a critical point, something that is by no means out of the question if the war continues. Social Democracy's task is to prepare the masses for revolution by explaining that the campaign for peace cannot achieve victory without revolution, and by creating illegal organizations in order to conduct unrestricted agitation.

Just as there can be no campaign for peace which is not at the same time revolutionary, so too the revolutionary peace campaign cannot content itself simply with the struggle for peace. In view of the sharpness of social contradictions, this struggle, once under way, *will take the road of socialism.*

The second task of the Social Democracy is, through our agitation and slogans, to make the most conscious workers aware of this essential characteristic of the struggle for peace. If the peace campaign is understood to be the first step in the revolutionary struggle for socialism then we do not need a so-called peace program that includes everybody's subjective wishes for redrawing the map of Europe. This is not at all an evasion. Rather it is an awareness that, under capitalism, the dangers of imperialism cannot be eliminated. We must topple capitalism in order, upon its ruins, to solve the problems that gave birth to the war.

All this must be said clearly to the masses. The campaign for peace cannot be carried out either in secret from the state prosecutors or without the masses' understanding its necessary character and its road forward.

The submission by Lenin and Radek on behalf of the Zimmerwald Left, printed below, included two documents: a resolution, intended for educational use among active Socialists, and a manifesto, intended for broader agitation.

Draft resolution on the World War and the tasks of Social Democracy

Submitted by the Zimmerwald Left

The World War, which in the last year has laid waste to Europe, is an *imperialist war.* It is being waged for the political and economic exploitation of the world: for export markets, sources of raw materials, areas for capital investment, and so on. It is the product of capitalist development, which has united the whole world into one global economy while at the same time maintaining independent national groups of capitalists, with conflicting interests, within the different states.

The bourgeoisie and the governments attempt to conceal the character of the war by asserting that it was forced upon them and that it is a war for *national independence*. But they mislead the *proletariat:* the war is really being fought for the subjugation of foreign peoples and countries. No less deceptive are the myths that this war is being fought for the defense of democracy, since imperialism signifies the unscrupulous tyranny of big business and political reaction.

Imperialism can be overcome only by abolishing the contradictions from which it sprang, through the *socialist reorganization of the leading capitalist countries*. Objective conditions are already ripe for this.

At the outbreak of the war, the majority of the leaders of the working-class parties did not raise this, the only slogan possible in opposition to imperialism. Possessed by nationalism and rank with opportunism, they *handed the proletariat over to imperialism when war came. They gave up the principles of socialism and thus any real struggle for the interests of the proletariat.*

In *Germany* both the openly patriotic majority current, made up of former Social-Democratic leaders, and also the party's "Center" current around Kautsky, which merely postures as an opposition, have gone over to social patriotism and social imperialism. This position is also held by a majority in France and Austria, and by some of the leaders in England and Russia (Hyndman, the Fabians, the trade unionists, Plekhanov, Rubanovich, the *Nashe Dyelo* [Our Cause] group). This current is a more dangerous enemy of the proletariat than the bourgeois advocates of imperialism. By misusing the banner of socialism, it can mislead the less conscious layers of the proletariat. *A ruthless struggle against social imperialism is the first prerequisite for the revolutionary mobilization of the proletariat and the restoration of the International.*

Both the Socialist parties and the Socialist oppositions within parties that have gone over to social imperialism must call and lead the workers to *revolutionary struggle* against the capitalist governments in order to conquer political power for the socialist organization of society.

Revolutionary Social Democrats do not give up the struggle for every single step forward, for every reform within the framework of capitalism that strengthens the proletariat; we do not renounce any method of organization and mobilization. We utilize every struggle and every reform demanded in our minimum program in order to *intensify the crisis of the war,* as we do with every political and social crisis of capitalism, and to broaden it into an attack on the foundations of capitalism. *Conducted under the banner of socialism,* this struggle will immunize the workers against calls for the enslavement of one people by another, for the domination of one nation over another, and for new annexations. This struggle will make the workers immune to the appeals to national solidarity that led the workers into the slaughter.

The prelude to the struggle is the *fight against the World War and for a rapid end to the mass human slaughter.* This fight demands *rejection of the war credits; resignation from government ministries;* denunciation of the capitalist and antisocialist character of the war from the parliamentary floor and in the columns of the legal and, where necessary, illegal press; and a merciless struggle against social patriotism. It demands *the utilization of every movement of the people called forth by the impact of the war (want, tremendous loss of life, etc.) in order to organize antigovernment street demonstrations,* carry out propaganda of *international solidarity in the trenches,* promote *economic strikes,* and, where conditions are favorable, to turn them into *political* strikes. "Civil *war*, not *'civil peace'*, is our slogan!"*

In opposition to all *illusions* that decisions of diplomats and governments can somehow create the *basis of a lasting peace* and *initiate disarmament*, the revolutionary Social Democrats must always explain to the masses that only *social revolution* can achieve a lasting peace and the liberation of humanity.

* These words are taken from the letter to the Zimmerwald Conference of an outstanding leader of the German opposition. [Footnote in original text.]

Draft manifesto

Submitted by the Zimmerwald Left

The war has already lasted for over a year. The battlefields are covered in millions of corpses. Millions of cripples will remain burdens to themselves and to society for the rest of their lives. The devastation caused by the war is monstrous, as is the tax burden it will leave behind.

The *capitalists of all countries*, who transform the blood of the proletariat into the gold of monstrous war profits, are demanding that the masses *hold out to the end*. They say that the war is being fought for the *defense of the fatherland* and in the interests of *democracy in all countries. They are lying!* In none of the countries did the capitalists enter the war because the independence of their country was threatened or because they wanted to free an oppressed people. They led the masses into the slaughter because they wanted to exploit and oppress other peoples. They could not reach agreement among themselves as to how to divide up the peoples of Asia and Africa who were still independent. Each one was suspicious that the other would be able to snatch away the spoils it had seized previously.

It is not for the cause of their own freedom or for the liberation of other peoples that the masses are bleeding in all corners of that huge slaughterhouse called Europe. This war will put new burdens and new fetters on both the European proletariat and the peoples of Asia and Africa.

That is why it is wrong to persist in this fratricidal war. Instead we must make every effort to put an end to it. The hour to do this has already struck. The first thing that you should demand is that your *Socialist deputies,* whom you sent to parliament to combat capitalism, militarism, and exploitation, should do their duty. With the exception of the Russian, Serbian, and Italian deputies and deputies Liebknecht and Rühle, they have all trampled upon this duty. They either gave assistance to the bourgeoisie in its rapacious war or shirked their responsibility by vacillating. You must demand that they either resign or else use parliament to explain the nature of this war before all the people. They must go outside the halls of parliament to help the working class take up the struggle. *Rejection of all war credits* and *withdrawal from the ministries in France, Belgium, and England* should be the first demand.

But that is not sufficient. The deputies alone cannot save you from that raging beast, the World War, which drinks your blood. *You yourselves must act.* You must make use of all your organizations and publications in order to rouse the broad masses, who suffer under the burden of the war, and lead them to oppose it. You must go out into the *streets* and fling in the face of the ruling class your rallying cry: *Enough of the slaughter!* Let the ruling class remain deaf to it. But the dissatisfied masses of the people will hear it and flock to your ranks to join you in the struggle.

It is necessary to demand vigorously the immediate cessation of the war. It is necessary to *protest loudly* against the partitioning of nations and against the subjugation of one people by another, which will all take place if any capitalist government wins and is able to dictate the terms of the peace to the others. If we let the capitalists conclude peace in the same way that they started the war—contemptuous of the wishes of the masses—then the *new conquests* will not only strengthen *reaction* and arbitrary police rule in the victorious country but will also *sow the seeds of new and more dreadful wars.*

The overthrow of the capitalist government must be the working class's goal in all the belligerent countries. Only when the power of life and death over whole peoples is taken out of the hands of capital will an end be put to wars and to the subjugation of one people by another. Only peoples freed from want, misery, and the domination of capital will be able to manage their mutual affairs through fraternal understanding and not war.

Great is the goal we have set. Great are the efforts you must make. Great are the sacrifices you must make, before the goal is reached. The road to victory is long. Peaceful pressure tactics will not suffice to bring the enemy to its knees. But if you decide to free yourselves from capitalism through struggle, and to accept in this fight only a small fraction of the immeasurable sacrifice you offer capitalism today on the battlefields—only then can you put an end to the war. Only then can you lay a real basis for a lasting peace which will transform you from slaves of capitalism to free human beings. If you let yourselves be held back from active struggle by the false phrases of the bourgeoisie and the Socialist parties that support them, if you content yourselves with yearnings for peace without being willing to take up the attack and give your heart and soul to the cause, then capital will continue to shed your blood and squander your wealth for as long as it pleases.

In every country, with every passing day, the number of workers who think as we do is growing. To serve their cause representatives from various countries have gathered here to call you to struggle. We want to lead the struggle and to support one another—for our interests are the same. The revolutionary workers of each country must see it as their honorable right and duty to be an example to others in struggle, an example of energy and self-sacrifice. Not anxiously awaiting what others will do, but leading through example: that is the way that a powerful International will arise which will put an end to war and capitalism.

The draft resolution and manifesto is signed by the delegations of the Central Committee of the Social Democratic Labor Party of Russia, the Regional Committee of the Social Democracy of Russian Poland and Lithuania, the Central Committee of the Social Democracy of Latvia, the Swedish and Norwegian Social Democratic Youth League, a representative of the revolutionary Social Democrats of Germany, and a Swiss delegate.

Discussion

HOFFMANN: Other resolutions have yet to be submitted. We can't begin the discussion until everything is in front of us.

GRIMM: First, we need to be clear what it is we want to achieve. Do we want a manifesto simply for the party comrades or for the broad masses of workers? In the latter case, the call will have to be of quite a different character. I believe we should issue a call to the entire proletariat. Let's first discuss this so we know what we want. In regard to Lenin's resolution, I would like to first of all say that it is directed exclusively to the organized party comrades, and not to the masses, and secondly, that it is inexpedient to reveal our tactical measures to the enemy. *(Approval)*

LEDEBOUR: *(Concerning the agenda)* Grimm's idea is completely correct. We have to start discussing the key question, that is, we have to discuss what the character of our appeal to the people should be. . . .

[Modigliani proposed that the conference refrain from adopting a manifesto and concentrate on establishing a continuing committee to direct the peace campaign. Ledebour convinced him to withdraw this proposal.]

LENIN: Grimm is wrong when he says that our resolution and manifesto are not aimed at the masses. (He proposes that the manifesto also be translated into French.) . . .

[On the request of Albert Bourderon, the conference adjourned briefly to permit the French and German delegates to consult together.]

LEDEBOUR: First, a few words on the agenda. The German delegation is submitting two documents to the conference. The first is a declaration drawn up jointly by the German and French delegations. You see from this that it is possible for German and French Socialists to work together.[25] *(Applause)*

The Berlin comrades, who gave me my mandate for the conference, all agreed that we should meet to complete what the International Socialist Bureau has left undone, and not to found the Third International. We want to discuss ways to carry out a demonstration for peace on as broad an international scale as possible. How must our manifesto be drawn up? To be most effective, we should concentrate on how best to build an international peace movement.

In this way we will dispel many prejudices and conduct propaganda for internationalist socialism. The significance of this conference lies in the educational actions it will generate. *("Very true!")* Lenin's resolution is unacceptable. We all hope that revolutionary action will take place, but a detailed call for it should not be trumpeted to the world. *(The speaker briefly enumerates the actions called for in the Lenin resolution.)* It may indeed come to revolutionary action, but not because we call for it in a manifesto. Whoever endorses such a manifesto has the responsibility to take the lead. *(Agreement)* We here should not direct such a call to other people. Those who are not in danger, such as several of the supporters of this resolution, should not make such an appeal.

In Berlin we have already had mass demonstrations, such as the big rally several years ago in the Tiergarten, held over the opposition of the police.[26] But we did not broadcast beforehand to the whole world what we were going to do.

Agitation in the trenches is certainly desirable. We're already working on that. However, it is being carried out in a more practical manner than is called for in the Lenin manifesto. Anybody who signed and disseminated such a manifesto in the belligerent countries would be done away with immediately. For this reason alone someone who wants genuine action cannot possibly agree to such an appeal. We cannot go further than to call for the resumption of the class struggle, and for its continuation by the traditional methods, the same ones that would also be employed in peacetime.

The proposed German-French declaration takes this concrete position, and also expressly raises the demand: No annexations! This obviously applies to Poland as well. The German Social Democratic opposition's view is that the Polish people have as much right to self-determination as do the German people, and so forth. If the Polish delegates wish to amend our resolution on this point, the German delegates will gladly agree.

The guiding principle of the manifesto we publish must therefore be the proletarian struggle for socialism. The struggle against the war is part of this struggle. It contains the seed of the new International and it constitutes the beginning of the struggle for the general renovation of our tactics. Great revolutionary struggles are approaching, and the campaign for peace should take us into this new period of the class struggle.

(Ledebour then read aloud the entire manifesto proposed by the German delegates.)

LENIN:[27] It was inevitable that things here should have come to a struggle of opinion between Ledebour and us. However, I must protest against the method used here by Ledebour in attacking Radek. The assertion that our manifesto has been signed only by men who are safe is inadmissible. It has also been signed by the Latvian delegates and Borchardt. Another old and hackneyed argument is saying that one should not call the masses to revolutionary action unless one is able to take a direct part in it oneself. Furthermore, I deny that there should be no mention of the means of struggle. That has occurred in all revolutionary periods. The means should be made known to the masses so that they could be explained and discussed. We in Russia have always acted in this way; in fact, the interpretation of the means of struggle had been the subject of arguments between Plekhanov and myself even in the pre-revolutionary years. When the objective historical situation of 1847 confronted Germany with revolution, Marx and Engels sent out an appeal from London calling for violence.[28] The German movement is faced with a decision. If we are indeed on the threshold of a revolutionary epoch in which the masses will go over to revolutionary struggle, we must also make mention of the means necessary for this struggle. According to the revisionist view taken by David and others, that is naturally something quite useless: after all, they do not believe that we are on the eve of a revolutionary epoch. We who believe this must act otherwise. You cannot make revolution without explaining revolutionary tactics. It was precisely the worst feature of the Second International that it constantly avoided explanations; and it is that which the Dutch *Tribune*-Marxists quite correctly called the German Centre's "passive revolutionary attitude."

Now on the question of persecutions. You in Germany should in general do more than legal work, if you want real action. You must combine legal and illegal activity. The old methods are no longer adequate to the new situation. You yourselves have said: we are going forward to an epoch of great class battles. In that case, you must also have the means for this. And it is not at all necessary for the manifesto to be signed, it could well be issued without signatures. At any rate, you should not act semi-legally, like Clara Zetkin, for instance. That calls for too much sacrifice.

Here is how things stand: either a truly revolutionary struggle or mere empty talk which will help no one but the deserters, against whom Liebknecht speaks out so sharply in this letter. Coming out for peace does not mean much in itself. David also writes: we are not for the war, but only against defeat. Everyone wants peace. Taking account of the new situation, we should use new and specific means of struggle which should not be similar in any way to the old German or Russian methods.

[Grimm proposed ending the discussion and referring the question of a resolution to a commission. Rakovsky opposed the proposal, and it was defeated.

[Speaking on the prospects for revolutionary struggle in

Germany, Meyer commented that "it is not possible right now to win any appreciable section of the German proletariat for the type of actions that are enumerated in Lenin's manifesto. . . . During the war imperialist notions have become widespread among workers," he added, recommending that the conference underline the intensive Socialist educational work required to overcome this.]

TROTSKY: The question has been raised whether we should address this manifesto to the masses or simply to the party. But this is a futile word game. For the boundary line between the party and the masses is not fixed for all time—it is fluid. In the German elections of 1912, four million voted for the Social Democracy. While the masses certainly are not yet thoroughly imbued with socialist ideas, and cannot yet be won to every form of antiwar action, nevertheless, they are not totally uneducated. Right now they are disoriented, infected with chauvinism. We cannot light the way forward and give them direction if we do not speak out explicitly and clearly on the most immediate practical questions. Because the masses listen not only to us, but also to David, we must tell them that we are the deadly enemy of David's policies.

Concerning revolutionary actions—I am not surprised at what Meyer has said. The party's left wing is disoriented. Events have shown that the broad masses had not grasped our basic ideas. Now it is said, "we must start all over again" and hold more educational courses, distribute more brochures, and so on. This conception is completely abstract. We have been doing all this now for fifty years. We have had a number of great revolutionary agitators in Germany—Lassalle and others. How can anyone say that really very little has been accomplished? Do not forget that the education of the masses was conditioned by the nonrevolutionary period that lies behind us. It would be very unfortunate if the left wing now went astray by underestimating all that was achieved in the previous period. We must clearly understand that the new conditions of the revolutionary period we are entering require new methods of struggle. If we understand this new situation well enough to see the need for new policies, then the change will certainly have progressed far enough to enable us to shape and express these policies.

I am in general agreement with Radek's resolution. As for the manifesto, it should not contain a detailed dissection of our program. This is not because, as Grimm believes, a resolution can be written discreetly. The problem is rather that if complete revolutionary programs are unfurled before the masses, they will not understand their practical implications. Nevertheless there is no way around making clear to the world, in one way or another, that the masses must do away with the "civil peace" once and for all.

This brings me to the question at the center of our discussion on tactics—the question of voting on the war credits. For the revolutionary proletariat of Europe today, there is only *one* parliamentary fraction that is revolutionary—Liebknecht's fraction. *(Agreement)* The French and Russian workers know that Liebknecht was not afraid of violating the policy of "civil peace" and that he placed himself clearly and unequivocally on the side of internationalist socialism. Narrow considerations of *party politics* have no validity in the present situation. Only *world politics* has any meaning now. Liebknecht's act has had a powerful impact on public opinion. In order to increase the impact, and in order to make our opponents feel it, however, he would have had to rally others along with him. When Liebknecht voted against the war credits in the Reichstag for the third time, he was greeted by the scornful laughter of the patriots. In him they were ridiculing the impotence of German radicalism.

In conclusion, I want to say a few words about the sudden

caving-in of French socialism. Of course, there are mitigating psychological circumstances for this collapse; however, from a political point of view I must reject them. France's unfavorable military situation makes the situation there much more difficult. The danger of social imperialism and chauvinism is much greater. For this reason, the courage that our comrades Merrheim and Bourderon have shown in coming here deserves recognition. *(Applause)* I would now like to read to you our draft of the manifesto. . .

[The draft, signed by Trotsky and Roland-Holst, served as the main basis for the final resolution. The draft contained the following slogans:

["Down with the yoke of 'civil peace'! Down with the war credits! Down with Socialist imperialism! Long live peace among the peoples! Long live the class struggle! Long live social revolution!"]

FRITZ PLATTEN (SWITZERLAND): In my opinion we are getting altogether too carried away with the desire for unity. It would be best to clearly formulate our principles in a resolution. The German minority should unambiguously express themselves.

(Hoffmann and Ewald Vogtherr interrupted the speaker; saying they completely agreed with him; nevertheless, for legal reasons, the German delegation could not formally declare themselves on the question of the war credits. They explained that German deputies do not have the right to formally commit themselves to anyone on how they will vote.)

MERRHEIM: We have agreed on a joint declaration with the Germans, which I would now like to read to you. We are starting from the premise that our most important task is to put forward a common understanding of the causes and consequences of the war. *(The speaker reads the German-French declaration, which receives prolonged applause.)*

Joint declaration of the French and German delegations

After a year of devastation the unequivocally *imperialist character* of this war has more and more revealed itself. This proves that the war was caused by the imperialist and colonial policy of *all* governments, that they are responsible for the outbreak of this carnage.

The masses of the people were drawn into this war through the *"civil peace"* being proclaimed in all countries by the profiteers of capitalism, who gave to the war the appearance of a racial struggle, a defense of rights and liberties. Under the pressure of these sentiments a considerable part of the organized and enlightened workers in each country were swept away by nationalism. Since then the press, at the command of the authorities, has unceasingly emphasized the alleged liberating character of the war.

Today the chauvinists of every nation ascribe to this war *the aim of conquering whole countries or territories.* These claims if realized *would cause future wars.*

Determined minorities in opposition to these ambitions have been formed in all nations. These minorities attempt to fulfill the tasks affirmed in the decisions of the International Socialist Congresses at Stuttgart, Copenhagen, and Basel.

It is their task, today more than ever, to oppose the *annexationist claims and to hasten the ending of the war,* a war which has already caused the loss of millions of human lives, produced so many cripples, and provoked such oppressive misery among the workers of all countries.

That is why we German and French Socialists and trade unionists declare: "This war is not our war!"

We *condemn* with all our energy the violation of Belgian

neutrality, which was solemnly guaranteed by international conventions recognized by all the belligerent countries. We demand and shall not stop demanding the restoration of Belgium to its complete integrity and independence.

We declare that we desire the ending of the war through an early peace established on conditions which will not violate the rights of any nation or people; that we will never agree to the plans of conquest of our respective governments, plans which must inevitably carry the seeds of new wars, that we shall work in our respective countries for a peace which would dispel hatred among the nations and make it possible for the peoples to unite in joint endeavor.

Such a peace, in our judgment, is possible only if *every thought of violating the rights and the liberties of the peoples is renounced.* The occupation of entire countries or provinces must not result in forcible annexation.

So, we say: no open or masked annexations; no forcibly imposed economic incorporation, which would be made still more intolerable by a further political disfranchisement of those involved. We say that the right of the peoples to determine their own destiny must be observed inviolably.

We take upon ourselves the explicit responsibility of acting unceasingly to this end in our respective countries so that the peace movement may become strong enough to force our governments to stop this slaughter.

By repudiating the policy of "civil peace" and by remaining faithful to the class struggle which serves as the foundation of the Socialist International we, German and French Socialists and trade unionists, will stand steadfastly among our countrymen in struggle against this horrible calamity and toward putting an end to this carnage which has disgraced humankind.

For the French delegation: A. Merrheim, A. Bourderon

For the German delegation: Adolph Hoffmann, Georg Ledebour

Discussion

[The debate was continued by Lazzari and Bourderon.]

VICTOR CHERNOV (RUSSIA, ZHIZN [LIFE] [SOCIALIST REVOLUTIONARIES]): I only want to make a few specific points. We are not forcing our viewpoint on you German comrades. Rather we want you to force yourselves to abide by resolutions that we and you both voted for. Remember the international congress in Amsterdam and Jaurès who submitted to international discipline and international considerations.[29] Today we have the right to demand you make a similar sacrifice.

What should the guiding idea of our joint declaration be? The struggle for peace exclusively, or the idea of transforming this struggle into one for the social revolution? I do not want to explain here the particular Russian viewpoint corresponding to our specific situation. Nevertheless I want to expressly state my opinion that the main idea of the manifesto must be the transformation of the war crisis into a revolutionary crisis. Our resolutions must be guided by this principle. That is the only way we can elevate the International's stature once again to a moral force and draw the masses out of their gloomy dejection. Therefore we declare ourselves in agreement in principle with Radek's resolution; not, however, with his manifesto. . . .

[Berta Thalheimer maintained that the manifesto should be directed to the masses. She held that for "strategic reasons" it was probably not possible to publish Radek's manifesto.]

ZINOVIEV: Almost all of the previous speakers have spoken in favor of our resolution. Trotsky's manifesto is a step forward compared to the German draft. What is missing is the struggle against Kautskyism. *(Turns to Ledebour)* During the time of the Anti-Socialist Laws the German party accepted both legal and illegal methods of struggle.

G.M. SERRATI (ITALY): If the war were not already a fact, I would agree to Lenin's resolution. But today it comes either too early or too late. When the war was launched, forced upon us by nothing more than very powerful minorities—then, had we been prepared to use force, we could have prevented it.

HENRIETTE ROLAND-HOLST (NETHERLANDS): . . . The workers of the belligerent countries are certainly tired of the war. However they lack the will to struggle because they have lost the belief in socialism due to the collapse of the International. It is necessary above all to win them to the struggle for peace, which can become the starting point for revolutionary struggles. Trotsky and I have prepared the draft now before you in this spirit.

The greatest encouragement comes from action, from the example of those of us willing to make sacrifices for our convictions. A revolutionary period requires sacrifices, but they do not take the same form for us all. Perhaps a greater sacrifice than putting your life on the line is breaking with deeply rooted traditions, renouncing what you used to be. The French comrades must now give up the old democratic idea of the liberating role of their country. You German comrades should give up the party traditions of strict adherence to legality and discipline above all. This is twice as hard because the German workers' movement has made such tremendous advances through legal activity and maintaining discipline. Nevertheless, as important as the weapons of discipline and unity are, one thing is more important: socialism.

To the German comrades I say this: We do not ever want to coerce you on the question of the war credits. We would like to convince you. We think you should reject the credits. Not only because of the international congress resolutions, but because you have understood how the revolutionary situation demands that you sacrifice stubborn party traditions.

JULIUS MARTOV (RUSSIA, ORGANIZING COMMITTEE): . . . The internationalism of the German Social Democracy was a mainstay for us Socialists in the backward countries. When the German party jumped on the bandwagon of national defense, the masses' belief in socialism began to waver. What can we say to our workers when the German parliamentary deputies here declare that they will not do anything different in the future? Either your policies or ours are false to the core. . . .

We are against acts of sabotage. But we have always said that the only way to fight the war is to sabotage it morally. And in this regard, approval or rejection of the war credits has a powerful influence. When I asked French parliamentary deputies why they did not vote against the credits, they responded: "Because it would quickly dampen enthusiasm in the trenches for the war." That shows how serious a step rejecting the credits is. It makes it clear to every enlisted soldier that the war is contrary to the interests of the people. Our duty is to see that the soldiers no longer fight with enthusiasm. It is not up to us to force the German comrades to adopt the same tactics as the Serbian comrades;[30] or to demand that the parliamentary fraction members follow Liebknecht's example. But if they do not they will increasingly demoralize the masses. The yoke of the policy of "civil peace" must be shattered. Whatever we do, nobody will be able to say that the German party minority gave in under pressure. Everyone knows that they were not for approving the credits. If we expressly demand rejection in our manifesto nobody will be able to say that they were coerced. . . .

RADEK: I am convinced we must have a resolution specifically laying down our political line of march. First, because we need to shed light on the struggle for peace in general, to make it clear why and for what we are fighting. It does not matter that some leaders want to sign because their authority is shaken, so long as the manifesto makes the perspective of the struggle clear to the masses. Already it is possible for the more conscious elements to draw the lessons of the war. The ferment among the masses is only just beginning, however. The contradictions have not yet come to a head. Therefore we must adopt a resolution as well as a manifesto.

It is illusory to think we can lead the struggle without the governments knowing how we are leading it. If we speak about revolutionary actions without saying anything else, without specifying anything further, the German comrades say that it is all only empty phrases. If we specify the actions, then they say that we are providing "evidence for the state prosecutor." On the contrary; we should incorporate the overall line of march in our statement, and thereby we will accelerate the struggle.

LENIN:[31] I do not agree with Serrati that the resolution will appear either too early or too late. After this war, other, mainly colonial, wars will be waged. Unless the proletariat turns off the social-imperialist way, proletarian solidarity will be completely destroyed; that is why we must determine common tactics. If we adopt only a manifesto, Vandervelde, *L'Humanité,* and others will once again start deceiving the masses; they will keep saying that they, too, oppose war and want peace. The old vagueness will remain.

LEDEBOUR: We have labored under a misunderstanding which now and again has taken an angry form. We do not agree on the purpose of the conference. We in Berlin are all agreed that the conference should make up for the collapse of the International Socialist Bureau, and that its task is to organize a Socialist peace movement. We should have concentrated on this task, but unfortunately we have taken a different road. Long speeches and recriminations—and we have almost lost sight of our goal. We are blamed for adhering too rigidly to legality; but the party has never accepted a strictly legal framework. Merely our presence here means we are breaking the laws of our country as well as the discipline of our party. We will act illegally where and when it appears to us necessary.

Comrades think that they have to continually lecture us on the stance of the party. Comrade Roland-Holst acts as if we were representatives of the majority or of the swamp. All this proves that they do not know us. Now it is my turn to be the schoolmaster. Follow the example of the sensitivity with which our French comrades have approached us! Our agreement will have great results in all countries. And this, after all, was the main point of the conference.

GIUSEPPE MODIGLIANI (ITALY): . . . We must write a manifesto so that it serves a concrete purpose. We will be ridiculed if we put too much into it. While there are very good things in Radek's resolution, you cannot renew the foundations of society through a proclamation. Our manifesto, which is aimed at everyone—the masses as well as the party comrades—must be modest, concrete, and clear. Our goal is to deal with the collapse of the International Socialist Bureau, to end that situation. We should set up a central bureau to work for peace. Above all the purpose of the manifesto must be to clearly put forward the founding of this central bureau.

HOFFMANN: I would have understood if the French delegates had attacked us. But no, all the others are doing it. Those of us who are here are not the guilty ones. Why hammer away at us all the time? Even the Austrians have not yet come under fire. It is inconceivable that we could act on behalf of Scheidemann and the others. Hammer at us as much as you want; just don't draw up any resolutions that will get us into hot water.

Comrade Thalheimer's remarks could lead you to think we did not stand behind Zetkin, Luxemburg, and Liebknecht. That is a mistake. We are united with them one hundred percent in our cause. We only think that Liebknecht should have come to an understanding with us. We are united on the rest—he cosigned all the leaflets and so forth.

Zinoviev said: "If you do it, then you must say it." But they say it because they are not in the country. Do not send us home with a directive, but rather help us create peace on earth.

MERRHEIM: Our Italian comrade expressed the views of the French delegation as well. Nevertheless I want to respond to some of Lenin's comments in order to clarify for him the difference between us and Vandervelde, Jouhaux, and so on.

Right now we want to limit ourselves to an action for peace. When peace comes there will be a great deal for all of us—including us syndicalists—to examine. We have been too content to confine our agitation to slogans, and have not dealt enough with the complexity of things and the realities of the world.

During the war when we wanted to undertake actions, the articles of Legien and the German trade union press were used against us with telling effect. We replied that, apart from the leaders, there must be workers who think exactly as we do. *(Prolonged applause)*

Comrade Lenin, you ask us to erect the foundation pillars for the future International. But that is a deadly serious task that can't be done through a resolution. I think of Hervé. It seems to me now that he exhausted the energy of the proletariat prematurely with his stirring speeches. Let us not blame others too much for mistakes when we ourselves have done much the same. And in anticipation of the hour when it will be time to resurrect the International, let us establish a publication for the struggle against the war.

In France we are confronted with a completely demoralized working class, which at the present moment has lost all faith. They will listen to us if we speak of peace, but not if we repeat the same old clichés.

TROTSKY: Monatte and Rosmer think otherwise.

MERRHEIM: Yes, Monatte thinks that the revolution will

arise out of the war. But we do not want to express that perspective in some narrow formula. A revolutionary movement can *only* arise out of the struggle for peace. You, Comrade Lenin, are concerned with the desire to lay the foundation of a new International, not with the demand for peace. This is what divides us. We demand a manifesto that will advance the struggle for peace. We do not want to emphasize what divides us, but what unites us. *(Enthusiastic applause)*

CHRISTIAN RAKOVSKY (ROMANIA): I am also speaking for Kolarov. It is impossible to act as if the International does not exist any more. In a certain sense it continues to exist as a political concept. How can we reach our goal of ending the slaughter? Would it not be worthwhile to orient ourselves to the International?

A large number of the parties belonging to the International are probably no longer internationalist at all. But another part vacillates back and forth—a house divided against itself. Our duty is to draw the vacillators over to our side. We are the embodiment of their socialist conscience. Should our manifesto not begin by appealing to this socialist conscience?

What unites us here are our common views. The old International nurtured these ideas within us; that is why we cannot cut ourselves off completely from it. Why do we not refer in our manifesto to the Stuttgart, Copenhagen, and Basel congress resolutions, which condemned the granting of war credits, collaboration with the bourgeoisie, and so forth? This is important. We want to be exact and concrete. . . .

The old International had many doors providing openings for class collaboration, especially in regard to national defense. What was prohibited by the resolutions from Basel and other congresses was accepted for this, the ultimate war. We must close these doors.

A third point: Not only is there an internationalist and socialist phraseology, but there is also a real corresponding sentiment. Our manifesto should awaken this sentiment everywhere, including in the trenches. We must make internationalism into a creed, a religion. It is this sentiment that will save the working class. The more concrete we are in these things, the better. The mere fact that we have held our conference here, in defiance of the bourgeoisie and its laws, will have a great impact.

GRIMM: We have now reached the end of the debate on the peace campaign. We have one draft resolution and three draft manifestos.[32] I propose that the manifestos be forwarded to the commission and the question of the resolution be left open, until we have created a permanent publication. . . .

[It was decided by a vote of nineteen to twelve[33] not to refer the Radek resolution to the commission, but to the continuing committee that was to be created. Voting with the eight delegates of the Zimmerwald Left to refer the resolution were Chernov, Natanson, Roland-Holst, and Trotsky.

[After a short discussion the following were elected as members of the commission: Ledebour, Lenin, Grimm, Martov, Merrheim, Meyer, Modigliani, Rakovsky, and Trotsky.

[Adjournment]

September 8: Discussion of commission report

GRIMM: *(Briefly explains the manifesto that has emerged from the debates in the commission, and reads the draft in German. After Merrheim has done the same in French,*

Grimm turns to Lenin.) For the sake of unity, I ask you not to magnify our tactical differences all out of proportion. The differences of opinion between you and the majority of the commission regard simply the question of explaining our methods of struggle; they are therefore not of a principled nature.

(The general discussion begins.)

ROLAND-HOLST: In the name of Borchardt, Höglund, Lenin, Nerman, Platten, Radek, Winter, and Zinoviev, I propose the following amendment: "And first and foremost we call on the parliamentary deputies of all the belligerent countries steadfastly to reject the granting of war credits to their governments." I think it is unnecessary to explain this proposal further. The proposal follows logically from the opinion expressed by a large majority of the conference, as the general course of the debate has shown. *(Voices: "Very true!")*

ODDINO MORGARI (ITALY): I greatly regret that I will have to abstain from the vote. The manifesto is in my opinion simplistic and unfair. Simplistic, because it only takes into consideration the economic factors and ignores all the others—the national, psychological, and so on—that also contributed to the outbreak of the war. Unfair, because it lays the blame for the war equally on all governments, while in reality the main responsibility lies with the Central Powers. They started the war, while France, Belgium, and Serbia found themselves in a defensive situation. Also it is not enough to demand no new annexations, in addition we should take a stand in favor of the liberation of all those nations and national groups that are oppressed by more powerful nations.

[Lenin then proposed an immediate vote; this was rejected.

[Martov proposed that the manifesto include a discussion of the conditions that workers would face after the end of the war.

[Herzfeld asked that the expression, "mass struggle against

the war," be removed from the draft for legal reasons.

[Chernov proposed mention of the role of dynastic ambitions as a cause of the war. He also moved that the phrase "the world of labor" or "the masses of working people" be used in place of "the proletariat" in reference to those who must pay the costs of war, since in Russia these are borne chiefly by the peasants. After further comments by Serrati and Rakovsky, delegates adjourned for dinner, and for formulation of written amendments.]

GRIMM: Those presenting the various amendments may now have the floor. There will be no debate on these. The bureau will decide on the final draft.

ROLAND-HOLST: *(Reads the following statement in the name of those who signed the amendment calling for rejection of war credits.)*

"Because the acceptance of our amendment would to some extent jeopardize the success of the conference and since Ledebour poses his opposition in terms of an ultimatum, we withdraw our amendment under protest. We will make do with Ledebour's statement in the commission that the essence of our amendment is already contained in the manifesto." Fritz Platten, Henriette Roland-Holst, V.I. Lenin, Gregory Zinoviev, Karl Radek, Zeth Höglund, Ture Nerman, Paul Winter, Leon Trotsky.[34]

LEDEBOUR: What I said was not accurately reported in the previous statement. In the commission I stated the following: "Since the position on the question of the war credits is explained perfectly clearly and unambiguously in the manifesto, any addition is superfluous." *(Ledebour's statement causes great commotion among a portion of the delegates.)*

(Following this statement by Ledebour, Trotsky declared that he also was signing the protest by Roland-Holst and other comrades.)

CHERNOV: *(Takes the floor to explain the following amendment.)* "The second most important cause of the war is the continued existence in modern Europe of the holdovers of past ages: monarchical dynasties, nobility, the junkers, which through their influence strengthen all of the most sinister sides of bourgeois society." [signed:] Chernov, Bobrov, Roland-Holst.

GRIMM (IN THE NAME OF THE COMMISSION): The commission cannot accept the amendment because the manifesto is concerned only with the most general causes of the war, which are applicable to all countries. *(Thereupon the amendment is rejected by a large majority.)* . . .

[Grimm further proposed on behalf of the commission that Martov's suggestion for a description of postwar conditions be referred to the continuing committee, who might utilize it in formulating a future statement. Ledebour emphasized that when Lenin's resolution was referred in this manner, there was no implication it would be the basis for a common resolution. Grimm agreed. Chernov declined to formulate his second amendment, explaining that with the rejection of his first, he would now have to vote against the resolution as a whole.]

(Lenin and five other comrades submitted the following statement for the record:)

Zimmerwald Left statement

The undersigned declare that:

We are not fully satisfied with the conference manifesto. It contains no characterization of opportunism—either when open or when disguised with radical phrases—which not only bears the main responsibility for the International's disintegration, but perpetuates that state of affairs. It contains no clear characterization of the methods of struggle against the war. As before, in the press of the International and in its meetings, we will argue for a firm Marxist position on the tasks of the proletariat in the epoch of imperialism. We are voting for the manifesto because we see it as a *call to struggle* and because we want to march forward in this struggle arm in arm with the other sections of the International.

We request that this statement be incorporated in the official report on the conference.

Lenin, Zinoviev, Radek,
Nerman, Höglund, Winter

Closing discussion

RAKOVSKY: . . . I would like to point out to Comrades Chernov and Morgari the great importance of unity in the vote. Even justifiable wishes and objections should be sacrificed for its sake. Like Morgari, I believe that *immediate* responsibility for the war does not rest equally with all countries. Nevertheless it is only necessary in the manifesto to explain the general, *underlying* responsibility of the capitalist classes and their governments.

I want to appeal to you, Morgari: you are the one who has contributed the most to bringing this conference about.

Vote for the manifesto with us. *(General agreement)*

MODIGLIANI: I agree with Rakovsky's statement and ask you, Morgari, to bear in mind what it would mean for the Italian party if you abstained on the manifesto. You should not forget that there are also vacillators and undecided elements among the ranks of the Italian Socialists. Your abstention will encourage these comrades to go against party discipline.

CHERNOV: . . . We must explain not only the underlying responsibility of capitalist society, but also the direct, personal responsibility of all the royal dynasties. So I ask myself, what is it that you really have against our text? I have not heard an actual objection from you. For this reason I would still like to ask you to accept our amendment.

GRIMM: The expression *imperialism* ties it all together for us. By imperialism, we also mean the royal dynasties, which are a tool of imperialism in this period. As is the case with Comrade Morgari, I have to tell you that we cannot accept your amendment. Otherwise everybody could raise special wishes and requests.

MORGARI: I know that various comrades must make sacrifices in order to vote for the manifesto. As you comrades see it, it is simply a matter of sacrificing your particular views on this or that point for the sake of agreement. However, I am being asked to sacrifice my political honor. Since the start of the war we have been accused of aiding the policies of Germany, and the wording of the manifesto lends credence to this accusation. It says: "no indemnities, no annexations." This formula measures everyone with the same yardstick, even though the sequence of the declarations of war makes it plain that immediate responsibility for the war lies with the Central Powers.

TROTSKY: *(Breaking in)* And Russian tsarism has no direct responsibility?

MORGARI: If you stipulate only the formula, "no annexations," then the right of nations to self-determination is jeopardized.[35]

MODIGLIANI: Let's keep calm.

MERRHEIM: *(Turns first to the Russians [Chernov and Bobrov])* We find ourselves in a similar situation to yours. The manifesto conforms just as inadequately to our wishes. Nevertheless, the manifesto is not a pamphlet, in which every particular point about the cause of the war can be brought forward. I ask you not to jeopardize the unity of the vote.

(Turns to Morgari) We are subjected to atrocious accusations just as you are. We are insulted in every imaginable way just as you are. Nevertheless we should endure all this for the sake of the great common goal of socialism.

MORGARI: *(Breaking in)* The German delegation insists on this wording because they are acting on behalf of their fatherland. *(With these words a great uproar breaks out. A large majority of the delegates shout out their disapproval of his remarks.)*

MERRHEIM: *(Speaks to Morgari)* I cannot possibly accept your view since it does not correspond to reality. Serbia was nothing more than a tool in the hands of Russia. All that the French government did in the last ten years was intended to lead to war. We shall remain firm as to the joint responsibility of all the capitalist states and reject making certain reservations regarding this or that imperialism. The war arises out of the totality of the policies of all the governments. Comrade Morgari has the duty to overcome his personal sensitivity. He must not allow his attitude to be determined by his bitterness toward the very demeaning accusations brought against him.

We only want to express general concepts. We French Socialists also could have requested that a special question be mentioned in the manifesto, namely that of Alsace-Lorraine. We have not done this because we do not attribute a lot of significance to this question. We think that it will be decided through peaceful agreement between free peoples and through socialism, not through arms. *(General agreement, shouts: "Very true, bravo!")* . . .

ANGELICA BALABANOFF (ITALY): I do not think that the differences are too great. Comrade Morgari knows that we fully understand his indignation at the slanders which are being propagated against him. I myself have had to endure similar slanders. But it has not kept me from remaining steadfast in the struggle against the war.

No matter what wording of the manifesto we publish, those slanders will not stop. The French comrades will be accused again and again of having sold themselves to the Germans and the German comrades of having been bribed with English gold. Comrade Morgari knows this just as much as I.

Our attitude should be determined solely by considering what the proletariat should expect from us, what will advance its unity and its strength. Simply tell us, Comrade Morgari, what is most important for you: That you will continue to be accused of having been bought by the Germans or that your abstention will be used against socialist internationalism? However much I sympathize with you, I think that you have a double responsibility to pay no attention to the slanders against you. What will be the consequences if you do not advance together with us? You are not just a delegate here. You also personify the aspirations of the international proletariat for unity.

(The conference moves on to the vote. Grimm requests that the delegates stand to indicate their endorsement of the manifesto. When Morgari stands up with the others, great jubilation breaks out. Only the representatives of the Russian Socialist Revolutionaries, Chernov and Bobrov, have not stood up. The delegates of various nationalities urge them to stand, shouting out pleas and requests. When they finally give in to the pleas for unity and stand, the jubilation breaks out anew.)

GRIMM: *(In the midst of great enthusiasm)* The manifesto has been unanimously adopted.

(All present join in singing "The Internationale.")

The Zimmerwald manifesto

Proletarians of Europe!

The war has lasted more than a year. Millions of corpses cover the battlefields. Millions of human beings have been crippled for the rest of their lives. Europe is like a gigantic slaughterhouse. All civilization, created by the labor of many generations, is consigned to destruction. The most savage barbarism is today celebrating its triumph over all that hitherto constituted the pride of humanity.

Irrespective of the truth about the direct responsibility for the war's outbreak, one thing is certain: the war that has produced this chaos is the product of imperialism, of the attempt on the part of the capitalist classes of every nation to feed their greed for profit by the exploitation of human labor and of the natural resources of the entire globe.

Economically backward or politically weak nations are thereby subjugated by the great powers who, in this war, are seeking to remake the world map with blood and iron in accord with their exploiting interests. Thus entire nations and countries like Belgium, Poland, the Balkan states, and Armenia are threatened with the fate of being torn asunder, annexed in whole or in part as booty in the game of compensations.

In the course of the war, its driving forces are revealed in all their vileness. Shred after shred falls the veil with which the meaning of this world catastrophe was hidden from the consciousness of the people. The capitalists of all countries, who are coining the gold of war profits out of the blood shed by the people, assert that the war is for defense of the fatherland, for democracy and the liberation of oppressed nations. They lie! In actual fact they are burying the freedom of their own people together with the independence of the other nations on the field of devastation. New fetters, new chains, new burdens are arising, and it is the proletariat of all countries, of the victorious as well as of the conquered countries, that will have to bear them. Improvement in welfare was proclaimed at the outbreak of the war—want and privation, unemployment and inflation, undernourishment and epidemics are the actual results. The burdens of war will consume the best energies of the peoples for decades, endanger the achievements of social reform, and hinder every step forward.

Cultural devastation, economic decline, political reaction—these are the blessings of this horrible conflict of nations.

Thus the war reveals the naked figure of modern capitalism which has become irreconcilable not only with the interests of the masses of workers, not only with the requirements of historical development, but also with the elementary conditions of human social existence.

The ruling powers of capitalist society, who held the fate of the nations in their hands; the monarchical as well as the republican governments; the secret diplomacy; the mighty business organizations; the bourgeois parties; the capitalist press; the church—all these bear the full weight of responsibility for this war which arose out of the social order fostering them and protected by them, and which is being waged for their interest.

Workers!

Exploited, disfranchised, scorned, they called you brothers and comrades at the outbreak of the war when you were to be led to the slaughter, to death. And now that militarism has crippled you, mutilated you, degraded and annihilated you, the rulers demand that you surrender your interests, your aims, your ideals—in a word, servile subordination to the "civil peace." They rob you of the possibility of expressing your views, your feelings, your pains; they prohibit you from raising your demands and defending them. The press is gagged, political rights and liberties trod upon—this is the way the military dictatorship rules today with an iron hand.

This situation that faces us, threatening the entire future of Europe and of humanity, cannot and must not be tolerated any longer without action. The Socialist proletariat has waged a struggle against militarism for decades. With growing concern, its representatives at their national and international congresses occupied themselves with the ever more menacing danger of war growing out of imperialism. At Stuttgart, at Copenhagen, at Basel, the International Socialist congresses indicated the course that the proletariat must follow.

Since the beginning of the war Socialist parties and workers' organizations of various countries that helped to determine this course have disregarded the obligations arising out of it. Their representatives have called upon the working class to give up the class struggle, the only possible and effective method of proletarian emancipation. They have granted credits to the ruling classes for waging the war; they have placed themselves at the disposal of the governments for the most diverse services; through their press and their messengers, they have tried to win the neutrals for the government policies of their countries; they have delivered up to their governments Socialist ministers as hostages for the preservation of the "civil peace," and thereby they have assumed the responsibility before the working class, before its present and its future, for this war, for its aims and its methods. And just as the individual parties, so the highest of the appointed representative bodies of the Socialists of all countries, the International Socialist Bureau, has failed them.

These facts are partly responsible for the failure of the international working class, which either did not succumb to the national panic of the first war period or which subsequently freed itself from it, to find ways and means of simultaneously beginning an energetic struggle for peace in all countries, even in the second year of the slaughter of the peoples.

In this unbearable situation, we, the representatives of the Socialist parties, trade unions, or of their minorities, we Germans, French, Italians, Russians, Poles, Latvians, Romanians, Bulgarians, Swedes, Norwegians, Dutch, and Swiss, we who stand not on the ground of national solidarity with the exploiting class, but on the ground of the international solidarity of the proletariat and of the class struggle, have assembled to retie the torn threads of international relations and to call upon the working class to come to its senses and to fight for peace.

This struggle is the struggle for freedom, for the reconciliation of peoples, for socialism. It is necessary to take up this struggle for peace, for a peace without annexations or war indemnities. Such a peace, however, is only possible if every thought of violating the rights and liberties of nations is condemned. Neither the occupation of entire countries nor of separate parts of countries must lead to their violent annexation. No annexation, whether open or concealed, and no forcible economic attachment made still more unbearable by political disfranchisement. The right of self-determination of nations must be the indestructible principle in the system of national relationships of peoples.

Proletarians!

Since the outbreak of the war you have placed your energy, your courage, your endurance at the service of the ruling classes. Now you must stand up for your own cause, for the sacred aims of socialism, for the emancipation of the oppressed nations as well as of the enslaved classes, by means of the irreconcilable proletarian class struggle.

It is the task and duty of the Socialists of the belligerent countries to take up this struggle with full force; it is the task and the duty of the Socialists of the neutral states to support their brothers in this struggle against bloody barbarism with every effective means.

Never in world history was there a more urgent, a more sublime task, the fulfillment of which should be our common labor. No sacrifice is too great, no burden too heavy in order to achieve this goal: peace among the people.

Workingmen and workingwomen! Mothers and fathers! Widows and orphans! Wounded and crippled! We call to all of you who are suffering from the war and because of the war:

Beyond all borders, beyond the reeking battlefields, beyond the devastated cities and villages:

PROLETARIANS OF ALL COUNTRIES, UNITE!

ZIMMERWALD, SWITZERLAND,
SEPTEMBER 1915

In the name of the International Socialist Conference

For the German delegation: Georg Ledebour, Adolph Hoffmann.

For the French delegation: A. Bourderon, A. Merrheim.

For the Italian delegation: G.E. Modigliani, Constantino Lazzari.

For the Russian delegation: N. Lenin, Paul Axelrod, M. Bobrov.

For the Polish delegation: St. Lapinski, A. Warski, Cz. Hanecki.[36]

For the Inter-Balkan Socialist Federation: In the name

of the Romanian delegation: C. Rakovsky; In the name of the Bulgarian delegation: Wassil Kolarov.

For the Swedish and Norwegian delegation: Z. Höglund, Ture Nerman.

For the Dutch delegation: H. Roland-Holst.

For the Swiss delegation: Robert Grimm, Charles Naine.

The establishment of the International Socialist Committee

[Following the adoption of the manifesto, the conference determined how it should be signed. It approved the final text of the German-French declaration. A statement of sympathy for the victims of the war was also adopted. In addition to the uncounted millions of war dead, it cited the sufferings of the Polish, Belgian, Jewish, and Armenian peoples. Among those persecuted for their Socialist convictions it singled out the assassinated Jean Jaurès; the exiled Russian Duma deputies; Karl Liebknecht and Pierre Monatte, held captive in the army; and the jailed comrades Rosa Luxemburg and Clara Zetkin.]

LEDEBOUR: . . . [The continuing committee] will develop over time, and its functions cannot be defined today. We must avoid above all anything that could create the appearance that we intend to replace or compete with the International Socialist Bureau, which still exists, although it has disappeared into the fourth dimension. We propose that the committee consist of Comrades Grimm, Naine, and Morgari, and Comrade Balabanoff as secretary. As you see, no government ministers are included. The committee's functions will include appointing correspondents in different countries that will maintain contact between it and the Socialist opposition as a whole.

[Pledges were made for the financial support of the center. The conference agreed on the name, "International Socialist Committee in Bern." Ledebour and Hoffmann insisted that Borchardt's vote not be counted in the minutes. Grimm resisted, and no decision was reached. The conference thanked its translators and secretaries, Balabanoff and Roland-Holst. Grimm closed the proceedings. Adjournment was at 2:30 a.m.]

Above, Alexandra Kollontai, Karl Radek; below, Gregory Zinoviev, Julius Martov.

Chapter 8

The discussion in the Zimmerwald Left

Reacting swiftly to the Zimmerwald conference, government authorities in France, Germany, Austria-Hungary, and Russia banned publication of its resolutions. The official Social Democratic parties of France, Germany, and Austria-Hungary also responded with hostility. The French party leadership exhorted its members that "a lasting peace can only be achieved through the victory of the allies and through crushing German militaristic imperialism, and that any other peace, any premature peace, could only be an illusion or a capitulation." It cautioned against any action that could give even an appearance of weakening national defense.[1]

An October 2, 1915, circular of the German SPD Executive Committee attacked the Zimmerwald conference for "raising in its verbose manifesto accusations of every kind against the party organizations of different countries." The German party was totally united in desiring peace, the Executive Committee said, and the party leadership was doing everything possible to achieve it, but had received no positive response from the other side. "The participation of German party comrades as individuals in so-called international conferences can only make the establishment of friendly relations outside the country harder, by giving the impression that only a small minority" of the German party is for peace. "The opposite is true," the circular explained, and the official party leadership had conveyed this united commitment to fraternal parties in other countries.

The SPD Executive Committee considered the Zimmerwald conference "meaningless," and expected that party organizations would not support the International Socialist Committee in Bern. "Party members can be confident that the party leadership will do everything to defend the interests of the proletariat insofar as war conditions permit, and will be more able to do this if party members reject the words of irresponsible advisors," the statement concluded.[2]

The pro-war Social Democratic press ignored the conference or dismissed it with brief disparaging remarks. Only a handful of Socialist publications printed the Zimmerwald manifesto, including the dailies *Avanti!* (Forward) in Italy, the *Berner Tagwacht,* and *Nashe Slovo*. It also appeared in *Sotsial-Demokrat* and in the British publications *Justice* and *Labour Leader.*

The manifesto was energetically distributed in leaflet form in many countries. The increasing suffering of working people fed their anger against the war and the governments pursuing it, thus winning a wider hearing for the Zimmerwald movement. Many centrist Socialist leaders, feeling the intense pressure of the rank and file, now began to publicly criticize their parties' pro-war course, although their objections remained limited.

Three months after the Zimmerwald conference, Georg Ledebour and seventeen other SPD Reichstag deputies joined Liebknecht and Otto Rühle in voting against war credits. A substantial part of the historic leadership of the German Socialist movement now stood in opposition to the SPD's most openly chauvinist wing.

In France, the Zimmerwaldists formed the "Committee for the Resumption of International Relations" in which both Leon Trotsky and Bolshevik leader Inessa Armand played an active role. The committee won the support of the General Confederation of Labor (CGT) teachers' union and local organizations of the French Socialist Party. Early in 1916 an influential Centrist current led by Jean Longuet and Adrien Pressemane broke with the party majority and adopted a stance of limited opposition.

The Swiss Social Democratic Party voted at its November 1915 convention to endorse the Zimmerwald manifesto, overturning the previous stand of its executive committee. It also adopted by a vote of 258 to 141 an amendment by Zimmerwald Left forces that specified that "peace can be achieved only through revolutionary actions by the working class."[3]

The Italian Socialist Party confirmed its stand of active support for the Zimmerwald movement. Both the Romanian Socialist Party and the Bulgarian left-wing Socialists (the Tesnyaki) lent their support. In Britain, the Independent Labour Party confirmed its stand for the Zimmerwald resolutions, while the British Socialist Party split, a majority adhering to Zimmerwald. The second issue of the International Socialist Committee's *Bulletin,* published November 27, 1915, reported the adherence as well of the Socialist Party and the Socialist Labor Party of the United States, the Socialist Party of Portugal, and the Socialist Federation of Salonika, Greece.

In the Netherlands, the *De Tribune* group, led by Hermann Gorter and David Wijnkoop, rejected signing the Zimmerwald manifesto. Wijnkoop criticized the manifesto's "socialist peace demands," its failure to specify opposition to war credits, and, in particular, its inclusion of the concept of national self-determination. A separate organization led by Henriette Roland-Holst, the Revolutionary Socialist League, built support for the manifesto. Later, the two groups united on the basis of support to the Zimmerwald Left.[4]

Trotsky wrote an extensive account of the Zimmerwald conference for *Nashe Slovo.* He praised the draft resolution presented by Lenin and Karl Radek, considering that it "represented a giant step forward for authentic revolutionary-socialist internationalism. It did not mention 'the defeat of Russia is the lesser evil' (one could imagine what a welcome this Russian national thesis would receive from the German opposition!); it did not elevate splitting the workers' organizations to a principle; and, finally, it recognized the revolutionary significance of the struggle for peace. In this framework everything separating the position of *Sotsial-Demokrat* from that of *Nashe Slovo* was absent from the draft resolution. It only remained for the representative of *Nashe Slovo* to declare his solidarity with the basic theses of the resolution and to propose it be transmitted to the commission for a happier formulation. Unfortunately, the resolution did not obtain a majority."[5]

Trotsky considered that the three draft manifestos placed before the conference reflected three separate currents of opinion among the delegates, which he analyzed in the following passage from his *Nashe Slovo* articles on Zimmerwald.

The work of the Zimmerwald conference[6]

by Leon Trotsky

The reports of the delegates from different countries revealed several tendencies among participants at the conference. This was especially true in the discussion of the main question on the agenda, the attitude toward the war and the struggle for peace.

One wing of the conference stood on the far left. It held that the old Socialist parties, such as those of Germany and

France, had politically liquidated themselves, not only in this critical period but forever, by tying their fate to that of the capitalist states in the most crucial period of European history. The workers' parties, it argued, could be regenerated only out of new forces, which had to raise the banner of split everywhere and break all organizational ties to the politics of the *Burgfrieden* [civil peace] and the *union sacrée* [sacred unity]. Lenin was the outstanding spokesperson for this group at the conference. More or less closely affiliated to him and his nearest friends were the Swedish deputy, Höglund, who leads a left-wing group, and the Norwegian leader of the youth leagues, Nerman.

Another group played, in a certain sense, the role of "center" at the conference. It was composed of a number of delegates who were no less hostile to the politics of the official Western European parties than was the first group. But they did not consider an immediate organizational split to be a mandatory precondition for all work in an internationalist spirit. This group's representatives, like those of the far left, proceeded from the position that the Second International's collapse resulted from an entire historical period of political stagnation and of immobility in international relations, at least in Western Europe. An entire generation in the workers' movement had been molded in an atmosphere of systematic adaptation to the parliamentary state, and at the critical moment joined their own fate to its.

The delegates of both this group and of the left agreed that after the war things could not go back to the way they were. Profound changes were occurring in the very heart of the Socialist parties. But the center did not consider an organized split to be politically necessary in the mass parties, such as those of Western Europe. Rather, an irreconcilable ideological and political struggle for influence over the masses within these organizations was needed. The left elements of the German delegation (the "Spartacists"),

Roland-Holst, Balabanoff, a section of the Italian delegates, and a section of the Russian, Balkan, and Swiss delegates belonged to this second group.

Finally, the third group was composed of the most moderate elements, who saw the conference's main purpose as being a demonstration for peace. Most of them hoped that after the war was over the present nationalist infection in the workers' movement would end and everything would return to the same old rut. This moderate group included a section of the German and the Italian delegates, and the French.

These three groupings clearly differentiated themselves by their opposing attitudes toward the tasks of the conference. In the name of a complete break with social nationalism, the first group inclined for the most part toward a narrow choice of cothinkers for the struggle within the old parties. The third group, meanwhile, wanted to limit the entire conference to the idea of a demonstration for peace.

The majority of the conference refused to draw up a programmatic tactical resolution. Thus it fell to the left wing to put the immediate task in reviving the International, the struggle against the war, on a revolutionary class track. We think that this goal, to the extent conditions permitted, was achieved. . . .

Three drafts of a manifesto were presented: from the editorial board of *Sotsial-Demokrat,* from the right wing of the German opposition, and from the *Nashe Slovo* delegation.

The draft of *Sotsial-Demokrat* tried to delineate specific methods of struggle along the lines of its previously rejected resolution. Leaving aside the question of *to what extent* it was appropriate to simply lift tactical prescriptions from a resolution and incorporate them into a manifesto, once the resolution was rejected there could be no hope of doing this.

The basic sin of *Sotsial-Demokrat*'s draft was an indecisive, evasive, and ambiguous attitude toward the slogan of the struggle for peace. Especially at the preliminary conference Comrade Lenin revealed clearly that, consistent with his earlier reports and articles, he personally had a completely *negative* attitude to the slogan of the struggle for peace. His political position on this question was summed up with the aphorism: our task is not to force the cannon to be silent, but rather to make them serve our ends.

Certainly revolutionists are distinguished from pacifists by the fact that we want to convert even military resources into instruments of the proletarian revolution. Counterposing this task to the struggle for peace, however, is entirely incorrect. Before the German proletariat will want to aim the big guns at its class enemies, it has to stop wanting to aim them at its class brothers. It must unite in opposition to *this* war, which is exterminating and bleeding white both itself and its social ally across the trenches.

The slogan of stopping the war is that of class self-preservation for the socialist proletariat. It is the slogan of international rapprochement, and therefore the precondition for revolutionary activity. But, in *Sotsial-Demokrat*'s draft, as in its entire platform, the slogan of peace appeared only as a half-hearted concession by pure revolutionary spirit to pacifist human flesh and not as the immediate central cry of the proletariat, mobilizing it against militarism and chauvinism.

On October 11, 1915, *Sotsial-Demokrat* published a double-sized issue containing documents and analyses of the Zimmerwald conference. It included the following assessment by Lenin of the conference's significance.

The first step[7]

by V.I. Lenin

The development of the international socialist movement is slow during the tremendous crisis created by the war. Yet it is moving towards a break with opportunism and social-chauvinism, as was clearly shown by the International Socialist Conference held at Zimmerwald, Switzerland, between September 5 and 8, 1915.

For a whole year, the socialists of the warring and the neutral countries vacillated and temporised. Afraid to admit to themselves the gravity of the crisis, they did not wish to look reality in the face, and kept deferring in a thousand ways the inevitable break with the opportunism and Kautskyism prevalent in the official parties of Western Europe.

However, the analysis of events which we gave a year ago in the Manifesto of the Central Committee (*Sotsial-Demokrat* No. 33)[8] has proved correct; the events have borne out its correctness. They *took* a course that resulted in the first International Socialist Conference being attended by representatives of the protesting elements of the minorities in Germany, France, Sweden, and Norway, who acted *against* the decisions of the official parties, i.e., in fact acted schismatically.

The work of the Conference was summed up in a manifesto and a resolution expressing sympathy with the arrested and persecuted. Both documents appear in this issue of *Sotsial-Demokrat.* By nineteen votes to twelve, the Conference refused to submit to a committee the draft resolution proposed by us and other revolutionary Marxists; our draft manifesto was passed on to the committee together with two others, for a joint manifesto to be drawn up. The reader will find elsewhere in this issue our two drafts; a comparison of the latter with the manifesto adopted clearly shows that a number of fundamental ideas of revolutionary Marxism were adopted.

In practice, the manifesto signifies a step towards an ideological and practical break with opportunism and social-chauvinism. At the same time, the manifesto, as any analysis will show, contains inconsistencies, and does not say everything that should be said.

The manifesto calls the war imperialist and emphasises two features of imperialism: the striving of the capitalists of *every* nation for profits and the exploitation of others, and the striving of the Great Powers to partition the world and "enslave" weaker nations. The manifesto repeats the most essential things that should be said of the imperialist nature of the war, and were said in our resolution. In this respect, the manifesto merely *popularises* our resolution. Popularisation is undoubtedly a useful thing. However, if we want clear thinking in the working class and attach importance to systematic and unflagging propaganda, we must accurately and fully define the principles to be popularised. If that is not done, we risk repeating the error, the fault of the Second International which led to its collapse, viz., we shall be leaving room for ambiguity and misinterpretations. Is it, for instance, possible to deny the signal importance of the idea, expressed in our resolution, that the objective conditions are mature for socialism? The "popular" exposition of the manifesto omitted this idea; failure has attended the attempt to combine, in one document, a clear and precise resolution based on principle, and an appeal.

"The capitalists of all countries . . . claim that the war serves to defend the fatherland. . . . They are lying . . .", the manifesto continues. Here again, this forthright statement that the fundamental idea of opportunism in the present war—the "defence-of-the-fatherland" idea—is a lie, is a repetition of the kernel of the revolutionary Marxists' resolution. Again, the manifesto regrettably fails to say everything that should be said; it is half-hearted, afraid to speak the whole truth. After a year of war, who today is not aware of the actual damage caused to socialism, not only by the capitalist press *repeating and endorsing* the capitalists' *lies* (it is its business as a capitalist press to repeat the capitalists' lies), but also by the greater part of the socialist press doing so? Who does not know that European socialism's greatest crisis has been brought about not by the "capitalists' lies", but by the *lies* of Guesde, Hyndman, Vandervelde, Plekhanov and *Kautsky*? Who does not know that the *lies* spoken by such leaders suddenly revealed all the strength of the opportunism that swept them away at the decisive moment?

Let us take a look at what has come about: To make the masses see things in a clearer light, the manifesto says that in the present war the defence of the fatherland idea is a capitalist lie. The European masses, however, are not illiterate, and almost all who have read the manifesto have heard, and still hear *that same lie* from hundreds of socialist papers, journals, and pamphlets, echoing it after Plekhanov, Hyndman, Kautsky and Co. What will the readers of the manifesto think? What thoughts will arise in them after this display of timidity by the authors of the manifesto? Disregard the capitalists' lie about the defence of the fatherland, the manifesto tells the workers. Well and good. Practically all of them will say or think: the *capitalists'* lie has long stopped bothering us, but the lie of Kautsky and Co. . . .

The manifesto goes on to repeat another important idea in our resolution, viz., that the socialist parties and the workers' organisations of the various countries "have *flouted* obligations stemming from the decisions of the

Stuttgart, Copenhagen and Basel congresses"; that the International Socialist Bureau too has *failed to do its duty;* that this failure to do its duty consisted in voting for war credits, joining governments, recognising "a class truce" (submission to which the manifesto calls *slavish;* in other words, it accuses Guesde, Plekhanov, Kautsky and Co. of substituting for propaganda of socialism the propaganda of *slavish* ideas).

Is it consistent, we shall ask, to speak, in a "popular" manifesto, of the failure of a number of parties to do their duty (it is common knowledge that the reference is to the strongest parties and the workers' organisations in the most advanced countries: Britain, France and Germany), without giving any explanation of this startling and unprecedented fact? The greater part of the socialist parties and the International Socialist Bureau itself have failed to do their duty! What is this—an accident and the failure of individuals, or the turning-point of an entire epoch? If it is the former, and *we* circulate that idea among the masses, it is tantamount to *our* renouncing the fundamentals of socialist doctrine. If it is the latter, how can we fail to say so forthright? We are facing a moment of historic significance—the collapse of the International as a whole, a turning-point of an entire epoch—and yet we are *afraid* to tell the masses that the whole truth must be sought for and found, and that we must do our thinking to the very end. It is preposterous and ridiculous to suppose that the International Socialist Bureau and a number of parties could have collapsed, *without* linking up this event with the long history of the origin, the growth, the maturing and *over*-maturing of the general European opportunist movement, with its deep economic roots—deep, not in the sense that it is intimately linked with the masses, but in the sense that it is connected with a certain stratum of society.

Passing on to the "struggle for peace", the manifesto states that: "This struggle is a struggle for freedom, the brotherhood of peoples, and socialism". It goes on to explain that in wartime the workers make sacrifices "in the service of the ruling classes", whereas they must learn to make sacrifices "*for their own cause*" (doubly underscored in the manifesto), "for the sacred aims of socialism". The resolution which expresses sympathy with arrested and persecuted fighters says that "the Conference solemnly undertakes to honour the living and the dead by *emulating their example*" and that its aim will be to "arouse the revolutionary spirit in the international proletariat".

All these ideas are a reiteration of our resolution's fundamental idea that a struggle for peace *without* a revolutionary struggle is a hollow and false phrase, and that a revolutionary struggle for socialism is the only way to put an end to the horror of war. But here too we find inconsistency, timidity, and a failure to say everything that ought to be said: it calls upon the masses to *emulate the example* of the revolutionary fighters; it declares that the five members of the Russian Social-Democratic Labour Duma group who have been sentenced to exile in Siberia have carried on "the glorious revolutionary tradition of Russia"; it proclaims the necessity of "arousing the revolutionary spirit", but *it does not specify* forthright and clearly the revolutionary methods of struggle.

Was our Central Committee right in signing this manifesto, with all its inconsistency and timidity? We think it was. Our non-agreement, the non-agreement, not only of our Central Committee but of the entire *international* Left-wing section of the Conference, which stands by the principles of *revolutionary Marxism,* is openly expressed in a special resolution, a separate draft manifesto, and a separate declaration on the vote for a compromise manifesto. We did not conceal a jot of our views, slogans, or tactics. A German edition of our pamphlet, *Socialism and War,* was handed out at the Conference. We have spread, are spreading, and shall continue to spread our views with no less energy than the manifesto will. It is a fact that this manifesto is a *step forward* towards a real struggle against opportunism, towards a rupture with it. It would be sectarianism to refuse to take this step forward *together* with the minority of German, French, Swedish, Norwegian, and Swiss socialists, when we retain full freedom and full opportunity to criticise inconsistency and to work for greater things.* It would be poor war tactics to refuse to adhere to the mounting international protest movement against social-chauvinism just because this movement is slow, because it takes "only" a single step forward and because it is ready and willing to take a step backward tomorrow and make peace with the old International Socialist Bureau. Its readiness to make peace with the opportunists is so far merely wishful thinking. Will the opportunists agree to a peace? Is peace *objectively* possible between *trends* that are dividing more and more deeply—social-chauvinism and Kautskyism on the one hand, and on the other, revolutionary internationalist Marxism? We consider it impossible, and we shall continue our line, encouraged as we are by its *success* at the Conference of September 5–8.

The success of our line is beyond doubt. Compare the facts: In September 1914, our Central Committee's Manifesto seemed almost isolated. In March 1915, an international women's conference adopted a miserable pacifist resolution, which was blindly followed by the Organising Committee. In September 1915, we rallied in a whole group of the international Left wing. We came out with our own tactics, voiced a number of fundamental ideas in a joint manifesto, and took part in the formation of an I.S.C. (International Socialist Committee), i.e., a practically new International Socialist Bureau, against the wishes of the old one, and on the basis of a manifesto that openly condemns the tactics of the latter.

The workers of Russia, whose overwhelming majority followed our Party and its Central Committee even in the years 1912–14, will now, from the experience of the international socialist movement, see that our tactics are being confirmed in a wider area, and that our fundamental ideas are shared by an ever growing and finer part of the proletarian International.

* We are not frightened by the fact that the Organising Committee and the Social-Revolutionaries signed the manifesto diplomatically, retaining all their links with—and *all their attachment* to *Nasha Zarya*, Rubanovich, and the July 1915 Conference of the Popular Socialists and the Social-Revolutionaries in Russia.[9] We have means enough to combat corrupt diplomacy and unmask it. It is more and more unmasking itself. *Nasha Zarya* and Chkheidze's group are *helping* us unmask Axelrod and Co. [Footnote by Lenin.]

The Zimmerwald Left elected a bureau of Lenin, Radek, and Zinoviev, who undertook an active correspondence, and distributed the left resolution and manifesto as widely as possible. Through various channels the resolution was published in English, French, German, Polish, and Russian. The Zimmerwald Left printed a small publication, *Internationale Flugblätter* (International Leaflets), containing the resolution and the draft manifesto. The following editorial by Karl Radek introduced the Zimmerwald Left to left Socialists in Western Europe.

The Zimmerwald Left[10]

by Karl Radek

In September 1915 a conference was held in Zimmerwald of Socialist parties, trade unions, and groups from Germany, France, Italy, Russia, Poland, Latvia, Bulgaria, Romania, Switzerland, the Netherlands, Norway, and Sweden to discuss the struggle against the war. It published a unanimously adopted *manifesto* and a declaration of solidarity with those victimized in the revolutionary struggle against the war, and established an *International Socialist Committee in Bern,* which is to maintain the ties among the affiliated parties and unify their struggle against the war. Since then the Independent Labour Party of England, the Socialist Party of Portugal, the Federation of Haute-Vienne [of the Socialist Party] in France, and other organizations have joined in endorsing the conference resolutions.

The Zimmerwald conference initiated the *reconstruction* of the International and the *resumption of the struggle* for the interests of the working class and for socialism. While we are pleased with this development, we cannot help but point out to the international working class that this initial step *was made very timidly.* It gives us no grounds for confidence that the majority of conference participants are conscious of what *must follow this first step.*

Official representatives of the biggest parties of the International, the German and French parties, were absent from the conference. Only oppositional minorities from these countries were represented. The International Socialist Bureau, primarily charged and obligated to lead the struggle against the war, was absent. Why? The manifesto of the Zimmerwald conference says that these forces "disregarded" the commitments undertaken at the Stuttgart, Copenhagen, and Basel congresses. Furthermore, they "gave up the class struggle," approved war credits, "placed themselves in various ways at the disposal of the governments for the most diverse services," and "delivered up Socialist ministers as hostages." And that puts it very mildly indeed.

The war represents the harshest form of exploitation and oppression of the working class. In the munitions factories the working day is being lengthened and the pace of the work increased without limit. Everywhere the capitalists hire women and reduce wages while food prices increase enormously. Democratic rights such as freedom of the press, of assembly, and of association are surrendered to the most brutal military dictatorship. Capital is no longer content with the workers' sweat; it demands their blood. Anyone who suspends the class struggle under such conditions and takes "responsibility for the war" is a *traitor who has abandoned the working class in face of the enemy, indeed, handed it over to the enemy*—regardless of the high-sounding phrases used to sweeten this abandonment of the class struggle. It was *politically necessary* to say this openly so that the workers could know *that there can be no peace with those who advocate the policy of holding out to the end.*

Why did the majority of the Socialist leaders ally with capital against the working class? Why do they demand that the proletariat hold out in a war in which millions lose their lives for the sake of the capitalists' profits? This question forces itself on every worker. Unless it is answered, the struggle cannot be carried out. The Zimmerwald Manifesto fails to provide an answer.

The onset of capitalism's stormy upsurge of the 1890s brought a period of high employment, filling the labor aristocracy with illusions about the peaceful evolution of national and world politics. *Opportunism* and *reformism* represented in part the interests of the labor aristocracy and in part the endeavors of the bourgeois intelligentsia to reconcile the proletariat with capital. Within the working class opportunism systematically fostered illusions of a peaceful growing-over into socialism. This made it harder for workers to recognize the signs of the times expressed in the ever-worsening inflation, the lack of progress in social policy, the attacks on democratic rights, the uninterrupted arms race, the repeated instances of imperialist conflicts, and the growing danger of war.

Opportunism also made it more difficult for workers to recognize that these new conditions required more militant tactics. The struggle against the newly dawning epoch of imperialism was limited to weak attempts at international protest. And these were not even capable of overcoming the *nationalist limitations* of the leading layers of the working class, although capital's international interpenetration and the migration of workers had laid the basis for international tactics. Instead of counteracting the narrow horizons of the working class, opportunism reinforced them. It worked systematically to reduce the significance of international solidarity in the eyes of the working class (the fight against the one-day strike on May Day),[11] opposed every attempt at international revolutionary actions, and transformed the International into an empty phrase for holiday occasions.

Opportunism also sought to nip in the bud any movement of revolutionary action. We need only recall its opposition to the mass suffrage demonstrations and the idea of the mass strike in Germany or the resistance to the stormy strike movement in England.[12] The German opportunists attempted to wangle some reforms from the government in return for restraining such activity. The English trade unionists also tried to paralyze the strike movement before it grew into a revolutionary mass struggle by wheeling and dealing with the bourgeoisie for peaceful arbitration.

The opportunists hoped their betrayal of socialism in the war would wring new concessions from the bourgeoisie. The labor aristocracy was also supposed to get a share in the imperialist booty (income derived from the colonies and from domination of world markets) through higher wages and certain rights. Even if this were possible, it would be at the expense of the broadest layers of the people both at home and abroad. But this was of no concern to the opportunists. They now step forward as *social patriots,* who proclaim "defense of the fatherland" in order to mask their traitorous alliance with their own bourgeoisie, which subjugates alien peoples.

The Zimmerwald conference was not able to explain all this to the working class. No matter how much it condemned the consequences of such politics, it still had not decided to break from them, clearly and resolutely. To lash out at the politics of opportunism would have entailed such a break, and the *counterposition of a clear revolutionary policy,* as outlined in our resolution. The Zimmerwald conference did not say, and say clearly, what had to be said about the past, the shameful present, or the future. Why? The *majority of the conference* consisted of two groups. First, comrades who, while they opposed the politics of social patriotism, still wanted at all costs to avoid a split with the big Socialist parties. They remain confused about the profound nature of the international collapse and maintain hopes that these parties as a whole can be won to socialism. Second, the majority included comrades who understood the necessity of a revolutionary policy. But considering that the disenchantment of the working class is just beginning, they thought it premature to proclaim the great objectives of our struggle and the paths of revolutionary action that lead to them.

The first group did not want a revolutionary struggle. The second either did not yet understand its necessity or else thought that it was premature.

The representatives of the Central Committee of Russian Social Democracy, the Regional Executive Committee of the Polish and Lithuanian Social Democracy, the Central Committee of the Latvian Social Democracy, a part of the German revolutionary Social Democrats, the revolutionary Social Democrats of Sweden and Norway, and a part of the Swiss delegation emerged as the *left* at *Zimmerwald*. They presented the conference with a draft resolution and a call to action and demanded a clear revolutionary policy along these lines. In answer to those who hesitated, who thought that a revolutionary policy was premature, they said that if we call on the workers to conduct an implacable, proletarian class struggle for peace and socialism, as the Zimmerwald Manifesto does; if we tell them that there is no sacrifice too great, then we must tell them *how this struggle is to be conducted.* Otherwise the social patriots will cry out: *Words without content! Impotent, stale phrases!* And they will be able in this way to *discourage* the awakening workers.

It may yet be a long time before the broad masses, bled white by the war, recover and renew the struggle. We can shorten this time, however, by explaining to the most conscious workers why the International collapsed, how they have to struggle, for what goals they must appeal to other workers, and how they must organize the struggle under conditions of military rule.

The more difficult the situation, the clearer must be the politics of socialism. It is never too early to tell workers their true situation.

To those who have not yet understood the profound nature of the collapse and the necessity of stepping up the struggle, the Zimmerwald Left said: "If you do not take the trouble to understand the dreadful lessons of the war, then your calls to struggle amount only to yearning for peace. The Scheidemanns, Renaudels, Plekhanovs, and Hyndmans will brand you as starry-eyed dreamers for peace, and rightly so. These agents of the bourgeoisie will take those who still hope they can be won over and wrap them around their little fingers, making them share the responsibility for their criminal policies."

The left wing remained a minority. Only four members of the majority supported the left's draft resolution, submitted by eight delegates, by calling for its submission to the editing commission. By a vote of nineteen to twelve, the conference decided that it was not yet time to adopt clear guidelines for proletarian politics. The left attempted to improve the majority manifesto, but with only limited success. In spite of this, the left decided to vote for the manifesto for the following reasons. It would be doctrinaire and sectarian to separate ourselves from forces that are beginning, to some extent, to struggle against social patriotism in their own countries while they fend off furious attacks from the social patriots. Their conduct justifies hopes they will draw the political conclusions from the struggle. The Zimmerwald Left voted for the manifesto, but differentiated itself from the text's weaknesses and half measures by making the following declaration for the minutes:

"We are not fully satisfied with the conference manifesto. It contains no characterization of opportunism—either when open or when disguised with radical phrases—which not only bears the main responsibility for the International's disintegration, but perpetuates that state of affairs. It contains no clear characterization of the methods of struggle against the war. As before, in the press of the International and in its meetings, we will argue for a firm Marxist position on the tasks of the proletariat in the epoch of imperialism. We are voting for the manifesto because we see it as a *call to struggle* and because we want to march forward in this struggle arm in arm with the other sections of the International."

Part of our predictions have already come true. The German social patriots scoff at the manifesto in their leading organ, *Internationale Korrespondenz* (International Correspondence), published by the trade union commission and used by most of the social-patriotic press, and in an article by Wilhelm Kolb in *Die Neue Zeit*. "You who preach so glibly of peace, how will you fight for it?" they mockingly ask. But at the same time the German party Executive Committee warns in a secret circular against the International Union of Socialist Youth Organizations' appeal summoning the proletarian youth vanguard to revolutionary struggle. They laugh at vague aspirations for peace, but take fright at calls to revolutionary struggle. For the servants of reaction are men of action. Pleas for peace go unheard. But every underground organization that spreads the idea of revolutionary struggle, every street demonstration, every hunger revolt, and every strike deals blows to the war cabal.

What do the social patriots say to the protestations by Zimmerwald conference organizers that they intend no break with social patriotism? The German and French party executive committees scream about a split! Hypocrites! It is the social patriots whose policies split the international proletariat. But they are right when they explain that you cannot at the same time both oppose social patriotism and work with it. Just as the Second International could not establish itself without breaking from *anarchism*, which rejected the parliamentary struggle, *the Third International will not be able to set up its line of battle without decisively breaking from social patriotism*. That is what we learn from the social patriots' howls of accusation, and it is necessary to take these lessons to heart.

Within the international framework laid down at Zimmerwald, on the basis of the parties affiliated to the Bern Commission and of the Zimmerwald Manifesto, it is necessary to support every revolutionary mass action and to energetically take up the *work of theoretical clarification* and of building an *underground organization.* To do this, the broadest layers of class-conscious workers must above all *clearly grasp the goals and methods* of our struggle both during the war and after. We are publishing the *resolution* and the *draft proposal for the call to action* of the Zimmerwald Left. We are calling on the workers to make these the basis for *discussion* and urging them to approach other opponents of social patriotism who have different views and clearly put forward their ideas. The question of the proletarian methods of struggle *cannot be confined to small conferences of leaders.* The liberation of the working class can only be accomplished through its own efforts! So now you must discuss how this is to be achieved.

We do not want to create the illusion that we are a powerful and homogeneous force. We represent a section of the international proletariat that is only gradually awakening. But, despite the obstacle of censorship, the voices that reach us every day from the warring countries show that the layer of internationalists that thinks and wants to act as we do is larger than we believed. With every day this layer will grow until it has become a great combative army. For the positions that we advocate and the means of struggle that we recommend to the proletariat are not miraculous potions we have invented. Rather they are points of view that will develop in the proletariat under the impact of the war's consequences, the growing burdens, the heightening social antagonisms, and the strengthening of reaction.

In spite of the social patriots' cries that there can be no international revolutionary movement during the war, we see political strikes in Russia, demonstrations against the high cost of living in Germany, strikes in England and Italy. These are only beginnings, it is true, but with the support of revolutionary forces they can develop into a mass struggle of the proletariat against the war and capitalism. The social patriots' blindness toward these facts only proves that they are afraid of them. They cry out that the revolution is impossible only so that they will not have to support its initial stages. But neither the treacherous phrases of the social patriots nor persecution by the state will succeed. Denounced today as revolutionary illusions, our slogans will become tomorrow the common property of the class-conscious proletariat within a growing revolutionary movement and the banner it carries into battle.

The Socialist groups in the Zimmerwald Left came from diverse political backgrounds, and held widely separated positions on many of the questions posed by the collapse of the old International. The Bolsheviks sought ways to exchange views with other currents that supported the Zimmerwald Left or that were attracted to it. Their participation in the mass workers' and peasants' upsurges in 1905–1907 and 1912–1914 gave the Bolsheviks experience in applying Marxist ideas other left-wing Socialist currents still lacked.

One of the groups the Bolsheviks addressed was the Socialist Propaganda League in the United States, a small revolutionary group influenced by the ideas of Anton Pannekoek and the Dutch Tribunists. Lenin received a copy of their October 1915 manifesto, and replied in November with the following letter in English, to which he attached copies of the resolution and the manifesto of the Zimmerwald Left. The Socialist Propaganda League eventually adopted the program of the Zimmerwald Left in January 1917.

Letter to the secretary of the Socialist Propaganda League[13]

by V.I. Lenin

Dear Comrades!

We are extremely glad to get your leaflet. Your appeal to the members of the Socialist Party to struggle for a new International, for clear-cut revolutionary socialism as taught by Marx and Engels, and against the opportunism, especially against those who are in favor of working class participation in a war of defence, corresponds fully with the position our party (Social-Democratic Labor Party of Russia *Central Committee*) has taken from the beginning of this war and has always taken during more than ten years.

We send you our sincerest greetings & best wishes of success in our fight for true internationalism.

In our press & in our propaganda we differ from your programme in several points & we think it is quite necessary that we expose you briefly these points in order to make immediate & serious steps for the coordination of the international strife of the incompromisingly revolutionary Socialists especially Marxists in all countries.

We criticise in the most severe manner the old, Second (1889–1914) International, we declare it dead & not worth to be restored on old basis. But we never say in our press that too great emphasis has been heretofore placed upon so-called "Immediate Demands", and that thereby the socialism can be diluted: we say & we prove that all bourgeois parties, all parties except the working-class revolutionary Party, are liars & hypocrites when they speak about reforms. We try to help the working class to get the smallest possible but real improvement (economic & political) in their situation & we add always that *no* reform can be durable, sincere, serious if not seconded by revolutionary methods of struggle of the masses. We preach always that a socialist party not uniting this struggle for reforms with the revolutionary methods of working-class movement can become a sect, can be severed from the masses, & that this is the most pernicious menace to the success of the clear-cut revolutionary socialism.

We defend always in our press the democracy in the party. But we never speak against the centralization of the party. We are for the democratic centralism. We say that the centralization of the German Labor movement is not a feeble but a strong and good feature of it. The vice of the present Social-Democratic Party of Germany consists not in the centralization but in the preponderance of the opportunists, which should be excluded from the party especially now after their treacherous conduct in the war. If in any given crisis the small group (for instance our Central Committee is a small group) can act for directing the mighty mass *in a revolutionary direction,* it would be very good. And in *all* crises the masses can not act immediately, the masses want to be helped by the small groups of the central institutions of the parties. Our Central Committee quite at the beginning of this war, in September 1914, has directed the masses not to accept the lie about "the war of defence" & to break off with the opportunists & the "would-be-socialists-jingoes" (we call so the "Socialists" who are *now* in favor of the war of defence). We think that this centralistic measure of our Central Committee was useful & necessary.

We agree with you that we must be against craft Unionism & in favor of industrial Unionism, i.e., of big, centralized Trade Unions & in favor of the most active participation of *all* members of party in *all* economic struggles & in *all* trade union & cooperative organizations of the working class. But we consider that such people as Mr. Legien in Germany &

Mr. Gompers in the U. St. are bourgeois and that their policy is not a socialist but a nationalistic, middle class policy. Mr. Legien, Mr. Gompers & similar persons are not the representatives of working class, they represent the aristocracy & bureaucracy of the working class.

We entirely sympathize with you when in political action you claim the "mass action" of the workers. The German revolutionary & internationalist Socialists claim it also. In our press we try to define with more details what must be understood by political mass action, as f. i. political strikes (very usual in Russia), street demonstrations and civil war prepared by the present imperialist war between nations.

We do not preach unity in the *present* (prevailing in the Second International) socialist parties. On the contrary we preach *secession* with the opportunists. The war is the best object-lesson. In *all* countries the opportunists, their leaders, their most influential dailies & reviews are *for* the war, in other words, they have in reality *united* with "their" national bourgeoisie (middle class, capitalists) against the proletarian masses. You say, that in America there are also Socialists who have expressed themselves in favor of the participation in the war of defence. We are convinced, that unity with such men is an evil. *Such* unity is unity with the national middle class & capitalists, and a *division* with the international revolutionary working class. And we are for secession with nationalistic opportunists and unity with international revolutionary Marxists & working-class parties.

We never object in our press to the unity of S.P. & S.L.P. in America. We always quote letters from Marx & Engels (especially to Sorge, active member of American socialist movement), where both condemn the sectarian character of the S.L.P.

We fully agree with you in your criticism of the old International. We have participated in the conference of Zimmerwald (Switzerland) 5–8.IX. 1915. We have formed there a *left wing*, and have proposed *our resolution* & our draught of a manifesto. We have just published these documents in German & I send them to you (with the German translation of our small book about "Socialism & War"), hoping that in your League there are probably comrades, that know German. If you could help us to publish these things in English (it is possible only in America and later on we should send it to England), we would gladly accept your help.[14]

In our struggle for true internationalism & against "jingo-socialism" we always quote in our press the example of the opportunist leaders of the S.P. in America, who are in favor of restrictions of the immigration of Chinese and Japanese workers (especially after the Congress of Stuttgart, 1907, & *against* the decisions of Stuttgart). We think that one can not be internationalist & be at the same time in favor of such restrictions. And we assert that Socialists in America, especially English Socialists, belonging to the ruling, and *oppressing* nation, who are not against any restrictions of immigration, against the possession of colonies (Hawaii) and for the entire freedom of colonies, that such Socialists are in reality jingoes.

For conclusion I repeat once more best greetings & wishes for your League. We should be very glad to have a further information from you & to *unite* our struggle against opportunism & for the true internationalism.

Yours N. Lenin

N.B. There are *two* Soc.-Dem. parties in Russia. Our party ("*Central* Committee") is against opportunism. The other party ("*Organization* Committee") is opportunist. We are *against* the unity with them.

You can write to our official address (Bibliothèque russe. For the C.K. 7 rue Hugo de Senger. 7. Genève. Switzerland). But better write to my personal address: Wl. Ulianow. Seidenweg 4a, *Berne*. Switzerland.

An opportunity to win a wider audience for the ideas of the Zimmerwald Left arose in late 1915. Henriette Roland-Holst offered to finance and publish a German-language journal as a collaborative effort of the Dutch, Polish, and Russian forces in the Zimmerwald Left; her own Dutch group; Leon Trotsky, with whom she had collaborated at Zimmerwald; and other revolutionary forces. The Zimmerwald Left agreed, and Trotsky received invitations from both Roland-Holst and Radek to participate in the journal, to be called *Vorbote* (Herald).

Trotsky was initially favorable, but soon withdrew on the grounds that the Zimmerwald Left would be the predominant force in the editorial board. Roland-Holst then decided to limit the editorial team to herself and Anton Pannekoek, enlisting the Zimmerwald Left bureau members not as editors but as collaborators.

On learning of this, and on seeing Pannekoek's editorial for the first issue, Lenin wrote Roland-Holst noting that this represented a change from the original conception of the journal. He stated, however, that the Bolsheviks would not refuse to participate on this new basis, provided that they could be assured that *Vorbote* would not exclude articles by them on topics where they disagreed with the two editors. Roland-Holst provided this assurance, and two issues of *Vorbote* were published with their collaboration.[15]

The first issue of *Vorbote* contained an editorial by Pannekoek and the resolution of the Zimmerwald Left,[16] and two articles that originally appeared in *Kommunist:* Lenin's "The Collapse of the Second International," and Pannekoek's "Imperialism and the Tasks of the Proletariat." Also included were articles by Radek on defense of the fatherland, by Zinoviev and Roland-Holst on the Russian and Dutch Socialist movements, and informational reports on the Austrian and French parties.

After receiving the first issue, Trotsky wrote the following letter to Roland-Holst explaining his refusal to join *Vorbote.*

Letter to Roland-Holst on 'Vorbote'[17]

by Leon Trotsky

Dear friend,

I received your renewed and insistent invitation to collaborate on *Vorbote* and, almost on the same day, the first issue of this journal. And I cannot but be startled at the crying discrepancy that exists between the journal itself and the character that you ascribe to it in your letter.

You write of a coalition paper in which all revolutionary internationalist forces should collaborate, and you mention the Lenin group, *Nashe Slovo,* the Internationale Group, Rakovsky's group, the French lefts, and so on. However, *Vorbote* appears as the organ of the so-called Zimmerwald Left, that is, of the Lenin group. Lenin's draft resolution is printed as the journal's basic platform, and the introductory article declares that it is precisely the resolution of the Zimmerwald Left that constitutes the journal's starting point. Moreover, aside from yourself, only Leninists figure among the collaborators in the first issue. What does this mean?

First of all, as to the principled side of the matter. The ideological poverty of the journal will surprise every critical reader. You and I could vote at the Zimmerwald conference to forward Lenin's draft resolution to the commission, although I personally declared at the time that its exposition of some very important questions was extremely inadequate. There it was a matter of political fighting unity, of an *action.* Here, however, it is a question of a journal, an organ of criticism and propaganda. If it was possible there, for the sake of immediate political impact, to conditionally sign a document written in a spirit of the most primitive vulgarization of social radicalism, making such a document the *platform of a journal* is a crime against theory, politics, and—literary taste.

When a certain group decided in the nineteenth month of the war to address a *German* audience, then this pretension had to be justified by the serious and striking character of what they have to say. The first issue had all the more to be composed with great consciousness of theoretical and political responsibility, in that it is published by non-Germans in the German language. However, as I said, issue number one startles me by the poverty of its theoretical contents. What it says was already printed nine months ago in the journal *Kommunist.* In general, instead of the coalition organ of which you write, we Russians see before us a translation into German of Lenin's journal *Kommunist.*

I do not believe that such a journal will be able to attract serious forces from the German and French workers' movement. I know only too well with what scorn the leaflet of the Zimmerwald Left was regarded here to have any doubt of this. You must not forget, after all, that the Leninists do not have cothinkers in Germany, or in France, or in Britain, and in my view they cannot have them. Russian and Dutch extremism cannot together create an International. Dutch extremism is the product of a rigid petty-bourgeois milieu; Russian extremism is the product of an amorphous and backward social milieu, where the initial historical movement of the proletariat naturally requires a simplification and vulgarization of theory and politics. To think that Russian and Dutch extremism, in publishing a German-language journal, will prove capable of organizing workers over the heads of the left forces, is to fall into a pure Leninist utopia. . . .

As to the question of inviting in Kautsky and others, I

personally made no such proposal, and I do not think that this would be necessary or attainable under present circumstances. On the other hand, if an editorial board existed that was left-wing not in the formal and extremist sense but in the sense of genuine revolutionary Marxism, the collaboration of Kautsky or Friedrich Adler, if it were achieved, would not pose any danger, for it would signify a capitulation of the German center to the left. The appearance of an article by Kautsky in a journal of the type of which I speak would of course be of huge agitational significance, impelling many people to a journal still controlled by the far left. But all indications are that this is the purest utopia. Things have not gone so far with Kautsky for him to decide on such a crucial step. And I would of course not agree to make any kind of principled concessions to his tendency in order to secure his collaboration.

The only concession that should be made, therefore, would be to maintain a more polite tone with regard to Kautsky, who has been steadily moving to the left throughout the last six months. Such a concession in tone, however, would not be a concession to Kautsky but to political tact and literary taste. But, I repeat, for me the question of the journal is not in any way linked to an invitation to Kautsky or to the left Germans or centrist Austrians in general. It is only a question of securing for the journal the kind of editorship and management for the whole publication in which collective work by the left and extremist forces would really be possible.

Do not forget that we are not so numerous and the individual authority of each of us in the International is not so great as the authority of those against whom we must conduct a hard struggle. For us, therefore, it is a question of counterposing to their authority as individuals collective authorities, which can be built on the basis of collective theoretical and political work. But Leninism is the exclusion of all collectivity. If Lenin cannot restrain himself from the pleasure of adding footnotes to your article,[18] what must we expect his attitude to be to collaborators who are not also the publishers of the journal? That is why I fully stand by my refusal to participate in the journal in its present form, and my closest friends, the French, are in complete agreement with me.

In conclusion permit me to tell you that on the question of your article (which of course bears no relationship to the subject of this letter) you have taken in my opinion a very large step toward extremism. Your formalistic posing of the question of organizational split seems to me to be false. Just as false, if not more so, although on another plane, is your opinion of the right of nations to self-determination. You say that this right is unrealizable under capitalism and superfluous under socialism. Why it is superfluous under socialism I cannot understand. One would think that our politics now proceed from the conviction that we are entering an epoch of social revolution. Therefore we must have a program for social revolution, a program of proletarian state power in Europe. Is it really superfluous to tell the Poles, the Serbs, and the Alsatians what government the European proletariat will secure for them, once it is in power? Do you really think that national frictions and disputes will disappear from the face of the earth, once the proletariat has achieved power? I believe the contrary to be true: only then will they unfold in their full depth and sharpness and demand a complete answer. And we must explain what content the right of nations to self-determination will have under conditions of proletarian power, and not simply sweep away the question like a petty-bourgeois illusion. . . .

I strongly shake your hand and wish you all the best.

Yours,
Trotsky

The question of self-determination also provoked an extensive debate within the Zimmerwald Left. There was firm agreement within it, on a general level, in counterposing revolutionary socialism to opportunism and chauvinism. But in their criticisms of the opportunists' preoccupation with the struggle for reform of capitalism, Pannekoek and others rejected many immediate demands and tactics that the Bolsheviks had successfully integrated into their revolutionary program and practice. A prominent example was the Bolsheviks' support for the democratic demand for the right of oppressed nations to self-determination, which was rejected by both the Dutch and Polish adherents of the Zimmerwald Left.

Such political disagreements lay behind the differences over the composition of the *Vorbote* editorial board and control over the journal. In letters to Bolshevik leaders, Lenin held Karl Radek responsible for the exclusion of Bolsheviks from the editorial board, which had converted the journal into the vehicle of only one wing of the Zimmerwald Left, the Dutch Marxists, with whom Radek had long been associated and who shared his views on national self-determination.[19]

The second issue of *Vorbote,* published in April 1916, contained an exchange of views between Polish and Russian Socialists on this question. The theses of *Gazeta Robotnicza* (Workers' Gazette), drafted by Radek in collaboration with other leaders of the Polish Social Democratic opposition and printed below, explained the underlying grounds for their opposition to the self-determination demand.

Imperialism and national oppression[20]

by 'Gazeta Robotnicza'

1. Imperialism represents the tendency of finance capital *to outgrow the limits of the national state,* to seize overseas sources of raw materials, food supplies, spheres for investment, and markets for national capital, and also to form *large state units in Europe,* by combining adjacent territories that complement each other economically, regardless of the nationality of the inhabitants. There are also military reasons for this tendency toward combination. By sharpening the antagonisms between states, imperialism necessitates a more powerful capacity for both attack and defense.

Imperialism's tendency toward colonial and continental annexation signifies an *increase and generalization of national oppression.* Hitherto this existed only in those states populated by many nationalities where one nationality ruled over several for historic and geographic reasons.

2. This national oppression *contradicts the interests of the working class.* The same imperialist bureaucracy that is the instrument of national oppression becomes as well the agent of the *class oppression of the proletariat of its own nationality.* All the *means* used in the struggle against the oppressed peoples are turned against the fighting proletariat of the oppressing nation. At the same time national oppression *checks the class struggle* of the working class of the oppressed nation by restricting its *freedom to organize* and by pressing down its cultural level. It also arouses in the working class *feelings of solidarity with its national bourgeoisie.* Tied hand and foot, bribed politically by nationalism, the proletariat of the oppressed nation becomes a *helpless object*

of exploitation and hence a dangerous rival (wage-cutter, strikebreaker) of the workers of the oppressing nation.

When nationally alien regions are forced inside the boundaries of a victorious state, this creates new causes of war. The vanquished state will endeavor to regain these territories because it needs them economically and militarily, or because a slogan for national revenge can best cover up its own imperialist policy.

3. The Social Democratic party, therefore, must *fight* most energetically *against imperialism's policy of annexation,* as well as against the *policy of national oppression* that flows from it. The imperialists assert that colonies must be acquired for the development of capitalism. The Social Democratic party, on the contrary, points out that in Central and Western Europe, as well as in the United States of North America, the time is ripe for transforming capitalism into socialism, which requires no colonies. That is because socialism will be able to offer to backward peoples so much unselfish cultural assistance that it will be able to obtain from them, in free exchange and without domination, all that the socialist peoples are themselves unable to produce for geographic reasons. . . .

4. The Social Democratic struggle against annexations, against holding oppressed nations forcibly within the boundaries of the state that annexed them, begins with *the renunciation of any defense of the fatherland.* In the imperialist era defense of the fatherland can only be defense of the right of one's own bourgeoisie to oppress and plunder foreign peoples. Social Democrats *denounce national oppression* as a blow directed against the interests of the proletariat of the oppressor nation. They demand *all democratic rights* for the oppressed, including freedom of agitation for political separation, because democratic principles demand that agitation, whatever it may be, should be countered only through intellectual methods and not through violence. Social De-

mocracy thus rejects any responsibility for the results of the imperialist policy of oppression and strongly fights against it. *But neither does it advocate the erection of new boundary posts in Europe or the re-erection of those already torn down by imperialism. . . .*

Social Democracy demands that European capitalism renounce colonial expansion. It *utilizes* the struggle of the young colonial bourgeoisie against European imperialism *to sharpen the revolutionary crisis in Europe.* Yet it supports the proletarian struggles in the colonial countries against European and native capital, in order to hasten the time when socialism's hour will strike outside Europe. It also seeks to promote the colonial proletariat's understanding that its own lasting interests demand its solidarity, not with its national bourgeoisie, but with the European proletariat fighting for socialism.

5. Under capitalism it is impossible to reshape imperialism in line with the interests of the working class, or to put an end to its arms race. *In the same way imperialism cannot be stripped of its tendency toward national oppression or be made to recognize the right of the peoples to self-determination.* Therefore *the struggle against national oppression must be conducted as a struggle against imperialism and for socialism.*

In order to reach its goal and liberate the nationally oppressed masses, Social Democracy *must struggle for a social revolution* and must strive to extinguish capitalist rule. For only by eliminating capitalist private property can the working class abolish the objective interest in national oppression, which is only a part of class rule. A socialist society will know no oppression. It will grant all peoples the right to decide collectively on all their needs, and will grant every citizen the freedom to *participate* in deciding upon the tasks that he will help to accomplish.

Guiding the struggle against national oppression into

the wide stream of revolutionary mass struggle for socialism does not signify an indefinite postponement of that struggle, nor does it signify empty promises to the oppressed peoples for the future. The imperialist epoch arouses peoples to revolution and therefore is a period of socialist revolution in which the proletariat will break all the chains that bind it.

II. The so-called right of nations to self-determination

The self-determination formula was left to us as an inheritance from the Second International. There it had played an ambiguous role, aiming, on the one hand, to express a protest against all national subjugation; and on the other, Social Democracy's readiness to "defend the fatherland." It was applied to specific national questions only to evade looking into their content and the direction of their evolution.

The policy of defense of the fatherland has brought results in the World War that very clearly show the counterrevolutionary nature of the self-determination formula. Yet many still do not understand its deceptive character when used in an attempt to sum up our struggle against national oppression. Since it expresses sharp opposition to the oppressive tendencies of imperialism, some revolutionary Social Democrats, for example those in Russia, regard it as a necessary part of our revolutionary agitation. While we recognize the revolutionary proletarian goals that they seek to advance through using the slogan of self-determination, nonetheless we cannot accept this formula as a correct expression of our struggle against imperialism, for the following reasons:

1. *The right to self-determination cannot be realized in capitalist society.*

Modern nations constitute the political and cultural form of bourgeois rule over masses of people who share a common language. Divided into classes as they are, these nations possess no common interests and no common will. "National" policies are those that correspond to the interests of the ruling class. . . . In the relations of nations with one another, the interest of the strongest bourgeoisie prevails, or that of an alliance of bourgeoisies of several nations. Capitalism cannot postpone its expansion into new territories until it has imposed its will on the masses there through economic and cultural influence. That process would require decades, and such a peaceful expansion often encounters and is rendered impossible by the opposition of other capitalist groups. *In questions of the annexation of foreign territories, therefore, the forms of political democracy are dispensed with and replaced by brute force.* A referendum can be utilized only as open deception, to ratify what has been achieved by use of force. It is therefore quite impossible to make the will of nations the deciding factor in changing boundaries in capitalist society, as stipulated by the so-called right to self-determination.

Insofar as it is interpreted as meaning that each part of a nation should itself decide whether it will belong to this or that state, the self-determination demand is utopian, because capitalism will never leave it to the people to decide on its state boundaries. In addition, it is also particularistic and undemocratic. For if the people of a state had it in their power to decide on its boundaries, this decision would be rendered for the entire state and not a single province. Moreover, when it is a matter of disputes between two countries, democracy requires an agreement between their democratically elected representatives. . . .

2. *The right to self-determination is inapplicable to socialist society.*

The so-called right to self-determination is also invoked with the explanation that it will only be achieved under socialism and therefore expresses our struggle for socialism. The following objection must be raised against this. We know that socialism will abolish all national oppression, because it eliminates the class interests that generate it. Further, we have no reason to assume that economic and political units in socialist society will be national in character. In all probability the nation will only have the character of a cultural and linguistic unit. For the territorial subdivisions of socialist society, insofar as they exist at all, can only be determined by the requirements of production. This division will of course not be made by individual nations, separately, as an expression of their sovereignty, as the *"right of self-determination"* would have it, but through *joint decision* of all concerned citizens. To carry over the formula of "the right to self-determination" to socialism is to fully misunderstand the nature of a socialist community.

3. *The tactical consequences of using the formula of the right to self-determination.*

This slogan, like all utopian slogans, can only spread false conceptions of the nature of both capitalist and socialist society, and mislead the proletariat struggling against national oppression. This slogan arouses *false hopes* that capitalism can accommodate the national interests of weak peoples. It must rather be openly explained that the proletariat can only free itself from the danger of having its fate determined arbitrarily according to the military and economic interests of a capitalism shot through with contradictions, just as it can only free itself from the danger of war, *by doing away with capitalism itself.* Thus, independently and even against the will of those employing it, this slogan substitutes a national, reformist perspective *for the social-revolutionary outlook* which is a most important result of the World War. As part of the program of the proletariat of the *oppressed nation,* the slogan of the right to self-determination could serve as a bridge to social patriotism. . . .

If, however, the slogan of the right to self-determination is to be used in agitation as something only to be achieved through the social revolution, that is as a slogan leading us over to the struggle for socialism, then it is not only impossible, . . .

but also insufficient. For in a transitional period, when socialism is economically already possible, but social-revolutionary class struggles have not yet begun, *correct tactics* require a sharp *emphasis on the clear, unobscured slogan of socialism, of socialist revolution, as the central notion that broadens and sharpens every partial struggle.*

The best-known spokesperson for Polish Social Democracy on self-determination was Rosa Luxemburg. Her view at this time, which was at variance with that of *Gazeta Robotnicza*'s theses, is contained in her "Junius Pamphlet," and is printed in Chapter 10 of the present collection. Socialists uphold the right of national self-determination, she maintained, but she argued that it could only be realized in a socialist society.[21]

Lenin noted that it was above all the Dutch and Polish left Socialists who raised objections to the demand for "self-determination." This "is not at all due to the especially bad subjective qualities of the Dutch and Polish comrades but to the *specific* objective conditions in their countries. Both countries are: (1) small and helpless in the present-day "system" of great powers; (2) both are geographically situated between tremendously powerful imperialist plunderers engaged in the most bitter rivalry with each other (Britain and Germany; Germany and Russia); (3) in both there are terribly strong memories and traditions of the times when they *themselves* were great powers: Holland was once a colonial power greater than England, Poland was more cultured and was a stronger great power than Russia and Prussia; (4) to this day both retain their privileges consisting in the oppression of other peoples: the Dutch bourgeois owns the very wealthy Dutch East Indies; the Polish landed proprietor oppresses the Ukrainian and Byelorussian peasant; the Polish bourgeois, the Jew, etc."

Lenin thought that the Polish Social Democrats were correct in not raising the demand for Polish independence, and in stressing instead the need for unity in action with the workers of Germany and Russia. But they went wrong in generalizing this attitude, and applying it to the workers of other nations—especially the dominant nations. "It is *not* indifferent to the Russian and German workers whether Poland is independent, or they take part in annexing her," he wrote.

"The situation is, indeed, bewildering, but there is a way out in which *all* participants would remain internationalists: the Russian and German Social-Democrats by demanding for Poland unconditional '*freedom* to secede'; the Polish Social-Democrats by working for the unity of the proletarian struggle in both small and big countries without putting forward the slogan of Polish independence for the given epoch or the given period."[22]

The following is excerpted from the theses drafted by Lenin and submitted by the editors of *Sotsial-Demokrat* to the exchange in *Vorbote.*

The socialist revolution and the right of nations to self-determination[23]

1. Imperialism, socialism and the liberation of oppressed nations

Imperialism is the highest stage in the development of capitalism. In the foremost countries capital has outgrown the bounds of national states, has replaced competition by monopoly and has created all the objective conditions for the achievement of socialism. In Western Europe and in the United States, therefore, the revolutionary struggle of the proletariat for the overthrow of capitalist governments and the expropriation of the bourgeoisie is on the order of the day. Imperialism forces the masses into this struggle by sharpening class contradictions on a tremendous scale, by worsening the conditions of the masses both economically—trusts, high cost of living—and politically—the growth of militarism, more frequent wars, more powerful reaction, the intensification and expansion of national oppression and colonial plunder. Victorious socialism must necessarily establish a full democracy and, consequently, not only introduce full equality of nations but also realise the right of the oppressed nations to self-determination, i.e., the right to free political separation. Socialist parties which did not show by all their activity, both now, during the revolution, and after its victory, that they would liberate the enslaved nations and build up relations with them on the basis of a free union—and free union is a false phrase without the right to secede—these parties would be betraying socialism.

Democracy, of course, is also a form of state which must disappear when the state disappears, but that will only take place in the transition from conclusively victorious and consolidated socialism to full communism.

2. The socialist revolution and the struggle for democracy

The socialist revolution is not a single act, it is not one battle on one front, but a whole epoch of acute class conflicts, a long series of battles on all fronts, i.e., on all questions of economics and politics, battles that can only end in the expropriation of the bourgeoisie. It would be a radical mistake to think that the struggle for democracy was capable of diverting the proletariat from the socialist revolution or of hiding, overshadowing it, etc. On the contrary, in the same way as there can be no victorious socialism that does not practise full democracy, so the proletariat cannot prepare for its victory over the bourgeoisie without an all-round, consistent and revolutionary struggle for democracy.

It would be no less a mistake to remove one of the points of the democratic programme, for example, the point on the self-determination of nations, on the grounds of it being "impracticable" or "illusory" under imperialism. The contention that the right of nations to self-determination is impracticable within the bounds of capitalism can be understood either in the absolute, economic sense, or in the conditional, political sense.

In the first case it is radically incorrect from the standpoint of theory. First, in that sense, such things as, for example, labour money, or the abolition of crises, etc., are impracticable under capitalism. It is absolutely untrue that the self-determination of nations is *equally* impracticable. Secondly, even the one example of the secession of Norway from Sweden in 1905 is sufficient to refute "impracticability" in that sense. Thirdly, it would be absurd to deny that some slight change in the political and strategic relations of, say, Germany and Britain, might today or tomorrow make the formation of a new Polish, Indian and other similar state fully "practicable". Fourthly, finance capital, in its drive to expand, can "freely" buy or bribe the freest democratic or republican government and the elective officials of any, even an "independent", country. The domination of finance capital and of capital in general is not to be abolished by *any* reforms in the sphere of political democracy; and self-determination belongs wholly and exclusively to this sphere. This domination of finance capital, however, does not in the least nullify the significance of political democracy as a freer, wider and clearer *form* of class oppression and class struggle. Therefore all arguments about the "impracticability", in the economic sense, of one of the demands of political democracy under capitalism are reduced to a theoretically incorrect definition of the general and basic relationships of capitalism and of political democracy as a whole.

In the second case the assertion is incomplete and inaccurate. This is because not only the right of nations to self-determination, but *all* the fundamental demands of political democracy are only partially "practicable" under imperialism, and then in a distorted form and by way of exception (for example, the secession of Norway from Sweden in 1905). The demand for the immediate liberation of the colonies that is put forward by all revolutionary Social-Democrats is also "impracticable" under capitalism without a series of revolutions. But from this it does not by any means follow that Social-Democracy should reject the immediate and most determined struggle for *all* these demands—such a rejection would only play into the hands of the bourgeoisie and reaction—but, on the contrary, it follows that these demands must be formulated and put through in a revolutionary and not a reformist manner, going beyond the bounds of bourgeois legality, breaking them down, going beyond speeches in parliament and verbal protests, and drawing the masses into decisive action, extending and intensifying the struggle for every fundamental democratic demand up to a direct proletarian onslaught on the bourgeoisie, i.e., up to the socialist revolution that expropriates the bourgeoisie. The socialist revolution may flare up not only through some big strike, street demonstration or hunger riot or a military insurrection or colonial revolt, but also as a result of a political crisis such as the Dreyfus case or the Zabern incident,[24] or in connection with a referendum on the secession of an oppressed nation, etc.

Increased national oppression under imperialism does not mean that Social-Democracy should reject what the bourgeoisie call the "utopian" struggle for the freedom of nations to secede but, on the contrary, it should make greater use of the conflicts that arise in this sphere, *too*, as grounds for mass action and for revolutionary attacks on the bourgeoisie.

3. The significance of the right to self-determination and its relation to federation

The right of nations to self-determination implies exclusively the right to independence in the political sense, the right to free political separation from the oppressor nation. Specifically, this demand for political democracy implies complete freedom to agitate for secession and for a referendum on secession by the seceding nation. This demand, therefore, is not the equivalent of a demand for separation, fragmentation and the formation of small states. It implies only a consistent expression of struggle against all national oppression. The closer a democratic state system is to complete freedom to secede the less frequent and less ardent will the desire for separation be in practice, because big states afford indisputable advantages, both from the standpoint of economic progress and from that of the interests of the masses and, furthermore, these advantages increase with the growth of capitalism. Recognition of self-determination is not synonymous with recognition of federation as a principle. One may be a determined opponent of that principle and a champion of democratic centralism but still prefer federation to national inequality as the only way to full democratic centralism. It was from this standpoint that Marx, who was a centralist, preferred even the federation of Ireland and England to the forcible subordination of Ireland to the English.

The aim of socialism is not only to end the division of mankind into tiny states and the isolation of nations in any form, it is not only to bring the nations closer together but to integrate them. And it is precisely in order to achieve this aim that we must, on the one hand, explain to the masses the reactionary nature of Renner and Otto Bauer's idea of so-called "cultural and national autonomy"[25] and, on the other, demand the liberation of oppressed nations in a clearly and precisely formulated political programme that takes special account of the hypocrisy and cowardice of socialists in the oppressor nations, and not in general nebulous phrases, not in empty declamations and not by way of "relegating" the question until socialism has been achieved. In the same way as mankind can arrive at the abolition of classes only through a transition period of the dictatorship of the oppressed class, it can arrive at the inevitable integration of nations only through a transition period of the complete emancipation of all oppressed nations, i.e., their freedom to secede.

4. The proletarian-revolutionary presentation of the question of the self-determination of nations

The petty bourgeoisie had put forward not only the demand for the self-determination of nations but *all* the points of our democratic minimum programme long *before,* as far back as the seventeenth and eighteenth centuries. They are still putting them *all* forward in a utopian manner because they fail to see the class struggle and its increased intensity under democracy, and because they believe in "peaceful" capitalism. That is the exact nature of the utopia of a peaceful union of equal nations under imperialism which deceives the people and which is defended by Kautsky's followers. The programme of Social-Democracy, as a counter-balance to this petty-bourgeois, opportunist utopia, must postulate the division of nations into oppressor and oppressed as basic, significant and inevitable under imperialism.

The proletariat of the oppressor nations must not confine themselves to general, stereotyped phrases against annexation and in favour of the equality of nations in general, such as any pacifist bourgeois will repeat. The proletariat cannot remain silent on the question of the *frontiers* of a state founded on national oppression, a question so "unpleasant" for the imperialist bourgeoisie. The proletariat must struggle against the enforced retention of oppressed nations within the bounds of the given state, which means that they must fight for the right to self-determination. The proletariat must demand freedom of political separation for the colonies and nations oppressed by "their own" nation. Otherwise, the internationalism of the proletariat would be nothing but empty words; neither confidence nor class solidarity would be possible between the workers of the oppressed and the oppressor nations; the hypocrisy of the reformists and Kautskyites, who defend self-determination but remain silent about the nations oppressed by "their own" nation and kept in "their own" state by force, would remain unexposed.

On the other hand, the socialists of the oppressed nations must, in particular, defend and implement the full and unconditional unity, including organisational unity, of the workers of the oppressed nation and those of the oppressor nation. Without this it is impossible to defend the independent policy of the proletariat and their class solidarity with the proletariat of other countries in face of all manner of intrigues, treachery and trickery on the part of the bourgeoisie. The bourgeoisie of the oppressed nations persistently utilise the slogans of national liberation to deceive the workers; in their internal policy they use these slogans for reactionary agreements with the bourgeoisie of the dominant nation (for example, the Poles in Austria and Russia who come to terms with reactionaries for the oppression of the Jews and Ukrainians); in their foreign policy they strive to come to terms with one of the rival imperialist powers for the sake of implementing their predatory plans (the policy of the small Balkan states, etc.).

The fact that the struggle for national liberation against one imperialist power may, under certain conditions, be utilised by another "great" power for its own, equally imperialist, aims, is just as unlikely to make the Social-Democrats refuse to recognise the right of nations to self-determination as the numerous cases of bourgeois utilisation of republican slogans for the purpose of political deception and financial plunder (as in the Romance countries, for example) are unlikely to make the Social-Democrats reject their republicanism.*. . .

6. Three types of countries with respect to the self-determination of nations

In this respect, countries must be divided into three main types.

First, the advanced capitalist countries of Western Europe and the United States. In these countries progressive bourgeois national movements came to an end long ago. Every one of these "great" nations oppresses other nations both in the colonies and at home. The tasks of the proletariat of these ruling nations are the same as those of the proletariat in England in the nineteenth century in relation to Ireland.**

Secondly, Eastern Europe: Austria, the Balkans and particularly Russia. Here it was the twentieth century that particularly developed the bourgeois-democratic national movements and intensified the national struggle. The tasks of the proletariat in these countries, both in completing their bourgeois-democratic reforms, and rendering assistance to the socialist revolution in other countries, cannot be carried out without championing the right of nations to self-determination. The most difficult and most important task in this is to unite the class struggle of the workers of the oppressor nations with that of the workers of the oppressed nations.

Thirdly, the semi-colonial countries, such as China, Persia and Turkey, and all the colonies, which have a combined population of 1,000 million. In these countries the bourgeois-democratic movements either have hardly begun or have still a long way to go. Socialists must not only demand the unconditional and immediate liberation of the colonies without compensation—and this demand in its political expression signifies nothing else than the recognition of the right to self-determination; they must also render determined support to the more revolutionary elements in the bourgeois-democratic movements for national liberation in these countries and assist their uprising—or revolutionary war, in the event of one—*against* the imperialist powers that oppress them. . . .

8. The concrete tasks of the proletariat in the immediate future

The socialist revolution may begin in the very near future. In this case the proletariat will be faced with the immediate task of winning power, expropriating the banks and effecting other dictatorial measures. The bourgeoisie—and especially the intellectuals of the Fabian and Kautskyite type—will, at such a moment, strive to split and check the revolution by foisting limited, democratic aims on it. Whereas *any* purely democratic demands are in a certain sense liable to act as a hindrance to the revolution, provided the proletarian attack on the pillars of bourgeois power has begun, the necessity to proclaim and grant liberty to *all* oppressed peoples (i.e., their right to self-determination) will be as urgent in the socialist revolution as it was for the victory of the bourgeois-democratic revolution in, say, Germany in 1848, or Russia in 1905.

It is possible, however, that five, ten or more years will elapse before the socialist revolution begins. This will be the time for the revolutionary education of the masses in a spirit that will make it impossible for socialist-chauvinists and opportunists to belong to the working-class party and gain a victory, as was the case in 1914–16. The socialists must explain to the masses that British socialists who do not demand freedom to separate for the colonies and Ireland, German socialists who do not demand freedom to separate for the colonies, the Alsatians, Danes and Poles, and who do not extend their revolutionary propaganda and revolutionary mass activity directly to the sphere of struggle against national oppression, or who do not make use of such incidents as that at Zabern for the broadest illegal propaganda among the proletariat of the oppressor nation, for street demonstrations and revolutionary mass action—Russian socialists who do not demand freedom to separate for Finland, Poland, the Ukraine, etc., etc.—that such socialists act as chauvinists and lackeys of bloodstained and filthy imperialist monarchies and the imperialist bourgeoisie. . . .

9. The attitude of Russian and Polish Social-Democrats and of the Second International to self-determination

The latest formulation of the position of the Polish Social-Democrats on the national question (the declaration of the Polish Social-Democrats at the Zimmerwald Conference) contains the following ideas:

The declaration condemns the German and other governments that regard the "Polish regions" as a pawn in the forthcoming compensation game, *"depriving the Polish people of the opportunity of deciding their own fate themselves"*. "Polish Social-Democrats resolutely and solemnly protest against the *carving up and parcelling out of a whole country"*. . . . They flay the socialists who left it to the Hohenzollerns *"to liberate the oppressed peoples"*. They express the conviction that only participation in the approaching struggle of the international revolutionary proletariat, the struggle for socialism, *"will break the fetters of national oppression* and destroy *all forms of foreign* rule, will ensure for *the Polish people* the possibility of free all-round development as an *equal* member of a concord of nations". The declaration recognises that *"for the Poles"* the war is *"doubly* fratricidal". (*Bulletin of the International Socialist Committee* No. 2, September 27, 1915, p. 15. Russian translation in the symposium *The International and the War*, p. 97.)

These propositions do not differ in substance from recognition of the right of nations to self-determination, although their political formulations are even vaguer and more indeterminate than those of most programmes and resolutions of the Second International. Any attempt to express these ideas as precise political formulations and to define their applicability to the capitalist system or only to the socialist system will show even more clearly the mistake the Polish Social-Democrats make in denying the self-determination of nations.

The decision of the London International Socialist Congress of 1896, which recognised the self-determination of nations, should be supplemented on the basis of the above theses by specifying: (1) the particular urgency of this demand under imperialism, (2) the political conventionalism and class content of all the demands of political democracy, the one under discussion included, (3) the necessity to distinguish the concrete tasks of the Social-Democrats of the oppressor nations from those of the Social-Democrats of the oppressed nations, (4) the inconsistent, purely verbal recognition of self-determination by the opportunists and the Kautskyites, which is, therefore, hypocritical in its political significance, (5) the actual identity of the chauvinists and those Social-Democrats, especially those of the Great Powers (Great Russians, Anglo-Americans, Germans, French, Italians, Japanese, etc.), who do not uphold the freedom to secede for colonies and nations oppressed by "their own" nations, (6) the necessity to subordinate the struggle for the demand under discussion and for all the basic demands of political democracy directly to the revolutionary mass struggle for the overthrow of the bourgeois governments and for the achievement of socialism.

The introduction into the International of the viewpoint of certain small nations, especially that of the Polish Social-Democrats, who have been led by their struggle against the Polish bourgeoisie, which deceives the people with its nationalist slogans, to the incorrect denial of self-determination, would be a theoretical mistake, a substitution of Proudhonism for Marxism implying in practice involuntary support for the most dangerous chauvinism and opportunism of the Great-Power nations.

Editorial Board of Sotsial-Demokrat
Central Organ of R.S.D.L.P.

* It would, needless to say, be quite ridiculous to reject the right to self-determination on the grounds that it implies "defence of the fatherland". With equal right, i.e., with equal lack of seriousness, the social-chauvinists of 1914–16 refer to any of the demands of democracy (to its republicanism, for example) and to any formulation of the struggle against national oppression in order to justify "defence of the fatherland". Marxism deduces the defence of the fatherland in wars, for example, in the great French Revolution or the wars of Garibaldi, in Europe, and the renunciation of defence of the fatherland in the imperialist war of 1914–16, from an analysis of the concrete historical peculiarities of each individual war and never from any "general principle", or any one point of a programme.

** In some small states which have kept out of the war of 1914–16—Holland and Switzerland, for example—the bourgeoisie makes extensive use of the "self-determination of nations" slogan to justify participation in the imperialist war. This is a motive inducing the Social-Democrats in such countries to repudiate self-determination. Wrong arguments are being used to defend a correct proletarian policy, the repudiation of "defence of the fatherland" in an *imperialist* war. This results in a distortion of Marxism in theory, and in practice leads to a peculiar small-nation narrow-mindedness, neglect of the *hundreds of millions* of people in nations that are enslaved by the "dominant" nations. Comrade Gorter, in his excellent pamphlet *Imperialism, War and Social-Democracy* wrongly rejects the principle of self-determination of nations, but correctly *applies* it, when he demands the *immediate* granting of "political and *national* independence" to the Dutch Indies and exposes the Dutch opportunists who refuse to put forward this demand and to fight for it. [Footnotes by Lenin]

The question of self-determination divided the exiled Bolsheviks as well. The Bolsheviks had decided in the spring of 1915 to supplement their newspaper *Sotsial-Demokrat* with a theoretical magazine, *Kommunist* (Communist). However, Yevgeniya Bosh and Yuri Pyatakov, the publishers of the Bolshevik journal, were won over in 1915 to Nikolai Bukharin's position of opposition to the self-determination demand. This led to disagreements over editorial control of *Kommunist*.[26]

Only one issue of *Kommunist* was published, and in 1916 the Bolshevik Central Committee withdrew from the journal and published two issues of *Sbornik Sotsial-Demokrata* (*Sotsial-Demokrat* Collection) under its exclusive control.[27]

Bukharin based his criticisms of the demand for self-determination on the nature of the imperialist epoch as shown by the war. He joined with Bosh and Pyatakov to forward the following theses to the Central Committee in November 1915.

Theses on the right of nations to self-determination[28]

by Yuri Pyatakov, Yevgeniya Bosh, and Nikolai Bukharin

1. The imperialist epoch is a period of the absorption of small states by large states and of a constant redrawing of the political map of the world toward greater state homogeneity. In this process of absorption many nations are incorporated into the state system of the victorious nations.

2. Modern capitalist foreign policy is closely bound up with the supremacy of finance capital, which cannot abandon the policy of imperialism without threatening its own existence.

Therefore, it would be extremely utopian to advance anti-imperialist demands in the field of foreign policy while remaining within the framework of capitalist relations.

The answer to the bourgeoisie's imperialist policy must be the socialist revolution of the proletariat; Social Democracy *must not advance minimum demands in the field of present-day foreign policy.*

3. It is therefore impossible to struggle against the enslavement of nations other than through a struggle against imperialism. *Ergo* a struggle against imperialism; *ergo* a struggle against finance capital; *ergo* a struggle against *capitalism* in general. To turn aside from this path in any way and advance "partial" tasks of the "liberation of nations" *within the limits* of capitalist society diverts proletarian forces from the true solution of the problem and unites them with the forces of the bourgeoisie of the corresponding national groups.

4. The slogan "self-determination of nations" is first of

all *utopian,* as it cannot be realized *within the limits* of capitalism. It is also *harmful,* as it is a slogan that *sows illusions.* In this respect it does not distinguish itself at all from the slogans of arbitration courts, disarmament, and so on, which presuppose the possibility of so-called peaceful capitalism.

5. We should not get carried away by the agitational side of the question and forget its connection to other questions. Advancing the slogan of "self-determination" in order to struggle against "the chauvinism of the working masses" would be making exactly the same kind of error as Kautsky does, when he advances the slogan of "disarmament" for the struggle against militarism. In both cases the error lies in a one-sided examination of the question. It overlooks the specific gravity of a given "social evil"; in other words, it examines the question from an entirely rational and utopian standpoint and not from the standpoint of revolutionary dialectics.

6. The major cases of a concrete application of the slogan of "the right of nations to self-determination" through state independence or secession are, first, the annexation of "foreign" territory in the course of an imperialist war, and second, the disintegration of an already formed state unit. In the first case the slogan of "self-determination" is only a different form of the slogan "defense of the fatherland," because unless an appeal is made for physical defense of the corresponding state boundaries, the "slogan" remains an empty phrase. In the second case we have essentially the same harmful consequences as with the slogan "defense of the fatherland." The attention of the proletarian masses is shifted to another plane; the international character of their action disappears; the forces of the proletariat are split up; the entire tactical line moves in the direction of national and not class struggle. Moreover, in this case the slogan also *implicite* [implicitly]

includes the slogan of "defense," for *after* the achievement of secession, and the slogan of "the right to self-determination" of course presupposes such a possibility, is it not necessary to *defend* "independence"? Otherwise, what with the constant dangers of the imperialist epoch, why "demand" it at all?

To struggle against the chauvinism of the working masses of a nation which is a great power by recognizing "the right of nations to self-determination" is the same as to struggle against this chauvinism by recognizing the right of the oppressed "fatherland" to defend itself.

7. Diversion of the proletariat's attention toward the solution of "national" problems becomes extraordinarily harmful, especially now, when the question of mobilizing the proletariat's forces on a world scale, in international struggle to overthrow capitalism, has been posed *for action*.

The task of Social Democracy at the present moment is *propaganda* for an attitude of *indifference* to "the fatherland," "the nation," and so on. This by no means presupposes a "state" formulation of the question (protests against "dismemberment"), but, on the contrary, poses it in a sharply pronounced revolutionary way with regard to state power and the entire capitalist system.

8. Therefore it follows that in no case and under no circumstances do we support the government of a great power that represses the insurrection or rebellion of an oppressed nation. At the same time, we do not mobilize proletarian forces under the slogan of "the right of nations to self-determination." Our task in this case is to mobilize the forces of the proletariat *of both nations* (jointly with others) under the slogan of civil, class war for socialism and to propagandize against mobilization of forces under the slogan of "the right of nations to self-determination."

9. In the case of *non-capitalist countries or countries with an embryonic capitalism* (for example, colonies), we

can *support* the uprising of the popular masses as something that weakens the ruling classes on the European continent and that does not split the proletarian forces. This is so because, in this case: (a) it is not a question of socialism; and (b) the forces mobilized here are not those of the international proletariat, but the national forces of the *bourgeoisie*, which objectively help the proletariat of the European continent.

10. Furthermore, the slogan of "the right to self-determination" does not concretely answer the question concerning a *given* nation.

11. An essential identity ("aid to imperialism") does not flow from a *formal* similarity between the position developed in these theses and the position of Cunow *und Konsorten* [and company]. To base an objection on "aid" in this case means to go down the road paved by Kautsky.[29]

P.S. Incidentally, is it possible that all the *far lefts* who have a well thought-out *theory* are all "traitors"?

Pyatakov developed this viewpoint more fully in an article submitted under the pen name Kievsky to the third issue of *Sbornik Sotsial-Demokrata*. Lenin wrote a reply in the late summer of 1916 for the same issue. The magazine could not be printed because of lack of funds, but the manuscripts of these articles were widely circulated and read among Bolsheviks in exile. Lenin's reply, which follows, argued that the rejection of the demand for self-determination implied, by extension, a rejection of all democratic demands, and emphasized that "a proletariat not schooled in the struggle for democracy is incapable of performing an economic revolution."

Reply to P. Kievsky (Y. Pyatakov)[30]

by V.I. Lenin

Like every crisis in the life of individuals or in the history of nations, war oppresses and breaks some, steels and enlightens others.

The truth of that is making itself felt in Social-Democratic thinking on the war and in connection with the war. It is one thing to give serious thought to the causes and significance of an imperialist war that grows out of highly developed capitalism, Social-Democratic tactics in connection with such a war, the causes of the crisis within the Social-Democratic movement, and so on. But it is quite another to allow the war to *oppress* your thinking, to stop thinking and analysing *under the weight* of the terrible impressions and tormenting consequences or features of the war.

One such form of *oppression* or *repression* of human thinking caused by the war is the contemptuous attitude of imperialist Economism towards *democracy*. P. Kievsky does not notice that running like a red thread through all his arguments is this war-inspired oppression, this fear, this refusal to analyse. What point is there in discussing defence of the fatherland when we are in the midst of such a terrible holocaust? What point is there in discussing nations' rights when outright strangulation is everywhere the rule? Self-determination and "independence" of nations—but look what they have done to "independent" Greece![31] What is the use of talking and thinking of "rights", when rights are everywhere being trampled upon in the interests of the militarists! What sense is there in talking and thinking of a republic, when there is absolutely no difference whatsoever between the most democratic republics and the most reactionary monarchies, when the war has obliterated every trace of difference!

Kievsky is very angry when told that he has given way to fear, to the extent of rejecting democracy in general. He is angry and objects: I am not against democracy, only against *one* democratic demand, which I consider "bad". But though Kievsky is offended, and though he *"assures"* us (and himself as well, perhaps) that he is not at all "against" democracy, his *arguments*—or, more correctly, the endless *errors* in his arguments—*prove* the very opposite.

Defence of the fatherland is a lie in an imperialist war, but not in a democratic and revolutionary war. All talk of "rights" seems absurd during a war, because *every* war replaces rights by direct and outright violence. But that should not lead us to forget that history has known in the past (and very likely will know, must know, in the future) wars (democratic and revolutionary wars) which, while replacing every kind of "right", every kind of democracy, by violence during the war, nevertheless, in their social content and implications, *served* the cause of democracy, and *consequently* socialism. The example of Greece, it would seem, "refutes" all national self-determination. But if you stop to think, analyse and weigh matters, and do not allow yourself to be deafened by the sound of words or frightened and oppressed by the nightmarish impressions of the war, then this example is no more serious or convincing than ridiculing the republican system because the "democratic" republics, the most democratic—not only France, but also the United States, Portugal and Switzerland—have already introduced or are introducing, in the course of this war, exactly the same kind of militarist arbitrariness that exists in Russia.

That imperialist war obliterates the difference between republic and monarchy is a fact. But to therefore reject the republic, or even be contemptuous towards it, is to allow oneself to be frightened by the war, and one's thinking to be *oppressed* by its horrors. That is the mentality of many supporters of the "disarmament" slogan (Roland-Holst, the younger element in Switzerland, the Scandinavian "Lefts" and others). What, they imply, is the use of discussing revolutionary utilisation of the army or a militia when there is no difference in this war between a republican militia and a monarchist standing army, and when militarism is *everywhere* doing its horrible work?

That is all *one* trend of thought, *one and the same* theoretical and practical political error Kievsky unwittingly makes at every step. He *thinks* he is arguing only against self-determination, he *wants* to argue only against self-determination, but the *result*—against his will and conscience, and that is the curious thing!—is that he has adduced *not a single* argument which could not be just as well applied to democracy in general!

The real source of all his curious logical errors and confusion—and this applies not only to self-determination, but also to defence of the fatherland, divorce, "rights" in general—lies in the *oppression* of his thinking by the war, which makes him completely distort the Marxist position on democracy.

Imperialism is highly developed capitalism; imperialism is progressive; imperialism *is* the negation of democracy—"hence", democracy is "unattainable" under capitalism. Imperialist war is a flagrant violation of all democracy, whether in backward monarchies or progressive republics—"hence", there is no point in talking of "rights" (i.e., democracy!). The "only" thing that can be "opposed" to imperialist war is socialism; socialism alone is "the way out"; "hence", to advance democratic slogans in our minimum programme, i.e., under capitalism, is a deception or an illusion, befuddlement or postponement, etc., of the slogan of socialist revolution.

Though Kievsky does not realise it, that is the real source

of all his mishaps. That is his *basic* logical error which, precisely because it is basic and is not realised by the author, *"explodes"* at every step like a punctured bicycle tire. It "bursts out" now on the question of defending the fatherland, now on the question of divorce, now in the phrase about "rights", in this remarkable phrase (remarkable for its utter contempt for "rights" and its utter failure to understand the issue): we shall discuss *not* rights, *but* the destruction of age-old slavery!

To say that is to show a lack of understanding of the relationship between capitalism and democracy, between socialism and democracy.

Capitalism in general, and imperialism in particular, turn democracy into an illusion—though at the same time capitalism engenders democratic aspirations in the masses, creates democratic institutions, aggravates the antagonism between imperialism's denial of democracy and the mass striving for democracy. Capitalism and imperialism can be overthrown only by economic revolution. They cannot be overthrown by democratic transformations, even the most "ideal". But a proletariat not schooled in the struggle for democracy is incapable of performing an economic revolution. Capitalism cannot be vanquished without *taking over the banks,* without repealing *private ownership* of the means of production. These revolutionary measures, however, cannot be implemented without organising the entire people for democratic administration of the means of production captured from the bourgeoisie, without enlisting the entire mass of the working people, the proletarians, semi-proletarians and small peasants, for the democratic organisation of their ranks, their forces, their participation in state affairs. Imperialist war may be said to be a triple negation of democracy (*a.* every war replaces "rights" by violence; *b.* imperialism as such is the negation of democracy; *c.* imperialist war fully equates the republic with the monarchy), but the awakening and growth of socialist revolt against imperialism are *indissolubly* linked with the growth of democratic resistance and unrest. Socialism leads to the withering away of *every* state, consequently also of every democracy, but socialism can be implemented only *through* the dictatorship of the proletariat, which combines violence against the bourgeoisie, i.e., the minority of the population, with *full* development of democracy, i.e., the genuinely equal and genuinely universal participation of the *entire* mass of the population in all *state* affairs and in all the complex problems of abolishing capitalism.

It is in these "contradictions" that Kievsky, having forgotten the Marxist teaching on democracy, got himself confused. Figuratively speaking, the war has so oppressed his thinking that he uses the agitational slogan "break out of imperialism" to replace all thinking, just as the cry "get out of the colonies" is used to replace analysis of what, properly speaking, is the *meaning*—economically and politically—of the civilised nations "getting out of the colonies".

The Marxist solution of the problem of democracy is for the proletariat to *utilise* all democratic institutions and aspirations in its class struggle against the bourgeoisie in order to prepare for its overthrow and assure its own victory. Such utilisation is no easy task. To the Economists, Tolstoyans, etc., it often seems an unpardonable concession to "bourgeois" and opportunist views, just as to Kievsky defence of national self-determination "in the epoch of finance capital" seems an unpardonable concession to bourgeois views. Marxism teaches us that to "fight opportunism" by renouncing utilisation of the democratic institutions created and distorted by the bourgeoisie of the *given*, capitalist, society is to *completely surrender* to opportunism!

The slogan of *civil war* for socialism indicates the quickest way out of the imperialist war and *links* our struggle against the war with our struggle against opportunism. It is the only slogan that correctly takes into account both war-time peculiarities—that war is dragging out and threatening to grow into a whole "epoch" of war—and the general character of our activities as distinct from opportunism with its pacifism, legalism and adaptation to one's "own" bourgeoisie. In addition, civil war against the bourgeoisie is a *democratically* organised and *democratically* conducted war of the propertyless mass against the propertied minority. But civil war, like every other, must inevitably replace rights by violence. However, violence in the name of the interests and rights of the majority is of a different nature: it tramples on the "rights" of the exploiters, the bourgeoisie, it is *unachievable* without democratic organisation of the army and the "rear". Civil war forcibly expropriates, immediately and first of all, the banks, factories, railways, the big estates, etc. But *in order* to expropriate all this, we shall have to introduce election of all officials and officers by the people, *completely merge* the army conducting the war against the bourgeoisie with the mass of the population, completely democratise administration of the food supply, the production and distribution of food, etc. The object of civil war is to seize the banks, factories, etc., destroy all possibility of resistance by the bourgeoisie, destroy *its* armed forces. But that aim cannot be achieved *either* in its purely military, *or* economic, *or* political aspects, unless we, during the war, simultaneously introduce and extend democracy among *our* armed forces and in *our* "rear". We tell the masses now (and they instinctively feel that we are right): "They are deceiving you in making you fight for imperialist capitalism in a war disguised by the great slogans of democracy. You must, you shall wage a *genuinely* democratic war *against* the bourgeoisie for the achievement of genuine democracy and socialism." The present war unites and "merges" nations into coalitions by means of violence and financial dependence. In our civil war against the bourgeoisie, *we* shall unite and merge the nations *not* by the force of the ruble, *not* by the force of the truncheon, not by violence, but by *voluntary* agreement and solidarity of the working people against the exploiters. For the bourgeoisie the proclamation of equal rights for all nations has become a deception. For us it will be the truth that will facilitate and accelerate the winning over of all nations. Without effectively organised *democratic* relations between nations—and, consequently, without freedom of secession—civil war of the workers and working people generally of all nations against the bourgeoisie is *impossible.*

Through utilisation of bourgeois democracy to socialist and consistently democratic organisation of the proletariat against the bourgeoisie and against opportunism. There is no other path. There is *no* other way out. Marxism, just as life itself, knows no other way out. In this path we must include free secession and free merging of nations, we must not fight shy of them, not fear that they will "defile" the "purity" of our economic aims.

A somewhat different position in the self-determination debate was advanced by Trotsky in the columns of *Nashe Slovo.* While not signing the resolution and manifesto of the Zimmerwald Left, Trotsky had supported it on some questions at the Zimmerwald conference. He had been invited to participate in the publishing of *Kommunist* and *Vorbote.* Although he declined both invitations, his views were closely followed by many in the Zimmerwald Left.

During the war Trotsky continued to advance the Russian Social Democrats' long-standing position for self-determination. In his view, however, during the imperialist epoch this slogan more and more took on significance only when linked to the perspective of a European-wide federation of socialist states. He wrote the following in the May 6, 1915, issue of *Nashe Slovo*.

Imperialism and the national idea[32]

by Leon Trotsky

According to petty-bourgeois ideologues, two "first principles" are in conflict in the present war: the principle of national rights and the principle of force, Good and Evil, Ormazd and Ahriman.[33] We materialists see the war as essentially imperialist in nature, expressing the fundamental striving of all capitalist states to expand and conquer. Where the direction of capitalist expansion coincides with the direction of national unification, there the imperialist Ahriman willingly leans for support on the national Ormazd, without thereby ceasing to be himself. . . .

Imperialism represents the predatory capitalist expression of a *progressive* tendency in economic development—to construct a human economy on a world scale, freed from the cramping fetters of the nation and the state. The national idea in its naked form, as counterposed to imperialism, is not only impotent but also *reactionary:* it drags the economic life of mankind back to the swaddling clothes of national limitedness. Its sorry political mission, conditioned by its impotence, is to create an ideological cover for the work of the imperialist butchers.

Demolishing the very foundations of economic life, the

present imperialist war, illuminated and embellished by the spiritual poverty or charlatanism of the national idea, is the most convincing expression of the dead end into which the development of bourgeois society has run. Only socialism, which must neutralize the nation economically, uniting humanity in the solidarity of cooperation, which liberates the world economy from confining national barriers and thereby liberates national culture itself from the clutches of the economic competition between nations—only socialism offers a way out from the contradictions which have revealed themselves to us as a terrible threat to all of human culture.

Two months later, Trotsky returned to the question of the limits within which he believed self-determination should be applied.

Nation and economy[34]

by Leon Trotsky

Recognition of every nation's right to self-determination, which has become part of the program of Russian Social Democracy, originates from the epoch of the revolutionary battles of national bourgeois democracy. In the final analysis, this demand means the recognition of every nation's right to state independence. Consequently there follows from this the duty of Social Democracy to oppose any regime that compels the cohabitation of nations or parts of nations, and to assist—depending on circumstances of place and time—the struggle of nations and parts of nations against a foreign national yoke.

But nothing more than that.

Social Democracy is by no means throwing overboard the program of national democracy, as the most unbridled social imperialists would like it to. It cannot and does not wish to reconcile itself to the use of state coercion for the forcible incorporation of national groups into large state bodies in the alleged interests of economic development paralyzed by fragmentation into national states. At the same time, Social Democracy does not take on the task of increasing this fragmentation; that is, it does not transform the national principle into some kind of absolute idea, standing above history. . . .

Capitalism strives to confine both nation and economy within the limits of the state. It created a mighty formation which served for a whole epoch as the arena of development of nation and economy. But nation and economy have come into contradiction—with the state and with each other. The state has become too narrow for the economy. Striving to expand, it tramples upon the nation. The economy, for its part, refuses to subordinate the natural movement of its forces and resources to the distribution of ethnic groups on the earth's surface.

The state, essentially an economic organization, is forced to adapt itself to the requirements of economic development. The place of the exclusive national state must inevitably he taken by a broad democratic federation of advanced states, based on the elimination of all customs barriers. The national community resulting from the needs of cultural development not only will not be destroyed by this, but, on the contrary, can find its full completion only on the basis of a republican federation of advanced countries. The conditions necessary for this presuppose the emancipation of the nation's limits from those of the economy, and vice versa. The economy will be organized on the broad arena of a union of European states, as the core of a world-wide organization. Its political form can only be a republican federation in whose flexible and elastic framework every nation can develop its cultural forces in the greatest freedom.

In contrast to the "socialist" annexationists in Germany and elsewhere, we do not intend to throw overboard the recognition of the right of nations to self-determination. On the contrary, we think that the epoch is approaching when this right can at last be realized. We are also infinitely distant from the idea of counterposing the "sovereign" rights of every national group and grouplet to the centralized needs of the economy. But in the very course of historical development we discover the dialectical reconciliation of both "elements," the national and the economic. For us, recognition of every nation's right to self-determination is necessarily complemented by the slogan of a democratic federation of all the advanced countries, the slogan of the *United States of Europe.*

The 1916 Easter Uprising in Ireland provided a practical test of Trotsky's, Radek's, and Lenin's divergent positions on self-determination. This was the first major rebellion in Europe since the outbreak of the war. The Irish rebels' stand, "We serve neither king nor kaiser, but Ireland," was in stark contrast to that of the majority Socialist leaders. The rebellion in Dublin was crushed after several days fighting, and James Connolly, Patrick Pearse, and thirteen other leaders were executed.

Trotsky's analysis appeared in the July 4, 1916, issue of *Nashe Slovo.*

Lessons of the events in Dublin[35]

by Leon Trotsky

Sir Roger Casement, formerly a prominent official in the British colonial service, but by conviction a revolutionary Irish nationalist who acted as intermediary between Germany and the rising in Ireland has been sentenced to death. "I prefer to be standing in the dock to being in the prosecutor's place," he cried before the sentence was passed on him, with its statement, in accordance with the time-honored pious formula, that Casement was to be "hanged by the neck until dead," after which God was invited to have mercy on his soul.

Will the sentence be carried out? This question must be giving Asquith and Lloyd George some anxious hours. To execute Casement would mean making more difficult the situation of the opportunist, purely parliamentary Irish Nationalist Party led by Redmond, which is ready to sign in the blood of the Dublin rebels a new compromise with the government of the United Kingdom. Reprieving Casement, however, after so many executions have already taken place, would mean openly "showing indulgence to a highly placed traitor." British social-imperialists of the Hyndman type are strumming their demagogic tunes on this string, with real hooligan blood-lust. But however Casement's personal fate may be settled, the sentence passed on him marks the close of this dramatic episode of the rising in Ireland.

So far as the purely military operations of the rebels were concerned, the government, as we know, proved to be rather easily the master of the situation. A nationwide movement, such as the nationalist dreamers had conceived of, completely failed to occur. The Irish countryside did not rise. The Irish bourgeoisie, together with the upper, more influential stratum of the Irish intelligentsia, held aloof. Those who fought and died were urban workers, along with some revolutionary enthusiasts from the petty-bourgeois intelligentsia.

The historical basis for a national revolution has disappeared even in backward Ireland. Insofar as the Irish movements in the last century were popular in character, they always drew their strength from the social antagonism between the rightless and starving pauper-farmers and their all-powerful British landlords. But whereas for the landlords Ireland was merely an object of exploitation by agrarian plundering, for British imperialism it was a necessary guarantee of domination of the seas. In a pamphlet written on the eve of the war, Casement, speculating on arousing Germany's interest,[36] showed that an independent Ireland would mean "freedom of the seas" and a mortal blow to Britain's naval supremacy. This is true, inasmuch as an "independent" Ireland could exist only as an advance post of some imperialist state hostile to Britain, and as its naval base against British command of the seaways.

It was Gladstone who first set the military and imperial interests of Britain quite clearly higher than the interests of the Anglo-Irish landlords, and inaugurated a broad scheme of agrarian legislation whereby landlords' estates were transferred, through the instrumentality of the state, to the farmers of Ireland—with, of course, generous compensation to the landlords. Anyhow, after the land reforms of 1881–1903 the farmers were transformed into conservative petty proprietors, whose attention the green flag of national independence could no longer distract from their small holdings. The surplus of Ireland's educated population flowed away in their masses to the cities of Britain, as lawyers, journalists, shop assistants, and so on, and in this they were, in the main, lost to the "national cause." The independent Irish bourgeoisie of trade and industry, to the extent that such a class was formed in the last few decades, at once took up a fighting stance toward the young Irish proletariat, and thereby removed itself from the national-revolutionary camp into that of imperial possibilism and Irish "conciliation."

The young working class of Ireland, formed as it was in an atmosphere saturated with heroic memories of national rebellion, and coming into conflict with the egoistically narrow and imperially arrogant trade unionism of Britain, has naturally wavered between nationalism and syndicalism, and is always ready to link these two conceptions together in its revolutionary consciousness. It has attracted to itself some young intellectuals and certain nationalist enthusiasts, who, in their turn have brought about the ascendancy of the green flag over the red in the labor movement. Thus, the "national revolution," in Ireland too, has amounted in practice to a workers' revolt and Casement's markedly isolated position in the movement merely gives sharper emphasis to this fact.

In a wretched, shameful article Plekhanov wrote recently of the "harmfulness" of the Irish rising to the cause of freedom and rejoiced that the Irish people had "to their honor," understood this and had not supported the revolutionary madmen. Only given complete patriotic softening of the brain can one imagine that the Irish peasants declined to take part in the revolution out of regard for the international situation and thereby saved the "honor" of Ireland. Actually, they were guided merely by the blind egoism typical of farmers and their utter indifference to everything that happens beyond the bounds of their bits of land. For this reason and this alone they made possible the swift victory of the London government over the heroic defenders of the Dublin barricades.

The experiment of an Irish national rebellion, in which Casement represented, with undoubted personal courage, the outworn hopes and methods of the past, is over and done with. But the historical role of the Irish proletariat is only beginning. Already it has brought its class anger against militarism and imperialism into this rising, under an out-of-date flag. This anger will not now subside. On the contrary, it will find echoes all over Britain. Scottish soldiers smashed down the barricades of Dublin. But in Scotland itself the miners have rallied round the red flag raised by MacLean and his comrades.

The hangman's work done by Lloyd George will be sternly avenged by those very workers whom the Hendersons are now trying to chain to the bloody war chariot of imperialism.

Writing two months earlier in the *Berner Tagwacht,* Radek also had argued that the land reform in Ireland had removed the social base for an Irish national revolt. The following is excerpted from his analysis of the Easter Rising.

The song is played out[37]

by Karl Radek

The thunder of cannon has solemnly laid to rest a specter that has kept the rulers of Britain awake nights throughout history since the eighteenth century. As something that could endanger Britain's international position, *the Irish question is played out.*

The Irish question was an *agrarian question.* The nobility's hunger for cultivable land drove England to conquer Ireland. To this reason for the conquest later came an additional cause to maintain British rule over the emerald isle: an independent Ireland could endanger at any time *Britain's sea lanes* just as Britain itself endangers Germany's. Yet the oppression of Ireland by the landlords did not lessen, but became more intense, as it came to be accompanied by the suppression of any industrial development. . . .

In the 1880s agrarian unrest surged fiercely across Ireland. The British bourgeoisie felt compelled to grant concessions to the Irish peasants. It was all the more able to do this now that it exploited the entire world. After the British bourgeoisie had granted Ireland a number of political concessions . . . it laid its axe against the roots of British landlord rule in Ireland. . . .

The peasants, who had until then constituted the social basis of every anti-British movement, were appeased, and turned their attention to questions of agriculture and of farmers' cooperative banks. "If such actions as boycott, mutilation of cattle, political murder, and refusal to pay rent have not entirely disappeared, they have not for some time been a factor in political life. . . . Today, after the great land reform, the Catholic population of Ireland consists *not of famished malcontents,* but overwhelmingly of small farmers, who are inclined around the world to a calm and conservative attitude." So wrote Professor Dibellins in his basic treatise on Britain's problem in Ireland published as the war broke out. His assessment only confirms what we heard during the Dublin unrest from such a competent judge of Britain as Comrade *T. Rothstein.*

Meanwhile the Irish nationalist movement has acquired *a new social foundation.* The economic ascent of the Irish peasants also promoted the *development of the urban petty bourgeoisie,* the intellectuals, who serve the peasant population as lawyers, teachers, and journalists. Since the petty bourgeoisie suffers from the competition of British capital, intellectuals began to dream of the complete independence of the country, which would put the government into their hands. Indeed they began to agitate for the establishment of Irish as a national language, which is spoken by perhaps seven percent of the population and remains at a medieval level of development. This movement, called "Sinn Fein,"[38] was a *purely urban petty-bourgeois movement,* and although it caused considerable commotion, it had little social backing. When its hopes for German assistance led it to revolt, this amounted only to a *putsch* that the British government easily disposed of.

The extinguishing of the blaze in Ireland reveals an *aspect of the so-called national question.* A national movement only wields real power when strong class interests stand behind it. In *Poland,* when the nobility gave way to the bourgeoisie, the latter found possibilities for economic development in the Russian Empire, despite the tsarist knout. In the long run the Polish bourgeoisie, too, would have been fettered by tsarism, but that would not be grounds for an effort to separate from Russia and establish a state, but for an attempt to be rid of tsarist rule. So it wanted to have nothing to do with an independence struggle.

As soon as the economic interests of the *Irish peasantry*

no longer stood opposed to British domination, it deserted the banner of the independence struggle. The peasantry was content to struggle for *home rule*. It was the tragic fate of the adherents of Sinn Fein that they, as petty bourgeois, did not understand this and were seduced by nationalist dreams.

In keeping with its predatory character, the British bourgeoisie will punish them with the gallows for this error. They fall as victims of the imperialist world war. Although the proletariat does not share their ideals, and indeed often confronts them as opponents, yet it will record their blood in the registry of the crimes of those who unleashed the war.

The first issue of *Sbornik Sotsial-Demokrata*, published in October 1916, presented quite a different appraisal of the Irish revolt by Lenin, contained in his article, "The Discussion on Self-Determination Summed Up."

The Irish Rebellion of 1916[39]

by V.I. Lenin

The views of the opponents of self-determination lead to the conclusion that the vitality of small nations oppressed by imperialism has already been sapped, that they cannot play any role against imperialism, that support of their purely national aspirations will lead to nothing, etc. The imperialist war of 1914–16 has provided *facts* which refute such conclusions.

The war proved to be an epoch of crisis for the West-European nations, and for imperialism as a whole. Every crisis discards the conventionalities, tears away the outer wrappings, sweeps away the obsolete and reveals the underlying springs and forces. What has it revealed from the standpoint of the movement of oppressed nations? In the colonies there have been a number of attempts at rebellion, which the oppressor nations, naturally did all they could to hide by means of a military censorship. Nevertheless, it is known that in Singapore the British brutally suppressed a mutiny among their Indian troops; that there were attempts at rebellion in French Annam (see *Nashe Slovo*), and in the German Cameroons (see the Junius pamphlet); that in Europe, on the one hand, there was a rebellion in Ireland, which the "freedom-loving" English, who did not dare to extend conscription to Ireland, suppressed by executions, and, on the other, the Austrian Government passed the death sentence on the deputies of the Czech Diet "for treason", and shot whole Czech regiments for the same "crime".[40]

This list is, of course, far from complete. Nevertheless, it proves that, *owing* to the crisis of imperialism, the flames of national revolt have flared up *both* in the colonies and in Europe, and that national sympathies and antipathies have manifested themselves in spite of the Draconian threats and measures of repression. All this before the crisis of imperialism hit its peak; the power of the imperialist bourgeoisie was yet to be undermined (this may be brought about by a war of "attrition" but has not yet happened) and the proletarian movements in the imperialist countries were still very feeble. What will happen when the war has caused complete exhaustion, or when, in one state at least, the power of the bourgeoisie has been shaken under the blows of proletarian struggle, as that of tsarism in 1905?

On May 9, 1916, there appeared in *Berner Tagwacht*, the organ of the Zimmerwald group, including some of the Leftists, an article on the Irish rebellion entitled "Their Song Is Over" and signed with the initials K.R.[41] It described the Irish rebellion as being nothing more nor less than a "putsch", for, as the author argued, "the Irish question was an agrarian one," the peasants had been pacified by reforms, and the nationalist movement remained only a "purely urban, petty-bourgeois movement, which, notwithstanding the sensation it caused, had not much social backing".

It is not surprising that this monstrously doctrinaire and pedantic assessment coincided with that of a Russian national-liberal Cadet, Mr. A. Kulisher (*Rech* No. 102, April 15, 1916), who also labelled the rebellion "the Dublin putsch".

It is to be hoped that, in accordance with the adage, "it's an ill wind that blows nobody any good", many comrades, who were not aware of the morass they were sinking into by repudiating "self-determination" and by treating the national movements of small nations with disdain, will have their eyes opened by the "accidental" coincidence of opinion held by a Social-Democrat and a representative of the imperialist bourgeoisie!!

The term "putsch", in its scientific sense, may be employed only when the attempt at insurrection has revealed nothing but a circle of conspirators or stupid maniacs, and has aroused no sympathy among the masses. The centuries-old Irish national movement, having passed through various stages and combinations of class interest, manifested itself, in particular, in a mass Irish National Congress in America (*Vorwärts*, March 20, 1916) which called for Irish independence; it also manifested itself in street fighting conducted by a section of the urban petty bourgeoisie *and a section of the workers* after a long period of mass agitation, demonstrations, suppression of newspapers, etc. Whoever calls *such* a rebellion a "putsch" is either a hardened reactionary, or a doctrinaire hopelessly incapable of envisaging a social revolution as a living phenomenon.

To imagine that social revolution is *conceivable* without revolts by small nations in the colonies and in Europe, without revolutionary outbursts by a section of the petty bourgeoisie *with all its prejudices,* without a movement of the politically non-conscious proletarian and semiproletarian masses against oppression by the landowners, the church, and the monarchy, against national oppression, etc.—to imagine all this is to *repudiate social revolution.* So one army lines up in one place and says, "We are for socialism", and another, somewhere else and says, "We are for imperialism", and that will be a social revolution! Only those who hold such a ridiculously pedantic view could vilify the Irish rebellion by calling it a "putsch".

Whoever expects a "pure" social revolution will *never* live to see it. Such a person pays lip-service to revolution without understanding what revolution is.

The Russian Revolution of 1905 was a bourgeois-democratic revolution. It consisted of a series of battles in which *all* the discontented classes, groups and elements of the population participated. Among these there were masses imbued with the crudest prejudices, with the vaguest and most fantastic aims of struggle; there were small groups which accepted Japanese money, there were speculators and adventurers, etc. But *objectively,* the mass movement was breaking the back of tsarism and paving the way for democracy; for this reason the class-conscious workers led it.

The socialist revolution in Europe *cannot be* anything other than an outburst of mass struggle on the part of all and sundry oppressed and discontented elements. Inevitably, sections of the petty bourgeoisie and of the backward workers will participate in it—without such participation, *mass* struggle is *impossible,* without it *no* revolution is possible—and just as inevitably will they bring into the movement their prejudices, their reactionary fantasies, their weaknesses and errors. But *objectively* they will attack *capital,* and the class-conscious vanguard of the revolution, the advanced proletariat, expressing this objective truth of a variegated and discordant, motley and outwardly fragmented, mass struggle, will be able to unite and direct it, capture power, seize the banks, expropriate the trusts which all hate (though for different reasons!), and introduce other dictatorial measures which in their totality will amount to the overthrow of the bourgeoisie and the victory of socialism, which, however, will by no means immediately "purge" itself of petty-bourgeois slag.

Social-Democracy, we read in the Polish theses (I, 4), "must utilise the struggle of the young colonial bourgeoisie against European imperialism *in order to sharpen the revolutionary crisis in Europe".* (Authors' italics.)[42]

Is it not clear that it is least of all permissible to contrast Europe to the colonies in *this* respect? The struggle of the oppressed nations *in Europe,* a struggle capable of going all the way to insurrection and street fighting, capable of breaking down the iron discipline of the army and martial law, will "sharpen the revolutionary crisis in Europe" to an infinitely greater degree than a much more developed rebellion in a remote colony. A blow delivered against the power of the English imperialist bourgeoisie by a rebellion in Ireland is a hundred times more significant politically than a blow of equal force delivered in Asia or in Africa. . . . The dialectics of history are such that small nations, powerless as an *independent* factor in the struggle against imperialism, play a part as one of the ferments, one of the bacilli, which help the *real* anti-imperialist force, the socialist proletariat, to make its appearance on the scene.

The general staffs in the current war are doing their utmost to utilise any national and revolutionary movement in the enemy camp: the Germans utilise the Irish rebellion, the French—the Czech movement, etc. They are acting quite correctly from their own point of view. A serious war would not be treated seriously if advantage were not taken of the enemy's slightest weakness and if every opportunity that presented itself were not seized upon, the more so since it is impossible to know beforehand at what moment, where, and with what force some powder magazine will "explode". We would be very poor revolutionaries if, in the proletariat's great war of liberation for socialism, we did not know how to utilise *every* popular movement against *every single* disaster imperialism brings in order to intensify and extend the crisis. If we were, on the one hand, to repeat in a thousand keys the declaration that we are "opposed" to all national oppression and, on the other, to describe the heroic revolt of the most mobile and enlightened section of certain classes in an oppressed nation against its oppressors as a "putsch", we should be sinking to the same level of stupidity as the Kautskyites.

It is the misfortune of the Irish that they rose prematurely, before the European revolt of the proletariat had *had time* to mature. Capitalism is not so harmoniously built that the various sources of rebellion can immediately merge of their own accord, without reverses and defeats. On the other hand, the very fact that revolts do break out at different times, in different places, and are of different kinds, guarantees wide scope and depth to the general movement; but it is only in premature, individual, sporadic and therefore unsuccessful, revolutionary movements that the masses gain experiences, acquire knowledge, gather strength, and get to know their real leaders, the socialist proletarians, and in this way prepare for the general onslaught, just as certain strikes, demonstrations, local and national, mutinies in the army, outbreaks among the peasantry, etc., prepared the way for the general onslaught in 1905.

Above, Irish Citizen Army in Dublin; below, wartime breadline in Russia.

Chapter 9

Russia: Toward revolution

By September 1915 the tsarist military machine was irreparably damaged. The mounting social crisis had driven even the bourgeois parties into opposition, leaving the government isolated. A new upsurge of workers' struggles was under way. The war raged on, with no end in sight.

Russian Social Democrats prepared for a revolutionary explosion. One aspect of their discussions that was to prove crucial to the course of the Russian revolution was the question of its social character and the tasks that it would pose for the proletariat.

The Bolsheviks and Mensheviks agreed that the revolution on the agenda in tsarist Russia was a bourgeois-democratic revolution. Its tasks were first and foremost to bring down the tsarist autocracy, establish a republic, abolish feudal obligations and privileges, destroy landlordism, and secure political liberties.

Despite this seeming agreement, however, the Bolsheviks and Mensheviks drew fundamentally opposing strategic political conclusions about the tasks of the Russian working class and its vanguard. Looking back on these differences the year following the October

1917 revolution, Lenin described the basic lines of cleavage. Since the tasks of the impending revolution were bourgeois-democratic, Lenin said, the Mensheviks argued that "the proletariat must not go beyond what is acceptable to the bourgeoisie and must pursue a policy of compromise with it."

The Bolsheviks, Lenin said, replied that "this was a bourgeois-liberal theory. The bourgeoisie were trying to bring about the reform of the state on bourgeois, *reformist,* not revolutionary lines, while preserving the monarchy, the landlord system, etc., as far as possible. The proletariat must carry through the bourgeois-democratic revolution to the end, not allowing itself to be 'bound' by the reformism of the bourgeoisie."

In contrast to the Mensheviks, the Bolsheviks looked to the peasantry, not to the liberal bourgeoisie, as a revolutionary ally. "The Bolsheviks formulated the alignment of *class* forces in the bourgeois revolution as follows," Lenin wrote in the 1918 pamphlet. "The proletariat, winning over the peasants, will neutralise the liberal bourgeoisie and utterly destroy the monarchy, medievalism and the landlord system.

"It is the alliance between the proletariat and the peasants *in general* that reveals the bourgeois character of the revolution, for the peasants in general are small producers who stand on the basis of commodity production.

"Further, the Bolsheviks then added, the proletariat will win over *the entire semi-proletariat* (all the working and exploited people), will neutralise the middle peasants and *overthrow* the bourgeoisie; this will be the socialist revolution, as distinct from a bourgeois-democratic revolution."[1]

Exactly how this revolutionary process would unfold in practice, the Bolsheviks said, how protracted or how condensed its different stages would be, could not be determined in advance. That would depend on the relative strength of the various class forces and capacities of the proletarian vanguard, as well as what was happening in the international class struggle.

The aim of Bolshevik activity in Russia was to organize the

proletariat so that it could lead the peasant majority in the overthrow of the tsarist autocracy and the establishment of a provisional revolutionary government. In its class character and tasks, the Bolsheviks said, such a revolutionary government would be a revolutionary democratic dictatorship of the proletariat and peasantry.

As Russia headed into a prerevolutionary situation at the end of 1915, these longstanding differences between the Bolsheviks and Mensheviks had been sharpened by the deep divisions over the war and the Second International.

Not all those in the Russian Social Democracy who were to join with the Bolsheviks in leading the October 1917 insurrection and subsequently launching the Communist International, however, agreed with them in the prewar period on the strategy and class forces in the Russian revolution. Leon Trotsky had differed with Lenin on this fundamental question since the early years of the century, adopting a position between the two fundamental trends that were most influential in the Russian proletariat.

Writing in *Nashe Slovo* at the beginning of September 1915, Trotsky argued that capitalist expansion in Russia since 1905 had reduced the capacity of any class other than the proletariat to play a revolutionary role, and that the empire's majority peasant population would be far less of a revolutionary factor in years to come than it had been during the 1905–07 events. The aim of Social Democratic politics, he argued, thus could no longer be a "national bourgeois revolution," but rather only the "international revolution of the proletariat."

The social forces in the Russian revolution[2]

by Leon Trotsky

The basic contradiction in the historically belated revolution of 1905 was that while the immediate objective task of that revolution was to open the road to bourgeois development of the nation, the principal driving force of the revolution turned out to be the proletariat. The classic [French] bourgeois revolution of 1789–93 relied upon the Third Estate, with the urban petty bourgeoisie led by the intelligentsia as its nucleus. In Russia profound objective and subjective antagonisms divided this "third estate," even before its historical emancipation. The proletariat confronted the big bourgeoisie, while the social weight and political importance of the petty bourgeoisie constituted an insignificant quantity.

What has changed in this picture during the past decade?

The years of reaction and economic crisis saw a relative Europeanizing of our industry; the level of technique was raised, and more intensive methods of exploiting labor-power were introduced. The three years before the war were a time of mighty economic upsurge. Revolution, counter-revolution, and economic crisis had deadly effects primarily on the petty and middle bourgeoisie, while the industrial boom enriched mainly the big capitalists. This resulted in a further deepening of the social contradictions which, in the revolution of 1905, had already ruled out the possibility of a protracted joint, or parallel, struggle against the old regime by the proletariat and the bourgeoisie. During this period the proletariat grew, became still more concentrated in production, and took its strongest steps forward in class organization and class consciousness. Thus, the fundamental contradiction of our past revolution expresses itself today more deeply and in a more clearly defined form.

The proletariat is the only independent force that can now exist in the revolutionary movement. In its very first moves the proletariat will find arrayed against it the mighty forces of the bourgeois nation, from the reactionary landlord forces right through to the liberal intellectual forces.

Today, based on the experience of the Russian revolution and of the reaction, we can expect the *peasantry* to play a less independent, not to mention decisive, role in the development of revolutionary events than it did in 1905. To the extent that the peasantry has remained in the grip of "estate" and feudal slavery, it continues to suffer from economic and ideological disunity, political immaturity, and cultural backwardness and helplessness. Despite its elemental opposition to the old regime, in every movement the peasantry's social energy is always paralyzed by these weaknesses. They force it to halt precisely where really revolutionary action begins.

The economic and cultural progress made by the peasantry in this period has proceeded entirely along the line of bourgeois development, and has further developed the class contradictions within the peasantry itself. For the industrial proletariat, therefore, it is now—immeasurably more so than in 1905—a question of attracting to its side the rural proletarian and semiproletarian elements rather than the peasantry as an "estate." In these circumstances, the revolutionary movement acquires an incomparably less "national" and an incomparably greater "class" character than it had in 1905.

In recent years, both before and during the war, the sharper class differentiation and greater maturity of social relations have been vividly expressed in Russian political activity.

The 1905 strike wave stirred up wide circles of bourgeois society, especially its left wing. While the revolutionary strike wave just before the war was incomparably more systematic and conscious than that of ten years ago, this time the strikes faced the almost total apathy of the intermediate groups, the so-called "bourgeois democracy."

And while at the beginning of the century the urban movement found a confused but noisy echo in the agrarian unrest among the peasantry that had been intensifying since 1902, the 1912–13 proletarian strike wave met with no response at all in the countryside.

The Russian intelligentsia had played a disproportionate role in the old revolutionary movement. But in recent years it underwent earnest training in the service of capital as it got itself caught up in the process of the country's capitalist development. The intelligentsia became extremely susceptible to the imperialist aims and suggestions of capital, and has covered them up with the garbage of its radical-democratic or "socialist" ideology.

During the Russo-Japanese War the first steps in the mobilization of the ponderous Zemstvo opposition were accomplished under the slogan of popular representation.[3] In the subsequent period the intelligentsia waged its campaign by holding mass meetings and forming associations under the banners of peace and a constituent assembly.

Now the property-owners' "opposition" is mobilizing under the slogan of organizing for victory, and takes responsibility for the war and its continuation. At the same time, the "opposition" as a whole, and its left, Cadet wing in an especially demonstrative way, has refused to raise elementary domestic problems, since these cannot be solved, according to the liberal press, without a struggle.

In 1904–1905, too, the bourgeois classes were neither able nor inclined to carry on a revolutionary struggle. But their "irresponsible" opposition exposed the state power, and in the first period of the revolution they were benevolently neutral toward the revolutionary popular masses. Today the bourgeois parties, including the social-patriotic rabble, see the revival of revolutionary struggle as a service to the kaiser and a betrayal of national interests. In order to isolate the revolutionary opposition they refuse to mobilize the bourgeois classes, even if only to call for a responsible ministry, let alone universal suffrage. They insist on a business-like reshuffling of ministers, and close ranks around the government, thus becoming a buffer between it and the popular masses.

However wretched the liberal-democratic press may have been in the 1904–1905 "spring" period, its politically amorphous oppositional attitude fostered the growing revolutionary excitement of the popular masses. Today the entire liberal press consciously strives to divert the popular masses' social and political discontent into a national-patriotic unification with the government and the ruling parties of June 3.

All these changes are summed up in the isolation of the proletariat that is now very pronounced indeed.

Between the monarchy and militarism, on the one hand, and the popular masses on the other, now stands a complex mechanism of bourgeois parties, newspapers, and public organizations and congresses of all kinds. They are bound to the monarchy by a unity of imperialist schemes and a community of political responsibility. The revolutionary mobilization of the proletariat now runs up against not only the state police system, as in the days of Plehve and Svyatopolk-Mirsky, but also against the "social" police of patriotism, whose police function is now being carried out by all the bourgeois parties, with the assistance of the guerrilla bands of social patriotism.

These factors together determine the general direction of revolutionary Social Democratic politics in Russia.

A national or an international course?

The revolution of 1905 was historically belated in the sense that it involved the struggle of bourgeois society as a whole against the "serf-holding" state, that is, a national revolution. In another sense it was a historical anticipation, because its principal driving force was the proletariat. The struggle was carried out not only under the benevolent neutrality of bourgeois society, as in the revolution's first period, but also in opposition to bourgeois society, as in its second.

This dual standpoint explains why the revolution of 1905 was not carried through to completion. The causes of defeat lay, on the one hand, in the insufficient strength of bourgeois democracy and the insufficient revolutionary "preparedness" of the peasantry. And on the other hand, they lay in the working class's lack of revolutionary strength and in the absence of support from the European proletariat in the form of a parallel revolutionary movement, at a time when tsarism was wholly reliant upon the stock exchanges and capitalist governments of Europe.

These two explanations cannot be united in a mechanical way. The very factor that strengthens the Russian proletariat, increases its numbers, raises its consciousness, and heightens its connection with the world proletariat—the development of capitalism in its modern, concentrated form—is leading to the final disappearance of urban bourgeois democracy as a political force and to the further social disintegration of the peasantry as an "estate."

But it is precisely this factor—capitalism—that has been at work in the entire post-revolutionary period. Our social relations in this decade have developed toward a further reduction of the potential revolutionary role of the petty bourgeoisie and the peasantry and a further growth in the numbers and productive importance of the industrial proletariat. If a "national" revolution could not be *completed* in 1905, then a second national revolution, that is, a revolution that unites "the nation" against the old regime, cannot now even be *posed*.

Social Democracy, of course, takes into account and makes good use in its struggle of every oppositional movement of other social forces. But the major, fundamental question is: Do we consider the bourgeois classes of Russia, which have finally revealed their reactionary imperialist nature in foreign policy, to be capable of a revolutionary role in internal affairs? Should the development of the Russian revolution, the movement of the Russian proletariat, in practice be made dependent on the revolutionary movement of the Russian intelligentsia, the urban petty bourgeoisie, and the peasantry? Or should we rather subordinate the movement of the Russian proletariat to the tasks and aims of the movement of the entire proletariat of Europe and make the Russian revolution dependent on the proletarian struggle throughout the capitalist world? In short: should the basic course of all our politics be toward a national bourgeois revolution or toward an international revolution of the proletariat?

This is precisely the main dividing line between us, the revolutionary internationalists, and the Russian social patriots. They do not simply float along blindly with the current, but rather, in a politically dubious way, "accept" the war and participate in "the organization of victory." They do this in the name of the fictitious and essentially reactionary idea of creating a national basis for the revolution, one that embraces the entire people. . . .

From this follows the entire enormous task that today falls to the Russian proletariat and its party.

In 1905 the slogan "Down with the war!", along with "Down with the autocracy!", became a popular watchword that brought the proletariat closer to the other classes in society. Today, however, this same cry of "Down with the war!", the initial slogan of the whole subsequent movement of the proletariat, puts the Social Democrats in hostile opposition to all the parties of bourgeois society. Now the proletariat's mobilization assumes a revolutionary class character from the very outset.

No firm assumptions are possible about the extent to which the proletariat's Socialist vanguard can rally the lower classes, the rural and urban poor, around itself in this struggle. How far it will be able to lead them is unclear. Without a doubt, however, Social Democracy is now more than ever the only destined leader of these masses. It is summoned by its historical duty to raise among them its banner of peace and revolution.

But here, as everywhere, we shall proceed from a profound conviction of the necessity of the European proletariat's revolutionary struggle against their own capitalist reaction, against militarism, and against private ownership of the means of production. Only this struggle, a period of direct offensive by the proletariat of Western Europe against the state power, only an international socialist revolution can create the conditions and advance those forces with whose aid the revolutionary struggle of Russia's proletariat can be carried through to the end.

However, the revolutionary struggle of the Russian proletariat, the aim of all our political work, will itself quickly become the most important factor in the relationship of social forces in Europe. Whatever powerful national obstacles stand in its way, it will give a mighty impetus to the revolutionary offensive of the European proletariat against the foundations of capitalist society.

Our recognition that hopes of a national revolution are illusory does not imply any rejection of the revolution but, on the contrary, the extension of its historical basis and its social aims, and the intensification of its class methods.

Gregory Zinoviev replied to Trotsky's articles in the October 11, 1915, issue of *Sotsial-Demokrat.*

War and the revolutionary crisis[4]

by Gregory Zinoviev

In the camp of the platonic internationalists *(Nashe Slovo)*, vacillations continue even in the face of the approaching decisive events. *Nashe Slovo* arrives at the liquidation of revolutionary tactics in Russia by yet another route.

From the *correct* and *important* thesis that the destiny of the Russian revolution is now *tied more closely than ever* to the fortunes of the international proletarian revolution, they draw a profoundly incorrect conclusion. They proceed as though the task of the bourgeois-democratic revolution in Russia should be dropped from the agenda. They proclaim that there is no bourgeois-democratic movement in Russia, that the peasantry cannot play a revolutionary role, that the Russian proletariat has to wait until, along with the proletariat of other countries, it is able to bring about a revolution on an international scale. (*Nashe Slovo,* numbers 181–182, a series of editorial articles entitled, "The War Crisis").[5]

The same old Trotskyist tune in a new key! What a profoundly harmful *liquidationist* idea! Only the liquidators—none other than Potresov and Larin—can benefit from posing the question in this way. It leads in fact to renouncing the struggle for a new revolution in Russia, to abdicating from the proletariat's task of rousing the masses of the urban and rural petty bourgeoisie to the struggle for a republic and for the confiscation of the landlords' estates. This is indeed the ideological umbilical cord that ties Trotsky to the liquidators.

No, revolutionary Social Democracy struggles as before for the democratic revolution in Russia. The imperialist World War has indissolubly bound the revolutionary crisis in our country to the growing proletarian socialist revolution in the West. Even ten years ago revolutionary Russian Social Democracy conceived of the democratic revolution in Russia as the prologue to the socialist revolution in the West. Developments have taken a strong step forward. The time of the prologue is approaching that of the epilogue. The tie between the democratic revolution in Russia and the socialist revolution in the West has become closer still.

But that means neither renouncing the "three pillars" nor dismissing the slogans of the democratic revolution in Russia,[6] but rather a still more energetic struggle for this revolution. The interests of tens of millions of petty bourgeois and semiproletarians in Russia have not been reconciled with either the monarchy or with the great feudal landlords. The conflict of these interests stares us in the face. The petty bourgeoisie has wavered and will waver again; yesterday it generally followed the liberals, today the bourgeois patriots. The task of the proletariat is not to dismiss the democratic interests of the masses out of hand, but to help the masses escape from the influence of the bourgeoisie, to make good use of life's lessons to expose yesterday's liberal and today's patriotic illusions.

Long live the second democratic revolution in Russia, opening the era of world proletarian revolution! Victory over the tsarist monarchy, not for "victory" over Germany, but for the development of the proletarian socialist revolution in the West! Such is the banner of revolutionary Social Democracy in Russia.

The Bolsheviks argued that the proletariat should not abandon to the bourgeoisie the banner of a national-democratic revolution. Lenin explained the difference between the political line proposed by the proletariat for the revolution and that advanced by the bourgeoisie, as illustrated by the 1905–1907 upsurge, in the November 20, 1915, issue of *Sotsial-Demokrat*. These opposing class perspectives, Lenin wrote, underlay the strategic and programmatic divisions between Bolshevism and Menshevism.

On the two lines in the revolution[7]

by V.I. Lenin

The experience of the 1905 Revolution and of the subsequent counterrevolutionary period in Russia teaches us that in our country *two* lines of revolution could be observed, in the sense that there was a struggle between two classes—the proletariat and the liberal bourgeoisie—for leadership of the masses. The proletariat advanced in a revolutionary fashion, and was leading the democratic peasantry towards the overthrow of the monarchy and the landowners. . . .

The first line of the Russian bourgeois-democratic revolution, as deduced from the facts and not from "strategic" prattle, was marked by a resolute struggle of the proletariat, which was irresolutely followed by the peasantry. Both these classes fought against the monarchy and the landowners. The lack of strength and resolution in these classes led to their defeat (although a partial breach was made in the edifice of the autocracy).

The behaviour of the liberal bourgeoisie was the second

line. We Bolsheviks have always affirmed, especially since the spring of 1906, that this line was represented by the Cadets and Octobrists as a *single* force. The 1905–15 decade has proved the correctness of our view. At the decisive moments of the struggle, the Cadets, together with the Octobrists, betrayed democracy and went to the aid of the tsar and the landowners. The "liberal" line of the Russian revolution was marked by the "pacification" and the fragmentary character of the masses' struggle so as to enable the bourgeoisie to make peace with the monarchy. . . .

The Bolsheviks helped the proletariat consciously to follow the first line, to fight with supreme courage and to lead the peasants. The Mensheviks were constantly slipping into the second line; they demoralised the proletariat by adapting its movement to the liberals. . . .

Only these trends—the Bolshevik and the Menshevik—manifested themselves in the politics of the *masses* in 1904–08, and later, in 1908–14. Why was that? It was because only these trends had firm class roots—the former in the proletariat, the latter in the liberal bourgeoisie.

This state of affairs patently indicates the task of the proletariat. That task is the waging of a supremely courageous revolutionary struggle against the monarchy (utilising the slogans of the January Conference of 1912,[8] the "three pillars"), a struggle that will sweep along in its wake all the democratic masses, i.e., mainly the peasantry. At the same time, the proletariat must wage a ruthless struggle against chauvinism, a struggle in alliance with the *European* proletariat for the socialist revolution in Europe. The vacillation of the petty bourgeoisie is no accident; it is inevitable, for it logically follows from their class stand. The war crisis has *strengthened* the economic and political factors that are impelling the petty bourgeoisie, including the peasantry, to the left. Herein lies the objective foundation of the full possibility of victory for the democratic revolution in Russia. There is no need here for us to prove that the objective conditions in Western Europe are ripe for a socialist revolution; this was admitted before the war by all influential socialists in all advanced countries.

To bring clarity into the alignment of classes in the impending revolution is the main task of a revolutionary party. This task is being shirked by the Organising Committee, which within Russia remains a faithful ally to *Nashe Dyelo,* and abroad utters meaningless "Left" phrases. This task is being wrongly tackled in *Nashe Slovo* by Trotsky, who is repeating his "original" 1905 theory and refuses to give some thought to the reason why, in the course of ten years, life has been bypassing this splendid theory.

From the Bolsheviks Trotsky's original theory has borrowed their call for a decisive proletarian revolutionary struggle and for the conquest of political power by the proletariat, while from the Mensheviks it has borrowed "repudiation" of the peasantry's role. The peasantry, he asserts, are divided into strata, have become differentiated; their potential revolutionary role has dwindled more and more; in Russia a "national" revolution is impossible; "we are living in the era of imperialism," says Trotsky, and "imperialism does not contrapose the bourgeois nation to the old regime, but the proletariat to the bourgeois nation."

Here we have an amusing example of playing with the word "imperialism". If, *in Russia,* the proletariat already stands contraposed to the "bourgeois nation", then Russia is facing a *socialist* revolution (!), and the slogan "Confiscate the landed *estates*" (repeated by Trotsky in 1915, following the January Conference of 1912), is incorrect; in that case we must speak, not of a "revolutionary workers'" government, but of a "workers' *socialist*" government! The length Trotsky's muddled thinking goes to is evident from his phrase that by their resoluteness the proletariat will attract the "*non*-proletarian [!] popular masses" as well (No. 217)![9]

Trotsky has not realised that if the proletariat induce the non-proletarian masses to confiscate the landed estates and overthrow the monarchy, then that will be the consummation of the "national bourgeois revolution" in Russia; it will be a revolutionary-democratic dictatorship of the proletariat and the peasantry!

A whole decade—the great decade of 1905–15—has shown the existence of two and only two class lines in the Russian revolution. The differentiation of the peasantry has enhanced the class struggle within them; it has aroused very many hitherto politically dormant elements. It has drawn the rural proletariat closer to the urban proletariat (the Bolsheviks have insisted ever since 1906 that the former should be *separately* organised, and they included this demand in the resolution of the Menshevik congress in Stockholm). However, the antagonism between the peasantry, on the one hand, and the Markovs, Romanovs and Khvostovs, on the other, has become stronger and more acute. This is such an obvious truth that not *even* the thousands of phrases in scores of Trotsky's Paris articles will "refute" it. Trotsky is in fact helping the liberal-labour politicians in Russia, who by "repudiation" of the role of the peasantry understand a *refusal* to raise up the peasants for the revolution!

That is the crux of the matter today. The proletariat are fighting, and will fight valiantly, to win power, for a republic, for the confiscation of the land, *i.e.*, to win over the peasantry, make *full* use of their revolutionary powers, and get the "*non*-proletarian masses of the people" to take part in liberating *bourgeois* Russia from *military-feudal* "imperialism" (tsarism). The proletariat will at once utilise this ridding of bourgeois Russia of tsarism and the rule of the landowners, not to aid the rich peasants in their struggle against the rural workers, but to bring about the socialist revolution in alliance with the proletarians of Europe.

The Bolsheviks ran candidates in the September 1915 Petrograd elections for the "workers' group" in the War Industries Committees, but they continued their call for a boycott of these committees. Their candidates presented the Bolshevik program to a broad range of working people and succeeded in turning the elections into a workers' demonstration against the war and the government. The internationalist candidates received 93,000 votes compared to 80,000 for candidates who supported participation in the War Industries Committees. After the elections the Bolsheviks issued instructions to their delegates, which were also distributed as a leaflet in the factories.

"In the advanced capitalist countries the objective requirements for socialist revolution have already ripened," the Bolshevik leaflet said. "In Russia the proletariat must still secure a democratic state structure, that is, a *democratic republic*. The revolution will sweep away the remains of the feudal epoch and so free the development of productive forces. It will therefore swiftly create in Russia the conditions for a purely socialist revolution. However not only the proletariat but also the peasantry and other bourgeois democratic layers have a stake in the destruction of the tsarist monarchy and of its social base: the landed proprietors.

"Therefore the proletariat turns to the bourgeois revolutionary democracy appealing for a joint struggle against the tsarist government. The proletariat calls for the creation of a provisional government after the overthrow of the autocracy, to convoke an all-peoples constituent assembly on the basis of universal, direct, and secret ballot without distinction of sex, nationality, or religion."

The Petrograd Bolshevik leaflet went on to call for a boycott of the War Industries Committees. The elected workers' representatives, however, should be prepared to meet separately, it said, when circumstances required—as a soviet of workers deputies, acting under the political direction of the Bolsheviks' Petrograd Committee.[10]

The October 13, 1915, issue of *Sotsial-Demokrat* contained reports on the work of the Petrograd party and extracts from many of its leaflets, accompanied by the following discussion article, drafted by Lenin.

Several theses[11]

Proposed by the editors

The material published in this issue shows the tremendous scope of the work being done by the St. Petersburg Committee of our Party. To Russia, and indeed to the entire International, this is indeed a model of Social-Democratic work during a reactionary war and in most difficult conditions. The workers of St. Petersburg and Russia will bend every effort to give support to that work and will continue it along the same road ever more energetically and extensively.

Complying with advice from comrades in Russia, we have drawn up several theses on current problems of Social-Democratic work:

(1) The slogan of a "constituent assembly" is wrong as an independent slogan, because the question *now* is: who will convene it? The liberals accepted that slogan in 1905 because it *could* have been interpreted as meaning that a "constituent assembly" would be convened by the tsar and would be in agreement with him. The most correct slogans are the "three pillars" (a democratic republic, confiscation of the landed es-

tates and an eight-hour working day), with the addition (cf. No. 9) of a call for the workers' international solidarity in the struggle for socialism and the revolutionary overthrow of the belligerent governments, and against the war.

(2) We are opposed to participation in the war industries committees, which help prosecute the imperialist and reactionary war. We are in favour of utilising the election campaign; for instance, we are for participation in the first stage of the elections for the *sole* purpose of agitation and organisation. There can be no talk of boycotting the Duma. Participation in the second ballot is *essential.*

While we have no Duma deputies from our Party, we must utilize everything that happens in the Duma so as to advance the aims of revolutionary Social-Democracy.

(3) We consider that the consolidation and extension of Social-Democratic work among the proletariat and its extension to the rural proletariat, the rural poor and the army are the immediate and pressing tasks. It is revolutionary Social-Democracy's most pressing task to develop the incipient strike movement, and to conduct it under the slogan of the "three pillars." The demand for the immediate cessation of the war should be given due attention. Among other demands, the workers must not lose sight of the demand for the immediate reinstatement of the workers' deputies, members of the R.S.D.L. Duma group.

(4) Soviets of Workers' Deputies and similar institutions must be regarded as organs of insurrection, of revolutionary rule. It is only in connection with the development of a mass political strike and with an insurrection, and in the measure of the latter's preparedness, development and success that such institutions can be of lasting value.

(5) Only a revolutionary-democratic dictatorship of the proletariat and the peasantry can form the social content of the impending revolution in Russia. The revolution cannot be victorious in Russia unless it overthrows the mon-

archy and the feudal-minded landowners, and these cannot be overthrown unless the proletariat is supported by the peasantry. The step forward made in the differentiation of the rural population into wealthy "homestead farmers" and rural proletarians has not done away with the oppression of the rural areas by the Markovs and Co. We have urged and still urge the absolute need, in all and any circumstances, for a *separate* organization for rural *proletarians.*

(6) The task confronting the proletariat of Russia is the consummation of the bourgeois-democratic revolution in Russia *in order* to kindle the socialist revolution in Europe. The latter task now stands very close to the former, yet it remains a special and second task, for it is a question of the *different classes* which are collaborating with the proletariat in Russia. In the former task, it is the petty-bourgeois peasantry of Russia who are collaborating; in the latter, it is the proletariat of other countries.

(7) As hitherto, we consider it admissible for Social-Democrats to join a provisional revolutionary government together with the democratic petty bourgeoisie, but *not* with the revolutionary chauvinists.

(8) By revolutionary chauvinists we mean those who want a victory over tsarism so as to achieve victory over Germany, plunder other countries, consolidate Great-Russian rule over the other peoples of Russia, etc. Revolutionary chauvinism is based on the class position of the petty bourgeoisie. The latter always vacillates between the bourgeoisie and the proletariat. At present it is vacillating between chauvinism (which prevents it from being consistently revolutionary, even in the meaning of a democratic revolution), and proletarian internationalism. At the moment the Trudoviks, the Socialist-Revolutionaries, *Nasha Zarya,* Chkheidze's Duma group, the Organising Committee, Mr. Plekhanov and the like are political spokesmen for this petty bourgeoisie in Russia.

(9) If the revolutionary chauvinists won in Russia, we would be opposed to a defence of *their* "fatherland" in the present war. Our slogan is: against the chauvinists, even if they are revolutionary and republican—*against* them, and *for* an alliance of the international proletariat for the socialist revolution.

(10) To the question of whether it is possible for the proletariat to assume the leadership in the bourgeois Russian revolution, our answer is: yes, it is possible, *if* the petty bourgeoisie swings to the left at the decisive moment: it is being pushed to the left, not only by our propaganda, but by a number of objective factors, economic, financial (the burden of war), military, political, and others.

(11) To the question of what the party of the proletariat would do if the revolution placed power in its hands in the present war, our answer is as follows: we would propose peace to *all* the belligerents on the condition that freedom is given to the colonies and *all* peoples that are dependent, oppressed and deprived of rights. Under the present governments, neither Germany, nor Britain and France would accept this condition. In that case, we would have to prepare for and wage a revolutionary war, i.e., not only resolutely carry out the whole of our minimum programme,[12] but work systematically to bring about an uprising among all peoples now oppressed by the Great Russians, all colonies and dependent countries in Asia (India, China, Persia, etc.), and also, and first and foremost, we would raise up the socialist proletariat of Europe for an insurrection against their governments and despite the social-chauvinists. There is no doubt that a victory of the proletariat in Russia would create extraordinarily favourable conditions for the development of the revolution in both Asia and Europe. *Even* 1905 proved that. The international solidarity of the revolutionary proletariat is a *fact,* despite the scum of opportunism and social-chauvinism.

We now present these theses for discussion among the comrades, and shall develop our views in the next issues of the Central Organ.

The main Menshevik forces, for their part, played the role of agents of the bourgeoisie in the elections to the War Industries Committees. Their attempts to rally the workers to participate in the pro-war committees increased the estrangement between the majority of the *Nashe Slovo* editorial board and those, like Martov, who clung to their ties to the chauvinist forces.

Writing in *Nashe Slovo* in November 1915, Trotsky explained that the War Industries Committees elections provided further proof of the need to break organizational ties with the chauvinists.

All the conclusions must be drawn[13]

by Leon Trotsky

How were the social patriots able to mobilize tens of thousands of workers in the briefest period—without political authority, without an organization, without a propaganda apparatus? Very simply: lacking their own base among the masses, the social patriots relied on an apparatus itself not based on the masses, the most powerful apparatus of all—all the organs of bourgeois public opinion and, to a significant degree, even the military and police organizations of the state. . . .

The monarchy's Black Hundreds never recruited more than the most benighted or corrupt dregs of the working class. Russian liberalism attracted only a few individuals from among the most privileged workers in the factory hierarchy. Social patriotism proved to be a more suitable political instrument of the propertied classes and the government for the ideological and political subjection of the backward workers. If Khvostov, Guchkov, and Milyukov had racked their brains for seven days and seven nights they couldn't have thought up anything better for their needs than the Plekhanovite appeal. But they didn't have to think it up; they got this document for a song, ready-made and with the added bonus of more or less authoritative names and "signatures." Where the ruling class on its own, without the aid of the compromisers, could have mobilized only thousands of workers, thanks to the assistance of the social patriots they mobilized tens of thousands.

Social patriotism has come out openly, in a broad arena, as the political instrument of the mortal enemies of socialism and of the class enemies of the proletariat. This conduct must henceforth determine not only our political, but also our organizational attitude toward it.

When the Duma deputy Mankov went over from political vacillations to half-hearted patriotism, abstaining in the vote on war credits, the Social Democratic fraction expelled him from its ranks.[14] We approved of its decision as the only course that corresponded to the seriousness and depth of the contradiction between socialism and nationalism. Today the inspirers of Mankov have come out *en masse* into the arena of political struggle. Against revolutionary socialism and our party organization, they advance their own anti-revolutionary banner, *organizationally* leaning on the class enemies of the proletariat and *politically* serving these enemies. By these actions the contradiction between us and them is definitively passing out of the realm of principled "discussion" or the struggle of tendencies within the party; it is becoming a component part of the class struggle of the proletariat against bourgeois society.

Organizational contact with the social-nationalist general staffs is therefore becoming intolerable for Social Democracy and its organizations. We cannot involve ourselves in collaboration with social patriots who openly link themselves with the bourgeoisie's struggle against us. We cannot use the authority of the workers' party to cover up for these poisoners of proletarian consciousness and we cannot allow any organizational ties whatsoever to restrict our struggle with them, which must be and will be taken *to the very end!*

An organizational break with the militant social patriots all down the line—that is the conclusion we draw from the latest Petrograd experience.

Popular discontent continued to rise in the winter of 1915–16. In Petrograd, 100,000 workers went on strike in January to commemorate "Bloody Sunday," the start of the 1905 revolution. Tsarist military authorities confined most soldiers to their barracks for fear they would join the workers' protest.

Under the pressure of the mass upsurge, cleavages in the ruling classes grew wider. While the tsarist regime rejected pleas for reform, the "Progressive Bloc" sharpened their criticisms of the government. The Menshevik currents in Russia, including the Duma deputies who claimed to oppose the war, sought an alliance with these pro-war capitalist forces. Although the Menshevik Duma fraction led by Chkheidze gave formal support to the Zimmerwald movement, Trotsky noted in April 1916, its real course was far removed from consistent internationalism.

The Social Democratic Duma fraction[15]

by Leon Trotsky

Even before the last Duma session we repeatedly spoke about the inadequately defined position of the Social Democratic Duma fraction under Chkheidze's leadership. In view of the widening gulf in the workers' movement between the partisans of national defense and those of revolutionary internationalism, maintaining this vagueness any longer could place the fraction in an altogether desperate situation. It is impermissible to shut one's eyes to this danger. . . .

Karl Liebknecht is giving us an example of driving revolutionary initiative, using socialist tactics in an imperialist parliament to mount an untiring offensive. . . . Our deputies lack such a tactic of revolutionary offense. It is pointless to deceive ourselves with their energetic denunciations of the government on questions of domestic policy. The central life-or-death question for the popular masses, and the central phenomenon of the whole period, is *the war*. However, the closer our fraction gets to this central question, the more their energy and determination evaporates.

The *"revolutionary"* social patriots, at least those few of them who sincerely consider themselves revolutionary, *accept the war.* They therefore seek to further the development of a "national revolution" by assuming the role of critic of the *government's conduct* of the war. It is understandable that from their standpoint, that of a national revolution under the patriotic banner, it is necessary to seek a common language with the "Progressive Bloc" and to limit the sphere of "revolutionary" criticism to questions of domestic policy and military technique. Such a point of view, while internally logical, represents politically the most pathetic and barren of utopias. During the latest session Milyukov once again mobilized all his resources of philistine realism and political shamelessness to drum into even the stubbornest head the total hopelessness of combining patriotism with revolution.

But, to its credit, our Duma fraction, with the exception of Chkhenkeli, is not involving itself with such a combination.[16] This is the main *negative* virtue of its position. However, this is entirely inadequate. After rejecting a pseudorevolutionary mobilization of the proletariat on the basis of the "national undertaking" (the war), two possibilities remain. The first is the revolutionary mobilization of the proletariat *against* the "undertaking," which implies a class break with the "Progressive Bloc." The other is a *passive, wait-and-see* policy, which neither involves itself in the patriotic current, nor, in Liebknecht's words, finds "the desire or courage to give the proletariat a revolutionary slogan." Our Duma fraction's activity runs between these two alternatives, while obviously approaching passive internationalism. The prospect of a *revolutionary* mobilization of the proletariat against the "national undertaking," which would be not only against the monarchy and the nobility, but also against the imperialist bourgeoisie, undoubtedly frightens the fraction with its political "desperation."

In the national framework such a prospect actually does end up in a blind alley. The proletariat's revolutionary opposition not only to "reaction," but to the imperialist bloc as well is possible only with a clear understanding that this war means "a period of big social battles" for all of Europe. The political action of the Russian proletariat, "isolated" from the imperialist classes, is only one of these battles. The fate of militant anti-imperialist politics in Russia depends, in the final reckoning, not on the relationship of forces within the national framework, but on the course and outcome of the revolutionary struggle across the entire breadth of Europe. Our deputies do not have a clear conception of international revolution. If, with the exception of Chkhenkeli, they reject the national-patriotic conception, at the same time they far too often find themselves disarmed before it. That is the *fundamental* cause of the lack of adequate political definition in the fraction's activity and the passive, temporizing character of its internationalism.

But besides this there is another cause working more directly and therefore more sharply to this end: the organizational connection of the fraction with the leaders of the social patriots. For the deputies to be able to appeal openly from the rostrum of the Duma to the workers not to tie their hands with the chains of defensist policy, the hands of the deputies themselves must be completely free of organizational ties with the defensists, whether they are called Potresov or Chkhenkeli.

In August 1916, one month before he was deported by the French government, Trotsky wrote a general assessment of the different currents of Russian Social Democracy. He now said that the "August Bloc" (the Menshevik forces officially headed by the Organizing Committee), by politically subordinating the working class forces to the bourgeoisie represented "the greatest danger." While recognizing the need for coordinated action with the Bolsheviks, however, he still maintained his political criticisms of their positions on the war question.

Groupings in Russian Social Democracy[17]

by Leon Trotsky

Two years of war and crisis have sufficiently clarified the situation within the Russian Social Democracy to permit us to sum up the overall results. This should now prompt the internationalist groupings that do not occupy defined organizational niches in the party to draw the necessary practical conclusions and determine more precisely their future course inside the party, in closest association with groupings in the Socialist International as a whole.

1. *Prizyv* (The Call). This group has provided a banner to all the renegade, politically corrupt, and chauvinist elements of the intelligentsia and the clearly antirevolutionary elements of the working class. In this period it has slid further and further into liberal-militarist falsifications of socialism and into unbridled chauvinist baiting of revolutionary Social Democracy. Internationalists can have no doubt whatsoever

about their attitude to this scab outfit, which in itself has no future in the Russian workers' movement.

2. The *Samozashchita* (Self-Defense) group (Potresov and others) represents an incomparably more serious formation. This group stands between the "August Bloc," with which it is organizationally linked, and *Prizyv,* from which it is ideologically and politically distinguished only by its less unbridled methods. It has significant ties to both the most opportunist elements in the upper layers of the working class and to bourgeois "society" (the bourgeois press and publishing houses, the bourgeois "opposition" organizations).

The *Samozashchita* group represents the Russian variety of social patriotism (Scheidemann, Renaudel, Hyndman, and so on). Moreover, given Russia's social and political condition, this Russian variant has a most malignant character.

3. The "August Bloc" represents a far more complex political formation.

The political work of the "August Bloc" in Russia takes place almost entirely in the context of participation in the defensist War Industries Committees. The Petersburg Initiative Group and the Moscow Group base their tactics principally on coordination of activities with the liberal-imperialist bourgeoisie.

Within this milieu disagreements are breaking out regarding an *appraisal* of their participation in the actual work of the War Industries Committees. Some, the open social patriots, demand that this participation proceed under the banner of *defense*. Others—while in fact subordinating the proletariat's policy to the bourgeoisie's defensist, "opposition" policy—supplement this with a purely verbal internationalism, with platonic declarations of solidarity with Zimmerwald and so on.

The internal struggle of these two tendencies is, in fact, paralyzing the Organizing Committee. Despite this, they remain tied to the framework of a single "August Bloc" organization on the common ground of defensist practice, even after the entire international and Russian experience of two years.

The center of the day-to-day work of the "August Bloc," its focal points, remain the central, Petersburg, and Moscow war industry groups, with their battle flag of patriotism.

4. The Duma fraction is in a state of chronic breakdown. From the rostrum Chkheidze and Skobelev declare their solidarity with Zimmerwald and decline all political responsibility for the Organizing Committee. But not once have they come out against participation in the War Industries Committees. Nor have they publicly protested that the "August Bloc" press writes about the fraction as if they and Gvozdev's group were politically related institutions. Nor have they protested Chkhenkeli's proclamation of solidarity with Gvozdev's declaration.

The speeches and declarations of the fraction, more precisely those by Chkheidze and Skobelev, give a certain degree of support to the German, French, and Italian Zimmerwaldists, and in that sense play a progressive role. However, the fraction's position on questions of domestic policy, and particularly on internal party questions, is being presented not only formlessly, but ambiguously. The longer it goes on, the more it threatens to turn into a parliamentary screen for the cooperation of the proletariat with the liberal bourgeoisie in the War Industries Committees.

5. Outside the country the "August Bloc" is represented by the so-called Secretariat Abroad. In its positions at international conferences on the politics of the International, the Secretariat Abroad is by and large moving toward the right-wing Zimmerwaldists (Ledebour, Bourderon, and others). Nonetheless, the Secretariat Abroad is tied to a faction whose work is being carried out on the basis of the War Industries Committees. The Secretariat Abroad has displayed a complete inability and unwillingness to free itself from this tie and openly mobilize the revolutionary elements of Menshevism

against the social patriots—both open and unconscious.

On the contrary, the Secretariat Abroad has guarded the unity of the "August Bloc" in every way it can. As far as possible it conceals its own internal contradictions; thereby strengthening the position of the social patriots. Having in fact reconciled itself with the defensist activities of its co-thinkers in Russia (see *Izvestia* [News] No. 5), the Secretariat Abroad struggles with the greatest energy against the revolutionary internationalists, in particular against *Nashe Slovo*.

As a result, the entire right wing of the "August Bloc" takes the position of social patriotism *(Samozashchita)*. In the form of its "left" groupings (Dan and others), the "August Bloc" draws near the position of Longuetism in France and other such tendencies, which combine actual collaboration with the parties of national defense and internationalist declarations. Since blatant social patriotism of the Plekhanov and Potresov models cannot last long in the ranks of the proletariat under the conditions of the Khvostov-Stürmer regime, *the policy of the "August Bloc" presents the greatest danger.* It is here, under the formal cover of the Zimmerwald banner, that the task of politically subordinating the upper layers of the working class to the imperialist bourgeoisie is being carried out. Under such conditions a coordinated and energetic struggle of all the internationalists against the politics of the "August Bloc" is needed to minimize the antirevolutionary influence of nationalism and opportunism in the Russian workers' movement.

6. In the camp of the Russian internationalists we find first of all the *Sotsial-Demokrat* group. It has been our lot, time and again, to point out those traits of this organization which, not to detract from its role as a weighty revolutionary factor in the present time of crisis, prevent it at this moment from including all the revolutionary elements of the movement. From the very beginning of the war *Sotsial-Demokrat*

showed hostility to the slogan of the struggle for peace. But experience shows that the mobilization of proletarian opposition everywhere has taken place and is taking place precisely under this slogan. Only on this basis can revolutionary internationalists today successfully carry out their work. The formula of *civil war* expresses in an essentially correct way the inevitable exacerbation of all forms of class struggle in the coming period. But they counterpose it to the struggle for peace, which causes the formula to hang in mid-air and lose its meaning for the period we are living through.

Finally, the paradoxical and internally contradictory formula "the defeat of Russia is the lesser evil," creates difficulties for our German cothinkers and does not enrich but rather hampers our agitation. It has provided the social patriotic demagogues with a most important weapon in their struggle against our common banner. Such an exaggeration of revolutionary slogans is all the more dangerous since *Sotsial-Demokrat* is quick to turn these formulas into the absolute test of internationalism.

The negative traits mentioned here have never prevented us—and still less can they prevent us now—from recognizing the urgent necessity for coordinated action with *Sotsial-Demokrat.*

7. In fact, this coordination can be seriously accomplished only if there is preliminary political and organizational agreement among the independent groups now scattered abroad and in Russia itself that stand on revolutionary internationalism, and intransigently combat the national and liberal policy of domesticating the proletariat. This policy is now being carried out not only under the banner of *Prizyv* and *Samozashchita* but also under the cover of the "August Bloc" as a whole.

Such an agreement is all the more necessary inasmuch as it could also meet the same kind of needs of the grouping in the International. The Zimmerwald Left has undoubtedly played a progressive role in the broad Zimmerwald current as a whole. However, at present it does not include all the revolutionary groupings and factions that have emerged. Only by creating firm ideological and organizational ties among all the revolutionary internationalist forces and by strengthening and broadening this revolutionary unification can we create a solid guarantee against the unexpected and against backward motion in the process of evolving the Third International.

Noting the evolution of Trotsky's position, Lenin commented in December 1916: "The pressure of facts has increasingly compelled *Nashe Slovo* and Trotsky, who reproach us for our 'factionalism', to take up the struggle against the O.C. [Organizing Committee] and Chkheidze. The trouble, however, is that it was only 'under pressure' (of our criticism and the criticism of the facts) that the *Nashe Slovo* supporters retreated from position to position; but they *have not yet said* the decisive word. Unity or a split with the Chkheidze faction? They are still afraid to decide!" [18]

Trotsky was associated with a small group in Petrograd known as the Mezhrayontsi (Interdistrict Committee) which included former members of both the Bolshevik and Menshevik currents. Alexander Shlyapnikov recalled that "from the very beginning of the war this organization took an internationalist position. It maintained contact with the Petersburg [Bolshevik] Committee during the war, but worked separately, not wishing to 'dissolve' into our mass organization. At first they had some objections to our 'defeatism,' but the war and the tsarist war policy educated the Mezhrayontsi, and toward the end of 1916 they adopted all of our slogans, beginning with that of civil war and ending with that of the Third International." [19]

A Mezhrayontsi leaflet dated October 1916 reflects the degree to which they had adopted aspects of Bolshevik policy in the final months before the outbreak of revolution.

Mezhrayontsi appeal for revolutionary unity[20]

In the third year of the World War, just as on its first day, we raise our slogan of the struggle for peace, for a democratic republic.

We know that the International, the international brotherhood of the workers, will come to life again. The socialist conferences in Zimmerwald and Kienthal, the strikes in Russia and Britain,[21] the demonstrations in Germany, are laying the unshakable foundation of a new International. Against the slogan of the government and the liberals—"all for victory"—we counterpose the slogan of civil war, of armed insurrection. The sufferings of the people, who stagger under the burden of taxes and military dictatorship, must be ended. The tsarist autocracy's pleas for "unity" deceive no one. Let the Gvozdevs walk into the trap of "unity." We also call for unity, but for the unity of the workers, the unity of the revolutionary forces of Social Democracy. We call upon you, comrades, to struggle for the unity of the party. Great tasks stand before Russian Social Democracy, but it has no united will, no common decisions, no authoritative Central Committee; and a pitiful sectarianism exists, which strives to substitute its small circles for the party. It is time to end this collapse, time to rally around a powerful goal.

We, unified Social Democrats—Bolsheviks and Mensheviks—pose for the coming days the need to convene an all-Russian conference in which all revolutionary Social Democrats must participate. Comrades! Organize meetings and protests against the war: organize collections for the illegal press and those hit by repression. Rally to the workers' organizations! The proletariat must proclaim a mobilization of its strength. A mighty cry must escape from the breasts of millions of workers:

Down with the war! Down with the autocracy! Long live civil war! Long live the Russian revolution! Long live the international brotherhood of the workers! Long live the Third International! Long live the United Russian Social Democratic Labor Party! Long live socialism!

Petersburg Interdistrict Committee

A new wave of workers' strikes broke out in Russia in October 1916. Overall, there were twice as many strikes in 1916 as in 1915, and many raised political slogans as well as demanding wage increases to keep up with soaring prices. The shortages of food and other items erupted into food riots. More and more, soldiers called out to quell protests showed sympathy for the demonstrators.

Rural discontent boiled over in the summer of 1916, fed by the toll of casualties at the front, by the peasants' lack of bread, seed, and draft animals, and by the bitter letters from their inadequately fed and supplied sons in the army. Tsarist officials counted 294 instances of large-scale peasant action during the course of the year. Some manor houses were burned; in other cases whole villages refused to pay rent. Tsarist officials compared peasant unrest with that of 1905–1907. Protests by oppressed nationalities also broke out in wide areas of the tsarist empire.

In the fall of 1916 the liberal opposition to the tsar struck a more radical tone, aiming to win popular support for its proposals to reform the tsarist regime. A leaflet was distributed to factory workers in the capital calling on them to rally around the Duma majority in seeking a "Government of National Salvation." The leaflet mentioned no measures to end the war or to ease the burdens on working people.

The Petersburg Bolshevik Committee responded in November 1916 with a leaflet warning workers against bourgeois attempts to seize the fruits of the mounting mass struggles and impose a new form of capitalist rule. The struggle to overthrow tsarism must aim for "genuine people's rule," the leaflet said, "for a provisional revolutionary government of the workers and poor peasants." Workers must set their course for socialism, the only solution for the people's suffering. While preparing for the showdown with tsarism, the Petrograd worker-Bolsheviks thus anticipated the great questions placed before the workers' movement by the February 1917 revolution.

For genuine people's rule[22]

"Workers of the World, Unite!"

Comrades! During the entire course of the war the State Duma at its opening sessions has sworn allegiance to the tsarist government and embraced its ministers as an expression of the Duma's loyal sentiments. Now the militant deputies, lackeys of the tsar as before, have nonetheless raised a ruckus and fallen out with the government. Over what? They declare that a change of ministry is required to continue the war to the end. Now that the popular masses, exhausted by the excessive burdens of a war blessed by the capitalists, begin to lose patience and are ready to move against their oppressors, the liberal wheeler-dealers are trying to use this popular movement to satisfy their own predatory appetites. They need, they say, a ministry enjoying public confidence. What can it bring to the tormented people? A Milyukov instead of a Stürmer. They talk about the salvation of the country, but they are ready to lead it to new deaths, and they demand more and more sacrifices.

No! We must always remember that those who call on us to carry the war to the end consider us least of all and worry least of all about the fate of the people. The replacement of one group of murderers by another will not lead us to break off our struggle against a reconstituted government.

A few chauvinist workers, who up to now have found words only to condemn our revolutionary activity, place special hopes on the longings of the liberals. They are addressing an appeal to us to fight for a "government of national salvation." These "worker politicians" deserted us at the most difficult moment, the outbreak of the war, in order to help the government and the bourgeoisie conduct it; they condemned our revolutionary efforts not to lay down the weapons of struggle against the war and the oppressors; they kept silent about the kidnapping of our deputies, who were torn from us. Now they call on us to march behind their slogans! To place the salvation of the country in the hands of the men who want to turn long months of bloodshed into years and who mercilessly strangle the workers' movement!

Comrades! Surely decades of bloody experience in the

workers' movement show clearly who is really able to fight against this piratical monarchy.

By gathering our forces, spreading agitation in the ranks of the poor peasants and the army, we can forge a true hammer of revolution, which will finish off the government, the tormentor of the people.

That is the first task—overthrow the tsarist government and create a provisional revolutionary government of the workers and poor peasants!

We will demand from this government an immediate cessation of the war; the immediate convocation of a *constituent assembly;* the achievement of political freedoms, creating the conditions for the struggle to establish genuine people's rule—a democratic republic; the confiscation of the landlords' estates; and in order to put into the hands of the working class its strongest weapon—the shortening of its working time by the institution of the eight-hour day!

Now we must be on guard! Choking on the torrents of blood they have spilled, the governments and ruling classes will strain every nerve to ensure that the war's outcome will strengthen their power and deepen the enslavement of the peoples. The workers of the entire world, and first and foremost the workers of the warring countries, must aim their blows against their own governments. Only when the people have disarmed the governments and put an end to this war by carrying out political revolutions, will we be truly able to save the country from destruction.

But remember comrades! As long as the capitalists feed off the life of the workers, as long as they lord it over the world, they will not hesitate, in their pursuit of profits, to hurl the people again and again into the inferno of war. Only the annihilation of the capitalist system and its replacement by socialism will put an end to wars and human suffering.

Therefore, by developing the revolutionary might of the international proletariat, by creating the Third International, we Russian workers can devote all our strength to the realization of socialism. We will cast off the shackles of the tsarist monarchy and support the comrades of England, Germany, and France in their readiness to carry on a struggle for the overthrow of the capitalist governments.

Forward without rest! Down with the war! Down with the tsarist government! Long live the provisional revolutionary government! Down with the tsarist monarchy! Long live the democratic republic! Long live the revolution! Long live socialism!

Above, Friedrich Ebert, Philipp Scheidemann; below Hugo Haase.

Chapter 10

Germany: Toward a communist party

German imperialism scored several military successes in 1915, including the conquest of much Russian territory and all of Serbia. Yet none of these victories was decisive. Russia was not knocked out of the war; Italy entered the war on the Entente side; the British naval blockade was unbroken; and the growing shortages of food and essential raw materials in the Central Powers reflected the marked superiority of the Entente's productive resources.

By the end of 1915, German workers' resistance to the government's war policies was rapidly increasing. Widespread strikes and demonstrations, including a rally of 10,000 in the center of Berlin in late November, protested hunger and declining living standards and demanded an end to the war.

Under these pressures, and challenged by the growing influence of the Spartacists, eighteen SPD Reichstag members led by Georg Ledebour and Hugo Haase resolved to defy party discipline and joined Karl Liebknecht and Otto Rühle in voting on December 21, 1915, against the fifth set of war credits. Fritz Geyer declared on behalf of the SPD minority that their commitment to peace and against any plans for conquest was incompatible with support of the war appropriations.[1]

The government had failed to dissociate itself from those agitating for annexation, Geyer said. Yet "our national boundaries and our independence are secure. It is not the invasion of hostile armies that threatens us. Rather the continuation of the war threatens our land, like the rest of Europe, with the destruction of its most vigorous citizens, the impoverishment of the people and the ravaging of their civilization."

Because Germany and its allies enjoyed a more favorable military situation, it was up to the German government and its allies to take the first step toward peace, Geyer explained. The Social Democratic fraction had called on the government to make a peace offer; yet the chancellor had rejected this out of hand.[2]

Karl Liebknecht commented on the action of the eighteen SPD deputies in a Spartacist letter of January 27, 1916. In order to prevail, he wrote, opponents of the social-patriotic SPD majority had to display "public, tenacious opposition against the Reichstag fraction majority, constantly using every means to destroy the extraparliamentary 'civil peace.'" This spirit was utterly lacking in Geyer's December 21 declaration, Liebknecht explained. Indeed, the statement itself, he argued, held to the muffled tones of "civil peace" and avoided any sharp assessment of the government, let alone of the fraction majority.

The Geyer declaration's reference to the danger of enemy invasion was deliberately ambiguous, Liebknecht noted, coming close to affirming the correctness of the SPD's August 4, 1914, pro-war declaration, which had hinged on the same concept.

"A policy that rejects principled internationalism . . . adheres to the concept of national defense, and makes supporting or opposing the government and the war dependent on the current military situation or on some kind of declaration on war aims differs from that of the party majority only by being less consistent." Far from rejecting the course of the social chauvinists, he said, the December 21 statement made concessions to it all down the line.[3]

The Spartacists did not seek to submerge their current in that of the Haase-Ledebour forces. Rather, they aimed to build an independent, revolutionary current. Rosa Luxemburg had insisted on this course in a December 8, 1915, letter smuggled out of prison to Spartacist leader Leo Jogiches.

"I regret very much that I was not promptly informed at the time about the plan for Zimmerwald," Luxemburg wrote. "I believe the affair was not only unsuccessful, but a nearly catastrophic mistake that has placed the further development of the opposition and the International on the wrong track. . . . The problem is that our people believe that something must absolutely be done as soon as possible. So, in order to achieve this 'something,' they think it is vital not to scare away the flotsam and jetsam. This policy of going around and begging for crumbs makes genuine clarity and action impossible."[4]

Luxemburg proposed in this letter that programmatic theses be placed for adoption before a conference of Spartacist leaders. "Our goal at this conference should not be to bring the entire opposition under one roof, but rather to pull out of this mush the small, solid kernel that is capable of action, and unite it around our platform."[5]

About fifteen leading Spartacists from across Germany met January 1, 1916, and founded the Internationale Group, named after their banned journal. They adopted the following theses, written by Luxemburg while still in prison, and edited by Liebknecht, Clara Zetkin, and Franz Mehring.

Theses on the tasks of international Social Democracy[6]

A large number of comrades from different parts of Germany have adopted the following theses, which constitute an application of the Erfurt program to the contemporary problems of international socialism.[7]

1. The World War has annihilated the work of forty years of European socialism, by destroying both the revolutionary proletariat as a political force and the moral prestige of socialism; by breaking up the workers' International and setting its sections one against the other in fratricidal massacre; and by tying the aspirations and hopes of the masses of the people in the main developed capitalist countries to the destinies of imperialism.

2. By their vote for war credits and their proclamation of "civil peace," the official leaderships of the Socialist parties in Germany, France, and England (except for that of the Independent Labour Party) have strengthened imperialism. They have induced the masses of the people to suffer patiently the misery and horror of the war; contributed to the unleashing of unrestrained imperialist frenzy, the prolongation of the massacre, and the multiplication of its victims; and assumed their share in the responsibility for the war itself and for its consequences.

3. This policy of the official party leaderships in the belligerent countries, above all of the German party that until recently led the International, signifies a betrayal of the elementary principles of internationalist socialism, of the vital interests of the working class, and of all the democratic interests of the peoples. This has condemned Socialist policy to impotence even in those countries where the leaders have

remained faithful to their principles: Russia, Serbia, Italy and—with one exception—Bulgaria.[8]

4. By abandoning the class struggle in wartime and adjourning it until after the war, official Social Democracy in the principal countries has guaranteed the ruling classes everywhere a delay in which to enormously strengthen their economic, political, and moral positions at the proletariat's expense.

5. The World War serves neither the national defense nor the economic or political interests of any layer of the masses. It is precisely the monstrous progeny of imperialist rivalries among the capitalist classes of the different countries for world hegemony and for a monopoly in the exploitation and oppression of areas still not under the heel of capital. National wars are no longer possible in this era of raging imperialism. National interests serve only as the means to trick the laboring masses, putting them at the service of their mortal enemy, imperialism.

6. The imperialist war and the policies of the imperialist states cannot bring a single oppressed nation its liberty and its independence. The ruling classes of the small nations are mere appendages and accomplices of their partners in the great powers. These nations are no more than pawns on the great powers' chessboard. Just like the working masses, they are pliant tools to be abused in war and sacrificed to capitalist interests when it ends.

7. Therefore, whether it brings "defeat" or "victory," the present World War signifies a defeat for socialism and democracy. Whatever its outcome—excepting the revolutionary intervention of the international proletariat—it strengthens militarism, international antagonisms, and world economic rivalries. It accentuates capitalist exploitation and internal reaction, weakens popular control, and reduces parliaments more and more to obedient tools of militarism. The present World War develops all the conditions that will bring new wars.

8. World peace cannot be assured by utopian or basically reactionary projects like international arbitration courts made up of capitalist diplomats, diplomatic agreements for "disarmament," "the freedom of the seas," "outlawing maritime seizure," "the European federation of states," a "customs union for Central Europe," "national buffer states," and other such illusions. Imperialism, militarism, and war can never be abolished nor attenuated so long as the capitalist class exercises uncontested class hegemony. The sole means of successful resistance, and the only guarantee of world peace, is the international proletariat's capacity for action and its revolutionary determination to hurl its full weight onto the balance.

9. Imperialism is the last phase of capital's world political hegemony, when this hegemony achieves its greatest expansion. Imperialism is therefore the common mortal enemy of the proletariat of all countries. Just as in the preceding stages of capitalism, imperialism increases the forces of its mortal enemy in pace with its own development. It accelerates the concentration of capital, the grinding down of the middle classes, and the growth of the proletariat, arousing more and more resistance from the masses and so leading to an intensified sharpening of class antagonisms. In peacetime as in war, the proletarian class struggle must be focused first of all against imperialism. Its international struggle against imperialism is at the same time a struggle for state power, the decisive showdown between socialism and capitalism. The international proletariat will realize the final goal of socialism only if it opposes imperialism all along the line, making the slogan "war against war" the guiding line in the application of its policy, deploying all its forces, and displaying the greatest courage and self-sacrifice.

10. To this end, socialism's principal mission today is to unite the proletariat of all countries into a living revolutionary force. This requires a powerful international organization

with a homogeneous conception of its interests and tasks, a homogeneous tactical policy, and a common striking power in peace and war alike, so that it may become a decisive factor in political life and thus fulfill its historic mission.

11. The war has smashed the Second International. Its inability to effectively prevent its forces from being broken apart in wartime along national lines and its incapacity to lead the proletariat in carrying out a common policy and common actions in all countries demonstrated that the Second International was inadequate.

12. The official representatives of the Socialist parties in the main countries have betrayed the aims and interests of the working class. They have passed from the camp of the proletarian International to the political camp of the imperialist bourgeoisie. It is therefore vitally necessary for socialism to build a new workers' International, which will take into its own hands the leadership and coordination of the revolutionary class struggle in all countries against world imperialism.

To accomplish its historic mission, socialism must be guided by the following principles:

1. Class struggle against the ruling classes within the bourgeois states; solidarity of the workers of all countries internationally: these are the two indissoluble basic principles of the historic working-class struggle for world liberation. There is no socialism without international proletarian solidarity, and there is no socialism without class struggle. For the socialist proletariat to renounce the class struggle and international solidarity, in time of peace as in time of war, is to commit suicide.

2. As a class the proletariat's activity in all countries, in peacetime as in war, must take as its supreme goal the fight against imperialism and the prevention of war. Parliamentary and trade union action, like every activity of the workers' movement, must be subordinated to setting the proletariat

of each country in the sharpest opposition to its national bourgeoisie. In this way the political and spiritual antagonism between the two is always brought to the fore, and international solidarity between the workers of all countries is emphasized and put into practice.

3. The center of gravity of the proletariat's class organization is the International. The International decides the tactics of the national sections in time of peace on the questions of militarism, colonial policy, trade policy, and the celebration of May Day, and in addition, the entire tactical policy to be applied in wartime.

4. The duty to carry out the International's decisions takes precedence over all other organizational obligations. National sections that violate these decisions place themselves outside the International.

5. Only the mobilized masses of the proletariat in all countries can exert decisive power in the struggle against imperialism and against war. Thus the policy of the national sections aims above all to prepare the masses for political action and resolute initiative; to ensure the international cohesion of the masses in action; and to build the political and trade union organizations so that they can always guarantee prompt and effective collaboration of all the sections and so that the will of the International takes shape in actions by the broadest masses of workers of all countries.

6. The immediate task of socialism is to liberate the proletariat spiritually from the tutelage of the bourgeoisie, as expressed in the influence of nationalist ideology. The national sections must agitate in the parliaments and the press, denouncing the traditional phraseology of nationalism as an instrument of bourgeois rule. The revolutionary class struggle against imperialism is today the sole defense of all real national independence. The workers' fatherland, to the defense of which all else must be subordinated, is the Socialist International.

These theses were distributed across Germany as an underground leaflet and were also submitted to the February conference of the International Socialist Committee in Bern (ISC). Formation of the Internationale Group and circulation of its program unleashed a sharp debate among the opposition forces in the SPD.

The centrist Haase-Ledebour current called on the revolutionists to draw back from separate activity as a tendency in the opposition, to set aside their particular views, and to turn their entire energy toward a united struggle to win a majority in the SPD around Haase and Ledebour's program.

Replying to the Spartacist theses in the *Bulletin* of the ISC, Ledebour and Adolph Hoffmann took exception to the opening words of the theses. In their view, these implied that the theses were a common statement of the SPD opposition, when they represented in fact the views of only a small minority. Rather than take up the central assertion of the Spartacists' theses—the call for a new workers' International—Ledebour and Hoffmann concentrated on the claim that the Spartacists advocated an exaggerated level of international centralization.

Reply to the Spartacists[9]

by Adolph Hoffmann and Georg Ledebour

We must also express reservations concerning the specific content of the publication in question. By leading in the direction of a fusion of all the Socialist parties into a united and centralized body, the provisions go far beyond the Erfurt program and the statutes of the Social Democratic Party of Germany. They also contradict the basic points of the *Zimmerwald manifesto,* upon which we base ourselves.

In fact, the twelve provisions are accompanied by a founding draft for a new, third International summarized in six paragraphs, the two most important of which state the following:

"3. The center of gravity of the proletariat's class organization is the International. The International decides the tactics of the national sections in time of peace on the questions of militarism, colonial policy, trade policy, and the celebration of May Day, and in addition, the entire tactical policy to be applied in wartime.

"4. The duty to carry out the International's decisions takes precedence over all other organizational obligations. National sections that violate these decisions place themselves outside the International."[10]

If they carried this program out, the Socialist parties of various countries would be reduced to the status of subordinate bodies of a centralized International. Until now the national Socialist parties were sovereign organizations which, in the final analysis, determined their own statutes and activity and joined together in a federated manner for international tasks.

In addition, the decisions of international congresses had to be ratified by the national organizations before being carried out in the different countries. To avoid any split, the international congresses tried as much as possible to achieve unanimity in their decisions.

But the national parties were never subordinate bodies of a great international party. The international bureau had no functions except those of an initiator and intermediary. It never had the functions of a general staff commanding the troops of the international proletariat.

This organizational basis would have to be completely changed in order to carry out the Spartacus plan. It is clearly the draft's intention that in the future the International would make decisions that were absolutely binding on all the member national sections.

In their relationship to the centralized International, the parties or sections would then find themselves in a situation analogous to the relationship of the regional organizations to the Social Democratic Party of Germany.

Within the framework of the decisions of the international congress, leadership and control of the national sections would rest in the hands of a central institution. Therefore, *the international bureau would be turned into a central executive committee.* All the faults of uniformity and bureaucratization that experience has shown go with a national executive committee would be multiplied in an international executive committee.

The fundamental democratic concept of our proletarian party, that all decisions should flow from bottom to top, would almost completely disappear in this centralized International. Such plans could not be carried out even in the period when a Marx or an Engels created the First International, which dealt only with weak groups of activists. Now, when the movement in various countries has reached such great development, this kind of attempt would soon flounder in the face of the *differing degrees of maturity* of these parties and the multiplicity of economic, social, and legal conditions.

And this is all the more true *during the war*! How could anyone want every tactic to be directed by a central International in that situation? Even if it were possible to bring together the representatives of the Socialists in all countries, including the belligerent countries, to carry this out, this body would very quickly lose all contact with those it represents and would then be condemned even to impotence.

So from whatever angle one examines this plan, it is totally impractical.

Naturally any comrade is free to work out any plan he wants, and to submit it to the discussion in the party. But we do not believe that the period of a state of siege is particularly propitious for carrying out organizational plans of such scope. Moreover, the authors of this plan have made a completely nondemocratic attempt to win approval for it in an international conference *even before* they made it public in Germany. . . .

So much for the proposal to form a new International.

We will say a few words on the rest of the material distributed by the Spartacists. . . . They try to show that the twenty deputies who voted against the war credits on December 21 are, with only two glorious exceptions, unreliable people whom comrades ought to watch like a hawk. Their fiery zeal leads them to conclusions that are objectively false and to unwarranted personal attacks.

This policy of the Spartacists is simply grist for the mill of the Reichstag fraction majority and the official party leadership.

The effort to reestablish in the party a policy based on socialist principles cannot be successful unless its defenders unite firmly in common action, setting aside for now disputes over past differences. If, on the other hand, the Spartacists' policy were to gain support among comrades, that would inevitably disorganize and paralyze the opposition movement. We want a quick and decisive victory, which can only be assured by cooperation based on the mutual confidence of all the friends of our cause. . . .

The Spartacists replied that Ledebour and Hoffmann had entirely misunderstood their conception of the International, which was based not on mechanical centralization by commands from the top, but on involvement of the masses as a "living revolutionary force." The fundamental difference, they said, was that Ledebour and Hoffmann "cannot recognize that the old International has definitively collapsed. They still do not understand that it is precisely now, in wartime, in the struggle against imperialism and war, that the future International must demonstrate its existence and develop its forces. They have not understood that the future International must be an International in reality and not merely in appearance."[11]

Despite differences on this and other questions, the Spartacists explained, they wished to collaborate with Ledebour and Hoffmann in areas where they agreed, as they had been doing since early summer 1915. They insisted only that they must be free to speak and act independently. Ledebour and Hoffmann turned this offer down, and in February 1916 the centrist and revolutionary currents on a national leadership level and in Berlin parted company.

The next major publication of the Internationale Group was a pamphlet by Rosa Luxemburg, *The Crisis in the Social Democracy.* She had completed it in prison in April 1915, and the Spartacists smuggled the manuscript out of prison, but had not found a way to print it. Shortly after Luxemburg's release in January 1916 a printer was found, and her essay was illegally circulated among Socialist workers, who, from her pseudonym, knew it as the "Junius Pamphlet."

The crisis in the German Social Democracy[12]

by Junius (Rosa Luxemburg)

Things are not as they were. The scene has thoroughly changed. The six weeks' march on Paris has burgeoned into a world drama. Mass slaughter has become tiresome and routine, without bringing a solution one step closer. Bourgeois statesmanship is caught in its own trap, and cannot lay to rest the spirit that it has invoked.

Gone is the first mad delirium. Gone is the patriotic clamor in the streets, the chase after suspicious-looking automobiles, the phony telegrams, the cholera-poisoned wells. Gone, the mad tales of Russian students hurling bombs at every railway trestle in Berlin, of French planes over Nürnberg; gone, the spy-hunts in every alley, the teeming throngs in the cafes where deafening music and patriotic songs drowned all else out; gone, the lynch mobs, looking for victims, harassing women, ready to whip themselves into a delirious frenzy over every wild rumor; gone, the atmosphere of ritual murder, the pogrom atmosphere that left the policeman on the corner as the only remaining representative of human dignity.

The show is over. The German scholars, the "wavering spirits of the dead," have long been housebroken. The troop trains no longer get joyous sendoffs from eager young maidens. The reservists' faces no longer smile cheerily from the train windows. Quietly they trudge through the streets, with their duffel bags upon their shoulders. And the public, with an annoyed look, goes about its daily business.

Into the sober atmosphere of pale daylight echoes a

different chorus: the hoarse croak of the vultures and hyenas of the battlefield. Ten thousand tents, guaranteed to specifications! 100,000 kilos of bacon, cocoa powder, coffee substitute—cash only, for immediate delivery. Grenades, lathes, cartridge belts, marriage bureaus for war widows, leather straps, war orders—serious bids only, please! And the cannon fodder that was loaded upon the trains in August and September rots on the battlefields of Belgium, the Vosges, and the Masurian Lakes, while profits shoot up from the fields of the dead. The crop is ready to harvest. Thousands of greedy hands reach over the ocean to grasp their part.

Business is flourishing upon the ruins. Cities are turned into rubble, villages into cemeteries, whole countries into deserts, entire nations into beggars, churches into stables; civil rights, treaties, alliances, the holiest words, and the highest authorities have been ripped in tatters; every sovereign by the grace of God is called an idiot, a lying cheat, by his cousin on the other side; every diplomat calls his opposite number a desperate rogue; each government looks upon the other as a fateful curse on its own people, worthy of universal contempt. Hunger riots in Venice, Lisbon, Moscow, Singapore; pestilence in Russia; misery and desperation everywhere.

Shamed, dishonored, wading in blood, and dripping with filth—this is capitalist society. Not preened and proper, feigning culture, philosophy, and ethics, order, peace and lawfulness, but a roaring beast, an orgy of anarchy, a pestilential breath, devastating culture and humanity—so it appears in all its hideous nakedness.

And in the midst of this orgy a world tragedy has occurred: the capitulation of the international Social Democracy. To close one's eyes to this fact, to try to hide it, would be the most foolish, the most dangerous thing that the international proletariat could do. . . .

The August 4 declaration

The fundamental fact cited in the declaration of our Reichstag fraction was . . . simply an echo of the speech from the throne and of the chancellor's speech of August 4. "We are not driven by the desire for conquest," affirms the speech from the throne, "We are inspired by the unalterable determination to preserve for Ourselves and for all coming generations the land upon which God has placed us. From the documents that have been presented to you, you will see how Our government, and above all Our chancellor strove to the very last to avert the worst. We grasp the sword in self-defense, with a clear conscience and clean hands."

And Bethmann-Hollweg declared: "Gentlemen, we are acting in self-defense, and necessity knows no law. . . . Threatened as we are, fighting for the highest stakes, we can be guided by but one consideration, how best to beat down our foes. We are fighting for the fruits of our peaceful labor, for the heritage of our great past, for the future of our nation."

That is precisely the message of the Social Democratic declaration. (1) We have done everything to preserve peace, the war was forced upon us by the other side. (2) Now that the war is here we must act in self-defense. (3) In this war the German people are in danger of losing everything. The statement of our Reichstag group is an obvious rehashing of the government declarations. Just as the government based its claims upon Bethmann-Hollweg's diplomatic endeavors and the kaiser's telegrams, the Socialist fraction points to Social Democracy's peace demonstrations before the outbreak of war. Where the speech from the throne denies all aims of conquest, the Reichstag group repudiates a war of conquest by standing upon its socialism. And when the kaiser and chancellor cry out, "We are fighting for the highest principles. We know no parties, we know only Germans," the Social Democratic declaration echoes: "Everything is at stake now for our people. We will not desert our fatherland in its hour of need."

The Social Democratic declaration differs from its government model in only one point: in the forefront of its orientation it places Russian despotism as a danger to German freedom. The speech from the throne says, regarding Russia: "With a heavy heart We have been forced to mobilize against a neighbor alongside whom We have fought upon so many battlefields. With honest sorrow We have seen a friendship faithfully kept by Germany fall to pieces." The Social Democratic group changed this sorrowful rupture of true friendship with Russian tsarism into a fanfare for liberty against despotism. This is the one point on which it showed some independence vis-à-vis the government declaration. The Social Democracy used the revolutionary heritage of socialism to give the war a democratic mantle, a popular halo. . . .

The nature of German imperialism

In Germany the development of imperialism, crowded as it was into the shortest possible span of time, can be studied in its purest form. The unprecedented rise of German large-scale industry and commerce since the empire's foundation brought out during the eighties two characteristic features peculiar to capitalist accumulation: the most pronounced growth of monopoly in Europe and the best developed and most concentrated banking system in the whole world. The monopolies have organized heavy industry, that is, the branch of capitalist endeavor most interested in government orders, in military equipment, and in imperialistic undertakings (railroad building, the exploitation of mineral deposits, and so on) into the most influential force in the state. The banks have cemented finance capital into a firmly organized power, with the greatest, most intensive energy. Thus they have created a power that imperiously rules the nation's industry, commerce, and credit. It dominates private as well as public affairs, boundless and fitful in its powers of expansion, ever hungry for profit and activity, impersonal, and therefore, grandiose, reckless and unscrupulous, by its very nature international and ordained to use the world as its stage.

Germany is further characterized by the strongest form of personal rule, marked by the kaiser's quite erratic political initiatives, and by the weakest kind of parliamentarism, incapable of any opposition. All bourgeois strata stand united behind the government in sharp opposition to the working class. Thus it could be foreseen that this young, boisterous imperialism, unhampered by any inhibitions, and stepping onto the world stage with a monstrous appetite just when the world had been almost entirely carved up, would quickly become an incalculable factor of general unrest. . . .

By developing its naval might and raising the banner of its world policies, German imperialism signaled its plans for new and wide-ranging forays in the world. By means of a first-class, offensive navy, and an army that increased by leaps and bounds, the apparatus for a future policy was established whose perspectives and goals threw open the doors to unlimited possibilities. Naval construction and armaments became the grand and glorious business of German heavy industry, opening up boundless prospects for further operations by trust and bank capital around the world.

This assured that all bourgeois parties would fall into line behind the flag of imperialism. The Center [party] followed the example of the National Liberals, the palace guard of imperialist heavy industry. Once the Naval Bill of 1900 was adopted, the Center, which had so loudly denounced it, immediately rallied to the government. The Progressives trotted after the Center when the successor to the naval bill, the high-tariff bill, came up. Bringing up the rear were the Junkers, transformed from the staunchest opponents of the "horrid navy" and of the Rhine-Elbe canal into the most enthusiastic porkers and parasites of naval militarism, colonial robbery, and the related tariff policy. The Reichstag election of 1907, the so-called Hottentot Elections, revealed the whole of bourgeois Germany in a paroxysm of imperialistic fervor, firmly united under one flag, the Germany of von Bülow, which felt itself called on to play the role of world enforcer. These elections, marked by the intellectual atmosphere of a pogrom, prefigured the Germany of August 4. They were a challenge not only to the German working class, but to the other capitalist nations as well, a challenge directed to no one in particular, but rather a clenched fist shaken in the face of the entire world. . . .

Defense of the fatherland

"But since we have been unable to prevent the war, since war has come and our country is facing enemy invasion, should we leave our country defenseless? Should we deliver it into the hands of the enemy? Germany to the Russians, or France and Belgium to the Germans, or Serbia to the Austrians? If socialism supports the right of nations to determine their own destinies, does this not mean that every people is justified—even more, is duty bound—to defend its freedom and independence? When the house is burning, should we not first put out the fire before trying to discover who set it?"

This argument about the "burning house" has been invoked by Socialists on both sides of the fronts, by Socialists in Germany and in France to justify their stand. . . .

To be sure. It is an unworthy people that capitulates before the external foe and an unworthy party that capitulates before the enemy within. But there is one thing that the fire brigade of the "burning house" has forgotten: in the mouth of a Socialist, the phrase "defending one's fatherland" means something other than playing the role of cannon fodder under the command of an imperialist bourgeoisie.

Is "invasion" really the horror of horrors, which paralyzes

and conjures away all class conflict within the country as though by some supernatural witchcraft? . . .

In the history of capitalism, invasion and class struggle are not opposites, as the official legend would have us believe. Rather, one is the means and the expression of the other. Just as invasion is a proven weapon in the hands of capital against the class struggle, so on the other hand the fearless pursuit of the class struggle has always been the most effective deterrent to foreign invasions. . . .

The classic example of all time is the Great French Revolution. If ever a people was surrounded by enemies, then it was the French in 1793, and its heart—Paris![13] And yet Paris and France did not succumb to the storm tide of the coalition of European reaction, to invasion from all sides. On the contrary, in face of the growing danger, and through a titanic struggle, it welded its forces in ever more gigantic resistance. If France, at that critical time, was able to pummel every new enemy coalition with a new, miraculous and inexhaustible fighting spirit, it was only because the internal forces of society were completely unleashed in the great class struggles of France.

Today, with a century's hindsight, it is clearly discernible that only the starkest expression of this struggle, only the popular dictatorship of Paris and its fearless radicalism, could call forth means and forces from the nation's soil sufficient to defend and sustain the newborn bourgeois society against a world of enemies, against the intrigues of the dynasty, against the traitorous machinations of the aristocrats, against the plots of the clergy, against the Vendée insurgency, against the treachery of their generals, against the opposition of sixty departments and provincial capitals, and against the united armies and navies of the monarchical coalition of Europe. The centuries have proven that not the state of siege, but relentless class struggle, is the power that arouses the self-confidence, the spirit of sacrifice, and the moral strength of the masses; that the class struggle is the nation's best protection and best defense against foreign enemies.

National self-determination

This same tragic *quid pro quo* victimized the Social Democracy when it based its conduct in this war upon the doctrine of the right of national self-determination.

It is true that socialism grants every people the right of independence and freedom, of autonomous control of its own destiny. But it is a veritable perversion of socialism to present the modern capitalist states as the expression of this right of nations to self-determination. In which of these states has the nation determined the forms and conditions of its national, political, or social existence?

The meaning of self-determination for Germany was formulated by the revolutionary democrats of 1848; by the first fighters of the German proletariat—Marx, Engels, Lassalle, Bebel, and Liebknecht. They proclaimed and fought for *a united pan-German republic.*[14] For this ideal the revolutionary fighters in Berlin and in Vienna shed their blood upon the barricades in March [1848]. Marx and Engels demanded that Prussia take up arms against tsarism to carry out this program. They called for the liquidation of "the heap of organized decay"—the Hapsburg monarchy[15]—as well as the abolition of the Prussian military monarchy and the two dozen dwarf monarchies within Germany, as the first precondition for the achievement of this national program. The defeat of the German revolution, the German bourgeoisie's betrayal of its own democratic ideals, led to the Bismarck regime and its creation: present-day Greater Prussia, twenty fatherlands under one steel helmet, named the German Empire.

Modern Germany is built upon the grave of the March revolution of 1848, upon the ruins of the right of self-determination of the German people. The present war, aimed at holding on to Turkey, maintaining the Hapsburg monarchy, and strengthening the Prussian military autocracy, is a second burial of the March revolutionists, and of the German national program. It is a fiendish jest of history that the Social Democrats, the heirs of the German patriots of 1848, should go forth in this war with the banner of "self-determination of nations" held high!

But, perhaps the Third French Republic, with its colonial possessions on four continents and its colonial horrors on two, is the expression of the "self-determination" of the French nation? Or the British Empire, with its India, with its South African rule of a million whites over a population of five million colored people? Or perhaps Turkey, or the empire of the tsar?

Only a bourgeois politician, in whose eyes the master races are humanity and the ruling classes are the nation, can speak of "national self-determination" in such colonizing states. To the socialist, no nation is free whose national existence is based upon the enslavement of another people, for colonial peoples, too, count as peoples and as parts of the state. International socialism recognizes the right of nations to freedom, independence, and equality. But socialism alone can create such nations, can bring self-determination of the peoples. This slogan of socialism is, like all its others, not an apology for the status quo, but a guidepost, a spur for the revolutionary, innovative, active policy of the proletariat. So long as capitalist states exist, that is, so long as the internal and international life of the nation is determined and regulated by imperialist world policy, the right of national self-determination has nothing at all in common with any expression of imperialist policy in peacetime or in war.

In the present imperialist context, moreover, there can be no wars of national self-defense. Any Socialist policy that abstracts from this overriding historical context, that is willing in this global whirlpool to be guided by the isolated point of view of a single country, is built upon a foundation of sand. . . .

Revolutionary defense of the German people

What do these considerations mean for the attitude of the Social Democracy in practice in the present war? Should it declare: since this is an imperialist war, since this state does not correspond to the national ideal or to the socialist norm of the right to self-determination, we are indifferent to it, and we surrender it to the enemy? Passive fatalism can never be the guideline for the conduct of a revolutionary party like the Social Democracy. It must neither take its stand in defense of the existing class state, under the command of the ruling classes, nor can it stand silently by to wait until the storm is past. It must adopt a policy of *independent class politics,* a policy that will whip the ruling classes *forward* in every great social crisis and that will drive the crisis itself far beyond its original extent. That is the role that the Social Democracy must play as the vanguard of the fighting proletariat. Instead of falsely disguising this imperialist war in the cloak of national self-defense, the Social Democracy should have demanded the right of national self-determination and of national self-defense *in earnest,* and used these demands as a lever *against* the imperialist war.

The most elementary demand of national defense is that the nation takes its defense into its own hands. The first step in this direction is the militia; not only the immediate arming of the entire adult male populace, but above all, popular decision-making in all questions of peace and war. It requires, furthermore, the immediate elimination of every limitation on political rights, since the greatest political freedom is required as a basis for the people's defense. The first duty of the Social Democracy was to proclaim these genuine measures of national defense and to demand their realization.

For forty years we have demonstrated to the ruling classes as well as to the masses of the people that *only* the militia is really capable of defending the fatherland and making it invincible. And yet, when the first test came, with no hesitation we turned over the defense of the country to the hands of the standing army, made up of cannon fodder under the club of the ruling classes. When our parliamentary deputies sent this cannon fodder to the front with their "fervent good wishes," they openly acknowledged the royal Prussian standing army as the real savior of the fatherland in its hour of need. Apparently they did not notice that by this admission they sacrificed the fulcrum of our political program, the militia, and dissolved into thin air the meaning in practice of forty years of agitation against the standing army. Our military program became a utopian, doctrinaire whim, that no one could possibly take seriously. . . .

Yes, Socialists are obligated to defend their country in great historical crises. Here lies the great fault of the German Social Democratic Reichstag fraction. When it announced on August 4, "We will not forsake our fatherland in its hour of need," it denied its own words in the same breath. For truly it did desert its fatherland in its hour of greatest danger. The first duty of the Social Democracy toward its fatherland was to expose the real background of this imperialist war, to tear away the web of imperialist and diplomatic lies that conceals this assault on the fatherland.

It was their duty to speak loudly and distinctly, to proclaim to the people of Germany that in this war victory and defeat would be equally fatal; to oppose to the utmost the gagging of the fatherland by the state of siege; to proclaim the necessity of the arming of the people; to demand that the people alone decide on war and peace; to demand that the people's representatives meet in permanent session while the war continued, in order to assure a watchful control over the government by parliament, and over parliament by the people; and to demand the immediate removal of all limitations on political rights, since only a free people can adequately defend its country. It was their duty, finally, to combat the imperialist war program aimed at maintaining Austria and Turkey, that is, reaction in Germany and in Europe, by counterposing the old, truly national program of the patriots and democrats of 1848, the program of Marx, Engels, and Lassalle, the slogan of the united pan-German republic.

That was the banner that should have been carried before the country—truly national, truly free, and in accord with the best traditions of Germany and the international class politics of the proletariat. . . .

An alternative course for the SPD

What, then, should our party do to give weight and emphasis to our opposition to the war and to our demands? Should it proclaim a general strike? Should it call on the soldiers to refuse military service? That is how the question is often posed. To simply answer "yes" would be just as ridiculous as if the party were perhaps to decide: "When war breaks out we will make the revolution." Revolutions are not "made" and great people's movements are not produced according to technical recipes that party leaders pull out of their pockets. Small circles of conspirators may "prepare" a putsch for a certain day and a certain hour, can signal their few dozen supporters to "cut loose" at the appointed hour. Mass movements in great historical crises, however, cannot be initiated by such primitive methods. . . .

What the leaders of the Social Democracy, as the vanguard of the class-conscious proletariat, should have been able to give was not ridiculous precepts and technical recipes, but *a political guide, clarity on the political tasks and interests of the proletariat* in times of war. . . .

Far more important than the outward, technical form of the action is its political *content*. For example, parliament, as the only free, far-reaching, and internationally conspicuous platform, could have become a mighty tool for the awakening of the people, had it been used by the Social Democratic deputies to proclaim loudly and clearly the interests, the tasks, and the demands of the working class in this crisis.

"Would the masses have supported the Social Democracy in its attitude against the war?" That is a question that no one can answer. But neither is it decisive. Did our parliamentary deputies demand an absolute assurance of victory from the generals of the Prussian-German army before voting in favor of war credits? What is true of military armies is equally true of revolutionary armies. They go into battle, where it is offered, without previous assurance of success. At worst, the party's voice might at first have had no visible impact. . . .

Our party's courageous voice would nevertheless have put a heavy damper on the chauvinistic intoxication and insensibility of the masses. It would have saved the more conscious sectors of the people from delirium, and made it more difficult for imperialism to poison and stupefy the minds of the people. The resulting crusade against the Social Democracy would have sobered the masses in a very short time.

And as the war went on, as the horror of endless massacre and bloodshed in all countries grew and grew, as its imperialistic character became more and more evident, as the chorus of bloodthirsty speculators became more and more shameless, every vital, honest, progressive, and humane force would have rallied to the banner of the Social Democracy. And above all, the German Social Democracy would have stood in the midst of this mad whirlpool of collapse and decay, like a great rock in a stormy sea. It would have remained the shining beacon of the whole International, giving leadership to the workers' parties of every country on earth. The enormous moral prestige that the German Social Democracy enjoyed up until August 4, 1914, would quickly have wrought a change in the pattern of general international confusion. The longing for peace and the masses' pressure to achieve it would have mounted in all countries, hastening the end of the slaughter and decreasing the number of its victims.

The German proletariat would have remained the beacon of socialism and of human emancipation—truly this is a patriotic task not unworthy of the disciples of Marx, Engels, and Lassalle.

The socialist road to peace

Despite military dictatorship and press censorship, despite the failure of the Social Democracy, despite the fratricidal war, the class struggle arises with elemental force from the "civil peace"; the international solidarity of the workers arises from the blood and smoke of the battlefields. Not in feeble attempts to artificially patch up the old International, not in pledges rendered now here, now there, to stand together *after* the war is over. No—here, in the war, out of the war, with new power and intensity, the fact asserts itself that the proletarians of all lands have one and the same interest. The World War itself utterly dispels the myth it has created. . . .

For the European proletariat as a class, victory or defeat of either of the two warring camps would be equally disastrous. For *the war* as such, whatever its military outcome, signifies the greatest conceivable defeat for the European proletariat. The international action of the proletariat to force a halt to the war and a speedy peace, is the only way the proletarian cause can gain a victory. And this victory, alone, can truly rescue Belgium and bring democracy to Europe.

The class-conscious proletariat cannot identify its cause

with either military camp in this war. Does that mean that proletarian policies now demand a return to the prewar status quo, and that we have no plan of action beyond the fond hope that everything remain as it was before the war? On the contrary, the existing conditions have never been our ideal; they have never expressed the self-determination of the people. Moreover, prewar conditions no longer exist and cannot be reinstated, even if the old national boundaries remain unchanged. For even before the final balance sheet is drawn up, this war has brought a prodigious shift in the relationship of forces, in mutual assessments of strength, in alliances, and in antagonisms. It has so thoroughly altered relations between countries and between classes within society, destroyed so many old illusions and powers, and created so many new impulses and new tasks that to return to the old Europe that existed before August 4, 1914, is as impossible as to return to prerevolutionary conditions, even after a defeated revolution. Proletarian politics knows no turning back. It can only forge ahead, beyond what exists, beyond even what has just been created. Only in this manner can it oppose its own policy to both camps in the imperialist World War.

But this policy cannot consist of working up ingenious blueprints for capitalist diplomacy, either by individual Social Democratic parties acting alone, or by their competition with each other at international conferences, on how to conclude peace and assure future peaceful and democratic development. All demands for complete or partial "disarmament," for the abolition of secret diplomacy, for the dissolution of the great powers into smaller national entities, and the like, are absolutely utopian so long as the capitalist class remains in the saddle. For capitalism on its present imperialist course to dispense with present-day militarism, with secret diplomacy, with great centralized multinational states is so impossible that these demands might, much more consistently, be united into the simple slogan, "abolition of the capitalist class state." The proletarian movement cannot regain its rightful place by means of utopian advice and proposals for limited reforms to mollify, tame, or subdue imperialism within the framework of the bourgeois state.

The real problem that the World War has placed before the Socialist parties, and upon whose solution the future of the working-class movement depends, *is the capacity of the proletarian masses to act in the fight against imperialism.* The international proletariat does not suffer from a lack of proposals, programs, and slogans, but from one of deeds, of effective resistance, of the capacity to attack imperialism at the decisive moment, precisely in time of war. It has been unable to put into actual practice its old slogan, "war against war." Here is the Gordian knot of the proletarian movement and of its future.

Certainly imperialism, with all its brutal policy of force, with the chain of incessant social catastrophes that it provokes, is a historical necessity for the ruling classes of the present capitalist world. Nothing could be more detrimental than the proletariat deriving from the present war the slightest hope or illusion of the possibility of an idyllic and peaceful development of capitalism. But the historical inevitability of imperialism does not imply that the proletariat must capitulate before it, and live forever in its shadow, feeding off the crumbs that fall from the tables of its victories.

The dialectic of history moves in contradictions, and for every necessity puts its opposite into the world as well. Bourgeois class rule is doubtless a historic necessity, but so also is the revolt of the working class against it. Capital is a historic necessity, but so too in the same measure is its gravedigger, the socialist proletariat. The world rule of imperialism is a historic necessity, but likewise its overthrow by the proletarian international. Side by side the two historic necessities exist in constant conflict with each other. And ours, the necessity of socialism, is more enduring. Our necessity is validated at the moment bourgeois class rule ceases to be the motor of historical progress, when it becomes a hindrance, a danger to the further development of society. The present World War has revealed that the capitalist social order has now reached this point. . . .

But today's horrors of imperialist bestiality on the fields of Europe have had another effect, for which the "civilized world" has no horror-stricken eyes, no agonized heart. *This is the mass destruction of the European proletariat.* Never has a war killed off whole nations to this degree; never, within the past century, has it so seized all of the great and established lands of civilized Europe. Millions of human lives are being annihilated in the Vosges, in the Ardennes, in Belgium, in Poland, in the Carpathians, and on the Sava; millions have been rendered cripples. But nine-tenths of these millions come from the working people of the cities and the countryside. It is our strength, our hope that is mowed down there, day after day, like grass by the sickle of death. The workers of England, France, Belgium, Germany, and Russia who are being gagged and butchered in droves were the best, the most intelligent, the best trained forces of international socialism, the bearers of the most sacred traditions and the staunchest heroism of the modern workers' movement, the vanguard of the whole world proletariat. The workers of the leading capitalist countries of Europe are precisely those who have the historic mission of carrying out the socialist revolution.

Only from Europe, only from the oldest capitalist nations, when the hour is ripe, can the signal come for the social revolution that will free all humanity. Only the English, the French, the Belgian, the German, the Russian, the Italian workers together can lead the army of the exploited and oppressed of the five continents. And when the time comes they alone can call capitalism to account for centuries of crimes committed against primitive peoples; they alone can avenge its work of destruction over a whole world. But for the advance and victory of socialism we need a strong, educated proletariat, capable of acting; we need masses whose strength lies in knowledge as well as in numbers. And these very masses are being decimated by the World War. The flower of our manhood and our youthful strength, hundreds of thousands whose socialist education in England, in France, in Belgium, in Germany, and in Russia was the product of decades of education and propaganda, and other hundreds of thousands who could have been won to socialism, have fallen, and are rotting upon the battlefields. The fruit of the decades-long sacrifices and toil of generations is destroyed in a few short weeks; the choicest troops of the international proletariat are torn out by the roots.

The bloodletting of the June [1848] battle laid low the French workers' movement for a decade and a half. The bloodletting of the Commune massacre threw it back again for more than a decade.[16] What is happening now is a massacre such as the world has never seen before, which is reducing the working population in all of the leading nations to the aged, the women, and the maimed; a bloodletting that threatens to bleed white the European workers' movement.

Another such war, and the hope of socialism will be buried under the ruins of imperialist barbarism. That is more serious than the ruthless destruction of Louvain and of the Rheims Cathedral. That is a blow, not against the capitalist civilization of the past, but against the socialist civilization of the future, a deadly blow against the force that carries the future of humankind in its womb and that alone can rescue the precious treasures of the past for a better society. Here capitalism reveals its death's head, here it betrays that it has forfeited its historic right of existence, that its rule is no longer compatible with the progress of humanity.

But here is proof also that the war is not only a grandiose slaughter, but also the suicide of the European working class as well. It is soldiers of socialism, the workers of England, of France, of Germany, of Italy, of Belgium who are slaughtering each other at the bidding of capital, who are thrusting the cold steel of death into each other's breasts and tumbling together into the grave locked in a murderous embrace.

"Deutschland, Deutschland über alles!" "Long live democracy!" "Long live the tsar and the Slavs!" "Ten thousand tent cloths, guaranteed to specifications!" "A hundred thousand pounds of bacon; coffee substitute for immediate delivery!" Dividends are rising—proletarians falling. And with each one a fighter of the future, a soldier of the revolution, a savior of humanity from the yoke of capitalism, falls into the grave.

This madness will not stop, and this bloody, hellish specter will not disappear until the workers of Germany, France, Russia, and England wake up out of their drunken torpor, clasp each others' hands in brotherhood, and drown the bestial chorus of warmongers and the hoarse cry of capitalist hyenas with the mighty cry of labor, "Proletarians of all countries, unite!"

The first issue of the Bolsheviks' new journal, *Sbornik Sotsial-Demokrata*, published in October 1916, contained the following assessment by Lenin of Luxemburg's pamphlet. He gave special emphasis to the question of national self-determination, which had provoked a debate inside the Zimmerwald Left and among the Bolsheviks in Western Europe.

The Junius pamphlet[17]

by V.I. Lenin

At last there has appeared in Germany, illegally, without any adaptation to the despicable Junker censorship, a Social-Democratic pamphlet dealing with questions of the war! The author, who evidently belongs to the "Left-radical" wing of the Party, takes the name of Junius (which in Latin means junior) and gives his pamphlet the title: *The Crisis of Social-Democracy.* Appended are the "Theses on the Tasks of International Social-Democracy", which have already been submitted to the Berne I.S.C. (International Socialist Committee) and published in No. 3 of its *Bulletin;* the theses were drafted by the *Internationale* group, which in the spring of 1915 published one issue of a magazine under that title (with articles by Zetkin, Mehring, R. Luxemburg, Thalheimer, Duncker, Ströbel and others), and which in the winter of 1915–16 convened a conference of Social-Democrats from all parts of Germany where these theses were adopted.

The pamphlet, the author says in the introduction dated January 2, 1916, was written in April 1915, and published "without any alteration". "Outside circumstances" had prevented its earlier publication. The pamphlet is devoted not so much to the "crisis of Social-Democracy" as to an analysis of the war, to refuting the legend of it being a war for national liberation, to proving that it is an imperialist war on the part of Germany as well as on the part of the other Great Powers, and to a revolutionary criticism of the behaviour of the official party. Written in a very lively style, Junius's pamphlet has undoubtedly played and will continue to play an important role in the struggle against the ex-

Social-Democratic Party of Germany, which has deserted to the bourgeoisie and the Junkers, and we extend our hearty greetings to the author.

To the Russian reader who is familiar with the Social-Democratic literature in Russia published abroad in 1914–16, the Junius pamphlet does not offer anything new in principle. In reading this pamphlet and comparing the arguments of this German revolutionary Marxist with what has been stated, for example, in the Manifesto of the Central Committee of our Party (September–November 1914), in the Berne resolutions (March 1915) and in the numerous commentaries on them, it only becomes clear that Junius's arguments are very incomplete and that he makes two mistakes. Before proceeding with a criticism of Junius's faults and errors we must strongly emphasise that this is done for the sake of self-criticism, which is so necessary to Marxists, and of submitting to an all-round test the views which must serve as the ideological basis of the Third International. On the whole, the Junius pamphlet is a splendid Marxist work, and its defects are, in all probability, to a certain extent accidental.

The chief defect in Junius's pamphlet, and what marks a definite step backward compared with the legal (although immediately suppressed) magazine, *Internationale*, is its silence regarding the connection between social-chauvinism (the author uses neither this nor the less precise term social-patriotism) and opportunism. The author rightly speaks of the "capitulation" and collapse of the German Social-Democratic Party and of the "treachery" of its "official leaders", but he goes no further. The *Internationale*, however, did criticise the "Centre", i.e., Kautskyism, and quite properly poured ridicule on it for its spinelessness, its prostitution of Marxism and its servility to the opportunists.[18] This same magazine *began* to expose the true role of the opportunists by revealing, for example, the very important fact that on August 4, 1914, the opportunists came out with an ultimatum, a ready-made decision to vote *for* war credits in *any* case. Neither the Junius pamphlet nor the theses say *anything* about opportunism or about Kautskyism! This is wrong from the standpoint of theory, for it is impossible to *account for* the "betrayal" without linking it up with opportunism as a *trend* with a long history behind it, the history of the whole Second International. It is a mistake from the practical political standpoint, for it is impossible either to understand the "crisis of Social-Democracy", or overcome it, without clarifying the meaning and the role of *two trends*—the openly opportunist trend (Legien, David, etc.) and the tacitly opportunist trend (Kautsky and Co.). This is a step backward compared with the historic article by Otto Rühle in *Vorwärts* of January 12, 1916, in which he directly and openly pointed out that a split in the Social-Democratic Party of Germany was *inevitable* (the editors of *Vorwärts* replied by repeating honeyed and hypocritical Kautskyite phrases, for they were unable to advance a single material argument to disprove the assertion that there were *already* two parties in existence, and that these two parties could not be reconciled). It is astonishingly inconsistent, because the *Internationale's* thesis No. 12 *directly* states that it is necessary to create a "new" International, owing to the "treachery" of the "official representatives of the socialist parties of the leading countries" and their "adoption of the principles of bourgeois imperialist policies". It is clearly quite absurd to suggest that the old Social-Democratic Party of Germany, or the party which tolerates Legien, David and Co., would participate in a "new" International.

We do not know why the *Internationale* group took this step backward. A very great defect in revolutionary Marxism in Germany as a whole is its lack of a compact illegal organisation that would systematically pursue its own line and educate the masses in the spirit of the new tasks; such an organisation would also have to take a definite stand on opportunism and Kautskyism. This is all the more necessary now, since the German revolutionary Social-Democrats have been deprived of their last two daily papers; the one in Bremen *(Bremer Bürger-Zeitung)*, and the one in Brunswick *(Volksfreund)*, both of which have gone over to the Kautskyites. The International Socialists of Germany (I.S.D.) group *alone* clearly and definitely remains at its post.

Some members of the *Internationale* group have evidently once again slid down into the morass of unprincipled Kautskyism. Ströbel, for instance, went so far as to drop a curtsey in *Die Neue Zeit* to Bernstein and Kautsky! And only the other day, on July 15, 1916, he had an article in the papers entitled "Pacifism and Social-Democracy", in which he defends the most vulgar type of Kautskyite pacifism. As for Junius, he strongly opposes Kautsky's fantastic schemes like "disarmament", "abolition of secret diplomacy", etc. There may be two trends within the *Internationale* group: a revolutionary trend and a trend inclining to Kautskyism.

The first of Junius's erroneous propositions is embodied in the fifth thesis of the *Internationale* group. "National wars are no longer possible in the epoch (era) of this unbridled imperialism. National interests serve only as an instrument of deception, in order to place the working masses at the service of their mortal enemy, imperialism." The beginning of the fifth thesis, which concludes with the above statement, discusses the nature of the *present* war as an imperialist war. It may be that this negation of national wars generally is either an oversight, or an accidental overstatement in emphasising the perfectly correct idea that the *present* war is an imperialist war, not a national war. This is a mistake that must be examined, for various Social-Democrats, in view of the false assertions that the *present* war is a national war, have likewise mistakenly denied the possibility of *any* national war.

Junius is perfectly right in emphasising the decisive influence of the "imperialist atmosphere" of the *present* war, in maintaining that behind Serbia stands Russia, "behind Serbian nationalism stands Russian imperialism", and that the participation of, say, Holland in the war would *likewise* be imperialist, for, first, Holland would be defending her colonies and, second, would be allied with one of the *imperialist* coalitions. That is irrefutable in respect to the *present* war. And when Junius stresses what for him is most important, namely, the struggle against the "phantom of national war", "which at present holds sway over Social-Democratic policies", then it must be admitted that his views are both correct and fully to the point.

The only mistake, however, would be to exaggerate this truth, to depart from the Marxist requirement of concreteness, to apply the appraisal of this war to all wars possible under imperialism, to ignore the national movements *against* imperialism. The sole argument in defence of the thesis, "national wars are no longer possible", is that the world has been divided among a small group of "great" imperialist powers and for that reason any war, even if it starts as a national war, is *transformed* into an imperialist war involving the interest of one of the imperialist powers or coalitions.

The fallacy of this argument is obvious. That all dividing lines, both in nature and society, are conventional and dynamic, and that *every* phenomenon might, under certain conditions, be transformed into its opposite, is, of course, a basic proposition of Marxist dialectics. A national war *might* be transformed into an imperialist war *and vice versa*. Here is an example: the wars of the Great French Revolution began as national wars and indeed were such. They were revolutionary wars—the defence of the great revolution against a coalition of counter-revolutionary monarchies. But when Napoleon founded the French Empire and subjugated a number of big, viable and long-established national European states, these national wars of the French became imperialist wars and *in turn* led to wars of national liberation *against* Napoleonic imperialism.

Only a sophist can disregard the difference between an imperialist and a national war on the grounds that one *might* develop into the other. Not infrequently have dialectics served—and the history of Greek philosophy is an example—as a bridge to sophistry. But we remain dialecticians and we combat sophistry not by denying the possibility of all transformations in general, but by analysing the *given* phenomenon in its concrete setting and development.

Transformation of the present imperialist war of 1914–16 into a national war is highly improbable, for the class that represents *progressive* development is the proletariat which is objectively striving to transform it into a civil war against the bourgeoisie. Also this: there is no very considerable difference between the forces of the two coalitions, and international finance capital has created a reactionary bourgeoisie everywhere. But such a transformation should *not* be proclaimed *impossible: if* the *European* proletariat remains impotent, say, for twenty years; *if* the present war *ends* in victories like Napoleon's and in the subjugation of a number of viable national states; *if* the transition to socialism of non-European imperialism (primarily Japanese and American) is also held up for twenty years by a war between these two countries, for example, then a great national war in Europe would be possible. It would hurl Europe *back* several decades. That is improbable. But *not* impossible, for it is undialectical, unscientific and theoretically wrong to regard the course of world history as smooth and always in a forward direction, without occasional gigantic leaps back.

Further. National wars waged by colonies and semi-colonies in the imperialist era are not only probable but *inevitable.* About 1,000 million people, or *over half* of the world's population, live in the colonies and semi-colonies (China, Turkey,

Persia). The national liberation movements there are either already very strong, or are growing and maturing. Every war is the continuation of politics by other means. The continuation of national liberation politics in the colonies will *inevitably* take the form of national wars *against* imperialism. Such wars *might* lead to an imperialist war of the present "great" imperialist powers, but on the other hand they might not. It will depend on many factors.

Example: Britain and France fought the Seven Years' War for the possession of colonies. In other words, they waged an imperialist war (which is possible on the basis of slavery and primitive capitalism as well as on the basis of modern highly developed capitalism). France suffered defeat and lost some of her colonies. Several years later there began the national liberation war of the North American States against Britain alone. France and Spain, then in possession of some parts of the present United States, concluded a friendship treaty with the States in rebellion against Britain. This they did out of hostility to Britain, i.e., in their own imperialist interests. French troops fought the British on the side of the American forces. What we have here is a national liberation war in which imperialist rivalry is an auxiliary element, one that has no serious importance. This is the very opposite to what we see in the war of 1914–16 (the national element in the Austro-Serbian War is of no serious importance compared with the all-determining element of imperialist rivalry). It would be absurd, therefore, to apply the concept imperialism indiscriminately and conclude that national wars are "impossible". A national liberation war, waged, for example, by an alliance of Persia, India and China against one or more of the imperialist powers, is both possible and probable, for it would follow from the national liberation movements in these countries. The transformation of such a war into an imperialist war between the present-day imperialist powers would depend upon very many concrete factors, the emergence of which it would be ridiculous to guarantee.

Third, even in Europe national wars in the imperialist epoch cannot be regarded as impossible. The "epoch of imperialism" made the present war an imperialist one and it inevitably engenders new imperialist wars (until the triumph of socialism). This "epoch" has made the policies of the present great powers thoroughly imperialist, but it by no means precludes national wars on the part of, say, small (annexed or nationally-oppressed) countries *against* the imperialist powers, just as it does not preclude large-scale national movements in Eastern Europe. Junius takes a very sober view of Austria, for example, giving due consideration not only to "economic" factors, but to the peculiar political factors. He notes "Austria's intrinsic lack of cohesion" and recognises that the "Hapsburg monarchy is not the political organisation of a bourgeois state, but only a loose syndicate of several cliques of social parasites", and that "the liquidation of Austria-Hungary is, from the historical standpoint, only the continuation of the disintegration of Turkey and, at the same time, a requirement of the historical process of development". Much the same applies to some of the Balkan countries and Russia. And if the "great" powers are altogether exhausted in the present war, or if the revolution in Russia triumphs, national wars and even victorious national wars, are quite possible. Practical intervention by the imperialist powers is *not* always feasible. That is one point. Another is that the superficial view that the war of a small state against a giant is hopeless should be countered by the observation that even a hopeless war is a war just the same. Besides, certain factors operating within the "giant" countries—the outbreak of revolution, for example—can turn a "hopeless" war into a very "hopeful" one.

We have dwelt in detail on the erroneous proposition that "national wars are no longer possible" not only because it is patently erroneous from the theoretical point of view—it would certainly be very lamentable if the "Left" were to reveal a light-hearted attitude to Marxist theory at a time when the establishment of the Third International is possible only on the basis of unvulgarised Marxism. But the mistake is very harmful also from the standpoint of practical politics, for it gives rise to the absurd propaganda of "disarmament", since it is alleged that there can be no wars except reactionary wars. It also gives rise to the even more ludicrous and downright reactionary attitude of indifference to national movements. And such an attitude becomes chauvinism when members of the "great" European nations, that is, the nations which oppress the mass of small and colonial peoples, declare with a pseudo-scientific air: "national wars are no longer possible"! National wars *against* the imperialist powers are not only possible and probable; they are inevitable, *progressive* and *revolutionary though* of course, to be *successful*, they require either the concerted effort of huge numbers of people in the oppressed countries (hundreds of millions in our example of India and China), or a *particularly* favourable conjuncture of international conditions (e.g., the fact that the imperialist powers cannot interfere, being paralysed by exhaustion, by war, by their antagonism, etc.), or the *simultaneous* uprising of the proletariat against the bourgeoisie in one of the big powers (this latter eventuality holds first place as the most desirable and favourable for the victory of the proletariat).

It would be unfair, however, to accuse Junius of indifference to national movements. At any rate, he remarks that among the sins of the Social-Democratic parliamentary group was its silence on the death sentence passed on a native leader in the Cameroons on charges of "treason" (evidently he attempted to organise an uprising against the war). Elsewhere Junius especially emphasises (for the benefit of the Legiens, Lensches and the other scoundrels who are still listed as "Social-Democrats") that colonial peoples must be regarded as nations along with all the others. Junius clearly and explicitly states: "Socialism recognised the right of every nation to independence and freedom, to independent mastery of its destinies"; "international socialism recognises the right of free, independent and equal nations, but it is only socialism that can create such nations, and only it can realise the right of nations to self-determination. And this socialist slogan," Junius justly remarks, "serves, like all other socialist slogans, not to justify the existing order of things, but to indicate the way forward, and to stimulate the proletariat in its active revolutionary policy of transformation". It would be a grave mistake indeed to believe that all the German Left Social-Democrats have succumbed to the narrow-mindedness and caricature of Marxism now espoused by certain Dutch and Polish Social-Democrats who deny the right of nations to self-determination even under socialism. But the *specific,* Dutch-Polish, roots of *this* mistake we shall discuss elsewhere.

Another fallacious argument is advanced by Junius on the question of defence of the fatherland. This is a cardinal political question during an imperialist war. Junius has strengthened us in our conviction that our Party has indicated the only correct approach to this question; the proletariat is opposed to defence of the fatherland in this imperialist war *because* of its predatory, slave-owning, reactionary character, *because* it is possible and necessary to oppose to it (and to strive to convert it into) civil war for socialism. Junius, however, while brilliantly exposing the imperialist character of the present war as distinct from a national war, makes the very strange mistake of trying to drag a national programme into the *present, non*-national, war. It sounds almost incredible, but there it is.

The official Social-Democrats, both of the Legien and of the Kautsky stripe, in their servility to the bourgeoisie (who have been making the most noise about foreign "invasion" in order to deceive the mass of the people as to the imperialist character of the war), have been particularly assiduous in repeating this "invasion" argument. Kautsky, who now assures naïve and credulous people (incidentally, through Spectator [M.I. Nakhimson], a member of the Russian Organising Committee) that he joined the opposition at the end of 1914, continues to use this "argument"! To refute it, Junius quotes extremely instructive examples from history, which prove that "invasion and class struggle are not contradictory in bourgeois history, as official legend has it, but that one is the means and the expression of the other". For example, the Bourbons in France invoked foreign invaders against the Jacobins; the bourgeoisie in 1871 invoked foreign invaders against the Commune. In his *Civil War in France,* Marx wrote:

"The highest heroic effort of which old society is still capable is national war; and this is now proved to be a mere governmental humbug, intended to defer the struggle of classes, and to be thrown aside as soon as that class struggle bursts out into civil war."

"The classical example for all times," says Junius, referring to 1793, "is the Great French Revolution." From all this, he draws the following conclusion: "The century of experience thus proves that it is not a state of siege, but relentless class struggle, which rouses the self-respect, the heroism and the moral strength of the mass of the people, and serves as the country's best protection and defence against the external enemy."

Junius's practical conclusion is this: "Yes, it is the duty of the Social-Democrats to defend their country during a great historical crisis. But the grave guilt that rests upon the Social-Democratic Reichstag group consists in their having given the lie to their own solemn declaration, made on August 4, 1914, 'In the hour of danger we will not leave our fatherland unprotected'. They *did* leave the fatherland unprotected in the hour of its greatest peril. For their first duty to the fatherland in that hour was to show the fatherland what was really behind the present imperialist war; to sweep away the web of patriotic and diplomatic lies covering up this encroachment on the fatherland; to proclaim loudly and clearly that both victory and defeat in the present war are equally fatal for the German people; to resist to the last the throttling of the fatherland due to the state of siege; to proclaim the necessity of immediately arming the people and of allowing the people to decide the question of war and peace; resolutely to demand a permanent session of the people's representatives for the whole duration of the war in order to guarantee vigilant control over the government by the people's representatives, and control over the people's representatives by the people; to demand the immediate abolition of all restrictions on political rights, for only a free people can successfully defend its country; and finally, to oppose the imperialist war programme, which is to preserve Austria and Turkey, i.e., perpetuate reaction in Europe and in Germany, with the old, truly national programme of the patriots and democrats of 1848, the programme of Marx, Engels and Lassalle—the slogan of a united, Great German Republic. This is the banner that should have been unfurled before the country, which would have been a truly national banner of liberation, which would have been in accord with the best traditions of Germany and with the international class policy of the proletariat. . . . Hence, the grave dilemma—the interests of the fatherland or the international solidarity of the proletariat—the tragic conflict which prompted our parliamentarians to side, 'with a heavy heart', with the imperialist war, is purely imaginary, it is a bourgeois nationalist fiction. On the contrary, there is complete harmony between the interests of the country and the class interests of the proletarian International, both in time of war and in time of peace; both war and peace demand the most energetic development of the class struggle, the most determined fight for the Social-Democratic programme."

This is how Junius argues. The fallacy of his argument is strikingly evident, and since the tacit and avowed lackeys of tsarism, Plekhanov and Chkhenkeli, and perhaps even Martov and Chkheidze, may gloatingly seize upon Junius's words, not for the purpose of establishing theoretical truth, but for the purpose of wriggling, covering up their tracks and throwing dust into the eyes of the workers, we must in greater detail elucidate the *theoretical* source of Junius's error.

He suggests that the imperialist war should be "opposed" with a national programme. He urges the advanced class to turn its face to the past and not to the future! In France, in Germany, and in the whole of Europe it was a *bourgeois*-democratic revolution that, *objectively*, was on the order of the day in 1793 and 1848. Corresponding to this *objective* historical situation was the "truly national", i.e., the national *bourgeois* programme of the then existing democracy; in 1793 this programme was carried out by the most revolutionary elements of the bourgeoisie and the plebeians, and in 1848 it was proclaimed by Marx in the name of the whole of progressive democracy. *Objectively*, the feudal and dynastic wars were then opposed by revolutionary-democratic wars, by wars for national liberation. This was the content of the historical tasks of that epoch.

At the present time, the *objective* situation in the biggest advanced states of Europe is different. Progress, if we leave out for the moment the possibility of temporary steps backward, can be made only in the direction of *socialist* society, only in the direction of the *socialist revolution*. From the standpoint of progress, from the standpoint of the progressive class, the imperialist bourgeois war, the war of highly developed capitalism, can, *objectively*, be opposed only with a war *against* the bourgeoisie, i.e., primarily civil war for power between the proletariat and the bourgeoisie; for *unless* such a war is waged, serious progress is *impossible;* this may be followed—only under certain special conditions—by a war to defend the socialist state against bourgeois states. That is why the Bolsheviks (fortunately, very few, and quickly handed over by us to the *Prizyv* group) who were ready to adopt the point of view of conditional defence, i.e., defence of the fatherland on condition that there was a victorious revolution and the victory of a republic in Russia, were true to the *letter* of Bolshevism, but betrayed its *spirit;* for being drawn into the imperialist war of the leading European powers, Russia would *also* be waging an imperialist war, even under a republican form of government!

In saying that the class struggle is the best means of defence against invasion, Junius applies Marxist dialectics only half way, taking one step on the right road and immediately deviating from it. Marxist dialectics call for a concrete analysis of each specific historical situation. It is true that class struggle is the best means of defence against invasion *both* when the bourgeoisie is overthrowing feudalism, and when the proletariat is overthrowing the bourgeoisie. Precisely because it is true with regard to *every* form of class oppression, it is *too general,* and therefore, *inadequate* in the present *specific* case. Civil war against the bourgeoisie is *also* a form of class struggle, and only this form of class struggle would have saved Europe (the whole of Europe, not only one country) from the peril of invasion. The "Great German Republic", had it existed in 1914–16, would *also* have waged an *imperialist* war.

Junius came very close to the correct solution of the problem and to the correct slogan: civil war against the bourgeoisie for socialism; but, as if afraid to speak the whole truth, he turned *back,* to the fantasy of a "national war" in 1914, 1915 and 1916. If we examine the question not from the theoretical angle but from the purely practical one, Junius's error remains just as evident. The whole of bourgeois society, all classes in Germany, including the peasantry, were *in favour* of war (in all probability *the same* was the case in Russia—at least a majority of the well-to-do and middle peasantry and a very considerable portion of the poor peasants were evidently under the spell of bourgeois imperialism). The bourgeoisie was armed to the teeth. Under such circumstances to "proclaim" the programme of a republic, a permanent parliament, election of officers by the people (the "armed nation"), etc., would have meant, *in practice, "proclaiming" a revolution* (with the *wrong* revolutionary programme!).

In the same breath Junius quite rightly says that a revolution cannot be "made". Revolution was on the order of the day in the 1914–16 period, it was hidden in the depths of the war, was *emerging* out of the war. This should have been *"proclaimed"* in the name of the revolutionary class, and *its* programme should have been fearlessly and fully announced; socialism is impossible in time of war without civil war against the arch-reactionary, criminal bourgeoisie, which condemns the people to untold disaster. Systematic, consistent, practical measures should have been planned, which *could be carried out no matter at what* pace the revolutionary crisis might develop, and which would be in line with the maturing revolution. These measures are indicated in our Party's resolution: (1) voting against war credits; (2) violation of the "class truce"; (3) creation of an illegal organisation; (4) fraternisation among the soldiers; (5) support for all the revolutionary actions of the masses. The success of *all* these steps *inevitably* leads to civil war.

The promulgation of a great historical programme was undoubtedly of tremendous significance; not the old national German programme, which became obsolete in 1914, 1915 and 1916, but the proletarian internationalist and socialist programme. "You, the bourgeoisie, are fighting for plunder; we, the workers of *all* the belligerent countries, declare war upon you for, socialism"—that's the sort of speech that should have been delivered in the parliaments on August 4, 1914, by socialists who had not betrayed the proletariat, as the Legiens, Davids, Kautskys, Plekhanovs, Guesdes, Sembats, etc., had done.

Evidently Junius's error is due to two kinds of mistakes in reasoning. There is no doubt that Junius is decidedly opposed to the imperialist war and is decidedly *in favour* of revolutionary tactics; and all the gloating of the Plekhanovs over Junius's "defencism" cannot wipe out this *fact*. Possible and probable calumnies of this kind must be answered promptly and bluntly.

But, first, Junius has not completely rid himself of the "environment" of the German Social-Democrats, even the Leftists, who are afraid of a split, who are afraid to follow revolutionary slogans to their logical conclusions.* This is a false fear, and the Left Social-Democrats of Germany must and *will* rid themselves of it. They *are sure to do so* in the course of their struggle against the social-chauvinists. The fact is that they are fighting against *their own* social-chauvinists resolutely, firmly and *sincerely*, and this is the tremendous, the fundamental difference in principle between them and the Martovs and Chkheidzes, who, with one hand (*à la* Skobelev) unfurl a banner bearing the greeting, "To the Liebknechts of All Countries", and with the other hand tenderly embrace Chkhenkeli and Potresov!

Secondly, Junius apparently wanted to achieve something in the nature of the Menshevik "theory of stages", of sad memory; he wanted to *begin* to carry out the revolutionary programme from the end that is "more suitable", "more popular" and more acceptable to the *petty bourgeoisie*. It is something like a plan "to outwit history", to outwit the philistines. He seems to say, surely, nobody would oppose a *better* way of defending the real fatherland; and the real fatherland is the Great German Republic, and the best defence *is* a militia, a permanent parliament, etc. Once it was accepted, that programme would automatically lead to the next stage—to the socialist revolution.

Probably, it was reasoning of this kind that consciously or semi-consciously determined Junius's tactics. Needless to say, such reasoning is fallacious. Junius's pamphlet conjures up in our mind the picture of a *lone* man who has no comrades in an illegal organisation accustomed to thinking out revolutionary slogans to their conclusion and systematically educating the masses in their spirit. But this shortcoming—it would be a grave error to forget this—is not Junius's personal failing, but the result of the weakness of *all* the German Leftists, who have become entangled in the vile net of Kautskyite hypocrisy, pedantry and "friendliness" for the opportunists. Junius's adherents have managed, *in spite* of their isolation, to *begin* the publication of illegal leaflets and to start the war against Kautskyism. They will succeed in going further along the right road.

* We find the same error in Junius's arguments about which is better, victory or defeat? His conclusion is that both are equally bad (ruin, growth of armaments, etc.). This is the point of view not of the revolutionary proletariat, but of the pacifist petty bourgeoisie. If one speaks about the "revolutionary intervention" of the proletariat—of this both Junius and the theses of the *Internationale* group speak, although unfortunately in terms that are too general—one *must* raise the question from *another* point of view, namely: (1) Is "revolutionary intervention" possible without the risk of defeat? (2) Is it possible to scourge the bourgeoisie and the government of one's *own* country without taking that risk? (3) Have we not always asserted, and does not the historical experience of reactionary wars prove, that defeats help the cause of the revolutionary class? [Footnote in original]

A revolutionary voice in parliament

The German Reichstag after August 1914 was a showpiece of the "civil peace." Its key proceedings were negotiated in advance among party leaders in order to preserve the appearance of national unity. Karl Liebknecht set out to break through this facade. He utilized parliament to give voice to a revolutionary workers' program by asking pointed questions and delivering speeches that were publicized by the underground circulars of the Spartacists.

On August 20, 1915, he rose to ask a question of great concern to German workers, on which the SPD Reichstag fraction had maintained a studied silence:

"Is the government prepared to enter into immediate peace negotiations on the basis of repudiation of any form of annexation, should a corresponding readiness exist among the other belligerent powers?" Foreign Secretary von Jagow responded that it would be inappropriate to reply. "That is ambiguous; that is an admission," cried Liebknecht, before he was drowned out by catcalls and ruled out of order.[19]

The SPD Reichstag fraction formally censured Liebknecht for asking a question without its permission. But he continued over the next several months to pose similar pointed questions, provoking growing tumult from the right-wing deputies and the hostility of both right-wing and centrist deputies of his own party. On January 12, 1916, the SPD fraction made Liebknecht's use of parliamentary questions its formal grounds for expelling him from the fraction's ranks.

On March 16, 1916, Liebknecht utilized a discussion of educational policy in the Prussian state parliament, of which he was also a deputy, to speak on the German government's responsibility for the war and on the need for soldiers to turn their weapons against the ruling class. The following is from the official report of his speech, which the Internationale Group distributed across Germany.

War and education[20]

by Karl Liebknecht

Deputy von Campe spoke of a weakening of moral backbone that must be countered by pro-war propaganda in the schools, and welcomed the decree along these lines enacted in Hannover. If, however, the first duty of education is to tell the truth, and if you are to teach the truth in the schools, then you must teach something totally different than what is being taught today in conformity with the views of Deputy von Campe, this decree, and the will of the government.

Teach the truth about martial law! Teach what the "new orientation" really means![21] Teach whose interests this war serves and how it came about! Herr von Campe would have it taught that the Sarajevo murder was an atrocity. But don't stop there. Add that certain circles in Germany and Austria welcomed this murder as a gift from God *("Very true!" from the Social Democrats),* since it gave them the pretext they needed for the war. *(Loud cries of "Shame!"; the president rings the bell to call the speaker to order.)* That is the truth! *(Continuing noisy commotion and cries of "Shame."; the president rings the bell.)* That is the truth! It was a pretext! We must tear off the mask. . . . *(Continuing uproar, cries of*

"Shame!"; the president rings the bell.)

THE PRESIDENT: Deputy Liebknecht, I must ask you to stop.

LIEBKNECHT: That is the truth! *(Continuing loud commotion and shouts: "Get out!")* You refuse to listen. Yet justice will prevail. *(Continuing noisy interruptions. The Conservatives, Free-Conservatives, the Center, and the National Liberals leave the hall.)* Flee from the truth! Leave! You cannot face the truth! *(The president rings the bell.)*

THE PRESIDENT: Deputy Dr. Liebknecht, I call you to order on account of this outrageous offense to the national sentiment of this house and of the entire nation, and bring to your attention the sanctions for breach of procedure. If you provoke another call to order, I will ask the house if it wants to continue listening to you. I ask you to proceed. *(Loud commotion. Shouts: "Get out!" Protests by the Social Democrats.)*

LIEBKNECHT: Gentlemen, these facts that I have reported arouse the deepest indignation in me as well. But I have heard them with my own ears and they are the truth. . . .

It is our task in this moment to call out to the working class of all countries: "On with the job!" Whether in the trenches or inside the country, they should lower their weapons, and turn them against their common foe, who robs them of life and breath. *(Loud commotion from the right; the president rings the bell.)*

THE PRESIDENT: Deputy Dr. Liebknecht, you are out of order. I call you to order for the third time and I will now ask the house if it wishes to continue to hear you. *(Stormy applause from the right and center. Loud commotion. Vigorous protests from the Social Democrats. Deputy Dr. Liebknecht tries in vain to continue speaking. The deputies of the Conservative, Free Conservative, Center, and National Liberal parties return to the hall.)*

[Amid the continuing uproar, the vote was taken and Liebknecht was denied the right to finish his address.]

A second national conference of the Internationale Group in the middle of March adopted the following resolutions on the question of the International, the tasks of Social Democratic parliamentary deputies, and an outline of class struggle policy in wartime.

Three resolutions of the Internationale Group[22]

I

With the collapse of the old International on August 4, 1914, a new International must rise again, which can only be born of the revolutionary class struggle of the proletarian masses in the most important capitalist countries. The existence and effectiveness of the International is neither a question of organization nor one of agreement in a small circle of people acting as representatives of opposition-minded layers of the working class. It is a question of the proletarian mass movement in all countries returning to socialism. The International that dissolved on August 4, 1914, was a purely formal institution, existing only through loose ties among small groups of party and trade union leaders. In contrast, the new International, in order to become a real political force, must be rooted in the understanding, the capacity for action, and the daily experience of the broadest proletarian masses. The International will arise from below by the same process and to the same degree that the working class in all the belligerent countries frees itself from the fetters of "civil peace" and from the poisonous influences of the official leaders and throws itself into the revolutionary class struggle. The main slogan of the struggle must be systematic mass action to forcibly bring about peace. This alone can bring about the birth of the new, living, and effective International.

The conference of the "Internationale" tendency, the opposition in the German Social Democracy that stands on the "Theses," greets the second International Socialist Conference.[23] This conference is a sign that Socialist circles in many countries are already moving in the direction outlined here and feel a growing need to unite internationally. We are confident that its declarations will give further impulse toward launching the new International as a product of the vigorous will of the proletarian masses.

II

The situation in Germany, after almost two years of war, indicates that imperialism is now already bankrupt. The war has reached an impasse on the battlefield, so that a purely military settlement of the World War is even more unlikely today than when this genocidal slaughter began. Increasing inflation has meant nothing less than literal starvation for the broad masses. The horrendous toll of dead and crippled has now reached millions. Ever-increasing taxes have thrust an immense and crushing financial burden upon working people. Industrial activity now rests entirely on the purely artificial mechanism of war contracts and must break down immediately when the slaughter ends. Germany's exclusion from the world market results in growing raw material shortages, and it is more and more difficult to continue even the extortionate system of financing the war through loans.

All this is a product of the nearly two years of imperialist slaughter. It reveals the ghastly economic ruin of Germany, and of all the other belligerent nations as well. The official campaign of the warmongers and a lying and servile press on both sides of the front are inadequate to conceal this ruin. These conditions produce a mood among the broad masses, both at home and on the battlefield, that culminates in a passionate longing for peace and in a growing hatred of the endless human slaughter.

This situation requires the Social Democracy in Germany, as well as that in other belligerent nations, to act in the spirit of the International's Stuttgart resolution. No stone must be left unturned in efforts to shape the masses' antiwar sentiment into a clear and purposeful political understanding and into a strong will capable of action.

For that purpose, parliamentary representatives of Social Democracy who are determined to cast off the chains of "civil peace" must do the following:

1. On grounds of socialist principle, reject war credits in all the belligerent countries, regardless of the military situation;

2. Deny the belligerent governments all taxes and financial support;

3. Untiringly utilize every avenue offered by existing parliamentary procedures and activities to persistently harass and sharply criticize the imperialist majorities and their governments. In this way they can arouse the masses and encourage them to vigorously demonstrate their will against the war and in favor of international socialist solidarity.

III

The collapse of German Social Democracy only demonstrated its long-existing weakness. It must undergo a complete internal transformation if it is to lead the masses of proletarians in their historic mission.

It cannot develop into an active revolutionary force through mere programs and manifestos, mechanical discipline, or lifeless organizational forms, but only through propagating living class consciousness and resolute initiative among the masses.

The bureaucratic system of party and trade union organizations now stifles the resolution and strength of the masses in a chaos of official party institutions. It must be transformed into a democratic system in which the functionaries are the instruments of the masses. Party and trade union institutions now obstruct and betray the masses by misusing the slogans of "discipline" and "unity" and by utilizing the organizational apparatus to subordinate the workers to the interests of the imperialist classes. Instead, what is needed is for the clear and purposeful will of the proletarian masses to be resolutely carried out at every opportunity, from the bottom upwards. Only in this way can the organization be led back to its original purpose—to serve as a spirited weapon of class struggle.

The activity of women, called upon to play a particularly important political role in war, and of the youth must be greatly emphasized. The autonomy of the youth movement must be strongly supported.

Propaganda must be conducted among the organized workers above all. But it must strive to go further and reach the unorganized, who under the impact of the World War offer extremely good prospects for recruitment to socialism.

Clarification of principles, firmness on strategic and tactical stance, stubborn execution of the class struggle in the spirit of proletarian internationalism, these are life and death questions for socialism, especially in wartime. All tendencies toward opportunism in principles, tactics, or action, even where these masquerade as opposition to the party establishment's policy, must be firmly opposed.

The existence of the World War dominates and determines the entire international and internal political and economic situation today.

Working-class policy everywhere must orient itself to this fact and oppose the World War as the strongest and most ruinous manifestation of capitalist class rule. It is in this struggle that the socialist movement must establish its right to exist. Class struggle in wartime is the most important revolutionary school for the class struggle in peacetime, giving it strength and historic significance. Having failed to prevent the World War, the Socialist movement's task, in accordance with the Stuttgart congress decision, is to utilize the war and the conditions it creates and arouse the masses, in order to impose peace and hasten a socialist reconstruction of society.

This government represents imperialist war, martial law, neglect of social duties, extortionate prices for basic necessities, deception of the masses, and abrogation of their rights. It must be denied any material and moral support. Every form of taxation, "just" or "unjust," promotes and lengthens the war. Our war against the war requires that we reject all war taxes and bar all the government's financial appropriations, in order to undermine governmental power in every way.

We must go over to the offensive along this entire front.

We must consistently denounce to the masses the political and social effects war has on proletarian class interests: the food supply; social policy; the tax system; freedom of association, assembly, and travel; freedom of the press; personal freedom; justice; education; and so on. We must respond by asserting the demands of the socialist program more vigorously. To combat the militarism of the World War we must demand the abolition of the standing army. To combat secret diplomacy and the absolutism of martial law we must demand a republic, democracy in domestic and foreign policy, and the people's right to decide on war and peace.

We must use every opportunity both inside and outside parliament to break through the state of siege and shatter the "civil peace"—the illusion of national class solidarity during the war. The deceptive phrase about the duty to defend one's country must be refuted. The international identity of the proletariat's class interests has not been negated by the war but has risen to its highest level, and we must proclaim it as a basic political principle.

The feelings of political and social discontent and indignation must be increased by every possible means of agitation and demonstration.

The aim of all propaganda must be to develop the preconditions for large-scale revolutionary mass actions and to give them, wherever they originate, a political content and aim. It must drive them forward and shape them into a conscious opposition against the war and capitalist class rule.

On March 24, 1916, the opposition SPD Reichstag deputies voted once more against war credits. The majority leadership responded by expelling from the fraction the group of deputies led by Haase and Ledebour. The expelled deputies formed a new parliamentary caucus, the Social Democratic Working Group *(Sozialdemokratische Arbeitsgemeinschaft),* which maintained relations with the quickly growing opposition groupings in the membership.

This current came to encompass a wide range of Socialist viewpoints: from Eduard Bernstein, a right-wing revisionist and proimperialist, to revolutionary-minded worker militants. Karl Kautsky, one of its best-known adherents, explained why he joined the Working Group in an August 7, 1916, letter to the pro-war Austrian Socialist Victor Adler.

"The question is no longer whether the opposition will triumph," Kautsky said of the struggle within the party, "but what kind of opposition will win." The Spartacus group represents a very real danger, he continued. "Their radicalism corresponds to the present needs of the broad, uneducated masses. Liebknecht is today the most popular man in the trenches. Everyone who has been there unanimously assures us of that. The discontented masses understand nothing of his particular political policies, but they see in him the man who is acting to end the war, and for them, that is the main question."

The Spartacists want to build a new party, Kautsky asserted. The party leadership, for their part, would be glad to be rid of them. "As curious as it may seem to you," Kautsky told his old associate, "the Working Group is, in contrast to these two extremes, the bond that actually still holds the party together. . . . We are the center, and our strength will determine whether the party can overcome the centrifugal forces from the right and the left."[24]

Despite the efforts of the Working Group, the SPD's majority leadership was moving to secure exclusive control over the party. Opposition-minded newspapers were taken over. Where the opposition had a majority in membership organizations, rival structures were established. The Spartacists responded by proposing that membership organizations stop dues payments to the party center, and use the funds instead for the party's urgent class-struggle tasks.

A conference of opposition youth, held April 23–24, 1916, and organized and led by adherents of the Internationale Group, elected a provisional national leadership. Its tasks were to maintain contact with the local opposition youth groups, establish an independent publication, and collaborate with the Socialist Youth International—an important step toward a separate revolutionary youth movement.

On May Day, 1916, the Spartacists organized an illegal demonstration of some 10,000 working people in Berlin. The SPD and the trade unions no longer held May Day celebrations and the Spartacists had been unable to convince the Working Group to participate.

Thus, they had proceeded on their own.

The action was publicized by a leaflet written by Liebknecht, and by small slips of paper that read: "All those opposed to the war will come to the Potsdamer Platz (Potsdam Square) at 8 p.m. May First. Bread! Freedom! Peace!" The following Spartacus circular described the action.

May Day in Berlin, 1916[25]

At precisely 8 p.m. a crowd of workers, including a great many women and young people, gathered in the Potsdamer Platz to demonstrate. They were so numerous that the usual skirmishes with the police began right away. The cops and their officers in particular quickly became very nervous and began to drive the crowd back and forth with blows.

Suddenly, at the head of the crowd, right in the middle of the Potsdamer Platz, the loud sonorous voice of Karl Liebknecht rang out: "Down with the war! Down with the government!"

He was immediately overpowered by a knot of policemen who separated him from the crowd and led him away to the police headquarters at the Potsdam railway station. The cry, "Hurrah for Liebknecht!" rang out after the arrested leader, whereupon the police plunged into the crowd and made still more arrests.

After Liebknecht had been taken away, the police, inflamed by their officers, who behaved with the greatest brutality, began to push the throng off onto the side streets. In this way three large contingents of demonstrators were formed in Köthener Strasse, Link Strasse, and in Königgrätzer Strasse. Slowly they surged forward amid continual clashes with the police. Cries of "Down with the war!," "Long live peace!," "Long live the International!" rang out one after the other and were repeated by many thousands of voices. But loudest of all was the cry, "Hurrah for Liebknecht!" which was taken up by the masses again and again.

Word of his arrest spread rapidly among the demonstrators. Thousands had seen him at the head of the demonstration and had heard his loud voice urging them on. The bitterness and pain over the loss of the beloved leader, whom everyone knew to be in the cops' clutches, filled every heart and were on everyone's lips. Women in particular lamented loudly, breaking into curses against the police, the war, and the government. The demonstration lasted until ten o'clock, with the three main contingents of the crowd attempting again and again to flow back together through the side streets. But this was prevented time and again by the swarming, leaping, charging police. Songs resounded, the "Workers' Marseillaise," the Socialists' march, alternating with revolutionary chants. Only toward ten thirty, in some cases later, did the mass of demonstrators disperse—flushed and in excellent spirits. The number of demonstrators is conservatively estimated at ten thousand.

The demonstration gave the government a terrible fright. The entire area around Potsdamer Platz was flooded with mounted police right up until midnight. In the precinct station at the Potsdam railway depot, where the command post was set up, patrols nervously ran to and fro, and agitated instructions and reports went on ceaselessly until almost one o'clock at night.

The May Day demonstration in Berlin must therefore be described as a complete success. Of course this was achieved at great cost through the loss of Karl Liebknecht. Liebknecht was yanked from our midst, and for the near future will be away from his post where he is irreplaceable.

Liebknecht did not allow his arrest to stop him from continuing to publicize the basic ideas of the Internationale Group. He wrote as follows to the court where he was to be tried, laying out the political reasons for his actions on May 1, and the class-struggle orientation of the Spartacist current.

Statement to the Royal Military Court[26]

by Karl Liebknecht

BERLIN, MAY 3, 1916

I wish to clarify my statements in the transcript of the investigation of the case against me, as follows:

1. The German government is socially and historically an instrument to oppress and exploit the working masses; at home and abroad it serves the interests of junkerism, capitalism, and imperialism.

It is the most reckless champion of expansionism in world politics, the most ardent promoter of the arms race, and consequently one of the most important agencies in developing the causes of this war.

In partnership with the Austrian government it has engineered the war and must therefore carry the main immediate responsibility for its outbreak.

It has staged this war by deceiving the masses, and even the Reichstag (for example, the concealment of the ultimatum to Belgium, the makeup of the German White Book, the censorship of the tsar's telegram of July 29, 1914, and so on).[27] By reprehensible means, it tries to maintain the war fever among the people.

It carries on the war with methods that are monstrous even by standards of previous practice. . . .

The German government has used martial law to enormously intensify the economic exploitation of the masses and the suppression of their political rights. It tries to keep the masses obedient to its imperialist war policy through phrases about supposed equal treatment of all parties, the discontinuation of political and social discrimination, and the "new orientation," but it rejects every serious political and social reform.

Out of concern for landlord and capitalist interests, the German government has completely failed to meet the population's economic needs during the war, and so has opened the way for outrageous extortion and misery among the people.

Holding fast to this day to its war aims of conquest, it thereby constitutes the main obstacle to immediate peace negotiations on the basis of renunciation of all annexations and violations of national rights. By illegally maintaining martial law (censorship, and so on), the government prevents the public from learning disturbing facts and also blocks socialist criticism of government measures. Its seeming legality and sham popularity are thus revealed to be nothing more than a cover for a system of violence, hostility, and malevolence towards the masses.

The call "Down with the government!" brands this entire government policy as disastrous for the masses of the people. It also signifies that the duty of every Socialist, of every champion of working-class interests, must be the most determined struggle—the class struggle—against the government.

2. This war is not a war to defend national sovereignty, liberate oppressed nations, or improve the well-being of the masses.

For the proletariat the war simply means concentrated and intensified political repression, economic exhaustion, and military slaughter of its life and limb for the benefit of capitalism and absolutism.

The working class of all countries has only one answer: to intensify the international struggle against the capitalist governments and ruling classes of all countries, to end all oppression and exploitation, and to terminate the war through a peace based on socialist principles. The International is the Socialist's fatherland and everything that a Socialist is obliged to defend can be defended through the class struggle.

The call "Down with the war!" signifies that I totally condemn and oppose this war—because of its historical nature, both its underlying social causes and the immediate reasons for its outbreak, the way it is waged, and the goals it pursues. Every champion of working-class interests has the duty to participate in the international class struggle to terminate the war.

3. As a Socialist, I absolutely oppose this war and the existing military system. To the best of my ability, I have consistently supported the struggle against militarism as an especially important task—a life-or-death question—for the working class of all countries (see my book: *Militarism and Antimilitarism* published 1907, and the international youth conferences in Stuttgart, 1907, and Copenhagen,

1910). The war requires us to redouble our efforts against militarism.

4. Since 1889 the First of May has been dedicated both to education in and demonstration for the principles of socialism and against all exploitation, oppression, and violation of human rights. It has proclaimed the solidarity of workers of all countries, a solidarity which is not negated but strengthened by war. May Day stands against fratricidal slaughter among workers, against war, and for peace.

Educating and demonstrating in this spirit is an especially sacred duty of every Socialist in time of war.

5. The policy I advocate is outlined in the resolution adopted by the International Socialist Congress held in Stuttgart (1907). It requires Socialists of all countries, if they fail to prevent war, to work by every means for its speedy termination. It obliges them to utilize the economic and political crisis created by the war to hasten the downfall of the capitalist social order.

This policy is internationalist through and through. It establishes the same duty for Socialists of other belligerent nations toward their governments and ruling classes that I and others have followed against the government and ruling classes in Germany.

Carried out internationally, this policy will inspire workers in every nation with the achievements in other lands, and so promote the international class struggle against the war.

Together with others, I have advocated and defended this policy in public since the beginning of the war. I have also made contact with my cothinkers in other countries, for example, through my journey to Belgium and Holland in September 1914; my Christmas letter in 1914 to the *Labour Leader* of London; the International Socialist Conferences in Switzerland, although I was unfortunately prevented by the state power from myself participating, and so on.[28]

6. I will stand by this policy whatever the cost. It is not mine alone but also the policy of a steadily increasing proportion of the population of Germany and the other belligerent and neutral nations. I hope that it will soon be the policy of the working class of all countries. I am determined to work for that goal. The working class will then possess the power to break the imperialist will of the classes that rule today and to permit humankind to freely shape social relations and conditions for the common good.

Liebknecht, Soldier—
Engineering Corps
[Armierungssoldat]

Liebknecht was put on trial on June 28 and sentenced to two and a half years in prison. On June 29, in the first mass protest strike of the war, 55,000 metalworkers in Berlin downed tools to protest against his prosecution. Twenty-five thousand demonstrated in the Potsdamer Platz. The government struck back with new repressive measures, jailing Rosa Luxemburg, Julian Marchlewski, Franz Mehring, Ernst Meyer, and other Spartacist leaders.

In September 1916 the last national conference of the united SPD took place. The right-wing leadership arranged representation to assure itself a clear majority, and the conference had no authority in the eyes of the opposition. The conference did, however, afford all currents an opportunity to explain their program. Käte Duncker took the floor to present the perspectives of the Internationale Group.

Use workers' strength to end the war[29]

by Käte Duncker

Comrades! The Internationale Group asked me to speak here, not only because we sharply oppose the majority's policy, but also because we are critical of the Social Democratic Working Group on certain essential points, above all on the International and defense of the fatherland. To the extent that they go beyond simple rejection of the war credits, the Working Group and its followers seek to return the party and the International to their pre–August 4 positions, thus resuming the supposedly well-tested and triumphant policies of that period. In fact, August 4 clearly revealed that these policies failed precisely when put to the test. *("Very true!")* They did not lead to victory but rather to devastating defeat.

We consider that the Second International collapsed irretrievably on August 4, 1914. Despite all the fine speeches and resolutions at international congresses it could only collapse, because it was not an organic whole, but only a loose structure without internal cohesion. The national parties were autonomous and the German party in particular would never allow its freedom of action to be restricted by binding international decisions. Every attempt to make the International a real power ran aground when the German delegation replied, "Unacceptable."

We are striving for an International that stands above the national parties. It must be the central goal and pivot of the proletarian class organization. It must decide on all questions whose significance extends beyond national frontiers, for example, the question of militarism and expansion of the navy, colonial policy, and above all what course of action to adopt in case of war. We want to build the International after the war on a sounder basis and make it into a real political force. The concept of internationalism, together with the idea of class struggle, must therefore become the very essence of our informational and educational work in the nation. Every party member in every village must sense and realize that the proletarians beyond our borders are our brothers and class comrades. We are closer and more committed to them than to the ruling classes of our own country. We counterpose internationalist ideology to the nationalist ideology to which the party capitulated on August 4.

Organizationally we do not conceive of the new International as a loose structure of autonomous parties with some office in Brussels or The Hague where comrades gather for non-binding discussions of international questions. However, contrary to the criticisms made by a Working Group publication, we do not envision the International as a commanding general staff reigning above the clouds and sending down orders from on high to the troops of the international proletariat. Rather we seek a permanent and much tighter organizational structure, one equipped with decision-making power. Resting on the internationalist consciousness of the masses in all capitalist countries, its decisions will therefore be binding for the Social Democracy in all these countries. *("How will you bring this about?")* You might say that we demand the transformation of the present loose confederation of provinces into a federal state.

Our stand on national defense flows from this position on the International and from our understanding of the imperialist nature of the war. As you know, every war begins with the battle cry, "The fatherland is in danger!" because it is such an excellent way to mislead the less informed masses. In previous wars this slogan was usually a conscious deception. It is all the more clearly a deception today, in the age of imperialism, when war is waged to determine relationships among the great imperialist states.

Between the big imperialist states there are no longer any defensive wars. The claim that one goes to war to preserve borders and national sovereignty is today an outright swindle of the people. *("How's that again?")* When one pirate ship attacks another to take away its loot, we do not talk about justified self-defense. The imperialist powers always aim for expansion and plunder, and from the outset their wars are wars of conquest. *("Very true!")* It makes absolutely no difference on whose territory the war is fought. Of course, when there's a war, it has to be fought somewhere. *(Laughter)* Just where, is a question of military fortune; it is not the basis for our judgment of the war. *("Very true!")*

As a human being and a Socialist I find it just as painful and shocking to see French, Belgian, and Russian proletarians killed as to see the massacre of German proletarians. "Sound the alarm, they're killing our brothers!"—that must be the approach of internationalist Socialists, wherever war strikes. For that reason we cannot derive our position on this war and on approval of war credits from the military situation at any given moment, as the Working Group did in its statement of December 21 and influential comrades have done in various reports. If Germany faced the same situation as France does today, if large parts of its territory were occupied by foreign troops, who knows if the Social Democratic Working Group would even exist at all. *(Spirited laughter)* I repeat, we will not deduce our position on this war from the conjunctural military situation.

United action by the international proletariat against the war can never be achieved in this way. On this basis Social Democrats would deduce their policies in every war from the success of their country's armies. Those in one country would follow a policy directly contrary to those in the other. That would signify an admission of the bankruptcy of any internationalist proletarian policy.

A member of the Working Group employed the term defensive nihilism against us. This is entirely incorrect. We base ourselves on the Stuttgart resolution, which requires us, in the event we fail to prevent the war, not to defend the fatherland but to work by every possible means for the war's rapid termination, and to utilize the political and economic crisis created by the war to hasten the destruction of the capitalist social order. Of course, should the Socialists gain power in any country they would defend this hard-won stronghold, including against any invader. They would do this just as the partisans of the French Revolution defended their bourgeois freedom against feudal Europe, and just as the fighters of the Commune of 1871 defended it against the Prussian troops.

ALFRED HENKE: And that is just what our program says!

DUNCKER: I will refrain from discussing here the other disagreements we have with the Working Group, such as our differences on the tax question, on submarine warfare, and on the peace petition of the party Executive Committee. On the tax question I will say only that we reject all requests for money for the war, regardless of whether the taxes are indirect (taken from the paltry purses of the large masses), or direct (taken from the pockets of the property owners). They still fuel the war.

We have briefly pointed out the line that separates us from the Working Group, not to immerse ourselves in a polemic with them but to show how necessary it is for our group to make its way on its own, and to shatter the myth that there is one homogeneous opposition. While we will march separately, we will strike our common enemy together, and today dealing that blow is the main thing. *("Aha!" and laughter from the majority)*

We too have to settle accounts with the party Executive Committee, the so-called majority. But not with the social imperialists. We do not intend to discuss here with Kolb,

Lensch, Cohen, Heine, Heilmann, and so on. Not even with the people who, like Konrad Haenisch, sing the "Workers' Marseillaise" to the tune of "Deutschland, Deutschland, über alles." *("Very good!" and laughter from the minority)* It is increasingly clear to every comrade in this country that these people have moved outside the framework of the party program and congress decisions. *("Very true!" from the minority)* They know that themselves. The party program would have to be transformed from top to bottom to keep them in the party. *("Very true!")* Or, as a quicker procedure, we could simply adopt the party program of the National Liberals, fitted out with a few socialist flourishes. As long as our present party program exists the social imperialists and their followers will stand outside of the party framework. Between them and us there can be no common framework.

GEORG LEDEBOUR: Not with us either!

DUNCKER: They belonged long ago in the camp of the bourgeoisie. They are intruders in the house of socialism, and when the day of reckoning comes, those who stand on the party's program, tradition, and congress resolutions will be entitled to throw the intruders out. *(Laughter. "Very good!" from the minority)* These people desecrate the temple of socialist ideas and the socialist world outlook.

CHAIRMAN FRIEDRICH EBERT: I must ask the speaker to express herself in the manner customary in deliberations among party comrades.

LEDEBOUR: You should follow the example of Heine and Timm, and then the chairman would not call you to order!

EBERT: Silence, please. What I said applies to all party members and has always been the procedure at party congresses. *("Very true!")*

DUNCKER: Today we must deal above all with those comrades who claim to stand completely on the program and statutes, but in reality trample them into the ground. We must deal with those who misuse the words "internationalism," "party unity," and "party discipline" to consciously mislead our comrades. The comrades of the party Executive Committee and official [majority] fraction champion "holding on to the end." They approve the credits despite the war's unambiguously imperialist nature. These comrades support and defend the government despite its open declarations in favor of annexation. They have no right to claim they are striving to reestablish international ties and build peace. *("Oho!" and "Very true!")* The first requirement for the reestablishment of international relations is not to reproach the parties of other nations, but to clean up your own backyard *("That means the defeat of Germany!")*—to break with the policy of August 4. . . .

We call on all those who uphold the class struggle and international socialism to defend the integrity of our principles and display discipline in defending our world outlook. They must not be intimidated because of the protests of these fanatics over violations of party unity and discipline.

That means we must openly renounce obedience to the policy of the party establishment. We must break with the politics of half-measures and abandon the illusion that the crisis begins and ends with the purely parliamentary question of granting or rejecting the war credits. It means summoning the masses to a mighty struggle against imperialism and the war. Let us be clear on one thing: if the war ends as it began, as a gift from on high, as a result of diplomatic dealings, and without the intervention of the proletariat, then this peace will seal the defeat that socialism suffered in the war. If this peace is won through employing all the proletariat's instruments of power, it is an entirely different matter. Such a peace will then prepare the victory of socialism and shape the International into a power that would forever prevent the reoccurrence of such a horrible genocidal slaughter.

Not all the revolutionary Social Democrats of Germany adhered to the Internationale Group. The most important independent current, centered in Bremen, was linked with Anton Pannekoek and was now aligned with the Zimmerwald Left. In July 1916 Karl Radek analyzed Socialists' experience in the SPD during two years of war in the newly established Bremen revolutionary weekly, *Arbeiterpolitik* (Workers' Politics). Explaining the deep social antagonisms driving the SPD toward a split, he noted the political progress of the Internationale Group, and projected building a united revolutionary party of German workers around this nucleus.

Launching this party proved to be a difficult process. In early 1917, when the SPD majority leadership drove all opposition forces out of the party, thereby consummating the split in the SPD, the Bremen current urged the Internationale Group to take the initiative in organizing a new, revolutionary party. The Spartacists decided against this course, however, and instead joined the Independent Social Democratic Party (USPD) launched by the Haase-Ledebour forces in April 1917. While the Spartacists continued their independent activity, the revolutionary Socialists in Germany did not possess a common party framework in which to hammer out their program and organize their cadres during the decisive months before the outbreak of the German revolution in November 1918.

The appeal by Radek, Lenin, and others of the Zimmerwald Left to the Spartacists to build a revolutionary party was not fulfilled until December 1918, when the Communist Party of Germany was launched. This party, together with the Russian Bolsheviks, constituted two decisive building blocks of the new Communist International formed the following year.

The passage below is excerpted from Radek's 1916 article in *Arbeiterpolitik*.

The SPD: Unity or split?[30]

by Karl Radek

The politics of August 4, of "civil peace" with the bourgeoisie and support for its imperialist ventures, is an international phenomenon. And it is not only a cruel and hard fact of the past two years, but also a program for the future. A policy carried out simultaneously from London to Petersburg and from Paris to Vienna must, after all, have a common source. What is it?

Paul Lensch's most recent book, *The Social Democracy, Its Goal and Its Fortunes,* fuses the insights of the radical left with imperialist views in order to fabricate arguments in defense of the politics of August 4. In it Lensch explains the attitude of the British trade unionists and the British Labour Party as follows:

"Britain's domination of the world market, which in the last decades has not gone entirely unchallenged, has brought advantages to all social classes in Great Britain, and not least of all to the working class. Its privileged minority, the workers organized into trade unions, took the biggest share, but the great unorganized mass of workers sometimes temporarily got a share also. This unravels the mystery of why the British trade unionists became the staunchest supporters of the British war effort. They knew very well what was at stake and that by defending Britain's domination of the world they would be defending only their own privileges, their own exceptional position in the international trade union movement. Their wages are still considerably higher than those on the continent, and their living conditions are better on the average. This superiority is sustained by British world domination, and any challenge to it is an attack on these workers."

Lensch's view is not new. It is one of many he has borrowed from the radical Social Democrats. But it is doubtless correct. The politics of the British trade unions have always been those of the labor aristocracy, namely, chasing the crumbs that fall from the table of the internationally dominant British bourgeoisie. Both Marx and Engels saw it that way. And it is clear that the outbreak of the war did not suddenly transform the British labor aristocracy from short-sighted beneficiaries of the British bourgeoisie's privileged position into an idealistic group willing to shed their blood for the liberation of the "small nations."

But how is it that the same policy is also being carried out by both the German Social Democracy and the German unions, which until 1914 held a world reputation as the antithesis of the British trade unionists? What is the answer to this puzzle? It was actually revealed long before the war, and Lensch was then part of the ongoing work of explaining it. Even before the war, the difference between the British trade unions and the German "Social Democratic" labor aristocracy lay only in the different political phraseology.

Thanks to the rapid development of German industry, the top layer of the German working class received relatively high wages. The state and trade union social security systems offered them a certain measure of stability. They also took part to some extent in bourgeois culture. Through its trade union leaders and revisionist spokespersons in the party, this upper layer of the working class made known more and more frequently over the last fifteen years that it had more to lose than its chains, and that its long struggle had already brought victories. While the petty-bourgeois elements from southern Germany played a significant role in the revisionist camp, revisionism's growing power in party life came from the support given by the trade union leaders to these same petty-bourgeois ideals.

In the last analysis, the labor aristocracy's politics are purely petty bourgeois. They do not challenge the foundations of capitalism, but rather attempt to secure as many of its advantages as possible. Naturally the German trade unionists and revisionists professed to be for socialism. In contrast to the British trade unionists, who grew up with liberal views, the Germans were educated with socialist ideas. And much more important, the broad masses of German workers were steeped in socialist ideology. But for these leaders socialism became a far-off ideal or simply an empty slogan. Their daily work was limited to a struggle for minor gains. They judge politics on how it affects this struggle. They resist every attempt at constructing a mass movement that would enable the broad masses of the working class to secure political rights and improvements in living conditions. They protest against such "revolutionary romanticism," claiming that such actions are impossible. But in reality *they are afraid of jeopardizing the previous gains of the labor aristocracy.* The labor bureaucracy does not want to *generalize* these benefits through a mass movement, but only to *increase* them for the labor aristocracy, from which it is recruited and whose interests it represents.

For this reason the entire labor bureaucracy supported the revisionist policy of rapprochement with the bourgeoisie. They hoped the capitalists would make concessions to forces that acted in a "peaceful and business-like manner," and they feared that "radical phrases" would only frighten the bourgeoisie and drive them into the arms of reaction.

The trade union leaders and revisionists also had no objection to the bourgeoisie granting them *concessions made at the expense of the masses in other countries.* Without exception these trade union leaders and revisionists supported colonialist policy, which is nothing other than the exploitation of alien peoples for capitalist ends. Does their support prove that colonialism serves the interests of the German workers? No, in the case of the masses of the workers, that is, the working class *as a whole,* it does not. But their support does reflect the benefits that accrue to a thin layer of the most qualified workers who snare the crumbs that fall from the capitalists' superprofits. Securing these tidbits is not merely a goal for the future for the German trade unions. Even before the war, they provided the butter for the labor aristocracy's bread in Germany, just as in Britain. The only difference was that in Germany, the layer receiving these crumbs was narrower.

German capital has taken giant strides toward achieving the position previously attained by British capital. Before the war German industrial exports were almost equal to Britain's and its capital exports were growing every year. German capital had already secured the second-largest share of world plunder, next to Britain. And the German labor aristocracy had also secured a position very close to that of the British labor aristocracy. The German bourgeoisie is trying through this war to achieve a position at least equivalent to Britain's through winning "freedom of the seas" and through founding "Central Europe" *(Mitteleuropa).*[31] The trade unions too are dreaming of the fleshpots of Egypt.

In Germany just as in Britain, it is the labor aristocracy and labor bureaucracy who sustain the politics of August 4. . . .

The politics of August 4 represent the crowning achievement of opportunism as it developed in the Second International, where it was known as revisionism and reformism. In 1903, *Parvus,* then at his most radical, called the politics of the labor aristocracy *National Liberal labor politics.* Just as the National Liberals attempted to achieve the goals of the bourgeoisie not in struggle against the junkers but in alliance with them, the labor aristocracy and bureaucracy try to reach their goals in alliance with the bourgeoisie. Before the war we already knew that this policy was incompatible with socialism. But we thought that it resulted merely from the illusions of the leaders and that it would fade away under pressure of heightening class contradictions. Experience has shown that we were wrong. First *it was not just the policy of the leadership.* It was backed by a body of workers who entirely shared their leaders' goals. And it would be a fatal illusion for us to think that today these leaders enjoy no mass support or that they enjoy it only where workers are not sufficiently enlightened. *This split runs through the working masses themselves.* Everywhere a sector of the workers stands by the social patriots, not because they lack education, but because they want nothing more than reforms. If we do not recognize this, we will be condemned to carry out a party policy founded on illusion, which underestimates the enemy's strength.

The dreams of the social patriots will undoubtedly *go unfulfilled.* The costs of the war, the competitive struggle for the world market that will ensue after it, the increasing concentration of capital, and growing political reaction will not incline the bourgeoisie anywhere to make significant concessions to the labor aristocracy. The tragicomedy of social imperialism is that it betrayed socialism in order to obtain reforms through an alliance with the bourgeoisie, and to this end it supported the bourgeoisie in the war. But the war itself destroys all the illusory hopes of social imperialism. . . .

For split!

The social patriots and social imperialists represent the politics of the labor aristocracy. Through trade union and political activity this layer achieved a relatively high and secure standard of living in the last quarter century. But it was economic prosperity that made this possible. And the same process of capitalist evolution that brought this layer an improved standard of living will remove its basis. The perfection of technology and the rationalization of production (Taylor and similar systems),[32] the growing concentration of capital, the growing number of laborers brought in from the East, and the increasing use of female labor will endanger the position of the labor aristocracy. The immediate results of the war will do the rest.

Socialism's victory requires the existence of an intelligent layer of workers who are not entirely physically worn down and who can take the leadership of the working class as a whole. But as this privileged layer of the workers arose it acquired petty-bourgeois attitudes. This contradiction will be overcome through the development of capitalism itself. This bourgeoisified layer of workers will be pushed down into social living conditions that force it to abandon these petty-bourgeois methods of compromise with the bourgeoisie. To avoid being hurled down to the lowest rungs of society and becoming outcasts they will be forced to conduct a principled class struggle. In this way the evolution of imperialism, which gave birth to social imperialism, will also prepare its demise.

But this evolution cannot be completed in a year or even in a decade. Social-imperialist ideology has deeply rooted antecedents, and, during the course of half a century, it has firmly embedded itself among a layer of workers. It is nourished among them by the bourgeois environment. In and of itself such an ideology will have a tenacious life. We must also remember that the bourgeoisie knows only too well what an asset it has in social imperialism.

For decades the bourgeoisie all over the world spared no efforts in creating the Christian, liberal, and scab workers' organizations whose task it was to thwart the proletariat's independent movements in the interests of capital.[33] All of this did not have much success. Once imbued with the spirit of socialism, the workers recognized only too easily the goal of all of these "workers' movements." Social imperialism, on the other hand, arose within the socialist movement itself. At its head were men who through decades of work had acquired great standing in the socialist workers' movement. The bourgeoisie hopes that Scheidemann and Legien will influence the workers' movement in its favor more successfully than did Lebius and Stegerwald. For this reason they give Scheidemann's and Legien's policies their complete approval and support. . . .

Our task cannot consist only in fighting the social imperialists. They are merely the puppet troops of capitalism, and our struggle against them cannot be viewed as anything more than a precondition for the class struggle as a whole. If the party's formal unity is maintained and the social imperialists continue to dominate it and its politics, then we will be forced either to give up the real struggle against the class enemy for years, or to conduct it while disregarding the slogans of the social-imperialist officials. In the first case, if we abandon the real struggle against the external enemy and content ourselves with criticizing the social imperialists, then this criticism will lose all meaning. It will be nullified and destroyed by the actions we will be obliged to conduct together with the social imperialists in the Reichstag and in the trade union movement and by the absence of any actions that could prove to the masses of workers that our criticisms are correct.

In the second case, the social imperialists will throw *us* out of the party on the spot. For in the long run, no party majority can tolerate a closed group which castigates their politics as a betrayal of party principles. And even less can it tolerate a group that thwarts all of its activity and calls on the masses to carry out actions headed in the opposite direction. A party with two Reichstag fractions at war with one another and party groups that are locked everywhere in mutual hostility, cannot long endure.

But supposing that despite all the factors mentioned, we

succeed in winning a majority at the party congress. What then? Will we be content to thunder against the politics of August 4 with a mere resolution, adopt radical theses, as we have often done, and then entrust Scheidemann and Legien with its execution? Of course it is not excluded that these "skillful politicians" or some of their underlings would take on this task in order to retain the reins of the party in their hands. This happened at the 1904 *Dresden* congress, where the revisionists accepted the radical resolution, even though it rejected their politics, in order to better be able to carry out their line.

Although bound by the Dresden resolution, the party Executive Committee and the Reichstag fraction trampled its firm principles underfoot on August 4. Any worker who understands this will say that opportunist leaders heading a revolutionary party will constantly obstruct every party action and at the decisive historical moment hand the party over to the class enemy. After the experience of August 4, anyone who still thinks that we can tolerate Ebert and Scheidemann, Legien and August Müller at the head of the workers' movement is either a good-natured nincompoop (if they really believe that these people serve the cause of socialism) or is consciously preparing the road for social imperialism, that is, for the bourgeoisie. But anyone who sees that we must oust the men of August 4 from the party leadership must understand that they will not obediently submit. *They* will split the party.

Some comrades assume that if we have the majority and the social imperialists refuse to submit, only a small group will split away. We must dismiss such childish nonsense. It does not display a cool and prudent assessment of the situation. Behind the social imperialists stands a large section of the workers in the small towns who are strongly influenced by their petty-bourgeois environment. A section of the unionized workers will also back them. From whatever side the split may come, it will inevitably be a split in the working masses themselves.

No matter how you dance around the question, *the split is unavoidable.* If we form a majority, the social imperialists will split the party. If we form the minority, then we must split it, unless we submit nobly, take responsibility for the politics of August 4, and haggle only over incidental points. But the split is *not only historically necessary,* it is *directly useful* to the workers' cause. Without a split from the social imperialists, it is impossible to achieve unity in Social Democratic agitation, and to act. Only when we have rejected responsibility for the politics of August 4, through a split, will we be able to do effective work on the results of the war. Only after separating from the social imperialists will it be possible to reconstruct the International. Its purpose will not be accommodation with those who reconciled themselves with capital during the war, but rather unification of the proletariat for a common struggle. We can only defeat social imperialism when the split gives free rein for a ruthless socialist struggle against it. . . .

Arguing in favor of a split does not mean that we should now leave the party. On the contrary, we must try to get as many organizations and organs of the party as possible into our hands. They were created by half a century of effort as weapons for our struggle, and they belong to us by historical right. We must do all we can to compel the social imperialists to create new organizations for their new bourgeois purposes. Our duty is to hold out at our posts as long as possible, for the longer we do this, the greater will be the proportion of workers who go with us if we are expelled. The social imperialists will of course perfectly understand our intentions, even if we are discreet. But while it is correct to save the party's instruments of power from the grasp of the social imperialists, so they can be used for their historical goals, this must not become an end in itself.

We must not renounce any essential political activity, even if it should bring on a split earlier than we might perhaps wish. This activity is the source of our strength and our reason for being. And where the social imperialists seize the local committees, independent local organizations must be set up immediately.

The task of the hour is to *unite the local party organizations that adhere to the opposition with the oppositional minorities within the majority-controlled organizations, and set up a provisional leadership of the militant oppositionists.* Comrade *Luxemburg's* proposal to this end was rejected by the assembly of the Berlin party organization.[34] But the local organizations that stand with the militant lefts must carry this out. If we are isolated in local groups and not united, we will be a plaything in the hands of the social imperialists. We must therefore use every opening to centralize the opposition. . . .

Tasks of the radical left

The radical lefts began their struggle on the historic day when the "old policies, tried and true" collapsed. It was not the Ledebours, Haases, and Kautskys who raised the banner of rebellion, but the radical lefts. Later, when the workers began to move, a left wing of the old "center" current felt required to protest in the name of the old tactics against the new social-imperialist policy. A section of the radical lefts then believed that they could lead these centrist malcontents further by linking up with them.

The well-known protest of the thousand in July 1915 was the common project of a section of the radical lefts and the left wing of the center.[35] And at the Zimmerwald conference you could see the spectacle of a section of these radical lefts, representatives of the group that in March 1915 published the first issue of *Die Internationale,* voting together with Ledebour to defeat the radical lefts of Russia, Poland, Sweden,

Holland, and the delegate from the other, more consistent wing of the German radical lefts.[36]

That led to the formation of the *International Socialists of Germany* (ISD), an ideological association that from the outset demarcated itself from the center and pressed the radical lefts to adopt an independent political course. It was small and its numerical influence not broad. But the left wing of the center pursued a course so pitiful that, in December 1915, the majority of the radical lefts, grouped around the journal *Die Internationale*, were forced to differentiate themselves from it. This resulted in the *"Theses"* of the Internationale Group and the *Spartacusbriefe* (Spartacus Letters). Only then did it come to a break with the Ledebour people. Some leaders of the Internationale Group continued to suffer under the illusion that the break was not final and others, fearful of the weight of the old order, wished to avoid isolation. But the next months proved them wrong. The politics of the centrist Social Democratic Working Group proved that you cannot make a sword for the proletarian mass struggle out of the cardboard of the old leadership.

Furthermore, everywhere that the radical lefts turned directly to the masses and carried on tenacious educational work, a capable band of proletarians gathered round who had worked their way theoretically through all the confusion and fog. Speaking only for ourselves, we are of the opinion that *many of the contradictions that led to the formation of the ISD and that caused the Bremen radical lefts not to join the Internationale Group have now been overcome.* Through their tireless struggle against social patriotism, their fearless and far-ranging activity, and the great sacrifices that they have made for the cause, the comrades from the Internationale Group have won honor as one of the best vanguard contingents in action for the new International. By calling on party members to stop paying dues, by advocating more militant forms of struggle, and by the tenor of their "Theses," they have shown that they do not see the task of the radical left as returning to the old methods or passive protest, but as a real fight to mobilize the workers in struggle for a new International. . . .

While subjecting the Internationale Group to some friendly criticism, we also recognize that they are the nucleus of the German radical left. Our criticisms do not reflect any desire to compete with them. Rather they flow from our understanding that in this time of deep crisis, the necessary new orientation can be achieved only through an open discussion and an unrestrained exchange of opinions.

But in view of the courageous practical work of the Internationale Group, this exchange of opinions should not be grounds for struggle against it. On the contrary, in our opinion this discussion should open the road for our friends to consistently support the Internationale Group in its struggle against the social patriots and the center. The greater their losses, the more we must rally round them in practical activity and join with them in carrying out the tasks before the radical left wing.

For the moment these tasks are to struggle to win over the workers within the party and to move outward with the forces we have gathered. As we carry out these tasks we will find it necessary and possible to build our own structure for proletarian socialism by creating a socialist party that will implement the politics of the radical left wing.

Our opponents sneer that this party will be a sect. Not so! Dark clouds on the horizon herald a time of historical tempests, in which this party, armed with its courage, single-mindedness, and clear orientation on the aims and methods of our struggle, will take the leadership of the working masses. It already passed a historic test when it courageously raised its banner at the time of the great collapse. It is now experiencing the most difficult period. Not yet cut loose from the social patriots, it lacks its own organizational and cadre structure. It functions in the chaos left by the collapse of the old Social Democracy, surrounded by the relics of a dying era in which its efforts were opposed by the entire machine of the old party. Like Hercules it must combat the Hydra while still in the cradle.[37]

But it will emerge triumphant out of these struggles. Wiser through the historic lessons of the collapse and of the years of shame, the workers, forming up in their multitudes, will press toward independent political activity. Robbed of their old leaders, they will strive on their own to fight their way through the historical labyrinth, and their forces will grow with every passing day.

The split in the party and the struggle with the center, in which those who long for peace see only chaos, are the *birth pangs of a new party*. Through this the proletariat will become conscious of its tasks in the imperialist epoch. The greater the tasks, the greater the obstacles, and the greater the pressure, so too the greater must be our efforts and the harder will be the steel from which we forge our weapons.

Above, Rosa Luxemburg, Karl Liebknecht; below, Käte Duncker, Clara Zetkin, Georg Ledebour.

Chapter 11

The social roots of the split in the Second International

The schism between the revolutionary and opportunist wings of the Second International widened steadily during 1915 and 1916 in step with a growing class polarization. The opportunists in the chauvinist wing of the Social Democracy remained firmly lined up behind the capitalist ruling classes in their program of prosecuting the war and attacking the rights and living standards of working people. The Marxist forces, for their part, advanced a diametrically opposed program, as they sought to rally workers against these attacks and to chart a course toward the revolutionary conquest of power by the workers in alliance with other exploited producers. By the beginning of 1917 the major Social Democratic parties of Europe had either undergone a split or were clearly headed in that direction.

Among Socialists who opposed the outright chauvinist party leaderships there was substantial disagreement on the meaning and source of this split. In Germany, for example, the Haase-Ledebour forces held that it had resulted from the strains of wartime, and could be healed. The revolutionaries disagreed. "Before the war . . . we thought that (opportunism) resulted merely from the illusions of the leaders and that it would fade away under pressure of heightening class contradictions," explained Karl Radek in his article, "The SPD, Unity or Split."[1] "Experience has shown that we were wrong," he continued. The split was to be definitive.

Marxists sought during the war to develop a deeper understanding of the social roots of opportunism, in order to be better able to explain its influence and its staying power within the workers' movement. Radek's article contributed to this discussion, emphasizing that "it would be a fatal illusion to think that today these leaders enjoy no mass support."

V.I. Lenin and Gregory Zinoviev took up this question briefly in their pamphlet, "Socialism and War," published in 1915. "Not one Marxist has ever doubted that opportunism expresses bourgeois policies within the working-class movement," they wrote. It "expresses the interests of the petty bourgeoisie and the alliance of a tiny section of bourgeoisified workers with their *'own'* bourgeoisie, against the interests of the proletarian masses, the oppressed masses.

"The objective conditions at the close of the nineteenth century greatly intensified opportunism, converted the utilisation of bourgeois legality into subservience to the latter, created a thin crust of a working-class officialdom and aristocracy and attracted numerous petty-bourgeois 'fellow travellers' to the Social-Democratic parties.

"The war has speeded up this development and transformed opportunism into social-chauvinism, transformed the secret alliance between the opportunists and the bourgeoisie into an open one. Simultaneously, the military authorities have everywhere instituted martial law and have muzzled the mass of the workers, whose old leaders have nearly all gone over to the bourgeoisie.

"Opportunism and social-chauvinism stand on a common economic basis—the interests of a thin crust of privileged workers and of the petty bourgeoisie, who are defending their privileged position, their 'right' to some modicum of the profits that their 'own' national bourgeoisie obtain from robbing other nations, from the advantages of their Great-Power status, etc."[2]

Zinoviev, collaborating with Lenin, undertook a more extensive study of this question in 1916 in his work, *The War and the Crisis of Socialism,* excerpted below. Utilizing the example of the Social Democratic Party of Germany, he analyzed how petty-bourgeois layers, the labor bureaucracy, and a privileged layer of the working class interrelate in providing a material basis for the growth of opportunism in the workers' movement.

The social roots of opportunism[3]

by Gregory Zinoviev

The camp-followers

At the outbreak of the war the opportunists in the working class of all the most important countries became social chauvinists.

The evolution of the individual persons, of the individual representatives of the Second International cannot be fully explained as flowing from the struggle of the two tendencies. It is not correct to maintain that *all* the present social chauvinists were previously opportunists. It is true beyond a doubt, however, that all the former opportunists are today social chauvinists. Individual, isolated exceptions merely prove the rule. The most important elements of modern social chauvinism were always latent in the old theory of opportunism. The war came, and everything that was still unclear in the ferment of opportunism took on sharply defined forms. All the bourgeois muck that until then had been concealed by the mask of socialism came suddenly out into the limelight. All the potential (bourgeois) energy took on kinetic form—what had been kept secret until then was now openly expressed.

But here the question arises: where does opportunism in the Socialist movement come from? How, by which path, and through which channels does this bourgeois influence penetrate the workers' parties?

One of the causes of opportunism are the so-called camp-followers, that is, those strata of the electorate which are mainly recruited from the petty bourgeoisie, which do not belong to the Social Democratic Party and are not convinced socialists, but nevertheless join with the Social Democracy occasionally under the influence of one accidental circumstance or another, contributing their voting strength in the elections.

This phenomenon has its deeper causes and is rooted, above all, in the entire development of the bourgeois parties and of bourgeois liberalism. In all countries in which—one way or another—a bourgeois revolution has taken place, the bourgeoisie has long been—in Germany, ever since 1848—counterrevolutionary and inimical to the people. The historical experiences accumulated by the bourgeoisie have had their effect. Even in a country which is going through the state of development that present-day Russia is, the bourgeoisie has become a thoroughly counterrevolutionary factor.

Bourgeois liberalism has lost its attractive power and is continuing to lose it ever more, from year to year. In Germany, for instance, for some time now no genuine people's party has existed outside of the Social Democracy. There is no large bourgeois-democratic party to take into its ranks, not proletarians, but millions of the small people, those people who are dissatisfied with the existing order, who feel that they are at a disadvantage in modern society, who long for a radical economic and political improvement of their situation. All the dissatisfied, all the distressed, all the disadvantaged elements are forced to go to the Social Democracy. No matter how moderate in its demands, how opportunistic the German Social Democracy was even before the war, it was the only democratic people's party in Germany. It alone defended, for better or for worse, the interests of the small people and the middle classes. Thus it became a refuge for all the nonproletarian elements who could not stomach the practices of counterrevolutionary and antidemocratic liberalism, already fast in the grip of the imperialist claws. Under the influence of one or another aggressive measure on the part of the bourgeoisie or of the junkers, many hundreds of thousands of petty-bourgeois camp-followers came over and gave their votes to the Social Democracy.

Therein lay the strength as well as the weakness of the German Social Democracy. Its strength consisted in the fact that the German Social Democracy had become the only people's party, that all the dissatisfied in the country sought its protection, that almost the entire democratic population flocked to its banner. Its weakness consisted in the fact that the petty-bourgeois camp-followers brought with them into the workers' party the political spinelessness, the indecision, the bourgeois mode of thinking, and all those other characteristics inherent in the strata that stand between the classes. Socialism became infected with opportunism.

In a country that has universal suffrage a particularly intensive vote-chasing is inevitable. In the chase after electoral successes, the German Social Democracy adapted itself to its possible allies, to its camp-followers recruited among the nonproletarian strata. A whole category of people arose who voted for the Social Democracy but only reluctantly joined the Social Democratic organization, who interested themselves exclusively in the general democratic and reformist work of the Social Democracy.

The world of the "camp-followers" also carried to the surface the corresponding leaders, Heine, Südekurn, Landsberg, David—these are the typical representatives and leaders of such strata. One such stratum, for instance, the innkeepers, is strongly represented in the Social Democratic fraction of the Reichstag. Among the Social Democratic deputies to the Reichstag there were four innkeepers (out of thirty-five deputies) in 1892; six (out of eighty-one) in 1905; twelve (out of 110) in 1912. Basing themselves upon the more backward layers of the working class, these ideological-political leaders of the camp-followers create a whole tendency inside the Social Democracy. Gradually a state within a state is formed. The petty-bourgeois influences grow constantly stronger. The Social Democracy itself becomes *a camp-follower of the camp-followers.* It is not the camp-followers who adapt themselves to the Social Democracy, but the Social Democracy that adapts itself to them. In the critical moments of history it is the petty-bourgeois and not the proletarian tendencies in the Social Democracy that win the upper hand. The petty bourgeoisie, due to its social situation, is doomed forever to vacillate between two camps. Thus it is not at all surprising that in the course of such a crisis as was created by the outbreak of the World War, the pendulum swung over to the bourgeois-imperialist side and remained stationary there. The bourgeoisie thus achieved a signal victory inside the German Social Democracy against the working-class elements.

Even in Germany's biggest cities, in the chief fortresses of the Social Democracy, more than a third of its voters do not belong to the working class but to the bourgeoisie. To the petty bourgeoisie, for the greatest part; to those strata which are on their way toward proletarianization and stand close to the working-class population—but in any case, to the bourgeoisie. . . .

By and large, the voters coming from bourgeois circles naturally only form a minority inside the German Social

Democratic electorate. The majority of the Social Democratic voters consists of workers. (Among these, the better-situated workers, the so-called labor aristocracy, play a big role) By the force of their numbers, the working-class element could impose their majority will upon the nonproletarian elements. But in reality this does not normally happen. The party *wants as many camp-followers as possible.* In practice, the party exerts all its energy to draw these bourgeois camp-followers to its side, not to do anything that might displease them very much. Consequently, a whole series of concessions to petty-bourgeois psychology, moderation of the proletarian demands, the opening of the road to opportunist unclarity.

Immediately after the abolition of the Anti-Socialist Laws, the German Social Democracy doubled its vote The total number of participants in the election fell in 1890 by 312,400 votes (1887, 7,540,900; 1890, 7,228,500). The number of Social Democratic votes, on the other hand, rose by some 664,200 votes (1887, 763,100; 1890, 1,427,300). Whoever followed German public affairs attentively could have observed even at that time that this growth in the size of the vote was not simply due to the influx of many thousands of petty-bourgeois camp-followers. There was some talk, even then, about a certain kind of *coalition* between bourgeois democracy and the workers' party. . . .

Many of these camp-followers are not only poor Socialists but also very inconsistent democrats. Many of them are shaky recruits, unreliable allies of the working class even in the purely parliamentary contests. Bourgeois demagogy—particularly that demagogy which rests upon a "patriotic" base—can always count upon a certain amount of success among these alleged adherents of Social Democracy. In this connection the official German Social Democracy was given a sound lesson by the elections of 1907.

These elections, which have gone down into political history as the "Hottentot Elections," took place under the sign of "patriotism." Under the slogan of "saving the country," of strengthening the "military power" of Germany, of fighting for the "rightful interests of the nation" in the field of colonial policy, Prince Bülow succeeded in uniting all the bourgeois parties against the Social Democracy. And by uniting their forces, these parties succeeded in administering an electoral defeat to the Social Democracy. The German Social Democracy lost thirty-eight seats in parliament at the elections of 1907. To be sure, the absolute number of votes cast for the Social Democracy had risen by some 248,000. But the total number of voters participating in the elections had risen by about two million. In other words, *relatively* speaking, the German Social Democracy lost votes as well in these elections.

The petty-bourgeois camp-followers of the Social Democracy had been taken in by the bait of "patriotism," and thus the opponents of the Social Democracy were assured of success. The workers received an imposing lesson. The dependence of the official German Social Democracy upon its camp-followers was distinctly proved. . . .

In the elections of 1912 the camp-followers were once again on the side of the Social Democracy. On the one hand, they had become disillusioned with the policy of the bourgeoisie: the promises of mountains of gold had remained mere promises. The burdens of militarism were growing. Taxes were continually on the increase. The so-called financial reform brought about a deterioration in the condition of the middle class. On the other hand, the official leaders of the Social Democratic Party became even more opportunist. For them the chief lesson of the elections consisted in this: *that it was necessary to adapt themselves even more to the camp-followers.* If the mountain refuses to come to Mohammed, Mohammed must go to the mountain.

As a result, we see in 1912 a new and very strong influx of petty-bourgeois camp-followers toward the German Social Democracy. . . .

The official German Social Democracy has actually avoided an open struggle against bourgeois "patriotism." It took up the struggle against the bourgeoisie *on the latter's own grounds.* The official opposition of the German Social Democracy on this question was exhausted by the thesis: "We are also patriots, we are even better patriots than you are." Instead of a struggle between two principles—internationalism against nationalism—there appeared an unprincipled rivalry over the question who the greater "patriots" were. And there can remain no doubt: *this position of the official German Social Democracy was determined to a very important degree by opportunist considerations as to how to hold the camp-followers to the party.* It suffices to recall the fact that in 1911 Molkenbuhr (one of the pillars of the party leadership and officially a "Marxist" and not an opportunist) proposed that the International Socialist Bureau should not be convoked and that no alarm should be sounded over the Morocco conflict.[4] He based this position upon the grounds that Reichstag elections were approaching in Germany and that it would not be favorable for the Social Democracy to have international politics debated at every election meeting and in every village in place of the questions of internal policy.

Immediate success in the elections, even if it had to be paid for at the price of concessions to national prejudice—that was always the aim of the opportunist wing of the German Social Democracy. The greatest possible number of seats in parliament—that is the beginning and end of the policy of opportunism.

The old leaders of the Social Democracy attempted to combat this tendency which was steadily gaining the upper hand. But not always with success. On the eve of the elections of 1912 Bebel made a speech in Hamburg in which he postulated the following thesis: Better fifty deputies and 4 million votes than 100 deputies and 3 million votes. In other words: what is important for us is not the number of seats in parliament, but the number of sympathizers we have among the population. This was a feeble attempt to enter into a struggle against the policy of adaptation to the camp-followers. Only a feeble attempt, for in order to speak out clearly it would have been necessary to say: better 2 million votes of *convinced Socialists* than 4 million votes at the price of an adulteration of socialism; better twenty deputies who are really *Socialists* than a hundred deputies of whom half are still deeply immersed in the petty bourgeoisie. But even for this feeble attempt Bebel was fiercely attacked by the opportunists. And to tell the truth, the elections of 1912 actually proceeded far more under the banner of Südekum than under that of old Bebel. . . .

Naturally, we do not wish to contend that the opportunism inside of the German Social Democracy arose only and exclusively because of the camp-followers. No, opportunism is the product of a whole series of facts. The camp-followers, however, constitute *one of the channels* through which opportunism penetrates the workers' party.

The opportunists achieved victory over the Marxists in the German Social Democracy and not in the German alone. *That signifies,* among other things, that the policy of adaptation to the petty-bourgeois camp-followers defeated the other policy. The official German Social Democracy has itself become a camp-follower, an agent, a tool of imperialism.

The labor bureaucracy

The term *"labor bureaucracy"* was long ago legitimized in scientific and political literature. When we spoke of labor bureaucracy before the war we understood by that almost exclusively the British trade unions. We had in mind the fundamental works of the Webbs, the caste spirit, the reactionary role of the bureaucracy in the old British trade unionism, and we said to ourselves: How fortunate that we have not been created in that image, how fortunate that this cup of grief has been spared our labor movement on the continent!

But we have been drinking for a long time out of this very cup. In the labor movement of *Germany*—a movement which served as a model for Socialists of all countries before the war—there has arisen just as numerous and just as reactionary a caste of labor bureaucrats. The present crisis has revealed this fact with unsparing clarity.

Up to now little has been known of the numerical composition of the labor bureaucracy, of its influence, of its income, of its corporative organizational strength. Just as a great many things are concealed from the public eye and wrought in secrecy within the circle of the leaders of the capitalist trusts, so it is in that closed caste of the labor bureaucracy, a unique functionaries' job trust that directs the mass organization of the workers in all countries with an advanced labor movement. It is a characteristic attribute of every caste to be shut off from the entire world outside of it, to be accessible only to the initiated. That is why it is so extraordinarily difficult to obtain factual data about the role of the labor bureaucracy.

Let us first of all turn our attention to the labor movement in *Germany*. How strong is the labor bureaucracy there? How big is the influence of the "leaders" on the mass movement? Let us dwell for a while on the quantitative side of the matter. Some exceptionally interesting information on the role of the labor bureaucracy, that is, the role of the functionaries in the Social Democratic Party and in the free trade unions may be found in the *Handbuch des Vereins Arbeiterpresse* [Workers' Press Association Manual].[5] This manual has been appearing only for the past three years and is accessible only to functionaries of the labor movement. It cannot be obtained in bookstores. With great effort we succeeded in getting a copy of it for the purposes of this work. (We received this rare material on the situation of the German Social Democracy through the gracious aid of Comrade Julian Borchardt, to whom we express our thanks here.)

At the very end of the book there is an alphabetical index of all the paid officials working for the party and the free trade unions. This register of names alone occupies twenty-six pages of three columns each in print of the very smallest petit type. According to our calculation, the entire number of paid officials working for the party and the trade unions in 1914 amounts to 4,010. In Greater Berlin alone it amounts to 751, in Hamburg to 390. . . .

A large majority of these "upper" four to five thousand were originally *workers*. . . . The purely bourgeois elements (merchants, academicians, literary men, etc.) are more strongly represented in the opportunist center, Munich, and in part also in Frankfurt and Stuttgart. Generally, however, it may be said that workers constitute the absolutely preponderant element among the "upper" four thousand functionaries of the German labor movement. This fact cannot be disputed and in this respect our data here correspond with all the other data.

But the concept "worker," in and of itself, must be applied with the greatest care in this case. It would be better perhaps in this case not to say "worker" but "worker in his origin." For such party leaders as Scheidemann, Ebert, Kolb, Legien, Pfannkuch, etc., also belong in the category of worker-functionaries. Scheidemann is a compositor, Ebert a saddler, Legien a turner, Pfannkuch a carpenter, Molkenbuhr a tobacco worker. In reality, however, these people are no longer workers and have not been for decades. They have incomes bigger than that of middle-level bourgeois and have long ago given up their trades. They are workers in the same sense as the well-known "labor" ministers John Burns, Henderson,

Fisher, etc. . . . And that holds true not only for people in the center who stand on the highest rung of the bureaucratic ladder and direct all the affairs, like Legien, Scheidemann, etc. It holds true also for the *great majority of all the four thousand functionaries* of the German labor movement. In the provinces the picture is the same: the functionaries have long ago given up their original trade. They are workers in name only. In reality they are bureaucrats with a standard of living quite unlike that of the average worker.

The worker-functionaries very often hail from the circles of the labor aristocracy. The labor *bureaucracy* and the labor *aristocracy* are blood brothers. The group interests of the one and of the other very often coincide. Nevertheless, labor bureaucracy and labor aristocracy are two different categories. (The role of the latter is discussed below.) . . .

According to our calculation, four thousand functionaries occupy at least twelve thousand—if not more—important party and trade union posts. Every more or less efficient functionary takes care simultaneously of two or three and often even more offices. He is at the same time a Reichstag deputy and an editor; a member of the Landtag [regional parliament] and a party secretary; the president of a trade union, an editor, a cooperative functionary, a city councilman; etc. Thus all power in the party and trade unions accumulates in the hands of this upper four thousand. (The salaries accumulate, too. Many of the officials of the labor movement receive ten thousand marks per year and more.[6]) The whole business depends upon them. They hold in their hands the whole powerful apparatus of the press, of the organization, of the mutual-aid societies, the entire electoral apparatus, and so on.

The reactionary role of the trade union bureaucracy is confirmed even by such moderate critics as the historians of the British trade union movement, the Webbs. But we cannot here go into the role of the labor bureaucracy in

England more thoroughly (the number of *top* functionaries in the trade unions in 1905 was 1,000; more recent figures are, unfortunately, not available). That would be too much of a digression.

In the land of "unlimited possibilities," in America, the leaders of the labor unions sell themselves quite openly to the bourgeoisie. There the material dependence of the leaders upon the bourgeoisie is not even particularly concealed. There it is a common practice for the capitalists and labor leaders, and their respective wives, to exchange valuable "gifts" after the conclusion of a wage agreement with the trade unions. Naturally, this is simply common bribery. The labor leaders there are often pure and simple handymen of the bourgeoisie, *"labor lieutenants of the capitalist class,"* [7] as they say in America. That is no longer a matter of petty-bourgeois hangovers or of the group interests of the labor aristocracy, but venality pure and simple. There, the trade unions do a wholesale and retail trade with workers' votes before the presidential elections. The leaders of the labor unions over there take a prominent part in various capitalist associations.

One example: the notorious Samuel Gompers. He is simultaneously the president of the American Federation of Labor and first vice-president of the Civic Federation, that is, the most important capitalist organization for the combating of socialism. When Gompers came to Europe in 1909, Karl Kautsky extended to him this mocking greeting: "Welcome, brother—president of the American labor unions; begone, Mr. Vice-President of the National Federation of American Capitalists!"

However, the reactionary role of the "socialist bureaucracy" appears nowhere so ostentatiously as in Australia, that veritable promised land of social reformism. The first "labor ministry" in Australia was formed in Queensland in December 1899. And ever since then the Australian labor movement has been a constant prey of leaders on the make for careers. Upon the backs of the laboring masses there arise, one after another, little bands of aristocrats of labor, from the midst of which the future labor ministers spring forth, ready to do loyal service to the bourgeoisie. All these Holmans, Cooks, and Fishers were once workers. They act the part of workers even now. But in reality they are only agents of the financial plutocracy in the camp of the workers.

The caste of the "leaders" here appears quite openly as a unique type of job trust for functionaries. The labor party as such comes to the surface only during the parliamentary elections. Once the elections are over, the party disappears again for three whole years. The party conventions are only conventions of party functionaries. They are not in any sense composed of real representatives of the mass of labor. The party leader is elected by the convention and functions as such until the next election at the succeeding convention. If he is elected to Parliament, he also becomes the leader of the parliamentary fraction. If the party gets a majority in Parliament, the leader becomes prime minister and forms a "labor ministry." The powers of this leader are almost unlimited. It went so far that the "labor" minister of New South Wales, Holman (a former carpenter), proposed at the party conference of 1915 that the leader be given the power to change the *program of the party* at his own discretion, if this should be necessary for its "salvation." We have recently had quite a striking example of the means whereby Fisher, Holman, and Company "save" the labor party. These "leaders" have proved to be the worst sort of chauvinists. The majority of the workers pronounced themselves against the introduction of conscription in Australia. But Fisher and his friends continue to represent the views of the bourgeoisie.

When the Danish Socialist, Stauning, not so long ago became a minister, Huysmans congratulated him on his success and noted with joy the fact that Stauning is the tenth Socialist to become a minister. It would be interesting to know whether Huysmans counts Fisher among the ten ministers.

There is one consolation for the opponents of Fisher, nevertheless. Namely, that even in distant Australia it has come to an open break between Fisher and the genuine labor organizations. "Every cloud has its silver lining." The present crisis has sharpened the situation tremendously and it will lead to a good and healthy cleansing of the democratic ranks.

The most far-sighted of the German reactionaries knew long before the war that the official organization of the German Social Democracy had become thoroughly "bourgeoisified." And they said quite openly that at the critical moment they would appeal to the leaders, to the heads of the Social Democratic Party against *the laboring masses*. . . .

Naturally, the Socialists as well long ago recognized the reactionary role of the labor bureaucracy, but not quite so clearly as they did after the salient lesson of August 4, 1914. . . .

Objectively the labor bureaucracy—the so-called leaders—betrayed the cause of the workers in Germany on August 4. And not only in Germany. But that must not be taken to mean that every one of these leaders said to himself at the decisive moment: I had better go over to the side of the bourgeoisie, else I am going to lose my bread and butter, my position in public life, and so on. Not at all! Subjectively, many members of this caste are still convinced to this day that they have been acting exclusively in the interests of the working class, that their conduct was dictated by their better understanding of the proletarian interests. When we speak of the "treachery of the leaders" we do not mean to say by this that it was all a deep-laid plot, that it was a consciously perpetrated sell out of the workers' interests. Far from it. But consciousness is determined by existence, not *vice versa*. The entire social character of this caste of labor bureaucrats led inevitably, *given the previous tempo of the movement in the "peaceful" prewar period,* to complete bourgeoisification of their "consciousness." The entire position into which this numerically strong caste of leaders had climbed over the backs of the working class made of them a social group which objectively must be regarded as an agency of the imperialist bourgeoisie.

In his dispute with the leader of the opportunists, Vollmar, Bebel repeatedly pointed out that the social position of the former (von Vollmar belonged to the upper strata and was fabulously rich) prevented him from understanding the griefs of the working class and *therefore made him into an opportunist* tending toward a National-Liberal policy. Although this may not always be true for every person (an individual can raise himself above the milieu of his class, above his social group), it is absolutely true for the entire social stratum of the labor bureaucracy.

The rise of an entire, numerically strong stratum of labor bureaucrats—just like the mass influx of electoral camp-followers—is, at one and the same time, a symptom of strength as well as of weakness in the labor movement. Of strength—because it testifies to the enormous *numerical* growth of the movement. An organization with only a few thousand members can get along without paid functionaries. When it begins to have hundreds of thousands and millions of members it necessarily needs a big and complex organizational apparatus. But the rise of this stratum becomes a symptom of weakness in the movement when the leaders of the workers' organizations degenerate into officials in the negative sense of the word, when it shows that the movement is bogged down, and lacks the broad proletarian impetus necessary to the given stage of development. Every people, so the saying goes, has the government it deserves. This can be amplified by adding that every labor movement also has the kind of leadership it deserves.

During the crisis when the war broke out, the labor bureaucracy played the role of a reactionary factor. That is undoubtedly correct. But that does not mean that the labor movement will be able to get along in the future without a big organizational apparatus, without an entire stratum of people devoted specifically to the service of the proletarian organization. We do not want to go back to the time when the labor movement was so weak that it could get along without its own employees and functionaries, but rather to go forward to the time in which the labor movement itself will be something different; in which the stormy mass movement of the proletariat will *subordinate* the stratum of functionaries to itself; in which the routine will be destroyed, bureaucratic corrosion swept out; which will bring new people to the surface, infuse them with fighting courage, fill them with a new spirit.

The association of the "leaders" has dealt a heavy blow to the cause of the workers. Not only those labor leaders who hail from the bourgeoisie but also those who hail from the working class, who were elected by the workers and who owe their positions to working-class democracy. That is undoubtedly true. But that does not mean that the idea of democracy has therefore collapsed. . . .

The poisonous weed of labor bureaucracy grew in the soil of the "peaceful" epoch, not because of, but despite, the democratic organization. Only opportunism—a form of expression corresponding to that period—and not the democratic organizational principle, has suffered bankruptcy. New times will come and we shall hear new songs. As soon as the masses themselves enter the historical arena they will put an end to the uncontrollable dealings of the labor bureaucracy. The coming new epoch will bring forth a new generation of leaders and new forms of control by the working masses themselves over their deputies and representatives.

We do not at all wish to contend that the entire crisis can

be explained by the treachery of the leaders. The treachery of the leaders in itself can only be explained by more profound causes inherent in the period. But not everything can be unshouldered on the period. The fact of the betrayal by the leaders must not be passed over in silence. Treachery has been committed. It is necessary to call things by their name. It is our task not only to explain the causes of opportunism but also to *combat* opportunism. It is our duty not only to trace down the causes of the treachery, but also to unmask the traitors and to render them harmless.

The betrayal by the official leaders of the German Social Democracy, the counterrevolutionary role of the party and trade union bureaucracy during the war, was so infamous that in the periodical of the people forming the Social Democratic "Center," in *Die Neue Zeit* of 1916, may be found such lines as the following, the pen products of Kautsky's cothinker, the lately deceased Gustave Eckstein: "The leaders were constrained to remain radical in words, in order to hold the masses behind them. In actuality, however, they aimed above all at obtaining petty reforms that could be achieved without great struggles. Out of habit the leaders developed a wise smile. The organization became more and more of an end in itself, which more and more dislodged the thought of achieving the final goal from their heads and from their hearts."

After two years of war the honest representatives of the "center" also had to admit that the present official organization of the German Social Democracy had become a counterrevolutionary factor, that the leaders had become "wise men." That is exactly what Rosa Luxemburg had said in her polemics against Kautsky as far back as 1912. . . .

In its essence this caste has become the tool of an enemy class. The members of this caste who formally wield the full power of the working class are in reality *the emissaries of bourgeois society in the camp of the proletariat.*

Opportunism and the labor aristocracy

Until very recently the question of the labor aristocracy and its conservative role in the labor movement has been treated as a problem almost unique to the *British* labor movement. The epoch of modern imperialism and the events in the labor movement of the entire world in connection with the World War have posed this question on a much wider scale. It has become one of the most basic questions of the labor movement *as a whole.* The victory of opportunism and social chauvinism in Germany—and not in Germany alone—is intimately bound up with the victory of the narrow, group interests of the relatively small group of labor aristocrats over the genuine interests of the many-millions-strong mass of workers, that constitutes *the working class.*

For many years Britain was the promised land of bourgeois influence upon the proletariat and consequently the promised land of opportunism. It has become commonplace in Socialist literature to recognize this circumstance as being conditioned by the monopolistic position of Britain in the world market. The surplus profits which the British bourgeoisie has derived thanks to this monopolistic position, have enabled it to bribe "its" workers and thereby to tear them loose from the socialist movement. But it would be false to believe that the magnanimity of the British capitalists was extended in equal measure to the entire working class. No, with these crumbs they bought off mainly the upper stratum of the working class—the labor aristocracy. That sufficed, under conditions otherwise favorable for the bourgeoisie, to demoralize the British labor movement.

Among the great masses of the *unskilled* proletariat indescribable poverty prevails even in Britain. Their condition has not been much better than the condition of their brothers in other countries. Even in the heyday of British capitalism there were in Britain considerable strata of unskilled workers who lived in circumstances not much better than those described by Frederick Engels in his *The Condition of the Working-Class in England*. . . .

The great mass of the unskilled workers led a lamentable existence. But a minority, the aristocrats of labor, were bribed with small crumbs. Thus the bourgeoisie beheaded the movement of the British proletariat, so to speak. In Britain *organized* workers and skilled workers for a long time were synonymous. In the epoch of the old trade unionism the better-situated skilled workers constituted the main mass of the trade union membership. But even in the epoch of the new trade unionism this state of affairs has remained the same by and large.[8] The British trade unions still do not embrace more than a fifth of all the workers today. Many millions of women workers and of the most poorly paid unskilled workers are still unorganized, still outside the trade unions.

In 1902 Kautsky wrote, in characterizing the "upper strata of the British working class" (i.e., the labor aristocracy), that "today indeed they are scarcely more than little bourgeois and are distinguished from them only by a somewhat greater lack of culture. Their highest ideal consists in aping their masters and in imitating their hypocritical respectability, their admiration for wealth, however it may be obtained, and their spiritless manner of killing their leisure time. The emancipation of their class appears to them as a foolish dream. Consequently, it is football, boxing, horse racing, and gambling which move them the most deeply and to which their entire leisure time, their individual powers, and their material means are devoted."[9]

These "little bourgeois"—the labor aristocracy—served the big bourgeoisie as the best means of introducing bourgeois ideas into the laboring mass. By throwing down to these "little bourgeois" a few crumbs from their richly decked imperialist table, the big bourgeoisie made of them faithful watchdogs of the capitalist system. With the aid of a thin golden thread it bound them firmly to the bandwagon of imperialism, made them into *agents of the bourgeoisie*, destined to demoralize systematically the labor movement and to inculcate it with the virus of opportunism. The "little bourgeois" became the most reliable advance guards of the imperialist bourgeoisie in the camp of the working class.

When Kautsky speaks of the bourgeois "respectability" of these British "little bourgeois," he is only continuing in the tradition of Marx and Engels. Both of the founders of scientific socialism, who lived in England for a long time and therefore had the opportunity of acquainting themselves at first hand with the reactionary role of the labor aristocrats, advised their disciples continually to make just such an evaluation of the "little bourgeois" as we have found in Kautsky's passage above.

"The most repugnant thing here (in Britain—G.Z.) is the bourgeois 'respectability', which has grown deep into the bones of the workers! The division of society into innumerable strata, each recognised without question, each with its own pride but also its inborn respect for its 'betters' and 'superiors', is so old and firmly established that the bourgeois still find it fairly easy to get their bait accepted. I am not at all sure, for instance, that John Burns is not secretly prouder of his popularity with Cardinal Manning, the Lord Mayor, and the bourgeoisie in general than of his popularity with his own class. And Champion—an ex-lieutenant—has always intrigued with bourgeois and especially conservative elements, preaching socialism at the parsons' Church Congress, etc. And even Tom Mann, whom I regard as the best of the lot, is fond of mentioning that he will be lunching with the Lord Mayor."[10] That is what Frederick Engels wrote as far back as 1889.

Even earlier, in 1882, Engels wrote in a letter to Kautsky, which is devoted particularly to the question of the attitude of the British workers toward colonial policy, as follows: "You ask me what the English workers think about colonial policy. Well, exactly the same as they think about politics in general: the same as the bourgeoisie think. There is no workers' party here, there are only Conservatives and Liberal-Radicals, and the workers are cheerfully consuming their share of England's monopoly of the world market and the colonies."[11]

Here we see a direct indication of the fact that the bourgeoisie *bribes* the workers by leaving them little tidbits from among the multitude of benefits which the British monopoly on the world market and in the colonies nets them. . . .

In 1877 Marx writes of the "shameful trades union congress at Leicester . . . where the bourgeois played the role of patrons, among them a certain Mr. Th. Brassey, a multimillionaire . . . and the son of the notorious Brassey of the railroads, whose 'enterprise' is all Europe and Asia."[12]

In 1893 Engels upbraids the "socialist" Fabians in the following words: "The Fabians are a gang of careerists here in London who have understanding enough to realise the inevitability of the social revolution, but who could not possibly entrust this gigantic task to the raw proletariat alone and are therefore kind enough to put themselves at the head. Fear of the revolution is their fundamental principle. . . . Hence their tactics of not resolutely fighting the Liberals as adversaries but of pushing them on towards Socialist conclusions and therefore of intriguing with them, of permeating Liberalism with Socialism. . . . These people have of course many bourgeois followers and therefore money. . . .

"It is a critical moment for the movement here. . . . There was a moment when it nearly came under the wing of Champion—who consciously or unconsciously works just as much for the Tories as the Fabians do for the Liberals. . . . [But] socialism has penetrated the masses in the industrial districts enormously in the last few years and I am counting on these masses to keep the leaders in hand."[13]

These were the views of Marx and Engels on the "little bourgeois," the labor aristocracy. They stigmatized the antirevolutionary position of these strata unsparingly, whether it expressed itself in the policies of trade unionism or in the socialist organization of the Fabians. From every word uttered by Marx and Engels on this question, it is clearly evident how fatal for the cause of the workers, how disastrous for the socialist struggle of the proletariat, they considered the particular attitude of the labor aristocracy.

Marx and Engels derived their generalizations regarding the role of the labor bureaucracy mainly from their observations of the process of development of the working class in Britain. It was in Britain, moreover, that Marx made his studies of capitalism in general. In his *Capital,* also, Marx draws above all else from the experiences of British capitalism. But a great deal of water has passed under the bridge since then. The conservative role of the labor aristocracy may be observed today, not only in Britain, but in a large number of other countries.

Let us take the Netherlands, for example. Here is a small country that does not dream today of dominating the world market. But in this country there is a bourgeoisie bursting with wealth, whose few remnants of past colonial grandeur still bring it annually a golden shower of enormously large profits. Of these unheard-of profits of the Dutch imperialist bourgeoisie, only the "upper" strata of the workers enjoy a crumb or two, but that suffices to constitute them into a labor aristocracy and a conservative, counterrevolutionary force.

And in America? Do we not witness the spectacle there of a tiny group of labor aristocrats, bought out and nurtured by the financial oligarchy, rising on the backs of a millions-strong mass of oppressed workers—particularly of immigrants and Negroes? Are not Gompers and Company agents of the bourgeoisie in the circles of the "aristocrats of labor," and are not the latter, in turn, agents of Gompers in the camp of the working class? On the one hand, workers are shot down in the course of purely economic strikes; on the other, Gompers and the other "knights of labor" are decorated with ever greater honors, almost with the title of government minister.

Or in Australia. The social-liberals treasure Australia as the promised land, in which a coal miner can become a minister. But what has actually happened? Here too, a small parasitic band of labor leaders—Messrs. Fisher, Hughes, and Company—rise upon the shoulders of the oppressed mass of unskilled workers. Brought to the surface by a little group of labor aristocrats, they are betraying the interests of the working class with a cynicism unprecedented in history. The crisis created by the outbreak of the World War has thrown a particularly strong light upon this despicable treachery of the "labor leaders."

This same sort of bribery took place among the "upper strata" of the workers in Germany as well. Under different conditions, in a somewhat different form, it ran its course in the land of the "classic Social Democracy." But the historical meaning of the transformation undergone by the heads of the German working class, in the persons of the leaders of their trade unions and of their so-called Social Democratic Party, is not the same. There is no serious difference between Legien, Gompers, Fisher, and Henderson. Legien is not a minister as yet, but for reasons entirely outside his control. In the period immediately ahead of us he may not get any further than the ministerial antechamber. The Prussian junkers will continue to extend only one finger at a time to him. But he is, nevertheless, only a "labor lieutenant of the capitalist class." And not only Legien, but naturally also Scheidemann and Südekum, as well as all their doubles who speak a different language.

The process of the transition of the German labor aristocracy to the side of the bourgeoisie naturally did not begin yesterday. The corruption of the labor aristocracy began with the entrance of German imperialism into the world arena. . . .

What indeed, is the basic thesis of Cunow, Legien, Winnig, Lensch, Scheidemann, and the like? We, they say, support "our" government and "our" bourgeoisie, not at all because we like its looks. No, the interests of the German *working class* demand an ever stronger development of "our" fatherland's capitalism, demand that the economic progress of our country proceed as rapidly and as freely as possible, that "we" find a sufficiently great number of export markets, of sources of raw materials, of spheres of influence of "our" capital, and so on. Only then will the demand for labor power be big enough, only then will the living standard of the workers rise. When our capitalists make more profits there will be something left over for the workers as well.

But the same picture unfolds before us on the opposite side. It is not only "we" alone that are interested in the profits of "our" bourgeoisie; the workers of other countries that compete with "us" have identical interests in relation to "their" bourgeoisie. As soon as the contest for colonies, for the "freedom of the seas," has been sharpened to its highest pitch, war breaks out. What is to be done? It is a tragic necessity. The workers would naturally prefer to settle such matters peacefully, but that is not always possible. War has become a fact. What should the German workers do? Should they refuse to support their government and their bourgeoisie? But in that case, Germany will suffer defeat. And that will mean that the development of capitalism in Germany will be retarded, that the demand for labor power will decline, that the German workers will be forced to emigrate in order to earn their bread on foreign shores, to content themselves with low wages. What else can the German workers do if they are to avoid this misfortune? Only one thing: support "their" government, "their" imperialism. We know—Legien, Lensch, and Winnig say—that imperialism has its bad features, that it is bound up with wars, and so on. But these are far outweighed by its good features. Thanks to imperialism the living standard of our working class has been rising. We know, say these leaders of the official German Social Democracy, that when we support our imperialism, we thereby take up arms against the workers of other countries. That is truly very sad—but we have no choice in the matter. A tragic necessity remains a necessity nevertheless.

And what does this tragic necessity really prove? Only that in practice, in living reality, the actual interests of the workers of the various countries do not at all coincide. Often the interests of the workers in one country stand in an irreconcilable conflict with the interests of the workers of another country. "Workers of all countries, unite!" That sounds very good, but what can be done if the economic interests, practically speaking, do not unite the proletarians of the various countries, but rather divide them? . . .

One small question, however, must still be examined. *Is it true,* as the social chauvinists contend, that the whole working class benefits, and their wages and living standards rise, when the imperialism of their country is flourishing? Or have not Legien, Lensch (as well as their imitators) perhaps *confused the working class with the labor aristocracy?* And, in the case of the latter, have they not also confused a transitory material advantage with much more profound and more permanent interests? . . .

It is clear that imperialism does not result in any advantages whatsoever *for the working class as a whole.* But it cannot be denied that for a *certain minority* of skilled workers, for the *labor aristocracy,* a few crumbs may fall off from the imperialist table. . . .

But it is a *dwindling minority* of the working class. The experience of the World War has proved this in particularly striking fashion. The condition of the great mass of workers has—due to the frightfully high cost of living and the suspension of the protective labor laws, etc.—become considerably more *miserable.* Millions of women and children working at starvation wages have been drawn into the process of production. In these two years of war, the economic situation of the entire great mass of, let us say, the British workers, has undergone an absolute deterioration. Only a small minority—some two million workers—have succeeded in retaining their former real wages (i.e., an increase in wages corresponding to the rise in the prices of the necessities most in demand); only in the rarest cases are present-day wages higher than those of prewar days.

Yet there can be no doubt as to the existence of a small layer of labor aristocrats to whom the cannon and munition kings do throw a bone occasionally from their rich feast of war profits. This minority made good wages even before the war and has enjoyed still higher wages during the war. All kinds of privileges were granted this minority before the war, also. During the course of the war these privileges have become far more valuable for these aristocrats of labor. It is sufficient to point out that this labor aristocracy *has not been sent to the front* in most cases. The industrialists need them at home; they are indispensable as the element under whose direction the ordinary workers, the women, the youth, and the children are carrying on their work in the factories and in the mills and mines.

It is these very narrow, group interests of this minority of privileged labor aristocrats that the social chauvinists have confused with the interests of the working class. This confusion is quite understandable when we grasp the fact that the leaders of the trade unions and of the official Social Democracy hail, in their majority, from that very same environment of the labor aristocracy. The labor aristocracy and the labor bureaucracy are two blood brothers. When the social chauvinists speak of the interests of the working class, they have in mind—often quite unconsciously—the interests of the labor aristocracy. But here too, it is not really a matter of genuine interests in the broader meaning of the word, so much as of immediate material advantages. This is absolutely not one and the same thing. Marxists have never held the view that the realization of the interests of the workers means to fill their pockets as much as possible. From the point of view of interests, understood in the more profound sense of the term, when the labor aristocracy goes over to the side of the bourgeoisie, it is committing *treason against itself*. For the "aristocrats of labor" remain wage slaves, after all. Temporarily they do enjoy a slight advantage, to be sure, but they thereby undermine their own position and violate the unity of the working class. They sell their birthright for a mess of pottage. They retard the erection of a new order in society which will of necessity free them, the "aristocrats" themselves, from wage slavery. They become a tool of reaction. . . .

To foster splits between the various strata of the working class, to promote competition among them, to segregate the upper stratum from the rest by corrupting it and by making it an agency for bourgeois "respectability"—that is entirely in the interests of the bourgeoisie. Even if we were to disregard the *political* interests of the working class, the social chauvinists would still be traitors to the cause of the workers. For even in the field of protecting the *economic* interests they cannot see further than the end of their noses. They identify economic interests with a temporary advantage amounting to a few more pennies. They split the working class inside of every country and thereby intensify and aggravate the split between the working classes of different countries. Thanks to the common efforts of the bourgeoisie and the social chauvinists, the world proletariat is being split both horizontally and vertically, if we may be permitted to use these terms.

We have said that the official "European" labor organizations—particularly its leading strata—are recruited in the main from the better-paid workers, the labor aristocracy. Is that correct? Is there sufficient objective and well-founded evidence to substantiate this contention? These proofs are, beyond a doubt, at hand.

Let us turn once more to the *German* labor movement as the classic example of a labor movement in this past epoch. The composition of the German Social Democratic Party and of the German trade unions is certainly more proletarian than that of any other "European" party. And what do we see? The German Social Democracy possesses no extensive statistics regarding the social composition of its whole party organization. But such statistics do exist for the city of Berlin and may, to a certain extent, be regarded as typical for the entire party.

We have before us an excellent piece of statistical research regarding the composition of the Berlin Social Democratic organization; it was compiled some eight or nine years ago, but may still be considered as quite valid even today.

Berlin is the largest labor center and the strongest pillar of German Social Democracy. The data relates to the years 1906 and 1907; they encompass some 53,106 organized members of the Social Democratic Party (81 percent of all the members organized into the Social Democratic Party in Berlin at that time). At first glance two circumstances command our attention in this extremely interesting piece of statistical research. First, the existence of a numerically strong group of nonworkers in the Social Democratic organization, who are designated as "self-employed." Second, the relatively *small* percentage of party members recruited from the mass of unskilled workers. The group of "self-employed," that is, people who do *not* live by the sale of their labor power, consists of some 5,228 (out of 53,106), i.e., amounts to 9.8 percent of all the party members under investigation. Nearly 10 percent of all the organized Social Democrats in the city of Berlin and its environs are, therefore, not workers. . . .

Undoubtedly a distinct petty-bourgeois current is introduced into the Social Democratic Party by this stratum of the self-employed. Thousands of innkeepers, hundreds of owners of small factories, merchants, and independent tradesmen—these are not individual persons who have adopted the point of view of the proletariat. This is an entire, distinct stratum which has retained its own interests, its own psychology, its own mode of thinking.

On the other hand, we find the following things worthy of note in these Berlin statistics: The authors of the work have segregated the unskilled workers into a separate category under the classification of "workers"—without any further supplementary description. And what is the result? The unskilled workers amounted to 14.9 percent, all told, of the entire number of members surveyed of the Berlin Social Democratic organization. . . . Thus it follows that the bulk of the membership of the Berlin Social Democratic organization is composed of *trained*, of *skilled workers*. In other words, *the predominant mass of the membership of the Social Democratic organization consists of the better-paid strata of labor—of those strata from which the greatest section of the labor aristocracy arises.*

This conclusion is also confirmed by the statistics regarding the trade unions, which are particularly thoroughgoing in the research work we have mentioned. What branches show the highest percentage in trade union organization? Among the compositors and pressmen, 90.6 percent are organized (of the 10,986 printers employed in Berlin, 9,850 are members of the free trade unions). Among the lithographers, 90.5 percent are organized; among the engravers, 75.6 percent; among the metalworkers, 68.7 percent. In the textile industry, on the other hand, the organized workers are only 21.4 percent of the total. Of the garment workers, only 10 percent are organized; of the transport workers, only 25.3 percent; of the tobacco workers, 34.3 percent; of the bakers, 34.1 percent; of the shoe workers, 34.7 percent. The picture is the same throughout. No matter how big the membership of the free trade unions may be (before the outbreak of the war they comprised over 3 million organized workers)—they do *not* include in their ranks the great mass of the unskilled workers. The free trade unions have succeeded in organizing only a small minority (one-fifth) of the workers. The predominant mass of their workers are likewise recruited from among the skilled, better-paid category of workers.

Returning once more to the statistics covering the membership of the Social Democratic Party of Greater Berlin, we can draw the following balance sheet: The great mass of the unskilled workers, of the most exploited and most oppressed section of the proletariat, is very feebly represented in the German Social Democratic Party. It constitutes within it a group of no more than 15 percent in strength, at best. On the opposite pole to this group we have a group of nonworkers, namely, innkeepers, barbers, merchants, and so on, that is numerically almost as strong (10 percent). This group may be smaller in number than that of the unskilled workers. But its influence on party affairs—that may be said a priori—is incomparably bigger. The self-employed are far more mobile; far less preoccupied with physical labor; dispose of a far greater amount of free time; are in a position to offer the party material services; their social position is on a much higher plane; they are the ones that are put up as the party's candidates in the elections, etc. *Between* these two groups, which represent opposite poles, stand the better situated, more skilled workers, the real props of the Social Democratic Party organization. The main body, the central organism of the party, is thus formed of these strata of *skilled* workers.

In the previous section we have acquainted ourselves with the social composition of the electorate of the German Social Democracy and discovered the existence of a large group of petty bourgeois among it. The same symptoms—even though of a different numerical relationship, perhaps—can be established in the composition of the party organization as well. . . .

The official German Social Democracy has actually become more and more of a radical-democratic coalition party. That is just what the opportunists wanted and they have led the party on this path with full consciousness. Bernstein was right in one respect, when he said at the beginning of his campaign against Marxism: We need not fear to call things by their right names—to say that we are simply a party of democratic reforms.

The petty-bourgeois elements have pitched their tents in the ranks of the official Social Democracy—they constitute one of the sources of opportunism. The labor aristocracy—that is the second source, the second channel, through which the contagion of opportunism penetrated the party. . . .

In the course of its development the German Social Democracy is losing more and more of its revolutionary "venom." Its need for peace and for order is becoming constantly greater. It is becoming a *conservative* party. . . .

The crisis of the World War has proved that the official German Social Democracy is not only not revolutionary, but directly counterrevolutionary. Only in *opposition* to this official Social Democracy, only in the struggle against the specific "interests" of the labor aristocracy, can the road be paved for a truly socialist movement in Germany, as well as in the other countries.

In the spring of 1916 Lenin wrote *Imperialism, the Highest Stage of Capitalism,* a scientific examination of the nature of modern imperialism and its place in history, which ranks among his central works of the 1914–17 period.[14] It was written for publication in tsarist Russia, and carefully formulated with an eye to the censor. Its key political conclusions on the relationship of imperialism to the growth of opportunism and the crisis in the Socialist movement are spelled out in the following article, published in December 1916 in the second issue of *Sbornik Sotsial-Demokrata*.

Imperialism and the split in socialism[15]

by V.I. Lenin

Is there any connection between imperialism and the monstrous and disgusting victory opportunism (in the form of social-chauvinism) has gained over the labour movement in Europe?

This is the fundamental question of modern socialism. And having in our Party literature fully established, first, the imperialist character of our era and of the present war, and, second, the inseparable historical connection between social-chauvinism and opportunism, as well as the intrinsic similarity of their political ideology, we can and must proceed to analyse this fundamental question.

We have to begin with as precise and full a definition of

imperialism as possible. Imperialism is a specific historical stage of capitalism. Its specific character is three-fold: imperialism is (1) monopoly capitalism; (2) parasitic, or decaying capitalism; (3) moribund capitalism. The supplanting of free competition by monopoly is the fundamental economic feature, the *quintessence* of imperialism. Monopoly manifests itself in five principal forms: (1) cartels, syndicates and trusts—the concentration of production has reached a degree which gives rise to these monopolistic associations of capitalists; (2) the monopolistic position of the big banks—three, four or five giant banks manipulate the whole economic life of America, France, Germany; (3) seizure of the sources of *raw material* by the trusts and the financial oligarchy (finance capital is monopoly industrial capital merged with bank capital); (4) the (economic) partition of the world by the international cartels has *begun*. There are already over *one hundred* such international cartels, which command the *entire* world market and divide it "amicably" among themselves—until war *re*divides it. The export of capital, as distinct from the export of commodities under non-monopoly capitalism, is a highly characteristic phenomenon and is closely linked with the economic and territorial-political partition of the world; (5) the territorial partition of the world (colonies) *is completed.*

Imperialism, as the highest stage of capitalism in America and Europe, and later in Asia, took final shape in the period 1898–1914. The Spanish-American War (1898), the Anglo-Boer War (1899–1902), the Russo-Japanese War (1904–05) and the economic crisis in Europe in 1900 are the chief historical landmarks in the new era of world history.

The fact that imperialism is parasitic or decaying capitalism is manifested first of all in the tendency to decay, which is characteristic of *every* monopoly under the system of private ownership of the means of production. The difference between the democratic-republican and the reactionary-monarchist imperialist bourgeoisie is obliterated precisely because they are both rotting alive (which by no means precludes an extraordinarily rapid development of capitalism in individual branches of industry, in individual countries, and in individual periods). Secondly, the decay of capitalism is manifested in the creation of a huge stratum of *rentiers*, capitalists who live by "clipping coupons". In each of the four leading imperialist countries—England, U.S.A., France and Germany—capital in securities amounts to 100,000 or 150,000 *million* francs, from which each country derives an annual income of no less than five to eight thousand million. Thirdly, export of capital is parasitism raised to a high pitch. Fourthly, "finance capital strives for domination, not freedom". Political reaction *all along* the line is a characteristic feature of imperialism. Corruption, bribery on a huge scale and all kinds of fraud. Fifthly, the exploitation of oppressed nations—which is inseparably connected with annexations—and especially the exploitation of colonies by a handful of "Great" Powers, increasingly transforms the "civilised" world into a parasite on the body of hundreds of millions in the uncivilised nations. The Roman proletarian lived at the expense of society. Modern society lives at the expense of the modern proletarian. Marx specially stressed this profound observation of Sismondi. Imperialism somewhat changes the situation. A privileged upper stratum of the proletariat in the imperialist countries lives partly at the expense of hundreds of millions in the uncivilised nations.

It is clear why imperialism is *moribund* capitalism, capitalism in *transition* to socialism: monopoly, which grows *out of* capitalism, is *already* dying capitalism, the beginning of its transition to socialism. The tremendous *socialisation* of labour by imperialism (what its apologists—the bourgeois economists—call "interlocking") produces the same result.

Advancing this definition of imperialism brings us into complete contradiction to K. Kautsky, who refuses to regard imperialism as a "phase of capitalism" and defines it as a *policy* "preferred" by finance capital, a tendency of "industrial" countries to annex "agrarian" countries.* Kautsky's definition is thoroughly false from the theoretical standpoint. What distinguishes imperialism is the rule *not* of industrial capital, but of finance capital, the striving to annex *not* agrarian countries, particularly, but *every kind* of country. Kautsky *divorces* imperialist politics from imperialist economics, he divorces monopoly in politics from monopoly in economics in order to pave the way for his vulgar bourgeois reformism, such as "disarmament", "ultra-imperialism" and similar nonsense. The whole purpose and significance of this theoretical falsity is to obscure the *most profound* contradictions of imperialism and thus justify the theory of "unity" with the apologists of imperialism, the outright social-chauvinists and opportunists. . . .

Neither Marx nor Engels lived to see the imperialist epoch of world capitalism, which began not earlier than 1898–1900. But it has been a peculiar feature of England that even in the middle of the nineteenth century she already revealed at least *two* major distinguishing features of imperialism: (1) vast colonies, and (2) monopoly profit (due to her monopoly position in the world market). In both respects England at that time was an exception among capitalist countries, and Engels and Marx, analysing this exception, quite clearly and definitely indicated its *connection* with the (temporary) victory of opportunism in the English labour movement.

In a letter to Marx, dated October 7, 1858, Engels wrote: ". . . The English proletariat is actually becoming more and more bourgeois, so that this most bourgeois of all nations is apparently aiming ultimately at the possession of a bourgeois aristocracy and a bourgeois proletariat *alongside* the bourgeoisie. For a nation which exploits the whole world this is of course to a certain extent justifiable."[16] In a letter to Sorge, dated September 21, 1872, Engels informs him that

Hales kicked up a big row in the Federal Council of the International and secured a vote of censure on Marx for saying that "the English labour leaders had sold themselves". Marx wrote to Sorge on August 4, 1874: "As to the urban workers here [in England], it is a pity that the whole pack of leaders did not get into Parliament. This would be the surest way of getting rid of the whole lot." In a letter to Marx, dated August 11, 1881, Engels speaks about "those very worst English trade unions which allow themselves to be led by men sold to, or at least paid by, the bourgeoisie". . . . In a letter [by Engels], dated April 19, 1890: "But *under* the surface the movement [of the working class in England] is going on, is embracing ever wider sections and mostly just among the hitherto stagnant *lowest* [Engels's italics] strata. The day is no longer far off when this mass *will* suddenly *find itself*, when it will dawn upon it that it itself is this colossal mass in motion." [17] On March 4, 1891: "The failure of the collapsed Dockers' Union; the 'old' conservative trade unions, *rich* and therefore cowardly, remain lone in the field. . . ." September 14, 1891: at the Newcastle Trade Union Congress the old unionists, opponents of the eight-hour day, were defeated "and the bourgeois papers recognise the defeat of the *bourgeois labour party*" (Engels's italics throughout). . . .

That these ideas, which were repeated by Engels over the course of decades, were also expressed by him publicly, in the press, is proved by his preface to the second edition of *The Condition of the Working Class in England*, 1892.[18] Here he speaks of an "aristocracy among the working class", of a "privileged minority of the workers", in contradistinction to the "great mass of working people". "A small, privileged, protected minority" of the working class alone was "permanently benefited" by the privileged position of England in 1848–68, whereas "the great bulk of them experienced at best but a temporary improvement". . . . "With the breakdown of that [England's industrial] monopoly, the English working class will lose that privileged position. . . ." The members of the "new" unions of the unskilled workers, "had this immense advantage, that their minds were virgin soil, entirely free from the inherited 'respectable' bourgeois prejudices which hampered the brains of the better situated 'old unionists'". . . . "The so-called workers' representatives" in England are people "who are forgiven their being members of the working class because they themselves would like to drown their quality of being workers in the ocean of their liberalism". . . .

We have deliberately quoted the direct statements of Marx and Engels at rather great length in order that the reader may study them *as a whole*. And they should be studied, they are worth carefully pondering over. For they are the *pivot* of the tactics in the labour movement that are dictated by the objective conditions of the imperialist era. . . .

Secondly, why does England's monopoly explain the (temporary) victory of opportunism in England? Because monopoly yields *superprofits*, i.e., a surplus of profits over and above the capitalist profits that are normal and customary all over the world. The capitalists *can* devote a part (and not a small one, at that!) of these superprofits to bribe *their own* workers, to create something like an alliance (recall the celebrated "alliances" described by the Webbs of English trade unions and employers) between the workers of the given nation and their capitalists *against* the other countries. England's industrial monopoly was already destroyed by the end of the nineteenth century. That is beyond dispute. But *how* did this destruction take place? Did *all* monopoly disappear?

If that were so, Kautsky's "theory" of conciliation (with the opportunists) would to a certain extent be justified. But it is *not* so, and that is just the point. Imperialism *is* monopoly capitalism. Every cartel, trust, syndicate, every giant bank *is* a monopoly. Superprofits have not disappeared; they still remain. The exploitation of *all* other countries by one privileged, financially wealthy country remains and has become more intense. A handful of wealthy countries—there are only four of them, if we mean independent, really gigantic, "modern" wealth: England, France, the United States and Germany—have developed monopoly to vast proportions, they obtain *super*profits running into hundreds, if not thousands, of millions, they "ride on the backs" of hundreds and hundreds of millions of people in other countries and fight among themselves for the division of the particularly rich, particularly fat and particularly easy spoils.

This, in fact, is the economic and political essence of imperialism, the profound contradictions of which Kautsky glosses over instead of exposing.

The bourgeoisie of an imperialist "Great" Power *can economically* bribe the upper strata of "its" workers by spending on this a hundred million or so francs a year, for its *super*profits most likely amount to about a thousand million. And how this little sop is divided among the labour ministers, "labor representatives" (remember Engels's splendid analysis of the term), labour members of war industries committees, labour officials, workers belonging to the narrow craft unions, office employees, etc., etc., is a secondary question.

Between 1848 and 1868, and to a certain extent even later, only England enjoyed a monopoly: *that is why* opportunism could prevail there for decades. *No* other countries possessed either very rich colonies or an industrial monopoly.

The last third of the nineteenth century saw the transition to the new, imperialist era. Finance capital *not* of one, but of several, though very few, Great Powers enjoys a monopoly. (In Japan and Russia the monopoly of military power, vast territories, or special facilities for robbing minority nationalities, China, etc., partly supplements, partly takes the place of, the monopoly of modern, up-to-date finance capital.)

This difference explains why England's monopoly position *could* remain *unchallenged* for decades. The monopoly of modern finance capital is being frantically challenged; the era of imperialist wars has begun. It was possible in those days to bribe and corrupt the working class of *one* country for decades. This is now improbable, if not impossible. But on the other hand, *every* imperialist "Great" Power can and does bribe *smaller* strata (than in England in 1848–68) of the "labour aristocracy". Formerly a *"bourgeois labour party"*, to use Engels's remarkably profound expression, could arise only in one country, because it alone enjoyed a monopoly, but, on the other hand, it could exist for a long time. Now a *"bourgeois labour party" is inevitable* and typical in *all* imperialist countries; but in view of the desperate struggle they are waging for the division of spoils, it is improbable that such a party can prevail for long in a number of countries. For the trusts, the financial oligarchy, high prices, etc., while *enabling* the bribery of a handful in the top layers, are increasingly oppressing, crushing, ruining and torturing the *mass* of the proletariat and the semi-proletariat.

On the one hand, there is the tendency of the bourgeoisie and the opportunists to convert a handful of very rich and privileged nations into "eternal" parasites on the body of the rest of mankind, to "rest on the laurels" of the exploitation of Negroes, Indians, etc., keeping them in subjection with the aid of the excellent weapons of extermination provided by modern militarism. On the other hand, there is the tendency of the *masses,* who are more oppressed than before and who bear the whole brunt of imperialist wars, to cast off this yoke and to overthrow the bourgeoisie. It is in the struggle between these two tendencies that the history of the labour movement will now inevitably develop. For the first tendency is not accidental; it is "substantiated" economically. In *all* countries the bourgeoisie has already begotten, fostered and secured for itself "bourgeois labour parties" of social-chauvinists. The difference between a definitely formed party, like Bissolati's in Italy, for example, which is fully social-imperialist, and, say, the semi-formed near-party of the Potresovs, Gvozdyovs, Bulkins, Chkheidzes, Skobelevs and Co., is an immaterial difference. The important thing is that, economically, the desertion of a stratum of the labour aristocracy to the bourgeoisie has matured and become an accomplished fact; and this economic fact, this shift in class relations, will find political form, in one shape or another, without any particular "difficulty".

On the economic basis referred to above, the political institutions of modern capitalism—press, parliament, associations, congresses, etc.—have created *political* privileges and sops for the respectful, meek, reformist and patriotic office employees and workers, corresponding to the economic privileges and sops. Lucrative and soft jobs in the government or on the war industries committees, in parliament and on diverse committees, on the editorial staffs of "respectable", legally published newspapers or on the management councils of no less respectable and "bourgeois law-abiding" trade unions—this is the bait by which the imperialist bourgeoisie attracts and rewards the representatives and supporters of the "bourgeois labour parties".

The mechanics of political democracy works in the same direction. Nothing in our times can be done without elections; nothing can be done without the masses. And in this era of printing and parliamentarism it is *impossible* to gain the following of the masses without a widely ramified, systematically managed, well-equipped system of flattery, lies, fraud, juggling with fashionable and popular catchwords, and promising all manner of reforms and blessings to the workers right and left—as long as they renounce the revolutionary struggle for the overthrow of the bourgeoisie. I would call this system Lloyd-Georgism, after the English Minister Lloyd George, one of the foremost and most dexterous representatives of this system in the classic land of the "bourgeois labour party". A first class bourgeois manipulator, an astute politician, a popular orator who will deliver any speeches you like, even r-r-revolutionary ones, to a labour audience, and a man who is capable of obtaining sizable sops for docile workers in the shape of social reforms (insurance, etc.), Lloyd George serves the bourgeoisie splendidly,** and serves it precisely *among* the workers, brings its influence *precisely* to the proletariat, to where the bourgeoisie needs it most and where it finds it most difficult to subject the masses morally.

And is there such a great difference between Lloyd George and the Scheidemanns, Legiens, Hendersons and Hyndmans, Plekhanovs, Renaudels and Co.? Of the latter, it may be objected, some will return to the revolutionary socialism of Marx. This is possible, but it is an insignificant difference in degree, if the question is regarded from its political, i.e., its mass aspect. Certain individuals among the present social-chauvinist leaders may return to the proletariat. But the social-chauvinist or (what is the same thing) opportunist *trend* can neither disappear nor "return" to the revolutionary proletariat. Wherever Marxism is popular among the workers, this political trend, this "bourgeois labour party", will swear by the name of Marx. It cannot be prohibited from doing this, just as a trading firm cannot be prohibited from using any particular label, sign or advertisement. It has always been the case in history that after the death of revolutionary leaders who were popular among the oppressed classes, their enemies have attempted to appropriate their names so as to deceive the oppressed classes.

The fact is that "bourgeois labour parties", as a political phenomenon, have already been formed in *all* the foremost capitalist countries, and that unless a determined and relentless struggle is waged all along the line against these parties—or groups, trends, etc., it is all the same—there can be no question of a struggle against imperialism, or of Marxism, or of a socialist labour movement. The Chkheidze faction, *Nashe Dyelo* and *Golos Truda* in Russia, and the O.C. supporters abroad are nothing but varieties of one *such* party. There is not the slightest reason for thinking that these parties will disappear *before* the social revolution. On the contrary, the nearer the revolution approaches, the more strongly it flares up and the more sudden and violent the transitions and leaps in its progress, the greater will be the part the struggle of the revolutionary mass stream against the opportunist petty-bourgeois stream will play in the labour movement. Kautskyism is not an independent trend, because it has no roots either in the masses or in the privileged stratum which has deserted to the bourgeoisie. But the danger of Kautskyism lies in the fact that, utilising the ideology of the past, it endeavours to reconcile the proletariat with the "bourgeois labour party", to preserve the unity of the proletariat with that party and thereby enhance the latter's prestige. The masses no longer follow the avowed social-chauvinists: Lloyd George has been hissed down at workers' meetings in England; Hyndman has left the party; the Renaudels and Scheidemanns, the Potresovs and Gvozdyovs are protected by the police. The Kautskyites' masked defence of the social-chauvinists is much more dangerous.

One of the most common sophistries of Kautskyism is its reference to the "masses". We do not want, they say, to break away from the masses and mass organisations! But just think how Engels put the question. In the nineteenth century the "mass organisations" of the English trade unions were on the side of the bourgeois labour party. Marx and Engels did not reconcile themselves to it on this ground; they exposed it. They did not forget, firstly, that the trade union organisations directly embraced a *minority of the proletariat*. In England then, as in Germany now, no more than one-fifth of the proletariat was organised. No one can seriously think it possible to organise the majority of the proletariat under capitalism. Secondly—and this is the main point—it is not so much a question of the size of an organisation, as of the real, objective significance of its policy: does its policy represent the masses, does it serve them, i.e., does it aim at their liberation from capitalism, or does it represent the interests of the minority, the minority's reconciliation with capitalism? The latter was true of England in the nineteenth century, and it is true of Germany, etc., now.

Engels draws a distinction between the "bourgeois labour party" of the *old* trade unions—the privileged minority—and the *"lowest* mass", the real majority, and appeals to the latter, who are *not* infected by "bourgeois respectability". This is the essence of Marxist tactics!

Neither we nor anyone else can calculate precisely what portion of the proletariat is following and will follow the social-chauvinists and opportunists. This will be revealed only by the struggle, it will be definitely decided only by the socialist revolution. But we know for certain that the "defenders of the fatherland" in the imperialist war *represent* only a minority. And it is therefore our duty, if we wish to remain socialists, to go down *lower* and *deeper,* to the real masses; this is the whole meaning and the whole purport of the struggle against opportunism. By exposing the fact that the opportunists and social-chauvinists are in reality betraying and selling the interests of the masses, that they are defending the temporary privileges of a minority of the workers, that they are the vehicles of bourgeois ideas and influences, that they are really allies and agents of the bourgeoisie, we teach the masses to appreciate their true political interests, to fight for socialism and for the revolution through all the long and painful vicissitudes of imperialist wars and imperialist armistices.

The only Marxist line in the world labour movement is to explain to the masses the inevitability and necessity of breaking with opportunism, to educate them for revolution by waging a relentless struggle against opportunism, to utilise the experiences of the war to expose, not conceal, the utter vileness of national-liberal labour politics.

* "Imperialism is a product of highly developed industrial capitalism. It consists in the striving of every industrial capitalist nation to subjugate and annex ever larger *agrarian* territories, irrespective of the nations that inhabit them" (Kautsky in *Die Neue Zeit,* September 11, 1914).

** I recently read an article in an English magazine by a Tory, a political opponent of Lloyd George, entitled "Lloyd George from the Standpoint of a Tory". The war opened the eyes of this opponent and made him realise what an excellent servant of the bourgeoisie this Lloyd George is! The Tories have made peace with him! [Footnotes in original]

V.I. Lenin

Chapter 12

Toward the new International

The Zimmerwald conference came under sharp criticism from right-wing leaders linked to the old International Socialist Bureau (ISB). One of the first such attacks came from the Dutch Social Democrats Hendrick van Kol and Willem Vliegen. They charged that the Zimmerwald conference had been made up only of representatives of small groups, who came together accidentally, and that it possessed no authority to set up a continuing body rival to the ISB.

On September 29, 1915, the International Socialist Committee in Bern (ISC), which had been elected by the Zimmerwald conference, issued a reply.

The delegates at Zimmerwald had included official Socialist representation from seven countries, the ISC reply explained, and these had done everything possible to reactivate the International Socialist Bureau. "Only when all these efforts failed did the Italian party take the initiative in calling the conference" that elected the ISC.

"This committee is not a competitor of the ISB," the ISC declaration continued. "It has a provisional character and will be dissolved as soon as *the ISB begins to struggle against the war in conformity with the decisions of Stuttgart, Copenhagen, and Basel,* and no longer makes its activity dependent on the accord of those Socialist parties that still support the war policy of the ruling class in their countries."[1]

This offer to dissolve the ISC had not been authorized by the Zimmerwald conference. It reflected the desire of the Zimmerwald majority to reunite with the social chauvinists in the old Second International framework.

Meanwhile, the challenge of Zimmerwald stirred the ISB leaders into activity. "The International is not dead," announced ISB secretary Camille Huysmans on January 9, 1916, to the congress of the Dutch Social Democratic Workers Party. Sharply attacking the Zimmerwald conference, he claimed that the official Socialist parties of the warring powers still recognized the ISB. Furthermore, Huysmans stated, separate gatherings of Socialist parties of neutral nations and of each warring bloc had come to common conclusions on the basis on which to seek peace. This basis, he said, was the right of all nations to self-determination, the democratization of diplomacy, compulsory arbitration of international conflicts, and progressive steps toward disarmament.[2]

Huysmans promised that a meeting of the ISB would be called as soon as all the main Socialist parties in the belligerent powers agreed on a policy of mutual amnesty. This would mean, for example, French Social Democrats agreeing to ignore German Social Democratic leaders' actions in supporting their own ruling class against France in the war. But such an amnesty proved to be impossible. Despite a flurry of activity promoting convocation of the ISB, the French and British official parties responded that an ISB meeting was inappropriate.

The only solid result of Huysmans's maneuver was to strengthen the will of the International Socialist Committee to function more independently. Acting on a suggestion made by the Zimmerwald Left in September 1915, it established an enlarged ISC, including representatives of each country—a structure similar to that of the ISB in the old International.

The first meeting of this body, held February 5–9, 1916, drew up a circular letter to all its affiliates, and called a new international conference.

At the February ISC meeting, "the relationship of ideological tendencies was proportionally much the same as at Zimmerwald," reported Gregory Zinoviev in *Sotsial-Demokrat*. "Yet the programmatic appeal was very much closer to what the Zimmerwald Left wanted. This appeal is not programmatically complete and does not give a clear and systematic evaluation of opportunism and Kautskyism. But it indicates the necessity of a 'revolutionary intervention' by the working class, evoking examples of 'fraternization in the trenches,' and calling for 'strikes, demonstrations, and people's movements.' It condemns 'any voluntary participation by workers in institutions serving national defense' and demands 'voting against the war credits regardless of the military situation.' it declares that 'every attempt to reestablish the International through a mutual amnesty by the discredited opportunist leaders is . . . a plot against socialism.' It says that 'so-called defense of the fatherland in this war is nothing other than a means of crass deception aimed at subjugating the peoples to imperialism.' When it says all this, it takes a step forward, away from Ledebour's 'swamp,' which had its way at Zimmerwald, toward revolutionary Social Democracy."[3]

Zinoviev did not believe that the majority in the ISC had changed its centrist orientation since the Zimmerwald conference. In a letter to other Bolshevik leaders, he posed the question: How could it happen that such a manifesto originated in a body with a membership like this?

"*The logic of the situation* works for us. Since people wish to expose Huysmans, Scheidemann, Renaudel—nothing else can be said except what we have said, and by so doing these people incidentally hit Kautsky and Co., although (in spite of us) they issue ardent 'invitations' to Kautsky and Haase, make advances to them, etc."[4]

The most important decision of the February ISC meeting was to call a new international conference in April. Among the many proposals prepared for the consideration of this conference was one of the Bolshevik Central Committee, drafted by Lenin. It gave a full reply to the "peace program" of Huysmans and Kautsky. It also underlined the vacillation of the ISC majority on the central issue of breaking with the social chauvinists and building a new International.

'We must explain that split is inevitable'[5]

Submitted by the RSDLP Central Committee

The question of the convocation of the International Socialist Bureau boils down to a fundamental question of principle, i.e., whether the old parties and the Second International can be united. Every step forward taken by the international labour movement along the road mapped out by Zimmerwald shows more and more clearly the inconsistency of the position adopted by the Zimmerwald majority; for, on the one hand, it identifies the policy of the old parties and of the Second International with *bourgeois* policy in the labour movement, with a policy which does not pursue the interests of the proletariat, but of the bourgeoisie (for example, the statement in the Zimmerwald Manifesto that the "capitalists" lie when they speak of "defence of the fatherland" in the present war; also the still more definite statements contained in the circular of the International Socialist Committee of February 10, 1916); on the other hand, the International Socialist Committee is afraid of a break with the International Socialist Bureau and has promised officially to dissolve when the Bureau reconvenes.

We state that not only was such a promise never voted on, but it was never even discussed in Zimmerwald.

The six months since Zimmerwald have proved that *actual* work in the spirit of Zimmerwald—not empty phrases but work—is bound up throughout the world with the split that is becoming deeper and wider. . . .

Actually, there is already a split throughout the world; two entirely irreconcilable working-class policies in relation to the war have crystallised. We must not close our eyes to this fact; to do so would only result in confusing the masses of the workers, in befogging their minds, in hindering the revolutionary mass struggle with which all Zimmerwaldists officially sympathise, and in strengthening the influence over the masses of those leaders whom the International Socialist Committee, in its circular of February 10, 1916, openly accuse of "misleading" the masses and of hatching a "plot" *(Pakt) against* socialism.

It is the social-chauvinists and Kautskyites of all countries who will undertake the task of restoring the bankrupt International Socialist Bureau. The task of the socialists is to explain to the masses the inevitability of a split with those who pursue a bourgeois policy under the flag of socialism.

The Internationale Group in Germany submitted two resolutions from its March conference for the upcoming gathering—one on the building of a new International and the other on Socialist action in parliament on the war question.[6] These were included along with the document submitted by the Bolshevik Central Committee and other conference materials in an issue of the ISC *Bulletin* published on the eve of the conference.

The Second International Socialist Zimmerwald Conference met April 24–30, 1916, in Kienthal, near Bern, Switzerland.[7] More than a dozen delegates, including Trotsky, Roland-Holst, Merrheim, and Bourderon, were denied travel documents and thus prevented from attending. Haase and Kautsky once again declined to come. The minutes record forty-three delegates representing Socialists in France, Germany, Italy, Poland, Portugal, Russia, Serbia, and Switzerland. There were two observers, one of whom was from Britain.

While the range of political currents represented was similar to that at Zimmerwald, the revolutionary left wing exerted a greater influence over the debates at Kienthal. The resolution of the Zimmerwald Left on the peace question was supported by twelve delegates, including three Bolsheviks and three members of the Polish-Lithuanian Social Democratic opposition. The support of three Swiss delegates reflected the left's growing influence in that party. The three other supporters, each of them new to the Zimmerwald Left, were Paul Frölich of the Socialist left in Bremen, Germany; G.M. Serrati, editor of *Avanti!* and a leader of the left current in the Italian party; and the Serbian Socialist Triša Kačlerović.

The left also joined forces on certain questions during the conference with Willi Münzenberg of the Socialist Youth International, the delegations of the German Spartacists and the Polish-Lithuanian Social Democracy's Central Executive Committee, the French delegate Henri Guilbeaux, and M.A. Natanson of the Russian Socialist Revolutionary Party.

The following resolution was submitted by the Zimmerwald Left to the conference.

Social Democracy and the question of peace[8]

I. The slogans of defense of national independence and of democracy have been used in an attempt to conceal the true character of the World War. As the war goes on, however, its true nature is more and more revealed. The war is a struggle among the capitalist great powers for a new division of the undeveloped countries, which are to become objects of exploitation by the various cliques of finance capital. But the division of these countries that results from the war will not be final.

Finance capital, strengthened during the World War by government borrowing and by the powerful concentration of capital, will rearm anew after the war in order to continue its plunder. It will thus prepare new world wars to divide up the Near East, the territories bordering on the Pacific Ocean, and those colonies belonging to weaker capitalist powers. Secret negotiations are now under way and treaties have already been concluded to expand the economic spheres of the existing alliances and thus serve these new goals of plunder (for example, plans for Central Europe [*Mitteleuropa*], the economic conference of the Entente powers, the new division of spheres of influence, the Anglo-Japanese and Russo-Japanese treaties, and so forth).

II. The imperialist bandits are forging in the inferno of the World War a peace that represents only a temporary agreement for the division of the spoils, and one that will therefore conjure up the danger of new wars. Yet petty-bourgeois forces, opportunists, and social pacifists (the center current of the German party, the Independent Labour Party, and so on) try to blind themselves and the masses to this reality. They chase after the mirage of a democratic peace, which is supposed to bring us the United States of Europe, compulsory arbitration courts, disarmament, democratized diplomacy, and so on. In fact all this amounts to a deception of the people, concealing and disguising the cruel reality of world politics.

The capitalist bourgeoisie of every great power is concerned only with its own profits. It uses its power to amass the greatest possible profits, and not to share them with weaker capitalist states. Each gang of capitalists draws extra profits from armaments, protective tariffs, and its own particular colonies. Capitalism's future, like its present reality, does not lie in disarmament, reconciliation, or democratic control over its plundering forays, but rather in strengthening and expanding the tyranny of finance-capitalist cliques and of their world imperialist politics. The utopian vision of a peaceful capitalism, free of war, serves to mislead the masses about the real state of affairs and divert them from the path of revolutionary struggle. For that reason the politics of social pacifism only fuels the fires of opportunism. Just as the imperialist bourgeoisie itself must conceal its real goals, opportunism must conceal its determination to weaken the revolutionary struggle and share in the spoils with the bourgeoisie.

III. While it threatens the proletariat with the gravest dangers, imperialism is digging its own grave. It is based upon a high concentration of production, control by a few banks, monopolization, and a highly developed technology. But these are the economic prerequisites for socialism, and they show that its time has come. At the same time, imperialism spurs the masses of workers into action through the enormous suffering brought on by the World War and its consequences: inflation, a worsening of the conditions for the trade union struggle, political reaction. In this way the alternative is placed before the workers: the struggle for socialism or degeneration and general exhaustion.

IV. The proletariat's revolutionary mass struggle for socialism will flare up out of the struggles of masses of workers against all the misery that the imperialist epoch has burdened them with: inflation, unemployment, increasing tax burdens, colonial adventures, and national oppression. This struggle will be carried out under the slogans of abolishing all the burdens of imperialism (cancellation of government debts) and winning unemployment relief, the democratic republic, repudiation of all annexations, liberation of the colonies, abolition of state boundaries, and national equality. All of these struggles will flow together into a mighty current—the struggle for political power, for socialism, and for the unification of the socialist peoples.

The only peace program of the Social Democracy is to call on the international proletariat to take up these struggles and to organize it for the assault against capitalism. Lower your weapons, and turn them against our common enemy—the capitalist governments. This is the International's message for peace.

For the delegation of the Central Committee of the Russian Social Democracy: V.I. Lenin, Gregory Zinoviev, Petrov [Inessa Armand].

—of the Regional Executive Committee of the Social Democracy of Russian Poland: Karl Radek, Mieczyslaw Bronski, Dabrowski [Wladislaw Stein].

—of the Bremen Opposition: Paul Frölich.[9]

Reports from each country were the first major item on the Kienthal conference agenda. The three parliamentary deputies present from France represented the centrist Longuet-Pressemane current. They were still voting for war credits, and delegates questioned them closely on their policies. The following statement on the war credits was initiated by the Zimmerwald Left and signed by nineteen left-wing delegates.

"Just as we declared at the Zimmerwald conference that the *abstention* of 'oppositional' German Social Democratic deputies on war credits was *inadequate* and discredited German Social Democracy, so we declare that *the conduct of the minority of the French parliamentary fraction, which approves war credits, is completely incompatible with socialism and with opposition to the war.*

"This stance converts all these deputies' *protests* against the war and the politics of the *union sacrée* (sacred unity) into impotent protest. It tends to *undermine all confidence in the Socialist Party* among the oppositional masses. It enormously weakens all the efforts of internationalist parties to establish international unity against the World War.

"(Signed:) Paul Graber, H. Guilbeaux, Serrati, Bobrov, T. Kačlerović, Lenin, Zinoviev, Radek, Bronski, Dabrowski, Nobs, Platten, Robmann, Münzenberg, Frölich, Savalyev, Vlasov, Petrov, Peluso." [10]

After this statement had been read, Pierre Brizon, one of the French deputies, threatened to walk out of the conference. The minutes then record "tumult," and the adoption of a resolution to strike the protest of the nineteen from the record (which was not done). Later in the conference Brizon made a speech with strong chauvinist overtones, which was followed by another uproar. The left viewed such incidents as evidence that the Zimmerwald resolutions had failed to draw a sharp line between consistent internationalism and chauvinism.

The debate on the second major agenda item, the proletariat's position on the peace question, centered on the submissions of Robert Grimm and the Zimmerwald Left, and the second of the Internationale Group resolutions. The final resolution, printed below, was based on Grimm's draft, but incorporated proposals of the left delegates.

Kienthal conference resolution: The attitude of the proletariat toward the question of peace[11]

I

1. The modern development of bourgeois property relations gave rise to imperialist antagonisms, which led in turn to the present World War. Unresolved national problems, dynastic aspirations, and all the historical relics of feudalism are being utilized for the war's purposes. It aims at a new division of existing colonial possessions and at the subjugation of economically backward countries to the power of finance capital.

2. Since the war eliminates neither the capitalist economy nor its imperialist form, it cannot do away with the causes of future wars. It reinforces finance capital, leaves unresolved the old national and world-power antagonisms, complicates them, and creates new frictions. This leads to mounting economic and political reaction, to new armaments, and to the danger of further military embroilments.

3. Therefore, when the governments and their bourgeois and social-patriotic agents assert that the war's purpose is the creation of a lasting peace, they lie or they disregard the conditions necessary to realize this goal. Annexations and economic and political alliances of imperialist states cannot bring a lasting peace on a capitalist basis any more than can compulsory arbitration courts, the reduction of armaments, the so-called democratization of foreign policy, and so on.

4. Annexations, that is, the forcible incorporation of foreign nations, stir up national hatred and increase the

points of friction between states. The political alliances and the economic treaties of the imperialist powers are a direct method of extending economic wars, which lead to new world conflicts.

5. Plans to eliminate the danger of war through the general limitation of armaments and compulsory arbitration courts are mere utopias. They presuppose a generally recognized authority, a material force standing above the opposed interests of the states. No such authority, no such force, exists. Capitalism's tendency to sharpen the antagonisms between the bourgeoisie of various countries and their coalitions prevents its appearance. Democratic control over foreign policy presupposes a complete democratization of the state. Such control may be a weapon in the proletariat's hands in its struggle against imperialism, but cannot be a means for transforming diplomacy into an instrument of peace.

6. For these reasons the working class must reject the utopian demands of bourgeois or socialist pacifism. The pacifists evoke new illusions in place of the old. They try to force the proletariat to serve these illusions, which in the end only mislead the masses, divert them from the revolutionary class struggle, and favor the "hold out to the end" policy of continuing the war.

II

7. The conditions for a lasting peace, which cannot exist under capitalism, will be provided by socialism. By abolishing capitalist private property, together with the national oppression and exploitation of the masses by the propertied classes, socialism eliminates the causes of war. The struggle for lasting peace therefore can be only a struggle for the realization of socialism.

8. Every workers' action that renounces class struggle, sub-

ordinates proletarian aims to those of the bourgeois classes and their governments, or solidarizes with the exploiting class of the nation works against the conditions necessary for a lasting peace. Such actions entrust the capitalist classes and the bourgeois governments with a task they cannot fulfill. Moreover, actions like these consign the best forces of the working class to being slaughtered in vain. The strongest and most capable forces of the proletariat, who would be in the first ranks of the struggle for socialism in war as in peace, are thus handed over to destruction.

III

9. The resolutions of the Stuttgart, Copenhagen, and Basel congresses of the International have already stated that the proletariat's attitude toward the war cannot be determined by the current military and strategic situation. Therefore, it is vitally necessary for the proletariat to call for an immediate truce and the prompt opening of peace negotiations.

10. The working class will succeed in hastening the war's end and in gaining influence over the character of the coming peace only to the extent that this call for peace finds a response in the ranks of the international proletariat and leads to vigorous action directed toward the overthrow of the capitalist class. Any other position permits the governments, the diplomats, and the ruling classes to decree the conditions for peace.

11. In the revolutionary mass struggle for the aims of socialism and thus for the liberation of humankind from the scourge of militarism and of war, the proletariat should struggle against the belligerent powers' drive for annexations. Likewise it should reject all attempts, made under the false pretext of liberating oppressed peoples, to establish pseudo-independent states that are not really viable. The proletariat's struggle against annexations does not flow from a convic-

tion that the prewar map of the world corresponds with the peoples' interests and is therefore sacrosanct. Socialism strives to eliminate all national oppression by unifying the nations economically and politically on a democratic basis, something which cannot be realized in the framework of capitalist state boundaries. Annexations, in whatever form they occur, make it more difficult to reach this aim, because forcibly partitioning nations, arbitrarily subdividing them and incorporating them in foreign states, worsens the conditions of the proletarian class struggle.

12. So long as socialism has not achieved freedom and equal rights for all nations, the proletariat has the unfailing duty to wage its class struggle against all national oppression, to oppose any violation of the rights of weaker nations, and to promote the protection of national minorities and the autonomy of peoples on the basis of real democracy.

13. The demand for war indemnities for the imperialist powers is just as incompatible with the interests of the proletariat as are annexations. In the same way that the ruling classes in every country try to put the burden of war costs upon the shoulders of the working class, so in the end war indemnities will be paid by the working class of the vanquished country. This harms the working class of the victorious country as well, because the deterioration of economic and social conditions of the working class of one country affects the working classes of other countries and thereby makes the conditions for the international class struggle more difficult. We oppose the transfer of the economic burdens resulting from the war from one people to the other, and demand that these burdens be laid on the propertied classes by means of an annulment of state war debts.

14. The struggle against the war and against imperialism, arising from the misery of human slaughter, will grow with increasing force in the future out of the calamities with which the imperialist era scourges the masses. The Interna-

tional will expand and deepen the mass movements against inflation and unemployment, for the agrarian demands of the rural working classes, against new taxation and political reaction, until all these movements unite into one general international struggle for socialism.

The Zimmerwald Left voted for this resolution with the following statement:

"The undersigned vote for the theses as a step toward rejection of social-pacifist utopias, although this is not done with sufficient firmness on some important points, such as rejection of the possibility of *alleviation* of the war danger through arbitration courts.

"(Signed:) Radek, Dabrowski, Frölich, Zinoviev, I. Petrov, Lenin, Fritz Platten, Kačlerović, Bronski."[12]

The next major question on the agenda, that of reconvening the International Socialist Bureau, was not so easily resolved. The majority of the commission on this topic brought in the following draft resolution favoring a meeting of the ISB.

For reconvening the ISB[13]

Whereas since the outbreak of the war the International Socialist Bureau has not met to launch a common campaign against the war and has thus seriously evaded the responsibilities laid on it by the congresses of the International;

The sections affiliated to the Zimmerwald campaign demand that the Executive Committee of the International Socialist Bureau convoke the bureau so that it may carry out its duty, and make the following suggestions to this end:

1. The Executive Committee of the ISB, which has shown itself incapable of defending and applying the principles of the International during the war, should be replaced by a committee drawn from the nonbelligerent countries.

2. The sections of the International must expel from their ranks members belonging to a government taking part in the war.

3. Parliamentary representatives of sections of the International must reject war credits.

4. The policy of "civil peace" must everywhere be broken and the class struggle energetically resumed all down the line.

5. The sections are invited to use all means to speed the achievement of peace, a peace without annexations or indemnities and recognizing the right of nations to self-determination.

If the International Socialist Bureau refuses to meet, the adherents of the Zimmerwald resolutions reject all responsibility for the consequences.

The Zimmerwald Left joined forces with the German Spartacists to formulate the minority resolution. It was introduced by the representative of a third important current, Adolf Warszawski of the Polish-Lithuanian Social Democracy's Central Executive Committee. The resolution, which follows, consists of the main part of the document submitted by the Internationale Group (Spartacists), plus three additional paragraphs.

Against reconvening the ISB[14]

by Adolf Warszawski, Berta Thalheimer, and V.I. Lenin

With the collapse of the old International on August 4, 1914, a new International must rise again, which can only be born of the revolutionary class struggle of the proletarian masses in the most important capitalist countries. The existence and effectiveness of the International is neither a question of organization nor one of agreement in a small circle of people acting as representatives of opposition-minded layers of the working class. It is a question of the proletarian mass movement in all countries returning to socialism. The International that dissolved on August 4, 1914, was a purely formal institution, existing only through loose ties among small groups of party and trade union leaders. In contrast, the new International, in order to become a real political force, must be rooted in the understanding, the capacity for action, and the daily experience of the broadest proletarian masses. The International will arise from below by the same process and to the same degree that the working class in all the belligerent countries frees itself from the fetters of "civil peace" and from the poisonous influences of the official leaders and throws itself into the revolutionary class struggle. The main slogan of the struggle must be systematic mass action to forcibly bring about peace. This alone can bring about the birth of the new, living, and effective International.

The Second International Socialist Conference therefore considers the idea of convoking the International Socialist Bureau to be completely mistaken and harmful. It could serve to deceive the Socialist workers of all countries as to their international tasks.

In the opinion of this conference, convocation of the International Socialist Bureau is all the more likely to be harmful since both the bureau's Executive Committee and also the majority of the official parties in the belligerent countries affiliated to it were precisely the agents of the collapse of the International. They trampled upon the decisions of the international congresses of Stuttgart, Copenhagen, and Basel and replaced the class struggle with "civil peace." In this way they tore apart the ties of international working-class solidarity, enlisted the workers on the side of the bourgeoisie, and encouraged nationalist hatred. They have thus become accomplices of imperialism.

The conference calls upon the class-conscious workers of all countries to resolutely turn their backs on social patriotism and, through the revolutionary struggle against the war and imperialism, to create the theoretical and organizational preconditions for preparing the launching of the new International.

The discussion revealed a sharp cleavage between the Zimmerwald Left and its closest allies, who favored a new International free of social chauvinism, and the French adherents of Longuet, the German supporters of Ledebour, and the Russian Menshevik Axelrod, who wished to reunify all the currents coming out of the old International. The Italian delegation proposed a variant of this latter position: fighting to win a majority within the old ISB and using that majority to reform it. Italian, French, and German centrists all indicated that they would leave the conference if it decided to break with the ISB.

When the five draft resolutions were ultimately put to a vote, none received a majority. The commission majority resolution received only ten votes; the left-wing minority received twelve; a resolution with an intermediate position, submitted by Lapinski of the Left Polish Socialist Party, received fifteen. To avoid a deadlock, the Zimmerwald Left and Spartacist commission members then proposed the acceptance of the Lapinski text, submitting the following explanation.

"The undersigned members of the resolutions commission declare that they must maintain their opinion, previously expressed in their draft resolution, against the demand for convening of the International Socialist Bureau. However the vote in the plenary session, although it was only indicative, has shown that the Lapinski resolution has obtained a plurality. We therefore are abstaining from voting in the commission so that the Lapinski resolution can be adopted as the basis for work on a resolution, in the plenary session we intend to vote in favor of the commission's resolution or abstain from voting.

"(Signed:) Thalheimer, Lenin, Zinoviev, Nobs."

The Lapinski resolution was adopted, with one vote against and one abstention. Delegates, noting the resolution's detailed description of the misdeeds of the ISB, jokingly referred to it as an "arrest warrant." Yet its conclusion evaded taking any stand on the road ahead. The text of this resolution follows.

Kienthal conference resolution on the ISB and the war[15]

I

Whereas the Executive Committee of the International Socialist Bureau utterly failed to carry out the tasks clearly and expressly assigned to it by resolutions of the International Socialist congresses;

Whereas it obstinately refused to call a meeting of the bureau in spite of repeated demands by several national sections;

Whereas the Executive Committee has thus not only done nothing to overcome the sharp crisis the war has caused for the International but, on the contrary, has sharpened this crisis by becoming an accomplice in the policy of the so-called defense of the fatherland, and of "civil peace," that is, a policy that denies our principles and leaves the working class in a state of wretched weakness;

Whereas this complicity was most trenchantly expressed by the chairman of the Executive Committee's conviction that he could serve as a government minister in a belligerent country while continuing as chairman of the International Socialist Bureau, thus degrading the central organization of the Workers' International to the unworthy role of a servile tool and a weapon in the hands of one of the imperialist coalitions;

Whereas the Executive Committee has examined the question of calling a meeting of the bureau only after twenty months of war and only when faced by the growing indignation of the masses, who are freeing themselves from the nightmare of chauvinism;

Whereas these efforts go hand in hand with the Executive Committee's previously established approval of this fratricidal war, and its efforts to justify the war in terms of so-called national defense;

Whereas the Executive Committee, at the same time it absolves all those who have renounced the socialist banner, makes every effort to combat the revolutionary forces of the International, forces that have found each other across the bloody chaos and joined hands in the struggle against the imperialist war;

Whereas the attempt to resume relations between national sections therefore takes on the nature of a separate peace between the social patriots;

Whereas the relations established during the war between the governments and the social-patriotic leaders in most countries, relations that violate all socialist principles, pose the danger that the Executive Committee could call a meeting of the International Socialist Bureau under circumstances and at a time favorable to the political interests of one or both of the great-power coalitions;

The Second Zimmerwald International Socialist Conference therefore recommends that all the organizations that belong to the International Socialist Committee in Bern monitor carefully all the activities of the Executive Committee of the International Socialist Bureau.

The conference is deeply convinced that the International can recover from its collapse and arise again as a genuine political force only to the extent to which the proletariat is able to liberate itself from all imperialist and chauvinist influences and reenter the road of class struggle and mass action.

If a plenary meeting of the bureau takes place, delegates of the parties and the organizations that stand on the positions of the Zimmerwald conference who participate in this plenary meeting must pursue a special aim. They must expose the real intentions of nationalist socialism—to divert the working class from its goals. They must also ruthlessly oppose this coalition's attempt at deception to the hilt by affirming the fundamental principles on which the international opposition has formed in all countries.

II

If the Executive Committee of the International Socialist Bureau decides to call a meeting of the bureau, then the International Socialist Committee should if possible call a meeting of its Enlarged Committee and discuss the question of joint action by the representatives who adhere to the Zimmerwald resolutions.

III

The conference recognizes the right of the national sections adhering to the International Socialist Committee to demand themselves the convocation of the International Socialist Bureau.

The conference also adopted a statement of solidarity with all those struggling against capitalism under the difficult conditions of the war, and with the many victims of capitalist persecution.

In addition, the Zimmerwald Left introduced the following resolution of solidarity with the embattled Socialist youth of Sweden. Although the Swedish government had remained neutral in the war, capitalist circles were preparing for its possible entry into the conflict. In 1916 they responded to Socialist youth agitation against this danger by jailing Zeth Höglund, Erik Heden, and Lars Oljelund, three youth leaders who were also left supporters of Zimmerwald and members of the bureau of the Socialist Youth International.

Solidarity with Swedish Socialist Youth[16]

The Second International Socialist Conference congratulates the Swedish Socialist Youth League on its correct and courageous decision to respond to the warmongers with agitation for a mass strike and for insurrection in case of imminent war. The enthusiasm of the forty thousand organized workers that stand behind this decision and have welcomed it and the fear shown by the Swedish government in arresting the leaders of the movement, comrades Höglund, Heden, and Oljelund, show that this is not a matter of idle threats but of earnest revolutionary will of the vanguard of the Swedish working class.

The conference congratulates the Dutch revolutionary Socialists and syndicalists on taking up the mass struggle against the danger of war.[17]

By violating the parliamentary immunity of Deputy Höglund, the Swedish government only showed to the world that when capitalist interests are at stake, the governments of small nations regard the constitution as merely a scrap of paper, just as the great powers act toward neutrality treaties. The conference pillories the Swedish social patriots, led by Branting, who so strongly support the bourgeoisie in its struggle against the revolutionary Social Democrats that they have ejected comrade Höglund from his position on the party's paid staff, even as he sits in prison. In this way the Swedish social patriots only demonstrate that they are defenders of capitalism, just as much in the neutral as in the warring countries.

The conference recommends the action of the Swedish youth league and of the Dutch comrades to revolutionary Social Democrats in all the neutral countries as an example of revolutionary courage and consistency in the struggle against the dangers of war and against social patriotism.

(Signed:) Münzenberg, Frölich, Radek, Dabrowski, Bronski, Zinoviev, Lenin, Kačlerović, Agnes Robmann.

The conference manifesto, which resulted from a number of compromises with the French delegates, was regarded by the left wing as the weakest of the Kienthal resolutions. It demanded rejection of any form of support for the governments' war policies, including rejection of war credits, but otherwise did not go beyond the framework of the Zimmerwald manifesto.

The Kienthal manifesto[18]

Proletarians of all countries, unite!

Two years of World War! Two years of devastation! Two years of bloody sacrifice and raging reaction!

Who is responsible? Who is behind those who threw the burning torch into the powder keg? Who wanted this war and prepared it for so long?

The ruling classes!

In September 1915, amid the unrestrained passions of war, we Socialists from the belligerent and neutral countries joined hands across the bloody chaos and united together in Zimmerwald. Our manifesto explained, "The ruling powers of capitalist society, who held the fate of the nations in their hands; the monarchical as well as the republican governments; the secret diplomacy; the mighty business organizations; the bourgeois parties; the capitalist press; the church—all these bear the full weight of responsibility for this war which arose out of the social order fostering them and protected by them, and which is being waged for their interest."

"Every nation," said Jaurès a few days before his death, "rushed with a burning torch through the streets of Europe."

*

Millions of men have sunk into their graves, millions of families have been made to mourn, and millions of women and children have been turned into widows and orphans. Ruins have been heaped upon ruins and irreplaceable achievements of civilization have been destroyed. Yet after all this, the war is at a dead end.

In spite of untold millions of victims on all fronts, there are no decisive gains. To move these fronts even slightly the governments would have to sacrifice more millions of men.

Neither victors, nor vanquished—or rather, all are vanquished, all bleeding, all ruined, and all exhausted. That will be the balance sheet of this gruesome war. That is how the ruling classes will be able to establish that their fantastic dreams of global imperialist rule have not been fulfilled.

Once again it has been shown that the only Socialists who have served the interests of their peoples are those who, in spite of persecution and slander, have opposed the nationalist hysteria and demanded an immediate peace without annexations.

Therefore join us in our battle cry: "Down with the war! Long live peace!"

Workers in town and country:

The governments, the imperialist cliques, and their press tell you that it is necessary to hold out in order to free the oppressed nations. Of all the methods of deception that have been used in this war, this is the crudest. For some, the real aim of this universal slaughter is to maintain what they have seized over centuries and conquered in many wars. Others want to divide up the world over again, in order to increase their possessions. They want to annex new territories, tear whole peoples apart and degrade them to the status of common serfs and slaves.

Your governments and press tell you that the war must be continued in order that militarism may be destroyed.

Do not be deceived! Militarism in a nation can only be abolished by that nation itself and this must be done in all countries.

Your governments and press also tell you that the war must be continued so that it may be the last war.

This is also a deception. Never has war done away with war. On the contrary, it arouses the desire for revenge. Violence begets violence.

Thus after each sacrifice your tormentors will demand further ones. Neither do the bourgeois peace zealots offer a road leading out of this vicious circle.

There is only one effective way to prevent future wars: the seizure of political power by the working classes and the abolition of capitalist property.

Lasting peace can only result from victorious socialism.

Proletarians! Who is it that preaches to you the policy of "holding out until victory"?

It is preached by the masterminds who are responsible for the war—the venal press, the war contractors, the war profiteers, the social patriots who parrot the bourgeois war slogans, and the reactionaries. They are secretly pleased with the death on the battlefields of those who just yesterday threatened the rulers' privileges—the Socialists, the trade unionists, and all who sowed the seeds of socialism in town and field.

These are the politicians who demand we hold out!

They control governmental power; they dominate the lying press, which poisons the people; they have the freedom to agitate for the continuation of the war and for increasing the toll of bloody sacrifice and devastation.

But you are the victims. You have only the right to starve and to keep silent. You face the chains of the state of siege, the fetters of censorship, and the stale air of the dungeon.

*

You, the people, the working masses, are sacrificed in a war which is not your war.

You, toilers from town and country, are in the trenches, in the front lines; while behind the lines you can see the rich and their accomplices, the shirkers, hiding in security.

For them, war means the death of others!

While they conduct their class struggle against you more intensely than ever before, they preach to you about "civil peace." While they relentlessly exploit your suffering and misery, they try to incite you to betray your class duty and tear out of your heart your greatest strength, your hope of socialism.

Social injustice and class rule are even more evident in war than in peace.

In peacetime the capitalist system robs the worker of the joy of life. In wartime it robs the worker of everything, including life itself.

Enough killing! Enough suffering!

*

Likewise, enough of devastation!

Today and in the future these accumulated ruins will fall upon you, the toilers.

Hundreds of billions are today thrown into the maw of the god of war. Thus they are lost to the people's welfare, to cultural activities, and to social reforms, all of which could improve your lot in life, promote people's education, and lessen misery.

And tomorrow heavy new taxes will fall upon your stooped shoulders.

Therefore, let us put an end to the squandering of your labor, your money, and your energy! Join the struggle for an immediate peace without annexations.

*

Working men and women in all the belligerent countries must turn against the war and its consequences, against misery and deprivation, against unemployment and inflation. They must raise their voices to demand restoration of the civil liberties that have been swept away, and in favor of social legislation and of the demands of the working classes in town and in country.

Let the proletarians of the neutral countries aid the Socialists of the belligerent states in their difficult struggle and oppose the expansion of the war with all their strength.

Let the Socialists of all countries act according to the decisions of the international congresses, which declared it the duty of the working class to make every effort to bring about a speedy end to the war.

Exercise the maximum pressure possible upon your deputies, your parliaments, and your governments.

Demand that the representatives of the Socialist parties reject at once every form of support to the war policies of the governments. Demand that the Socialist members of parliament vote against all war credits from now on.

Use every means at your disposal for a quick end to the human slaughter!

Immediate cease-fire, that is your slogan! Peoples subjected to ruin and murder: rise up and fight!

Courage! Remember that you are the majority and that if you so desire the power can be yours.

The governments should know that in all countries hatred against the war and the desire for social retribution are growing, and so the hour of peace among the peoples of the world is approaching.

Down with the war!

Long live peace—immediate peace, without annexations!

Long live internationalist socialism!

MAY 1, 1916
The Second International Socialist Zimmerwald Conference

The left debates disarmament

Although the resolution on peace unanimously adopted by the Kienthal conference denounced disarmament schemes as "mere utopias," there was no such unanimity among antichauvinists as a whole. Indeed some of the most militant Socialist currents had taken stands in support of the disarmament demand.

One such grouping was the Socialist Youth International. Its magazine, *Jugend-Internationale,* was among the most influential publications supporting the Zimmerwald and Kienthal conferences. Circulation of its first two issues, of September and December 1915, reached 40,000 copies each, and 120,000 people took part in the first international day of antimilitarist action it organized on October 3, 1915.

The December 1915 issue of *Jugend-Internationale* contained an article by the Dutch Socialist A. van Amstel critical of the youth international's position defending the disarmament slogan. Capitalism necessarily generated the danger of war and a heightened arms race, van Amstel wrote. "In view of this, what is the significance of the resolution of our Bern youth conference on disarmament," he asked. "The concept of 'disarmament' is nothing but a humanitarian fantasy, which harms the development of proletarian class consciousness. The demand for 'disarmament' expresses the deceptive hope that capitalist society can peacefully grow over into socialism. . . .

"If in the future the bourgeoisie is really going to press weapons into the hands of the entire proletariat . . . then our slogan should be: use the weapons, when challenged by the bourgeoisie, but only to defend proletarian interests."[19]

The March 1, 1916, issue of *Jugend-Internationale* contained two further articles on this topic, under the heading, "People's Army or Disarmament?"

A contribution from the Norwegian youth reported favorably on the Norwegian party's position for "immediate and resolute disarmament," saying it had helped the party score significant gains in the 1915 Norwegian elections. In addition, an unsigned article, excerpted below, defended the Bern youth conference disarmament demand.

Disarmament![20]

We are against every war!

Not only because every war means a world of misery, suffering, and injustice and a sea of blood and tears;

Not only because every new war increases by millions the toll of those slaughtered and killed, and creates millions of widows and orphans, and millions of cripples and invalids;

Not only because every war turns countless villages and cities, even whole countries, into wasteland, annihilates peoples or leads them into the abyss, and pounds into the mud culture, customs, in short, all that separates human beings from animals.

No, we are against every war above all because *every war* in the imperialist stage of capitalism strikes first at the working class, unbearably worsening its conditions. Brother van Amstel excellently described this in the second issue of *Jugend-Internationale.* No significant social reform is possible since everything is sacrificed on the altar of the bloodthirsty god, expansionism, and its tools, militarism and war preparations. In the eyes of the capitalist profit-seekers the value of the workers' lives sinks to zero. The soldiers, poisoned by compulsory school military training in their youth and mentally deadened and brutalized by participation in wars stretching over many years, easily allow themselves to be misused to suppress strikes and revolutionary propaganda.

We therefore demand opposition to all tendencies toward war, rejection of all funds for war and war preparations, abolition of all armies, and abolition of everything used for military purposes.

We therefore demand disarmament!

By combating the system and its characteristics, the proletariat also combats war and its consequences. When the proletariat says, do not allow one man or one penny for military purposes, it strikes the system at its most important and most vulnerable spot. . . .

In opposition to the disarmament slogan some comrades counterpose the conquest of militarism. They demand that the army be revolutionized so that in the future, in response to a challenge by the bourgeoisie, it can assist in dealing capitalism a death blow. But what is there in the world that could lead to such a development? It was none other than Brother van Amstel who graphically and convincingly explained to us that events were heading in the other direction. More and more, he explained, the army is turning into a powerful tool in the hands of the imperialists for the suppression of every movement for socialist liberation. And the present war and the development of militarism in all states, including even democratic Britain and America, prove him correct.

The period of imperialist wars that is now beginning can only engender *militarism,* the complete subjugation of the individual by military force, and the ruthless use of this violence in the interests of capital. Suppose it were possible to create such a revolutionary army against the will of the power that still rules today. Do our comrades then really believe that the bourgeoisie would blithely and calmly look on until, one day, history had reached the point where they were put up against the wall and breathed their last in a hail of bullets from the "revolutionary soldiers"?

If the demand for disarmament is a dream, then the idea of revolutionary militarism is even more so. . . .

Based on these facts and our understanding, which we unfortunately could only sketch out here in brief outline, we also must put forward the demand of disarmament as a slogan for the daily political struggle:

Because only this demand clearly implies the abolition of any form of defense of the fatherland;

Because this demand puts an end in all countries to all forms of deception and conceptual word games;

Because this demand, raised simultaneously in all countries, is the only way to eliminate the mistrust produced by the Socialist parties' stand on the World War among the workers of different lands;

Because this demand, when given a revolutionary socialist explanation and constant emphasis, most clearly shows the contradictions between the proletariat and the bourgeoisie;

And because after all that has happened and in view of this slogan's clarity, it provides the only way to mobilize the masses and rouse them to a stubborn and passionate struggle against the war, the arms race, militarism, and thus also against the system that creates them.

The Norwegian and Swedish Socialist Youth League, which was influenced by this pacifist position, was an important component of the Zimmerwald Left current. Moreover, the Zimmerwald Left forces in Switzerland achieved a close collaboration during 1916 with Willi Münzenberg and other leaders in Switzerland of the youth International, which had adopted this demand. Lenin contributed an article on disarmament to *Jugend-Internationale,* which it published in late 1917.[21] The Bolsheviks also pursued the discussion in the second issue of their journal, *Sbornik Sotsial-Demokrata,* published in December 1916, printing contributions by two Scandinavian revolutionary Socialists that took up this question. The following passage describes the position of the Norwegian party.

Norwegian Social Democrats on disarmament[22]

by Arvid Hansen

Antimilitarism is deeply rooted in the Norwegian working class, whose hatred of the military is as intense as the cold of a Russian winter night. The question of the *arming of the proletariat* has often been officially discussed, but it is *disarmament* that has become the official slogan of the party. The antimilitarist outlook of the Norwegian Social Democracy was most clearly expressed at the party congress in May 1915, which advanced the programmatic demands of disarmament, permanent neutrality, and compulsory international courts of arbitration. The main official features of the program were as follows:

"For Social Democracy, the system of militarism represents a vivid expression of a social structure based on private capital. Militarism is disguised in all countries as 'armed defense.' We have seen, however, that this armed defense is just what contributes to drawing a country into war. Thus our struggle against militarism must inevitably lead toward disarmament. We are *opponents of armed defense,* for it brings with it such immense burdens and demands such great sacrifices from the conscripted as to destroy the well-being of both the state and individual citizens. These expenses are met by the direct and indirect exploitation of productive labor, that is, by depriving the workers of the fruit of their labor. Moreover, this exploitation impedes the working-class struggle for social liberation and the conquest of society. Since the majority of regular state income is used for military expenditures, the state is forced to pursue a policy of borrowing that makes the state very dependent on local and foreign capital. If the millions that are now spent on defense could be used to realize our party's cultural and material program, it would have tremendous significance for the welfare and happiness of the entire people.

"We are opponents of militarism because in the hands of the ruling class it is a dangerous weapon against the actions of the working class to better its lot.

"We are opponents of armed defense because we are convinced that the military strength that our country can muster cannot really protect it, and that it is on the contrary a menace to the country's independence and neutrality. . . .

"It stands to reason that our party will work with all its strength to secure the regulation of our neutrality and independence by international agreements on the basis of disarmament. In the same way there is no reason to presume that such an agreement will run up against insurmountable difficulties. But disarmament must not be tied to the condition of simultaneous agreements. These agreements might be attained sooner if our country would carry out the program of disarmament in complete earnestness."

It would be incorrect to deny that there are some pacifist features in Norwegian antimilitarism. The desire to abolish militarism by parliamentary action is only a logical consequence of the conviction that capitalism itself can be abolished in the same way.

In an accompanying reply, Lenin argued that the disarmament demand was "an evasion of all the concrete questions of revolution."

The 'disarmament' slogan[23]

by V.I. Lenin

In a number of countries, mostly small and not involved in the present war—Sweden, Norway, Holland and Switzerland, for example—there have been voices in favour of replacing the old Social-Democratic minimum-programme demand for a "militia", or the "armed nation", by a new demand: "disarmament". An editorial article in favour of disarmament appeared in No. 3 of *Jugend-Internationale* (The Youth International), organ of the international youth organisation. In R. Grimm's "theses" on the military question drawn up for the Swiss Social-Democratic Party Congress we find a concession to the "disarmament" idea. In the Swiss magazine *Neues Leben* (New Life) for 1915, Roland-Holst, while ostensibly advocating "conciliation" between the two demands, actually makes the same concession. Issue No. 2 of *Vorbote* (The Herald), organ of the International Left, carried an article by the Dutch Marxist Wijnkoop in defence of the old armed-nation demand. The Scandinavian Lefts, as is evident from the articles printed below, accept "disarmament", though at times they admit that it contains an element of pacifism.

Let us take a closer look at the position of the disarmament advocates.

I

One of the principal premises advanced, although not always definitely expressed, in favour of disarmament is this: we are opposed to war, to all war in general, and the demand for disarmament is the most definite, clear and unambiguous expression of this point of view.

We showed the fallacy of that idea in our review of Junius's pamphlet, to which we refer the reader. Socialists cannot be opposed to all war in general without ceasing to be socialists. We must not allow ourselves to be blinded by the present imperialist war. Such wars between "Great" Powers are typical of the imperialist epoch; but democratic wars and rebellions, for instance, of oppressed nations against their oppressors to free themselves from oppression are by no means impossible. Civil wars of the proletariat against the bourgeoisie for socialism are inevitable. Wars are possible between one country in which socialism has been victorious and other, bourgeois or reactionary, countries.

Disarmament is the ideal of socialism. There will be no wars in socialist society; consequently, disarmament will be achieved. But whoever expects that socialism will be achieved *without* a social revolution and the dictatorship of the proletariat is not a socialist. Dictatorship is state power based directly on *violence*. And in the twentieth century—as in the age of civilisation generally—violence means neither a fist nor a club, but *troops*. To put "disarmament" in the programme is tantamount to making the general declaration: We are opposed to the use of arms. There is as little Marxism in this as there would be if we were to say: We are opposed to violence!

It should be observed that the international discussion of this question was conducted mainly, if not exclusively, in the German language. The Germans, however, use two words, the difference between which is not easily rendered in Russian. One [Abrüstung], strictly speaking, means "disarmament", and is used by Kautsky and the Kautskyites, for instance, in the sense of reduction of armaments. The other [Entwaffnung], strictly speaking, means "disarming", and is used mainly by the Lefts in the sense of abolishing militarism, abolishing all militarist systems. In this article we speak of the *latter* demand, which is current among certain *revolutionary* Social Democrats.

The Kautskyite advocacy of "disarmament", which is addressed to the present governments of the imperialist Great Powers, is the most vulgar opportunism, it is bourgeois pacifism, which *actually*—in spite of the "good intentions" of the sentimental Kautskyites—serves to distract the workers from the revolutionary struggle. For this advocacy seeks to instil in the workers the idea that the present bourgeois governments of the imperialist powers are *not* bound to each other by thousands of threads of finance capital and by scores or hundreds of corresponding *secret treaties* (i.e., predatory, plundering treaties, preparing the way for imperialist war).

II

An oppressed class which does not strive to learn to use arms, to acquire arms, only deserves to be treated like slaves. We cannot, unless we have become bourgeois pacifists or opportunists, forget that we are living in a class society from which there is no way out, nor can there be, save through the class struggle and the overthrow of the power of the ruling class.

In every class society, whether based on slavery, serfdom, or, as at present, on wage-labour, the oppressor class is always armed. Not only the modern standing army, but even the modern militia—and even in the most democratic bourgeois republics, Switzerland, for instance—represent the bourgeoisie armed *against* the proletariat. That is such an elementary truth that it is hardly necessary to dwell upon it. Suffice it to recall that in all capitalist countries without exception troops (including the republican-democratic militia) are used against strikers. A bourgeoisie armed against the proletariat is one of the biggest, fundamental and cardinal facts of modern capitalist society.

And in face of this fact, revolutionary Social-Democrats are urged to "demand" "disarmament"! That is tantamount to complete abandonment of the class-struggle point of view, to renunciation of all thought of revolution. Our slogan must be: arming of the proletariat to defeat, expropriate and disarm the bourgeoisie. These are the only tactics possible for a revolutionary class, tactics that follow logically from, and are dictated by, the whole *objective development* of capitalist militarism. Only *after* the proletariat has disarmed the bourgeoisie will it be able, without betraying its world-historic mission, to consign all armaments to the scrap-heap. And the proletariat will undoubtedly do this, but only when this condition has been fulfilled, certainly not before.

If the present war arouses among the reactionary Christian socialists, among the whimpering petty bourgeoisie, *only* horror and fright, only aversion to all use of arms, to bloodshed, death, etc., then we must say: Capitalist society is and has always been *horror without end*. And if this most reactionary of all wars is now preparing for that society an *end in horror*, we have no reason to fall into despair. But the disarmament "demand", or more correctly, the dream of disarmament, is, objectively, nothing but an expression of despair at a time when, as everyone can see, the bourgeoisie itself is paving the way for the only legitimate and revolutionary war—civil war against the imperialist bourgeoisie.

A lifeless theory, some might say, but we would remind them of two world-historical facts: the role of the trusts and the employment of women in industry, on the one hand, and the Paris Commune of 1871 and the December 1905 uprising in Russia, on the other.

The bourgeoisie makes it its business to promote trusts, drive women and children into the factories, subject them to corruption and suffering, condemn them to extreme poverty. We do not "demand" such development, we do not "support" it. We fight it. But *how* do we fight? We explain that trusts and the employment of women in industry are progressive. We do not want a return to the handicraft system, pre-monopoly capitalism, domestic drudgery for women. Forward through the trusts, etc., and beyond them to socialism!

That argument takes account of *objective* development and, with the necessary changes, applies also to the present militarisation of the population. Today the imperialist bourgeoisie militarises the youth as well as the adults; tomorrow it may begin militarising the women. Our attitude should be: All the better! Full speed ahead! For the faster we move, the nearer shall we be to the armed uprising against capitalism. How can Social-Democrats give way to fear of the militarisation of the youth, etc., if they have not forgotten the example of the Paris Commune? This is not a "lifeless theory" or a dream. It is a fact. And it would be a sorry state of affairs indeed if, all the economic and political facts notwithstanding, Social-Democrats began to doubt that the imperialist era and imperialist wars must inevitably bring about a repetition of such facts.

A certain bourgeois observer of the Paris Commune, writing to an English newspaper in May 1871, said: "If the French nation consisted entirely of women, what a terrible nation it would be!" Women and teenage children fought in the Paris Commune side by side with the men. It will be no different in the coming battles for the overthrow of the bourgeoisie. Proletarian women will not look on passively as poorly armed or unarmed workers are shot down by the well-armed forces of the bourgeoisie. They will take to arms, as they did in 1871, and from the cowed nations of today—or more correctly, from the present-day labour movement, disorganised more by the opportunists than by the governments—there will undoubtedly arise, sooner or later, but with absolute certainty, an international league of the "terrible nations" of the revolutionary proletariat.

The whole of social life is now being militarised. Imperialism is a fierce struggle of the Great Powers for the division and redivision of the world. It is therefore bound to lead to further militarisation in all countries, even in neutral and small ones. How will proletarian women oppose this? Only by cursing all war and everything military, only by demanding disarmament? The women of an oppressed and really revolutionary class will never accept that shameful role. They will say to their sons:

"You will soon be grown up. You will be given a gun. Take it and learn the military art properly. The proletarians need this knowledge not to shoot your brothers, the workers of other countries, as is being done in the present war, and as the traitors to socialism are telling you to do. They need it to fight the bourgeoisie of their own country, to put an end to exploitation, poverty and war, and not by pious wishes, but by defeating and disarming the *bourgeoisie.*"

If we are to shun such propaganda, precisely such propaganda, in connection with the present war, then we had better stop using fine words about international revolutionary Social-Democracy, the socialist revolution and war against war.

III

The disarmament advocates object to the "armed nation" clause in the programme also because it more easily leads, they allege, to concessions to opportunism. The cardinal point, namely, the relation of disarmament to the class struggle and to the social revolution, we have examined above. We shall now examine the relation between the disarmament demand and opportunism. One of the chief reasons why it is unacceptable is precisely that, together with the illusions it creates, it inevitably weakens and devitalises our struggle against opportunism.

Undoubtedly, this struggle is the main, immediate question now confronting the International. Struggle against imperialism that is not closely linked with the struggle against opportunism is either an empty phrase or a fraud. One of the main defects of Zimmerwald and Kienthal—one of the main reasons why these embryos of the Third International may possibly end in a fiasco—is that the question of fighting opportunism was not even raised openly, let alone solved in the sense of proclaiming the need to break with the opportunists. Opportunism has triumphed—temporarily—in the European labour movement. Its two main shades are apparent in all the big countries: first, the avowed, cynical, and therefore less dangerous social-imperialism of Messrs. Plekhanov, Scheidemann, Legien, Albert Thomas and Sembat, Vandervelde, Hyndman, Henderson, et al.; second, the concealed Kautskyite opportunism: Kautsky-Haase and the Social-Democratic Labour Group in Germany; Longuet, Pressemane, Mayéras, et al., in France; Ramsay MacDonald and the other leaders of the Independent Labour Party in England; Martov, Chkheidze, et al., in Russia; Treves and the other so-called Left reformists in Italy.

Avowed opportunism is openly and directly opposed to revolution and to incipient revolutionary movements and outbursts. It is in direct alliance with the governments, varied as the forms of this alliance may be—from accepting ministerial posts to participation in the war industries committees. The masked opportunists, the Kautskyites, are much more harmful and dangerous to the labour movement, because they hide their advocacy of alliance with the former under a cloak of plausible, pseudo-"Marxist" catchwords and pacifist slogans. The fight against both these forms of prevailing opportunism must be conducted in *all* fields of proletarian politics: parliament, the trade unions, strikes, the armed forces, etc.

What is the main distinguishing feature of *both* these forms of prevailing opportunism?

It is that the concrete question of the *connection between the present war and revolution, and the other concrete questions of revolution,* are hushed up, concealed, or treated with an eye to police prohibitions. And this despite the fact that before the war the connection between *this* impending war and the proletarian revolution was emphasised innumerable times, both unofficially, and officially in the Basel Manifesto.

The main defect of the disarmament demand is its evasion of all the concrete questions of revolution. Or do the advocates of disarmament stand for an altogether new kind of revolution, unarmed revolution?

IV

To proceed. We are by no means opposed to the fight for reforms. And we do not wish to ignore the sad possibility—if the worst comes to the worst—of mankind going through a second imperialist war, if revolution does not come out of the present war, in spite of the numerous outbursts of mass unrest and mass discontent and in spite of our efforts. We favour a programme of reforms directed *also* against the opportunists. They would be only too glad if we left the struggle for reforms entirely to them and sought escape from sad reality in a nebulous "disarmament" fantasy. "Disarmament" means simply running away from unpleasant reality, not fighting it.

Incidentally, certain Lefts fail to give a sufficiently concrete answer on the defence of the fatherland issue, and that is a major defect of their attitude. Theoretically, it is much more correct, and in practice immeasurably more important, to say that in the *present* imperialist war defence of the fatherland is a bourgeois-reactionary deception, than to take a "general" stand against defence of the fatherland under "all" circumstances. That is wrong and, besides, does not "strike" at the opportunists, those direct enemies of the workers in the labour parties.

In working out a concrete and practically necessary answer on the question of a militia we should say: We are not in favour of a bourgeois militia; we are in favour only of a proletarian militia. Therefore, "not a penny, not a man", not only for a standing army, but even for a bourgeois militia, even in countries like the United States, or Switzerland, Norway, etc. The more so that in the freest republican countries (e.g., Switzerland) we see that the militia is being increasingly Prussianised, and prostituted by being used against strikers. We can demand popular election of officers, abolition of military law, equal rights for foreign and native-born workers (a point particularly important for those imperialist states which, like Switzerland, are more and more blatantly exploiting larger numbers of foreign workers, while denying them all rights). Further, we can demand the right of every hundred, say, inhabitants of a given country to form voluntary military-training associations, with free election of instructors paid by the state, etc. Only under these conditions could the proletariat acquire military training for *itself* and not for its slave-owners; and the need for such training is imperatively dictated by the interests of the proletariat. The Russian revolution showed that every success of the revolutionary movement, even a partial success like the seizure of a certain city, a certain factory town, or winning over a certain section of the army, inevitably *compels* the victorious proletariat to carry out just such a programme.

Lastly, it stands to reason that opportunism can never be

defeated by mere programmes; it can only be defeated by deeds. The greatest, and fatal, error of the bankrupt Second International was that its words did not correspond to its deeds, that it cultivated the habit of unscrupulous revolutionary phrase-mongering (note the present attitude of Kautsky and Co. towards the Basel Manifesto). In approaching the demand for disarmament from this aspect we must first of all raise the question of its *objective* significance. Disarmament as a social idea, i.e., an idea that springs from, and can affect, a certain social environment, and is not the invention of some crackpot or group, springs, evidently, from the peculiar "tranquil" conditions prevailing, by way of exception, in certain small states which have for a fairly long time stood aside from the world's path of war and bloodshed, and hope to remain that way. To be convinced of this, we have only to consider the arguments advanced, for instance, by the Norwegian advocates of disarmament. "We are a small country," they say. "Our army is small; there is nothing we can do against the Great Powers (and, consequently, nothing we can do to resist forcible involvement in an imperialist *alliance* with one or the other Great-Power group!). We want to be left in peace in our backwoods and continue our backwoods politics, demand disarmament, compulsory arbitration, permanent neutrality, etc." ("permanent" after the Belgian fashion, no doubt?).

The petty striving of petty states to hold aloof, the petty-bourgeois desire to keep as far away as possible from the great battles of world history, to take advantage of one's relatively monopolistic position in order to remain in hide-bound passivity—this is the *objective* social environment which may ensure the disarmament idea a certain degree of success and a certain degree of popularity in some of the small states. That striving is, of course, reactionary and is based entirely on illusions, for, in one way or another, imperialism draws the small states into the vortex of world economy and world politics.

Let us cite the case of Switzerland. Her imperialist environment objectively prescribes *two* courses to the labour movement. The opportunists, in alliance with the bourgeoisie, are seeking to turn the country into a republican-democratic monopolistic federation that would thrive on profits from imperialist bourgeois tourists, and to make this "tranquil" monopolistic position as profitable and as tranquil as possible. Actually, this is a policy of alliance between a small privileged stratum of the workers of a small privileged country and the bourgeoisie of that country *against* the mass of the proletariat. The genuine Swiss Social-Democrats are striving to use Switzerland's relative freedom, her "international" position (proximity to the most cultured countries, the fact that Switzerland, thank God, does not have "a separate language of her own", but uses three world languages) to extend, consolidate and strengthen the *revolutionary* alliance of the revolutionary elements of the proletariat of the whole of Europe. Let's help our own bourgeoisie retain as long as possible its monopoly of the supertranquil trade in the charms of the Alps; perhaps a penny or two will fall to our share—such is the *objective* content of the Swiss opportunists' policy. Let us help weld the alliance of the revolutionary sections of the French, German and Italian proletariat for the overthrow of the bourgeoisie—such is the objective content of the Swiss revolutionary Social-Democrats' policy. Unfortunately, it is still being carried out far from adequately by the Swiss "Lefts", and the splendid decision of the 1915 Aarau Party Congress (acceptance of the revolutionary mass struggle) is still largely a dead letter. But that is not the point we are discussing at the moment.

The question that interests us now is: Does the disarmament demand correspond to this revolutionary trend among the Swiss Social-Democrats? It obviously does not. Objectively, the "demand" for disarmament corresponds to the opportunist, narrow national line of a labour movement, a line that is restricted by the outlook of a small state. Objectively, "disarmament" is an extremely national, specifically national programme of small states; it is certainly not the international programme of international revolutionary Social-Democracy.

P.S. In the last issue of the English *Socialist Review* (September 1916), organ of the opportunist Independent Labour Party, we find, on page 287, the resolution of the party's Newcastle Conference—refusal to support *any* war waged by *any* government even if "nominally" it is a war of "defence". And in an editorial on page 205 of the same issue we read the following declaration: "In no degree do we approve the Sinn Fein rebellion [the Irish Rebellion of 1916]. We do not approve armed rebellion at all, any more than any other form of militarism and war."

Is there any need to prove that *these* "anti-militarists", that *such* advocates of disarmament, not in a small, but in a big country, are the most pernicious opportunists? And yet, theoretically, they are quite right in regarding insurrection as one "form" of militarism and war.

The ISC after Kienthal

After the Kienthal conference the International Socialist Bureau Executive Committee undertook another round of attempts to call an international conference of the right-wing Social Democratic leaderships. The Socialist parties of the United States and Argentina had called on the ISB Executive Committee to convene a conference of Socialist parties of the nonbelligerent countries. The paralysis of the bureau endangered the unity of the International, they maintained, for it threatened to provoke the ISC into declaring itself an autonomous body.[24]

A May Day appeal of the discredited International Executive Committee called such a conference and also asked all Socialist parties to make proposals for the future peace treaties. This renewed attempt to reactivate the ISB tested the real intentions of those who voted at Kienthal for the "arrest warrant" against the ISB. Gregory Zinoviev summed up the outcome of Kienthal and the response to this new ISB initiative as follows in the June 10 issue of *Sotsial-Demokrat*.

Zimmerwald-Kienthal[25]

by Gregory Zinoviev

Two points of view; two policies. Some consider that the Second International has collapsed and that the fire of world war is forging the preconditions for the Third International, freed from opportunism and nationalism. Others do not understand the character either of the war or of the crisis socialism is now undergoing. The whole contemporary period appears to them to be an episode that will pass away together with the war. The old organization will arise again, with its international bureau at its head. The wayward brothers will once more return to their senses; the "misunderstandings" will be set straight, and then "why not indeed have everyone grant each other an amnesty?", as P. Axelrod said to the commission. . . .

Without a doubt the second Zimmerwald conference represents a *step forward.* The influence of the left was greater by far than at Zimmerwald. The prejudices against the Left have diminished. Is it correct to say, however, that the die is cast, that the Zimmerwaldists are finally on the road to a split with the official "Socialists," and that Zimmerwald *represents* the embryo of the Third International? No, we cannot say that in clear conscience. We can only say that the *chances* of such a turn of events, which would be so favorable for socialism, are *greater* than they were after Zimmerwald. But renewed wavering and renewed concessions to the social chauvinists are very possible, particularly after the war, when their masters, the bourgeoisie, will permit them to talk in more "left-wing" terms. No illusions! There is a large right wing among the Zimmerwaldists. There is no guarantee that it will stay with us through to the end.

The enlarged International Socialist Committee in Bern, charged by the conference with the resolution of a number of important questions, met after its conclusion. Among other items, it took up how to deal with the conference of neutrals that Huysmans and company are calling for the middle of June. Martov proposed *to recommend participation.* And his motion received five votes, half of the gathering. Another five votes went to Zinoviev's motion to stand by the position of the Kienthal resolution.

What does this signify? It means that as soon as a small chance appears of being "seduced," half of the Zimmerwaldists willingly offer themselves for seduction. . . .

Two programs, two camps, two worlds, two Internationals. That is how the movement is developing; that is where the current crisis is taking us. The workers of Russia can make a significant contribution to speeding up the achievement of this goal.

There can be no unity between Socialists and the servants of the bourgeoisie. Muranov and Petrovsky in Russia, Liebknecht in Germany, Höglund and Heden in Sweden, MacLean in Britain: they are our real comrades, thrown in prison by the governments of their "fatherlands"—they are the authentic representatives of the idea of a new workers' International.

For the Third International!

The conference of the official Socialist parties of nonbelligerent countries called by the ISB's May Day appeal was held July 31 in The Hague. It was small and lacked authority. In addition to Dutch delegates, it was attended only by one delegate each from Sweden, Denmark, the United States, and Argentina. The pacifist appeal issued by the conference was rebuffed by the chauvinist leaderships in the Entente countries. These forces held firm to the "win the war" policies of their ruling classes, and maintained their refusal to meet with the Socialist parties of Germany or Austria-Hungary.

The social chauvinists in the camp of German imperialism, confronted with the military impasse faced by German imperialism and the menacing growth of workers' unrest, adopted a more flexible policy. In August 1916 they called in the Reichstag for a compromise peace. They also favored reconvening the ISB.

Analogous demands were advanced by the Pressemane-Longuet opposition current in the French Socialist Party. It won growing support during 1916 for the reconvening of the ISB. The

French majority was able, however, to win the approval of the party's national council on August 7 for a proposal for a conference limited to the Socialist parties in the Entente countries. The ISB Executive Committee endorsed this move and undertook to organize it for January 1917. Once again the Zimmerwald forces divided: the Bolshevik Central Committee decided to boycott the conference, while the Italian Socialist Party initially decided to attend.[26]

The costly and exhausting military campaigns of 1916 still gave no clear advantage to either side of the imperialist conflict. On December 12 the four Central Powers offered to begin peace negotiations immediately. They said nothing, however, of the conditions they would demand for the conclusion of peace, and bolstered their "offer" with a boastful reference to their military gains and their determination to hold out until victory. This so-called peace offer was not designed to obtain a favorable response from the Entente, and its rejection duly followed in January.

On December 18 President Woodrow Wilson of the United States invited both warring camps to declare their war aims, and suggested a compromise peace. Both the Entente and German governments couched their replies to ensure that nothing came of Wilson's overture. Both sides conducted maneuvers over peace terms in order to mobilize even greater strength in the drive for military victory. The German "peace offer" was part of the preparations for its campaign of unrestricted submarine warfare, launched in 1917. Wilson's move, in turn, was a further step to prepare for the U.S. government's entry into the war on the side of the Entente. Only four months later, on April 6, 1917, the U.S. government declared war on the Central Powers.

Among the masses of working people in the warring countries, however, the peace maneuvers and Wilson's statement evoked a wave of hope and illusion that the war could end rapidly. They also had a strong effect on the pacifist wing of the Zimmerwald movement.

Lenin commented on the new turn of events as follows in the January 31, 1917, issue of *Sotsial-Demokrat.*

A turn in world politics[27]

by V.I. Lenin

There is something of a holiday atmosphere in the pacifist camp. The virtuous bourgeois of the neutral countries are rejoicing: "We've made our little pile out of war profits and high prices; isn't it time to stop? We can't make more profits anyway, and the people's patience may not last to the very end."

Why shouldn't they rejoice when Wilson "himself" "paraphrases" the pacifist declaration of the Italian Socialist Party, which only just recently passed an official and solemn resolution in Kienthal to the effect that social-pacifism is utterly unsound?

Is it surprising that in *Avanti!* Turati exults at Wilson's having paraphrased *their,* Italian, "pseudo-socialist" pacifist phrases? Is it surprising that, in *Le Populaire,* the French social-pacifists and Kautskyites lovingly "unite" with Turati and Kautsky, who published in the German Social-Democratic press five particularly foolish pacifist articles, which also, of course, "paraphrase" the talk events have brought to the fore about a nice little democratic peace?

And the present talk does differ from the previous talk in that there is some *objective* ground for it. This ground was created by the turn in world politics from *imperialist war,* which brought the peoples utter misery and the greatest betrayal of socialism by Messrs. Plekhanov, Albert Thomas, Legien, Scheidemann, etc., towards an *imperialist peace,* which will bring the peoples the greatest deception in the form of pious phrases, semi-reforms, semi-concessions, etc.

This turn has taken place.

One cannot know at the present moment—even those who direct imperialist policy, the financial kings and the crowned robbers, are not in a position to determine this exactly—when this imperialist peace will come, what changes in the course of the war will precede it, what the details of that peace will be. Nor is that important. What is important is the *fact* that a turn towards peace has been made; the important thing is the *fundamental character* of that peace. And these two circumstances have been made sufficiently clear by the preceding development of events.

Kautsky's response to these maneuvers is expressed in his resolution on the peace question, printed below, which was adopted by the January 7, 1917, conference of the opposition in the German SPD.

For a peace of reconciliation[28]

by Karl Kautsky

Comrades!

The International calls on the Socialist parties, in keeping with the *Stuttgart, Copenhagen, and Basel* congress decisions, to intervene upon the outbreak of war for its speedy termination.

Accordingly, the German Social Democratic Opposition has always opposed the slogan of holding out for victory, and demanded that the government make known its *desire for peace.* The Opposition did not wait for the government's blessing to begin its propaganda for peace.

The Opposition has not demanded willingness to accept peace at any price. Neither has it favored a mere statement of readiness for peace, without any further specification of its conditions. What the Opposition has demanded is willingness to accept a peace in which there is *neither victor nor vanquished;* a peace of reconciliation without violation of rights.

The German Social Democratic Opposition regards the imperial chancellor's December 12 declaration on his government's desire for peace as a symptom of a budding desire for peace in ruling circles. However, we cannot recognize the form of this declaration as an appropriate means to achieve the goal of peace.

The imperial chancellor proclaimed Germany the victor in the World War. Such boasting about victories achieved, like announcements of victories to come, can only make the conclusion of peace more difficult. In addition the imperial chancellor refrained from any *detailed exposition of Germany's war aims.* Neither of the two great-power alliances has yet made known war aims that could facilitate the opening of negotiations. This fateful default flows from the power the parties of war still hold in the ruling classes. Their influence must be broken before peace can be achieved. That will not be done by diplomatic transactions behind the scenes, but only by *the pressure of the masses on their governments.* Genuine readiness for peace will emerge not from respect for the "civil peace" but only from this political struggle. It requires lifting the state of siege and implementing freedom of the press and association.

The struggle for peace must also be waged *internationally* to be victorious. It cannot remain one-sided. The new situation created by the chancellor's peace offer and by Wilson's intervention requires more than ever *the international unity of the parties of proletarian socialism,* who are called on to be the foremost champions of peace. Those who have never abandoned the spirit of international unity and have already utilized every opportunity to emphasize its urgency, as for example at Zimmerwald and Kienthal, must unambiguously proclaim their common stand today. This is all the more necessary since expressing this unity is inhibited by government power and by the attitude of many Socialist party majorities.

We consider that in all the belligerent countries *the time has come for the Socialist parties* to insistently demand that their governments make known the precise goals for which they are waging war. They must oppose all goals that would signify the humiliation of any of the affected peoples or any injury to their conditions of existence. Socialists everywhere must struggle against all parties and governments that wish to prolong the war to achieve such goals.

As a democratic and an international party, the Social Democracy affirms the principle of the right of all peoples to self-determination. But the German Social Democratic Opposition *does not have enough confidence in any bourgeois government* to confer on it the mission of liberating nationalities through war. *That can be achieved only by the victorious proletariat.*

Yet we are not indifferent to the freedom and self-determination of nations within the bourgeois order. We must work resolutely to prevent this situation from being worsened in comparison to prewar conditions. *We reject any transfer of territory* that has not been approved by the affected population. In keeping with its congress decisions, the International must above all demand an international agreement for the resolution of all conflicts through *arbitration courts* and *universal arms limitation.*

The arms race is one of the most powerful causes of this war and stamping it out is the first precondition for preventing future ones. Here is an opening to advance beyond the prewar status quo, and to achieve progress for all, without disadvantage to any of the belligerents. Here the material advantage, which some seek in vain to obtain through reparations, can indeed be achieved in a superior form: each billion saved through reduction in war expenditures is equivalent to the interest from a war indemnity of twenty billion.

A treaty for disarmament and arbitration courts will also provide the strongest guarantee against future aggression that is possible under capitalism through the shaping of the conditions of peace.

The most solid rampart in defense of peace, of course, can only be *a politically powerful and intellectually independent proletariat,* playing a most vital role in foreign policy, which should be conducted in the full view of public opinion.

Proletarian power and class independence; openness and clarity in its policies; internal unity and international solidarity—that is what will bring peace and secure the peace.

The Internationale Group assailed Kautsky's pacifist position in one of its underground Spartacus letters, printed below.

Wilsonian Socialism[29]

"What the Opposition has demanded is willingness to accept a peace in which there is *neither victor nor vanquished;* a peace of reconciliation without violation of rights." Here we have the cornerstone of the manifesto. "A peace of reconciliation"! This "reconciliation" is indeed the prime achievement of Kautsky's intellectual labor, and he has been promoting it ever since he recovered from having caved in when the war began and wriggled back to the "middle position."

"Be reconciled, be reconciled!" the Working Group and Kautsky call out to the warring powers, just like a peace-loving little Philistine admonishing his quarreling neighbors to be reasonable. But what does such a "reconciliation" mean in this World War? Nothing other than a reconciliation between Bethmann, Lloyd George, Sazonov or Miliukov, and Ribot on the political make-up of Europe for the next decade. That signifies turning everything over to the same bourgeois secret diplomacy, the same governmental cabinet magicians toward whom we have expressed the deepest mistrust in countless resolutions, articles, and speeches. Indeed we have laid them with the blame for the war, and demanded that they be swept away. And "oppositional" Social Democrats are now keen for such a reconciliation, and call for it, and recommend it to the proletariat as the goal of its peace policy!

The goal of Haase, Ledebour, and Kautsky in this is merely to ensure that things are done "without violation of rights" and that there are "no victors and no vanquished." But the "victors and vanquished" that Haase and Ledebour refer to are the same thing that the *Deutsche Tageszeitung* [German

Daily News] and the militarists designate with the words, victorious and vanquished *governments.* Yet our farseeing politicians, under the leadership of their profound theoretician, have not noticed that if bourgeois diplomacy shapes the peace, if the international and, above all, the German proletariat do not arise from their present terrible defeat to impose a peace and shape it through revolutionary class action, then the proletariat as a class, then socialism as a policy can only emerge the losers and capitalism the winner in this war.

They have not noticed that *every* reconciliation of the bourgeois governments is a conspiracy against the European proletariat, and even if international state boundaries were to be completely restored after the war as they were before, the national and international political situation and social *class relationships* will, nonetheless, be fully transformed.

The only concern of these people is that no national contingent of imperialism triumph decisively over any other. For them, the "reconciliation" of the imperialists over the body of international socialism and the return to prewar conditions is sufficient. They long for the political status quo of Europe of the past and do not understand that it was precisely this status quo that led to the unprecedented upsurge of imperialism and the outbreak of the World War.

Italy was another country where bourgeois "peace" maneuvers drove a wedge between right-wing and left-wing Zimmerwaldists. Lenin cited a speech of the centrist party leader Filippo Turati to show how Socialist pacifism could slide over into support of outright imperialist expansionism.

Turati favors 'rectification of frontiers'[30]

by V.I. Lenin

On December 17, Turati delivered a speech in Parliament, one passage of which caused an unusual and deserved sensation. This is the passage, quoted from the report in *Avanti!*:

"Let us assume that a discussion similar to the one proposed by Germany is able, in the main, to settle such questions as the evacuation of Belgium and France, the restoration of Rumania, Serbia and, if you will, Montenegro; I will add the rectification of the Italian frontiers in regard to what is indisputably Italian and corresponds to guarantees of a strategical character". . . . At this point the bourgeois and chauvinist Chamber interrupts Turati, and from all sides the shout goes up: "Excellent! So you too want all this! Long live Turati! Long live Turati!". . .

Apparently, Turati realised that there was something wrong about this bourgeois enthusiasm and tried to "correct" himself and "explain".

"Gentlemen," he said, "there is no occasion for irrelevant jesting. It is one thing to admit the relevance and right of national unity, which we have always recognised, but it is quite another thing to provoke, or justify, war for this aim."

But neither Turati's "explanation", nor the articles in *Avanti!* in his defence, nor Turati's letter of December 21, nor the article by a certain "B.B." in the Zurich *Volksrecht* can "correct" or explain away the fact that *Turati gave himself away!* . . . Or, more correct, not Turati, but the whole of socialist pacifism represented by Kautsky, and, as we shall see below, the French "Kautskyites", gave itself away. The Italian bourgeois press was right in seizing upon and exulting over this passage in Turati's speech.

The above-mentioned "B.B." tried to defend Turati by arguing that the latter referred only to "the right of nations to self-determination".

Poor defence! What has this to do with "the right of nations to self-determination", which, as everyone knows, the Marxist programme regards—and the programme of international democracy has always regarded—as referring to the defence of *oppressed* nations? What has it to do with the imperialist war, i.e., a war for the division of colonies, a war for the *oppression* of foreign countries, a war *among* predatory and oppressing powers to decide *which* of them shall oppress *more* foreign nations?

How does this argument about self-determination of nations, used to justify an imperialist, not national, war, differ from the speeches of Alexinsky, Hervé and Hyndman?

Events in France also showed a widening split in the Zimmerwald movement. The centrist current in the French Socialist Party led by Jean Longuet and Adrien Pressemane grew throughout 1916, and won the support of almost half the delegates at the December 1916 party congress. Its positions were more conservative than those of the Ledebour-Hoffmann forces at Zimmerwald: it supported national defense, voted for war credits, and in its majority opposed the Zimmerwald movement. Its pacifist orientation, however, distinguished it from the "win the war" chauvinism of the party majority.

While the majority forces refused to countenance any meeting with German SPD representatives, the Longuet current campaigned for reconvening the International Socialist Bureau. One of its adherents explained that "we must go to The Hague if we don't want others to go back to Zimmerwald."[31]

Among the French Zimmerwaldists organized in the Committee for the Resumption of International Relations, Merrheim and Bourderon were attracted to the centrist current of Longuet and Pressemane, while others like Rosmer and Monatte fought for a revolutionary orientation. In August 1916 Trotsky presented a resolution to the Zimmerwald committee in Paris calling for a sharp political fight against the Longuet current.

How could Longuet call for Socialists to withdraw from the government, Trotsky asked, while continuing to advocate national defense and the *union sacrée,* the French version of "civil peace"? "The anti-ministerialism of the Longuet forces, inconsistent from beginning to end, aims only to appease workers' aroused socialist consciousness through concessions on secondary issues, and to divert them from a genuine struggle against the war."

"From the point of view of Zimmerwald, which is that of the revolutionary class struggle," Trotsky's resolution continued, "there is no principled difference between the positions of Longuet and of Renaudel. And if we really want to combat the social-patriotic corruption and abasement of the workers' movement, we must tell workers everywhere the plain truth about Longuetism. It is an indispensable weapon of the bourgeois state, a harmless and tame socialism that uses inoffensive scraps of the phraseology and program of internationalism to politically exploit the masses."[32]

After an extended debate, a modified version of Trotsky's resolution was adopted. Its predictions were fulfilled in December, for just as the Longuet current came close to winning a majority at the party congress, a realignment took place, which found minority and majority alike voting together for a pacifist position inspired by Woodrow Wilson and his December 18 "peace" maneuver. Merrheim, Bourderon, Brizon, and other right-wing Zimmerwaldists were caught up in the wave of Wilsonian pacifism, and quit the French Zimmerwald committee in early 1917. Renaming itself in 1919 the "Committee for the Third International," it was to be instrumental in building the French Communist Party.[33]

A similar evolution took place in Switzerland. While the center and left currents had joined at the November 1915 convention of the Swiss Social Democratic Party to win a majority for Zimmerwald, at the November 1916 convention the Zimmerwald Left, acting alone, won a majority for its key resolution on asserting party control over its parliamentary fraction. In January 1917 Robert Grimm allied with right-wing forces to postpone a key party congress on the war question, against the left-wing opposition of Nobs, Platten, Münzenberg, and Naine.

In Sweden, three left Socialists withdrew from the Socialist parliamentary fraction in May 1916, beginning a split that was to lead in May 1917 to the formation of the Left Socialist Party, which was to become the Swedish Communist Party.

The International Socialist Committee took up the peace maneuvers of the imperialist powers at its December 27, 1916, meeting. Surveying the actions of each government, the statement asked:

"What about *the note of the President of the United States?* It cannot lose the character, scarcely disguised, of a war note. Very well, if Wilson wishes peace, America should stop every individual, without any exception, from gaining billions on war deliveries and, with *that* as proof, appear before the world as an apostle of peace.

"Truly, even today the governments do not want peace, because the leaders of the war fear the inevitable *settling of accounts* which must follow, and others find war *profits* more attractive than the highest interests and human rights. There is only one power that can force them to conclude peace: *the awakened force of the international proletariat, the firm will to turn one's weapons not against one's own brothers but against the internal enemy in every country."*[34]

Yet despite the militant phrases of this appeal, the ISC was no closer to agreement on how to reconstruct the international workers' movement. The December ISC meeting divided sharply once again on proposals for international conferences that would include chauvinist-led Socialist parties.

When the Russian revolution broke out in March (February) 1917, the crisis of the Zimmerwald movement remained as one of the problems of international socialism to be resolved by revolutionary Socialists.

Lenin singled out this crisis in the seventeenth of his "April Theses," written on his arrival in revolutionary Petrograd after the February revolution. "From the very outset," he wrote, "the Zimmerwald International adopted a vacillating, 'Kautskyite', 'Centrist' position, which immediately compelled the *Zimmerwald Left* to dissociate itself, to separate itself from the rest, and to issue *its own* manifesto (published in Switzerland in Russian, German and French).

"The chief shortcoming of the Zimmerwald International, and the cause of its *collapse* (for politically and ideologically it has already collapsed), was its vacillation and indecision on such a momentous issue of *crucial* practical significance as that of breaking completely with social-chauvinism and the old social-chauvinist International, headed by Vandervelde and Huysmans at The Hague (Holland), etc."[35]

Just before the Russian February revolution, Lenin wrote draft theses summarizing his conclusions on the work of the Zimmerwald Left and the experience of the Zimmerwald movement, and indicating the next stage in the struggle to launch the Third International.

Theses for an appeal to the International Socialist Committee and all Socialist parties[36]

by V.I. Lenin

ROUGH DRAFT

1. The turn in world politics, from imperialist war to open appeals by a number of bourgeois governments for an imperialist peace, coincides with a turn in the development of world socialism.

2. The first turn has produced a spate of pious and sentimental pacifist phrases, promises and pledges, with which the imperialist bourgeoisie and the imperialist governments seek to deceive the peoples and "peacefully" condition them to obediently bear the whole cost of the predatory war, peacefully disarm the millions of proletarians and cover up, by paltry concessions, the preparation for a deal to divide up the colonies and financially (also politically if possible) strangle weak nations. This deal comprises the sum and substance of the projected imperialist peace and is a direct continuation of the existing secret predatory agreements, particularly those concluded during the war, between *all* the powers of *both* warring imperialist coalitions.

3. The second turn consists in a "reconciliation" between the social-chauvinists, who have betrayed socialism and defected to bourgeois nationalism or imperialism, and the *Zimmerwald Right wing*, as represented by Kautsky and Co. in Germany, Turati and Co. in Italy, Longuet-Pressemane-Merrheim in France, etc. By uniting on a basis of empty,

meaningless and non-committal pacifist phrases, which in practice serve to *disguise* imperialist policy and imperialist peace, *embellish* them instead of exposing them, these two trends are taking a decisive step towards the greatest deception of the workers, towards consolidating the domination in the labour movement of a bourgeois labour policy veiled by socialist phraseology, the domination of leaders and privileged sections of the working class that have helped the governments and the bourgeoisie wage this predatory imperialist war on the pleas of "defending the fatherland".

4. Social-pacifist policy, or the policy of social-pacifist phraseology, now predominates in the socialist parties of the chief European countries (see Kautsky's five pacifist articles in the German Social-Democratic press and, appearing at the same time, the statement of the social-imperialist leaders in the Chemnitz *Volksstimme* that they are fully prepared for peace and unity with the Kautskyites on a basis of pacifist phrases; the January 7, 1917 pacifist manifesto of the German Kautskyite opposition[37]; the Longuetists and Renaudel and Co. voting together at the French Socialist Party Congress, and Jouhaux and Merrheim, also Broutchoux, at the General Confederation of Labour Congress, *for* resolutions composed of misleading pacifist phrases; a similar pacifist statement by Turati on December 17, 1916, and the defence of his position by the entire Socialist Party of Italy). *Whatever the terms* of the peace now being prepared between the present, i.e., *bourgeois*, governments of *both* imperialist coalitions, this policy signifies the conversion of socialist and syndicalist (Jouhaux and Merrheim) organisations into a *tool* of government intrigue and secret imperialist diplomacy. . . .

7. That being the objective state of affairs, it is the obvious and imperative task of every sincere socialist policy, every honest proletarian policy (not to speak of conscious Marxist policy) first of all and above all consistently, sys-

tematically, boldly and unreservedly to *expose the pacifist and democratic hypocrisy of one's own government and one's own bourgeoisie.* Lacking that, all talk of socialism, syndicalism, internationalism is a sheer deception of the people. For exposure of annexations by one's imperialist rivals (regardless of whether they are named or merely implied, by denouncing annexations "generally" or by similar "diplomatic" methods of concealing one's thoughts) is the direct concern, the direct business, of *all* venal journalists, all imperialists, including those that parade as socialists, such as Scheidemann and Co., Sembat and Co., Plekhanov and Co., etc. . . .

9. A policy designed not to mislead the workers, but to open their eyes to reality, should consist in the following:

(a) Socialists in every country must now, when the question of peace is so directly posed, unfailingly and more vigorously than usual expose their *own* government and their *own* bourgeoisie. They must expose the secret agreements *they* have concluded, and are concluding, with *their* imperialist allies for the division of colonies, spheres of influence, joint financial undertakings in other countries, buying up of shares, monopoly arrangements, concessions, etc.

For in this, and in this *alone,* lies the real, not deceptive, *basis* and substance of the imperialist peace now being prepared. Everything else is meant to deceive the people. Those who vow and swear by these catchwords are not really supporting a democratic peace without annexations, etc., for *real* support means exposing, *in practice,* one's *own* bourgeoisie, which by its *actions* is destroying these principles of true socialism and true democracy. . . .

For the Socialist of *another* country cannot expose the government and bourgeoisie of a country at war with "his own" nation, and not only because he does not know that country's language, history, specific features, etc., but also because *such* exposure is part of imperialist intrigue, and not an *internationalist* duty.

He is not an internationalist who vows and swears by internationalism. Only he is an internationalist who in a really internationalist way combats his *own* bourgeoisie, his *own* social-chauvinists, his *own* Kautskyites.

(b) In every country the Socialist must above all emphasise in all his propaganda the need to distrust not only every political phrase of his *own* government, but also every political phrase of his *own* social-chauvinists, who *in reality* serve that government.

(c) In every country the Socialists must above all explain to the masses the indisputable truth that a genuinely enduring and genuinely democratic peace (without annexations, etc.) can now be achieved *only* if it is concluded *not* by the present bourgeois governments, or by *bourgeois* governments in general, but by *proletarian* governments that have overthrown the rule of the bourgeoisie and are proceeding to expropriate it. . . .

(d) In every country the socialist must explain to the masses the indisputable truth that, if the phrase "democratic peace" is to be taken seriously, sincerely and honestly, and not merely used as a false *Christian* phrase meant to conceal an *imperialist* peace, then the workers have only one means of really achieving such a peace *right now.* That means is to *turn their weapons against their own government* (i.e., follow the advice of Karl Liebknecht, for which he has been sentenced to hard labour. He urged, in other words, what our Party manifesto of November 1, 1914 defined as turning the imperialist war into a civil war of the proletariat against the bourgeoisie and for socialism).[38]

To what extent such an attempt is feasible, from the standpoint of the *sentiment* of the broad masses, can only be *proved* by launching this type of agitation and propaganda everywhere and in the most resolute and energetic way; by giving the most sincere and devoted support to all revolutionary manifestations of the mounting mass resentment, to the strikes and demonstrations that are forcing the Russian bourgeoisie frankly to admit that the revolution is on the march, and have forced Helfferich to declare in the Reichstag: "Better to keep the Left Social-Democrats in prison than to have Potsdam Square littered with corpses," i.e., to admit that the masses *are* responding to agitation by the Left.

In any case, the alternative which socialists must clearly place before the masses is this: either continue to kill each other for capitalist profits, put up with the high cost of living, hunger, the burden of a debt running into billions, and accept the farce of an imperialist *truce* veiled by democratic and reformist promises, or rise in revolt against the bourgeoisie.

A revolutionary party which openly, before the whole world, threatened the governments with "proletarian revolution" in the event of *such* a war as is now being waged, would be committing moral suicide if it did not urge the workers, and the masses generally, to direct all thought and effort towards revolt, now that the masses are so excellently armed, so excellently trained in the art of warfare, and fed up with the absurdity of this criminal imperialist shambles, which up to now they have been helping.

(e) Socialists must centre their activity on the struggle against reformism, which has always corrupted the revolutionary labour movement by injecting bourgeois ideas, and has now assumed a somewhat special form, namely: "reliance" on the reforms the bourgeoisie is supposed to carry out after the war! Reformists argue that in urging, popularising and preparing the socialist revolution of the proletariat, we are "losing sight" of the "practical" aspect, "forfeiting" our chances to win reforms.

That argument, customary both to social-chauvinists and supporters of Kautsky, who has even denounced street demonstrations as "adventuristic", is thoroughly unscientific, fundamentally false, a bourgeois lie.

In the course of the war world capitalism has taken a forward step not only towards concentration in general, but also towards transition from monopoly in general to *state capitalism* on a much broader scale than before. Economic reforms in this direction are inevitable.

In the political sphere, the imperialist war has demonstrated that from the imperialists' standpoint it is *sometimes* much more advantageous to have as war ally a politically independent but financially dependent small nation rather than risk Irish or Czech "incidents" (i.e., uprisings or the defection of whole regiments) during a war. It is quite possible, therefore, that parallel with its policy of strangling small nations—a policy it can never wholly abandon—imperialism will in individual cases follow a policy of "voluntary" alliance (i.e., resulting exclusively from financial strangulation) with new small national states, or with mongrel states, such as Poland.

However, it does not follow from this that Social-Democrats can, without betraying their cause, "vote" for or support such imperialist "reforms".

Only bourgeois reformism, which *in substance* is the position of Kautsky, Turati and Merrheim, poses the question thus: *either* renunciation of revolution and that means reforms, *or* no reforms at all.

Yet all the experience of world history, like the experience of the 1905 Russian Revolution, teaches us the very opposite: *either* revolutionary class struggle, of which reforms are *always* a by-product (when the revolution is not completely successful), *or* no reforms at all.

For the *only effective* force that compels change is popular revolutionary energy, providing it does not remain on paper, as has been the case in the Second International, but finds expression in comprehensive mass revolutionary propaganda, agitation and organisation conducted by parties marching at the head of the revolution, not limping along in its tail.

Only by openly proclaiming revolution, by purging the workers' parties of all who oppose revolution or "sceptically" accept it—only by giving *every* aspect of party activity a revolutionary content, can Social-Democracy, in such *"critical"* eras of world history as the present one, guarantee the masses either complete success of their cause if the revolution is supported by very broad masses, or reforms, i.e., concessions by the bourgeoisie, if the revolution is only partially successful.

Otherwise, if the Scheidemann and Kautsky policy prevails, there is *no* guarantee that the reforms will not be reduced to naught, or carried out with police and reactionary restrictions that will *rule out* the very possibility of the proletariat using them in a repeated fight for the revolution.

(f) Socialists must make a serious effort to bring to reality Karl Liebknecht's slogan. The popularity that name enjoys among the masses is a *guarantee* that revolutionary activity is both possible and likely to succeed. The attitude of Scheidemann and Co., Kautsky and Co. towards that name is an example of hypocrisy: *in words* they swear by the "Liebknechts of all countries"; *in deeds* they combat Liebknecht's tactics.

Liebknecht broke not only with the Scheidemanns (Renaudels, Plekhanovs, Bissolatis), but also with the Kautsky *trend* (Longuet, Axelrod, Turati).

Liebknecht declared, as early as *October 2, 1914,* in his letter to the Party Executive:

"I have declared my deep conviction that, if it does not want to forfeit the right to call itself a Social-Democratic party, if it wants to restore its prestige in the eyes of the world, now so thoroughly undermined, the German party must be *regenerated* from top to bottom." (*Class Struggle Against the War!* Materials in the "Liebknecht Case", p. 22.) (Printed secretly in Germany: Published as a manuscript.)

All parties should take up Liebknecht's slogan and it would certainly be ridiculous to even think of being able to turn it into effect without ridding the party of the Scheidemanns, Legiens, Renaudels, Sembats, Plekhanovs, Vanderveldes and Co., or without denouncing the policy of concessions to the trend represented by Kautsky, Turati, Longuet and Merrheim.

*

10. We therefore suggest a conference of Zimmerwald supporters to discuss the following proposals:

(1) Socialist pacifism of a definite trend—Longuet-Merrheim, Kautsky, Turati, etc.,—already rejected in principle at Kienthal, and its concrete defence by these representatives of the afore-mentioned *trends* should be decisively and unconditionally rejected as bourgeois reformism (on the basis of the theses formulated above).

(2) A similarly decisive organisational break with social-chauvinism.

(3) Explain to the working class its immediate and urgent revolutionary tasks, precisely in connection with the fact that the masses have lost patience with the war and the lying milk-and-water pacifist phrases of the bourgeoisie.

(4) Openly brand as a complete break with the spirit and decisions of Zimmerwald and Kienthal, and condemn as such, the policy of the Italian Socialist Party, which is following a patently pacifist path, and the policy of the Swiss Social-Democratic Party, which on November 4, 1916 in Zurich voted to permit indirect taxes, and on January 7, 1917, through an alliance between the "Centrist" R. Grimm and the social-patriots Greulich, G. Müller and Co., secured indefinite postponement of the special party congress called for February 11, 1917 to discuss the war issue, and which now meekly accepts the outright ultimatum of these same social-patriot leaders, who openly threaten to resign from

parliament if the party rejects fatherland defence.

The sad experience of the Second International has clearly demonstrated the immense damage caused by combining, in *actual practice,* "general" revolutionary decisions, formulated in general phrases, with reformist actions—when professions of internationalism are attended by refusal *jointly* to discuss, in a truly internationalist manner, fundamental problems of the tactics of each individual party as a component part of the international union.

Prior to the Zimmerwald Conference and at the Conference itself, our Party considered it its duty to acquaint the comrades with our irrevocable condemnation of pacifism and abstract preachment of peace as a bourgeois deception (a German translation of our Party's resolution, in the pamphlet *Socialism and War,* and a French translation, in a separate leaflet, were circulated at the Conference). The *Zimmerwald Left,* in whose organisation we shared, was formed as a separate group at the Conference for the express purpose of showing that we support the Zimmerwald group *insofar* as it combats social-chauvinism.

It has now been definitely established—of this we are profoundly convinced—that the Zimmerwald majority, or the Zimmerwald Right, has made a *roundabout turn* not towards struggle against social-chauvinism, but towards complete surrender to it, towards merger with it on a platform of empty pacifist phrases. And we consider it our duty openly to state that to support, in these circumstances, the illusion of Zimmerwald unity and Zimmerwald struggle for the Third International would cause the greatest damage to the labour movement. We declare, not as a "threat" or "ultimatum", but as an open notification of our decision, that unless the situation changes we shall not remain a member of the Zimmerwald group.

Notes

1. The Stuttgart Congress of 1907

1. *The International Working-Class Movement* (Moscow: Progress Publishers, 1981), vol. 2, p. 526.

2. Ibid., pp. 528–29.

3. Hélène Carrère d'Encausse and Stuart R. Schram (eds.), *Marxism in Asia* (Baltimore: Penguin Press, 1969), pp. 125–26.

4. The resolutions and proceedings from the Stuttgart congress are excerpted from *Internationaler Sozialistenkongress zu Stuttgart, 18. bis 24. August 1907* (Berlin: Buchhandlung Vorwärts, 1907). Selections on colonialism are on pages 24–40 and 110–13. This German-language edition of the proceedings was based on accounts printed in *Vorwärts* (Forward), the official daily newspaper of the German Social Democratic Party. The texts of speeches made in German were submitted to the speakers for revision

The translation for the present volume has been revised on the basis of a comparison with the French-language edition of the congress proceedings, *VIIe Congrès socialiste international tenu à Stuttgart du 16 au 24 août 1907* (Brussels: Veuve Désiré Brismée, 1908).

5. The "Congo Free State," whose territory today comprises the state of Zaïre, was established in the 1880s as the personal possession of Belgian King Leopold. One measure of the brutality of Leopold's rule is that the population of the Congo decreased by an estimated three million over a period of just ten years.

In 1906 the Belgian parliament debated transferring rule over the Congo from the king to the Belgian state as a whole. Socialist leaders did not advocate granting self-government to the Congo, which they felt would only return its people to the domination of "Arab slave traders." A majority of the Socialist Party opposed the transfer and counterposed transferring sovereignty to an international consortium of capitalist powers. A minority, led by Emile Vandervelde, believed that Belgian annexation of the Congo and reform of the colonial administration represented the lesser evil and deserved support.

6. The German bourgeois parties concentrated fire in the 1907 elections on the SPD's opposition to colonialism, and succeeded in cutting down the Socialists' representation in parliament. See Chapter 2 of the present work.

7. The passage from Marx's *Capital* cited by Bernstein reads: "From the standpoint of a higher socioeconomic formation, the private property of particular individuals in the earth will appear just as absurd as the private property of one man in other men. Even an entire society, a nation, or all simultaneously existing societies taken together, are not the owners of the earth. They are simply its possessors, its beneficiaries, and have to bequeath it in an improved state to succeeding generations, as *boni patres familias* [good heads of the household]." (Karl Marx, *Capital* [New York: Vintage Books, 1981] vol. 3, p. 911).

Ferdinand Lassalle was the founder of the General Association of German Workers. After his death in 1864, his followers continued this organization, and in 1875 it fused with the Marxist Social Democratic Workers Party, led by Wilhelm Liebknecht and August Bebel, to form the united party.

Marx and Engels had sharply criticized many aspects of Lassalle's ideology, especially his reliance on the reactionary Prussian state as the central force to bring about the unification of Germany. Lassalle also denied the need for trade union activity and economic struggle by the working class. For him, the main purposes of the working-class struggle were the fight for universal suffrage and the formation of state-aided producers' cooperatives. Social change was to be achieved by peaceful means.

In his *Critique of the Gotha Programme,* Marx pointed out the Lassallean errors in the compromise program that was proposed for the 1875 fusion congress. Marx's critique, however, was not made public at the time. It was ultimately published on Engels's insistence as part of the SPD programmatic discussion of 1891, which led to the adoption of the Erfurt program, in which the influence of Marxism was stronger.

Nevertheless, the Lassalleans remained a current of opinion within the SPD and later merged into its revisionist wing.

8. Marx and Engels considered it possible, under certain circumstances, for precapitalist societies to bypass an extended stage of capitalist development of the European type, particularly in the event of a successful proletarian revolution in the advanced countries of Western Europe. For an examination of their views with regard to Russia, see: Karl Marx and Frederick Engels, "Preface to the Russian Edition of 1882," in Marx and Engels, *Selected Works* (Moscow: Progress Publishers, 1977), vol. 1, pp. 99–101; Engels, "On Social Relations in Russia," in Marx and Engels, *Selected Works*, vol. 2, pp. 387–410; Marx, "Letter to Vera Zasulich," in Marx and Engels, *Selected Correspondence* (Moscow: Progress Publishers, 1975), pp. 319–20. An instructive initial draft of this letter appears in Teodor Shanin (ed.), *The Late Marx and the Russian Revolution* (New York: Monthly Review Press, 1983), pp. 97–127.

9. Ira Kipnis, *The American Socialist Movement 1897–1912* (New York: Columbia University Press, 1952), pp. 278–79.

10. From a July 1910 letter to George D. Brewer, published in *Speeches of Eugene V. Debs* (New York: International Publishers, 1928), pp. 49–52.

11. Kipnis, *American Socialist Movement*, p. 277.

12. Extracted from *Internationaler Socialistenkongress zu Stuttgart*, pp. 113–20.

13. Japanese immigration to the United States began in the 1880s and these immigrants, like those from China, were immediately subjected to severe government harassment. The U.S. Congress adopted exclusion laws against Asian immigration in 1875, 1885, and 1887. The California legislature passed an anti-Japanese immigrant law in 1905, and in 1906 the children of Japanese immigrants were excluded from California schools. These measures were accompanied by riots and lynch attacks against Chinese and Japanese.

In 1907 Japan and the United States arrived at a "gentlemen's agreement" limiting immigration from Japan.

Many Socialist publications joined in the attacks on Asian immigrants. The virulence of such attacks in the West Coast Socialist press between 1904 and 1907 rose to such heights that the Japanese Socialist Party appealed to American party leaders "to be true to the exhortation of Marx—'Workingmen of all countries, unite.'" There is no record of a reply being sent to Japan.

14. Jürgen Kuczynski, *Der Ausbruch des ersten Weltkrieges und die deutsche Sozialdemokratie* (Berlin: Akademie-Verlag, 1957), p. 177.

15. G.Y. Zinoviev, *Der Krieg und die Krise des Sozialismus* (Vienna: Verlag für Literatur und Politik, 1924), p. 196.

16. Kuczynski, *Der Ausbruch*, pp. 178–79. The International Peace Conference, a meeting of representatives of capitalist governments, was convened in 1899 in The Hague, the Netherlands; a second conference was held there in 1907. No progress was made toward its announced purpose of reducing armaments levels. Several conventions on the laws of war were signed, prohibiting for example, poison gas and aerial bombardment; most of these conventions were disregarded when war broke out.

17. *Internationaler Sozialistenkongress zu Stuttgart*, pp. 85–87.

18. Excerpted from *Internationaler Sozialistenkongress zu Stuttgart*, pp. 81–105 and 64–66.

19. At the 1891 international congress at Brussels, Nieuwenhuis introduced a resolution proposing that "a threatened declaration of war should be answered by an appeal to the people for a general cessation from work." (Julius Braunthal, *History of the International, Vol. 1: 1864–1914* [New York: Frederick A. Praeger Publishers, 1967], p. 287). It was voted down overwhelmingly. At the 1893 congress at Zurich he accused the SPD of chauvinism for its position that Germany should be defended in a possible war with tsarist Russia, a position also held at the time by Frederick Engels and later defended by the Bolsheviks.

20. Commenting in 1916 on the Stuttgart militarism discussion, Gregory Zinoviev noted that this sentence presumably refers to positions on the national question of Marx and Engels, "although Bebel's meaning here is far from clear." As to the preceding reference to the students of Marx and Engels, "Bebel is quite wrong. In 1905 Plekhanov, one of these 'students,' defended very energetically

the thesis that 'the workers have no fatherland.'" See Zinoviev, *Der Krieg*, p. 612.

21. Luxemburg strongly opposed the influence of nationalism in Poland, most of which was ruled by Russia, and held that none of the social classes with decisive weight in Poland had an interest in pursuing the struggle for independence. She criticized the demand for national self-determination, which had been adopted by the International in 1896. See her article elsewhere in this collection, "The Crisis of German Social Democracy."

22. The Prussian king and the French ambassador met at Ems in 1870 to discuss the dispute between their countries over influence in Spain. When German Chancellor Otto von Bismarck received a dispatch summarizing their meeting, he edited it so as to discredit French Emperor Napoleon III, and published his truncated version, an act which provided the immediate pretext for the Franco-Prussian War of 1870–71.

23. Karl Liebknecht's book, *Militarism and Anti-Militarism*, was published in February 1907; two months later the authorities ordered the seizure of all copies. In October of that year Liebknecht was charged with high treason. He was accused of having advocated in his book the "abolition of the standing army by means of the military strike, if needs be conjointly with the incitement of troops to take part in the revolution." The charge also referred to his "making use of the Social-Democratic Young People's Organizations for the purpose of organically disintegrating and demoralizing the militarist spirit." Liebknecht explained that he proposed no actions outside the limits of the law; nevertheless, he was convicted and held in jail until 1908.

See Liebknecht, *Militarism and Anti-Militarism* (Cambridge, Great Britain: Rivers Press, 1973), pp. xi–xii.

24. The congress of French Socialists at Nancy, held the week before the Stuttgart congress, witnessed a full debate on militarism between the currents led by Jaurès, Hervé, and Guesde. In the voting, Hervé supported the Jaurès resolution and it was adopted, 1,960 to 1,174.

25. The "Anti-Socialist Laws" were adopted in 1878 on Bismarck's initiative. They banned all Social Democratic organizations and pub-

lications, allowing only parliamentary activity. During the following years of severe government repression, the Socialists conducted vigorous underground activity and continued to expand their mass influence and electoral support. More than 1,500 party members, including Bebel and Wilhelm Liebknecht, were imprisoned before the laws were repealed in 1890.

26. Luxemburg had been sentenced to three months' imprisonment in Germany in July 1904 for "insulting the emperor." The authorities had taken exception to her remark during the SPD's 1903 election campaign that "a man who talks about the security and good living of the German workers has no idea of the real facts." She had also served time in Russian Poland for her activity in the 1905–6 revolution. Luxemburg was jailed again during June and July of 1907 for making allegedly seditious remarks at the SPD's 1905 congress at Jena.

27. The French expression, "working for the king of Prussia," refers to labor from which one draws no benefits while others reap the advantage. The term originates in the peace of 1748, which brought France no gains while France's ally Prussia annexed the rich province of Silesia.

28. The Fashoda incident grew out of a challenge by France to British control of the Nile Valley. In September 1898 a French expedition occupied Fashoda, a village on the Nile River. Faced with the threat of a military defeat by British forces, the French withdrew in November. In March 1899 an agreement between the two countries was signed, excluding France from the Nile Valley, although a part of the Sudan was given as compensation to France. Subsequently, several meetings were held between French and British trade unionists as a demonstration against their governments' war policies.

29. At the SPD's September 1905 congress at Jena, August Bebel introduced a resolution on the question of the mass strike, declaring: "The party congress considers the broadest utilization of mass work stoppage under certain circumstances one of the most effective weapons to defend itself against such a criminal political act against the working class, or to acquire an important basic right for its liberation." (Carl E. Schorske, *German Social Democracy 1905–1917* [New York: John Wiley & Sons, Inc., 1955], p. 43.) The

adoption of this resolution was viewed as a victory for the left-wing forces within the SPD, and a rebuff for the revisionist wing of which Vollmar was a leader.

The impact of this victory was sharply reduced at the party congress the next year in Mannheim, when Bebel sponsored a resolution declaring that the call for protest strike action could only come from the trade unions, and asserting the independence of the trade unions from the party. The union leadership was strongly opposed to mass protest strikes.

30. This amendment was later introduced by Luxemburg, Lenin, and Julius Martov.

31. During the spring and summer of 1907 Belfast was rocked by a militant dockworkers' strike, led by James Larkin, which spread to other sections of the working class. On August 12 British troops fired on a crowd of 300–500 people in Belfast's Catholic district, killing two and wounding twelve.

32. The Trieste conference of Italian and Austrian Socialists, held May 23–24, 1905, dealt chiefly with the movement for union with Italy within Italian-populated areas of the Austrian Empire. Socialists opposed this movement, believing that it was being used to promote militarism. The Austrian Socialists agreed at Trieste to support autonomy for the Trentino (southern Tyrol) and the establishment of an Italian-language university in Trieste; both parties denounced militarism and imperialist expansion.

33. In 1905 the Norwegian parliament declared the country's independence from Sweden. When the Swedish monarchy threatened armed intervention, the Swedish Social Democratic Party called on workers to respond to such action with a general strike. In addition, the Social Democratic youth organization called on the Swedish proletariat to refuse military service in case of war, for which their leader, Karl Zeth Höglund, was sentenced to nine months' imprisonment. The Swedish government eventually decided to recognize the dissolution of the union between the two countries and war was averted.

34. See Karl Kautsky, "Der Stuttgarter Kongress," in *Die Neue Zeit*, year 25, vol. 2, pp. 724–30.

35. The sweeping condemnation of revisionism by the SPD's 1904

Dresden congress helped win the adoption of an antirevisionist resolution by the International's Amsterdam congress that same year.

36. V.I. Lenin, "The International Socialist Congress in Stuttgart," in Lenin, *Collected Works* (hereinafter *CW*) (Moscow: Progress Publishers, 1974), vol. 13, pp. 85–86.

37. Lenin, *CW*, vol. 15, pp. 194–95.

38. G.Y. Zinoviev, "Lenin i Komintern," *Sochineniya* (Leningrad: State Publishing House, 1924), vol. 15, p. 252.

39. Lenin, "The International Socialist Congress in Stuttgart," in Lenin, *CW*, vol. 13, pp. 75–81. First published October 20, 1907.

40. The Mensheviks held the majority at the fourth (unity) congress of the RSDLP, held in Stockholm, April 23–May 8 (April 10–25), 1906. The fifth RSDLP congress was held in London May 13–June 1 (April 30–May 19), 1907. The Bolsheviks held the majority there. For events relating to countries using the Julian calendar at that time, the date according to the modern calendar is given first, followed in parentheses by the date according to the Julian calendar.

41. Excerpted from Zinoviev, "Vtoroi Internatsional i problema voiny," in Zinoviev and Lenin, *Protiv techeniya* (Moscow: State Publishing House, 1923), pp. 484–98.

42. The term "Marxist Center" came to designate the dominant wing of the German party in the years before the First World War. Its central leader was Bebel, and chief theorist was Kautsky.

2. Resisting the threat of imperialist war: 1907–1914

1. Excerpted from *Stenographische Berichte der Verhandlungen des deutschen Reichstages* (Berlin: 1907), vol. 128, pp. 1062–99.

2. *Dokumente und Materialien zur Geschichte der deutschen Arbeiterbewegung* (Berlin: Dietz Verlag, 1958), series 1, vol. 4, p. 220.

3. Excerpted from *Dokumente und Materialien*, series 1, vol. 4, pp. 221–23, 224–26.

4. In 1859 French Emperor Napoleon III concluded a pact with the Kingdom of Sardinia (Piedmont), the largest independent state among the many states into which Italy was then divided, to wage war on Austria. Austria was then the dominant power in Italy and ruled the Italian provinces of Lombardy and Venice. Napoleon III

demagogically presented his war as one of Italian liberation against Austrian oppression, and many Italian nationalists supported the Sardinian-French alliance for that reason. In fact, Napoleon aimed to annex the Italian territories of Nice and Savoy to France and to weaken the popular revolutionary movement for Italian unity.

Marx and Engels supported the Italian struggle for national unification, but did not think that this fight could be advanced by supporting Napoleon III, whose regime was one of the bulwarks of reaction in Europe. To the contrary, they explained that the revolutionary democratic struggle of the Italian patriots was the road to Italian unity.

They urged workers and other democratic forces in Germany to press the German governments, especially Prussia, to enter the war on the Austrian side against Bonapartist France. They said that this would turn the war, independently of the will of the governments of those states, into a revolutionary war. If successful, this revolutionary war would result in the destruction not only of Bonapartism, but also of the reactionary regimes in Austria, Prussia, and the other states of Germany. In this way the national unification of Germany (including both Prussia and Austria) would be advanced in a revolutionary democratic way.

Fearing an upsurge in Germany if the German states joined in the war, the Prussian rulers remained neutral. Marx and Engels said this policy aided and abetted Bonapartism.

Lensch is not correct in identifying the views of Marx and Engels with those of Lassalle. Lassalle advocated a neutralist stance by Prussia, and in fact described Louis Napoleon's policy as progressive and portrayed the French emperor as a benefactor not only of Italy, but also of Germany. He saw the defeat of Austria as an advance for German unification and advocated war with France only in the event that Napoleon tried to keep the Austrian war booty for itself.

The two pamphlets Lensch refers to which summarize these opposing views are Engels's "Po and Rhine" (in Marx and Engels, *Collected Works*, vol. 16 [New York: International Publishers, 1980], pp. 211–55, and Lassalle's "The Italian War and Prussia's Tasks.").

5. Excerpted from D. Bozorgue (ed.), *Asnad-e Tarikhi: Jonbesh-e Kargari, Sosial Demokrasy va Kommunisti-e Iran 1903–1963* [His-

torical Documents: The Workers' Social Democratic and Communist Movement in Iran, 1903–1963] (Florence, Italy: Mazdak, 1977), vol. 6, pp. 26–30.

6. Carl Schorske, *German Social Democracy 1905–1917* (New York: John Wiley & Sons, 1955), p. 192.

7. Excerpted from "Two Worlds," Lenin, in *Collected Works* (hereinafter *CW*) (Moscow: Progress Publishers, 1974), vol. 16, pp. 305–13.

8. A reference to the January 9 (22), 1905, murderous attack by the tsarist government on a mass demonstration in St. Petersburg which sparked the 1905–6 revolutionary upsurge in Russia.

9. *Dokumente und Materialien,* series 1, vol. 4, pp. 317–18. A different English translation of the entire resolution appears in O.H. Gankin and H.H. Fisher (eds.), *The Bolsheviks and the World War* (Stanford: Stanford University Press, 1976), pp. 72–73.

10. Gregory Zinoviev, "Lenin i Komintern," in *Sochineniya* (Leningrad: State Publishing House, 1924), vol. 15, p. 253. A recent Soviet study, however, concludes that "the participants included Lenin, Rosa Luxemburg, Marchlewski, Braun, Wurm, de Brouckère, Blagoev, Guesde, Rappaport, Iglesias, Plekhanov, Ryazanov, and possibly Kolarov, Kirkov, Kabakchiev, David Wijnkoop, W. van Ravestejn, and others. Most of them supported Lenin's ideas and declared that opportunists should be rebuffed," and "although no decisions were taken . . . on the whole the conference helped consolidate the revolutionary wing." (*The International Working-Class Movement* [Moscow: Progress Publishers, 1983], vol. 3, p. 476.)

11. Excerpted from Rosa Luxemburg, *Gesammelte Werke* (Berlin: Dietz Verlag, 1972), vol. 2, pp. 491–504.

12. Britain, long the world's dominant naval power, responded to the challenge of Germany's ambitious naval construction program with various proposals for naval arms limitations. Since Britain still would hold decisive naval superiority, this would only perpetuate its advantage. No arms reduction was achieved.

13. In March 1911 a revolt broke out in the formally independent country of Morocco, which was a French "sphere of influence." A French expedition was sent to crush the rebellion and to "rescue" Europeans.

14. An army uprising in Turkey in 1908, led by the Young Turk

movement, limited the sultan's power and proclaimed constitutional rule. The ferment in China led to the 1911 national revolution that overthrew the Manchu dynasty and proclaimed a republic The Mexican revolution begun in 1910 overthrew the dictator Porfirio Díaz in May 1911. India and Egypt witnessed growing nationalist movements against British rule; nationalism in Arabia was directed against the Turkish sultan.

15. Negotiations between representatives of Germany and Russia at Potsdam in November 1910 failed to reconcile conflicting claims to "spheres of influence" in the Persian and Turkish empires. Several Russian-Japanese accords in these years aimed to adjust their rival claims within and on the borders of China.

16. In a speech to the House of Commons on March 13, 1911, Grey, the British minister for foreign affairs, proposed that Britain and Germany limit military expenditures and renounce any increase in their naval armament, in order to avoid the danger of financial ruin.

17. Excerpted from *Dokumente und Materialien*, series 1, vol. 4, pp. 348–50.

18. Gen. Georges Boulanger, the leading promoter of a French war of revenge against Germany, was appointed French minister of war in 1886. Bismarck used the occasion to launch a campaign of chauvinist agitation against France and to submit a new military law bill to the Reichstag. When the proposed law met with objections, Bismarck dissolved the Reichstag and called new elections, in which the Social Democrats suffered a severe setback.

19. Excerpted from Rosa Luxemburg, "Um Marokko," in *Gesammelte Werke* (Berlin: Dietz Verlag, 1973), vol. 3, pp. 5–11.

20. The junkers were the landed aristocracy of Germany east of the Elbe River, many of whom became capitalist farmers in the latter half of the nineteenth century. The junkers of Prussia retained a decisive grip on political power under the German Empire of 1871–1918.

21. *Protokoll über die Verhandlungen des Parteitages der Sozialdemokratischen Partei Deutschlands abgehalten in Chemnitz vom 15 bis. 21. September 1912* (hereinafter *SPD 1912 Congress*) (Berlin: Buchhandlung Vorwärts, 1912), pp. 411–12.

22. Ibid., pp. 429–30.

23. Ibid., pp. 415–19 and 421–22.

24. Ibid., pp. 529–30.

25. Lenin, *CW*, vol. 41, pp. 262–66.

26. Italy waged war against Turkey in 1911, conquering the Turkish possession of Tripoli (now Libya). Thousands of Arabs were massacred by Italian troops.

27. On April 17 (4), 1912, a demonstration of thousands of striking miners in the Lena goldfields of Siberia was fired on by troops. Some 500 miners were killed or wounded, and the massacre set off protests across Russia.

28. *Ausserordentlicher Internationaler Sozialisten-Kongress zu Basel am 24. und 25. November 1912* (Berlin, 1912), pp. 36–37.

29. Gankin and Fisher, *The Bolsheviks and the World War*, p. 86.

30. Excerpted from *Dokumente und Materialien*, series 2, vol. 1, pp. 3–8. A different English translation of the entire text appears in Gankin and Fisher, *The Bolsheviks and the World War*, pp. 81–85.

31. L.B. Kamenev, "Na bazelskom kongresse," *Sotsial-Demokrat*, January 25, 1913, no. 30.

32. *Protokoll über die Verhandlungen des Parteitages der sozialdemokratischen Partei Deutschlands abgehalten in Jena vom 14. bis 20. September 1913* (hereinafter *SPD 1913 Congress*) (Berlin: Buchhandlung Vorwärts, 1913), p. 174.

33. Luxemburg, *Gesammelte Werke*, vol. 2, p. 338.

34. Excerpted from *SPD 1913 Congress*, pp. 476–77.

35. Ibid., pp. 495–96.

36. The Progressives were the political party of liberal reform in imperial Germany.

37. Marx's April 1850 article, a review of the book *Le Socialisme et l'impôt*, is contained in Marx and Engels, *Collected Works*, vol. 10, pp. 326–37.

38. Excerpted from Luxemburg, *Gesammelte Werke*, vol. 2, pp. 340–41.

39. Excerpted from *Dokumente und Materialien*, series 1, vol. 4, pp. 477–80.

40. In the Convention, the revolutionary assembly that ruled France

from 1792 to 1795, the radical deputies sat on the high benches to the left of the speaker (the "Mountain"), and the conservative forces to the right (the "Gironde"). The deputies vacillating between them sat in the center of the hall and were designated the "Swamp."

41. The German phrase is literally "the old tactic, tried and true." The German word *die Taktik,* often employed in the documents in this collection to designate the party's entire line of march, is usually rendered as "policies."

42. Excerpted from a letter dated January 3, 1911, and reprinted in Lenin, *CW,* vol. 34, p. 437.

43. Excerpted from Lenin, *CW,* vol. 19, pp. 85–86. First published May 20 (7), 1913.

44. Excerpted from Lenin, *CW,* vol. 19, pp. 99–100. First published May 31 (18), 1913.

45. Lenin, *CW,* vol. 18, pp. 582–85. First published March 14 (1), 1913, on the thirtieth anniversary of Marx's death.

46. Excerpted from Zinoviev, "Vtoroi Internatsional i problema voiny," in Zinoviev and Lenin, *Protiv techeniya* (Moscow: State Publishing House, 1923), pp. 507–19.

3. 1914: The collapse of the Second International

1. Excerpted and translated from the official account of the proceedings of the ISB, an abbreviated stenographic record published in Georges Haupt, *Le Congrès manqué* (Paris: Maspéro, 1965), pp. 251–67. A different English translation of the entire abbreviated record appears in Georges Haupt, *Socialism and the Great War* (Oxford: Clarendon Press, 1972), pp. 250–65.

2. Angelica Balabanoff, *My Life as a Rebel* (New York: Harper & Brothers, 1938), p. 117.

3. Carl Grünberg, "Die Internationale und der Weltkrieg. Materialien," in *Archiv für die Geschichte des Sozialismus und der Arbeiterbewegung* (hereinafter *Grünberg Archiv*) (Leipzig: C.L. Hirschfeld), vol. 6 (1916), p. 406.

4. Ibid., pp. 429–30.

5. Ibid., p. 432.

6. Excerpted from *Dokumente und Materialien zur Geschichte*

der deutschen Arbeiterbewegung, (Berlin [GDR]: Dietz Verlag, 1958), series 2, vol. 1, pp. 17–18.

7. Walter Bartel, *Die Linken in der deutschen Sozialdemokratie im Kampf gegen Militarismus und Krieg* (Berlin [GDR]: Dietz Verlag, 1958), p. 163.

8. Ibid., p. 168.

9. "Der Krieg im Land! Europa in Flammen!" *Erzberger Volksstimme,* August 1, 1914, printed in Grünberg, "Die Internationale," in *Grünberg Archiv,* vol. 6, p. 439.

10. Eugen Prager, *Geschichte der U.S.P.D.* (Glashütten im Taunus: Verlag Detlev Auvermann, 1970), p. 34.

11. Originally published in *Vossische Zeitung,* May 5, 1916. This English translation is from Edwyn Bevan, *German Social Democracy During the War* (London: George Allen & Unwin, 1918), p. 15.

12. Alexandra Kollontai, *Selected Writings* (New York: W.W. Norton & Co., 1977), pp. 84–85.

13. Liebknecht, "Concerning August 4," in *Dokumente und Materialien,* series 2, vol. 1, pp. 19–21. Kautsky's statement in *Sozialisten und Krieg* (Prague: 1937), p. 460 is cited by Bartel, *Die Linken,* p. 177.

14. Bartel, *Die Linken,* p. 181.

15. *Dokumente und Materialien,* series 2, vol. 1, pp. 22–23.

16. William Walling, *The Socialists and the War: A Documentary Study* (New York: Henry Holt, 1915), p. 177.

17. Ibid., p. 165.

18. Grünberg, "Die Internationale", in *Grünberg Archiv,* vol. 7, pp. 140–43.

19. *The International Working-Class Movement,* Volume 3 (Moscow: Progress Publishers, 1983), pp. 515–16.

20. Excerpted from "Rabochii Peterburg i voina," *Kommunist,* no. 1–2, 1915, pp. 161–67. The tsarist capital, officially called "St. Petersburg," was referred to in the workers' movement as "Petersburg," or, simply, "Piter." When the war began, the government changed the official name to the more Russian-sounding "Petrograd"; the workers' movement took no notice of the change. The city was renamed Leningrad in 1924.

21. A.Y. Badayev, *Bol'sheviki v Gosydarstvennoi dyme* (Moscow: Partizdat, 1932), pp. 301–302.

22. Grünberg, "Die Internationale", in *Grünberg Archiv,* vol. 7, pp. 119–120.

23. A. Shlyapnikov, *Kanun semnadtsatogo goda* (Moscow: State Publishing House, 1923), vol. 1, pp. 28–29.

24. Bashibazouks was a term used to refer to irregular, ill-disciplined auxiliaries of the army of the Turkish Ottoman Empire.

25. Excerpted from K. Pechak, "The Social-Democracy of Latvia (Communist Party of Latvia) in the Period 1909–1915," *Proletarskaya revolyutsiya,* no. 12 (1922), pp. 79–81.

26. Grünberg, "Die Internationale," in *Grünberg Archiv,* vol. 7, pp. 121–25.

27. The opposition current in the Polish Social Democracy, called the "National Executive Committee" in Grünberg's Polish text, is designated as the "Regional Executive Committee" in his German translation of the text and in most other sources. In the Lenin *Collected Works* it is sometimes called the Warsaw opposition.

28. Lenin, *CW,* vol. 21, pp. 15–19.

29. Among the Socialists who became ministers in bourgeois governments were Emile Vandervelde in Belgium and Jules Guesde in France.

30. In four letters to Shlyapnikov written in October 1914, Lenin assessed more fully the responsibility of Kautsky and the Center current of the SPD in the party's position on the war. In his October 27 letter Lenin stated, "Rosa Luxemburg was right when she wrote, long ago, that Kautsky has the 'subservience of a theoretician'—servility, in plainer language, servility to the majority of the Party, to opportunism. Just now there is *nothing* in the world more harmful and dangerous for the *ideological* independence of the proletariat. . . ." See Lenin, *CW,* vol. 35, pp. 161–72.

4. National defense or social revolution

1. Eugen Prager, *Geschichte der U.S.P.D.* (Glashütten/Taunus: Detlev Auvermann, 1970), p. 50.

2. As quoted in the *Berliner Tageblatt,* February 23, 1915, no. 98.

From *Dokumente und Materialien*, series 2, vol. 1, p. 106.

3. Quoted in V.I. Lenin, *Collected Works* (hereinafter *CW*) (Moscow: Progress Publishers, 1974), vol. 21, p. 95.

4. Karl Kautsky, "Der Krieg," *Die Neue Zeit*, year 32, vol. 2, p. 846.

5. Karl Kautsky, "Die Sozialdemokratie im Kriege," *Die Neue Zeit*, year 33, vol. 1, pp. 3–8.

6. Excerpted from Karl Kautsky, "Die Internationalität und der Krieg," *Die Neue Zeit*, year 33, vol. 1, pp. 245–250.

7. Excerpted from Leon Trotsky, *Voina i revoliutsiya* (Moscow: State Publishing House, 1923), vol. 1, pp. 75–81, 147–151.

8. The Great French Revolution began in 1789; the wars related to it ended with the defeat of Napoleon in 1815; 1848 was a year of democratic revolutionary uprisings across much of Europe; wars in 1859, 1864, 1866, and 1870 were related to the process of German and Italian unification.

9. In the early 1880s, a wing of the French Socialist movement emerged that sought to win majorities on the French municipal councils as its main aim. Through this they hoped to gradually introduce public ownership, in alliance with progressive capitalists. This "policy of possibilities" led to the term *Possibilists*, which for many years came to signify the reformist wing of the French workers' movement.

10. This is a reference to Marx's statement, "The weapon of criticism cannot, of course, replace criticism by weapons, material force must be overthrown by material force." (Marx and Engels, "Contribution to the Critique of Hegel's Philosophy of Law," in Marx and Engels, *Collected Works*, [New York: International Publishers, 1976], vol. 3, p. 182.)

11. A. Shlyapnikov, *On the Eve of 1917* (London: Allison & Busby, 1982), p. 26.

12. Lenin, *CW*, vol. 21, pp. 27–34.

13. Excerpted from Lenin, *CW*, vol. 21, pp. 38–41.

14. Martov later resisted pressure from Trotsky and other editors for a break from the chauvinist Mensheviks, and retreated from his initial leading role in the paper. He resigned from *Nashe Slovo* in April 1916.

15. Gregory Zinoviev, "Patsifizm ili marksizm," Lenin and Zinoviev, *Protiv techeniya* (Moscow: State Publishing House, 1923), p. 124.

16. Zinoviev, "Rossiiskaya sotsial-demokratiya i russkii sotsial-shovinism," Lenin and Zinoviev, *Protiv techeniya,* p. 248.

17. Lenin, "Under a False Flag," in *CW,* vol. 21, pp. 151–53.

18. Lenin, *CW,* vol. 21, pp. 275–80. First published in *Sotsial-Demokrat,* July 26, 1915.

19. The term "social-chauvinists" was used to describe those who mouthed socialist words but practiced chauvinist deeds.

20. Trotsky's "Open Letter to the Editorial Board of 'Kommunist'" is included in Chapter 5 of the present collection.

21. The Bern resolution is included in Chapter 6 of the present collection.

22. This refers to the impetus to victory given the Austrian suffrage movement by the 1905 Russian revolution.

23. Excerpted from Trotsky, "Voyennaya katastrofa i politicheskiye perspektivy," *Voina i revoliutsiya,* vol. 1, pp. 242–47. First published between August 26 and September 4, 1915, in *Nashe Slovo.*

24. The "Moor" in this case is a character in the play *Die Räuber* (The Robbers) by Friedrich von Schiller. The "Moor" performs an unsavory task for the king and, on its completion, is then curtly and cynically dismissed.

25. Jürgen Kuczynski, *Der Ausbruch des ersten Weltkrieges und die deutsche Sozialdemokratie* (Berlin: Akademie-Verlag, 1957), pp. 214–16.

26. *Spartakusbriefe* (Berlin [GDR]: Dietz Verlag, 1958), pp. 7–8.

27. Lenin, "The Collapse of the Second International," in *CW,* vol. 21, pp. 251–52.

28. *Dokumente und Materialien zur Geschichte der deutschen Arbeiterbewegung* (Berlin: Dietz Verlag, 1958), series 2, vol. 1, pp. 64–65.

29. Excerpted from *Dokumente und Materialien,* pp. 165–66.

30. Alfred von Tirpitz, the architect of German naval expansion, was secretary of state for the German navy; Erich von Falkenhayn was chief of staff of the German army.

31. Internationale sozialistische Kommission zu Bern, *Bulletin,*

November 27, 1915, no. 2, p. 8.

32. Lenin, *CW*, vol. 21, pp. 181–82.

33. Excerpted from Kautsky, "Der Imperialismus," *Die Neue Zeit*, year 32, vol. 2, pp. 919–22.

34. Lenin, "The Collapse of the Second International," in *CW*, vol. 21, p. 225.

35. Heinz Wohlgernuth, *Burgkrieg, nicht Burgfriede!* (Berlin [GDR]: Dietz Verlag, 1963), pp. 228–29.

36. The Turkish Ottoman Empire in 1914 included territories presently occupied by Turkey, Syria, Lebanon, Iraq, Jordan, Israel, and the countries of the Arabian peninsula.

37. Rosa Luxemburg, "Der Wiederaufbau der Internationale," *Die Internationale*, no. 1, (Frankfurt: Verlag Neue Kritik, 1971), pp. 4–14.

38. Austro-Marxism was an opportunist trend in the Social Democracy associated with the leadership of the Austrian Social Democratic Party. Its leading spokesmen were Otto Bauer, Victor Adler, Friedrich Adler, Max Adler, Rudolf Hilferding, and Karl Renner. They became especially noted for their position on the national question, counterposing cultural autonomy for national minorities to the right of nations to self-determination.

39. The "Center" was the name of the Catholic party of imperial Germany; it was also a term for Kautsky's current in the SPD.

40. *Die Post* was a reactionary Berlin newspaper, organ of the Imperial Free Conservative Party.

41. The Copenhagen conference of Socialist parties of neutral countries was held January 17–18, 1915. It was attended by representatives from the parties of Sweden, Denmark, Norway, and Holland, with a guest from the Polish-Lithuanian Bund. The conference called on the Socialist parliamentary representatives in the belligerent countries to appeal to their governments for mediation to end the war.

42. P. Kievskii (Y.L. Pyatakov), "Sobrat po oruzhiyu," *Kommunist*, 1915, no. 1–2, p. 182.

43. Excerpted from Lenin, *CW*, vol. 21, pp. 205–59.

44. "Struvist" refers to P.B. Struve (1870–1944), a Russian Marxist in the 1890s, who later became a liberal and finally a monarchist.

45. The Brussels bloc was formed at the Brussels "unity" conference of Russian Social Democratic groups, convened by the International Socialist Bureau on July 16–18, 1914. A majority of representatives at this conference united around a resolution proposed by Kautsky, which purported to provide for the unification of the RSDLP. The Bolsheviks and the Latvian Social Democracy sent representatives to this meeting, but refused to take part in the vote.

46. "Gaponade" is derived from the name of Gapon, a priest of the Russian Orthodox Church. Acting as an agent of the tsarist secret police, Gapon founded and led an organization claiming to represent workers' interests and organized a workers' demonstration before the tsar's palace in St. Petersburg on January 9, 1905. By order of the tsar, troops fired on the unarmed demonstrators. The incident aroused workers' indignation throughout the country, and served as the starting point of the 1905 Russian revolution.

47. Lenin, "The Social-Chauvinists' Sophisms," in *CW*, vol. 21, pp. 185–86. First published May 1, 1915. According to a footnote in Lenin's *Collected Works*, October–December 1906 "refers to the October all-Russia political strike and the December armed uprising in Moscow, in 1905." (Lenin, *CW*, vol. 21, p. 475.)

48. Excerpted from Lenin, *CW*, vol. 21, pp. 295–338.

49. Marx and Engels led a protracted struggle to free the First International from the influence of anarchism, and the Second International shortly after its formation clarified its position on the anarchist movement and maintained a firm organizational separation from the anarchist movement.

5. Russian internationalists discuss unity: 1914–15

1. For a Bolshevik view of their differences with the Mensheviks since 1903, see V.I. Lenin, "Socialism and War," *Collected Works* (hereinafter *CW*) (Moscow: Progress Publishers, 1974), vol. 21, pp. 331–39.

2. Lenin, "The Question of the Unity of Internationalists," in *CW*, vol. 21, p. 188.

3. Gregory Zinoviev, "Vazhnyi dokument," *Protiv techeniya* (Moscow: State Publishing House, 1923), pp. 19–20.

4. Ibid., p. 20.

5. Alexander Shlyapnikov, *On the Eve of 1917* (London: Allison & Busby, 1982), pp. 45–46.

6. Shlyapnikov, *Kanun semnadtsatogo goda* (Moscow: State Publishing House, 1923), vol. 1, pp. 41–43.

7. Excerpted from Shlyapnikov, *Kanun semnadtsatogo goda,* vol. 1, pp. 57–61.

8. Lenin, "The Kind of 'Unity' Larin Proclaimed at the Swedish Congress," in *CW,* vol. 21, pp. 116–17.

9. Excerpted from Lenin, *CW,* vol. 21, pp. 108–14.

10. The reference is to the debate over Eduard Bernstein's revisionist book, *Evolutionary Socialism.*

11. Excerpted from "Doklad Organizatsionnago Komiteta R.S.D.L.P. kopengagenskoi konferentsii," *Izvestiya Zagranichnogo Sekretariata Organizatsionnago Komiteta Rossiiskoi Sotsial-Demokraticheskoi Rabochei partii,* February 22, 1915, no. 1.

12. Lenin, "To Alexander Shlyapnikov," in *CW,* vol. 35, p. 167.

13. Excerpted from Lenin, *CW,* vol. 21, pp. 125–27.

14. Quoted by Lenin, "The Question of Unity," in *CW,* vol. 21, p. 189.

15. Lenin, *CW,* vol. 21, pp. 165–68.

16. "Pis'mo redaktsii 'Nashego Slova'—TSK RSDLP," *Leninskii Sbornik,* vol. 17, pp. 204–6.

17. The "narrow" sense of the word Russian is its application to the ethnic Russians who made up less than 50 percent of the population of the tsarist empire.

18. The reference is to the Menshevik deputies in the Duma.

19. On March 20, 1915, Otto Rühle joined Liebknecht in voting against war credits, the first SPD Reichstag deputy to do so. Both had voted for the war credits in August 1914.

20. Trotsky, "Otkrytoye pis'mo v redaktsiyu zhurnala 'Kommunist,'" *Nashe Slovo,* June 4, 1915, no. 105.

21. For the opinion of the Bolshevik leadership on the statements, see Lenin's article, "What Has Been Revealed by the Trial of the RSDLP Duma Group," in Chapter 6 of the present collection.

22. Lenin, "The Question of the Unity of Internationalists," in *CW,* vol. 21, pp. 190–91.

6. The Bolsheviks in the first year of war

1. V.I. Lenin, *Collected Works* (hereinafter *CW*) (Moscow: Progress Publishers, 1974), vol. 21, pp. 171–77.

2. The prosecution gave special emphasis at the trial to a report on two supposedly incriminating documents of the arrested deputies, a notebook of Muranov and a personal diary of Petrovsky. The report, in fact, gave a picture of the deputies' tireless work promoting the struggles of working people across the country.

3. O.H. Gankin and H.H. Fisher, *The Bolsheviks and the World War* (Stanford: Stanford University Press, 1976), pp. 187–88.

4. "Bernskaya Konferentsiya 1915 g.," *Proletarskaya Revolyutsiya,* 1925, no. 5 (40), pp. 170–72.

5. This article is printed in Lenin, *CW,* vol. 21, pp. 35–41. Excerpts are printed in Chapter 4 of the present collection

6. This declaration was drafted by Maxim Litvinov, and printed in no. 40 of *Sotsial-Demokrat.* An English translation is printed in Gankin and Fisher, *The Bolsheviks and the World War,* pp. 282–84.

7. The reference is to an unsigned lead article by Gregory Zinoviev, "The War and the Destiny of our Emancipation," *Sotsial-Demokrat,* February 12, 1915, reprinted in *Protiv Techeniya* (Moscow: State Publishing House, 1923), pp. 52–59. In this article Zinoviev wrote, "Yes, we are for the defeat of 'Russia,' for that will facilitate the victory of *Russia,* emancipating it, liberating it from the fetters of tsarism."

8. "Bernskaya Konferentsiya," *Proletarskaya Revolyutsiya,* 1925, no. 5 (40), pp. 187–88.

9. Gankin and Fisher, *The Bolsheviks in the World War,* p. 182.

10. Ibid., p. 178.

11. Lenin, "The Conference of the R.S.D.L.P. Groups Abroad," in *CW,* vol. 21, pp. 158–64.

12. The quoted sentences are from the November 1914 Central Committee statement, "The War and the Russian Social Democracy," printed in Chapter 4 of the present collection. See Lenin, *CW,* vol. 21, p. 34.

13. Ibid., pp. 339–43. First published in *Sotsial-Demokrat* no. 44, August 23, 1915.

14. Proudhonism is a reference to Pierre-Joseph Proudhon (1809–

1865), the French petty-bourgeois socialist and precursor of anarchism. Proudhon envisioned a society based on fair exchange between independent producers, and proposed the replacement of the state by the free association of these producers.

15. *Partiya bol'shevikov v gody mirovoi imperialisticheskoi voiny* (Moscow: State Publishing House, 1963), pp. 233–35.

16. The "Italian" strike was a "work to rule" slowdown. In February 1905 Italian railway workers, facing a harsh antistrike law, undertook a form of strike in which they formally observed the work rules while doing everything possible to disorganize the functioning of the railways. This special kind of strike became known among workers of various countries as "Italian."

17. The lack of elementary social legislation forced Russian workers to establish their own insurance funds; these institutions also provided a useful vehicle for legal political work.

18. The "three whales" were the three primary Bolshevik slogans for the democratic revolution: the democratic republic, the eight-hour working day, and the confiscation of the landlords' estates. These slogans were popularly referred to as the "three pillars of Bolshevism," and sometimes as the "three whales of Bolshevism," after the ancient myth according to which the world rested upon three whales.

19. "Takticheskiye zadachi proletariata v demokraticheskoi revolyutsii," in *Partiya bol'shevikov*, p. 137. Lenin took up the problems in demanding a Constituent Assembly and the formation of Soviets in his October 1915 article "Several Theses," printed in Chapter 9 of the present collection.

20. "Listovka Peterburgskogo Komiteta . . . ," in *Partiya bol'shevikov*, pp.181–82.

21. Lenin, *CW*, vol. 21, pp. 367–69.

22. Carol Eubanks Hayden, "Feminism and Bolshevism: The *Zhenotdel* and the Politics of Women's Emancipation in Russia, 1917–1930" (Ph.D. diss., University of California, Berkeley, 1979), pp. 76–83.

23. "Proklamatsiya Kiyevskogo Komiteta RSDRP," in *Partiya bol'shevikov*, pp. 178–80.

24. Lenin, *CW*, vol. 21, pp. 378–82.

7. Birth of the Zimmerwald Left

1. Arnold Reisberg, *Lenin und die Zimmerwalder Bewegung* (Berlin [GDR]: Dietz Verlag, 1966), p. 140.

2. V.I. Lenin, *Collected Works* (hereinafter *CW*) (Moscow: Progress Publishers, 1971), vol. 41, pp. 347–48.

3. *Dokumente und Materialien zur Geschichte der deutschen Arbeiterbewegung* (Berlin [GDR]: Dietz Verlag, 1958), series 2, vol. 1, pp. 125–27.

4. Richard Schüller, *Von den Anfängen der proletarischen Jugendbewegung bis zur Gründung der KJI (Geschichte der Kommunistischen Jugendinternationale,* vol. 1) (Munich: Verlagskooperative Trikont, 1970), p. 104.

5. Midway through the conference, the number of voting delegates was increased to encompass representatives from Russia of both the Mensheviks and Bolsheviks.

6. *Berner Tagwacht,* April 17, 1915.

7. Jean Maxe, *De Zimmerwald au Bolchévisme* (Paris: 1920), pp. 27–28, quoted in Merle Fainsod, *International Socialism and the World War* (New York: Anchor Books, 1969), p. 88.

8. Gregory Zinoviev, "Otchet delegata TSK RSDRP o predvaritel'nom soveshchanii," in *Leninskii Sbornik,* vol. 14, pp. 161–64.

9. The question mark is in the original text. Balabanoff attended the conference as a representative of the Italian Socialist Party.

10. The Dutch Marxists refers to the left Socialists around the newspaper *De Tribune* (The Tribune), who formed a separate organization, the Social Democratic Party, in 1909. Their main theorist was Anton Pannekoek, who lived in Germany after 1909, and was particularly influential in the Bremen SPD organization.

11. In addition to being editor of *Die Gleichheit,* Zetkin was also a leader of the Stuttgart left Socialists, and a prominent figure in the Spartacist *(Die Internationale)* current.

12. Zinoviev, "Pervaya mezhdunarodnaya konferentsiya," in *Protiv techeniya* (Moscow: State Publishing House, 1923), p. 293. First published October 24 (11), 1915.

13. This resolution, adopted in October 1913, is printed in Lenin, *CW,* vol. 19, pp. 427–29. The prewar discussion among Polish and

Russian Social Democrats also includes Rosa Luxemburg, "The National Question and Autonomy," in Luxemburg, *The National Question* (New York: Monthly Review Press, 1976), pp. 101–287; Lenin, "Critical Remarks on the National Question," in Lenin, *CW*, vol. 14, pp. 17–51; Lenin, "The Right of Nations to Self-Determination," in Lenin, *CW*, vol. 14, pp. 393–454.

14. Lenin, "The Draft Resolution Proposed by the Left Wing at Zimmerwald," in *CW*, vol. 21, p. 345.

15. Ibid., p. 347.

16. The following delegates registered for the Zimmerwald conference (countries and organizations are listed as given in the conference minutes): Charles Naine, Switzerland; Fritz Platten, Switzerland; Robert Grimm, Switzerland; Karl Moor, Switzerland; V.I. Lenin, Central Committee, Russian Social Democratic Labor Party; Gregory Zinoviev, CC, RSDLP; Winter [Jan Berzin], Central Committee, Latvian Social Democracy; Leon Trotsky, *Nashe Slovo*, Russia; Pavel Axelrod, Organizing Committee, RSDLP; Julius Martov, Organizing Committee, RSDLP; Lemansky, Secretariat of the "Bund" Abroad; Marc Natanson, Delegation Abroad of the Central Committee of the Socialist Revolutionary Party of Russia; Victor Chernov, *Zhizn*, Russia; Adolph Hoffmann, Berlin, Germany; Minna Reinhart, Berlin, Germany; Berta Thalheimer, Stuttgart, Germany; Ewald Vogtherr, Deputy, Dresden, Germany; Ernst Meyer, *Vorwärts* editorial board, Berlin, Germany; Georg Ledebour, Deputy, Berlin, Germany; Heinrich Berges, Frankfurt am Main, Germany; Josef Herzfeld, Deputy, Berlin, Germany; Gustav Lachenmayer, Schwäbisch Gmünd, Germany; Julian Borchardt, Berlin, Germany; Warski [Adolf Warszawski], Social Democracy of Poland and Lithuania; Stanislaw Lapinski, Polish Socialist Party; Karl Radek, Poland; Constantino Lazzari, Italy; Angelica Balabanoff, Italy; Giacinto Menotti Serrati, Italy; Oddino Morgari, Italy; Giuseppe Emmanuele Modigliani, Italy; Christian Rakovsky, Romania; Vasil Kolarov, Deputy, Bulgaria; Henriette Roland-Holst, *De Internationale*, Holland; Arthur Merrheim, Brotherhood of Metalworkers and minority of the General Confederation of Labor (CGT), France; A. Bourderon, Brotherhood of Coopers and CGT minority, France; Zeth Höglund, Executive Committee, Social Democratic Youth League of Sweden

and Norway; Ture Nerman, Executive Committee, Social Democratic Youth League of Sweden and Norway.

(Horst Lademacher [ed.], *Die Zimmerwalder Bewegung* [The Hague: Mouton, 1967], vol. 1, pp. 45–48. This work contains the complete proceedings of the Zimmerwald and Kienthal conferences, and of related meetings of the Zimmerwald movement.)

17. Zimmerwald conference proceedings are exerpted from Horst Lademacher (ed.), "Zimmerwalder Konferenz," in *Die Zimmerwalder Bewegung*, vol. 1, pp. 43–179.

18. Ernst Meyer later recalled that this letter "called forth a storm of enthusiasm from all the members of the Conference except Ledebour and Adolf Hoffmann, who felt hurt, not without reason, and whispered something about 'eccentricity.' Lenin liked especially the passage: 'Civil war and not civil peace.' He said, 'Civil war—that is excellent!' and repeated this sentence over and over again." Quoted in O.H. Gankin and H.H. Fisher, *The Bolsheviks and the World War* (Stanford: Stanford University Press, 1976), p. 326.

19. The SPD's Executive Committee sent Hermann Müller, one of its members, to Brussels and Paris on July 31 (not September 2, as Ledebour says) in an attempt to arrive at a joint course of action by French and German Socialists in face of the impending war. He arrived in Paris the day after the assassination of Jaurès, and had a long discussion with French Socialist leaders. Their views on the nature of the war diverged completely from those of the German leaders, and all that could be agreed was that it would be desirable for both parties to abstain on the war credits vote, although neither party was then intending to do so.

20. The reference is to the minority vote within the SPD Reichstag fraction advocating opposition to each successive war credits vote in the Reichstag (August 4, 1914; December 2, 1914; March 20, 1915; and August 20, 1915). On the third occasion, the war credits were combined for the vote with appropriations for the regular imperial budget. Except for Liebknecht and Rühle, none of these minority deputies actually voted against war credits in the Reichstag until December 1915.

21. When the fourth set of war credits were voted, August 20, 1915, about thirty SPD deputies left the Reichstag chamber and did

not take part in the vote. Liebknecht alone voted against the war credits; Otto Rühle later declared that this had been his intention, but the vote had been taken without warning when he happened to be absent.

22. Ministerialism refers to Socialists accepting posts as ministers in bourgeois governments, as Millerand had done in France in 1899 and Guesde in 1914.

23. On June 3 (16), 1907, the tsar dissolved the second State Duma, and issued an electoral decree changing election laws to increase ruling-class representation. A landlord's vote now had the same weight as that of 500 workers; workers and peasants together elected one quarter of the deputies. This guaranteed a progovernment majority in the third Duma, regardless of the will of the majority of the people.

24. As the war progressed, the German government indicated that its war aims included annexation of additional Polish territory, as well as frontier "rectifications" in the west, maintenance of some form of domination over Belgium, and other demands. Ledebour proposed that the SPD attack these annexationist plans in the August 20, 1915, war credits debate. This was rejected by the party's Reichstag fraction by a vote of 49 to 48. David, speaking for the party in the Reichstag August 20, reiterated the party's general stand for self-determination and against wars of conquest, but said nothing about the government's statements on its plans for annexation. (Lademacher, *Die Zimmerwalder Bewegung*, p. 99.)

25. The second document of the German delegation was a draft manifesto, presented by Ledebour at the close of his remarks. The text of this draft is unavailable. Leon Trotsky reported in *Nashe Slovo* that the German proposal focused on the conditions of a future peace—no annexations, no forced economic integration, the right to self-determination—but failed to link them to a criticism of the conduct of the Socialist parties and to a projection of the need for revolutionary struggle. (Trotsky, "Raboty konferentsii," in *Voina i revolyutsiya* [Moscow: State Publishing House, 1924], vol. 2, p. 49.)

26. The reference is to the "suffrage promenade" of March 6, 1910, discussed in Chapter 2 of the present collection.

27. The translation of these remarks is from Lenin, *CW*, vol. 41, pp. 353–54.

28. The *Manifesto of the Communist Party*, published in February 1848, on the eve of the outbreak of the revolutionary upsurge of 1848, stated in its final paragraph that "The Communists disdain to conceal their views and aims. They openly declare that their ends can be attained only by the forcible overthrow of all existing social conditions." (Karl Marx and Frederick Engels, *Collected Works* [New York: International Publishers, 1976], vol. 6, p. 519.)

29. The Amsterdam congress of 1904 adopted a resolution against revisionism, strongly supported by Jules Guesde and opposed by Jean Jaurès. It also passed a motion for the unification of the two organizations led by Guesde and Jaurès, which was achieved the following year.

30. On July 31 (18), 1914, Serbian Socialist deputies voted against the war credits proposed by the Serbian government.

31. The translation of these remarks is from Lenin, *CW*, vol. 41, pp. 354–55.

32. The three draft manifestos were those submitted by Radek and Lenin, by the German delegation, and by Trotsky and Roland-Holst. The resolution was that submitted by Radek and Lenin.

33. Because of pressure from Ledebour, the official minutes did not count the vote of Borchardt, and gave the total as nineteen to eleven.

34. Trotsky's later statement indicates that he added his signature to this declaration following its submission.

35. France proposed to annex Alsace-Lorraine from Germany, and Italy wished to annex territory from Austria. Both justified their claims as reflecting the exercise of self-determination of national minorities in these territories, and also as corresponding to German and Austrian responsibility for the war.

36. Radek declared that according to the statutes of his party only members of its executive body could sign statements, and that he was therefore signing on behalf of Cz. Hanecki, a member of the Regional Executive Committee of the Social Democracy of the Kingdom of Poland and Lithuania.

8. The discussion in the Zimmerwald Left

1. Internationale sozialistische Kommission zu Bern, *Bulletin,* November 27, 1915, no. 2, p. 5.

2. Ibid.

3. Alfred Erich Senn, *The Russian Revolution in Switzerland 1914–1917* (Madison: University of Wisconsin Press, 1971), p. 121.

4. Henriette Roland-Holst, "Der Kampf um Zimmerwald in Holland," *Vorbote,* January 1916, no. 1, pp. 64–68.

5. Leon Trotsky, "Vyvody," in *Voina i revolyutsiya* (Moscow: State Publishing House, 1924), vol. 2, pp. 55–56.

6. Excerpted from Trotsky, "Raboty konferentsii," ibid., pp. 43–49.

7. V.I. Lenin, *Collected Works* (hereinafter *CW*) (Moscow: Progress Publishers, 1974), vol. 21, pp. 383–88.

8. See "The War and Russian Social Democracy" in Chapter 4 of the present collection.

9. The Conference of the Popular Socialists and the Socialist Revolutionaries in Russia adopted a resolution for active participation in the war on the side of tsarism.

10. Karl Radek, "Zur Einführung," *Internationale Flugblätter,* November 1915, no. 1.

11. One-day strikes to celebrate May 1, the international workers' holiday, had become a tradition among militant workers. Opportunist leaders of the German trade unions moved before the war to end these strikes, and the issue became a point of confrontation between right and left wings in the German party and the International.

12. British miners launched a general strike in 1912 for a guaranteed minimum wage. One million workers eventually participated and much of British industry was brought to a standstill. With the help of right-wing union leaders, the government secured an end to the struggle with minimal concessions.

13. Lenin, *CW,* vol. 21, pp. 423–28.

14. The resolution of the Zimmerwald Left was published as the lead article in the May 1916 issue of the *International Socialist Review,* a publication of the left wing of the U.S. Socialist Party. The article by Dutch Socialist S.J. Rutgers that presented the left resolution was entitled, "The Battle Cry of a New International."

It noted that "the resolution adopted by the majority of this Zimmerwald Conference proved to be a compromise, was confusing by its statement that the right of self-determination of peoples must be the indestructible foundation of national relations. And what was still worse, the accepted resolution did not indicate a definite method of fighting, did not come to a clear understanding that our only hope is in a series of mass actions on the industrial as well as on the political field."

After presenting the Zimmerwald Left resolution, Rutgers concluded: "American Comrades! This resolution breathes the fighting spirit of a new generation. . . . It means the social revolution as a practical issue of the class struggle; civil war till the final victory. . . . This always has been the spirit of our *International Socialist Review*."

15. Lenin's letter to Roland-Holst reads, in part:

"Comrade Radek has just shown us Comrade Pannekoek's letter and the 'Introduction'.

"This letter and the 'Introduction' substantially *change* the previously adopted constitution of *Vorbote*. It had been agreed that *Vorbote* would appear as the organ of *two* groups, namely, (1) the Roland-Holst and Trotsky group (or Roland-Holst and her friends without Trotsky, if Trotsky is unwilling to join); (2) the Zimmerwald Left group (whose bureau consists of three comrades: Radek, Lenin and Zinoviev). Comrade Pannekoek was appointed representative of the latter group.

"Now the above-mentioned documents (the letter and the 'Introduction') change the constitution: *Vorbote* appears as the organ of *two comrades*, Pannekoek and Roland-Holst.

"If Comrades Pannekoek and Roland-Holst have decided to make this change, we take note of it. The owner of *Vorbote* had the full right to do so.

"We do not refuse to co-operate in these new conditions, but must require certain guarantees." (Lenin, *CW*, vol. 36, pp. 363–64.)

See also Lenin's letter of March 8, 1916, to Roland-Holst, in Lenin, *CW*, vol. 43, pp. 513–16.

16. A translation of Pannekoek's "Introduction" was printed under the title "The Third International," in the *International Socialist*

Review, February 1917, vol. 17, no. 8, pp. 460–64.

17. Excerpted from L.J. van Rossum, "Ein unveröffentlichter Brief Trockijs von Anfang 1916," *International Review of Social History,* 1969, vol. 14, part 2, pp. 251–66.

18. Appended to Roland-Holst's article on the differences of evaluation of the Zimmerwald conference between her group (the Revolutionary Socialist League) and the Dutch Tribunists was an editors' note, stating that this presentation "appears to us to be in part already superseded," since members of both groups had now declared their agreement with the Zimmerwald Left. It also stated that the viewpoint of the Russian Marxists, who defended the demand for national self-determination, would appear in the next issue. *Vorbote* listed its editors as Pannekoek and Roland-Holst.

19. In a May 23, 1916, letter to Alexander Shlyapnikov, discussing disagreements between the Bolshevik Central Committee and the publishers of *Kommunist,* Lenin wrote the following on the *Vorbote* dispute:

"You may not know that Radek pushed us out of the *Vorbote* editorial board. It was initially agreed that there would be a joint editorial board composed of two groups: (1) the Dutch (maybe + Trotsky) and (2) us (i.e., Radek, *Grigory and me*). This condition gave us equal rights on the editorial board.

"Radek intrigued for months, and got the 'missus' (Roland-Holst) to *cancel* this plan. We were demoted to the position of contributors. It's a fact!

"Is it proper to reward Radek for this feat by giving him the *right* to 'discuss', and the publishers, the *right* to hide behind Radek? That will be not discussion, but dissension and intrigue. (1) *Gazeta Robotnicza* (February 1916), in which Radek participates, carried some purely factional attacks on us, and a resolution on *Nashe Slovo* lines. (2) Now on the question of assessing the Irish insurrection (a most important question, is it not? Not abstract 'theory'!) *both* Radek *and* Kulisher (the Cadet in *Rech*) are in *full agreement,* stupidly calling it a 'putsch'.

"This is incredible, but it's a fact!" (Lenin, *CW,* vol. 36, pp. 394–95.)

20. Excerpted from "Thesen über Imperialismus und nationale Unterdrückung," *Vorbote,* April 1916, no. 2, pp. 44–51. A different

English translation of the full text is printed as an appendix in Rosa Luxemburg, *The National Question* (New York: Monthly Review Press, 1976), pp. 303–319.

21. Rosa Luxemburg, "Die Krise der Sozialdemokratie," in *Gesammelte Werke,* (Berlin [GDR]: Dietz Verlag, 1974), vol. 4, pp. 135–36.

22. Lenin, "The Discussion on Self-Determination Summed Up," in *CW,* vol. 22, pp. 348–51.

23. Excerpted from Lenin, *CW,* vol. 22, pp. 143–56.

24. The Dreyfus case refers to the frame-up trial instituted in 1894 by reactionary circles in the French military against Alfred Dreyfus, a Jewish officer of the general staff. Dreyfus was falsely accused of espionage and high treason; a court-martial sentenced him to life imprisonment. A public movement for a review of the case took the form of a fierce struggle between republicans and royalists and led to his eventual release in 1906.

The Zabern incident refers to the outburst of indignation among the local, mainly French, inhabitants of Zabern in Alsace-Lorraine against the Prussian militarists caused by the brutality of a Prussian officer in November 1913.

25. "Cultural and national autonomy" refers to a scheme advanced by Austrian Social Democracy whereby every citizen in the state would register as part of one of its constituent nationalities, each of which would have its own parliament, controlling its own schools and other cultural institutions. Lenin condemned this proposal, which he said purported to treat nations on an equal basis, but in fact denied to the oppressed the political right, self-determination, that they required to combat centuries-old oppression. This proposal, moreover, institutionalized the backward exclusiveness of bourgeois nationalism. See "Critical Remarks on the National Question," in Lenin, *CW,* vol. 20, pp. 33–40.

26. Another area of disagreement between Lenin and Bukharin concerned the question of the state under imperialism. At first they shared a common position and Lenin wrote a favorable introduction to Bukharin's 1915 article, "Imperialism and the World Economy." Lenin's celebrated 1916 work, *Imperialism, the Highest Stage of Capitalism,* summarized the Bolshevik position, and is available today in many editions. Bukharin published a subsequent article,

"The Imperialist Pirate State," in *Jugend-Internationale* and elsewhere. In reply, Lenin criticized Bukharin for making concessions to an anarchist view of the state. Lenin further developed his views on this topic in "State and Revolution."

See Bukharin, "Mirovoye khozyaistvo i imperialism," in *Kommunist,* 1915, no. 1–2, pp. 4–48 (after 1917, Bukharin published an expanded version of this essay which is available in English translation, *Imperialism and World Economy* [New York: Monthly Review Press, 1973]); Lenin, "Preface to N. Bukharin's Pamphlet, Imperialism and World Economy," in *CW,* vol. 22, pp. 103–7; Lenin, *Imperialism, the Highest Stage of Capitalism,* in *CW,* vol. 22, pp. 185–304; Bukharin, "Der imperialistische Raubstaat," *Jugend-Internationale,* December 1, 1916, no. 6, translated as "The Imperialist Pirate State," in O.H. Gankin and H.H. Fisher, *The Bolsheviks and the World War* (Stanford: Stanford University Press, 1976), pp. 236–39; Lenin, "The Nascent Trend of Imperialist Economism," in *CW,* vol. 23, pp. 13–21; Lenin, "The Youth International," in *CW,* vol. 23, pp. 163–66.

27. See Lenin's letter to Gregory Zinoviev of May 21, 1916, (Lenin, *CW,* vol. 35, pp. 218–22) and other letters of this period to Shlyapnikov and Inessa Armand.

28. "Tezisy Stokgol'mskoi gruppy bol'shevikov o lozunge prava natsii na samoopredeleniye," *Proletarskaya Revolyutsiya,* 1930, no. 1 (96), pp. 45–46.

29. In a debate with Karl Kautsky in the pages of *Die Neue Zeit* in 1915, Heinrich Cunow, a right-wing SPD leader, maintained that imperialism was an inevitable stage of capitalist development, and moreover, that it displayed capitalism's vigor and continued potential for growth. The logic of this position was to justify imperialist denial of national rights in the name of progress. Kautsky responded that imperialism was an economic policy, was not in any sense inevitable, and should therefore be opposed. Kautsky continued to defend, in words, the right of all peoples to self-determination.

30. Lenin, *CW,* vol. 23, pp. 22–27.

31. Entente troops occupied Salonika, Greece in 1915 with the agreement of the Greek government. When a new government repudiated this agreement, the Entente organized a rival regime in Salonika, which declared war on the Central Powers. Entente

pressure was ultimately to secure the triumph in 1917 of its Greek supporters.

32. Excerpted from Leon Trotsky, "Imperializm i natsional'naya ideya," in *Voina i revolyutsiya* (Moscow: State Publishing House, 1924) vol. 1, pp. 160–162.

33. In the Zoroastrian religion of pre-Islamic Iran, Ormazd was the spirit of good, and Ahriman, of evil.

34. Excerpted from Trotsky, "Natsiya i khozyaistvo," in *Sochineniya* (Moscow: State Publishing House, 1927), vol. 9, pp. 209–16.

35. *Voina i revolyutsiya*, vol. 1, pp. 189–92.

36. Sir Roger Casement sought German support for the Irish rising, a position not endorsed by the rebel movement as a whole. He was executed by British authorities.

37. Excerpted from Karl Radek, "Ein ausgespieltes Lied," *Berner Tagwacht*, May 9, 1915.

38. Sinn Fein (Ourselves Alone), the nationalist political party, grew rapidly in the wake of the 1916 revolt. In January 1919 the nationalist armed forces launched an independence war and formed the Irish Republican Army. The British government, unable to crush the revolt, reached an agreement in 1921 with bourgeois leaders of the nationalist movement to partition Ireland. A semi-independent "Irish Free State" was established in the south; six northern counties remained under direct British rule. The Irish republican forces split, as one wing opposed the agreement with London and advocated continuation of the fight for an independent, united Ireland. A bloody two-year civil war developed between the two wings of the nationalist movement.

39. Excerpted from Lenin, *CW*, vol. 22, pp. 353–58.

40. Indian Sikh soldiers mutinied in Singapore on January 15, 1915, and controlled the city for seven days. They hoped with German help to occupy the Malay peninsula and drive the British from the Far East. Britain suppressed the revolt with help from Japan and France, court-martialing 400 Sikh soldiers and executing forty-one.

Vietnamese emperor Duy Tan led a rebellion against French rule in May 1916, which was quickly suppressed.

The Douala people of Cameroon had resisted land seizures by

their German rulers for many years. With the outbreak of war, their king, Rudolph Douala Manga Bell, sought to gain foreign assistance and organize an uprising. He was executed by German authorities in 1914.

Deputies of the Young Czech party were sentenced to death for treason on June 3, 1916; this was later commuted to imprisonment. There were many demonstrations and mutinies by Czech regiments in the Austro-Hungarian army, and on some occasions entire regiments defected to Russia or Italy. The Austrian command often arranged to have entire Czech regiments eliminated in battle.

41. Excerpts from Radek's article are published in this chapter under the title, "The Song is Played Out."

42. See the *Gazeta Robotnicza* theses printed in this chapter.

9. Russia: Toward revolution

1. V.I. Lenin, "The Proletarian Revolution and the Renegade Kautsky," in Lenin, *Collected Works* (hereinafter *CW*) (Moscow: Progress Publishers, 1974), vol. 28, pp. 294–95. For a selection of writings by the Mensheviks on these questions, see Abraham Ascher (ed.), *The Mensheviks in the Russian Revolution* (Ithaca: Cornell University Press, 1976).

2. Excerpted from Leon Trotsky, "Voyennaya katastrofa i politicheskiye perspektivy," in *Voina i revolyutsiya* (Moscow: State Publishing House, 1924), vol. 1, pp. 247–53.

3. The Zemstvos were local government bodies in tsarist Russia. In late 1904, under the impact of Russia's defeat in a war with Japan, liberal bourgeois forces in the Zemstvos began a petition campaign for a constitution and representative government.

4. Excerpted from Gregory Zinoviev, "Voina i revolyutsionnyi krizis v Rossii," in Zinoviev and Lenin, *Protiv techeniya* (Moscow: State Publishing House, 1923), pp. 287–88.

5. Trotsky's articles are excerpted above under the title, "The Social Forces in the Russian Revolution."

6. The "three pillars" were the demands for the democratic republic, the confiscation of landlords' estates, and the eight-hour working day.

7. Excerpted from Lenin, *CW,* vol. 21, pp. 416–20.

8. The January conference of 1912 was the Prague conference of the Russian Social Democratic Labor Party organized by the Bolsheviks. Its resolutions are printed in Lenin, *CW,* vol. 17, pp. 451–86.

9. This refers to Trotsky's article "Basic Problems" in issue no. 217 of *Nashe Slovo,* October 17, 1915. In this article Trotsky says that "the less the proletariat waits upon the appearance of bourgeois democracy, the less it adapts itself to the passivity and limitations of the petty bourgeoisie and peasantry, the more resolute and irreconcilable its fight becomes, the more obvious becomes its preparedness to go to 'the end', i.e., to the conquest of power, the greater will be its chances at the decisive moment of carrying with it the non-proletarian masses."

The peasants and the soldiers will not be won over by slogans like "confiscation of the land," Trotsky continues, unless they sense that the workers are "fighting for power and have some chance of winning it." Victory in this struggle for power "must transfer power to the class that has led the struggle, i.e. the Social-Democratic proletariat," he says.

Trotsky concludes that "the question, therefore, is not simply one of a 'revolutionary provisional government'—an empty phrase to which the historical process will have to give some kind of content, but of a *revolutionary workers' government.*"

When Trotsky's 1906 work *Results and Perspectives* was republished in 1919, he included this 1915 article as an appendix. It can be found in Leon Trotsky, *The Permanent Revolution and Results and Prospects* (New York: Pathfinder Press, 1974), pp. 116–22.

10. "Nakaz upolnomochennym po vyboram v tsentral'nyi voyenno-promyshlennyi komitet . . . ," in *Partiya bol'shevikov v gody mirovoi imperialisticheskoi voiny* (Moscow: State Publishing House, 1963), pp. 142–43.

11. Lenin, *CW,* vol. 21, pp. 401–4.

12. The program of the RSDLP adopted at the Second Congress of the party in 1903 consisted of two parts: a minimum program calling for the overthrow of tsarism, a democratic republic, the eight-hour day, and other demands attainable through a democratic revolution, and a maximum program, formulating the goal of the

dictatorship of the proletariat, the socialist revolution and the building of a socialist society.

13. Excerpted from Trotsky, *Voina i revolyutsiya,* vol. 2, pp. 135–39.

14. Mankov was expelled from the Menshevik fraction; the Bolshevik deputies had been arrested in November 1914.

15. Excerpted from Trotsky, *Voina i revolyutsiya,* vol. 2, pp. 175–78.

16. In another article from April 1916, Trotsky quotes the Menshevik deputy Chkhenkeli as saying, "At a time when the road has been opened for our French and Belgian comrades to participate freely in the defense of their country, the working class of Russia confronts the impenetrable wall of the feudal order, which does not permit it to carry out self-defense. Reaction is sooner prepared to give over the country to military disaster, to sell it and betray it, than to permit the people to act for self-defense." (Trotsky, "Logika plokhogo polozheniya," *Nashe Slovo,* April 9, 1915; printed in *Voina i revolyutsiya,* vol. 2, p. 175.)

17. Trotsky, ibid., vol. 2, pp. 194–97.

18. Lenin, "The Chkheidze Faction and Its Role," in *CW,* vol. 23, p. 171.

Lenin also took up Trotsky's position in "An Open Letter to Boris Souvarine," written in December 1916. "I have never branded Trotsky's position as chauvinistic," Lenin stated. "What I have reproached him with is that all too often he has represented the 'Centre' policy in Russia. . . . Having broken with Martov's party, he continues to accuse us of being splitters. Little by little he is moving to the Left, and even calls for a break with the Russian social-chauvinist leaders. But he has not definitely said whether he wants unity or a break with the Chkheidze faction. And that is one of the key issues." Lenin, *CW,* vol. 23, pp. 203–4.

19. Alexander Shlyapnikov, *Kanun semnadtsatogo goda* (Moscow: State Publishing House, 1923), vol. 2, p. 133.

20. Ibid., vol. 2, pp. 136–37.

21. The Kienthal conference is discussed in Chapter 11.

The first large wartime strike in Britain was conducted by Scottish workers of the Clyde valley in February and March 1915. Work stoppages spread across the country; 448,000 workers participated in strikes in 1915. The government responded in July 1915 with a law virtually banning strikes in essential war industries, and this was gradually extended to cover 80 percent of all workers. Yet the strike movement continued, and in 1916 276,000 workers participated in strike action.

22. Shlyapnikov, *Kanun semnadtsatogo goda*, vol. 2, pp. 252–54.

10. Germany: Toward a communist party

1. Geyer presented his statement in the name of all twenty deputies. Liebknecht had worked on early drafts of the statement, but no agreement had been reached and he had not seen the final version. Liebknecht declared that he disagreed with the statement and took no responsibility for it.

2. *Dokumente und Materialien zur Geschichte der deutschen Arbeiterbewegung* (Berlin [GDR]: Dietz Verlag, 1958), series 2, vol. 1, pp. 263–64.

3. Karl Liebknecht, "Die Dezembermänner von 1915," in *Spartakusbriefe* (Berlin [GDR]: Dietz Verlag, 1958), pp. 86–92.

4. Walter Bartel, *Die Linken in der deutschen Sozialdemokratie im Kampf gegen Militarismus und Krieg* (Berlin [GDR]: Dietz Verlag, 1958), p. 257.

5. Ibid., p. 270.

6. *Dokumente und Materialien*, series 2, vol. 1, pp. 279–82.

7. The program adopted by the German SPD at its 1891 congress in Erfurt was a major step by the party toward Marxism and served before 1914 as the model for the programs of most parties of the Second International.

8. There were two Social Democratic parties in Bulgaria. The revolutionary Social Democrats (Tesnyaki) opposed Bulgaria's participation in the war, while the opportunist group (Shiroki) went over to a chauvinist, pro-war position.

9. Excerpted and translated from the French text in Commission socialiste internationale à Berne, *Bulletin*, April 22, 1916, no. 4.

10. The Spartacists themselves emphasized the importance of these two theses by printing the first sentence of each as part of the masthead of their illegal newspaper, *Spartacus,* first published in September 1916.

11. "Die Gegensätze in der 'Opposition,'" *Spartakusbriefe,* pp. 118–21.

12. Excerpted from Rosa Luxemburg, *Gesammelte Werke* (Berlin [GDR]: Dietz Verlag, 1974), vol. 4, pp. 51–164. Subheads have been supplied by the editor. A different English translation of the entire text can be found in Rosa Luxemburg, *Rosa Luxemburg Speaks* (New York: Pathfinder Press, 1970), "The Junius Pamphlet: The crisis in the German Social Democracy."

Luxemburg took the pseudonym Junius from an anonymous British political writer of the late eighteenth century, who sought to unify the democratic opposition to King George III led by John Wilkes.

13. In 1793, revolutionary France was under attack by a counterrevolutionary coalition of Britain, Austria, Prussia, Holland, Spain, and Sardinia. By the end of the year the invaders had been driven out of France, and in 1794 France took the offensive.

14. A pan-German republic would have included not only Prussia and the many small German principalities and city states, but also the extensive German territories in the Austrian Empire.

15. The Hapsburgs were the royal house of Austria.

16. The reference is to the Paris Commune of 1871.

17. V.I. Lenin, *Collected Works* (Moscow: Progress Publishers, 1974), vol. 22, pp. 305–19.

18. See Rosa Luxemburg, "The Reconstruction of the International," in Chapter 4 of the present collection.

19. *Dokumente und Materialien,* series 2, vol. 1, p. 208.

20. Karl Liebknecht, *Gesammelte Schriften und Reden* (Berlin [GDR]: Dietz Verlag, 1958), vol. 8, pp. 538–44.

21. The "new orientation" referred to the government's vague promise to adopt a new attitude to the workers' movement and to introduce unspecified social and political reform measures after the war.

22. *Dokumente und Materialien,* series 2, vol. 1, pp. 316–20.

23. This resolution was submitted for adoption to the second International Socialist Conference at Kienthal, held in April 1916. See

Chapter 12 of the present collection.

24. *Dokumente und Materialien,* series 2, vol. 1, p. 431.

25. Excerpted from "Die Maifeier," in *Dokumente und Materialien,* series 2, vol. 1, pp. 376–78.

26. Excerpted from "Erklärung Karl Liebknechts vom 3. May 1916 . . . ," in *Dokumente und Materialien,* pp. 380–83.

27. The reference is probably to a July 28, 1914, telegram of Nicholas II calling on Kaiser Wilhelm II to restrain Austria-Hungary from its moves toward war.

28. Liebknecht made contact with Socialists in the Entente states during his trip to Belgium and Holland. The *Labour Leader* was the publication of the British Independent Labour Party, which opposed the war policies of the British government. Liebknecht's Christmas letter affirmed his stand against the German government and for the reconstitution of the International on a new basis through the struggle against the war. The International Socialist Conference referred to is that held at Zimmerwald.

29. Excerpted from *Dokumente und Materialien,* series 2, vol. 1, pp. 457–63.

30. Excerpted from Karl Radek, "Einheit oder Spaltung der Partei," in *In den Reihen der deutschen Revolution 1909–1919* (Munich: Kurt Wolff Verlag, 1921), pp. 319–38.

31. The establishment of *Mitteleuropa,* a tariff-free zone economically dominated by Germany, was one of the German government's war aims. In addition to Germany and Austria-Hungary, it was to include France, Belgium, the Netherlands, Denmark, Poland, and perhaps other territories.

32. U.S. management specialist F.W. Taylor pioneered in the late nineteenth century the introduction of mass production techniques. These destroyed old crafts that had afforded workers some control of quality and work pace, introduced a more detailed division of labor, and subjected workers to greater management control and more intensive exploitation.

33. In Germany in 1912, 2.5 million workers belonged to trade unions aligned with the Social Democracy, while 1.1 million belonged to unions subject to Catholic, liberal, or direct employer control.

34. Rosa Luxemburg's proposal was contained in a resolution of the Spartacists to the June 25, 1916, assembly of the SPD organization in Berlin and vicinity. Citing the attacks by the majority leadership on membership rights in many areas of Germany, the resolution proposed that the opposition leaders in Berlin "enter into contact with the districts affected by the Executive Committee's brutal policies, in order to consider defensive organizational measures to save the party." Hugo Haase rejected the proposal as not clearly defined and capable of leading to actions outside the party's existing statutes and structures. (*Dokumente und Materialien,* series 2, vol. 1, pp. 412–14.)

35. The July 9 protest statement of 1,000 oppositional SPD members was a combined project of the Spartacist current and the Ledebour wing of the centrist forces. A limited collaboration of these two currents lasted until early 1916.

36. Ernst Meyer and Berta Thalheimer of the Spartacist current voted with the Ledebour forces at Zimmerwald; Julian Borchardt voted with the Zimmerwald Left.

37. According to Greek myth, Hercules, a few months after his birth, strangled two serpents laid in his cradle by the goddess Hera. In a different exploit, Hercules later slew Hydra, the many-headed serpent.

11. The social roots of the split in the Second International

1. This article is printed in Chapter 10 of the present collection.

2. V.I. Lenin and Gregory Zinoviev, "Socialism and War," in Lenin, *Collected Works* (hereinafter *CW*) (Moscow: Progress Publishers, 1974), vol. 21, pp. 309–10.

3. Excerpted from Zinoviev, *Der Krieg und die Krise des Sozialismus* (Vienna: Verlag für Literatur und Politik, 1924), pp. 483–553. A more extensive English translation is printed in *New International,* Winter 1983–84, vol. 1, no. 2, pp. 97–137.

4. See "The Molkenbuhr Letter on Morocco" in Chapter 2 of the present collection.

5. The main German trade union federation, which was associated with the Socialist movement, was designated "free" to distinguish it from unions dominated by the employers, the Catholic church, or the liberal bourgeoisie.

6. The German mark was then worth approximately US$.25; by today's official price index it would be worth about $2.50.

7. These words are in English in the original text.

8. During the late 1880s, a wave of workers' struggles in Britain brought thousands of unskilled workers, previously unorganized, into the trade unions. The idea that the unions should organize these layers was dubbed the "new trade unionism"—as opposed to the "old trade unionism," where the trade unions were viewed as the exclusive domain of the skilled crafts.

9. Karl Kautsky, *The Social Revolution* (Chicago: Charles H. Kerr and Co., 1902), pp. 101–02.

10. Karl Marx and Frederick Engels, *Selected Correspondence* (Moscow: Progress Publishers, 1975), p. 386.

11. Ibid., pp. 330–31.

12. *Briefe und Auszüge aus Briefen von J.P. Becker, Jos. Dietzgen, Friedrich Engels, Karl Marx u. a. an F.A. Sorge u. a.* (Stuttgart: Dietz Verlag, 1906), p. 156.

13. Karl Marx and Frederick Engels, *On Britain* (Moscow: Foreign Languages Publishing House, 1953), pp. 532–33.

14. See Lenin, *Imperialism, The Highest Stage of Capitalism* (New York: International Publishers, 1977). Also printed in Lenin, *CW*, vol. 22, pp. 185–304.

15. Excerpted from Lenin, *CW*, vol. 23, pp. 105–120.

16. Marx and Engels, *Selected Correspondence*, p. 103.

17. Ibid., p. 390.

18. Karl Marx and Frederick Engels, *Selected Works* (Moscow: Progress Publishers, 1977), vol. 3, pp. 440–452.

12. Toward the new International

1. Internationale sozialistische Kommission zu Bern, *Bulletin*, November 27, 1915, no. 2, p. 2.

2. Arnold Reisberg, *Lenin und die Zimmerwalder Bewegung* (Berlin [GDR]: Dietz Verlag, 1966), p. 198; Merle Fainsod, *International Socialism and the World War* (New York: Anchor Books, 1969), pp. 115–16.

3. Gregory Zinoviev, "Posle Tsimmerwal'd," in *Protiv techeniya*

(Moscow: State Publishing House, 1923), p. 350.

4. O.H. Gankin and H.H. Fisher, *The Bolsheviks and the World War* (Stanford: Stanford University Press, 1976), p. 382. This volume also contains an English translation of the ISC's February 1916 circular letter.

5. Excerpted from V.I. Lenin, "Proposals Submitted by the Central Committee of the R.S.D.L.P. to the Second Socialist Conference," in Lenin, *Collected Works* (hereinafter *CW*)(Moscow: Progress Publishers, 1974), vol. 22, pp. 178–79.

6. See "Three Resolutions of the Internationale Group," parts I and II, in Chapter 10 of the present collection.

7. The official proceedings of the Kienthal conference are printed in Horst Lademacher (ed.), *Die Zimmerwalder Bewegung* (The Hague: Mouton, 1967), vol. 1, pp. 263–390.

8. Ibid., pp. 322–23.

9. The other delegates supporting the Zimmerwald Left resolution were Triša Kačlerović (Serbia); Ernst Nobs, Fritz Platten, and Agnes Robmann (Switzerland); and Giacinto Serrati (Italy).

10. Lademacher, *Die Zimmerwalder Bewegung,* vol. 1, pp. 307–8.

11. Angelica Balabanoff, *Die Zimmerwalder Bewegung 1914–1919* (Frankfurt am Main: Verlag Neue Kritik, 1969), pp. 41–44.

12. Lademacher, *Die Zimmerwalder Bewegung,* vol. 1, p. 379.

13. Ibid., pp. 353–54.

14. Ibid., pp. 356–57.

15. Balabanoff, *Die Zimmerwalder Bewegung 1914–1919,* pp. 44–45.

16. Lademacher, *Die Zimmerwalder Bewegung,* vol. 1, pp. 381–82.

17. Although neutral during the war, the Dutch government nonetheless maintained its army fully mobilized and built up the strength of its army and navy. When the majority Socialist Party failed to combat this, the small Tribunist group (Social Democratic Party) organized a committee that united representatives of 20,000 workers. Many mass meetings of workers were held in a campaign for demobilization of the army, against the expansion of militarism, and against attacks on workers' living standards. Willem van Ravestejn, "Die Lage in Holland nach einem Jahr Weltkrieg,"

Jugend-Internationale, July 1, 1916, no. 4, p. 5.

18. Balabanoff, *Die Zimmerwalder Bewegung 1914–1919,* pp. 45–49.

19. *Jugend-Internationale,* December 1, 1915, no. 2, p. 3.

20. Excerpted from "Entwaffnung!," *Jugend-Internationale,* March 1, 1916, no. 3, pp. 7–8.

21. See Lenin, "The Military Programme of the Proletarian Revolution," in *CW,* vol. 23, pp. 77–87.

22. Excerpted from Arvid Gansen [Hansen], "Nekotorye momenty sovremennago rabochago dvizheniya v Norvegii," *Sbornik Sotsial-Demokrata,* December 1916, no. 2, p. 43.

23. Excerpted from Lenin, *CW,* vol. 23, pp. 94–104.

24. Julius Braunthal, *History of the International Volume II 1914–1943* (New York: Frederick A. Praeger, 1967), p. 52.

25. Excerpted from Zinoviev, *Protiv techeniya,* pp. 362–63.

26. The Italian Socialist Party eventually joined the Bolsheviks in declaring it would not attend the proposed Paris conference of Entente "Socialist" parties. The February 1917 ISC meeting, in which the Zimmerwald Left forces held a majority, denounced the conference. The chauvinist leaderships then could not agree on who to invite, and the conference was not held.

27. Excerpted from Lenin, *CW,* vol. 23, pp. 262–63.

28. Eugen Prager, *Geschichte der U.S.P.D.* (Glashütten im Taunus: Verlag Detlev Auvermann, 1970), pp. 127–29.

29. Excerpted from "Wilsons Sozialismus," in *Spartakusbriefe* (Berlin [GDR]: Dietz Verlag, 1958), pp. 306–07.

Eugen Prager wrote in 1922 that Kautsky's resolution was unanimously adopted by the January 1917 conference, and that Spartacist speakers declared their wholehearted agreement with it. Walter Bartel wrote in 1958 that this was an error on Prager's part. Bartel cites a contemporary press report of a Spartacist statement that the manifesto was not unanimously adopted, and refers to the Spartacist criticism of it printed in this chapter.

(Prager, *Geschichte der U.S.P.D.,* p. 129; Walter Bartel, *Die Linken in der deutschen Sozialdemokratie im Kampf gegen Militarismus und Krieg* (Berlin [GDR]: Dietz Verlag, 1958), pp. 408–9.)

30. Excerpted from Lenin, "Bourgeois Pacifism and Socialist Pacifism," in *CW*, vol. 23, pp. 183–84.

31. Robert Wohl, *French Communism in the Making, 1914–1924* (Stanford: Stanford University Press, 1966), p. 71.

32. Leon Trotsky, "Deklaratsiya, vnesennaya v Komitet dlya vosstanovleniya internatsional'nykh svyazei," in *Voina i Revolyutsiya* (Moscow: State Publishing House, 1924), vol. 2, pp. 215–18. A French translation of this and of other wartime articles of Trotsky is printed in Leon Trotsky, *La guerre et la révolution* (Paris: Editions Tête de Feuilles, 1974).

33. For an account of the struggle of French Zimmerwaldists by a leading revolutionary participant, see Alfred Rosmer, *Le mouvement ouvrier pendant la première guerre mondiale* (Paris: Mouton & co, 1959), 2 vols.

34. Gankin and Fisher, *The Bolsheviks and the World War*, pp. 469–71.

35. Lenin, *CW*, vol. 24, pp. 80–81.

36. Lenin, *CW*, vol. 23, pp. 205–16. The draft appeal by Lenin was not submitted to the ISC; the Zimmerwald Left forces pursued their struggle with the centrists led by Robert Grimm in other forms inside the Swiss party and at the February ISC meeting. The written debate continued after the opening of the Russian revolution.

37. See "For a Peace of Reconciliation," included in this chapter.

38. See "War and Education," in Chapter 10 of the present collection.

Chronology

For countries where the Julian calendar was then in use, dates by the modern calendar are given first, followed by the dates according to the Julian calendar in parentheses.

1864

September 28 – First International founded.

1871

Paris Commune crushed in bloody massacre by French bourgeoisie.

1872

First International center moved to United States in wake of post-Commune wave of political reaction throughout Europe.

1876

July – First International dissolved.

1889

July 14–20 – Founding congress of Second International in Paris.

1898

April – Beginning of Spanish-American War. Spanish government surrenders in August.

September – Confrontation between French and British governments over Nile Valley, known as Fashoda incident.

1899

February – German Socialist leader Eduard Bernstein publishes revisionist attack on basic program and strategy of Marxism.

June 29 – French Socialist leader Alexandre Millerand accepts post in French bourgeois cabinet.

October – Beginning of British war against Boers in South Africa; ends in May 1902 with British victory.

1900

June – European powers and U.S. and Japanese governments send troops to crush anti-imperialist movement in China known as Boxer uprising.

September 23–27 – Fifth Congress of Second International in Paris.

1903

July 30–August 23 (July 17–August 10) – Second congress of Russian Social Democratic Labor Party in London. Party divides into Bolshevik and Menshevik factions.

1904

February 9 (January 27) – Beginning of Russo-Japanese War. Tsarist regime makes major concessions in peace treaty signed in September 1905.

August 14–20 – Sixth Congress of Second International at Amsterdam.

1905

January 22 (9) – Bloody Sunday in St. Petersburg as tsar's troops fire on demonstrators. General strike breaks out next day in Moscow.

March – First Morocco crisis threatens war between France and Germany.

June – Outbreak of Constitutional Revolution in Iran; shah grants constituent assembly in August 1906.

October – Strike wave develops into general strike in Russia. First meeting of Petersburg Soviet of Workers' Deputies.

1907

August 18–24 – Seventh Congress of Second International at Stuttgart.

August – Russian and British governments agree on division of zones of influence in Persia.

1908

June – Russian-led troops suppress Iranian parliament, setting off civil war which ends in July 1909 with victory of constitutionalist forces.

July – "Young Turk" rebellion forces sultan to reinstitute constitution in Ottoman Empire.

1909

April – Uprising in Turkey deposes Sultan Abdul-Hamid II and increases power of parliament.

1910

August 28–September 3 – Eighth Congress of Second International at Copenhagen.

1911

July 1 – Arrival of German warship in Agadir triggers new Morocco crisis.

September 29 – Italian government launches attack against Turkish-held Libya.

October – Revolution breaks out in China, leading to emperor's abdication in February 1912.

October–November – British and Russian governments send troops to occupy Iran.

1912

April 17 (4) – Massacre of workers in Lena goldfields sets off strike wave across Russia.

October 8 – Government of Montenegro declares war on Turkey beginning First Balkan War.

November 24–25 – Socialists hold special congress at Basel to protest danger of imperialist war.

1913

June 29–30 – Beginning of Second Balkan War.

1914

May–July – Escalating wave of strikes across Russia, reaching peak with strike of 300,000 St. Petersburg factory workers in July.

June 28 – Assassination of Archduke Ferdinand of Austria-Hungary at Sarajevo, Bosnia.

July 14–16 – French Socialist Party convention votes in favor of using general strike to avert war.

July 23 – Government of Austria-Hungary issues ultimatum to Serbia.

July 26 – Serbian government mobilizes armed forces.

July 28 – Government of Austria-Hungary declares war on Serbia.

July 29–30 – International Socialist Bureau meets in Brussels, calls for peace demonstrations.

July 31 (18) – Tsarist regime mobilizes armed forces against Austria-Hungary and Germany. German government demands that Russia demobilize in twelve hours. French Socialist leader Jaurès assassinated. Serbian Social Democrats vote against war credits.

August 1 (July 19) – German and French governments mobilize armed forces. German government declares war on Russia.

August 2 – German government issues ultimatum to Belgium, demanding passage for German troops. Belgian Labor Party directs its parliamentary deputies to vote for war credits. Italian government declares neutrality.

August 3 – German government declares war on France. SPD Reichstag fraction votes 78–14 to approve war credits.

August 4 – German troops invade Belgium. Social Democrats in Reichstag unanimously vote for war credits. British government declares war on Germany. War appropriations approved unanimously by French Chamber of Deputies. Belgian Labor Party pledges support to government and their leader Vandervelde enters cabinet.

August 8 (July 26) – Russian Bolsheviks and Mensheviks issue joint declaration against war and walk out of Duma without voting on war credits.

August 13 – British Socialist Party publishes chauvinist manifesto. Independent Labour Party of Britain issues antiwar manifesto.

August 14 – French Socialist Party issues manifesto explaining participation in government of party leaders Guesde and Sembat.

August 23 – Japanese government declares war on Germany.

September 4 – British, French, and Russian governments agree not to sign separate peace.

September 6–8 – Lenin's theses calling for revolutionary struggle against imperialist war and for new International accepted by Bolshevik conference at Bern, and forwarded for discussion by Bolshevik leaders in Russia.

September 5–12 – German offensive in France is turned back at Battle of the Marne.

September 27 – Italian and Swiss Socialist parties meet at Lugano, Switzerland, and condemn war as imperialist.

November 1 – Bolshevik Central Committee manifesto denounces chauvinist betrayal that has destroyed Second International and calls for a new proletarian International, freed from opportunism. Manifesto printed in first wartime issue of *Sotsial-Demokrat.*

November 18–19 (5–6) – Bolshevik representatives in Duma arrested at party conference near Petrograd.

November 23 – Larin and Shlyapnikov address convention of Swedish Social Democrats.

December 2 – Liebknecht votes in Reichstag against war credits, the only deputy to do so.

December – Revolutionary Socialists in Germany publish first underground circulars, known as "Spartacus Letters."

1915

January 17–18 – Conference of Socialist parties from nonbelligerent countries (Sweden, Norway, the Netherlands, and Denmark) held at Copenhagen.

February – Disorders in Berlin and other German cities because of food shortage.

February 6 – *Nashe Slovo* calls for united stand by Russian internationalists.

February 7 – Liebknecht drafted into army.

February 14 – London conference of official Socialist parties of Entente countries.

February 18 – Rosa Luxemburg imprisoned in Germany; held until January 22, 1916.

February 23–26 (10–13) – Trial and conviction of five Bolshevik Duma deputies; protest demonstrations and strikes in several Russian cities.

February 27–March 4 – Bern conference of Bolshevik groups abroad.

March 20 – Liebknecht and Rühle vote in Reichstag against war credits.

March 26–28 – International Conference of Socialist Women held at Bern.

April 4–6 – International Conference of Socialist Youth held at Bern.

April 14 – Spartacists in Germany publish *Die Internationale.*

April 30 – Official Socialist parties of Germany and Austria meet at Vienna.

May – U.S. Socialist Party votes to expel any member who approves war credits.

May 23 – Italian government declares war on Austria-Hungary. Italian Socialist Party maintains antiwar stand.

May–September – German offensive inflicts series of defeats on Russia and conquers most of Russian Poland.

June 4 – Trotsky declines invitation to become collaborator of *Kommunist.*

June 9 – Liebknecht, Ledebour, and more than 1,000 SPD members sign open letter opposing party's pro-war policy and calling for resumption by SPD of class struggle.

June 19 – Statement by Kautsky, Haase, and Bernstein attacks annexationist plans of Germany's rulers, calls for SPD to struggle for peace.

July 11 – Meeting to prepare Zimmerwald conference held at Bern.

July–August 1915 – Wave of political protest strikes in Russia.

August 2 – Russian troops evacuate Warsaw and continue retreat.

August 23 (10) – General political protest strike in Ivanovo-Voznesensk, Russia. Police attack, killing 100 and wounding 40 workers, sparking protest strikes across country.

August 28 (15) – Russian bourgeois parties form "Progressive Bloc" to press for domestic reforms and more effective war effort.

September 4 – Revolutionary Marxists form Zimmerwald Left.

September 5–8 – Zimmerwald conference.

September 11–12 – Bolsheviks publish new journal, *Kommunist*.

September 16–22 (3–9) – Renewed wave of political strikes; 150,000 strike in Petrograd, 90,000 in Moscow.

September 28 – Zimmerwald supporters in France launch Committee for the Resumption of International Relations in effort to renew ties among Socialists.

October 1 (September 27) – First meeting of Petrograd delegates to War Industries Committees votes 95–80 for Bolshevik proposal to boycott committees.

October 12 – Italian Socialist Party adopts Zimmerwald resolution as basis for action.

November – Zimmerwald Left publishes *International Flugblätter*, containing its resolution and manifesto for Zimmerwald conference.

December 12 (November 29) – Second election to War Industries Committees in Petrograd.

December 21 – Twenty SPD deputies vote against war credits in Reichstag; twenty-two abstain.

1916

January 1 – National conference of German Socialist left adopts "Theses," founds Internationale Group.

January – First issue of *Vorbote* published.

January 22 (9) – At least 100,000 strike in Petrograd in commemoration of 1905 Bloody Sunday massacre.

February 5–9 – Meeting of expanded International Socialist Committee in Bern calls Kienthal conference.

February – New wave of strikes in Petrograd demands higher wages and an end to the war and tsarism.

Mid-March – National conference of Internationale Group.

March 24 – Formation of Social Democratic Working Group in Germany by seventeen SPD deputies in Reichstag, led by Haase and Ledebour.

April – Second issue of *Vorbote* published, containing Bolshevik and *Gazeta Robotnicza* theses on self-determination.

April 23–29 – "Easter Uprising" in Ireland.

April 24–30 – Kienthal conference.

May 1 – Liebknecht arrested at May Day antiwar demonstration in Berlin.

May–June – Hunger riots in Germany.

June 27–30 – Strikes of 55,000 workers in Berlin, of 8,000 in Braunschweig, and of Krupp workers in Essen protest against trial and conviction of Liebknecht.

June 28 – Liebknecht sentenced to 2½ years in prison.

July – Uprising begins in Kazakhstan and Central Asia against tsarism and local rulers.

July 10 – Luxemburg re-arrested; held in jail until November 1918.

September 21–23 – SPD national conference in Berlin.

December 12 – German chancellor makes "peace" proposal to Entente powers.

December 18 – U.S. President Wilson calls on warring governments to state their terms for peace, laying the groundwork for U.S. entry into war.

1917

January 18 – SPD Executive Committee excludes from party membership the adherents of the Working Group, thus splitting the party.

March 8 (February 23) – Widespread strikes and demonstrations in Petrograd on occasion of International Women's Day begin the Russian revolution, leading to general strike, formation of soviets, and abdication of the tsar.

Glossary

Abbé, Ernst (1840–1905) – German scientist and capitalist; gave his factory to foundation to provide social benefits to workers.

Adler, Friedrich (1879–1960) – son of Victor Adler and secretary of Austrian Social Democratic Party, 1911–16; led centrist opposition to party's war policy; in 1916 assassinated Austrian prime minister as protest against war; sentenced to death, later commuted to imprisonment; freed by 1918 revolutionary upsurge; secretary of centrist Two-and-a-Half International, 1921–23, of Second International, 1923–39.

Adler, Victor (1852–1918) – central leader of Austrian Social Democratic Party; prominent leader of Second International; adopted chauvinist position during war; Austrian foreign minister, 1918.

Aladyin, A.F. (b. 1873) – Trudovik member of Russian Duma; served with counterrevolutionary White armies during civil war; later went into exile.

Alexinsky, G.A. (1879–1965) – Bolshevik member of 1907 Duma; later broke with party and became Menshevik, supporting Russia in war; joined counterrevolution after 1917.

Antonov-Ovseenko, V.A. (1884–1938) – Russian Social Democrat; during war collaborated with *Golos* and *Nashe Slovo* in Paris; joined Bolsheviks May 1917; headed Military Revolutionary Committee in October 1917 uprising; member of Bolshevik-Leninist opposition, 1923–27; executed during Moscow trials.

Armand, Inessa (1874–1920) – joined Bolsheviks 1904; participated in 1905–1907 revolution; Bolshevik Central Committee delegate in Petersburg, 1912–13; lived in Switzerland during war and represented Bolsheviks at conferences of Zimmerwald movement; became head of Russian CP women's department after 1918.

Asquith, Herbert (1852–1928) – British Liberal Party prime minister, 1908–16.

August Bloc – grew out of August 1912 conference in Vienna to unify Russian Social Democracy; various Russian Social Democratic groups opposed to Bolsheviks participated; key organizational role initially played by Trotsky although he broke with it thereafter; rapidly came under domination of right-wing Mensheviks.

Avanti! – daily newspaper published by Italian Socialist Party since 1896; remained organ of SP majority following split with Communist minority in 1921.

Axelrod, Pavel (1850–1928) – in 1883 a founder of Emancipation of Labor group, first Russian Social Democratic organization; leading Russian Menshevik after 1903; leader of Secretariat of the Organizing Committee Abroad during war; supporter of Zimmerwald right; opposed October 1917 revolution.

Badayev, A.Y. (1883–1951) – Bolshevik deputy to fourth Duma, 1912–14; arrested November 1914 for antiwar activities and exiled to Siberia; served in various Soviet posts after 1917.

Balabanoff, Angelica (1878–1965) – prominent figure in Italian SP before war; following Zimmerwald was secretary of International Socialist Commission and editor of its *Bulletin;* joined Bolsheviks in 1917; secretary of Communist International, 1919–20; expelled from Soviet CP in 1924 and broke with communism, becoming secretary of Italian SP.

Barrès, Maurice (1862–1923) – right-wing nationalist French writer and politician.

Bauer, Otto (1881–1938) – a leader and theoretician of Austrian Social Democratic Party; drafted in 1914, war prisoner in Russia until 1917; Austrian foreign minister, 1918–19; opposed Communist International and helped found centrist Two-and-a-Half International.

Bebel, August (1840–1913) – collaborator of Marx and Engels; a founder and the central leader of German SPD; played prominent role in Second International; opposed revisionist current in SPD but eventually adopted centrist positions.

Belenin – See Shlyapnikov, Alexander.

Belgian Labor Party – founded 1879 as Socialist Party of Belgium; in 1885 merged with trade unions and cooperative societies to form Labor Party; 270,000 members in 1913, of which only 16,000 belonged to political organizations within it; took chauvinist position during war.

Berger, Victor (1860–1929) – right-wing leader of U.S. SP from Milwaukee; partisan of extreme chauvinist, anti-immigrant position; first Socialist member of Congress in 1910; conviction for sedition during war was later reversed by Supreme Court.

Berner Tagwacht (Bern Reveille) – newspaper of Swiss Social Democratic Party founded in 1893; edited by Robert Grimm, 1909–18; after 1914 published statements of Zimmerwald movement and German Socialist left; following 1917 openly supported party right wing.

Bernstein, Eduard (1850–1932) – early German Social Democrat and Engels's literary executor; became leading advocate of revisionism in 1899; author of *Evolutionary Socialism;* adopted pacifist stand during war; briefly a member of split-off Independent Social Democratic Party, returned to SPD in 1918.

Berzin, J.A. (1881–1938) – Latvian Social Democrat; supported Bolsheviks and member of Zimmerwald Left; returned to Russia in 1917 and was elected to Bolshevik Central Committee; arrested during Moscow trials.

Bethmann-Hollweg, Theobald von (1856–1921) – German chancellor, 1909–17.

Bismarck, Otto von (1815–1898) – head of Prussian government, 1862–71; German chancellor, 1871–90; organized German national unification under Prussian domination.

Bissolati, Leonida (1857–1920) – a founder of Italian SP and co-editor of *Avanti!*, 1896–1903, 1908–10; expelled from party in 1912 for supporting Italy's war against Turkey; campaigned for Italy's entry into World War; government minister without portfolio, 1916–18.

Black Hundreds – monarchist gangs formed by tsarist police; murdered revolutionists and organized pogroms against Jews.

Blagoev, Dmitri (1859–1924) – founder of Bulgarian social democracy; after 1903 split headed left-wing Tesnyakis, which later became CP; became president of CP's Central Committee in 1919.

Bobrov – See Natanson, M.A.

Bolsheviks – formed in 1903 as majority faction of 1903 Second Congress of RSDLP; renamed Russian Communist Party (Bolsheviks), 1918.

Borchardt, Julian (1868–1932) – German left-wing Social Democrat before war; during war edited *Lichtstrahlen;* member of Zimmerwald Left and a founder of International Socialists of Germany; after 1916 shifted toward an anarchist position.

Bosh, Yevgeniya (1879–1925) – Russian Bolshevik; aligned with Bukharin and Pyatakov during war, in 1915 she was on editorial staff of *Kommunist;* participant in Bolshevik civil war effort in Ukraine.

Boulanger, Georges (1837–1891) – French war minister, 1886–87; headed chauvinist movement and aimed to establish military dictatorship.

Bourderon, Albert (1858–1930) – member of French SP and leader of CGT; took antiwar position and attended Zimmerwald conference; subsequently moved to right and broke with Zimmerwald movement.

Bracke, Alexandre (1861–1955) – foreign relations secretary of French SP and longtime member of Chamber of Deputies; took defensist position during war and supported party majority.

Branting, Karl (1860–1925) – longtime leader of Swedish Social Democrats and editor of central organ, *Social-Demokraten,* 1886–1917; opportunist; organized 1915 Conference of Socialists of Neutral Countries in Copenhagen; chairman of Bern Conference, 1919; Swedish prime minister, 1921–23; won Nobel Peace Prize, 1921.

Brassey, Thomas (1836–1918) – British secretary to the admiralty, 1883–85; governor of Victoria, Australia, 1895–1900.

Braun, Adolf (1862–1929) – Austrian Social Democrat and trade union leader; moved to Germany in 1910 and took centrist position within SPD before and during war.

Braun, Otto (1872–1955) – member of SPD Executive Committee and supporter of majority; became Prussian prime minister in 1920.

British Labour Party – founded in 1906 as federation of trade unions and Socialist organizations and societies; affiliated to Second International; 1.6 million members in 1914, predominantly through union affiliation; supported British war policy in 1914.

British Socialist Party – founded in 1911 out of fusion of Social Democratic Federation and other groups; 14,000 members in 1914; right-wing pro-war minority led by Henry Hyndman split off in 1916; in 1920 played leading role in founding British CP.

Bronski, Miecyslaw (1882–1941) – a leader of Polish SDKPiL opposition; member of Zimmerwald Left; moved to Russia in 1917 and held a number of positions in Soviet government.

Brouckère, Louis de (1870–1951) – a leader and theoretician of Belgian Labor Party; left-winger before war, became chauvinist in 1914 and subsequently entered Belgian government; president of Second International, 1937–39.

Broutchoux, Benoit (1879–1944) – French miner and anarcho-syndicalist; during war took centrist position within CGT; participated in left-wing split from it after war; returned to CGT in 1923.

Bukharin, Nikolai (1888–1938) – prominent Bolshevik leader and writer; emigrated to Western Europe in 1911; during war helped edit *Kommunist* in 1915 and *Novy Mir* (New World) in New York, 1916–17; returned to Russia in 1917 and was leading member of Bolshevik Central Committee; led Left Communists in 1918; editor of *Pravda*, 1919–29; prominent in Communist International; headed Right Opposition and was expelled from Soviet CP in 1929; later recanted and was readmitted; executed during Moscow trials.

Bukvoyed – See Ryazanov, David B.

Bulletin – official organ of Zimmerwald movement, 1915–17, published in Bern by International Socialist Committee.

Bülow, Bernard von (1849–1929) – German chancellor, 1900–1909.

Bund (General Jewish Workers' Union of Lithuania, Poland, and Russia) – founded in 1897; joined RSDLP as autonomous organization in 1898; split off in 1903; rejoined in 1906; within RSDLP supported Mensheviks; strong nationalist tendencies; supported Provisional Government in Russia following February 1917 revolution; opposed October revolution; majority joined Russian CP in 1920 split; continued functioning within Poland.

Burns, John (1858–1943) – British union leader; president of Local Government Board in Liberal Party government, 1906–14; resigned because of opposition to declaration of war.

Cadets (Constitutional Democrats) – party of Russian liberal bourgeoisie founded in 1905; supported World War I; leading counterrevolutionary party in 1917.

Cambon, Jules (1845–1935) – French ambassador to Germany, 1907–14.

Campe, Rudolf von (1860–1939) – German Reichstag member from National Liberal Party.

Casement, Roger (1864–1916) – Irish nationalist; attempted to join 1916 Easter Rebellion after having sought German support for Irish independence; captured by British and hanged.

Catholic Center Party – German bourgeois party, supported privileges for the Catholic hierarchy and opposed reform in general.

Cato (234–149 B.C.) – Roman statesman; attempted to restore what he considered high morals and simplicity of life of early days of Rome.

CGT – See General Confederation of Labor.

Champion, Henry H. (1857–1928) – British Socialist; publisher of *Labour Elector;* emigrated to Australia and helped form Australian SP.

Cherevanin, N. (F.A. Lipkin) (1868–1938) – Menshevik defensist during war; member of Menshevik Central Committee after 1917.

Chernov, Victor M. (1876–1952) – main theoretician of Russian

Socialist Revolutionaries; attended Zimmerwald conference; member of 1917 Provisional Government; opposed October revolution.

Chkheidze, N.S. (1864–1926) – head of Menshevik Duma fraction from 1908; first president of Petrograd Soviet in 1917; opponent of October revolution.

Chkhenkeli, A.I. (1874–1959) – Russian Menshevik; Duma member during war; foreign minister of Menshevik-led Georgian republic, 1918–21.

Clausewitz, Karl von (1780–1831) – Prussian general; author of books on science of war.

Cohen, Max (1876–1963) – SPD leader from Frankfurt; chauvinist during war.

Committee for Resumption of International Relations – formed January 1916 by French antiwar Socialists and syndicalists to work within French SP and CGT; leaders included Merrheim, Bourderon, Loriot, Monatte, Rosmer, and Rappoport; Trotsky, Armand, and Lozovsky were also among participants; became Committee for the Third International in 1919, which played instrumental role in founding of French CP.

Connolly, James (1870–1916) – founder of Irish Socialist Republican Party; leader of Irish Citizen Army and 1916 Easter Rebellion; executed by British.

Conservative Party – German party representing Prussian state and junker landlords, identified with junker-military caste of Prussian state.

Cook, Joseph (1860–1947) – leader of Australian Labor Party; prime minister, 1913–14.

Cunow, Heinrich (1862–1936) – part of SPD "Marxist Center" current before 1914; on editorial boards of *Vorwärts* and *Die Neue Zeit;* became chauvinist in 1914 and was main theoretician of Ebert-Scheidemann group within SPD right-wing leadership.

Dabrowski – See Stein, Wladislaw.

Dan, F.I. (1871–1947) – a central leader of Russian Mensheviks; took pacifist position during war; leading opponent of October revolution; deported in 1922 and edited emigré Menshevik journal.

David, Eduard (1863–1930) – right-wing SPD leader and outspoken apologist for German imperialism; widely published propagandist for majority policy during war; minister without portfolio, 1919–20; first president of National Assembly, 1919.

Debs, Eugene (1855–1926) – spokesman for U.S. SP and five-time presidential candidate; supporter of party's pre-World War I left wing; imprisoned for antiwar statements, 1918–21; solidarized with Bolshevik revolution but remained in SP following 1919 split by forces forming U.S. Communist movement.

Diner-Dénes, József (1857–1937) – Hungarian writer and journalist; leading Social Democrat.

Dittmann, Wilhelm (1874–1954) – member of SPD Reichstag fraction from 1912; joined centrist opposition in 1915 and later became co-chairman of Independent Social Democratic Party; returned to SPD in 1922.

Dix, Arthur (b. 1875) – German journalist and supporter of National Liberal Party.

Duncker, Käte (1871–1953) – SPD member and leader of socialist women's movement; Spartacist during war; founding member of German CP and elected to Central Committee; emigrated to U.S. in 1938; returned to Germany in 1947 and lived in German Democratic Republic.

Ebert, Friedrich (1871–1925) – elected co-chairman of SPD Executive Committee in 1911; became party's central leader following Bebel's death in 1913; chauvinist during war, together with Scheidemann presided over crushing of German revolution in 1918–19; president of Germany, 1919–25.

Eckstein, Gustav (1875–1916) – Austrian Social Democrat; contributor to *Die Neue Zeit* and *Der Kampf;* close collaborator of Kautsky; took centrist position during war.

Einem, Karl von (1853–1934) – German general; Prussian war minister, 1903–1909.

Ellenbogen, Wilhelm (1863–1951) – founding member and prominent leader of Austrian Social Democratic Party; took pacifist position during war and participated in Zimmerwald movement; entered Social Democrat-led Austrian government in 1919.

Fabian Society – British reformist-liberal organization founded in 1884; denied need for class struggle and advocated gradual transition to socialism through reform; affiliated to Labour Party, 1900; member of Second International; held chauvinist position during war.

Falkenhayn, Erich von (1861–1922) – Prussian war minister, 1913–15; chief of German general staff, 1914–16.

Fischer, Richard (1855–1926) – SPD member; became business manager of *Vorwärts* in 1902; supported party majority.

Fisher, Andrew (1862–1928) – three-time Australian prime minister between 1908 and 1915 at head of Labor Party government.

Frank, Ludwig (1874–1914) – leading right-wing SPD member from Baden; enlisted in German army at start of war and was killed.

Frölich, Paul (1884–1953) – German Social Democrat; member of Bremen left-wing opposition during war; participant in Zimmerwald Left at Kienthal conference; founding member of German CP; expelled in 1928; rejoined SPD after 1945; author of biography of Rosa Luxemburg.

General Confederation of Labor (CGT) – largest French trade union federation; 600,000 members in 1914; syndicalist orientation; pro-war majority after 1914; minority participated in Zimmerwald movement; growing differences led to split in 1921, with minority sympathetic to Communist Party.

Geyer, Friedrich (1853–1937) – long-time SPD member and leader of tobacco workers' union; member of party Control Commission; in 1915 joined SPD centrist opposition; became founding member of Independent Social Democratic Party; joined CP in 1920 but returned to SPD two years later.

Gladstone, Herbert (1854–1930) – prominent British politician and leader of Liberal Party.

Glasier, Bruce (1859–1920) – a founder of British Labour Party and leader of ILP; editor of *Labour Leader;* took pacifist position during war.

Die Gleichheit (Equality) – fortnightly published by German Socialist women's movement in Stuttgart and edited by Clara Zetkin from 1892 until it was taken over by SPD right wing in 1917.

Golos (The Voice) – Russian Socialist paper published in Paris, September 1914–January 1915; collaborators included Martov, Trotsky, Lunacharsky, and Kollontai; banned and replaced by *Nashe Slovo.*

Gompers, Samuel (1850–1924) – president of American Federation of Labor, 1886–1924 (except 1895); outspoken class collaborationist; advocate of U.S. entry into war; member of Council of National Defense, 1917.

Gorky, Maxim (1850–1936) – prominent Russian writer and Social Democrat; sympathizer of Bolsheviks and friend of Lenin; critical of Soviet regime in its early years; later publicly supported Stalin.

Gorter, Hermann (1864–1927) – Dutch left-wing Socialist; led Tribunist current; expelled from right wing–led Social Democratic Labor Party in 1909; opponent of war and member of Zimmerwald Left; a founder of Dutch CP; held ultraleft views in Communist International and split in 1921.

Graber, Ernst Paul (1875–1956) – Swiss Social Democrat; editor of *La Sentinelle,* 1915–25; signed Left statement at Kienthal conference; abandoned internationalist position and supported right wing in Swiss party after 1917.

Greulich, Hermann (1842–1925) – long-time leader of Swiss Social Democratic Party; right-wing opponent of Zimmerwald movement.

Grey, Edward (1862–1933) – British foreign secretary, 1905–16; member of Liberal Party.

Grimm, Robert (1881–1958) – leader of Swiss Social Democratic Party and editor of *Berner Tagwacht,* 1909–18, 1928–32; took centrist position during war; participated in Zimmerwald and Kienthal conferences; chairman of International Socialist Commission, 1915–17; helped organize Two-and-a-Half International in 1920; later returned to Second International.

Guchkov, A.I. (1862–1936) – Russian landowner and capitalist; head of Octobrists; Duma president, 1907–12; minister of war in Provisional Government, 1917.

Guesde, Jules (1845–1922) – a founder of French Socialist Party; leader of its Marxist wing before 1914; became defensist during war; minister without portfolio in French government.

Guilbeaux, Henri (1884–1938) – French SP member and anarcho-syndicalist; supported Zimmerwald Left at 1916 Kienthal conference; later active in Communist International; broke with CP in 1930s and became sympathetic to fascism.

Gurevich, E.L. (b. 1866) – right-wing Menshevik; defensist during war; later a member of Marx-Engels-Lenin Institute in Moscow.

Gvozdev, K.A. (b. 1883) – right-wing Menshevik; defensist during war; headed workers' group in War Industries Committee; minister of labor in 1917 Provisional Government; opposed October revolution; later held various posts in Soviet economy and trade unions.

Haase, Hugo (1863–1919) – elected SPD Reichstag member 1897; in SPD Center current before war; SPD co-chairman, 1911–16; opposed August 4, 1914, stand on war credits, but as head of SPD Reichstag fraction, read out affirmative declaration; member of centrist opposition; co-chairman of Independent Social Democratic Party; member of provisional government, November–December 1918; assassinated.

Haenisch, Konrad (1876–1925) – editor of SPD publishing house from 1911; in SPD left wing before 1914; chauvinist during war.

Hales, John (b. 1839) – British reformist trade union leader; secretary of General Council of First International.

Hammer, Julius (1874–1948) – wealthy physician; represented U.S. Socialist Labor Party at Stuttgart congress; later member of left wing of SP and founding member of Communist Labor Party in 1919.

Hanecki, Jakób (1879–1937) – a leader of Polish SDKPiL opposition; within RSDLP collaborated with Bolsheviks; member of Zimmerwald Left; held various posts in Soviet government after 1917; executed during Moscow trials.

Hansen, Arvid (b. 1894) – Norwegian left-wing Socialist; leader of Socialist Youth International; supported affiliation to Communist International by Norwegian Labor Party; after it broke with Comintern in 1923, became a central leader of Communist Party.

Hardie, Keir (1865–1915) – a central leader of British Independent Labour Party and founder of Labour Party; adopted pacifist stand in 1914.

Heden, Erik – member of left-wing minority within Swedish Social Democratic Labor Party that was expelled in 1917; imprisoned during war for antimilitarist agitation.

Heilmann, Ernst (1881–1940) – SPD member and editor of *Chemnitzer Volksstimme* (Chemnitz People's Voice), 1909–17; chauvinist during war.

Heine, Wolfgang (1861–1944) – leading German SPD right-winger; Reichstag member from 1898; contributor to *Sozialistische Monatshefte;* chauvinist during war; entered Prussian government in 1918.

Helfferich, Karl (1872–1924) – German secretary of state, 1915–17.

Henderson, Arthur (1863–1935) – British trade unionist and secretary of Labour Party, 1911–34; chauvinist during war; instrumental in securing Labour endorsement for government war policy; cabinet minister, 1916–17; foreign secretary, 1929–31.

Henke, Alfred (1868–1946) – SPD Reichstag member from Bremen; disagreed with August 4, 1914, vote on war credits; centrist; founder of Independent Social Democratic Party; later rejoined SPD.

Hervé, Gustave (1871–1944) – held ultraleft antimilitarist views within French SP before 1914; founded *La Guerre Sociale* in 1906; became extreme chauvinist in 1914 and changed name of paper to *La Victoire;* after war became a monarchist and organized profascist movement in 1927.

Herzfeld, Josef (1853–1939) – long-time SPD Reichstag member; took antiwar position in 1915; Independent Social Democratic Party founding member in 1917; joined CP in 1920 fusion.

Hilferding, Rudolf (1877–1941) – SPD member and author of *Finance Capital;* took pacifist position during war and joined Independent Social Democratic Party; returned to SPD in 1922; became German finance minister in 1922.

Hillquit, Morris (1869–1933) – initially member of U.S. Socialist Labor Party; founding leader of SP in 1901 and representative on International Socialist Bureau; centrist during war; opponent of Communist International.

Hindenburg, Paul von (1847–1934) – chief of German general staff, 1916–18; president, 1925–34; appointed Hitler chancellor.

Hoch, Gustav (1862–1942) – member of SPD majority fraction in Reichstag.

Hoffmann, Adolph (1858–1930) – long-time SPD member; attended Zimmerwald and Kienthal conferences; chairman of Berlin SPD, later Independent Social Democratic Party; Prussian minister of education, 1918–19; participated in 1920 fusion with CP; resigned the following year and eventually rejoined SPD.

Höglund, Karl Zeth (1884–1956) – a leader of Swedish Social Democratic Party; imprisoned 1905 and 1916 for antiwar propaganda; member of Zimmerwald Left; became central leader of Swedish CP; expelled in 1924 and rejoined Social Democrats.

Hohenzollern – royal house of Prussia.

Hughes, William M. (1864–1952) – Australian union official and Labor Party Leader; prime minister, 1915–23.

L'Humanité (Humanity) – daily newspaper founded by Jean Jaurès in 1904 as organ of French SP; during war became an organ of majority Socialist leadership; became CP organ following party's 1920 decision to affiliate to Communist International; during war edited by Pierre Renaudel and Compère Morel.

Huysmans, Camille (1871–1968) – a leader of Belgian Labor Party; secretary of International Socialist Bureau, 1904–19; centrist before war, became defensist in 1914; subsequently served in Belgian government.

Hyndman, Henry (1842–1921) – founder of British Social Democratic Federation in 1881; helped found British Socialist Party in 1911; became defensist in 1914 and led split from party; formed National Socialist Party in 1916.

Iglesias, Pablo (1850–1925) – founder of Spanish Social Democracy in 1879; head of trade union federation; supported Triple Entente during war.

Independent Labour Party (ILP) – British reformist party founded 1893; affiliated to Second International and Labour Party; advocated electoral alliances with Liberal Party; 30,000 members in 1912; pacifist stand during war, although some members voted for war credits; left-wing minority split in 1921 to join CP.

Die Internationale (The International) – Berlin journal published by Rosa Luxemburg and Franz Mehring; suppressed in 1915 after first issue; resumed publication in 1919 as organ of German CP.

Internationale Group – named after magazine *Die Internationale* published by revolutionary German Socialists in 1915; founded at conference of left Social Democrats on January 1, 1916; popularly called Spartacists after illegal publications signed "Spartacus"; forerunner of German Communist Party.

Internationale Korrespondenz (International Correspondence) – a weekly journal of SPD right wing, published September 1914 to October 1918.

International Socialist Bureau – formed in 1900 as executive body of Second International, headquartered in Brussels; moved to The Hague with outbreak of war.

International Socialist Committee – executive organ of Zimmerwald movement; initially composed of Robert Grimm, Oddino Morgari, Charles Naine, and Angelica Balabanoff; dominated by left wing after 1917 October revolution; in 1919 majority of ISC members joined Communist International and it was formally dissolved by first Communist International congress.

International Socialists of Germany – a group of left-wing German Social Democrats united around newspaper *Lichtstrahlen*, 1913–21.

Izvestia (News) – organ of Menshevik Secretariat of the Organizing Committee Abroad; published 1915–17.

Jaurès, Jean (1859–1914) – longtime leader of French Socialist movement, associated with reformist wing; founder and central leader of united SP from 1905; editor of *L'Humanité;* prominent antimilitarist; assassinated by nationalist on eve of war.

Jogiches, Leo (1867–1919) – a founding leader and central organizer of Polish SDKPiL; moved to Germany and became central organizer of Spartacist group; arrested in March 1919 and murdered by counterrevolutionaries.

Jouhaux, Léon (1879–1954) – secretary of CGT, 1909–47; antimilitarist and syndicalist before war; chauvinist during war.

Jowett, Frederick W. (1864–1944) – chairman of British ILP, 1914; longtime member of Parliament; member of cabinet in first Labour government, 1924.

Jugend-Internationale (Youth International) – began publishing in Zurich, 1915 as quarterly of reconstituted Socialist Youth International; strongly influenced by Zimmerwald Left; subsequently official organ of Communist Youth International.

Kabakchiev, Khristo (1878–1940) – a central leader of Bulgarian Tesnyaki and founder of CP; later worked in Communist International; imprisoned during Moscow trials.

Kačlerović, Triša (1879–1964) – founder of Serbian Social Democratic Party and its secretary, 1906–1907; voted against war credits in 1914; participant at Kienthal conference; secretary of Yugoslav CP, 1923–25; left political activity in 1926; held minor posts in Yugoslavia after revolution.

Kama, Bhikajee – representative of Indian National Congress at 1907 Stuttgart congress; in 1910 she moved to France and joined Socialist Party.

Kamenev, Leon (1883–1936) – joined RSDLP 1901 and became Bolshevik; representative to Copenhagen and Basel congresses of Second International; member of Bolshevik Central Committee; directed Duma fraction and editor of *Pravda*, 1914; deported to Siberia at beginning of war; opposed Bolshevik perspective of seizing power in October 1917; allied with Stalin and Zinoviev, 1923–25; part of United Opposition, 1926–27; capitulated, but was executed during Moscow trials.

Kamienska, Anna – represented Polish SDKPiL at 1915 International Socialist Women's Conference at Bern; later became prominent member of Polish and Soviet CP; imprisoned for supporting Left Opposition.

Der Kampf (The Struggle) – monthly theoretical journal of Austrian Social Democratic Party; published in Vienna, 1907–34.

Karski – See Marchlewski, Julian.

Kato Tokijiro – physician and social reformer; member of Japanese Socialist Party and representative to 1907 Stuttgart congress.

Kautsky, Karl (1854–1938) – Marxist theoretician and collaborator of Engels; founder and editor of *Die Neue Zeit* and author of numerous books; a leader of "Marxist Center" in SPD before 1914; adopted pacifist stand in 1914, making apologies for chauvinist majority; founding member of Independent Social Democratic Party and member of its right wing; rejoined SPD in 1922.

Khrustalev-Nosar, G.S. (1877–1918) – Menshevik; resigned from RSDLP in 1909; subsequently engaged in shady financial operations.

Khvostov, A.N. (1872–1918) – Russian interior minister in tsarist government, 1915–16; executed after revolution.

Kiderlen-Wächter, Alfred von (1852–1912) – German foreign secretary in 1910; negotiated with France during Morocco crisis.

Kirkov, Georgi (1867–1919) – left-wing Socialist; secretary of Central Committee of Bulgarian Tesnyaki.

Kolarov, Vasil (1877–1950) – prominent leader of Bulgarian Tesnyaki and its representative at Zimmerwald conference; a central leader of Bulgarian CP from its founding; became prime minister in 1949.

Kolb, Wilhelm (1870–1918) – right-wing SPD member and leader of Baden revisionists; social chauvinist during war.

Kollontai, Alexandra (1872–1952) – Russian Social Democrat since 1890s; active in international Socialist women's movement; Menshevik before 1914; collaborated with Bolsheviks during war while abroad; joined Bolsheviks in 1915 and elected to Central Committee in 1917; a leader of Workers' Opposition, 1920–22; later held Soviet diplomatic posts.

Kommunist (Communist) – Bolshevik journal launched in 1915; published by Pyatakov and Bosh under direction of Central Committee; only one double issue appeared in September 1915; discontinued because of disagreements between publishers and Central Committee.

König, Max (1868–1941) – member of SPD Reichstag fraction during war.

Kosovsky, V. (M.Y. Lewinson) (1868–1941) – founder of Jewish Bund; right-wing Menshevik within RSDLP; contributed to *Nasha Zarya* and *Luch;* during war defended position of German SPD; did not return to Russia in 1917.

Krupp – Family of leading German armaments manufacturers. During first world war, firm run by Gustav Krupp (1870–1950) and Bertha Krupp (1886–1957).

Krupskaya, N.K. (1869–1939) – Lenin's wife and collaborator; secretary of Bolshevik Central Committee Bureau Abroad while in exile; held a number of posts in Soviet government following 1917; briefly member of United Opposition in 1926.

Krylenko, N.V. (1885–1938) – joined Bolsheviks in 1904; lived in Switzerland, 1914–15, and collaborated with Bukharin at 1915 Bern conference of Bolshevik organizations abroad; after 1917 held posts in Soviet military and department of justice.

Labour Leader – weekly organ of British Independent Labour Party, published 1899–1922; replaced by *New Leader.*

Landsberg, Otto (1869–1957) – SPD Reichstag deputy; supported most openly pro-imperialist wing of party during war; became member of provisional government, 1918.

Lapčević, Dragiša (1864–1939) – Serbian Social Democrat and deputy in parliament from 1905; opposed war credits in 1914; sympathetic to left but remained in Social Democracy following war.

Lapinski, Stanislaw (Pawel Lewinson) (1879–1937) – leader of Polish Socialist Party (Lewica); attended Zimmerwald and Kienthal conferences; later became a leader of Polish CP; executed during Moscow trials.

Larin, Y. (1882–1932) – prominent Menshevik; joined Bolsheviks in August 1917; held various positions in Soviet economy.

Lassalle, Ferdinand (1825–1864) – participant in 1848 revolution; founder and president of General Association of German Workers; killed in duel; followers fused with Marxists in 1875 to form Social Democratic Party.

Lazzari, Constantino (1857–1927) – general secretary of Italian SP, 1912–19; attended Zimmerwald conference; favored adherence to Communist International but rejected conditions of admittance; joined Communist International along with Italian SP after 1919, but was expelled along with party majority, 1921.

Ledebour, Georg (1850–1947) – SPD member and Reichstag representative; opposed SPD pro-war majority in 1915 and led right wing of Zimmerwald movement; a leader of Independent Social Democratic Party and part of minority rejecting fusion with CP in 1920; later led a small split-off from Independent Social Democratic Party.

Legien, Carl (1861–1920) – Social Democratic head of German trade unions, 1890–1920; avowed reformist; supported SPD pro-imperialist right wing during war.

Leipziger Volkszeitung (Leipzig People's Gazette) – began publishing 1894; generally considered a voice of left wing within German SPD; editors included Mehring, Luxemburg, and Lensch.

Lemansky, P.L. (Girsh) (b. 1882) – a leader of Jewish Bund; member of its Committee Abroad after 1911; an editor of Bund organ *Die Zait* (The Times); attended Zimmerwald conference.

Lenin, V.I. (1870–1924) – founder of St. Petersburg League for the Emancipation of the Working Class, 1895; exiled to Siberia, 1896; went abroad and helped publish *Iskra*, 1900–1903; central leader of Bolsheviks from 1903; developed strategy for proletarian leadership in fight for provisional revolutionary government to establish revolutionary democratic dictatorship of proletariat and peasantry; participated in 1905–1907 Russian revolution; after 1907 defended revolutionary organization against liquidationism; RSDLP representative on International Socialist Bureau, 1908–12; issued call for new, revolutionary International, 1914; organized Zimmerwald Left to fight for this goal, 1915–17; returned to Russia and led Bolsheviks' struggle for Soviet power, 1917; Soviet chairman of people's commissars, 1917–24; central leader of Communist International.

Lensch, Paul (1873–1926) – left-wing SPD member; editor of *Leipziger*

Volkszeitung, 1905–13; chauvinist in 1914; eventually quit SPD and became editor for leading German industrialist.

Levitsky, V.O. (Tsederbaum) (b. 1883) – leading Menshevik; brother of Julius Martov.

Lichtstrahlen (Rays) – monthly organ of left-wing International Socialists of Germany, published 1913–21; chief editor, J. Borchardt.

Liebknecht, Karl (1871–1919) – son of Wilhelm Liebknecht; founding leader of Socialist Youth International in 1907; jailed that year for book *Militarism and Anti-Militarism;* only member of Reichstag to vote against war credits in December 1914; leading Spartacist; jailed in 1916 for antiwar propaganda; released by November 1918 revolution; arrested by troops of SPD government and murdered in January 1919.

Liebknecht, Wilhelm (1826–1900) – friend and collaborator of Marx and Engels; a founder of German Social Democracy in 1869; a leader of SPD until death.

Lilina, Zina (1881–1929) – Bolshevik; joined RSDLP in 1902; active in international Socialist women's movement and contributor to *Rabotnitsa* (Woman Worker); during war helped organize transport of illegal Bolshevik literature; held various posts in Soviet government after 1917.

Liquidators – name applied following 1907 to majority of Mensheviks, who advocated liquidating underground RSDLP organization and limiting party to legal work; the Bolsheviks considered that under conditions of tsarist repression, this would have meant abandoning all revolutionary activity.

Litvinov, Maxim (1876–1951) – joined RSDLP in 1898; prominent Bolshevik; secretary of united RSDLP delegation to 1907 Stuttgart conference; member of International Socialist Bureau after 1912; Soviet foreign minister, 1930–39.

Lloyd George, David (1863–1945) – British Liberal politician; prime minister, 1916–22.

Longuet, Jean (1876–1938) – grandson of Karl Marx; a leader of pacifist minority in French SP after 1916 although consistently voted for war credits in Chamber of Deputies; an opponent of party's affiliation to Communist International in 1920;

became an organizer of the Two-and-a-Half International; later returned to Second International.

Lozovsky, S.A. (1878–1952) – joined RSDLP in 1901; collaborated with *Golos* and *Nashe Slovo* as dissident Bolshevik during war; trade union leader after 1917; general secretary of Red International of Labor Unions, 1921–37; arrested in 1949 and died in prison.

Luch (The Ray) – right-wing Menshevik newspaper published in St. Petersburg.

Lunacharsky, A.V. (1875–1933) – joined Russian Social Democrats in 1890s; supported Bolsheviks after 1903; developed differences and split after 1908; contributed to *Golos* and *Nashe Slovo* during war; rejoined Bolsheviks along with Mezhrayontsi in 1917; people's commissar for education, 1917–29.

Luxemburg, Rosa (1871–1919) – founding leader of Polish Social Democracy in 1893; moved to Germany and joined SPD, 1898; leader of left wing against revisionist right and, after 1910, against "Marxist Center" led by Kautsky; Polish representative on International Socialist Bureau; after outbreak of war leader of Spartacus group; imprisoned by German government; founding leader of German CP; arrested by troops of SPD government and murdered in January 1919.

MacLean, John (1879–1923) – Scottish working-class leader; imprisoned for opposition to war; leader of left wing in British Socialist Party; supporter of Communist International, although never joined CP.

Mankov, I.N. (b. 1881) – Menshevik member of Fourth Duma; defensist during war; expelled from Menshevik Social Democratic fraction for not opposing war credits; withdrew from political activity in 1917.

Mann, Tom (1856–1941) – British trade union leader; served as secretary of ILP; took pacifist position during war; founding member of CP; a leader of the Red International of Labor Unions.

Mannesmann, Reinhard (1856–1922) – German capitalist and steel magnate.

Manuilsky, D.Z. (1883–1959) – Russian Social Democrat; split from Bolsheviks after 1908; wrote for *Nashe Slovo* during war; rejoined Bolsheviks in 1917 with Mezhrayontsi; leading Communist International functionary under Stalin.

Marchlewski, Julian (1866–1925) – member of German and Polish Social Democratic parties; during war, a leader of Spartacists; played a leading role in Communist International.

Markov, N.S. (b. 1866) – leader of extreme right-wing forces in Russian Duma.

Martov, L. (Julius) (1873–1923) – a central leader of RSDLP and of Mensheviks following 1903; initial editor of *Golos*, 1914; soon disagreed with majority of editors and ultimately resigned from *Nashe Slovo* in 1916; leader of Menshevik Secretariat of the Organizing Committee Abroad during war; backed centrists at Zimmerwald and Kienthal conferences; opposed October revolution; left Russia in 1920.

Martynov, A.S. (1865–1935) – Russian Social Democrat; a leader of Economists; after 1903 a Menshevik; took pacifist stand during war; joined Russian CP in 1923; prominent Communist International functionary under Stalin.

Maslov, P.P. (1867–1946) – prominent Russian economist; member of Menshevik right wing; defensist during war; left politics in 1917.

Mayéras, Barthélemy (1879–1942) – journalist and member of French SP; belonged to Chamber of Deputies during war and was a leader of centrist minority in SP; opposed affiliation to Communist International in 1920.

Mehring, Franz (1846–1919) – German Marxist historian and scholar; an editor of *Die Neue Zeit;* helped found *Die Internationale* in 1915; leader of Spartacus group and a founder of German CP.

Mensheviks – formed in 1903 as minority of Second Congress of RSDLP; increasingly moved to right after 1907; during war, contained defensist and nondefensist wings; opposed October 1917 revolution.

Merrheim, Alphonse (1881–1925) – French syndicalist and trade union leader; attended Zimmerwald conference; moved increasingly to the right and broke with Zimmerwald movement in 1917.

Meyer, Ernst (1887–1930) – left-wing SPD member; *Vorwärts* political editor, 1913–16; leading Spartacist; a founder of CP and chairman of its Political Bureau, 1921–22; active in Communist International.

Mezhrayontsi (Interdistrict Organization of United Social Democrats) – formed in St. Petersburg in November 1913 with stated object of uniting Bolsheviks and Mensheviks; took internationalist position during war; in 1917, its 4,000 members fused with Bolsheviks; leading members at time of fusion included Trotsky, Lunacharsky, Manuilsky, and Uritsky.

Milyukov, Paul (1859–1943) – leader of Russian Cadet Party; ardent supporter of war; foreign minister in 1917 Provisional Government; opponent of October revolution.

Modigliani, Giuseppe (1868–1947) – a leader of Italian SP; attended Zimmerwald and Kienthal conferences; supported reformist Unitary Socialist Party in three-way split in 1922.

Molkenbuhr, Hermann (1851–1927) – became secretary of SPD Executive Committee in 1904; represented SPD on International Socialist Bureau; supported party majority during war.

Monatte, Pierre (1881–1960) – French revolutionary syndicalist; one of first to publicly oppose war in 1914; member of CP, 1923–24; briefly sympathetic to Bolshevik-Leninist opposition.

Moor, Karl (1853–1932) – former German Socialist; became leading member of Swiss Social Democratic Party; editor of *Berner Tagwacht*, 1895–1907; attended Zimmerwald conference, 1915; moved to Soviet Union after October revolution.

Morgari, Oddino (1865–1929) – leader of Italian SP; became chief editor of *Avanti!* in 1908; member of International Socialist Committee elected at Zimmerwald; centrist; briefly supported Russian revolution, then moved to right.

Müller, August (b. 1873) – right-wing Social Democrat; in German government, 1918–19; joined bourgeois party, 1925.

Müller, Gustav (1860–1921) – right-wing leader of Swiss Social Democratic Party; during war a colonel in Swiss artillery.

Müller, Hermann (1876–1931) – member of SPD Executive Committee; supporter of majority during war; became editor of

Vorwärts in 1916; German foreign minister, 1919–20; chancellor, 1920, 1928–30.

Münzenberg, Willi (1889–1940) – German Socialist: moved to Switzerland 1910; secretary of reconstituted Socialist Youth International, 1915–19; editor of *Jugend-Internationale;* attended Kienthal conference in 1916 and later supported Zimmerwald Left; secretary of Communist Youth International, 1919–21; expelled from German CP in 1938; died in France under mysterious circumstances.

Muranov, M.K. (1873–1959) – Bolshevik Duma member, 1912–14; arrested November 1914; following 1917 member of Russian CP Control Commission.

Mussolini, Benito (1883–1945) – co-editor of Italian SP organ *Avanti!,* 1912–14, holding antiwar views; adopted chauvinist position in 1914 and expelled from party; founded fascist movement, 1919; Italian dictator, 1922–43.

Mysl (Thought) – Socialist Revolutionary daily published in Paris, November 1914–March 1915; edited by Victor Chernov.

Naine, Charles (1874–1926) – a leader of Swiss Social Democratic Party; member of International Socialist Committee elected at Zimmerwald; joined right wing of Swiss party after 1917.

Nakhimson, M.I. (1880–1938) – Russian economist and writer; member of Bund, 1899–1921; centrist during war.

Naoroji, Dadabhai (1825–1917) – longtime president of Indian National Congress; first Indian member of British House of Commons, 1892, elected on Liberal Party ticket.

Napoleon III (Louis Bonaparte) (1808–1873) – nephew of Napoleon Bonaparte; emperor of France, 1852–70.

Narodniks – movement of Russian intellectuals in late nineteenth century that saw the liberation of peasants and distribution of landed estates to peasantry as key to opening road to socialist development; later gave birth to Socialist Revolutionary Party.

Nasha Zarya (Our Dawn) – legal monthly of right-wing Mensheviks published in St. Petersburg, 1910–14; later replaced by *Nashe Dyelo;* main editor A.N. Potresov.

Nashe Dyelo (Our Cause) – began publishing in 1915 to replace

Nasha Zarya; organ of right-wing Mensheviks.

Nashe Slovo (Our Word) – published in Paris, January 1915–September 1916, replacing *Golos;* chief editor Trotsky.

Natanson, M.A. (Bobrov) (1850–1919) – a founder of Russian Narodniks, 1872; leader of Socialist Revolutionary Party; participated in Zimmerwald movement; supported October 1917 revolution as Left SR; headed "Revolutionary Communist" wing which later fused with CP.

National Liberal Party – German party of big industrial bourgeoisie.

Nerman, Ture (1886–1970?) – a leader of Swedish-Norwegian Socialist youth league before war; took antiwar stand in 1914; supporter of Zimmerwald Left; founding member of Swedish CP; left CP in 1929; later rejoined Social Democratic Party.

Die Neue Zeit (New Times) – theoretical journal of German SPD, published in Stuttgart, 1883–1923; edited by Kautsky until 1917; originally a voice of Marxism, then centrism; after 1914 took conciliationist stand toward social chauvinism; in 1917 Kautsky was ousted by SPD leadership and replaced by majority supporter Heinrich Cunow.

Nicholas II (1868–1918) – Russian tsar, 1894–1917; executed during civil war.

Nicod, René (1881–1950) – local leader of French SP; published open letter to party leadership in October 1914 opposing war; later a local CP leader; publicly opposed Stalin-Hitler pact in 1939 and rejoined SP.

Nieuwenhuis, Ferdinand Domela (1846–1919) – leader of Dutch Social Democrats from 1879; advocated general strike against war at 1891 and 1893 International congresses; became anarchist and led split from Second International in 1896.

Nobs, Ernst (1886–1957) – leading member of Swiss Social Democratic Party and editor of *Volksrecht* (People's Justice) during war; supported Zimmerwald Left at Kienthal conference; adopted centrist position in 1917 and became right-wing Social Democrat after 1920.

Norwegian Labor Party – founded 1887; 50,000 members in 1914; left-wing current won majority after war and party affiliated to Communist International in 1919; party majority disaffiliated from Third International in 1923 and minority founded Norwegian CP.

Noske, Gustav (1868–1946) – right-wing SPD leader and supporter of German colonial policy; German war minister, 1919–20; organized suppression of 1918–19 revolution.

Octobrists – members of Russian Union of October 17; formed after promulgation of tsar's manifesto of October 30 (17), 1905; represented big bourgeoisie and landlords; moderate bourgeois opposition before 1917; became ruling party in first stage of Provisional Government in 1917.

Oljelund, Lars (b. 1892) – member of left-wing minority of Swedish Social Democratic Labor Party; imprisoned during war for antimilitarist agitation.

Organizing Committee – set up by August 1912 conference of anti-Bolshevik Social Democrats; formed leading body of Mensheviks until 1917, when replaced by Menshevik Central Committee.

Pannekoek, Anton (1873–1960) – joined Dutch Social Democrats in 1902; leader of left-wing *Tribune* group expelled in 1909; lived in Germany for several years and active in SPD left; member of Zimmerwald Left during war; co-founder of Dutch CP; part of 1921 ultraleft split.

Parvus, A.L. (Alexander Helphand) (1867–1924) – active in Russian and German Social Democracy; along with Rosa Luxemburg initiated fight against revisionism in SPD in 1899; supported Mensheviks and collaborated with Trotsky; in years preceding war, enriched himself speculating on war deliveries to Balkans; became German social patriot.

Pearse, Patrick (1879–1916) – Irish nationalist; leader of Sinn Féin; commander of Irish forces in 1916 Easter Rebellion; executed by British.

Peluso, Edmondo (1882–1942) – Italian emigrant; represented Portuguese Socialist Party at Kienthal conference; moved to Germany and joined Spartacists; founding member of Italian Communist Party; active in Communist International; lived in Soviet Union after 1927.

Petrov – See Armand, Inessa.

Petrovsky, G.I. (1878–1958) – metal worker and Bolshevik deputy to Duma, 1912–14; arrested November 1914; later held posts in Soviet government.

Pfannkuch, Wilhelm (1841–1923) – longtime SPD leader; became a secretary of party Executive Committee in 1894; supported majority during war.

Pindar (522?–443 B.C.) – Greek lyric poet known for odes to victorious athletes.

Platten, Fritz (1883–1942) – secretary of Swiss Social Democratic Party, 1912–18; supported Zimmerwald Left; founding member of Swiss CP; moved to Soviet Union in 1923; imprisoned during Moscow trials, 1938.

Plehve, V.K. (1846–1904) – Russian interior minister, 1902–4; notorious for brutal repression; assassinated.

Plekhanov, Georgii (1856–1918) – founder of Russian Marxism; participated in founding of Second International in 1889; member of International Socialist Bureau until 1913; originally sided with Bolsheviks in 1903 split, soon after became Menshevik; formed group within Mensheviks that collaborated with Bolsheviks, 1909; took chauvinist position in 1914; opposed October revolution.

Poincaré, Jules (1860–1934) – French president, 1913–20.

Polish Socialist Party (PPS) – founded 1892; strongly marked by nationalist and reformist tendencies; right wing (PPS-Revolutionary Faction) was led by future dictator Josef Pilsudski; left wing majority founded PPS (Lewica) in 1906; latter group adopted internationalist position during war and merged with SDKPiL to form Polish CP in 1918.

Popular Socialists – split away from right wing of Socialist Revolutionary Party in 1906; politically close to Cadets.

Porte, Henri de la (1880–1924) – leading left-wing member of French SP before war; opposed colonialism at 1907 Stuttgart congress; took defensist position in 1914; joined bourgeois Radical Party in 1919.

Potresov, A.N. (1869–1934) – early Russian Marxist; right-wing Menshevik; member of *Nasha Zarya* editorial board; chauvinist during war; opposed October revolution and emigrated to Paris.

Pravda (Truth) – legal Bolshevik daily published in St. Petersburg, 1912–14; average circulation of 40,000; relaunched in 1917 as organ of Central Committee of Bolshevik Party.

Pressemane, Adrien (1879–1929) – French SP member of Chamber of Deputies; a leader of centrist minority after 1916; opposed affiliation to Communist International and was part of right-wing minority split in 1920 that retained name of SP.

Prizyv (The Call) – social chauvinist Paris weekly published by Mensheviks and Socialist Revolutionaries, October 1915–March 1917.

Progressive Party – German party of small and petty bourgeoisie, standing for liberal reform.

Proletarskii Golos (Proletarian Voice) – underground publication of Petrograd committee of Bolsheviks; four issues published, February 1915–December 1916.

Pyatakov, Y.L. (1890–1937) – Bolshevik since 1912; member of *Kommunist* editorial board in 1915; held positions in Soviet government following 1917; member of Bolshevik-Leninist opposition, 1923–28; executed following second Moscow trial.

Quelch, Harry (1858–1913) – leader of British Social Democratic Federation and British SP; editor of *Justice*, 1892–1913; member of International Socialist Bureau.

Quessel, Ludwig (1872–1931) – right-wing SPD member; Reichstag deputy during war.

Rabotnitsa (Woman Worker) – newspaper published by Bolshevik Central Committee, February–June 1914, and May 1917–January 1918; contributors included Krupskaya, Kollontai, and Lilina.

Radek, Karl (1885–1939) – joined Polish Social Democracy in 1904; moved to Germany in 1908 and active in German Socialist left; after 1915 a member of Zimmerwald Left bureau together with Lenin and Zinoviev; traveled to Russia with Lenin in April 1917 and joined Bolsheviks; played prominent role in Communist International; member of Bolshevik-Leninist opposition, 1923–29; expelled from CP, 1927; capitulated, 1929; arrested in 1937 during Moscow trials and died in prison.

Rakovsky, Christian (1873–1941) – prominent Romanian Social

Democrat since 1893; organized Balkan Socialist antiwar conference, 1915; left-centrist during war; attended Zimmerwald conference; imprisoned for opposing Romanian entry into war; joined Bolsheviks in 1918; chairman of Ukrainian Soviet republic, 1919; member of Bolshevik-Leninist opposition, 1923–34; expelled from party and arrested, 1927; capitulated 1934; died while in prison following Moscow trials.

Rappaport, Charles (1865–1941) – originally member of RSDLP; emigrated to France and supported left wing within French SP; founded newspaper *Contre la guerre* (Against War) in 1912; took antiwar position during war; a founding leader of French CP; resigned in 1938 and returned to SP.

Ravestejn, Willem van (1876–1970) – Dutch Tribunist and founding member of CP; expelled in 1926 with David Wijnkoop and retired from political activity.

Ravich, Olga (1879–1957) – Bolshevik living in Switzerland during war; active in public education following 1917; a supporter of Zinoviev and member of United Opposition, 1926–27.

Rech (Speech) – daily organ of Russian liberal-capitalist Cadet party, published in Petersburg, 1906–17.

Redmond, John (1856–1928) – longtime chairman of Irish Nationalist Party and member of British Parliament; supported Britain in war; opposed 1916 Easter Rebellion.

Reinhart, Minna – leader of Berlin SPD; attended Zimmerwald conference; founding member of Independent Social Democratic Party; later joined CP.

Renaudel, Pierre (1871–1935) – French Socialist; editor of *Le Peuple* prior to war; after 1914 a central leader of SP right-wing majority; editor of *L'Humanité*, 1914–18; part of 1920 split that took name of SP; led right-wing split from it in 1933.

Renner, Karl (1870–1950) – prominent revisionist in Austrian Social Democratic Party; adopted chauvinist position during war; Austrian chancellor, 1919–20, and president, 1931–33.

Ribot, Alexandre (1842–1923) – French finance minister, 1914–17; premier, 1917.

Robmann, Agnes (1876–1951) – member of Swiss Social Democratic Party; supported Zimmerwald Left at Kienthal conference, 1916.

Rohrbach, Paul (1869–1956) – influential German writer and politician; helped formulate imperialist foreign and colonial policy for German government.

Roland-Holst, Henriette (1869–1952) – Dutch left-wing Socialist; quit right-wing Social Democratic Labor Party in 1912; joined *Tribune* group in 1916; published *Vorbote;* founding member of CP in 1918; resigned several years later, eventually became Christian Socialist.

Romanov – Russian ruling dynasty, 1613–1917.

Rosmer, Alfred (1877–1964) – French revolutionary syndicalist; joined Zimmerwald movement during war; leader of French Committee for the Communist International; joined CP in 1920; editor of *L'Humanité;* leading member of Red International of Labor Unions; expelled from CP in 1924 as supporter of Bolshevik-Leninist opposition; broke with Bolshevik-Leninists in 1930 but collaborated with Trotsky and Fourth International after 1936.

Rothstein, Theodore (1871–1953) – Russian Socialist living in Britain; member of Social Democratic Federation and RSDLP; advanced pacifist position during war; helped found British CP; deported in 1920; worked in Soviet Commissariat of Foreign Affairs.

Rozmirovich, Yelena (1886–1953) – secretary of Bolshevik Duma fraction and of Russian Bureau of Central Committee after 1913; on editorial board of *Pravda* before war; lived in Switzerland during war; held various posts in Soviet government.

Rubanovich, I.A. (1860–1920) – a leader of Russian Socialist Revolutionary Party; member of International Socialist Bureau, 1907–1909; chauvinist during war.

Rühle, Otto (1874–1943) – German SPD member; in 1915 became second Reichstag member to oppose war credits; joined CP in 1919; helped lead ultraleft split in 1919; served on Dewey commission to investigate Moscow trial frame-up against Trotsky, 1937.

Russian Social Democratic Labor Party (RSDLP) – founded

1898; divided at 1903 congress into Bolshevik and Menshevik factions.

Rutgers, S.J. (1879–1961) – Dutch Tribunist; moved to U.S. during war and joined SP left; worked for Communist International, 1919–21; retired from politics in 1921; lived in Soviet Union until 1938.

Ryazanov, David B. (1870–1938) – Russian Marxist scholar; collaborator of *Nashe Slovo* during war; joined Bolsheviks in 1917 with Mezhrayontsi; later headed Marx-Engels Institute; arrested during Moscow trials and died in Siberian exile.

Sakazov, Janko (1860–1941) – central leader of right-wing Bulgarian Social Democratic party, the Shiroki ("broad"); opposed war credits in Bulgarian parliament during Balkan War in 1912; later supported Bulgaria's entry into First World War.

Samoilov, F.N. (1882–1952) – textile worker and Bolshevik deputy to Duma, 1912–14; arrested in 1914 and exiled to Siberia.

Samozashchita (Self-Defense) – a collection of articles by leading Menshevik chauvinists, including A.N. Potresov and P.P. Maslov; published 1916 in Petrograd.

Savalyev, M.A. (1884–1939) – Russian journalist; represented Socialist Revolutionary Party at Kienthal conference in 1916; wrote for *Pravda* after 1928.

Sazonov, S.D. (1866–1927) – tsarist foreign minister, 1910–16.

Sbornik Sotsial-Demokrata (*Sotsial-Demokrat* Collection) – journal of Bolshevik Central Committee; two issues published in 1916.

Scheidemann, Philipp (1865–1939) – German SPD member; elected to Reichstag, 1898; became a secretary of Executive Committee, 1911; following Bebel's death in 1913, was central leader of party along with Ebert; led SPD into supporting war in 1914; presided over suppression of 1918–19 revolution; German chancellor, 1919.

SDKPiL – See Social Democracy of the Kingdom of Poland and Lithuania.

Secretariat of the Organizing Committee Abroad – leadership of Mensheviks outside of Russia during war; leaders included Axelrod, Martov, and Semkovsky; published *Izvestia*.

Sembat, Marcel (1862–1922) – French SP leader; parliamentary deputy from 1893; chauvinist during war; minister of public works, 1914–16.

Semkovsky, S.Y. (Bronstein) (1882–1937) – leading Menshevik; leading member of Secretariat of the Organizing Committee Abroad during war; broke with Mensheviks in 1920 and joined Russian CP; executed during Moscow trials.

Serrati, Giacinto Menotti (1874–1926) – central leader of Italian SP during war; editor of *Avanti!*, 1915–20; attended Zimmerwald and Kienthal; led SP into Communist International but opposed break with Italian reformists and was expelled from International in 1921 with party majority; led SP left wing into fusion with CP in 1924.

Shagov, N.R. (1882–1918) – Bolshevik deputy to Duma, 1912–14; arrested in November 1914 and exiled to Siberia.

Shklovsky, G.L. (1875–1937) – joined Russian Social Democrats in 1898; Bolshevik delegate to 1912 Basel congress; lived in Switzerland after 1909 and attended 1915 conference of Bolshevik organizations abroad; held Soviet diplomatic posts 1918–25; removed from posts for supporting Bolshevik-Leninist opposition.

Shlyapnikov, Alexander (1883–1937) – metal worker and Bolshevik leader; active during war in maintaining Bolshevik international contacts; organized bureau of Central Committee inside Russia; commissar of labor following revolution; later became leader of Workers' Opposition, 1920–22; arrested during Moscow trials.

Singer, Paul (1844–1911) – chairman of SPD Executive Committee, 1890–1911; close collaborator of Bebel; opposed revisionist current within party and International.

Sismondi, Jean-Charles (1773–1842) – Swiss economist; petty-bourgeois critic of capitalism.

Skobelev, M.I. (1885–1939) – Menshevik deputy to Duma during war; minister of labor in Provisional Government, 1917; later broke with Mensheviks and joined CP.

Smart, Russell – long-time British Socialist and leader of Independent Labour Party; editor of *ILP News;* developed differences with ILP and participated in founding of British Socialist Party in 1911.

Smirnov, E. – See Gurevich, E.L.

Social Democracy of the Kingdom of Poland and Lithuania (SDKPiL) – founded 1893 as Polish organization, fused with Lithuanian organization in 1899; adopted position opposing demand for Polish independence and right to self-determination; became affiliated to RSDLP in 1906; split in 1911 between Central Committee and Warsaw Regional Committee; both wings fused with PPS (Lewica) to form Communist Party in 1918.

Social Democratic Labor Party of Austria – founded 1888; in 1914, 142,000 members in German Austria, 184,000 in Czech areas; functioned independently from Hungarian party; chauvinist stance during war; theoretical organ *Der Kampf*.

Social Democratic Labor Party of Sweden – founded 1889; 84,000 members in 1914; led by opportunists; left-wing split formed Left Social Democratic Party in 1917; majority of left-wing party became Swedish CP in 1921.

Social Democratic Labor Party of the Netherlands – founded 1894; opportunist majority leadership expelled Marxist *Tribune* group in 1909; 16,000 members in 1913; took chauvinist position during war; central leaders included Troelstra, van Kol, and Wibaut.

Social Democratic Party of Germany (SPD) – formed in 1875 as Social Democratic Workers Party, from fusion of Marxist party and Lassallean organization; changed name to SPD in 1891; split during war gave birth to centrist Independent Social Democratic Party in 1917 and to German Communist Party (Spartacus League) in 1918; Independent Social Democratic Party split in 1922, with majority joining CP and minority returning to SPD.

Social Democratic Party of the Netherlands – See Tribunists.

Social Democratic Working Group – formed March 1916 by seventeen German SPD Reichstag members who voted against government budget; forerunner of Independent Social Democratic Party.

Socialist Labor Party (SLP) – U.S. party founded 1876; during 1890s came under leadership of Daniel De Leon; increasingly adopted sectarian positions; took internationalist position during war; 2,000–3,000 members in 1916; initially sympathetic to October revolution; later rejected Soviet workers' state; degenerated into tiny sect.

Socialist Party of America – formed in 1901; 106,000 members in 1914; left wing split in 1919 to form Communist Party and Communist Labor Party, which united in 1921.

Socialist Party of France – founded 1905 by merger of Socialist Party of France led by Jules Guesde and French Socialist Party led by Jean Jaurès; 77,000 members in 1914; majority supported imperialist war; centrist minority current gained strength after 1916, eventually obtaining majority; in 1920 party voted to affiliate to Communist International at Tours congress, renamed itself Communist Party; right-wing minority continued name of SP; paper *L'Humanité*.

Socialist Party of Italy – founded in 1892; most outspoken reformists expelled at 1912 congress; 45,000 members in 1914; initiated Zimmerwald conference; voted to affiliate to Communist International in 1919, but was expelled for refusing to break with reformist wing of party; minority split off in January 1921 to form CP; *Avanti!* was central organ.

Socialist Propaganda League – formed 1915 in Boston by members of U.S. SP's Latvian Federation; strongly influenced by Pannekoek and Dutch Tribunists; held ultraleft views; published *New International*, renamed *Revolutionary Age*, with Louis Fraina as editor; played important role in birth of U.S. Communist movement in 1919.

Socialist Revolutionary Party – founded 1901–2 as expression of petty-bourgeois Narodnik current; affiliated to Second International; divided during war between internationalist and chauvinist wings; in 1917 had majority support of peasantry; split between supporters and opponents of Provisional Government; right SRs fought in civil war against Soviet rule; Left SRs split and participated in Bolshevik-led government until 1918, when majority of leadership led attempted coup; minority currents joined Soviet CP.

Sorge, Friedrich (1828–1906) – friend and collaborator of Marx and Engels living in United States; became secretary of First International, 1872; collaborator of *Die Neue Zeit* until death.

Sotsial-Demokrat – published 1908–17 as central organ of RSDLP; controlled by Bolsheviks after 1910; during war published in Switzerland; main editors, Lenin and Zinoviev.

Sozialistische Monatshefte (Socialist Monthly) – principal journal of German SPD opportunists, 1897–1933.

Spartacists – revolutionary current of German Socialists after December 1914 led by Luxemburg and Liebknecht; adopted name Internationale Group in 1916; many Spartacists participated in Independent Social Democratic Party, 1917–18; formed German CP in December 1918.

Spartakusbriefe (Spartacus Letters) – popular name for underground circulars of Spartacist tendency, issued from December 1914 to October 1918.

Spectator – See Nakhimson, M.I.

Stadthagen, Arthur (1857–1917) – became *Vorwärts* editor, 1893; SPD Reichstag deputy; member of Social Democratic Working Group during war; founding member of Independent Social Democratic Party.

Stampfer, Friedrich (1874–1957) – right-wing SPD member; chief editor of *Vorwärts*, 1916–33.

Stegerwald, Adam (1874–1945) – Reichstag deputy from German Center Party; later a government minister.

Stein, Wladislaw (A. Krajewski) (1886–1937) – joined Polish Social Democracy in 1904; a leader of SDKPiL opposition after 1911; supported Zimmerwald Left at 1916 Kienthal conference; founding leader of Polish CP; joined Soviet CP in 1931; executed during Moscow trials.

Ströbel, Heinrich (1869–1944) – SPD member; one of editors of *Vorwärts*, 1900–1916; opponent of SPD policy during war; worked briefly with Internationale Group, then moved to center, becoming founding member of Independent Social Democratic Party; rejoined SPD in 1922.

Struve, P.B. (1870–1944) – Russian economist; "legal Marxist" in 1890s; Cadet after 1905; emigrated after 1917.

Stürmer, B.V. (1849–1917) – Russian premier, 1916; arrested following revolution.

Südekum, Albert (1871–1944) – prominent right-wing SPD member; Reichstag member, 1900–1918; supporter of German imperialism before and during war; Prussian finance minister, 1918–20.

Svyatopolk-Mirsky, P.D. (1857–1914) – Russian interior minister, 1904–1905; considered a liberal by bourgeois oppositionists; ordered January 9, 1905, Bloody Sunday massacre.

Swiss Social Democratic Party – founded 1888; 33,000 members in 1913; leadership took centrist position during war, helping to lead Zimmerwald movement; had strong left-wing minority; central organ *Berner Tagwacht*.

Terwagne, Modeste (1864–1945) – right-wing Belgian Social Democrat and member of parliament, 1900–1918; headed government propaganda agency during war; led ultrachauvinist split from party after war to form rival "socialist" group.

Tesnyaki (literally "narrow") – revolutionary wing of Bulgarian Social Democratic Party, founded 1891; split with opportunist wing (Shiroki—"broad") in 1903; collaborated with Bolsheviks; 4,000 members in 1916; became Bulgarian CP in 1919.

Thalheimer, August (1884–1948) – left-wing German Social Democrat; joined SPD in 1904; Spartacist during war; crafted, 1914–16; leader of CP until expulsion in 1929 as supporter of Right Opposition.

Thalheimer, Berta (1883–1959) – German Spartacist; attended Zimmerwald conference; member of CP until expulsion in 1929 as supporter of Right Opposition.

Thiers, Louis-Adolphe (1797–1877) – French president, 1871–73; organized crushing of Paris Commune.

Thomas, Albert (1878–1932) – leading member of French SP right wing; a chauvinist during war; minister of armaments, 1915–17.

Thyssen, Fritz (1873–1951) – German steel magnate; helped finance Hitler's rise to power.

Timm, Johannes (1866–1945) – member of German SPD Control Commission, 1908–19; chauvinist during war.

Tirpitz, Alfred von (1849–1930) – German admiral; secretary of state for naval affairs, 1897–1916.

Tokijiro – See Kato Tokijiro.

Tolstoy, Leo (1828–1910) – Russian novelist; romanticized peasant life; developed extreme ascetic and pacifist ideas.

Treves, Claudio (1869–1933) – member of Italian SP; co-editor of *Avanti!*, 1908–12; took centrist position during war.

Tribunists – members of Dutch Social Democratic Party formed in 1909 by expelled left-wing members of Social Democratic Labor Party; named after newspaper *De Tribune;* 600 members in 1916; adopted internationalist position during war; formed Dutch CP in 1918.

Troelstra, Pieter (1860–1930) – founding leader of Dutch Social Democratic Labor Party in 1894; prominent opportunist within Second International; engineered expulsion of Dutch Tribunists in 1909; chauvinist during war.

Trotsky, Leon (1879–1940) – Russian Social Democrat; aligned with Mensheviks, 1903–1904; president of St. Petersburg soviet, 1905; took intermediate position between Bolsheviks and Mensheviks, 1904–17; helped publish *Nashe Slovo* during war; joined Bolsheviks with Mezhrayontsi in 1917 and elected to Bolshevik Central Committee; commissar of Red Army, 1918–25; leader of Communist International; led Bolshevik-Leninist opposition following 1923; expelled from party, 1927; exiled abroad, 1929; in 1933 launched fight for Fourth International, which was formed in 1938; main defendant, in absentia, at 1936–38 Moscow frame-up trials; assassinated by Stalinist agent.

Trudoviks – Russian party formed in 1906 of peasant deputies in State Duma; during First World War, most supporters took chauvinist stand.

Tulyakov, I.N. (1877–1920?) – Russian Menshevik; member of Duma during war.

Turati, Filippo (1857–1932) – a founder of Italian Socialist Party; avowed reformist; during war voted against war credits in Chamber of Deputies, but supported Woodrow Wilson's peace proposals; led right-wing split from SP in 1922.

Ugarte, Manuel (1874–1951) – represented Argentine SP on International Socialist Bureau; adopted anti-imperialist position not shared by Argentine party; publicly attacked by party in 1912 and later expelled; became prominent writer and Latin American nationalist.

Vaillant, Edouard (1840–1915) – longtime French Socialist; member, General Council of First International; participant in Paris Commune; prominent antimilitarist favoring general strike to oppose war; became chauvinist in 1914.

Vandervelde, Emile (1866–1938) – Belgian Socialist; opportunist chairman of International Socialist Bureau, 1900–1918; became chauvinist in 1914; minister of state, 1914–18; president of Socialist International, 1929–36.

Van Kol, Hendrick (1851–1925) – member of First International; lived many years in Dutch East Indies; founding leader of Dutch Social Democratic Labor Party; prominent opportunist on colonial and other questions within Second International; opponent of Zimmerwald movement.

Viviani, René (1863–1925) – left French SP in 1906 to enter government and become bourgeois politician; prime minister, 1914–15; minister of justice, 1915–17.

Vliegen, Willem (1862–1947) – a leader of Dutch Social Democratic Labor Party; editor of *Het Volk*, 1907–19; chauvinist during war; alternate member of International Socialist Bureau, 1915.

Vogtherr, Ewald (1859–1923) – member SPD Reichstag fraction; opposed majority policy; attended Zimmerwald conference; founding member of Independent Social Democratic Party; returned to SPD in 1922.

Voinov – See Lunacharsky, A.V.

Vollmar, Georg von (1850–1922) – former German army officer; became first open advocate of revisionism in SPD in 1890; helped form alliance with Catholic Center Party in Bavaria in 1898; chauvinist during war.

Vorbote (Herald) – organ of Zimmerwald Left, published in German in Bern; two issues appeared in 1916; official publishers were Roland-Holst and Pannekoek.

Vorwärts (Forward) – main daily organ of German SPD, began publishing, 1876; during first part of war was in hands of oppositional Berlin organization; closed by government in October 1916 on request of SPD majority leadership, and reopened under its control.

Walcher, Jacob (1887–1970) – SPD journalist; member of Spartacus League and German CP; expelled 1929 for supporting Right Opposition; joined centrist German Socialist Workers Party; later joined CP in German Democratic Republic and held minor government post.

Walecki, Henryk (1877–1937) – leader of left-wing Polish Socialist Party (Lewica); participated in Zimmerwald movement; founding leader of Polish CP; Communist International functionary from 1921; arrested during Moscow trials and died in prison.

Warszawski, Adolf (Warski) (1868–1937) – founding leader SDKPiL; collaborator of Luxemburg; allied with Zimmerwald Left at Kienthal 1916; founder of Polish CP; later moved to Soviet Union; executed during Moscow trials along with entire Polish CP leadership.

Webb, Sidney (1859–1947) and Beatrice (1858–1943) – wrote many books; leading figures in Fabian Society; supported British war policy; Sidney Webb later became colonial minister in Labour government, 1929–31.

Wibaut, F.M. (1859–1936) – leading member of Dutch Social Democratic Labor Party; centrist before 1914, then extreme right-winger; elected vice-president of Second International in 1919.

Wijnkoop, David (1877–1941) – founder and leader of left-wing Dutch Tribunists; founding leader of CP; supporter of ultraleft positions; expelled in 1926; reinstated several years later.

Wilhelm II (1859–1941) – German kaiser (emperor) and king of Prussia, 1888–1918.

Winnig, August (1878–1956) – German Social Democrat; president of construction workers' union; supporter of German annexationism during war; administered captured German territories in the Baltic territories in 1918–19; adviser to German war effort against Soviet republic; supported 1920 right-wing coup attempt and was expelled from SPD.

Winter – See Berzin, Jan Antonovich.

Wurm, Emanuel (1857–1920) – leading supporter of SPD "Marxist Center"; Reichstag deputy; in centrist opposition after 1915; founding member of Independent Social Democratic Party; Prussian food minister, 1918.

Yordansky, N.I. (1876–1928) – Menshevik writer; chauvinist during war; joined Russian CP, 1921.

Zetkin, Clara (1857–1933) – member of SPD left wing; secretary of International Bureau of Socialist Women; Spartacist during war; founding member of CP; elected to Executive Committee of Communist International, 1921.

Zinoviev, Gregory (1883–1936) – joined RSDLP, 1901; supporter of Bolsheviks; lived in exile in Western Europe 1908–17; member editorial board of *Sotsial-Demokrat* and Bolshevik Central Committee; member of Zimmerwald Left Bureau together with Lenin and Radek; opposed seizure of power in October 1917; president of Communist International, 1919–26; aligned with Stalin and Kamenev in 1923–25, aligned with Trotsky and Kamenev in United Opposition, 1926–27; capitulated in 1928; executed following first Moscow trial.

Further Reading

Below are English-language editions of Socialist writings from 1907 to 1916 and memoirs of this period related to the documents in this book.

Badayev, A. *The Bolsheviks in the Tsarist Duma.* Chicago: Proletarian Publishers, no date.

Balabanoff, Angelica. *My Life as a Rebel.* New York: Harper & Brothers, 1938.

Bobrovskaya, Cecilia. *Twenty Years in Underground Russia.* Chicago: Proletarian Publishers, 1976.

Bukharin, Nikolai. *Imperialism and World Economy.* New York: Monthly Review Press, 1973. An expanded version of his 1915 article for *Kommunist.*

Deutscher, Isaac, ed. *The Age of Permanent Revolution: A Trotsky Anthology.* New York: Dell Publishing Company, 1970.

Gankin, O.H., and Fisher, H.H., eds. *The Bolsheviks and the World War: the Origin of the Third International.* Stanford: Stanford University Press, 1940. Includes a wide selection of documents of Socialist conferences and debates during the war years.

Kautsky, Karl. *The Class Struggle.* New York: W.W. Norton and Company, 1971.

———— *The Road to Power.* Chicago: Charles H. Kerr and Company, 1909.

Kollontai, Alexandra. *Selected Writings.* New York: W.W. Norton and Company, 1977.

Krupskaya, N.K. *Reminiscences of Lenin.* New York: International Publishers, 1960.

Lenin, V.I. *Against Imperialist War.* Moscow: Progress Publishers, 1966.

———— *Collected Works.* Moscow: Progress Publishers. Translated from the fourth Russian edition, 1960–70.

———— *Imperialism: The Highest Stage of Capitalism.* New York: International Publishers, 1977.

———— *The National Liberation Movement in the East.* Moscow: Progress Publishers, 1952.

———— *The Right of Nations to Self-Determination.* Moscow: Progress Publishers, 1979.

———— *Socialism and War.* Moscow: Progress Publishers, 1977.

Liebknecht, Karl. *The Future Belongs to the People.* New York: Macmillan Company, 1918. Contains a selection of his wartime speeches.

———— *Militarism and Anti-Militarism.* Cambridge, Great Britain: Rivers Press, 1973.

———— *Speeches of Karl Liebknecht.* New York: International Publishers, 1927.

Looker, Robert, ed. *Rosa Luxemburg: Selected Political Writings.* New York: Grove Press, 1974.

Luxemburg, Rosa. *The National Question.* New York: Monthly Review Press, 1976. Includes "'Theses' of the Editors of Gazeta Robotnicza."

———— *Reform or Revolution.* New York: Pathfinder Press, 1970.

———— *Rosa Luxemburg Speaks.* New York: Pathfinder Press, 1970. Includes "Peace Utopias," "The Junius Pamphlet," and "The Mass Strike."

———— *Selected Political Writings.* New York: Monthly Review Press, 1971.

Shlyapnikov, Alexander. *On the Eve of 1917: Reminiscences from the Revolutionary Underground.* London: Allison and Busby, 1982.

Smart, D.A., ed. *Pannekoek and Gorter's Marxism.* London: Pluto Press, 1978.

Trotsky, Leon. *Leon Trotsky Speaks.* New York: Pathfinder Press, 1972.

———— *My Life.* New York: Pathfinder Press, 1970.

———— *The War and the International.* Colombo, Sri Lanka: Young Socialist Publishers, 1971.

———— *The War Correspondence of Leon Trotsky: The Balkan Wars, 1912–13.* New York: Pathfinder Press, 1980.

Walling, W.E. *The Socialists and the War: A Documentary Statement.* New York: Henry Holt and Company, 1915.

Walling, W.E., et al., eds. *The Socialism of To-day.* New York: Henry Holt and Company, 1916.

Zetkin, Clara. *Selected Writings. New York: International Publishers, 1984.*

Zinoviev, Gregory. *History of the Bolshevik Party: A Popular Outline.* London: New Park Publishers, 1973.

Index

THE RUSSIAN REVOLUTION'S WORLD EXAMPLE

Lenin's Final Fight

Speeches and Writings, 1922–23

V.I. LENIN

In 1922 and 1923, V.I. Lenin, central leader of the world's first socialist revolution, waged what was to be his last political battle—one that was lost after his death. At stake was whether that revolution, and the international communist movement it led, would remain on the revolutionary proletarian course that brought workers and peasants to power in October 1917. $17. Also in Spanish, Farsi, Greek.

The History of the Russian Revolution

LEON TROTSKY

How, under Lenin's leadership, the Bolshevik Party led millions of workers and farmers to overthrow the state power of the landlords and capitalists in 1917 and bring to power a government that advanced their class interests at home and worldwide. Unabridged, 3 vols. in one. Written by one of the central leaders of that socialist revolution. $30. Also in French and Russian.

The Revolution Betrayed

What Is the Soviet Union and Where Is It Going?

LEON TROTSKY

In 1917 workers and peasants of Russia were the motor force of one of the deepest revolutions in history. Yet within ten years a political counterrevolution by a privileged social layer, whose chief spokesperson was Joseph Stalin, was being consolidated. The classic study of the Soviet workers state and its degeneration. $17. Also in Spanish, Farsi, Greek.

COMMUNIST CONTINUITY AND PROGRAM

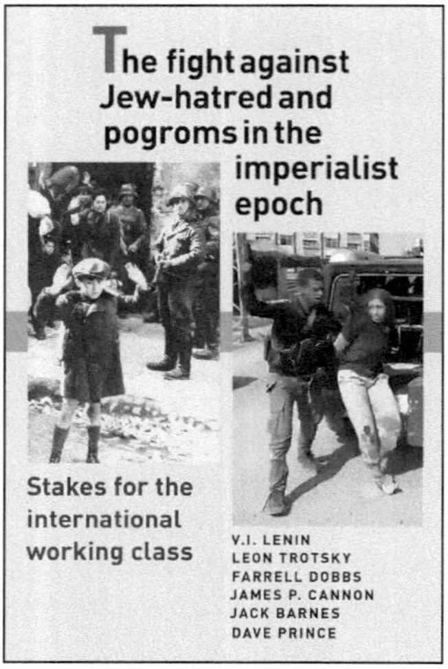

New!

The Fight against Jew-Hatred and Pogroms in the Imperialist Epoch

Stakes for the International Working Class

V.I. LENIN, LEON TROTSKY
FARRELL DOBBS, JAMES P. CANNON
JACK BARNES, DAVE PRINCE

Jew-hatred and pogroms—like Hamas carried out on October 7, 2023—are now part of the permanent social convulsions and wars of the imperialist epoch. That's why fighting Jew-hatred is of decisive importance to the working class and oppressed nations of the entire world. The authors answer the all-important question: *What is to be done to end it*—for all time. $10. Also in Spanish and French.

Are They Rich Because They're Smart?

Class, Privilege, and Learning under Capitalism

JACK BARNES

Exposes growing class inequalities in the US and the self-serving rationalizations of well-paid professionals who think their "brilliance" equips them to "regulate" working people, who don't know what's in our own best interest. $10. Also in Spanish, French, Farsi, Arabic, Greek.

The Struggle for a Proletarian Party

JAMES P. CANNON

"The workers of America have power enough to topple the structure of capitalism at home and to lift the whole world with them when they rise," Cannon asserts. On the eve of World War II, a founder of the communist movement in the US and leader of the Communist International in Lenin's time defends the program and party-building norms of Bolshevism. $20. Also in Spanish and Farsi.

The Low Point of Labor Resistance Is Behind Us

The Socialist Workers Party Looks Forward

JACK BARNES, MARY-ALICE WATERS
STEVE CLARK

The global order imposed by Washington after its victory in World War II is shattering. A long retreat by the working class and unions has come to an end. The bosses and their government are stepping up attacks on our wages, conditions, and constitutional rights. This book highlights opportunities for building a mass proletarian party able to lead the struggle to end capitalist rule, opening a socialist future for humanity. $10. Also in Spanish, French, Greek.

Revolutionary Continuity

Marxist Leadership in the U.S.

The Early Years, 1848–1917
Birth of the Communist Movement, 1918–1922

FARRELL DOBBS

"Successive generations of proletarian revolutionists have participated in the movements of the working class and its allies. . . . Marxists today owe them not only homage for their deeds. We also have a duty to learn what they did wrong as well as right so their errors are not repeated." —*Farrell Dobbs*
Two volumes, $17 each.

The Transitional Program for Socialist Revolution

LEON TROTSKY

The Socialist Workers Party program, drafted by Trotsky in 1938, still guides the SWP and communists the world over. The party "uncompromisingly gives battle to all political groupings tied to the apron strings of the bourgeoisie. Its task—the abolition of capitalism's domination. Its aim—socialism. Its method—the proletarian revolution." $17. Also in Farsi.

THE COMMUNIST INTERNATIONAL IN LENIN'S TIME

To See the Dawn

Baku, 1920—First Congress of the Peoples of the East

How can peasants and workers in the colonial world achieve freedom from imperialist exploitation? By what means can working people overcome divisions incited by their national ruling classes and act together for their common class interests? These questions were addressed by 2,000 delegates to the 1920 Congress of the Peoples of the East. $17

The First Five Years of the Communist International

LEON TROTSKY

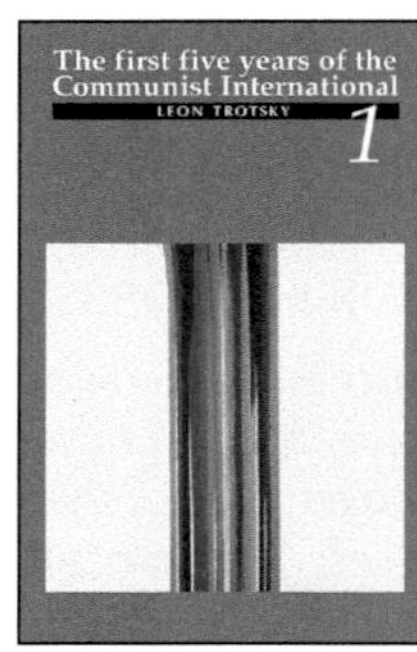

During its first five years, the Communist International, guided by V.I. Lenin, Leon Trotsky, and other central Bolshevik leaders, sought to build a world movement of Communist Parties capable of leading the toilers to overthrow capitalist exploitation and colonial oppression. This two-volume collection contains Trotsky's speeches and writings from the first four Comintern congresses. Volume 1, $22; volume 2, $22.

Workers of the World and Oppressed Peoples, Unite!

Proceedings and Documents of the Second Congress, 1920

The debate among delegates from 37 countries takes up key questions of working-class strategy and program and offers a vivid portrait of social struggles in the era of the October Revolution. 2 vol. set. $45

‘THE HISTORY OF EXISTING SOCIETY IS THE HISTORY OF CLASS STRUGGLES’

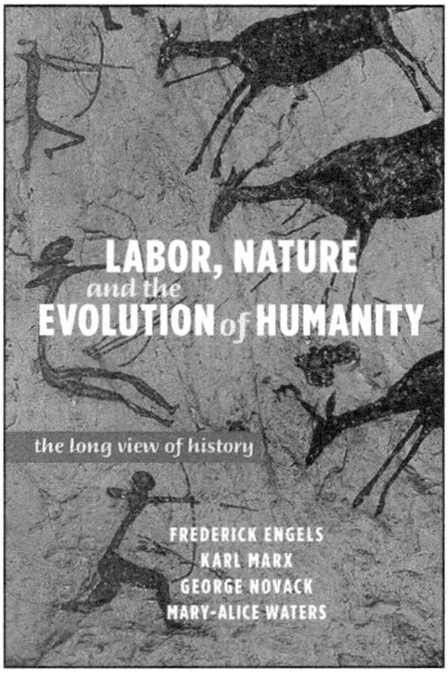

Labor, Nature, and the Evolution of Humanity

The Long View of History

FREDERICK ENGELS, KARL MARX
GEORGE NOVACK
MARY-ALICE WATERS

Without understanding that social labor, transforming nature, has driven humanity’s evolution for millions of years, working people are unable to see beyond the capitalist epoch of class exploitation that warps all human relations, ideas, and values. Only the revolutionary conquest of state power by the working class can open the door to a world free of capitalist exploitation, degradation of nature, subjugation of women, racism, and war. A world built on human solidarity. A socialist world. $12. Also in Spanish and French.

Woman’s Evolution

From Matriarchal Clan to Patriarchal Family

EVELYN REED

An expedition from prehistory to class society that reveals women’s still largely unknown contributions to civilization. Pinpointing the historical factors that led to the subordination of women as a sex, Reed offers fresh insights on the struggle against their oppression and for the liberation of humanity. $25. Also in Spanish, Farsi, Indonesian.

Understanding History

Marxist Essays

GEORGE NOVACK

How did capitalism arise? Why and when did this exploitative system exhaust its once revolutionary role? Why is revolutionary change fundamental to human progress? $15

The Teamster Series

FARRELL DOBBS

Four books on the strikes, organizing drives, and political campaigns that transformed the Teamsters across the Midwest in the 1930s into a militant industrial union movement. Written by Farrell Dobbs, the general organizer of these Teamster battles and leader of the Socialist Workers Party.

A tool for workers seeking to use union power in every workplace and advance the fight for an independent labor party. $16 each, series $50. Also in Spanish. *Teamster Rebellion* is available in French, Farsi, Greek.

Is Socialist Revolution in the US Possible?

A Necessary Debate among Working People

MARY-ALICE WATERS

An unhesitating "Yes"—that's the answer given here. Possible—but not inevitable. That depends on what working people *do*. $7. Also in Spanish, French, Farsi.

Capitalism's World Disorder

Working-Class Politics at the Millennium

JACK BARNES

The social devastation and financial panic, coarsening of politics, cop brutality, and imperialist aggression—all are products not of something gone wrong with capitalism but of its lawful workings. Yet the future can be changed by the united struggle of workers and farmers increasingly conscious of their capacity to wage revolutionary struggles for state power and to transform the world. $20. Also in Spanish and French.

CUBA'S SOCIALIST REVOLUTION

Women in Cuba: The Making of a Revolution within the Revolution

VILMA ESPÍN
ASELA DE LOS SANTOS
YOLANDA FERRER

The integration of women in the ranks and leadership of the Cuban Revolution was intertwined with the proletarian course of the leadership of the revolution from the start. This is the story of that revolution and how it transformed the women and men who made it. $17. Also in Spanish, Farsi, Greek.

Cuba and the Coming American Revolution

JACK BARNES

This is a book about the example set by the Cuban people that socialist revolution is not only necessary—it can be made. A book about the struggles of workers and other exploited producers in the imperialist heartland, and the youth attracted to them. About the class struggle in the US, where the revolutionary capacities of working people are as utterly discounted by the ruling powers as were those of the Cuban toilers. And just as wrongly. $10. Also in Spanish, French, Farsi.

Colombia: Fidel Castro on the Debate around Revolutionary Strategy and Lessons of the Cuban Revolution

FROM THE PAGES OF THE *MILITANT*

Fidel Castro describes the Cuban leadership's efforts to end decades of war between the FARC guerrilla movement and Colombia's brutal regime. He explains why Cuban revolutionaries, unlike FARC leaders, rejected taking hostages and organized Cuba's working people to win state power, not pursue a "prolonged people's war." $5. Also in Spanish.

New International

A MAGAZINE OF MARXIST POLITICS AND THEORY

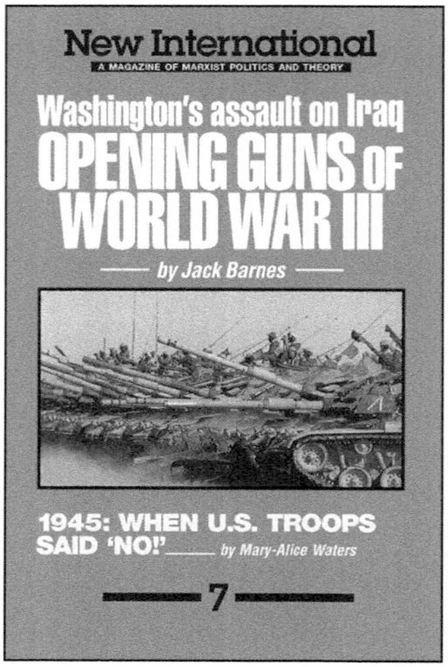

NEW INTERNATIONAL NO. 7

Opening Guns of World War III: Washington's Assault on Iraq

JACK BARNES

The murderous assault on Iraq in 1990–91 heralded increasingly sharp conflicts among imperialist powers, growing instability of capitalism, and more wars. Also includes:

1945: When US Troops Said No!
by Mary-Alice Waters

Lessons from the Iran-Iraq War
by Samad Sharif

$14. Also in Spanish, French, Farsi.

NEW INTERNATIONAL NO. 12

Capitalism's Long Hot Winter Has Begun

JACK BARNES

Today's global capitalist crisis is but the opening stage of decades of economic, financial, and social convulsions and class battles. Class-conscious workers confront this historic turning point for imperialism with confidence, Jack Barnes writes, drawing satisfaction from being "in their face" as we chart a revolutionary course to take power. $14. Also in Spanish, French, Farsi, Arabic, Greek.

NEW INTERNATIONAL NO. 11

U.S. Imperialism Has Lost the Cold War

JACK BARNES

The collapse of regimes across Eastern Europe and the USSR claiming to be communist did not mean workers and farmers there had been crushed. In today's sharpening class conflicts and wars, these toilers are joining working people the world over in the struggle against capitalist exploitation. $14. Also in Spanish, French, Farsi, Greek.

EXPAND YOUR REVOLUTIONARY LIBRARY

New Edition!

Che Guevara on Economics and Politics in the Transition to Socialism

CARLOS TABLADA

It's essential for working people to win state power, said Ernesto Che Guevara. "Then there's the second stage, maybe more difficult than the first"—the transition from dog-eat-dog capitalism to socialism. That includes moving from work as a condition for survival, to voluntary social labor through which we express our common humanity. Includes Fidel Castro's 1987 speech "Che's Ideas Are Absolutely Relevant Today." New edition with substantially expanded selections from Guevara's writings. $17. Also in Spanish, coming in French.

Thomas Sankara Speaks

The Burkina Faso Revolution, 1983–87

Under Sankara's guidance, Burkina Faso's revolutionary government led peasants, workers, women, and youth to expand literacy; to sink wells, plant trees, erect housing; to combat women's oppression; to carry out land reform; to join others worldwide to free themselves from the imperialist yoke. $20. Also in French.

Their Trotsky and Ours

JACK BARNES

To lead the working class in a successful revolution, a mass proletarian party is needed whose cadres, well beforehand, have absorbed a world communist program, are proletarian in life and work, derive deep satisfaction from doing politics, and have forged a leadership with an acute sense of what to do next. This book is about building such a party. $12. Also in Spanish, French, Farsi..

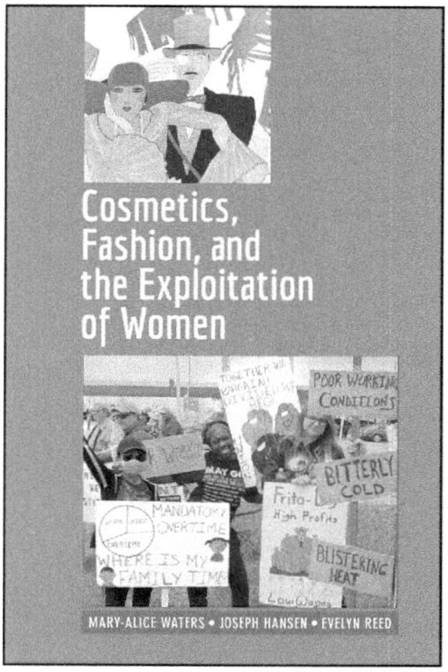

New Edition!

Cosmetics, Fashion, and the Exploitation of Women

JOSEPH HANSEN, EVELYN REED
MARY-ALICE WATERS

How big business reinforces women's second-class status and uses it to rake in profits. Where does women's oppression come from? How has the entry of millions of women into the workforce strengthened the battle for emancipation, still to be won? $12. Also in Spanish.

Malcolm X Talks to Young People

"The young generation of whites, Blacks, browns, whatever else—you're living at a time of revolution," said Malcolm in 1964. "And I for one will join with anyone, I don't care what color you are, as long as you want to change this miserable condition that exists on this earth." Four talks and an interview in the last months of Malcolm's life. $12. Also in Spanish, French, Farsi, Greek.

Pathfinder Press **accessible e-books** for the blind, those with low vision, or other challenges reading print books

For a list of current accessible titles, go to: pathfinderpress.com/collections/books-for-the-blind.

Visit bookshare.org for information on how to sign up.

BY KARL MARX AND FREDERICK ENGELS

The Communist Manifesto

KARL MARX
AND FREDERICK ENGELS

Communism, say the founding leaders of the revolutionary workers movement, is not a set of ideas or preconceived "principles" but workers' line of march to power, springing from a "movement going on under our very eyes." $5. Also in Spanish, French, Farsi, Arabic.

Socialism: Utopian and Scientific

FREDERICK ENGELS

"To make men the masters of their own form of social organization—to make them free—is the mission of the modern proletariat," writes Engels. A classic guide to the operations of capitalism and struggles of the working class. $10. Also in Farsi.

Capital

KARL MARX

Marx explains the workings of the capitalist system and how it produces the insoluble contradictions that breed class struggle. He demonstrates the inevitability of the fight for the revolutionary transformation of society into one ruled for the first time by the producing majority, the working class.

Three volumes, $18 each. Also in Spanish.

The Origin of the Family, Private Property, and the State

FREDERICK ENGELS

The emergence of class-divided society gave rise to repressive state bodies and the oppression of women to enable the ruling classes to pass along wealth and privilege. Engels discusses the consequences for working people of these class institutions—from their ancient forms to their modern versions. $15. Also in Spanish and Farsi.

Anti-Dühring and Dialectics of Nature

FREDERICK ENGELS

Anti-Dühring rebuts the dogma of a reformist professor, whose backers, Engels says, sought "to spread this doctrine in a popular form among workers" and turn the working-class party in Germany into a "little sect." Bolshevik leader V.I. Lenin called it "a handbook for every class-conscious worker" aiming to uproot exploitation and oppression.

A companion work, *Dialectics of Nature*, explains the interconnection between natural science and the evolution of human society.

Both are in Marx and Engels *Collected Works*, vol. 25, $35.

The Civil War in the United States

KARL MARX
AND FREDERICK ENGELS

Articles by the founding leaders of the communist workers movement on the Second American Revolution—which they followed closely as it unfolded—and why the overthrow of the slavocracy and abolition of slavery were in the interests of working people worldwide. $20

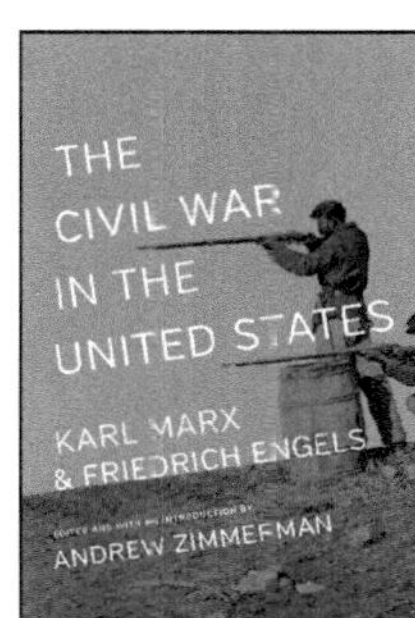